UNIX Developer's Tool Kit

J. Ranade Workstation Series

CHAKRAVARTY • *Power RISC System/6000: Concepts, Facilities, and Architecture,* 0-07-011047-6

DEROEST • *AIX for RS/6000: System and Administration Guide,* 0-07-036439-7

HENRY • *Solaris 2.0: System Administrator Guide,* 0-07-029368-6

JOHNSTON • *OS/2 Connectivity & Networking: A Guide to Communication Manager/2,* 0-07-032696-7

LAMB • *MicroFocus Workbench and Toolset Developer's Guide,* 0-07-036123-3

LOCKHART • *OSF DCE: Guide to Developing Distributed Applications,* 0-07-911481-4

SANCHEZ, CANTON • *Graphics Programming Solutions,* 0-07-911464-4

SANCHEZ, CANTON • *High Resolution Video Graphics,* 0-07-911646-9

SANCHEZ, CANTON • *PC Programmer's Handbook,* 2/e, 0-07-054948-6

WALKER, SCHWALLER • *CPI-C Programming in C: An Application Developer's Guide to APPC,* 0-07-911733-3

WIGGINS • *The Internet for Everyone: A Guide for Users and Providers,* 0-07-067019-8

UNIX Developer's Tool Kit

Kevin E. Leininger

McGraw-Hill, Inc.

New York San Francisco Washington, D.C. Auckland Bogotá
Caracas Lisbon London Madrid Mexico City Milan
Montreal New Delhi San Juan Singapore
Sydney Tokyo Toronto

Library of Congress Cataloging-in-Publication Data

Leininger, Kevin E.
Unix developer's tool kit / Kevin E. Leininger.
p. cm. — (J. Ranade workstation series)
Includes index.
ISBN 0-07-911836-4 —ISBN 0-07-911690-6 (pbk.)
1. UNIX (Computer file) 2. Operating systems (Computers)
I. Title. II. Series.
QA76.76.068L448 1994
005.4'3—dc20 93-44068
CIP

1 2 3 4 5 6 7 8 9 0 DOH/DOH 9 0 9 8 7 6 5 4

P/N 037143-1
PART OF ISBN 0-07-911836-4 (HC)

P/N 037142-3
PART OF ISBN 0-07-911690-6 (SC)

The sponsoring editor for this book was Jerry Papke, the editing supervisor was Nancy Young, and the production supervisor was Suzanne W. Babeuf. This book was set in Century Schoolbook. It was composed by Carol Woolverton Studio in cooperation with Warren Publishing Services.

Printed and bound by R. R. Donnelley & Sons Company.

Contents

Preface

There are many UNIX books on the market today with topics ranging from system administration to general introductions to internetworking. Many of these books are useful and fill a void for both veterans and people new to UNIX. However, there is a need to provide information to all UNIX users on what tools are available and how to use them on a UNIX platform.

The most difficult thing in learning about a new platform is not learning the editor or intricacies of the C compiler but instead is learning what you don't know. By this I mean discovering what is available to assist you in getting your work done in a timely and efficient manner. The entire paradigm of UNIX is very different from that of any other operating system platform. This book is an attempt to provide information which will assist you in accessing, installing, and using many UNIX tools which otherwise you may never have used.

I am not only a consultant on the use of information technology for competitive advantage but a daily UNIX user as well. While I have many books on system administration, introductions to environments and networking, I noticed a lack of books available which describe good tools which I can use to do my job better. This is really what this book is all about and the reason I felt it necessary to write it in the first place. I hope it is as valuable for you as it has been for me to write it.

There is a CD included with this book which contains many free software tools which are readily available from a variety of sources. None of these tools was written by me but instead by people much better at writing software than I am. I have chosen some of the tools that I use and that make me more effective on UNIX computers.

Neither I nor the authors warrantee these software systems or any aspect of the software on this CD. We do, however, encourage you to take a look at and even use these systems to perform your work more effectively and efficiently on UNIX computers. Most of the free software on the CD is from a group called GNU, who now call themselves the Free Software Foundation (FSF). This is a group of people who write very high-quality software systems which they license and distribute free of charge. Their license (called the GNU General Public License) is contained in full in App. B in the back of this book. Without these people, this book would not be possible, and more importantly, many UNIX users could not be as productive and effective on their computers as they are today. Their contribution to UNIX and the software industry in general is large. To them, I can only say—keep up the good work.

I want to emphasize again that *all* the software included on the accompanying CD is free and available to you through a variety of means. There are a variety of software providers such as UUNET and PSI as well as a variety of anonymous ftp machines directly on the Internet. The cost of this book is simply for the book and not the CD. I am not charging any money for the CD or for the work I put into building most of the systems on the CD. While the CD is not absolutely complete, there are Sun and IBM RS/6000 binaries for most of the software on the CD. If there is not a compiled system, there was a reason, and it is probably documented in the README file at the top of the distribution on the CD. I would have created more binaries, but no other machines were readily available to me. There is a support organization known as Ready to Run Software which will support and maintain these packages for you. See App. C for more information.

I take no responsibility for support or the stability of the codes on the CD. None of these systems was written by me and I guarantee nothing with respect to the software systems contained on the accompanying CD. There are various disclaimers in the appendixes of this book as well as with the individual pieces of software on the CD. See these if you have any more questions or comments.

Finally, if you like this book and you want more like it, feel free to drop me a line (on the Internet of course) at:

kevinl@devtech.com

or

uunet!devtech!kevinl

and I may consider putting some more stuff together (heaven help me).

Kevin E. Leininger

Acknowledgments

I would like to thank my wife, Karen, and my son, Alex, for their patience and understanding as I spent many hours and nights putting this book together. Because of them, I have done this. Because of me, I'll probably do this again.

UNIX Developer's Tool Kit

Part

1

UNIX: Getting Started

Chapter

1

The Paradigm of UNIX Power Tools

Paradigm is a term that has just recently come into vogue. It was invented by a historical philosopher named Thomas Kuhn in a book entitled *The History of Scientific Revolutions.* A paradigm is defined as "a fundamental set of beliefs or accepted rules." Today, management consultants are running around corporate executive's offices shouting about the paradigm shift that has occurred with respect to information technology. This shift has been primarily driven by UNIX and its associated ability to radically change people's use of information technology and, ultimately, their business.

1.1 The History of UNIX, at Least as of Today

UNIX was written at AT&T Bell Laboratories in the early 1970s as a spin-off of the MULTICS project that had occurred at M.I.T. in the late 1960s. AT&T withdrew from the MULTICS project and subsequently allowed several of their people who had been involved in this project to acquire a DEC PDP-7 and begin work on a new operating system. Because the system was a simplification of the MULTICS operating system, it became known as UNIX. Originally written in assembler on a DEC PDP-7, it was later rewritten in C on a DEC PDP-11 in an effort to increase portability as well as try out the new language C which some people at Bell Laboratories had invented.

Bell Laboratories began using the UNIX system internally, and it rapidly became the operating system of choice for word processing as well as turn-key systems for their switching equipment. Word gradually spread in the research community and soon copies of UNIX were being shipped to universities around the world. As universities began to use UNIX, they added their own enhancements and tools and began to ship them back to AT&T to be integrated into UNIX for future shipments.

One university, the University of California at Berkeley, decided that AT&T was not shipping and upgrading UNIX often enough and began distributing their own version of UNIX called Berkeley Software Distribution (BSD). AT&T realized that it might actually be able to make money on UNIX instead of giving it away and began charging for UNIX and focusing it toward the business community, while Berkeley dominated in the university and engineering communities.

AT&T originally named their UNIX versions *editions,* with the most well known being the Sixth and Seventh editions of UNIX. In the late 1970s, AT&T reorganized their UNIX support and called their version System III. System V superseded System III in the mid 1980s as the AT&T UNIX version of choice. System IV was never released for public use and support. There have been four major releases since the inception of System V, named 1 through 4. The current release is System V Release 4, commonly known as SVR4. This version has turned out to be a major standard in the UNIX community since most vendors have claimed support for it or at least are moving in that direction. In fact, this is proving to be the platform which may save UNIX as a commercial desktop operating system. It is forcing UNIX vendors to reconverge around a single specification for UNIX and, it is hoped, it will finally allow its users to realize true portability, scaleability, and all of the other purported virtues of UNIX.

While AT&T was developing their UNIX versions, Berkeley was continuing to develop and distribute their version (BSD) of UNIX. While Berkeley diverged from AT&T UNIX through most of the 1970s and 1980s, they reconverged with AT&T with the announcement of System V Release 4. This is a combined AT&T/Berkeley version of UNIX which should help to unite the once fragmented UNIX community. SVR4 was actually controlled and developed by a group called UNIX International (UI). UI was a consortium formed by vendors, including AT&T and Sun, in an effort to standardize UNIX and increase its market presence in the face of rapidly increasing competition and marketshare. UI was later spun off as a subsidiary of AT&T known as Unix Systems Laboratory (USL). The majority of this was sold to Novell in January of 1993. This sale is the biggest in the history for UNIX since it means a major competitor (namely Novell) owns the licensing rights to UNIX SVR4. Novell has since given the UNIX trademark to X/Open. It is yet to be determined how this will affect UNIX and the marketplace.

Because of the fragmentation of the UNIX community in the 1970s and 1980s and some large agreements between AT&T and vendors like Sun Microsystems, Inc., another group was formed, known as the Open Software Foundation, or more commonly OSF. This was a consortium of vendors such as DEC, IBM, and HP who joined together and formed standards for UNIX in an attempt to wrest control of the UNIX marketplace from Sun and AT&T. They released specifications for a UNIX kernel known as OSF/1; however, this has largely been ignored, even by the vendors themselves. OSF has become a specification body that works to define standards in the distributed network environment such as the Distributed Computing Environment (DCE) and the Distributed Management Environment (DME). There are still large gaps in offerings for networking monitoring and administration as well as system administration and security. These will be the focus of groups like OSF and UNIX International.

While there have been many battles between UNIX International and OSF, the SVR4 kernel and associated tools will, in all probability, be the standard for UNIX for the foreseeable future. As hardware technology progresses, technologies such as multiprocessing and new high-speed networks are going to redefine UNIX and all operating system environments; however, you can be sure that UNIX is going to be at the forefront of the utilization of this new technology. Companies like Novell and NeXt have jumped on the UNIX bandwagon and will continue to force innovation in the UNIX marketplace, only adding more power tools to the already large collection of them.

1.2 The UNIX Software Paradigm

In the 1970s, the United States government formed a group known as the Defense Advanced Research Project Agency (DARPA) which was responsible for building high-speed networks to foster communications between geographically dispersed groups of people working on defense-related projects. This network became known as the ARPAnet. As it matured and grew, many other networks attached to it, and the collective network became known as the Internet. Today there are literally millions of nodes and users with access to the Internet.

As the Internet grew, people began to use it to share information, including mail and software, they or their colleagues were working on. This user community consisted of software engineers working in research fields as well as at universities around the world. The computer expertise available on this network became and still is unavailable anywhere else. Today, virtually every major business as well as research lab and university is connected to the Internet. In fact most vendors are now distributing operating system patches and upgrades and providing technical support via the Internet. This is clearly the way of the future in the UNIX marketplace.

Because of the widespread distribution of UNIX throughout the academic and research communities as well as the presence of the Internet, many tools have been developed to enhance UNIX's usability. The paradigm for development of these tools has been very different from that of most other software. Graduate students and their professors working on a thesis, researchers trying to solve a particularly sticky research problem, or just people at home working on an idea to provide a tool which will make the UNIX platform more powerful are the people who create UNIX power tools. These tools are almost always free and most often of excellent quality. While corporations hire software engineers to build systems to sell, tremendous software innovation is occurring throughout the UNIX community.

Because of the modular nature of the UNIX platform, tools are necessary to perform even the most rudimentary of tasks. UNIX provides many single-function tools which, when linked together, perform complex and sophisticated tasks. This is very different from most proprietary systems which provide a smaller number of more powerful tools. This is limited because often you want something slightly different than is offered. With UNIX, you can simply connect the tools in a different order to change the outcome. Thus, the power of UNIX and the associated tool paradigm has developed over the years.

There are thousands of applications available today on the Internet which significantly enhance the value of the UNIX platform. Because of the paradigm of UNIX and the Internet, these tools have often been developed without consideration of their commercial applicability and are, therefore, relatively unknown and unused outside the veteran UNIX community. As commercial UNIX becomes more prevalent, these tools become more relevant to the everyday needs of new UNIX users.

1.3 UNIX as a Tool Platform

UNIX, at its simplest level, is a tool platform. It was designed and built in a modular fashion in order to allow everyone to provide their own tools easily and at low cost. The typical drawing which you see describing the UNIX operating system and its associated environment is that of an onion. I prefer to represent things as a layered approach similar to a networking protocol because this is really how UNIX was constructed (see Fig. 1.1).

The lowest layer is the computer hardware which runs all software and associated hardware peripherals. Above this is the UNIX kernel and its associated system calls. These are well documented and consist of a variety of services which a program can use. The layer above this

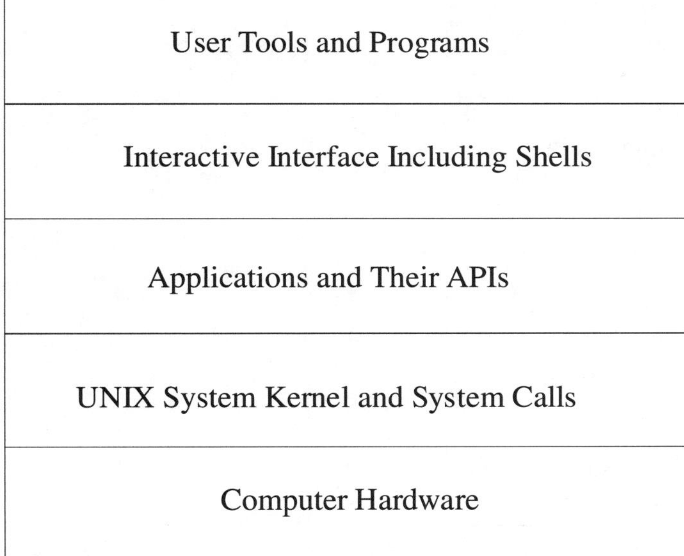

Figure 1.1 The structure of UNIX.

consists of applications and their associated application programming interfaces (APIs) which define how other programs can use the application through a function or subroutine reference. This layer relies on the lower two to provide the compute services it needs to get its tasks accomplished. A good example of this kind of tool is a database.

The next layer is the interactive access layer which typically amounts to a shell such as the Bourne or Korn shells. The final layer is user tools which may rely on all underlying layers to provide what it needs. It is important to note that any higher layer does not have to use the next lower layer but in fact can reference kernel calls directly. This is typically not done, however, since it requires a level of sophistication beyond a typical business programmer.

The new rage in the operating system arena is microkernel technology. This technology breaks the kernel and its associated services down even more and provides very small, highly specialized underlying kernels for a variety of operating systems. This means that by providing a variety of microkernel technologies along with different higher layers, you can run very different operating systems on the same microkernel and gain the benefits of building an environment which the customer is accustomed to while at the same time minimizing your investment in operating system design. This is clearly the wave of the future (see Fig. 1.2).

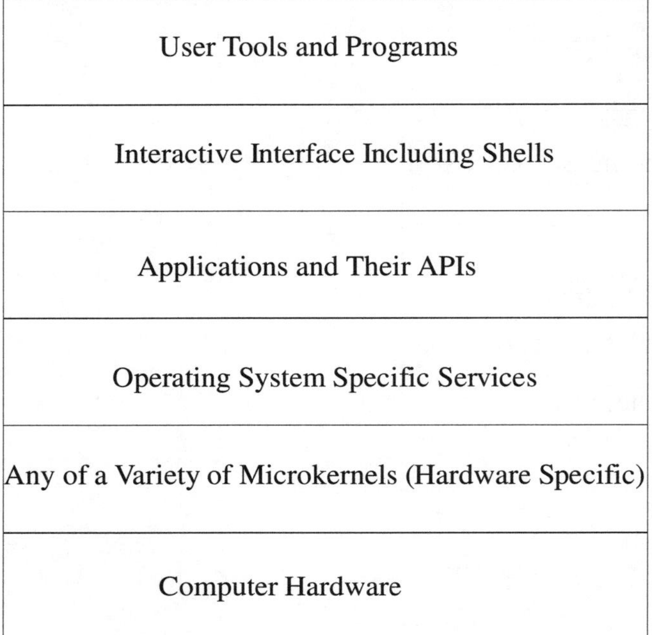

Figure 1.2 The coming structure of UNIX.

Above the hardware layer is the microkernel layer. This is a hardware-specific microkernel which is specifically tuned to run on that hardware platform. Because of its specificity, it performs extremely well on its particular hardware platform. The next higher layer is the OS-specific layer which consists of what, in large part, used to be the system kernel. The difference is that now the operating-system-specific layer is whatever operating system you would like. An example is running MacOS on top of a UNIX-like microkernel with its associated services. The layers above the OS-specific layer are identical to those in Fig. 1.1.

You can see the immediate benefits of this kind of operating system architecture since it provides an easy way to put virtually any operating system and associated services on any hardware platform. This model looks very similar to the OSI ISO network-layered model. The advantages of well-defined program interfaces has not gone unnoticed by the operating system developers, and the microkernel architecture is the result. Operating systems like Windows NT and a variety of UNIX variants will be microkernel based in the next 12 to 18 months.

Shells provide users with interactive access to the kernel as well as the ability to run tools from the command line and batch subsystem. Shells provide few actual tools as a part of their base functionality but instead provide a platform from which tools can be accessed and used.

The top layer of both models is the tool layer. This layer is where the power of UNIX really resides and is, in fact, what differentiates UNIX from other operating systems. The tool layer has access to both the shell and kernel layers. This allows a tool to be isolated from the intricacies of what lies underneath and instead to concentrate on interfaces between itself and lower layers. This is very similar to network protocol models which provide a layered approach to allow transparent change and evolution.

This is a very different model from most other operating systems, which have been built in a monolithic fashion with tools included. Operating systems such as MVS and VMS have "grown up" within corporations which developed them to sell for a profit. Because of this, they have restricted access to low layers of the operating system, including source code and specifications, to allow tool builders to produce innovative tools and products. Source code for UNIX is available for a minimal fee from either your vendor or any of a number of other vendors. In fact, most of the code for UNIX exists on the Internet and is available for free download any time you would like. There are no other major operating system platforms which exist in this form.

UNIX as a tool platform is what gives UNIX the flexibility and power while at the same time providing some of the well-known cryptic syntax and lack of elegance. With flexibility comes the requirement for more sophistication from the user and developer; power, of course, also comes. UNIX is seen as the ultimate development platform for precisely the reasons it is often criticized for being difficult to use. UNIX is the ultimate power tool development platform.

1.4 The UNIX Marketplace Today

The UNIX marketplace is by far the largest growth segment in the computer market today. With compound annual growth exceeding 20 percent, every vendor is writing software as well as developing hardware which relies on UNIX. Because of this tremendous growth in an essentially stagnant industry and the push by corporate users for "open systems," UNIX is exploding in the commercial marketplace.

The entire paradigm of open systems is at the heart of the debate as to how most corporations are moving ahead with their investments in information technology. While there are de facto desktop standards such as Microsoft Windows, what you must examine is their ability to be easily transitioned to another competitive product. In other words, the open systems movement is about the ability to change easily. By providing multiple vendors with very similar offerings, the client gains leverage on its hardware and software provider in the form of lower barriers to entry and exit of a particular information technology architecture. While Microsoft Windows and MacOS may have a large presence on the desktop today along with a large number of $99 software packages, you must examine your ability to change Windows out easily and quickly for a competitive technology. This is virtually impossible to do and is why Microsoft Windows is one of the most closed systems available today.

The entire discussion of open systems is religious in nature and is certainly not addressed in this book; however, suffice it to say that UNIX is at the heart of the open systems debate and is driving the marketplace to a very different place than it would have been without UNIX's existence.

With the realignment of UNIX into several camps, no longer really focusing on the kernel and associated services but instead focusing on complementary areas, UNIX is set to make another leap of marketshare in the next 5 years. While SVR4 has become the de facto standard for kernels and associated tools and system interfaces, coalitions like OSF have become specification providers with such technology as DCE, DME, and ANDF. This means that the technologies of UNIX are going to appear on a variety of nonUNIX platforms. Good examples are IBM's announcement of DCE support on MVS and DEC's OpenVMS, which is a POSIX (read UNIXlike) implementation of VMS. This wide adoption of UNIX and related technologies is redefining the computer marketplace as we know it.

Companies like The Santa Cruz Operation (SCO) have dominated the market for UNIX on the Intel architecture. Their operating system is SCO UNIX (known today as Open Desktop). Several vendors, in a rush to capture some of the money flowing into the UNIX marketplace, have either ported UNIX to their environments or taken pieces of UNIX and incorporated this into their own technology. A good example of this is Novell with their offering known as Novell Lite. This provides peer-like connectivity between DOS PCs on a LAN. Other companies have introduced their own versions of UNIX for the Intel architecture; the Sun Microsystems version is called Solaris. Meanwhile SCO is continuing to update their offerings and will offer SVR4 (code name Destiny, which is really SVR4.3). The battle for the UNIX desktop will occur between Novell, SCO, and Sun. Of course, Microsoft is releasing their own competitor to UNIX in the form of Windows NT, and there is no doubt this will be successful on the Intel desktop; however, UNIX has the opportunity to gain significant marketshare in the confusion on the desktop which will occur in 1994.

The other major player in this newly evolving market for power on the desktop is the PowerPC, which comes from the joint coalition of IBM, Motorola, and Apple. This platform runs Mac, DOS, Windows, and UNIX applications all on the same box. Binary compatibility is claimed as well. This means that you can go to your local PC software store, buy PC and Mac software on floppies, and bring it home and run it on your PowerPC. At the same time, you can run UNIX applications and display results on the same screen. If this really works, it will revolutionize the desktop marketplace in the 1990s. But don't forget, it runs UNIX under the covers.

The UNIX marketplace today is one of flux and change. While vendors such as IBM and Hewlett Packard still offer proprietary operating systems, it is clear that their focus is turning to UNIX and the open systems movement. The battle for the desktop between IBM, HP, Sun, SCO, Microsoft, and Novell as well as hardware architectures such as Intel, SPARC, PA-RISC and the soon-to-be released PowerPC will be an interesting one to watch. It is also difficult to predict. We'll just have to wait and see. However, two things are sure—UNIX will be a key player, and knowledge of tools and environments will be key to the successful implementation and use of desktop computing in the 1990s and beyond.

Chapter

2

The UNIX Environment

The UNIX environment is unique in its flexibility and power. In fact, UNIX is either loved or hated because of its flexibility. Flexibility requires responsibility and knowledge of a particular technology, which many computer users do not possess. Many environments have imposed rigid requirements and rules on users. UNIX imposes none of these. This causes dramatic culture shock to many nonUNIX computer users. However, when people become accustomed to using a tool such as UNIX, they quickly become enamored with its power and flexibility and begin to realize its true potential to provide virtually any capability they wish with a set of simple commands.

Because of UNIX's heritage of development at thousands of universities, research laboratories, and businesses, its tools were neither well documented as an entire environment nor were they well thought out in terms of an overall system design and integration. In other words, there is no overall philosophy as to the architecture provided or the underlying services accompanying it. What was done well, however, was UNIX's overall tool philosophy.

UNIX was developed as a platform to build tools and use them in a modular fashion. By combining tools together, functionality can be significantly enhanced well beyond any single tool in most other environments. This, as discussed earlier, is the tool paradigm on which UNIX was built. Because of the diversity of development work in the UNIX arena and the wide variety of applications running on UNIX, several different environments were developed and distributed. This chapter will discuss some of the major UNIX subsystems and issues related to the power tool paradigm. It is not intended to give an in-depth discussion of each of these topics but instead will present a basic background and the philosophy of each in order to help you understand how each is related to the UNIX power development paradigm that is the primary thesis of this book.

2.1 Shells and Processes

Shells provide the interactive interface to UNIX and supply command line interpretation, interfaces to file systems, and an interface to lower levels of the operating environment such as the kernel. There are three primary shells in use today: C, Bourne, and Korn. They all provide significantly different functionality and have strengths and weaknesses.

Shells are also what provide the shell script capability that makes UNIX famous. By creating files which contain shell commands, you can build programs which can be executed at any time to provide the desired functionality. Each shell has its own shell script language and syntax. In fact, several of the tools and utilities that are discussed in this book consist of either partial or entire shell script content. Scripts are most often used to create installation procedures but can also be used to create entire applications and utilities.

Because of the nature of shells, different ones can be used within the same session. Because of this flexibility, UNIX users typically shift back and forth between shells to accomplish different tasks. This capability is provided by UNIX's method for creating and destroying processes. A process within UNIX consists of what is known as a context. This describes what is in memory and the registers of the computer at any given time. When you issue a command, one of two things happens: A new process is created to execute your command, or your command is executed within your current process context. The latter is called an internal command and usually consists of a command that is contained within the shell executable itself. Examples are the alias command in the C and Korn shells and the export command in the Bourne shell. If there is not an internal command which matches the one typed, an external command is invoked. This is either a shell script or executable that exists in your path.

When an external command is typed, a new process is "forked," or created. The term *fork* comes from the way a process is created in UNIX. By creating a duplicate copy of everything in your current process context and then invoking the supplied command, UNIX provides a fork, or new process, which is very similar to the current one. The command used to load the new command into the newly forked process context is called an execl (which stands for execute on load). Fork and execl are the actual kernel-level calls which provide this new process, hence the names. The execl loads the program into memory and executes it. This is the way all external commands and programs are executed in UNIX. Figure 2.1 outlines the fork and execl process, which

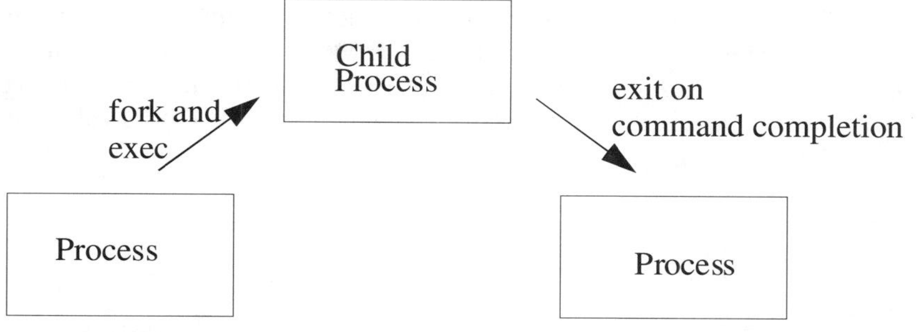

Figure 2.1 Process creation and completion.

leads to some of the flexibility of the UNIX architecture in that it allows you complete flexibility in creating new processes with entirely different contexts and behaviors. This child process is unable to communicate with its parent, but the reverse is not true. Information can be passed from the parent shell to the child shell when invoked. This leads to the ability to create and fork new shells by simply issuing the shell executable name. For example, to initiate a C shell from a Bourne shell you would type:

```
$ /bin/csh
```

and would then be in a C shell. To exit you would simply type:

```
% exit
$
```

Note the different prompts. This is one of the ways you can tell which shell you are in. The Bourne and Korn shells typically use the $ prompt, while the C shell uses the % prompt. The specific shells are described in more detail below. It should be noted that whenever you are logged in as root (also known as superuser), your prompt is the pound sign (#). This ensures that you always know when you are logged in as root; root can do anything and is the power user on any UNIX system. It is, therefore, critical that you know you are in root.

The other key aspect of shells is variables. Each shell has its own way of interacting and controlling variables, but they all have one thing in common: UNIX tools use them to determine their behaviors. Because this is so key to the use of power tools, a brief discussion is in order.

Variables allow for temporary storage of information which can be shared with subprocesses and tools and applications within the current process. Whenever a new environment is forked, the variables from the parent process are maintained and passed to the child process in order to communicate environmental and process information. There are several variables which are commonly used to control UNIX tools behaviors. They are:

SHELL

TERM

PATH

HOME

PROMPT

STATUS

These variables can be manipulated and controlled with the shells to provide environmental control not available any other way. These variables are standard and should be carefully used and controlled to control your overall environment better. You can create your own variables, and most UNIX power tools do just this. Variables are a key way to control tools and their interaction with the rest of the environment.

There are a variety of ways to manipulate these variables, which are mostly shell dependent. Because of this, the exact commands and methods are discussed in more detail in the individual shell sections.

2.1.1 The Bourne shell

The oldest and most common is the Bourne shell. It is often referred to as simply "the shell." This was the original shell and the one in which most shell scripts for system administration and software installation and maintenance are written. Because of this heritage, many regard it as the shell of choice. This shell is shipped with every UNIX box and consists of a single executable /bin/sh. Most system administration is still done in the Bourne shell, and, therefore, most software vendors deliver tools and software with Bourne shell scripts.

The Bourne shell was developed by AT&T and has been shipped with all but the earliest releases of UNIX. Because of its early development and distribution, it has become the standard across all UNIX platforms. If you use a Bourne shell on one platform, you can be very confident that the Bourne shell on another UNIX platform will be identical.

Environmental variables, as discussed above, are key to the operation of the Bourne shell and associated commands and programs. Environmental variables are passed between shells and their associated children with the export command.

A simple example of setting the TERM variable is:

```
$ TERM = vt100;export TERM
```

This sets the TERM variable to vt100, which tells your computer that your display is emulating a vt100. The semicolon separates two Bourne shell commands on a single line. The export command tells the shell to provide this definition of TERM to all child processes. Without it, the value of the TERM variable (in this case vt100) may not be exported to subsequently forked child processes. Use the export command if you want to ensure that variables will be defined for all external command and program executions. This technique will be important as you read about some of the tools and techniques described in the rest of this book, so keep it in mind.

Another common example of the use of environmental variables is to set the path. For many of the tools in this book, you will need to modify your path to include the binaries in your search order. As an example, if you create an executable file in /usr/local/gcc/bin, you would add this directory to your path with a command like:

```
$ PATH = $PATH:/usr/local/gcc/bin; export PATH
```

This appends the /usr/local/gcc/bin path to your current path. This can be placed in the initial login script for the Bourne shell, which is named .profile. If you place the above command in your .profile file, every time you log in, you will have this path correctly set.

To view the value of an environmental variable use the echo command. You can view the value of any environmental variable with a command like:

```
$ echo $PATH
```

This will display the current value of PATH. Note that you can also use the set command to see which variables are defined in your current working session. These commands are slightly different in the csh, so see the following section if you are running in the C shell.

The other subtlety with variables is their definition from within a shell script. If you define a variable within a shell script and execute the shell script by simply typing its name, you will not get the resultant variable set in your current process context. This is because when you execute the shell script, UNIX forks a new shell (the child process) and executes the shell script. When the shell script is finished executing, it kills itself and returns to its original parent process. In the process of killing itself, it removes all variables defined within its context. This occurs in all shells within UNIX.

The way to avoid this in the Bourne shell is with the . (period or dot) command. The basic syntax is:

```
$ . shellscript
```

This will execute the file shell script in the current process, and all definitions created within the shell script will be retained when the shell script is exited. This is often the way you edit your login file .profile.

As an example, if you want to make a permanent change to your TERM variable, you would simply edit the .profile file and save it with the appropriate set and export commands. Once you have done this, you can execute it with the command:

```
$ . .profile
```

This will allow you to define the new variable definitions as well as check your .profile syntax. It avoids many of the problems you may have with shell scripts and, at the same time, allows you to manipulate your current environment.

Finally, the Bourne shell is considered to be the most secure of all shells today and as such is still recommended and used for most issues related to security and root access. While the Korn shell is replacing the Bourne shell as the standard, there are still many vendors who do not deliver the Korn shell with their platform, and as such the Bourne shell remains the standard. Of course, it is safest to use the Bourne shell to develop techniques and scripts for heterogeneous architectures since this is still the most widely portable shell environment on UNIX today.

2.1.2 The C shell

The C shell was developed by Bill Joy (founding member of Sun Microsystems) at Berkeley when, as the UNIX power tool paradigm predicts, some UNIX users decided they could write a better shell than the Bourne shell. After Bill developed the C shell, Berkeley began to distribute it with the BSD distribution. Because of the wide popularity of the BSD solution, the C shell became widely used in place of the Bourne shell.

The C shell gained rapid popularity with software developers and novice users because of its C-like syntax, command line editing, and recall and job control capabilities which do not exist in the Bourne shell. The explosion of Sun Microsystems led to the widespread use of the C shell. Because of this, it is probably the most widely used interactive shell.

Environmental variables are manipulated in a slightly different way in the C shell than in the Bourne shell. The basic command to set the value of a variable is:

```
% setenv TERM vt100
```

This is equivalent to the combination of commands set and export in the Bourne shell. When you use the setenv command, the value of the variable is automatically exported to any child processes just as you would like. To view the value of these variables, use a command like:

```
% echo $TERM
```

To see the value of all variables set, use the command:

```
% setenv
```

This will display all variables and their associated values. If you use the set command in the C shell, you will see the values related to terminal and other process definitions instead of variable values, so watch out.

The C shell has the same subtlety that the Bourne shell has with respect to the definition of variables within a shell script. Just as you can run the shell script in your current process context with the . command in the Bourne shell, you can use the exec command in the C shell. The basic syntax of this command is:

```
% exec shellscript
```

where shellscript is any shell script which can be executed. When you exec the shell script, it does not fork and exec a new process but instead runs the shell script within the current process context. This, in effect, defines all variables and definitions defined within the shell script to the current process context. When the shell script is finished, all definitions are maintained in the current shell. This is similar to the . syntax of the Bourne and Korn shells and is often how you change your login file .cshrc and reexecute it.

For example, if you want to make a permanent change to your path, you should edit the .cshrc file and place the appropriate setenv command in it. Once you have made these changes and saved the new version of the file, you can execute with the command:

```
% exec .cshrc
```

This will define all new variables in the current shell and check your C shell syntax at the same time. There are other switches to the exec command. See your local C shell documentation for more details.

The other useful command in the C shell is the alias command. You can view all defined aliases with the command:

```
% alias
```

If you want to set an alias, use a command like:

```
% alias gcc /usr/local/gcc/bin/gcc
```

When you type % gcc, it will actually run the command /usr/local/gcc/bin/gcc. The alias is a way to define shorthand commands which will make you more efficient in your use of the shell. To remote an alias, type the command:

```
% unalias gcc
```

Note that gcc is an example and could be any defined alias as described above.

The final topic related to the C shell that will be of use to users of this book is command line recall and substitution. There is no command line substitution in the Bourne shell, but there is in the C shell. The basic syntax of the command line recall in the C shell is:

```
%![-]n
```

where n is the number of the previous command. The - represents the number of commands in the reverse order starting with the current command.

To save the previous commands, you need to set the history variable. To set the history to remember the last 25 commands, use the command:

```
% set history = 25
```

This creates a file named .history which stores up to 25 previously executed commands. There is no reason to store more than 25 other than the amount of disk space used by the .history file and the amount of memory used to cache some information.

Because the .history file is preserved, your commands are maintained between login instances. This means that you can log in and immediately have access to the previous 25 commands you executed in any number of previous sessions. To view the command history list, type the command:

```
% history [n]
```

where n is optional and lists the previous n commands you have saved in the history list. A typical example might look like:

```
% history 5
20 Mail
21 /usr/lpp/local/Xframe/bin/maker &
22 telnet uunet
23 compress /tmp/file
24 cat /tmp/.login
```

From this you can choose to reexecute command number 22 with a command like:

```
% !22
```

You can execute the same command with:

```
%!-3
```

Finally, you can execute this command by following the ! (better known as bang in the UNIX community) with a unique character string which identifies the command. To execute the telnet command, you might issue a command like:

```
%!t
```

You must be careful with this syntax, however, since it works through the history list in reverse chronological order. To execute the compress command, you would have to issue the command like:

```
% !co
```

This runs the compress command. If you simply entered !c, you would get the cat command and not the compress command.

Even with the C shell's widespread use, it has been criticized as buggy and so close to C without actually being C that many AT&T UNIX users did not consider it a viable alternative to the Bourne shell. However, it was tough to argue with the fact that it was more user friendly because of things like command line recall and aliases. Because of this, another shell known as the Korn shell was developed.

2.1.3 The Korn shell

The Korn shell was an attempt to use the best features of the Bourne and C shells. The security and reliability of the Bourne shell combined with the user friendliness of the C shell are its virtues. The script language is very similar to the Bourne shell, thus preserving all of those Bourne shell scripts. The Korn shell programming language is significantly enhanced beyond the Bourne shell and provides capabilities which enhance usability and speed over other shells. Features such as job control and command line editing, as in the C shell, are incorporated. Also, because many more of the commands are built-in, scripts and the shell execute more quickly.

The Korn shell supports the exact same syntax with respect to variable manipulation and definition as the Bourne shell, and you can reread the above section for more information if you would like. You can also use the alias command just as you do in the C shell as described above. The primary difference between the Korn shell and the other shells is its command line substitution mechanism.

The Korn shell uses either the vi or emacs editor as its command line substitution system. You set which editor and associated commands you want to use with the command:

```
$ set -o editor
```

where editor is either vi or emacs. So, for example, to set the command line editor to vi, you would use the command:

```
$ set -o vi
```

This will give you all the vi commands to edit your commands—commands like x for delete, i for insert, dw for delete word, etc. All line-oriented vi commands are supported. To cycle through the list of previous commands, you use the k and j keys prefaced by the ESC key. The ESC key toggles you between the command line edit and command line input modes.

When you are entering commands and want to recall one, simply press ESC, and then k to begin to cycle backward through the previous commands. To cycle forward in the saved commands from the current position, use the j key. To move the cursor to the left and right, use the h and l keys, respectively.

If you use the command:

```
$ set -o emacs
```

you have an associated set of commands such as CTRL-P to recall the previous commands, CTRL-R to move the cursor to the right, CTRL-B to move the cursor to the left, etc. Note that most line-oriented emacs commands are supported when in this mode. Choose either vi or emacs depending on your editor preference.

The Korn shell is not as widely distributed as either of the other shells and is therefore less portable. However, this is changing, and vendors such as IBM and Sun are beginning to ship the Korn shell with their operating systems. The Korn shell will become the de facto shell in the very near future.

This section is not a substitute for real documentation on each of the shells but instead introduces you to what you will need to know to use the tools in this book. This section merely scratches the surface when describing the functionality and power of each shell. There are other differences which are more subtle and require more experience which are not discussed here. See the appropriate documentation on the individual shells for more details. There are more examples and discussion of shell functions throughout this chapter.

2.2 Regular Expressions

A regular expression describes a set of one or more matching strings. Regular expressions are the foundation on which the UNIX command set and syntax are based. Utilities such as ed, vi, grep, awk, and others use regular expressions to generate commands within their environments. Shells such as C, Korn, and Bourne also use regular expressions to parse for filenames.

Almost everything in UNIX is a regular expression including strings, numbers, and special characters. In fact, a regular expression is defined as any string it matches. Many examples of regular expressions are described throughout this book. As you gain more experience with UNIX, you will come to understand what a regular expression is and how it is typically used.

Some examples of regular expression matching expressions are:

`character`	Matches any character against itself.
`.`	Matches a single character except newline.
`-`	Indicates a range of characters.
`[ ]`	[a–f] indicates abcdef.
`[ ]`	[A–Z] indicates entire uppercase alphabet.
`^`	When ^ is the first character in a string, it will match any character except the characters in the string and the newline character.
`*`	Matches zero or more occurrences of the string (e.g., ab*d matches the strings abcd, acd, and abbcd but not abd).
`\{k\}`	Matches exactly k occurrences of expression preceding.
`\{k,\}`	Matches at least k occurrences of expression preceding.
`\{k,l\}`	Matches any number of occurrences of the string matched by the expression preceding from k to l where k and l are 0–255.

Expressions can be combined with line addressing using the following constructs:

`$`	Denotes end of line
`/string`	Finds next occurrence of string and makes it the current line
`?string?`	Finds previous occurrence of string and makes it the current line
`+or-`	If used before the line address, specifies a range either forward or backward

A comma is used to separate line addresses by default. For example (2,8) would specify lines 2 through 8. A semicolon (2;8) specifies line 2, makes it the current address, and then uses the second number as an increment from the current line. In this example (2;8) would be equivalent to (2,10).

Since the . matches any character, you could represent the string abc with a.c. The string a.c would also match aac, acc, adc, and so on. However, the string abbc would not match since there are two characters between the a and c. Brackets are used to denote sets of which any can be a match. The string a[abc]c would match the strings aac, abc, and acc but not abbc since, again, there are too many characters.

Some simple examples are shown below:

`a.c`	Represents any string of three characters beginning with an a and ending with a c, for example, aac, abc, acc, adc, etc.
`a[bB]c`	Represents a string abc or aBc
`a[b-d]c`	Represents a string abc, acc, or adc
`a*c`	Represents any string of any length beginning with a and ending with c

There are an infinite number of regular expressions; however, the most common are those described above. The only way to understand regular expressions is to use them and begin to understand their power. The rest of this book discusses regular expressions to accomplish a variety of tasks.

2.3 Job Control

Job control is a key differentiator between the three shells.While the Bourne shell has no capabilities to control jobs as subprocesses, the other shells do. With the C and Korn shells, you can begin jobs, temporarily suspend them, and either restart them in the foreground or start them in the background. This gives you the ability to run multiple interactive jobs simultaneously, thus increasing your productivity at your workstation.

When you issue a command, it is given a job number by the shell, which allows you to track this job. This is not the same as the process id (PID) which is common to all operating systems and shells. With this job number, you can push jobs into the foreground or background as you wish. For example, in the C shell the following commands will run two jobs in the background:

```
% date & # The & executes the job in the background
[1] 101
% nroff -man date > /tmp/date.out &
[2] 103
[1] Done
% jobs
[1] - Running date
Wed Jan 27 08:00:00 CST 1993
[2] - Running nroff -man date > /tmp/date.out
```

As you can see, job 1 (designated by the 1 in square brackets) finished quickly and the results were printed to the screen along with a completion message for job 1. Job 2 on the other hand is running based on the output of the jobs command which reports on the status of all background processes.

To move jobs from the background into the foreground, issue the command:

```
% fg %x
```

where x is the job number. To put a job into the background from the foreground, issue the following commands:

```
% CTRL-Z
% bg
```

The CTRL-Z stops the current execution of the job and places it in a stopped state. The bg command starts the job running in the background. To stop a background job, issue the command:

```
% stop %x
```

where x is again the job number.

The background processes are still attached to the terminal as the input and output device unless redirected. To block a job when requesting I/O from the screen or keyboard, issue the command:

```
stty tostop
```

before executing the job.

The status of the background jobs is displayed randomly on your terminal screen with an associated job id in square brackets in front of it.

This is how you are kept informed about the status of all background jobs.

These functions exist for both the C and Korn shells. They significantly enhance the usability of the shells as an interactive environment.

2.4 Terminals

In UNIX, every file is simply a bit stream and every device is a file. This is one of the single most important concepts in UNIX. It creates the ability to generate programs and scripts which are independent of the type of device you are going to use. Because every I/O operation writes to a device which supports a stream of bits, it greatly simplifies all I/O operations as well as the applications which use them. This is very different from an operating system such as VMS, which uses a tool called Record Management Services (RMS) to access all record-oriented devices such as disk drives, and MVS, which uses file access methods such as VSAM to provide access to disk data. When you wish to instead use a tape or terminal device, you must change your code to support these changes. In UNIX, you simply redirect the output in any of a variety of ways and the code remains unchanged. It is this kind of flexibility which sets UNIX apart from the rest of the operating systems available today.

Because of the concepts of device-independent I/O, it is easy to write applications which take information from a file or device transparently. The terminal is simply another bit stream device which generates bit streams to the operating system. Tape devices are merely bit stream devices as well as network devices such as local area network (LAN) and wide area network (WAN) adapters. This is the power of UNIX and why programmers love it.

There are certain keys which control the execution of your current process context. To end a command line and execute the RETURN key is the standard. The RETURN key issues a CTRL-M which tells the shell to parse and execute any information on the current command line. To erase a command line, typically you would use the CTRL-H sequence, which is most often by default the BACKSPACE key. It may also be the DEL or DELETE key. Finally, you may want to interrupt execution of your current process. You typically issue a CTRL-C command, which interrupts your current process and places you back at the shell.

Many new UNIX users are confused in their initial interactions with UNIX because some or all of these terminal interaction commands are not set as they expect. The primary interface to control the interpretation of your keyboard commands is the stty command. To view the current settings type:

```
$ stty
```

You will see the results of many of the settings that determine how the UNIX environment reacts to your keystrokes. The primary variables of interest are the erase, intr, and kill. These control the erase, interrupt, and line keys, respectively. To change the settings to more commonly used variables, type the commands:

```
$ stty erase "^?"
$ stty intr "^C"
$ stty kill "^X"
```

The ^ denotes a CTRL keystroke. The doubles quotes are required to keep the shell from interpreting the variables before inputting them to the kernel for execution. Remember, the shell is first and foremost a command line interpreter and as such will interpret any information before passing it to the kernel for execution. To stop interpretation by the shell, simply enclose information in double quotes.

Terminals are described by a terminfo database as well as by a termcap subsystem. The terminfo is a System V attempt to describe the characteristics of most dumb ASCII terminals, and the termcap subsystem is Berkeley's attempt at the same sort of thing. When you are using dumb ASCII terminals, these still come into play. However, with the advent of bitmap high-resolution terminals, windowing systems are the primary interface to the UNIX operating environment. What the termcap and terminfo subsystems will still control are some of the behaviors of the terminals windows within the windowed environment.

Also, many of the more classic tools in UNIX examine the terminal and its characteristics and modify their behavior accordingly. The other attribute that is important is the variable TERM. Many UNIX tools examine this variable to determine which list of terminal characteristics in the terminfo or termcap databases they should access to control how they display on the screen and interact with the keyboard. This variable must be set and exported to all child processes for the terminal to work correctly.

To see your default terminal, type:

```
$ tty
```

This shows the default terminal device for your current interactive session. You will notice that terminals typically reside in the /dev directory and are most often named tty something. Since UNIX treats a device as just another bit stream file, you can treat this terminal as you would a file and use redirection to allow for interactive viewing and logging. This is a common technique used by UNIX users for debugging code once they become more accustomed to the tty interface subsystem.

2.5 Input and Output

In UNIX, all data is bitstream data and as such all devices and files are treated the same way. There are no special layers in between calls and accesses to data from a program or command as in other operating systems. This leads to maximum flexibility in application generation and portability.

In UNIX, input and output are referred to as standard input and standard output (or stdin and stdout). These are generic terms used to denote generic input and output data streams. Because of stdin and stdout, applications neither know or care where their input and output are going but instead simply issue calls to stdin and stdout and let the operating system handle the rest. By using simple redirection from the shell or redefining stdin and stdout from within a program, you can redirect the input to and output from an application to or from any device including networks, disk files, terminals, tape drives, and any other device that you might wish to attach to a UNIX computer.

Most often the terminal is stdin and stdout as shown in Fig. 2.2. However, stdin and stdout can be redirected and controlled with redirect symbols < and >, which allow you redirect input and output to any other bitstream file. For example, to list a directory to the screen, you would issue the command:

```
$ ls
```

To list a directory to a file, you would simply redirect stdout. For example:

```
$ ls > /tmp/output.dir
```

This creates a file called /tmp/output.dir which contains the same information that was printed to the screen in the previous command.

An example of stdin redirection is:

```
$ cat < /tmp/output.dir
```

This will print the results of the previous ls command to the terminal screen.

Figure 2.2 stdin and stdout.

You can use redirection to append with the >> symbol. This allows you to append information to the end of a file. For example:

```
$ date >> /tmp/output.dir
```

will append the current date to the end of the /tmp/output.dir file.

The final power tool related to I/O is the pipe. A pipe allows you to connect UNIX tools together into a chain that accomplishes an ultimately desired task. Because of the philosophy of UNIX, there are many small tools that do one thing very well. Often, to accomplish a task, you will want to take the output of one command and input (or pipe) it to the next. For example:

```
$ ls -l | grep ^d
```

will print out all directories within your current working directory. The output of the ls -l command is simply piped directly into the grep ^d command.

The power of stdin and stdout is one of the primary features of UNIX that make it so powerful. With the existence of many small powerful tools and the ability to redirect input and output at any time, there is almost no limit to what you can do with UNIX. As you examine the tools contained in this book, you will see that many of them are simply aggregations of tools that come with UNIX but need to be used together in some way to achieve a desired result. This will open up the possibility that you can do the same sorts of things to accomplish your tasks more quickly and efficiently. This is really the primary power of UNIX and is what makes it almost the universal choice of software developers.

2.6 Filesystems and Files

Much of our previous discussion has centered around bitstream files. Everything in UNIX is simply a stream of bits. This allows applications and tools to treat all different kinds of files and devices in the same manner. This is one of the fundamental advantages of the UNIX system.

UNIX consists of a hierarchical filesystem much like DOS (see Fig. 2.3). This provides the maximum flexibility and leads to several tools and utilities, such as Network File Systems (NFS), which would not be possible without this capability.

UNIX file naming conventions vary by release of the operating system but most allow 255-character filenames which can consist of all alphabetic characters(a–z, A–Z, 0–9) as well as the period (.), underscore (_), and comma (,). In UNIX, it is common to name a file without an extension. For example, the external commands such as sh and csh are simply files named /bin/sh and /bin/csh. Extensions are merely used to provide more information and have no bearing on file behaviors or characteristics. There are hidden files which are denoted by a period as the first character of the filename. They are called hidden since when you issue an ls command, you will not see them unless you issue the -a option on the ls command. For example:

```
$ ls
file1
file2
$ ls -a
.
..
.login
.cshrc
file1
file2
```

The .login and .cshrc are special hidden files which are yours to use and control just as you would any other file; however, they are hidden from other users unless they issue the -a option on the ls command. The . and .. files listed above are special files. The . file denotes the current directory and allows you to ensure execution of a file or com-

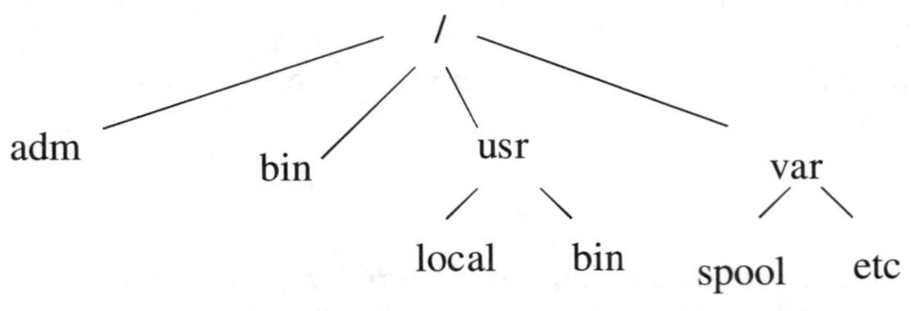

Figure 2.3 UNIX' hierarchical file system.

mand in the current directory by preceding the filename with a ./. For example:

```
./file1
```

will ensure that you reference the file1 file in your current directory and not another file1 in your path. The .. file denotes the directory above the current one. This allows you to access a file that resides in a directory a level above your current working directory. For example, to execute a file in a directory above your current working directory, issue the command:

```
$ ../file1
```

which will execute the file file1 in the directory above your current one.

Your path describes the directories and associated order of directories the shell will look in for executables. To examine your path, type the command:

```
$ echo $PATH
/bin:/usr/bin:/home/devtech/kevin
```

since your path is maintained by a variable called PATH. The above output denotes that when you issue a command, the directories /, /bin, /usr/bin, and /home/devtech/kevin will be searched in that order to find a file to execute. To change your path, you must use a syntax specific to each shell.

For the Bourne and Korn shells use:

```
$ PATH = /bin:/usr/bin:/home/devtech/kevin:/usr/devtech/kevin
$ export PATH
```

This adds the directory /usr/devtec/kevin to the end of the search path. The export command is necessary in the Bourne shell to export this PATH variable to all current and future child processes.

For the C shell, use:

```
$ setenv PATH /bin /usr/bin /home/devtech/keivn /usr/devtec/kevin
```

Note that the export command is unnecessary because "environmental" variables from the C shell are automatically propagated to child processes.

There are really three kinds of files in the UNIX environment. There are standard files which contain both binary and ASCII information and are the ones typically used and created by users of a UNIX system. The two other kinds of files typically relate to I/O devices such as disks and terminals. These are called device files and are typically placed in the /dev directory. They consist of two kinds of devices: block and character. This characteristic controls access to the files and devices. Block device files are primarily accessed as a block of data at a time, while a character device file is accessed a character at a time. Disks are typically block devices while terminals and printers are typically character devices, and their associated files therefore have the same characteristics.

To see what type of file or files you are working with, issue the command:

```
$ ls -l
-rw-r—r— 1 kevin author 1000 Jan 29 08:00 file1
drw-rx-r— 3 kevin author 512 Jan 28 12:00 dir1
crwxrwxrwx 1 root sys 1024 Jan 10 08:34 tty1
```

The first character is either -, d, b, or c to denote a standard file, a directory, a block file, or a character file. This becomes important when applications and tools utilize these files in a particular way.

The next pieces of information relate to file protections. The first three characters relate to file owner's permissions, the next three describe the group's permissions, and the last three describe the world's permission on the file. An r denotes read permission, a w denotes write, a - denotes that particular permission is not set, and an x denotes execute. Read and write permissions are obvious. The execute permission allows files to be executed by simply typing the name of the executable just as you do with external UNIX commands. Execute permission on a directory allows you to see the contents of the directory without specific read and write permissions if you list the contents of the directory explicitly. This means that if you know the exact name of the file or directory and it has the x privilege on it, you will be able to execute or view the contents of a directory even if you don't have read or execute permission on the directory above. This is a potential security problem, so be careful with the x privilege on a directory.

There are several other types of files known as the symbolic link, the named pipe, and the socket which are also related to files and filesystems. Each is discussed below.

The symbolic link is simply a pointer to a file. It allows you to create a placeholder file which points to the contents of another file. For example, let's assume you have a file named unix.txt which contained the following text:

```
UNIX is great, I just love it.
```

If you issued the following command:

```
$ ln -s unix.txt newunix.txt
```

and you now issued the ls command, you would see both files (unix.txt and newunix.txt) in the directory. If you list out both files, you will note that they are exactly the same; newunix.txt is in fact pointing to the same information on the disk as unix.txt. Issue the command:

```
$ ls -l
-rwxrw-rw- 2 kevin author 24 Jan 29 01:00 unix.txt
lrwxrw-rw- 3 kevin author 24 Jan 29 01:05 newunix.txt
```

The l denotes a symbolic link. Note that you must be careful using a symbolic link because if you remove the file unix.txt before newunix.txt, the newunix.txt file will point to nonexistent data on the disk, and you will get an error; newunix.txt is *not* a copy of unix.txt but instead simply points to the contents of unix.txt. Keep this in mind when you use symbolic links or see tools that use them.

Named pipes are typically used for interprocess communications and are denoted with a p in the first column of the ls -l command output. This is a System V construct which is used to provide a communication process between two unrelated processes and essentially functions as a queue. Named pipes are used less and less often and have been replaced by a concept known as a Transport Level Interface (TLI), which provides enhanced functionality.

A socket is a Berkeley construct which provides the ability to communicate between processes. This is often seen as a competitor to the named pipe from AT&T described above. The socket is denoted with an s in the first character of the ls -l command output. This has become the de facto standard for both interprocess and internode communications. Most UNIX tools and utilities use sockets to communicate with other processes on other machine on a network.

2.6.1 Network filesystems

Filesystems are groups of files contained within a physical or logical partition on a disk. They consist of an initial sector on a disk which maps all files contained within this filesystem into a place called the superblock. The superblock contains information about the filesystem, and there is exactly one superblock per filesystem. Until the last few years, a filesystem, much like a minidisk in VM, could not span more than one physical disk. With the advent of new tools such as the Logical Volume Manager (LVM) from IBM and equivalent tools from other UNIX vendors, you can now span multiple physical disks with a single filesystem. This is useful for performance and data integrity considerations.

The filesystem concept is roughly similar to the concept of a partition and associated filesystem on a DOS PC. By defining an area on one or more disks and creating a filesystem on this physical area (with the newfs command), you create a filesystem which is now accessible from the operating system.

Filesystems contain groups of files that are accessible as an entire unit by the UNIX kernel. Through the mount command, you can access all files in a filesystem based on where you mount the filesystem. This is, in fact, one of the tasks that UNIX performs when it boots. By reading a file containing "mount points," UNIX takes all filesystems and makes them available to all users of the system. This is essentially a mapping of physical partitions on the disk to a place called a mount point in the UNIX file hierarchy.

There is a file called /etc/fstab (/etc/filesystems on AIX) which contains all mount points for filesystems. An example is shown below:

```
/dev/sd0a / 4.2 rw 1 1
/dev/sd0g /usr 4.2 rw 1 2
/dev/fd0 /pcfs pcfs rw,noauto 0 0
devtech:/home/chicago /home/chicago nfs rw 0 0
devtech:/usr/local /usr/local nfs rw 0 0
devtech:/var/spool/mail /var/spool/mail nfs rw 0 0
devtech:/usr/share/man /usr/share/man nfs ro 0 0
istanbul:/usr/data1 /usr/data1 nfs rw 0 0
istanbul:/usr/data2 /usr/data2 nfs rw 0 0
istanbul:/usr/data3 /usr/data3 nfs rw 0 0
```

This is a line-by-line listing of which filesystems to mount. The first portion amounts to a physical partition or network filesystem to mount. The next contains a mount point which defines where to mount the filesystem in the current filesystem hierarchy. For example, the first line contains the line:

```
/dev/sd0a / 4.2 rw 1 1
```

/dev/sd0a defines an actual physical partition on a local disk to be mounted as the root (/) filesystem partition. It is to be mounted as a version 4.2 local filesystem in read/write (rw) mode. The last two numbers denote special characteristics having to do with dump frequency and fsck checking intervals. These parameters vary by both machine and filesystem type. See your local documentation for more details.

Some of the lines farther down in the example /etc/fstab file denote NFS filesystems. For example:

```
devtech:/home/chicago /home/chicago nfs rw 0 0
```

This denotes an NFS filesystem. The devtech:/home/chicago denotes a filesystem actually contained on a machine named devtech. The machine name is presented before the colon in the first column of the /etc/fstab file.

An NFS filesystem is a filesystem which is specifically created and exported from an NFS server machine for use by one or more machines on the network which support NFS. Keep in mind that it is a filesystem just like all other local filesystems, and the local machine, the one the NFS filesystem is mounted on, treats it just as if it were local. In fact, this capability is very reminiscent of the Novell disk-sharing mechanism. By creating a file server and exporting certain filesystems to the network, other client machines can access them, mount them, and treat them as if they were local to the machine itself. This is a very powerful concept and is often underutilized in most companies which have this capability. NFS is available on virtually every platform today, including mainframes, minis, and desktop machines. See your vendor for more information.

To see which partitions are mounted in your current working environment, issue the command:

```
$ df
```

which lists current mount points and their relation to physical disk partitions and capacities. This will list all filesystems, including local- and NFS-mounted filesystems. From this, you can learn what information is available to you on your local machine.

An example of df output might look something like:

```
Filesystem kbytes used avail capacity Mounted on
/dev/sd0a 23423 5943 15138 28% /
/dev/sd0g 297423 192314 15367 72% /usr
/dev/sd2g 904801 617625 196696 76% /usr/local
/dev/sd2e 56171 19 50535 0% /export
/dev/sd2h 551950 462589 34166 93% /usr/export/home
/dev/sd2a 37457 5444 28268 16% /var
swap 80516 24 80492 0% /tmp
istanbul:/usr/data1 368518 68566 263100 21% /usr/data1
istanbul:/usr/data2 149802 45399 89422 34% /usr/data2
istanbul:/usr/data3 149595 31924 102711 24% /usr/data3
amethyst:/export/usenet/spool/news
  192423 120986 52197 70% /var/spool/news
amethyst:/export/usenet/news
  192423 120986 52197 70% /usr/lib/news
amethyst:/export/usenet/newsbin
  192423 120986 52197 70% /usr/lib/newsbin
```

This denotes a machine with two local disks (SCSI id 0 and 2) and two machines acting as NFS file servers (istanbul and amethyst). You can learn a significant amount about your current working environment with the df command; it is the first command typed by many UNIX users to determine what information is available to them and how to get access to what they need.

By placing a physical disk partition at a mount point in the filesystem hierarchy, you can build an entire tree structure of files and filesystems starting with the root partition and filesystem known as /.

An NFS filesystem can exist anywhere within the filesystem hierarchy you would like. By creating a directory and issuing the mount command, you can mount any NFS filesystem from one machine to another. You can also mount a remote (network accessible) filesystem over the top of an existing directory or filesystem, so be careful. This may be something you want to experiment with.

Note that these filesystems are not accessible until they are mounted. Once mounted, they fit within the overall structure of the file structure transparently. The end user will notice no filesystems within the overall file structure as this is transparent by design.

Backup and restore procedures are also directly related to the filesystem structure on your disks. There are many tools which act on a particular filesystem, including dump, backup, and tar in addition to NFS.

Particularly relevant to this discussion is the CD-ROM included with this book. It contains a filesystem type called the High Sierra File System type, commonly known as HSFS. Most UNIX operating systems support this, and you must mount the CD filesystem just as you would mount any other filesystem. See Appendix A for more details.

Filesystems are important to the UNIX user since you may want to create your own filesystem to include all installed tools and utilities and then export it to other machines and users on your network. A typical structure for utilities and tools is to create a filesystem known as /usr/local. This is then typically mounted on /usr/local (see below) and often exported to other machines and users on the network with NFS.

```
$ ls /usr/local
X11R5
emacs
kermit
perl
```

This shows that directories for X11R5, GNU emacs, kermit, and perl were created on the filesystem /usr/local. These can now be exported and mounted on other systems for use; they can also be used as the local system.

There are several UNIX implementations that support commands that have both a System V version and a BSD version. To accomplish this, vendors often create a directory with a name like sysv. For example, on a Sun machine, you have a directory /usr/bin and a directory /usr/5bin. There are other systems which use a directory structure like

/usr/sysv or /usr/vsys for these systems. Keep in mind that your path is critical and determines which command is executed. There are a variety of commands which have subtle differences in them because of their different implementations on different flavors of UNIX. Two examples are lex and yacc. These are different in very subtle ways and, if you execute the wrong one, you will have unexpected and hard to solve problems. Keep this in mind, especially when you compile programs.

Finally, filesystems are changing in the UNIX environment. Until recently, filesystems had to reside on a single physical disk partition and could not dynamically change size. With the advent of new technologies such as the LVM from IBM and its adoption by other vendors as the standard, filesystems can now span multiple physical volumes and change size dynamically. This is a key enabling technology as you use power tools. When installing a tool or utility, if you need more space, you can simply increase the size of the filesystem to support your new needs instead of having to physically repartition the entire disk as was the case before.

2.7 Windowing Systems

Windowing systems are revolutionizing computing as we know it today. For years we have been using character-based terminals such as 3270 tubes for IBM mainframes or ASCII tubes such as DEC vt100 class terminals to interface with computers. This limited users to a single session and provided limited graphical capabilities. The new paradigm for interactive computing is windowing environments which provide graphical environments from which to use your computer. The most common example of this is Microsoft Windows, which is really nothing more than a windowing interface to a relatively simple operating system called DOS.

Instead of using a single terminal (or window) in your interactive session, windowing systems give you the ability to have multiple windows on the same screen and to have multiple sessions active at the same time. Windowing systems are one of the key ways in which an operating system like UNIX differentiates itself from something like Microsoft Windows.

While you can have multiple windows open in Windows, only one can be actively doing work at any time because of limitations in the underlying operating system. With windowing systems which come with UNIX and the underlying capabilities of UNIX itself, you can have multiple sessions active at the same time doing work while you focus on one particular session to accomplish a specific task. Windowing systems are the operating system access methods of the 1990s. After that, voice recognition systems and other more sophisticated computer interaction techniques will replace the windowed terminal. But for now, the UNIX X11 windowing workstation is the multitasking, multithreaded workstation of choice in many corporations.

The primary windowing system on UNIX platforms is X11. X11 began as a joint project between MIT, DEC, and others to provide a network-extensible windowing system that ran across many platforms using bitmapped displays. There are many windowing environments available today, including the clear desktop marketshare leader, Microsoft Windows. What differentiates X11 from technologies like Windows is network extensibility. With X11 you can display windows across the network and even share in the simultaneous display and control of windows on multiple machines.

The current standard which most vendors are shipping is their port of X11R4, which is X11 Release 4. X11R5 has been released from M.I.T. and is either ported or being ported by all major vendors for coming release. The primary advantages of X11R5 over X11R4 are authentication and security enhancements and scaleable fonts.

Above the core layer of technology known as X11, there is software known as the Graphical Use Interface (GUI). The GUI provides the "look and feel" of the windowing interface which the users see. There are two primary GUIs today: Motif and OpenLook. Motif is derived from Presentation Manager from IBM and is endorsed by the OSF. Vendors such as IBM, DEC, and HP use this GUI as their primary windowing interface. The competitor to Motif is OpenLook from Sun Microsystems. The only vendor of significance using OpenLook is Sun. While there are technical merits and advantages to each, this has largely degraded to a religious war which the user doesn't really care about. Most applications will run equally well on both, and if you need to get the competing GUI for a platform, you can buy it from a third-party vendor. It is significant only in that some tools will rely on one GUI or the other as their primary and will, therefore, expect that GUI to reside on the hardware platform you are running.

Many existing UNIX tools and those in this book are tuned for optimum performance when used with X11 and a particular GUI. See Chap. 8 for more details.

2.8 Where and How to Get Help

This is probably one of the most important sections of this book. Because of UNIX's heritage and marketplace, it is virtually impossible to present even a small portion of the information a user needs to be most productive in the UNIX environment. This book is focused on tools, utilities, and techniques which will enhance a user's productivity above and beyond what you can get from standard documentation and UNIX usage.

The primary utility for help with UNIX is the man (short for manual) system. There is no general help facility in UNIX that allows for general subject or title searches. However, there is a man subsystem which provides help on specific commands or system calls. UNIX documentation has traditionally been divided into eight sections broken down as follows:

Section 1	General User
Section 2	System Calls
Section 3	Subroutines
Section 4	File Formats
Section 5	Miscellaneous
Section 6	Games
Section 7	Special Files
Section 8	System Administration

To search for help on a particular command, issue the command:

```
$ man command
```

where command is the command you are interested in. For example, to see the manual page on the ls command, issue the command:

```
$ man ls
```

Several pages of text relating to the ls command will be written to your screen using the more command. At the bottom of the screen you will see the text (More 7%); you can hit the SPACE BAR to move forward a page and the RETURN key to move forward a line at a time.

Most manual pages are stored in the /usr/man subdirectories; however, you can install man pages in other areas and simply point to them with a command line option with the man command or with the environmental variable MANPATH.

Man uses the nroff utility and associated an macros to format the output for the selected output device. By choosing which output device you would like, man will format the text appropriately. For example, to get a rough listing of a manual page in a file, simply use redirection. For example:

```
$ man ls > /tmp/ls.man
```

will create a file called /tmp/ls.man, which contains the full manual page for the ls command. The manual input page format is a special format to be processed by the nroff utility and therefore cannot be simply listed. See Sec. 7.2 for more details on the input manual page format.

Some UNIX systems contain other tools which provide a more keyword-oriented help facility known as apropos. This searches a file called a permuted index. This is a keyword-sorted index against all UNIX commands. See your local system for the apropos command (use the command $ man apropos . . .).

There are other utilities which are graphically driven and often hypertext based which have been announced on UNIX platforms in the last year. Tools such as Answerbook from Sun Microsystems and InfoExplorer on AIX are just two of those available to assist you with subject searches and other more helpful methods for finding information.

2.9 Kernels

UNIX is written in C and is therefore relatively portable. This is one of the main reasons for UNIX's tremendous success. UNIX allows vendors to engineer new and exciting hardware and software more quickly by relying on a software platform that runs on virtually every hardware platform running today.

As was discussed in Chap. 1, UNIX is a layered environment consisting of tools and utilities which rely on an underlying core technology, known as a kernel, for services and access to the actual hardware on which the tools are running. Kernel architecture is a broad topic worthy of many textbooks and college graduate courses; however, there are a few basic things to remember when using power tools on UNIX that will be discussed here.

Many tools discussed here require significant amounts of processor power to function properly. The kernel is responsible for providing access and control of the hardware to these tools. Kernels can be tuned for particular behavior by adjusting certain parameters and recompiling the kernel itself. One of the remaining problems with UNIX is the relative static nature of the UNIX kernel. Most often, to change a characteristic such as number of users or to process table space, etc., you have to change a file somewhere and recompile the kernel, replacing the old executable, which was the kernel.

Issues such as dynamic loading of device drivers may or may not be relevant to utilities and tools you use. Most UNIX kernels now provide some dynamic capabilities for device drivers and kernel characteristics; however, you should check with your particular vendor before making any assumptions. Certainly HP, IBM, and Sun are providing these capabilities, while many of the smaller UNIX vendors are not.

The other technology directly affecting this aspect of UNIX is the microkernel movement described earlier in this chapter. While most vendors are moving toward a microkernel approach, UNIX vendors, in particular, are well prepared to move into this arena. By providing small, very focused operating system kernels, vendors will be able to provide more software and interfaces at a lower cost, thus enabling more software and hardware to be developed for the UNIX architecture. Microkernel technology is the key to the long-term success of UNIX and will be adopted by most vendors in the next 12 to 18 months.

By changing the configuration of the kernel, you change its size and therefore how much room it takes up in physical memory. Keep this in mind since it is always to your advantage to keep the kernel as small as possible to maximize its performance.

2.10 Tape Devices

Tape devices consist of a variety of supported devices in UNIX from the standard Quarter Inch Cartridge (QIC) that came with most UNIX computers to the new 8- and 4-mm Digital Audio Tape (DAT) tape devices more commonly used today. The interesting thing about tape drives is that, to UNIX, they look like any other device or file. This gives you the ability to use them just as you would use a disk file or terminal. By redirecting from stdin or stdout, you can use a tape device transparently with any program or script that you currently have.

All devices an in particular, tape devices are located in the /dev directory. They typically begin with st (scsi tape) or mt (magnetic tape) at the beginning of the filename. For example:

```
/dev/mt0
```

designates a tape drive at SCSI address 0. Often a tape device will have an r at the beginning, which designates a raw device. For example:

```
/dev/rmt0
```

designates the character-based device, which ensures that there is no blocking to the device occurring by the operating system. You generally use the raw interface to the device to minimize any changes from other files or devices you might use in UNIX.

There are basic characteristics of tape devices which include rewind on close and filemark sizes. These can often be controlled through the device chosen. For example, in AIX, you choose a device which rewinds at the end of an operation by appending a .1 or .5 to the end of the device name. For example, to issue a tar command and not rewind the tape at the end of the tar command, you might issue a command like:

```
$ tar cvf /dev/rmt0.1 /tmp
```

This will create a tar file and leave the tape positioned at the end of the tar file when the tar command is complete. This is *not* the default behavior of the tape device. If you choose the command:

```
$ tar cvf /dev/rmt0 /tmp
```

the tape will rewind when the tar command is finished. Therefore, if you issued a subsequent command to write to the tape, you would overwrite the results of the previous tar command. By choosing the appropriate device, you can control this. On some SVR4-based UNIX machines, you might use a command like:

```
$ tar cvf /dev/rmt0nr /tmp
```

where nr designates no rewind. There are other characteristics you can control through the choice of a device; see your local documentation for more details.

There are several commands, including tio and tape, which manipulate the tape device directly. However, the command most commonly used to monitor and control the tape device is the mt command. The syntax for this command is:

```
$ mt [-f device] command [count]
```

where -f device denotes which device you want to query and control. command comes from the following list:

`bsf`	Backspace counts number of files
`bsr`	Backspace counts number of records
`eof, weof`	Write end of filemarks equal to count
`fsf`	Spaces forward count number of files
`fsr`	Spaces forward count number of records
`rewind`	Rewinds tape to beginning
`status`	Prints current status of device

To rewind a tape to the beginning, issue the command:

```
$ mt -f /dev/rmt0 rewind
```

To skip forward to the fourth file use the command:

```
$ mt -f /dev/rmt0.1 fsf 3
```

Note that the device /dev/rm0.1 contains an additional suffix (.1) which describes the characteristics of the device behavior. In this case, it tells

AIX not to rewind the tape at the end of the tar operation. This only makes sense given that you are forward spacing the tape three files. If you chose the command:

```
$ mt -f /dev/rmt0 fsf 3
```

the tape driver would forward space the tape three files and then rewind the tape because the mt command was completed. Understanding the function of the proper choice of device files is critical to your successful use of tape devices in UNIX.

Always remember that tape devices are serial devices and must be manipulated from beginning to end through the use of commands like mt and tar as well as through the choice of the proper tape device. See the man pages on devices or tapes or mt for more information.

mt and other related commands are the most powerful ones related to tape devices, and once you understand them, they will save you hours of trouble and misunderstanding.

Part

2

Native UNIX Power Tools

While many books exist on UNIX and some of the tools and commands that exist within the UNIX environment, none really provides the correct set of tools for the power developer. Part 2 is an overview of some of the more powerful tools available in the UNIX environment which can help you immediately become more productive and efficient. With these tools and some of the ones mentioned in Part 3, there is very little you will need to do in a computer environment that you can't do in the UNIX environment.

Chapter

3

Native Editors

Editors are a fundamental part of any operating environment, and this is certainly no different in UNIX. There are two primary editors that come with UNIX: ed and vi—ed is the standard line mode editor that exists whenever UNIX is booted, and vi (short for visual editor) is the full-screen editor which supports commands from an editor called ex as well as a set of its own. Both of these editors will be discussed in this chapter.

It should be noted that both ed and vi are editors and not documentation or publishing systems. They will not provide sophisticated typesetting or font manipulation or support the integration of any non-ASCII text information. There are other tools such as troff, FrameMaker, TeX, and Interleaf which support these activities.

3.1 The ed Editor

3.1.1 Overview

ed is a line mode editor which creates a buffer and works exclusively on that buffer until changes are explicitly committed to a disk file. It is typically used when you only boot parts of UNIX for system administration purposes or when you have a dumb device that does not support full-screen mode. Since this is becoming infrequent, the discussion of ed will be brief.

3.1.2 Using ed

To invoke ed, issue the command:

```
$ ed [-p] [-s] [-] filename
```

where -p [string] sets the editor prompt to string, default is null.
-s is same as - switch.
- suppresses character counts and diagnostic messages.
filename is the name of the file you would like to edit.

ed works on the concept of a current line. The current line is the line which receives the default actions of all commands given within the editor. Typically, the editor commands work with addresses followed by a single-character subcommand. The addresses determine the lines to receive the command. If you don't use an address, the current line will be the default. In ed, the current line is known as ., and the last line is known as $.

When you enter ed, the current line is the last line of the file. You also receive status information which contains the number of characters in the file and the filename if the file is new.

3.1.3 Modes

ed has two modes: command and text input. Command mode is the default mode and the one you are in when you enter ed. Command mode recognizes and executes commands. Text input mode is used for inputting text but does not recognize commands. You enter text input mode by entering a c, a, or i and leave by entering a period (.) at the beginning of a line.

All UNIX editors and shells are driven by a technique known as a regular expression. A regular expression consists of both an operator and a context which controls the range of the operation. This is what allows for string substitution and manipulation. See the full discussion in Chap. 2; however, a brief discussion with examples is given below.

3.1.4 Regular expressions

ed, like many other UNIX tools, uses regular expressions to construct strings. Regular expressions form the foundation for all expressions and syntax in UNIX. ed is a tool which takes great advantage of regular expressions in its syntax. While ed is not widely used, the syntax demonstrated in the examples in this section is demonstrative of many similar tools, including sed and vi. Because of their widespread use, pay particular attention to the examples given below.

3.1.5 Subcommands

ed subcommands control the behavior of your ed editor. The most common commands are:

.=	Reports current line in the file.
$=	Reports last line number in the file.
NEWLINE	Moves the current line one forward.
-	Moves the current line one backward.
linenumber	Makes linenumber the current line.
/string	Searches forward from the current line for the first appearance of string and wrap.
?string	Searches backward from the current line for the first appearance of string and wrap.
/	Repeats the previous /string command.
?	Repeats the previous ? command.
!	Shell escape; you can issue any shell command following the ! (even sh, ksh, or csh).
H	Turns on verbose help mode.
P	Turns command mode prompt (*) on.
Q	Quits editor, ignoring changes to buffer.
a	Begins input mode following a line.
d	Deletes a line.
e [filename]	Edits a new file.
f [filename]	Changes the current default filename; useful with w and r commands.
i	Begins input mode preceding a line.
j	Joins contiguous lines.
k[x]	Marks line with alphanumeric character. You can later address this with 'x in an address range.
m	Moves line from one place to another.
p	Prints out a line.
r file	Reads in a new file after the current line.
q	Quits file checking for changes before exiting.
s/oldstring/newstring	Replaces oldstring with newstring.
u	Undoes the last command.
w [file]	Writes out changes to file.

Most commands in ed support the use of line numbers and other regular expressions before the command. This allows the above commands to work on lines other than the current line. For example, the following prints out lines 1 through 6:

```
: 1,6p
```

Using the . and $ notation, you can print out the entire file using:

```
:.,$p
```

You can also perform simple arithmetic on addresses. For example, the following prints out the line three back from the current line:

```
:.-3p
```

To begin inserting text after line 2, type:

```
:2a
```

To return to command mode, enter a . by itself in column 1.

String substitution is the most common use for ed. The s command can be used with line addresses and regular expressions to achieve almost any goal. For example,

```
:1,4s/oldstring/newstring
```

will replace oldstring with newstring for only lines 1 through 4. To delete a string, use:

```
:s/string//
```

To add a string to the beginning of a line, use:

```
:s/^/beginning stuff/
```

To add a string to the end of a line, use:

```
:s/$/ending stuff/
```

Note also that the / at the end of the string is optional; however, if you use it, you will normally get the changed line printed out, while if you don't, your changes will go unprinted.

The above substitution commands either explicitly use line ranges or operate only on the current line. Remember that all subcommands in ed operate on the current line and therefore must be prefaced with line ranges to operate on more than one line. For example, to change a string on all lines in a file, use:

```
:1,$s/oldstring/newstring
```

This will change one occurrence on each line in the file for all lines in the file. If you have more than one occurrence of oldstring on the same line in the file, only the first will be changed. To change multiple occurrences of oldstring to newstring on the same line, you must add the global switch to the end of the command. For example:

```
:1,$s/oldstring/newstring/g
```

will replace all occurrences of oldstring with newstring in the file.

To join contiguous lines, use the j command. For example, to join lines 3 and 4, use:

```
:3,4j
```

To include multiple files in one work buffer, you need to use the r command. To read in a new file after the current line, use:

```
:r new.file
```

new.file is now included in the line immediately after the current line. You can use a line number preceding the r subcommand to insert text at that point. To read in a file at the beginning of the work buffer, use:

```
:0r file.text
```

While ed is not often used, many of the commands as well as the structure of the command syntax is similar to many other tools, including vi. As you will see in the next section, you can enter the command mode in vi and use the commands described above to accomplish tasks that may be more convenient to perform in line mode.

3.2 The vi Editor

vi is the full-screen editor that ships with most versions of UNIX. While ed is the editor you use for line mode editing, vi is the editor you would use when you have full-screen capabilities. vi uses commands from another line editor known as ex. While ex is very standard on UNIX platforms, it is rarely used and will therefore not be discussed. However, all of the vi commands are ex commands, and you should investigate the ex editor further if you are interested in it.

vi reads a file into a temporary work buffer. All modifications are made in memory and are not saved until explicitly saved with the appropriate command. Keep this in mind when you are editing a file. This is particularly important because the UNIX filesystem does not version files, and when you save the buffer, it replaces the original file unless explicitly told to do otherwise.

3.2.1 Full-screen editors

Full-screen editors provide a sliding window into your file. They enable you to move around within the file and see the movements and changes reflected in the file. Editors rely on terminal definitions and characteristics to control their behavior. There are two things to check before proceeding with the use of a full-screen editor.

1. The TERM environment variable
2. The stty characteristics

The TERM variable needs to be set to a value which reflects the characteristics of your terminal. For example, many terminals emulate a vt100, and therefore the TERM variable should be set to vt100. For example, for the Bourne and Korn shells, use:

```
$ TERM=vt100;export TERM
```

For the C shell, use

```
% setenv TERM vt100
```

If you have a terminal type that is unknown, you will get default line mode and the following status message:

```
type: Unknown terminal type
I don't know what kind of terminal you are on - all I have is 'type'
[Using open mode]
"filename" [New file]
```

The cursor is placed below the filename line in line mode. From here you can issue line-oriented commands only. This is because the operating system doesn't know what type of terminal you are on and therefore chooses a default line mode terminal which doesn't support full-screen capabilities. To remedy this, type :q! to exit vi and use the following commands to set your terminal type for the Bourne shell, use:

```
$ set TERM=vt100;export TERM
```

For the Korn shell, use:

```
$ export TERM=vt100
```

And for the C Shell, use:

```
% setenv TERM vt100
```

This will set your terminal type to vt100, which is a widely used default. If you know your terminal type, try setting the TERM variable to it and see what happens. If you get the same set of messages as those described above, try a different value for the TERM variable.

Once you have set your TERM variable appropriately, reissue the vi command and begin editing as you normally would have.

There are many other terminal definitions described in the termcap and terminfo databases. Sometimes there is not a terminal definition which exactly matches your terminal. When this occurs you have two options:

1. Use a generic terminal definition or one which most closely matches your terminal
2. Define your own.

The other generic TERM setting which may work is ansi. This is a generic terminal definition which is included in most UNIX implementation and supports most full-screen operations used by vi. See your documentations on termcap and terminfo to determine which terminal characteristics are right for your device.

The stty characteristics can be viewed using:

```
$ stty
```

This will display many of the characteristics of your terminal and your terminal session. Issues such as terminal interrupt and escape sequences can be controlled from here. For more information, see the stty man pages. Below is an example of a reasonable stty definition:

```
$ stty
speed 2400 baud; evenp hupcl
brkint -inpck -istrip icrnl -ixany ixoff onlcr tab3
echo echoe echok
```

This is a dial-up terminal definition at 2400 baud. There are many values associated with the terminal line which can be modified or removed depending on your needs. See the man page on stty for more information.

Settings such as erase affect the behavior of your terminal and should be set carefully to reflect the type of terminal you are using. A generic command which will normally establish settings and will work on a terminal is:

```
$ stty sane
```

This sets default characteristics which will provide reasonable terminal characteristics for most terminals.

3.2.2 Entering the vi editor

To invoke the vi editor, issue the command:

```
vi [-c command] [-lLRv] [-r file] [-t tag] [+command] [file...]
```

where -c command executes an ex command before editing begins.
-l enters vi in LISP mode.
-L lists files saved in system or editor crash.
-R sets read-only option.
-v sets verbose mode.
-r file recovers file from editor crash.
-t tag edits the file containing the tag created with the ctag command.
+command executes an ex command before editing begins.
file consists of one or more files to be edited sequentially.

Note that not all options are supported on all UNIX machines, but most machines support the options listed above. There are other options which perform different functions. See your system documentation for more information.

When you invoke the vi editor, it looks for the environmental variable EXINIT. If this exists and points to a currently existing file, the vi editor reads this and performs the commands listed in the file before editing begins. If the EXINIT environmental variable does not exist, vi checks for the existence of a .exrc file in your home directory. If this exists, it again reads and executes commands in this file before beginning editing. This .exrc file is the initialization file for vi and allows you to set characteristics and behaviors of your editing environment before you begin your editing session.

3.2.3 Basic operation of the vi editor

vi begins with the cursor on the first line, unlike ed which begins on the last. You can use commands like the +command to position yourself at places other than the first line. For example:

```
$ vi +10 test
```

will invoke the file test and position the cursor at line 10. When you invoke vi, it fills all lines on the screen except the bottom with text from the file. The bottom line is the command line and will be used to execute commands not available from the screen. If your file does not fill the screen, empty lines will be represented with a tilde (~) in column 1. For example:

```
$ vi test
[new screen]
This is the file test
It contains information used to write Kevin's book.
~
~
~
~
~
~
"test" 2 lines, 74 characters
```

The tildes will fill your screen and represent unused lines.

3.2.4 vi modes of operation

vi has three modes of operation: text input, command line input, and last line mode. Command mode allows you to issue and execute commands anywhere on the screen and is controlled by cursor position. Text input mode allows you to enter text and is entered with the commands described in the "Input Mode Commands" section below. Last line mode allows you to execute file- and shell-level commands. These are documented in the "Last Line Mode Commands" section below. The first two modes are similar to those described in the ed section but use ex commands instead.

The ESC key switches you back to command mode. You will often see UNIX programmers hit the ESC key several times to make sure they are back in command mode. It doesn't hurt to press the ESC key multiple times to ensure that you are back where you want to be. It shouldn't be necessary; however, it can't hurt, so do it if you like.

The basic vi commands, broken down by mode, are as follows:

Input mode commands

i	Inserts text before cursor
I	Enters text at start of line
a	Inserts text after cursor
A	Enters text at end of line
o	Opens line below
O	Opens line above

Delete

dw	Deletes word
dd	Deletes line

D	Deletes to end of line
x	Deletes character under cursor

Change text

cw	Changes word
cc	Changes line
C	Changes to end of line
r	Replaces single character under cursor
J	Joins lines

Move cursor

e	Moves to end of word
w	Moves to next word
$	Moves to end of line
l	Moves one space right
k	Moves one line up
j	Moves one line down
h	Moves one space left
fx	Moves cursor to first occurrence of x
Fx	Moves cursor to last x character
;	Repeats the last f or F command
Number |	Moves cursor to column Number
H	Moves cursor to top line on screen
L	Moves cursor to bottom line on screen
M	Moves cursor to middle line on screen
^	Moves to beginning of line

Marking locations

mx	Marks current position with letter x
`x	Moves cursor to mark x
‘x	Moves cursor to beginning of line containing mark x

Screen control

CTRL-d	Scrolls forward one-half screen
CTRL-u	Scrolls backward one-half screen
CRTL-f	Scrolls forward one screen
CRTL-b	Scrolls backward one screen
CRTL-l	Refreshes screen
z	Redraws screen with current line at top

z-	Redraws screen with current line at bottom
[number]G	Places cursor at line number or at bottom if no number specified

Moving text

yy	Yanks line into buffer
p	Puts yanked lines below cursor position
P	Puts yanked lines above cursor position
"x[number]yy	Yanks number of lines into named buffer represented by x. Note that x can be any character a–z; number represents the number of lines to yank
"xp	Puts the yank buffer x after the cursor line
"x[number]dd	Deletes number of lines and yanks them into buffer x. Again x can be any character a–z
"X[number]yy	Same as "x[number]yy except when you use a capital letter for the named buffer, it appends the results of the command to the lowercase named buffer. This works the same for the dd command and any other vi command that follows the yank commands.

Last line mode

:w [file]	Writes current buffer as file
:q	Quits file
:q!	Quits file without saving changes
:wq	Writes changes to file and quits
:r [file]	Reads in file
:e [file]	Edits file
:!command	Executes command in the shell
:n	Moves to line n
:f	Prints out current line and filename

Getting information

CRTL-G	Shows size of file, current filename, and current line

Other functions

u	Undoes last command
/string	Searches forward for string
?string	Searches backward for string
n	Finds next string
.	Repeats last command
ESC	Moves from text input mode to command mode

CRTL-V	Inserts any character including a special character
~	Changes character to opposite case
ZZ	Saves file and exits

All of the above commands work relative to the current line, which is defined by the position of the cursor. In vi, you can work relative to positions other than the current line by preceding the command with a number. In fact the general syntax for a vi command is:

```
[named_buffer][operator][number]command
```

where buffer specifies the name of a buffer which is a temporary storage area.
operator specifies a vi command.
number is a number which represents lines relative to cursor position.
command is vi command to be executed.

For example, to delete five lines, you would execute the command:

```
5dd
```

Or to yank 10 lines into a temporary buffer, you would execute the command:

```
10yy
```

Finally, you can scroll down 10 lines by issuing the command:

```
10CRTL-d
```

More will be said about named buffers in Sec. 3.2.8. Suffice it to say that you can modify vi commands in an almost infinite number of ways to achieve the desired result by simply preceding the vi command with a number, operator, or buffer number.

3.2.5 Creating a new file

To create a new file with the name test, type:

```
$ vi test
```

This will place you in a full-screen mode where you can issue commands from the command line or use full-screen commands to insert and modify text. You are in command mode by default. To begin inserting text, type the i command. You can now begin entering text. When you are finished entering text, you must type ESCAPE. This will take you back to command mode and out of text input mode. For example:

```
i
This is the file test
ESCAPE
```

At this point you can issue any command to modify or insert text. To insert a line following the first line, type an o. This will create a blank line following the first line and position the cursor where you can begin typing:

```
o
This is the file test.
This is the second line in test.
ESCAPE
```

Note that you again use ESCAPE to exit the text input mode and reenter the command mode. You can now enter the last line mode by entering a :, !, or / command. In this case we will save the file and exit with a last line mode command:

```
This is the file test.
This is the second line in test.
:
```

When you press the :, you enter last line mode and a : appears in column 1 at the bottom of the screen. At this point you can type any of the commands listed in the last line mode section above. To save the file and quit, type wq. You are now back at the command prompt. Note that you could also have pressed ZZ (press and hold the SHIFT key and hit the Z key twice) while in command mode and accomplished the same thing. This is often the choice of more experienced vi users.

3.2.6 Editing an existing file

When you want to edit an existing file, you simply invoke vi with the filename, make your modifications, and save as before. To make modifications, you need to use the commands listed above in the "Move Cursor" section. Note that all single-position cursor move commands are located next to each other on the keyboard. This makes it relatively simple to move the cursor around on your screen with one hand. There are many other commands to move within a file; see the section above for more information.

You can use all the commands listed above to do things from changing words to deleting lines and words. You can also mark lines with the m command and find them later with the ' command. This is a nice feature since it allows you to quickly find a location in a file that you have marked for later use.

The yank feature allows you to use a temporary unnamed buffer to store and move lines of information. For example, take the following file:

```
this is line 1
this is line 2
this is line 3
```

If you want to move line 1 and place it after line 3, you would use the yy command as follows. Place the cursor on line 1 and type yy. This yanks the line into a temporary storage buffer. Move the cursor to line 3 and issue a p command. This places the contents of the temporary buffer after line 3. The file now looks like:

```
this is line 1
this is line 2
this is line 3
this is line 1
```

To yank multiple lines, simply precede the yy command with the number of lines you would like to yank. For example, to take the changed file above and move the first two lines to the bottom, place the cursor on line 1 and issue the command 2yy. This yanks two lines into the temporary buffer. Move the cursor to the bottom line with a G command and issue a p command. This places the contents of the buffer at the bottom of the file. The file now looks like this:

```
this is line 1
this is line 2
this is line 3
this is line 1
this is line 1
this is line 2
```

Note that each time you use the temporary buffer, all previous contents are replaced. To delete the two yanked lines, place the cursor on line 1 and issue the 2dd command. This will delete the first two lines. The final file looks like this:

```
this is line 3
this is line 1
this is line 1
this is line 2
```

Remember that in UNIX there are not multiple file versions, and when you save a file, you replace the contents of the previous file. If you edit a file and decide to save this as a new file, use the :w last line mode command. For example, to save the edited file test as the file test1, use:

```
:wq test1
```

This will save your edited file as test1 and quit the vi editor.

3.2.7 Changing the location of the temporary work file

One of the most annoying things that can happen to you when you invoke an editor is to have insufficient temporary working storage to edit a large file. When you invoke vi, it makes a temporary copy of the entire file you are editing against, where it makes changes. This means that you effectively double the disk space required to edit the file. When the file is large, this can cause a disk space problem.

There are a number of ways you can work around this including using split to split the file into smaller chunks and piping this into the vi editor or increasing the disk space in the temporary storage area. The other way is to move the location of the temporary storage file to a location other than the default. The easiest way to do this is by setting an environmental variable:

```
$ EXINIT = 'set dir /tmp.'
$ export EXINIT
```

where /tmp represents one possible choice for a temporary directory. You can choose any directory in which you have write permission.

The EXINIT variable is checked when vi is invoked for any initialization parameters to use. The set dir command allows you to choose the directory for the temporary working file. By choosing a large filesystem, you can avoid having problems with file space. Note that the file is removed when you exit vi, so there is no long-term storage issue. You can also place this in the vi initialization file $HOME/.exrc as the command:

```
set dir /tmp
```

This will be read when vi is invoked and will be executed before the file to be edited is read. This accomplishes the same as the EXINIT method described above.

These techniques can help you avoid one of the most common problems when working in a large file environment. Keep this in mind as you move forward with UNIX.

3.2.8 Working with multiple files

Often you will want to combine files and information from files into one buffer before saving. There are many ways to work with multiple files, but the most common one is to read a second file into the buffer in which you are currently working. To insert a file after the current cursor location, simply issue the last line mode command :r file, and the file will be read in following the line the cursor is on. The buffer can then be manipulated as you normally would.

More often, when working with multiple files, you would like to move lines of information between files. You must use the named buffer approach to do this. Let's use the following two files:

```
This is line 1 of file1
This is line 2 of file1
This is line 3 of file1

This is line 1 of file2
This is line 2 of file2
This is line 3 of file2
```

Let's assume we are going to move the first two lines of file1 into file2. First edit file1:

```
$ vi file1
```

Position the cursor on the first line and issue the command d2yy. This yanks the first two lines into a named buffer d. Issue the command :e file2. This reads in file2 into the work buffer. Type the command "dp to place the contents of the d buffer before the cursor. Now file2 looks like this:

```
This is line 1 of file1
This is line 2 of file2
This is line 1 of file2
This is line 2 of file2
This is line 3 of file2
```

You can now save the contents of this buffer exactly as you normally would. This is one of the most powerful techniques in vi for moving information between files. The named buffer can be any alphanumeric character between a and z. If you use the uppercase character, it appends the output of the command to the named buffer represented by the lowercase equivalent.

3.2.9 Issuing commands outside the editor

If you want to issue commands outside the editor, you simply invoke the shell escape sequence !. For example, to issue a command to look at the files in the current directory, issue the last command line command:

```
:!ls
```

This forks a shell and issues the ls command to your screen. You can invoke a subshell by simply invoking a shell. For example, to invoke a C shell, type:

```
:!/bin/csh
^%
```

You are now running in a C shell. To exit the shell and return to your editing session, type exit.

3.2.10 Entering nonprintable characters

If you need to enter an escape sequence or control character into a file, insert the nonprintable characters in vi with the command:

```
C-v
```

This denotes holding down the CTRL key and pressing v, which gives you the ability to enter a nonprintable character at the current location. For example, to place an ESC character in a file, simply position the cursor to the proper location and press C-v ESC. This allows you to enter one nonprintable character. If you need to string two or more together, simply depress the C-v sequence for each character.

3.3 Conclusion

This chapter discussed the two most commonly used editors for UNIX. There are many editors available from vendors such as IBM and HP as well as editors which are available from the Internet. The most commonly used editor other than vi is emacs. This editor is discussed in Chap. 10.

There are many other things you can do in the vi and ed editors. See system documentation or other books for more information on both of these. This chapter was intended to give you enough information to create and modify files related to the other power tools discussed in this book.

Chapter

4

Native Software Development Tools

This section discusses tools available with most versions of UNIX in native fashion. The tools discussed in this chapter provide significant function related to software development and the use of Power Tools in the UNIX environment without requiring much development effort to use them. For tools that require more scripting capabilities and offer subsequently more power, see Chap. 5.

4.1 dbx

dbx is the interactive command line debugger that comes with most UNIX implementations. It is a symbolic debugger which allows you to:

- Examine object and core files
- Control the execution of an application
- Set breakpoints and trace program execution and variables
- Use symbolic variables and display them in their correct formats
- Manipulate variables in virtual memory
- Use several languages in the same executable and debug session
- many more things

Languages most often supported are C, Fortran, Pascal, and COBOL. dbx is the Berkeley equivalent to sdb from AT&T. Most UNIX systems today use dbx as their standard debugger; sdb is not available on most machines today.

4.1.1 Using dbx

To invoke, dbx use:

```
dbx [-a pid] [-c commandfile] [-d nesting] [-I dir] [-k] [-u] [-f]
[-r] [objectfile [corefile]]
```

where -a pid attaches the debug process to the process with process id of pid.
-c commandfiles are dbx commands executed before beginning debug session.
-d nesting sets limit for nesting of program blocks; default is 25.
-I dir is the directory to look for associated source files; default is the current directory and directory where the executable is located.
-k maps memory addresses; it is useful for kernel debugging.
-u causes dbx to prepend symbols with an @ to avoid possible conflicting symbol names.
-f starts dbx, reading only a minimum number of symbols to minimize start-up time and memory requirements (useful for large programs).
-r runs object file immediately; if program terminates successfully, dbx is exited.
objectfile specifies object file to debug.
corefile specifies core file to debug.

To use dbx, the programs must have been compiled with the -g option to generate symbol information which dbx uses.

When dbx starts, it checks for the existence of an initialization file .dbxinit in the current directory and the user's HOME directory. Any commands in the .dbxinit file are executed before the debugging session begins.

When you invoke dbx, you are placed in an interactive session from which you can issue commands and examine variables inside the program. For example, the following simple C program will be compiled and debugged:

```
$ cat test.c
main()
{
printf("this is a test of the debugger\n");
}

$ cc -g test.c
$ dbx a.out
Reading symbolic information..
Read 31 symbols
(dbx)
```

You are now at the dbx interactive prompt. From this point you can issue dbx commands and examine variables, change values, and run the program line by line. Note that a.out is the default object name from most UNIX compilers.

4.1.2 The dbx language

dbx commands are C-like in syntax and function. dbx works with expressions which consist of constants, operators, procedure calls, and variables. Some of the most important of these are:

Constants, which consist of constants declared within the program:

Character constants must be enclosed in single quotes.
Octal format must be preceded with a '0'.
Hex format must be preceded with a '0x'.

Operators. The standard operators in most languages are:

+ add
– subtract
* multiply
/ divide
div remainder
<< bitwise shift left
>> bitwise shift right
& bitwise AND
| bitwise OR
~ bitwise complement
& address and content of operator
< less than
> greater than
<= less than or equal to
>= greater than or equal to
== equal to
!= not equal to
&& logical AND
| | Logical OR
sizeof(cast) size of variable or case
. field reference

4.1.3 Scope

Scope is a concept which defines the availability of constants and variables within procedures. The scope of variables is defaulted to within the current file and function. Values of variables are updated as functions are entered and exited. You can apply a specific scope with the file and func commands within dbx. Source files are expected to have the same name as the function with the proper language extension (.f, .c, etc.) to make it available to the compiler.

4.1.4 Running dbx

The basic dbx commands are:

`/[regular expression]`	Searches forward in current source code for regular expression. Most often used to match strings (e.g., /string).
`?[regular expression]`	Searches backward in current source code. Opposite of /.
`alias [name ["command"]]`	Creates aliases for dbx commands to make shorthand notation for commonly used commands. Note that the .dbxinit file is ideal for these commands. alias alone prints out all aliases.
`assign var=expression`	Assigns the value expression to the variable var. expression can be a string, logical type, or constant. See the examples for more information.
`call proc [params]`	Executes the procedure specified by the proc and passes parameters. Note that this procedure can be any standard procedure supported by the language (e.g., printf in the C language).
`case [default | mixed | lower | upper]`	Changes how dbx interprets symbols. Default is language dependent.
`catch [signum | signame]`	Sets a catch for the signal SIGNUM or SIGNAME before it reaches the program. If no parameters are used, all signals are trapped except SIGHUP, SIGCLD, SIGALARM, and SIGKILL.
`clear [line]`	Clears all breakpoints or only one on line if chosen. See set for more details. Line can be either a line number (integer) or a filename followed by a colon.
`cont [signum | signame]`	Continues program from the current stopping point. If either signum or signame is included, the program continues as if it had been sent the appropriate signal contained in signum or signame.
`delete { number ... | all }`	Removes traces and stops from the current session. All traces and stops have an associated number which can be viewed with the status command and established with the trace and stop commands.
`detach [signum | signame]`	Continues execution but exits dbx. Useful if you have seen all you need in the debugger and simply want to finish the program.
`display [expr]`	Print on the screen the value of expression where expression is a regular expression.

`down [num]`	Moves the current functions down one level or num levels in the call stack. This is relevant for scope and name resolution.
`dump [proc] [>file]`	Prints all variables local to the current procedure or named procedure. You can redirect your output to a specified file.
`edit [proc | file]`	Invokes an editor on the specific procedure or file. You can set the variable EDITOR to choose an editor other than vi.
`file [file]`	Changes the current source file to another. Simply type file to display the current source file.
`func [proc]`	Changes the current procedure to another. Simply type func to see your current context.
`help [cmd]`	Prints listing of dbx commands or more detailed description of command cmd.
`ignore [signum | signame]`	Ignores signals signum or signame sent to the current program.
`list [proc | line,line]`	Lists source lines either in the current procedure if no parameters are used, from proc if a procedure name is specified, or from line1 to line2 if a line expression is used. The default is 10 lines starting at the current line in the current procedure. The $ represents the current line, and you can use regular expressions to designate lines.
`multproc [on | off]`	Enables multiprocess debugging. (Not available on all dbx implementations.)
`next [num]`	Executes one line or num lines jumping *over* function calls. Note that this means that a function call will be executed in its entirety and treated as a single line. See step for an alternative.
`print [expr]`	Prints the value of an expression. The expression can be any expression supported by the language used in the program.
`quit`	Exits dbx. Program execution is terminated.
`rerun [args]`	Begins execution again passing args as command line input parameters.
`return [proc]`	Continues execution until the procedure proc is reentered. If you don't specify a proc, you will execute until you leave the current procedure. (This is not available on all implementations of dbx.)
`run [args]`	Begins execution of the program, optionally passing args as command line arguments. The arguments should be entered exactly as they would be on the command line.
`set var=expression`	Same as assign.
`sh [command]`	Executes a shell specified by the SHELL environmental variable. You can specify a command to execute within this shell with the optional command parameter. If you use command, when the command is finished, you are placed back in dbx.
`skip [num]`	Resumes execution skipping 1 or num breakpoints before honoring a breakpoint. This is not supported on all versions of dbx.

`source [filename]`	Executes dbx commands from the filename file.
`status [>file]`	Prints trace and breakpoint information which can be optionally placed in a file.
`step [num]`	Steps through one line of execution *into* calls. This means that if the next line of execution is a function call, you will stop at the first executable line in the function as a result of a step command. This is the opposite of the next command.
`stop {var | [var] { at line | in proc}} [if condition]`	sets breakpoints where program execution is halted. Execution is halted when: var—the variable var changes. at line—the source line is reached. in proc—the procedure is called. if condition—the condition is reached. dbx associates a number with each breakpoint. Use status to see these associations. You can use the delete function to remove them.
`trace [line | expression at line | proc | [var] | [at line | in proc]] [if condition]`	Prints tracing information specified on the dbx command line: at line—specifies a source line which contains the expression to be traced. if condition—specifies a condition for the trace to begin. in proc—specifies the procedure which contains the procedure or variable to be traced. See the examples sections for details.
`unalias name`	Removes the alias for name.
`unset var`	Removes the value of var.
`up [num]`	Moves the current function up the program stack. Default is 1.
`use [dir1 dir2 ...]`	Specifies which directories to use for source files separated by spaces. Used by itself, it displays which directories are currently being searched.
`where [>file]`	Displays list of active procedures. Output can be redirected to a file.
`which [name]`	Displays the fully qualified identifier name.
`whereis [name]`	Displays the fully qualified symbol name.
`whatis [name]`	Displays the declaration of name; name can be a function, procedure, variable, or constant.

Most dbx commands will print out the current status of associated variables or parameters if executed without any parameters (e.g., alias, case). There are also machine-level instructions which allow for low-level debugging at the machine instruction level. See your machine's specific dbx documentation since this is machine and debugger specific in many cases.

The above list is not all inclusive for all implementations of dbx but does include the majority of commands in dbx. If you use these commands fully, you will realize most of the power of dbx.

4.1.5 Example

The example below documents many of the dbx commands described above. The program test consists of three separate files test.c, test1.c, and test2.c. All three files reside in the same directory /tmp/book. The content of test.c is as follows:

```
main() {
int a=5;
printf("This is test and a is %d\n",a);
test1();
test2(a);
}
```

test1.c contains:

```
test1() {
printf("This is test1\n");
}
```

And test2.c contains:

```
test2(a) {
printf("This is test2 and a is %d\n",a);
}
```

The example is:

```
** Now compile the files to create a single executable a.out. **

% cc -g test.c test1.c test2.c
test.c:
test1.c:
test2.c:
Linking:

% dbx a.out # now invoke the debugging session

Reading symbolic information...
Read 80 symbols
(dbx) help /* printout help for SunOS dbx */
Command Summary

Execution and Tracing
 catch clear cont delete ignore next rerun
 run status step stop trace when

Displaying and Naming Data
 assign call display down dump print set
 set81 undisplay up whatis where whereis which

Accessing Source Files
 cd edit file func list modules pwd
 use / ?

Miscellaneous
 alias dbxenv debug detach help kill make
 quit setenv sh source
```

```
Dbxtool
 button toolenv unbutton unmenu menu

Machine Level
 nexti stepi stopi tracei

The command 'help <cmdname>' provides additional
 help for each command

** Now help on a specific command. **

(dbx) help print
print <exp>, ... - Print the value of the expression(s) <exp>, ...
(dbx) print a
bad data address

** List status of all breakpoints, traces, etc. Note there are none
set yet. **

(dbx) status
(dbx) list /* list source code of current procedure */
2 int a=5;
3 printf("This is test and a is %d\n",a);
4 test1();
5 test2(a);
6 }
(dbx) step /* execute the first executable command but can't because
I have invoked dbx yet */ can't continue execution

** Note that you must issue the run command before you can invoke
any dbx execution commands since the run command begins the execu-
tion of the program. What you typically do is set a breakpoint at
the first executable statement with the stop command and then type
run. **

(dbx) stop at 3
(dbx) run
Running: a.out
stop at 3
stopped in main at line 3 in file "test.c"
(dbx) list
3 printf("This is test and a is %d\n",a);
4 test1();
5 test2(a);
6 }
(dbx) status
(2) stop at "/tmp/book/test.c":3
(dbx) step
This is test and a is 5
stopped in main at line 4 in file "test.c"
4 test1();
(dbx) stop in test1

** Now set a breakpoint to stop at first executable line inside
test1 **

(4) stop in test1
(dbx) step /* step into test1, note next would have stepped over
  test1 */
stopped in test1 at line 2 in file "test1.c"
(dbx) list /* lists source code inside current procedure */
2 printf("This is test1\n");
3 }
(dbx) trace test2
(5) trace test2 /* notify me whenever we enter test2 */
(dbx) status
(2) stop at "/tmp/book/test.c":3
```

```
(4) stop in test1
(5) trace test2
(dbx) delete stop in test2
(6) stop in test2 /* set a breakpoint at the beginning of test2 */
(dbx) status
(2) stop at "/tmp/book/test.c":3
(4) stop in test1
(5) trace test2
(6) stop in test2
(dbx) delete 6 /* remove the stop in test2 */
(dbx) status
(2) stop at "/tmp/book/test.c":3
(4) stop in test1
(5) trace test2
(dbx) continue /* whoops */
unrecognized command/syntax "continue"
(Type 'help' for help)
(dbx) cont /* continue on until next breakpoint or end of execution
  */
This is test1
calling test2(a  =  5) from function main
This is test2 and a is 5
returning 5 from test2
execution completed, exit code is 1
program exited with 1
(dbx) rerun /* reexecute program maintaining all breakpoints, etc. */
Running: a.out
stopped in main at line 3 in file "test.c"
3 printf("This is test and a is %d\n",a);
(dbx) status
(2) stop at "/tmp/book/test.c":3
(4) stop in test1
(5) trace test2
(dbx) use /* which directory is everything in */
/tmp/book/
(dbx) file /* what source code file am I in now */
test.c
(dbx) func /* what is my current function name */
main
(dbx) list
4 test1();
5 test2(a);
6 }
(dbx) next /* step over test1 function call, see where we end up */
This is test and a is 5
stopped in main at line 4 in file "test.c"
4 test1();
(dbx) next
This is test1
stopped in main at line 5 in file "test.c"
5 test2(a);
(dbx) step
calling test2(a = 5) from function main
stopped in test2 at line 2 in file "test2.c"
(dbx) list
2 printf("This is test2 and a is %d\n",a);
3 }
(dbx) sh /* fork a shell, to get back to dbx type exit */
% ls
a.out test.c test1.c test2.c
book.script test.o test1.o test2.o
% exit
```

```
(dbx) where /* where is my current line position */
test2(a = 5), line 2 in "test2.c"
main(), line 5 in "test.c"
(dbx) quit /* quit dbx without finishing execution of my program */
```

The above example is all inclusive and demonstrates much of the power and functionality of the dbx debugger. While there are subtleties in this example which you may not understand, you can refer to it later as you learn more about UNIX.

4.1.6 Conclusion

This section has demonstrated a significant amount of the functionality of dbx. There are, however, more commands which can perform tasks which you may be interested in. See the man pages for your particular machine for more details. There is also a GNU version of dbx which provides enhanced functionality and commonality across platforms. The dbx session shown in this chapter was run on SunOS from within a terminal window. There are tools such as dbxtool on the Sun which provide a more sophisticated interface to dbx; however, these are all changing in the near future as UNIX vendors change their interface, so they will not be documented here. See your local system documentation for more information on GUI-based dbx tools and use them just as you would use dbx as show above.

dbx is a powerful tool for software developers and maintainers. In combination with other more sophisticated tools, it will help you to write and deliver better software.

4.2 lint

4.2.1 Introduction

The lint tool has been used for years to analyze C source code for syntax and possible run-time errors. lint can also check for nonportable and inefficient code. Some of the basic things you can do are:

Perform type-checking rules more strictly than most compilers

Identify variable and function problems

Identify flow control problems

Identify inefficiencies in constructs

Identify unused and unreferenced code

Identify nonportable code

Identify code and library incompatibilities

4.2.2 Usage

```
lint [-a] [-b] [-c] [-h] [-lkey] [-n] [-olibrary] [-p] [-u] [-v]
[-wclass [class  . . . ]] [-x] [-MA] [- Ndnumber] [-Nl dir] [-DName
  [-def]] [-U name]
file  . . .
```

where -a suppress messages concerning assignments of long variables to variables that are not defined as long.

-b suppress messages about unreachable break statements.

-c produces a .ln file for every C file which can be used later by lint for more thorough analysis.

-h suppress bug, style, and inefficiency checking.

-lkey includes a lint library for further cross checking. key can be any of:

key—includes the llib-lkey.ln lint library
m—includes the llib-lmath.ln lint library
dos—includes the llib-ldos.ln lint library

-n suppresses check for compatibility with standard and portable lint libraries.

-olibrary creates the llib-llibrary.ln library.

-p performs portability checks.

-u suppresses messages about unused variables and functions.

-v suppresses unused function messages.

-wclass [class] specifies warning classes which determine what is reported. Some of the classes are:

a—non-ANSI features
c—comparison with unsigned values
d—declaration consistency
h—heuristic complaints
k—use for Kernighan and Ritchie (K&R) style of C code
l—assignments of long variables to nonlong variables
p—portability concerns
r—return statement consistency
u—proper usage of variables and functions
A—disable all warnings
C—constants occurring in conditional statements
D—external declarations never used
P—function prototypes
S—storage capacity checks

-x suppress messages about variables that have external declarations but are never used.

-MA enforces ANSI standards constructs in C code.

-NdNumber changes table dimension.

-NlNumber changes number of type nodes.

-NnNumber changes symbol table size.

-NtNumber changes tree node numbers.
-Idir adds dir to directories to search for #include files.
-Dname=def is a macro definition similar to that used by cpp.
-Uname removes definition of name where name is a symbol used by the program.
file is any number of files to scan with lint.

lint has been in use for a long time and has a history of support for the K&R style of C code and only recently has begun to support the ANSI standard C. Keep this heritage in mind when you are using lint to analyze code.

There are a number of strings you can place within your source code to control lint's behavior. They are beyond the scope of this chapter. See other lint documentation for more information on these commands.

4.2.3 Examples

To check a simple program for syntax errors, issue the command:

```
$ lint kevin.c
```

To check a series of files, you should first run each file through with the -c option, which produces a .ln file. After performing this operation on each file, run lint on the result with the appropriate -l options to generate lint statements that reference the appropriate file. If you don't use this methodology, you will get lint messages from unknown file locations.

```
$ lint -c file1.c
$ lint -c file2.c
$ lint -lfile1 -lfile2 file1
```

Each lint -c command generates a file with a .ln extension, which is a lint library. This is then cross-referenced in the last command and will produce error messages which reference the appropriate file. This is particularly useful for makefiles since you can lint only those files that have changed and can issue the appropriate lint command with the correct -l options to regenerate the executable.

4.2.4 Conclusion

lint is a very powerful analysis tool for C code. Use this before compilation to check for inconsistencies and syntax and run-time errors. You can also search for unused and inefficient code before you waste time with more sophisticated performance analysis tools. lint is one of the most powerful tools available on the UNIX platform for code analysis and design.

4.3 prof and gprof

4.3.1 Introduction

Profiling consists of code analysis to understand where you are spending most of your resources, including CPU time, I/O, and memory. With profiling tools you can study how your program behaves and where it is burning the most resources. Once you have found the "hot spots" in your code where it spends most of its time, you can focus on fine tuning these areas to increase the performance of your overall system.

The general profiling and application tuning utilities available with UNIX are prof and gprof. While these tools do not offer the functionality of many performance and profiling tools that you can purchase, they do offer basic capabilities which will assist you in monitoring and analyzing the hot spots and other problems with your code.

To take full advantage of the profiling, you must compile your code with the -p option for use with the prof command and with -pg for use with the gprof command. See the sections below for more details.

Profiling your code will provide information on the percentage of time spent in each function, the number of times a particular function was called, and the number of milliseconds spent within each function. While the granularity of the statistics made available is not high, it will provide you with enough information to structure your code differently if necessary.

4.3.2 prof usage

The basic syntax for the prof command is:

```
prof [-t | -c | -a | -n] [-o | -x] [-g] [-z] [-h] [-s] [-S] [-v]
[-L path] [prog] [-m file...]
```

where -t sorts by decreasing percentage of total time (default).
-c sorts by decreasing number of calls.
-a sorts by increasing symbol address.
-n sorts by symbol name.
-o displays addresses in octal.
-x displays addresses in hex.
-g includes nonglobal symbols.
-z includes all symbols, even those not referenced or executed.
-h suppresses default heading.
-s produces a summary file in mon.sum.

-S displays statistics on standard error.
-v displays output graphically on standard output.
-L path uses alternate path for shared libraries.
prog is the program to execute.
-m file takes profiling data from file instead of mon.out.

To use prof effectively, you should first compile your codes with the -p option and execute normally. This produces a file named mon.out by default which contains information on that particular iteration of the code. Once that has been run, you would issue a command like:

```
$ prof -t
Name       %Time    Seconds    Cumsecs    #Calls    msec/call
.printf    52.0     0.02       0.02       6         2.
.main      42.0     0.02       0.04       2         1.
sub1        8.0     0.01       0.05       1         1.
```

As you can see, it produces a decreasing listing of times spent within a particular function call. The columns are self-explanatory and consist of the percentage of time spent in each routine, the total section in each routine, the accumulated time for the overall program, the number of calls from each routine, and the milliseconds per call for each subroutine or function. This will give you a good estimate of how much time your system is spending in each routine as a percentage of total execution time. You can issue the command:

```
$ prof -L/usr/share/lib kevin.out -Mkevin.mon
```

It will generate information using shared library files contained in /usr/share/lib, use the executable kevin.out, and the monitor data from the file kevin.mon instead of the default mon.out.

4.3.3 gprof usage

The basic syntax for the gprof command is:

```
gprof [-b] [-e name] [-E name] [-f name] [-F name] [-L path] [-s]
  [-z]
[a.out [gmon.out ...]]
```

where -b suppresses field descriptions.
-e name suppresses graph profile entry for name and all of its descendants.
-E name suppresses graph profile entry, time spent, and percentage time information for name.
-f name displays graph profile entry for name and its descendants.

-F name displays graph profile entry and time and percentage entries for name and its descendants.
-L path uses path for locating shared libraries instead of default.
-s produces gmon.sum which sums statistics for multiple gprof executions.
-z displays functions that have zero execution times.
a.out is the default executable name.
gmon.out is the default gprof statistics file.

The basic operation of gprof is the same as prof. After compilation of the source code with the -pg option, you invoke the resulting executable as you normally would. This results in a file named gmon.out, which contains information which is used by gprof. Once you have collected the information by running your program, use a command like:

```
$ gprof
# gprof
# @(#)64 1.4 com/cmd/stat/gprof/gprof.callg, bos, bos320 7/31/91
18:48:5
#
# COMPONENT_NAME: (CMDSTAT) gprof
#
# FUNCTIONS: N/A
#
# ORIGINS: 27
#
# (C) COPYRIGHT International Business Machines Corp. 1989
# All Rights Reserved
#
# US Government Users Restricted Rights - Use, duplication or
# disclosure restricted by GSA ADP Schedule Contract with IBM Corp.

call graph profile:
The sum of self and descendants is the major sort
for this listing.

function entries:

index the index of the function in the call graph
listing, as an aid to locating it (see below).

etc...

0.00 0.00 13/13 ._doprnt [5]
[1] 0.0 0.00 0.00 13 .fwrite [1]
0.00 0.00 13/13 .memchr [2]
0.00 0.00 3/7 ._xflsbuf [3]
0.00 0.00 1/2 ._wrtchk [20]
-----------------------------------------------
0.00 0.00 13/13 .fwrite [1]
[2] 0.0 0.00 0.00 13 .memchr [2]
-----------------------------------------------
0.00 0.00 1/7 .fflush [22]
0.00 0.00 3/7 ._flsbuf [7]
0.00 0.00 3/7 .fwrite [1]
[3] 0.0 0.00 0.00 7 ._xflsbuf [3]
0.00 0.00 7/7 .write [4]
```

```
-----------------------------------------------
etc.

# @(#)65 1.4 com/cmd/stat/gprof/gprof.flat, bos, bos320 7/31/91
18:49:52
#
# COMPONENT_NAME: (CMDSTAT) gprof
#
# FUNCTIONS: N/A
#
# ORIGINS: 27
#
# (C) COPYRIGHT International Business Machines Corp. 1989
# All Rights Reserved
etc.

% cumulative self self total
time seconds seconds calls ms/call ms/call name
0.0 0.00 0.00 13 0.00 0.00 .fwrite [1]
0.0 0.00 0.00 13 0.00 0.00 .memchr [2]
```

This will produce several outputs. The first is very similar to that produced by prof, including function times as a percentage of total execution time, number of times the functions are called, and the total execution time of each. Times are then propagated to a call graph as illustrated above. The second piece of output includes call graph execution times including time distribution to the descendants. Finally, cycles are shown including an entry for the cycle as a whole and a listing of the members of the cycle and their individual cycle and call count times. The above is a very limited presentation of the actual output of the gprof command. Run some examples on your local machine for more information.

4.3.4 Conclusion

prof and gprof provide basic profiling capabilities which allow for a certain level of analysis of code to occur, and included performance and analysis information. By using these tools, you can better understand the execution characteristics of your code and thereby perform the appropriate actions on the code to enhance performance and any other desired characteristics.

There are other commercial tools available which do far more than prof and gprof, but these two do provide the basics that you need to tune your code effectively and efficiently.

4.4 ar

4.4.1 Introduction

The ar command is used to create and manipulate archive files. These are libraries of files which are typically used for the link process. Files are created by a compiler into a format known as the object format and can then be stored as members in an archive file. These members are then used by the link editor to generate a final executable code.

4.4.2 Usage

```
ar [c][l][o][s][v]{m [a|b|i|] position | r [a|b|i|u] position |
{d|h|p|q|t|w|x}}
archivename [membername ...]
```

where c suppresses normal creation messages.
l places temporary files in current directory instead of default /tmp.
o sequentially orders and compresses archive file.
s regenerates symbol table.
v is verbose mode.
m moves members within an archive:
a position—moves to position following position
b position—moves to position preceding position
i position—same as b position
r replaces members within an archive; a position, b position, i position—same as m option.
u updates number.
d deletes member from archive.
h changes modification times of members to current date and time.
q displays contents of named members or entire archive if no member is specified.
t displays table of contents.
w displays symbol table.
x extracts members to current directory.
archivename is name of archive library.
membername ... is name or names of members to be manipulated.

The archive library consists of members generated by a compiler and a symbol table which is used by the link editor to create an executable. Most operations which affect members cause a regeneration of the symbol table; however, this is not always the case. See the examples below for more information.

The basic options for the ar command must be used as described above. You must select one of closv and one of dhpqtwx. The rest are optional and depend on the other options chosen. Keep in mind that the options must be placed sequentially on the command line with no intervening spaces.

4.4.3 Linking

The linking process generates a single executable file from a series of object files generated by a compiler. Most linkage editors are contained within the command used to invoke the compiler. For example, the cc command by default invokes both the compiler and the linkage editor. The same holds true for the f77 command.

When the linkage editor examines the link statement, it performs a single pass through all referenced files and archives to generate an executable file. The first discovered reference is used to build the executable. This means that if you have multiple references to the same member or object filename, the linkage editor will use the first. This implies that the order of members within the archive library is important to determine the final executable contents. Keep this in mind when generating the archive library and using the position commands like m and r to move members within an archive. See the examples below for more information. Also see Sec. 4.6, which describes the linkage editor in more detail.

Suffice it to say that most developers use archive libraries as function or subprogram libraries, especially when software systems get large. This provides an easy way to track and maintain groups of functions or subprograms.

4.4.4 Examples

These examples assume the existence of four object files (member1.o, member2.o, member3.o, and member4.o) in a single directory. To generate an archive library from these files, use the command:

```
$ ar vq members.a member1.o member2.o member3.o member4.o
```

This will create an archive file named members.a which contains four members named member1.o through member4.o.

If the archive file members.a already exists, it will add these four members to the end of the archive without checking for previous members of the same member name. This is important since the linkage editor will use the first occurrence of the member name to generate the executable. Keep this in mind as you create more archive libraries. It is generally *not* a good idea to create equivalent member names within an archive library; however, if you know what you are doing, this can be a powerful technique.

To view the results of your archive creation, issue the command:

```
$ar vt members.a
rw-r--r-- 0/0 4997 May 01 10:14 1993 member1.o
rw-r--r-- 0/0 5121 May 01 10:14 1993 member2.o
```

```
rw-r--r-- 0/0 4030 May 01 10:14 1993 member3.o
rw-r--r-- 0/0 10939 May 01 10:14 1993 member4.o
```

This generates a table of contents which is similar to ls -l.

To replace a member, use the command:

```
$ ar vr members.a member1.o
```

You can use the positioning command to affect the order of members in the archive. To add the contents of a modified members1.o file, you can use the command:

```
$ ar vq members.a member1.o
```

Note that this command creates a duplicate member. The results of the table of contents command show this:

```
$ar vt members.a
rw-r--r--     0/0     4997 May 01 10:14 1993 member1.o
rw-r--r--     0/0     5121 May 01 10:14 1993 member2.o
rw-r--r--     0/0     4030 May 01 10:14 1993 member3.o
rw-r--r--     0/0     10939 May 01 10:14 1993 member4.o
rw-r--r--     0/0     4128 May 02 10:24 1993 member1.o
```

This is dangerous; however, it does provide certain functionality that you may need. You can position files within the archive with a command like:

```
$ ar vma member3.o members.a member2.o
```

This moves the member member2.o to follow member3.o.

```
$ar vt members.a
rw-r--r--     0/0     4997 May 01 10:14 1993 member1.o
rw-r--r--     0/0     4030 May 01 10:14 1993 member3.o
rw-r--r--     0/0     5121 May 01 10:14 1993 member2.o
rw-r--r--     0/0     10939 May 01 10:14 1993 member4.o
rw-r--r--     0/0     4128 May 02 10:24 1993 member1.o
```

This command moves the member member2.o to follow the member member3.o. You may want to do this to place a global symbol contained in member3.o before the same global symbol contained in member2.o. This is related to linkage editor resolution requirements.

To extract a member, use the command:

```
$ ar vx members.a member2.o
```

This will place the contents of member2.o in a file named member2.o in the current working directory. Because of ar's use of standard input and output, you can use redirection and piping as you would with most other UNIX commands. For example, to rename the results of the above extraction to a file named something other than member2.o, use:

```
$ar vx members.a member2.o > cmember2.o
```

This will create a file named cmember2.o that contains the contents of the member member2.o.

You can delete a member in an archive with the command:

```
$ ar vd members.o member4.o
```

As you have made changes to the archive, its structure and order have changed. Because of the structure of the archive, it may have unused space and inefficiencies within itself. To reorder and compress the archive, use the command:

```
$ ar vo members.a
```

This sequentially orders and compresses the members.a archive. This is particularly useful after a number of delete operations since these often don't compress the archive file as efficiently as possible.

Finally, you can use the strip command (see Sec. 4.7 for more information on the strip command) to remove symbol and other information; this is related to the ar command. You may want to strip the archive library to remove many deleted symbols from deleted members. After you strip the archive library, rebuild the symbol tables with the command:

```
$ ar vs members.a
```

This will generate a clean up-to-date copy of the global symbols contained in the members within the archive. To view the new symbol table, use the command:

```
$ ar vw members.a
```

There are other commands related to archives such as strip and ld. See the sections on these commands for more details and more examples of how to use archive libraries.

4.4.5 Conclusion

The ar command is a powerful command that creates and manipulates archive libraries. These libraries can help you organize your development effort and control the generation of executables. There are special provisions in make and the linkage editor which take advantage of archive libraries. UNIX power developers take full advantage of the ar facility.

4.5 nm

4.5.1 Introduction

The nm facility generates a listing of the symbols in an object file. The file can be a simple object file, an executable file, or an archive file. Each symbol is preceded by a value which defines the characteristics of the symbol itself.

There are two versions of the nm command: Berkeley and AT&T. They use different syntax but perform the same basic tasks. Keep this in mind and examine the manual pages for your particular platform.

An example of a simple nm command is:

```
% nm bin/kermit | more
000227a4 d _ATT7300
000225c4 d _CERMETEK
0002277c d _CONCORD
000222f0 D _DELCMD
000225ec d _DF03
00022614 d _DF100
0002263c d _DF200
000222fc D _DIRCMD
00022d4c d _EXP_ALRM
000228ac d _F_reason
00022664 d _GDC
0002268c d _HAYES
000226b4 d _PENRIL
000222f4 D _PWDCMD
000226dc d _RACAL
00022304 D _SPACM2
00022300 D _SPACMD
000222f8 D _TYPCMD
00022704 d _UNKNOWN
0002272c d _USROBOT
00022754 d _VENTEL
00022308 D _WHOCMD
```

The characters preceding the symbol name designate the following:

A—absolute variable

B—BSS segment symbol

D—data segment variable

T—text segment symbol

U—undefined symbol

f—file name symbol

-—debugger symbol

Symbol information is sorted alphabetically by symbol.

The above listing comes from a Berkeley-based machine. The System V variant of this output is slightly different but represents essentially the same type of information. With the System V variation, the variable types and contents are generally described in a little more detail. Example output might look like:

```
$ nm transform
$ nm transform | more
Symbols from transform:

Name Value Class Type Size Line Section

.__start | 512|extern| | | |.text
__start | 648|extern| | | |.data
_adata | 216|unamex| | | |.data
TOC | 656|unamex| | | |.data
_adata | 692|unamex| | | |.data
errno | 696|unamex| | | |.data
...
```

The nm command is a very useful way to understand and determine both the scope and function of all variables in an object or executable file. For example, when you have an executable and you would like to understand which symbols are defined where, you can use the nm command to determine this. nm is also useful to better understand the structure of code that exists without source code. The command nm provides access to some information on the structure and content of object and executable files. This is one of the first things you may want to do when taking a look at someone else's code.

4.5.2 Berkeley usage

The basic syntax of the nm command is:

```
nm [-a] [-g] [-n] [-o] [-p] [- r] [-u] [file...]
```

where -a displays symbols inserted for debugging purposes.
-g displays global symbols.
-n sorts numerically rather than alphabetically.
-o displays file or archive name with each symbol rather than once.
-p displays symbols in order of file occurrence.
-r displays in reverse order.
-u displays undefined symbols.
file is one or more files for nm to analyze.

Examples. To list symbols inserted into a file kevin.a for debugging purposes, use the command:

```
$ nm -a kevin.a
```

To sort global symbols in reverse order, use:

```
$ nm -gr kevin.a
```

The usage for the AT&T System V version of the nm command is:

```
nm [-O] [-T] [-e] [-f] [-h] [- r] [-u] [-n | -v] [-o | -d | -x]
[file ...]
```

where -O displays file or archive name with each symbol rather than once.
-T truncates symbol names as necessary.
-e displays static and external symbols.
-f displays all symbols.
-h does not display header information.
-r displays in reverse order.
-u displays undefined symbols.
-n displays external symbols ordered by name; use with the -e option.
-v displays external symbols ordered by value; use with the -e option.
-o displays values in octal.
-d displays values in decimal.
-x displays values in hex.
file ... is one or more files to operate on.

4.5.3 Examples

To display symbol sizes and values in octal and sort by value, use:

```
$ nm -eov kevin.out
```

To display external symbols, use:

```
$ nm -e kevin.out
```

4.5.4 Conclusion

The nm command is well used by UNIX users to provide information on the structure and content of object and executable files. Both versions of the command (Berkeley and AT&T) provide similar functionality and can be used by anyone to learn more about binary files.

4.6 ld

4.6.1 Introduction

The ld command is the linker for UNIX; it is sometimes known as the linkage editor or binder. ld combines object files, archive libraries, and import lists into a single executable which can be invoked from the command line. It is the final component in the compilation process of most third-generation languages such as C and Fortran. Many so-called fourth-generation languages do not require a compiler and include an interpreter which is invoked every time you run the application. The problem with this is the often great loss of execution speed because of the interpretation. The clear advantage of compilation is speed.

ld is invoked by most precompilers such as cc and f77 as the last step in the generation of an executable. You can specify that the ld not be called with a switch such as -o on the cc or f77 command. This will cause an object file to be generated but not the final executable. If you do this, you will need to invoke ld later to build the final executable.

4.6.2 Usage

ld is one of the commands that varies between different flavors of UNIX. Because ld is tightly linked with the architecture of the machine, there are different switches and options for each different UNIX architecture. This chapter will not present all the options available on all implementation of ld since this would not only be lengthy but incorrect by the time this book went to print. Most of the options discussed in this chapter will, however, exist on most implementation of ld. They may have different option representation. See your local ld documentation for more information on your particular flavor of UNIX.

The basic syntax of ld for SunOS is:

```
ld [-A name] [-Bbind] [-d] [-dc] [- dp] [-D len] [-e entry] [-lx]
  [-Ldir] [- M] [-n]
[-N] [-o file] [-p] [-r] [-s] [-S] [-t] [-T[text]hex] [-Tdata hex]
  [-u name] [-x]
[-X] [-ysym] file ...
```

where -A name uses the file name to input additional symbols to ld to generate a reentrant executable which can be called from other executables. This option is not supported on many versions of ld.

-Bbind—binding keywords possible for bind are:
dynamic—allows dynamic runtime binding.
nosymbolic—doesn't perform symbol relocation.
static—performs static binding; no dynamic binding allowed.
symbolic—performs symbol relocation.
-d forces common storage for uninitialized variables and symbols.
-dc is the same as -d but also includes initialized data from shared objects.
-dp forces an alias definition of undefined procedures. Useful when using dynamic binding.
-D len pads the data segment with zeroes to a total of len hex bytes.
-e entry defines the entry point of the program as entry. This is usually main.
-lx designates a library named libx.a where the x in -lc represents the x in libx.a. ld searches first in directories specified by -Ldir, then in the standard directories /lib, /usr/lib and /usr/local/lib. See the examples for more detail.
-Ldir tells ld to search for libraries in the directory dir before the standard directories /lib, /usr/lib and /usr/local/lib. Typically used with -lx.
-M generates a load map which contains symbol and resolution information.
-n arranges executable as read-only data segment immediately followed by a text segment.
-N is the same as -n but text segment is not read-only.
-o file generates the executable with the name file instead of the default a.out.
-p places data segment on a page boundary.
-r generates relocation bits so that unresolved symbols are not flagged; also provides the ability to take resulting executable and reexecute an ld command against it.
-s strips output of symbols and relocation bits (same as strip command).
-S strips output except for local and global symbols (similar to -s).
-t traces each file as it is operated on.
-T[text]hex starts text segment at location hex.
-T[data]hex starts data segment at location hex.
-u name enters name as an undefined symbol.
-x places only global symbols in executable symbol table.
-X places local symbols in executable symbol table except those beginning with an L.

-ysym displays each file which references sym and information about its use.
file ... is one or more object files to be linked.

Most options are position independent; however, -lx and -B options do depend on their location on the command line. Typically, the -lx option specifies where to search for a library relative to the nearest -Ldir option if one exists. See the next section for more information.

4.6.3 The linking process

The linking process varies from UNIX flavor to UNIX flavor; however, the basics are the same on all platforms. Most UNIX linkers are called single-pass linkers. This means that as symbols and externals are referenced, the linker searches in its current symbol table for resolutions. If they are not found, you will get an undefined symbol error message, and the link may fail.

This means that you must have all symbols referenced by a piece of your executable defined after the reference in the link process; otherwise, the linker will not resolve the reference. In other words, because the linker is a single-pass linker, it will only load references currently outstanding when it examines something like an archive library. This even holds true within the archive library in that you must have all definitions of referenced functions and symbols follow all references to those symbols and functions, or the linker will not load that particular member from the archive library to the final executable. If and when ld attempts to build the final executable, you will get an unresolved symbol or function error message. The ld command is directly related to the single-pass nature of the loader/linker, and you must be aware of the order in which you link any files and/or libraries since this may affect your ability to create the final executable.

Because of the nature of the linker, filename and archive name order are critical on the command line. You must place all defined functions and external symbols after their reference so that they will be loaded. You will quickly discover how to do this as you practice.

4.6.4 Shared libraries and binding

One of the early limitations of UNIX was its inability to perform dynamic binding. Dynamic binding means that the instructions in a compiled function are not actually loaded into an executable but instead are referenced when the program is executed and are, in fact, executed from a different file than the invoked executable. This has the advantage of providing relatively small executable files; it also provides portability and flexibility in that you could change some function or have a function that behaves a little differently from machine to machine based on that particular machine's architecture. Because you are dynamically executing this external function, you don't have to worry about what it is doing but only that you are interfacing to it properly. This is commonly used for shared libraries.

Shared libraries consist of shared dynamically loadable functions that are used by more than one program. They are fully reentrant, which means they can be executed any number of times from any number of programs at the same time.

More recent versions of UNIX support dynamic binding and the ability to dynamically load libraries and other external functions at run-time. This provides the ability to build and distribute large applications with a relatively small executable and merely provide the shared libraries on each platform on which you wish to run the final executable. Of course, if you don't have the shared libraries or all the files necessary to dynamically bind on a different machine than you compiled the original executable on, you will need to use static binding so that all executable code is present on the different machine. For example, device drivers and graphics drivers are typically distributed as shared dynamic library systems.

4.6.5 Examples

The best way to see how ld works is to generate several examples. To load some simple object files and generate an executable named kevin.out, use:

```
$ ld -o kevin.out kevin1.o kevin2.o kevin3.o
```

This will generate kevin.out from the three object files kevin1.o, kevin2.o, and kevin3.o.

```
$ ld -L/usr/kevin/lib -lk file1.o file2.o archive.a
```

will generate an executable named a.out which contains file1.o, file2.o; something from a library named libk.a in the directory /usr/kevin/lib or one of the standard directories /lib, /usr/lib, and /usr/local/lib; and finally any references made to the archive library archive.a. Remember that most UNIX linkers are single pass; this means that if some member of archive.a references something in libk.a, it won't be loaded. To fix this, you would rearrange the command line to look something like:

```
$ ld file1.o file2.o archive.a -L/usr/kevin/lib -lk
```

To force static binding to ensure portability to other machines that may or may not have the dynamic libraries needed, use a command like:

```
$ ld -Bstatic file1.o file2.o archive1.a archive2.a
```

Note that anything in archive2.a that would require a reference in archive1.a will not be loaded unless something in archive1.a or file1.o or file2.o caused ld to load the member. This behavior leads to a command like:

```
$ ld -Bstatic file1.o file2.o archive1.a archive2.a archive1.a
```

When you see a command like this, you know that there are dependencies between both archive1.a and archive2.a which require linking as described above. This will force you to understand the structure of your archive libraries as well as your object files.

Remember that you can, and do by default, invoke ld when you issue a command like:

```
$ cc kevin.c
```

This generates a file named kevin.o and invokes ld to produce an executable a.out. This is why many of the options available to a precompiler system like cc or f77 are also available to ld. They are merely passed to the appropriate phase of the compilation system by the precompiler.

If you have fully debugged your code and don't need any symbol or relocation information, you can use a command like:

```
$ ld -s -o main.exe main.o sub.o files.a
```

which will generate an executable named main.exe without any symbol or relocation information. This makes main.exe smaller without sacrificing anything with respect to execution.

4.6.6 Conclusion

This section is certainly not an exhaustive discussion of the UNIX linker; however, it does introduce you to some of the basic capabilities of the ld command and how and why link statements must be structured as they are.

With ld, you can generate relocatable or static executables from object files and archive libraries while maintaining good control over the structure of the actual executable with powerful options like -T and -p.

4.7 strip

4.7.1 Introduction

The strip command removes symbols and relocation information from object files. Symbols and relocation information are placed in the executable for linking and debugging purposes. Many of the tools you use to debug and link and compile your code rely on this information in the executable file. Once you have finished debugging, however, you may want to remove this for a variety of reasons.

Removing this information is useful when you want to decrease the size of your executable and remove all unnecessary information from the binary file before using it in production mode. By doing this, you shrink all resources required to run it, including memory, disk, and CPU. This is often used by more advanced UNIX developers, particularly in real-time system development and embedded control systems where resources are tight.

It is generally used to make object files and subsequent executables smaller without sacrificing performance. This is generally used after a program has been completely debugged and is ready for distribution and use.

4.7.2 Usage

The basic syntax for strip is:

```
strip file ...
```

where file ... is one or more object code files.

Once you have compiled a file and debugged the application, you can issue the strip command on the resultant executable to remove all symbol table information and relocation bits. These are only used by the debugger and linker and are not relevant to the execution process. This allows you to minimize the size of your executable without affecting the execution of your program.

A simple example is:

```
$ strip file.o file1.o file2.o
```

Once you have stripped the object files, you can link as you normally would with an ld or some other precompiler command such as f77 or cc.

4.7.3 Conclusion

The strip command is useful when you want to minimize the size of your executable and, therefore, minimize disk space and memory requirements. You can invoke the strip functionality either with the strip command or with the -s option on the link (ld) command. See Sec. 4.6 for more information.

The strip command provides the flexibility to minimize executable size while not affecting the execution process of your program.

4.8 The r Commands

4.8.1 Introduction

The r commands consist of several commands which begin with an r. The r designates remote. These commands allow you to emulate local commands on a remote machine. Basic examples of the r commands are:

rsh

rcp

rlogin

These commands were traditionally shipped with the Berkeley derivative of the UNIX operating system. Because of this, most versions of UNIX, other than standard System V, come with the r commands. These commands allow you to execute the cp, sh, and login commands remotely without requiring a password. Because of this, they are often seen as inferior to the standard ftp and telnet sorts of operations. However, since these commands became widely used, they are still included with almost every UNIX operating system shipping today.

4.8.2 Usage

Security and the r commands. The r commands use three files to perform user authentication on the remote machine. The first is the global r security file called /etc/hosts.equiv. This file contains a global mapping of hostnames and usernames supported for remote access. If the remote machines contain a /etc/hosts.equiv file which equates the local and remote hosts and usernames, you will be allowed access if the remote machine is in the /etc/hosts file and you have an account in both /etc/passwd files.

The basic syntax of the /etc/hosts.equiv file is:

```
hostname username
hostname username username
...
```

where hostname is the hostname of a particular machine on the network and username is the name of a user that you want to allow access on the local machine. For example, if you place the line:

```
devtech kevin
```

in the /etc/hosts.equiv file on a machine named ibmgod and issue a rlogin, rsh, or rcp command from devtech to ibmgod and you are the account kevin, you will permitted access. Note that the username specifies that you can share usernames between machines. You can allow all users with entries in the /etc/passwd machine on both machines access with the line:

```
devtech +
```

in the /etc/hosts.equiv. This says that all users with matching ids on ibmgod and devtech will be allowed access to their exact account on the ibmgod machine from devtech. If you placed this line in the /etc/hosts.equiv file on ibmgod and executed the command:

```
$ rsh ibmgod ls
```

from the devtech machine, you would be logged on to ibmgod, and the command ls would be executed on your HOME directory just as if you had logged on and issued the ls command. Note that you must have the same account on both machines (but *not* the same password), and there must be a mapping in the /etc/hosts.equiv file for this to work correctly.

You can also allow only specific other accounts access to your account with the r commands by placing their account names and machines specifically in the .rhosts file. An example file might be:

```
ibmgod root kevin
devtech kevin glen
pegasus gch psm glen
```

This says that the root and kevin accounts can issue the r command in the current account from ibmgod, kevin and glen can execute commands from devtech, and gch, psm, and glen can execute commands from pegasus. This allows you to pick and choose who you give "paswordless" access to your account to. This is key to successfully controlling access to your account.

Given all of this discussion about the /etc/hosts.equiv file, it is important to note that it is generally not a good idea to use it. The better solution is to create a file named .rhosts in your HOME directory that contains the mapping information exactly as described in the /etc/hosts.equiv file but only for your account. This file is consulted after the /etc/hosts.equiv file to see if access is allowed. The syntax of the .rhosts file is exactly the same as that of /etc/hosts.equiv.

For example, if you want to allow access to your kevin account on devtech from your kevin account on ibmgod, you would create the following $HOME/.rhosts file on devtech:

```
ibmgod kevin
```

This would specifically allow the kevin account on ibmgod to access the kevin account on devtech without requiring a password for the r commands.

You can also allow others to access your account from this file by creating a .rhosts file like:

```
ibmgod
```

This will allow all users on ibmgod to access the kevin account on devtech without requiring a password. This is obviously a bit of a security issue and should be avoided if possible.

It is generally not a good idea to allow root to access other machines without a password. If you place the line:

```
ibmgod
```

in the /etc/hosts.equiv or /.rhosts file on devtech, root from ibmgod now has access to root on devtech without a password. Even if you maintain both systems, it is generally not a good idea to do this and should be avoided.

While there are a variety of security holes and problems associated with this methodology, it is generally used and is exceedingly powerful when it comes to saving time moving files and information around in a network.

The r commands and login scripts. Many times, people experience strange problems with the r commands which cause rcp to fail and rsh to work intermittently. Often this is caused by something in their login scripts issuing output to standard output. If your login scripts (.login, .profile,.cshrc, etc.) issue output to standard output, they may confuse the r commands and cause either intermittent or complete failure of the r command itself. Check your login scripts and ensure that you do not issue any reads or writes from within them, or code them such that they check your terminal type to ensure that you are local when executing them. If you are not local, you should not execute any I/O since you may have problems with your r command execution.

The rlogin command. The rlogin command allows you to log into a remote machine without typing a password. The basic syntax is:

```
rlogin [-l username] hostname
```

where -l username specifies a username which can be other than your current username.
hostname is remote machine hostname.

The rlogin command provides a virtual terminal session into a remote computer. From this you can execute applications and run just as if you were logged on to the remote machine directly. You can use the -l option to specify an account other than the matching account for your current login id on the remote machine.

The rsh command. The rsh command allows you to execute remote commands on machines without issuing a password. Using the /etc/hosts.equiv and .rhosts files as described above, you can transparently access and run remote commands and display the output locally.

The basic syntax of the rsh command is:

```
rsh [-l username] [-n] hostname [command]
```

where -l username allows you to specify a username other than your current one.
-n sends input to the null device (/dev/null).
hostname is the remote hostname you wish to connect to.
command is the command to execute on the remote machine.

The rsh command is used to execute remote commands from the local command line. A simple example is:

```
$ rsh ibmgod ls
```

This, as described earlier, will log you on to ibmgod with your current userid and will issue the ls command in your HOME directory. You can execute any command from this rsh command. Standard input and standard output are mapped and appear local as you expect them to if you were executing the command locally.

A more interesting example is:

```
# rsh -l kevin devtech ls;echo $PATH;cat .profile
```

If you execute this as root (denoted by the #) from the ibmgod machine, it will execute all three commands on the devtech machine as userid kevin. This assumes that you have specifically allowed access to root from ibmgod access to the kevin account as described above. If you have not allowed specific access, you will get an access denied error message.

Note also that sometimes the -l username option is after the hostname. See your local system for documentation on the exact syntax for your machine.

The rcp command. The rcp command allows you to do a remote copy of a file without requiring a password. The basic syntax is:

```
rcp [-r] file1 file2
```

where -r recursively copies any directories underneath the current one.
file1 is the file to copy from.
file2 is the file to copy to.

The syntax of the file is:

```
[username@]hostname:filename
```

where username is the name of the remote user (default is your current userid).
hostname is the name of the remote host.
filename is the filename either fully qualified or given a relative path from the HOME directory of the user.

Note that the username is not required and will default to your current userid on the local machine. The colon (:) is what tells rcp that you are manipulating a remote file. This provides you with the ability to transfer a file without requiring a password like ftp does. This is very commonly used by users of several machines in a network and is definitely a time-saving feature of UNIX.

A simple rcp command might look like:

```
$ rcp devtech:/tmp/file /tmp/file
```

If executed on ibmgod, this command will look for a file named /tmp/file on the remote machine devtech and attempt to copy it to the ibmgod machine and place it in /tmp/file. You can use a command like:

```
$ rcp devtech:.rhosts .rhosts
```

which will copy the remote machine's (devtech) .rhosts file in your HOME directory to your current directory on your local machine.

The filename can be a directory if you wish to place the file in a directory. This is particularly useful if you are copying a group of files. A simple example might be:

```
$ rcp file1 file2 file3 ibmgod:
```

This will copy three files and name them file1, file2, and file3 in your HOME directory on ibmgod.

You can use wildcards to match filenames as you normally would with UNIX. A simple example is:

```
$ rcp devtech:"*.txt" textfiles
```

Note that textfiles must be a directory. In fact, anytime you copy multiple files, you must use a directory; otherwise, what is the filename of the three files? Note also that if the wildcards are to be expanded on the remote systems, you must enclose them in quotes to prevent the local shell from interpreting them before passing them to the r command.

A recursive copy looks like:

```
$ rcp -r devtech:prog prog
```

This will copy all files, recursively, from devtech and the subdirectory prog to the current directory prog. Note also that symbolic links are not supported in this environment, and actual copies of the files will be made. Therefore, if you have symbolic links in some directories which you are copying, you will need more disk space. If you are interested in preserving the exact structure of the data, you need to issue a command like:

```
$ tar cvf - test | rsh devtech tar xBf -
```

This will copy the current directory structure test to a remote machine named devtech and place it in a test subdirectory in your account on devtech. Note that this is a very powerful way of moving files around in your network.

The final example of using r commands accesses and controls remote devices. To retrieve a tar file from a remote tape device on devtech from ibmgod, you might use a command like:

```
$ rsh devtech dd if=/dev/rmt0 obs=16b | tar xvfBb - 16
```

This will dump (dd) the files from the tape drive (/dev/rmt0) with a blocking size of 16 to standard output. The tar command will take input from standard input (-) and place it on the local disk in the tar format in which it is received.

To copy a file to a remote tape device, you might use a command like:

```
$ rsh tar cvfb - 16 file1 file2 group1 | rsh devtech dd of=/dev/rmt0
ibs=16b
```

This will take file1 and file2 files as well as the contents of the group1 directory and place them in a tar file on the remote tape device /dev/rmt0 on the remote machine devtech.

These types of tools represent the kind of tricks you can perform with UNIX, and they illustrate some of the things you can do without writing a single line of code.

4.8.3 Conclusion

The r commands are often used by people who want to increase their effectiveness with UNIX. Because of the security implications of using the r commands, however, it is important that you understand exactly what you are doing and ensure that you are not opening up security holes in your network. Keep this in mind as you begin to look at these tools more carefully.

4.9 Install

4.9.1 Introduction

The install command is used by many software packages to install into a particular directory or set of directories. It is often used by free software tools in the build process to place files in particular directories. Because of this, it is included in this section so that you understand what it does later on in this book.

4.9.2 Usage

There are two styles of syntax for the install command:

```
install [-c dir] [-b dir] [-imosS] [-M mode] [-O owner] file [dir...]
```

where -c dir installs file in dir only if it does not previously exist in dir.
- -b dir forces installation of file even if it already exists in dir.
- -i ignores default directory list and uses only command line directories.
- -m moves the file instead of copying.
- -M mode specifies mode of destination file.
- -o saves copy of file as OLDfile in the same directory.
- -O owner specifies a different final owner than your id.
- -s displays error messages only.

-S strips binary after installation (see strip for more information).
file is file to be moved.
dir is directory in which to move the file.

The install command searches the default directories /usr/bin, /etc/, and /usr/lib in that order for files to move unless a directory is specified in the command line. This is the System V syntax of the install command and is what the RS/6000 uses by default.

The Sun uses the Berkeley install command which has the syntax:

```
install [-c] [-m mode] [-o owner] [-g group] [-s] file dir
```

where -c copies the file to dir.
-m mode specifies the mode of the file (default 755).
-o owner specifies an owner other than your id.
-g group specifies a group other than your gid.
-s strips the file after installation.
file is the file to move (or copy).
dir is destination directory.

Note that the syntax of the two commands is different. You may encounter problems with your installation scripts with some of the free software. The error messages will display something about unable to move file dir, etc. This error message may be coming from the install command. Check the syntax of the makefile (or Makefile) as well as the syntax supported on your machine before you proceed.

Some very simple examples are:

```
$ install -c kevin /usr/bin (BSD style)
```

This will copy the file kevin into the /usr/bin directory. From then on, you can execute kevin just as if it were a system-level command.

```
$ install -c /usr/bin kevin (SYSV style)
```

will accomplish the same as the previous Berkeley command. Note the difference in syntax and the problems that this may cause and beware.

```
$ install -i kevin /usr/local/bin, /usr/bin, /usr/kevin
```

will install a copy of kevin in /usr/local/bin, /usr/bin, and /usr/kevin if the file kevin exists. Remember that install only replaces existing files unless you use the -f dir option on the command. To force kevin into all three directories above, you might use:

```
$ install -f /usr/bin -o kevin
$ install -f /usr/bin -o kevin
$ install -f /usr/bin -o kevin
```

Note that you must execute this command three times to place it in three directories. Note also that the -o preserves any other kevin command in these directories and renames it OLDkevin.

There are a variety of ways you can use the install command. See your local documentation for more details.

4.9.3 Conclusion

The install command is a tool which allows you to place or replace files in directories from the command line. It provides a capability used by many makefiles to move files in and out of directories relatively transparently. Keep this in mind as you read through this book.

Chapter

5

Native Software Development Scripting Tools

While Chap. 4 focused on native UNIX tools which provided functionality based on command sets and syntax, this chapter focuses on native tools which provide scripting and development capabilities well beyond those described in Chap. 4. The tools described in this chapter are very flexible and powerful ones to use to develop applications and tools on your own.

5.1 awk

5.1.1 Introduction

awk is an interactive programming language which provides significant function similar to a fourth-generation language in common business nomenclature. awk provides pattern recognition capabilities as well as manipulation capabilities. It is typically used to manipulate large pieces of text without actually having to modify or even edit the file. It is a very powerful tool and one that is certainly underutilized on most UNIX computers. The name awk says much about UNIX and the way in which it was developed. awk stands for the last names of each of the authors: Alfred Aho, Peter Weinberger, and Brian Kernighan. Modesty has never been a characteristic of most UNIX developers.

awk is really a programming language all by itself. It is one of the most powerful pattern recognition and manipulations languages available on UNIX. It is a language which is C-like in syntax but is optimized to search files for strings and perform subsequent operations on these input lines. It uses ed commands (discussed in a previous chapter) to search for regular expressions in strings within files and performs a specified action on them. While this chapter cannot begin to describe all the features and functions of awk, it does present the main areas of functionality and provides enough information to allow you to decide whether you should look into awk in more detail.

5.1.2 Usage

awk is invoked as follows:

```
awk [-Fx] -f program [file1 file2...]
```

where -Fx allows you to specify a separator x other than whitespace.
-f program specifies a file which contains the awk commands.
[file1 file2 ...] contains a list of input files separated by blanks.

awk contains many of the features you would find in third-generation languages such as conditional branching, looping, string and arithmetic variables, and output format statements. It also contains things that you don't see in most languages such as transparent typing of variables and very flexible syntax. This allows you to code very powerful awk programs without being concerned with variable typing, definition, and manipulation.

The awk program represented by the -f program in the awk command syntax contains the following general syntax:

```
pattern command {action}
```

where pattern command is an ed command which provides for string searching and manipulation, and the action part consists of C-like commands which perform actions on the output of the pattern command. awk performs all actions on all lines selected by the pattern part of the awk program. The best way to understand this is with an example. The example input file called data1:

```
1col1 1col2
2col1 2col2
3col1 3col2
4col1 4col2
```

corresponds to the file part of the awk command. In other words, this will be the file that awk performs its program against. Let's also assume that we have a program called awk1 which looks like:

```
/3col1/ {print $1, $2}
```

To invoke this program against the above file, you would type:

```
$ awk -f awk1 data1
3col1 3col2
```

The output of that command is 3col1 3col2. awk first looked at the file awk1 for a pattern or ed command to use when examining the file data1. The /3col1/ command is the ed command to search for the string 3col1. awk performed the search and action pair on each line in the input file. In other words, it scanned line 1 and didn't find a match. It scanned line 2 and didn't find a match. It scanned line 3 and did find a match. It then applied the action print $1, $2 (more about this later) to this line and produced the output shown below the awk command. Finally, it scanned line 4 and didn't find a match. Once it reached the end of the data1 file, awk exited. This basic model holds true for all awk invocations; however, the awk program (awk1) can get much more powerful.

You can also execute the awk command functions from the command line by surrounding them with single quotes to prevent shell interpretation. For example, to execute the above awk commands without using the awk1 file, type:

```
$ awk '/3col1/ {print $1,$2}'
3col1 col
```

If you place several files separated by blanks on the awk command line, awk will process one line at a time and step sequentially through each file on the command line. If you choose to use standard input, use a -. For example:

```
$ awk -f awk1 -
1col1 1col2
2col1 2col2
3col1 3col2
3col1 3col2
4col1 4col2
```

Note that as you type each line in, awk processes it and presents the results to standard output. In this case the awk1 program searched for 3col1 and thus matched the third line.

The awk language. The awk language is a very powerful one which consists of most functions you would expect in a procedural language. Patterns can be ed commands that match patterns within the data files and regular expressions as well. The regular expressions consist of objects and operators. awk statements can combine both string and arithmetic operations in the same statement. Statements are terminated by newline or a semicolon. Also, just as in C, awk treats all statements within curly braces as a single statement. This allows you to nest statements under conditional branches just as you would with most other procedural languages.

Looping and conditional statements. The if conditional statement looks like:

```
if (condition) [{ statement }]
```

If you have a single statement, the curly braces are unnecessary. However, if you have more than a single statement, you must enclose them in curly braces to ensure that all are executed under the condition. For example:

```
{if (i<10) {
     print i
     ++i }
}
```

Note that the outside curly braces are necessary to denote that this is the action part of the awk statement, and the inner braces are necessary to group the two statements together under the conditional statement. If you do not include an action statement, the default action {print} is performed. This merely performs a print of the entire matched line.

There is also a while loop which looks like:

```
while(condition) [{] condition [}]
```

where the condition is similar to the if conditional. The curly braces must be used to contain more than one statement if you want them treated as one statement group under the while command.

There is a do loop in nawk (see nawk section for more information). It looks like:

```
do [{] action [}] while (condition)
```

Finally, there is a for statement which looks like:

```
for (initcounter;test;increment) action
```

where initcounter sets initial value for a loop counter.
test is the condition that is tested.
increment is the number to increment initcounter each time.

An example is in the examples section.

There are two other commands that affect command execution and flow:

`break`	Breaks completely out of a loop and begins at first line outside of loop
`continue`	Begins at top of loop in next iteration of loop itself

Besides string manipulation, numeric operations are fully supported by awk. The standard arithmetic statements supported are:

=	Assignment
<	Less than
>	Greater than
++	Increment by one
--	Decrement by one
/	Divide
*	Multiply
+	Add
-	Subtract
+=	Adds expression following operator to variable preceding it
-=	Subtracts expression following operator to variable preceding it

All numbers are converted to floating point before being manipulated, which eases a lot of problems you normally experience when programming. There are also relational operators supported by awk which allow for comparisons within the condition section of the statement. The primary relational operators supported by awk are:

<	Less than
>	Greater than
<=	Less than or equal to
>=	Greater than or equal to
==	Equal to
!=	Not equal to
~	Matches
~!	Does not match

You can also separate multiple patterns with boolean operators such as:

&& AND

|| OR

, range

See the examples for more discussion of the boolean operators.

Variables do not need to be initialized. This allows you to set the value of a variable without declaring it. For example:

```
s = 3
```

assigns the value of 3 to the variable s. It is not necessary to declare s anywhere else in the awk program. There are several special variables which are predefined:

`$0`	Current record
`$1-$n`	Fields in the current record
`FILENAME`	Name of current datafile
`FS`	Input field separator (default space)
`NF`	Number of fields in current record
`NR`	Number of current record
`OFS`	Output field separator (default space)
`ORS`	Output record separator (default newline)
`RS`	Input record separator (default space)

Several of these can be changed either by invocation switches (-F) or within the awk program.

There are also standard string functions which are supported by awk:

`index(string1,string2)`	Returns index of string2 in string1
`length[(string)]`	Returns the length of string, without an argument returns line length
`split(string,arr,del)`	Places elements of string, delimited by del in array arr[]
`sprintf(fmt,args)`	Defines formatted output args in format defined by fmt
`substr(string,pos,length)`	Returns string that begins at pos and is length characters long

All string functions act like their C language equivalents. See help on sprintf or other functions for more details about exact syntax and usage. See also some examples of function usage.

Finally, there are arithmetic operators in awk:

cos(x)

sin(x)

int(x)

log(x)

sqrt(x)

It is rare that you will need functions like these, but it is nice to know they are there.

BEGIN and END functions. You can structure special clauses both before and after the actual awk program which are executed before and after the awk program reads the data input file. For example:

```
BEGIN {
      print "this is the beginning..."
      }
      {
      awk program commands...
      }
END   {
      print "all done now..."
      }
```

The BEGIN and END clauses can do computations based on numbers generated in the main body of the awk program. A classic example of using the END function is to calculate the sum and mean of a set of numbers in a column:

```
    {
    m += $1
    n++
    }
END {
    print "mean is",m/n, "number of items is",n
    }
```

Remember that the END is processed after all lines are read. This makes end perfect to perform numerical calculations on an entire set of numbers. You can use this much as you would a spreadsheet to perform calculations on columns of numbers.

Errors. awk is notorious for ignoring errors and simply producing garbage output. You have to be extremely careful when structuring and coding your awk program. This is why it is almost always recommended to create an awk command file instead of using the command line since this will allow you to change and iterate your program severals times to eliminate all possible errors. When you place the awk commands on the command line, you run the risk of the shell command interpreter doing something to them before routing them to the awk command. While there is nothing wrong with using the command line, experience dictates that the awk command file is a better way to go. To save space, this book uses most examples on the command line; however, this is not an endorsement of this technique.

Passing parameters into a script. You can pass variables into awk programs by placing assignment statements between the script and data filename. For example:

```
$ awk -f awk1 var1=1 var2=2 data1
```

Note that the var1 and var2 statements must not contain spaces. Once you have invoked the awk1 script, the variables var1 and var2 are accessible to the script itself. For example, if you invoked awk1 as above and awk1 looked like:

```
{print var1, var2}
```

your output would be:

```
1 2
1 2
1 2
1 2
```

Remember that each line is processed and the command executed.

Note that command line parameters are not available to the BEGIN section of the awk program. With nawk, there is a -v option that allows for command line parameters to be available to the BEGIN procedure through the ARGC and ARGV parameters (similar to argc and argv in C).

Arrays. In awk, all arrays are associative. This means that the array index can be a string or number. Arrays look like:

```
array[index] = value
```

where index represents a position within the array.
value assigns the value to array[index].

The structure to access and loop through this array structure is:

```
for (elem in array) action
```

where elem is a variable that takes on value of each array element.
array ia an array name.
action is the action taken for each element in array.

Some examples. There are almost an infinite number of possible examples for awk. Below are some examples which illustrate some uses of awk. Let's use the same data file as before (data1):

```
1col1 1col2
2col1 2col2
3col1 3col2
4col1 4col2
```

Example 1

```
$ awk '/1/' data1
1col1 1col2
```

This uses the default action of printing the entire line.

Example 2

```
$ awk '$1 ~ /1/' data1
1col1 1col2
2col1 2col2
3col1 3col2
4col1 4col2
```

Example 2 matches all 1s in the first column (~) and performs the default action (print).

Example 3. If you want to check for all matching strings which begin with a 1, use:

```
# awk '$1 ~ /^1/' data1
1col1 1col2
```

Example 4

```
$ awk '$1 == 2col1' data1
2col1 2col2
```

This example uses a boolean operator to compare the first column ($!) with the string 2col1. Remember that you can use any regular expression.

Example 5. You can combine any number of functions and regular expressions to accomplish what you want.

```
$ awk 'length > 11 {print NR}' data1
```

This will scan the data1 file for lines longer than 11 characters. Note that the length function returns the length of the entire line including separators.

```
$ awk '{print length}' data1
11
11
11
11
```

Example 6. To print out the middle two lines, you could use:

```
$ awk 'NR == 2, NR == 3 {print}' data1
2col1 2col2
3col1 3col2
```

Note that the print command is redundant since this is the default action.

Example 7. You can also redefine variables and fields on the fly before output. For example, create an awk file called rename as shown below:

```
BEGIN {
      print "Changing stuff...here we go..."
      }
      {
      if ($2 ~ /2col2/) $2 = "2column2"
      }
END   {
      print "Hope you're satisfied now..."
      }
```

Still operating on data1, you would see:

```
$ awk -f rename data1
2col1 2column2
```

Example 8. To see some examples of looping commands with flow control commands, use:

```
for (i=1;i<2;++i)
     if ($i == "2col2") {
     print i, $i
     break
     }
```

This example will loop through an input file looking at the first two fields until it finds a column match for 2col2; it then prints out the value of i and the column at i and breaks out of the loop.

Example 9. This example scans the passwd file for accounts without passwords and users with duplicate user id's. It demonstrates many of the features available in awk. (This example is taken from *A Practical Guide to the UNIX System* by Mark G. Sobell, Benjamin/Cummings, 1989.)

```
awk < /etc/passwd ' BEGIN{
uid[void] = " " #tell awk that uid is an array
}
{   # no pattern indicates process all records
dup = 0
split($0,field,":") #split fields delimited by :
if (field[2] == "") #check for null password field
{
if (field[5] == "") #check for null info field
{
print field[1] "has no password"
}
```

```
else
     {
     print field[1] " (" field[5]") has no password"
     }
}
for (name in uid) == field[3] #loop through uid array
{
     if (uid[name] == field[3]) #check for 2nd use of id
     {
     print field[1] "has the same UID as "\
     name " : UID = " uid[name]
     dup = 1 #set duplicate flag
     }
}
if (!dup) #same as if (dup==0)
     {
     uid[field[1]] = field[3]
     }
}'
```

There are many things to note about the above file including comments, standard input redirection, and arrays. See awk help and books such as the O'Reilly and Associates Nutshell books for more information. Generate a sample file in the structure of a standard password file and try the above program out for yourself. Note that you invoke it by simply typing its name. This is a complete awk invocation in itself. For example, if the file is named checkpasswd, simply type:

```
$ checkpasswd
```

to run this awk program.

nawk. nawk stands for new awk and was released with SVR3. Many UNIX machines treat awk as nawk and don't tell you. nawk contains a richer set of commands and functions. Some of the newer functions are:

Multidimensional arrays

ARGV and ARGC system variables

Arithmetic functions such as atan2, rand, srand

String substitution commands such as sub and gsub

Writing your own functions

System access via the system() call

Again, it should be said that many of these functions have been integrated into awk as awk has been replaced by nawk. However, you will still find awk out there, and you should be careful how you code your awk scripts if portability is an issue. Perhaps GNU's awk (gawk) may be of interest if you are concerned about portability.

gawk. This is GNU's version of awk. It contains functions not in awk or nawk and runs on almost all platforms running today. See Sec. 11.10 and the software included on the accompanying CD for more information on gawk.

awkcc. awkcc is a utility which converts awk programs to C programs which can then be compiled and executed. Because awk is an interpreted language, it is slow and relatively clumsy when it comes to execution and performance. The awkcc program is available from the AT&T System Toolchest. Call AT&T for more information.

5.1.3 Conclusion

awk is a very powerful language for file and string manipulation. Its strengths occur when data is formatted in such a way that it can be manipulated by column. You can treat data as type independent, and awk will behave as you would expect most of the time. Spend some time with awk, and you will begin to see some of its power. If you are interested in the GNU version of awk, see Sec. 11.10. gawk has the advantage of being the same awk on all platforms in your environment, while awk can vary from UNIX to UNIX implementation.

5.2 sed

5.2.1 Introduction

sed is an acronym for stream editor. It interprets scripts written in sed format. It supports the basic functions of ed while having an interactive capability of grep. ed reads in one line at a time and performs a sed command against it; it then reads in the next line and so on. If there is a match in the current line, the substitution is made and the resulting line printed out. If there is no match, the current line is printed out unchanged.

sed is most often used to perform substitutions into medium- and large-size files. Because of the ability to act on one line at a time, you can alter very large files without invoking an editor or worrying about memory or disk space requirements. Many editors, including vi and ed, read a file from the disk into virtual memory and create a temporary, or working, file. This essentially doubles the disk space required and may cause problems when working with large files. sed helps you avoid this, and many UNIX developers use sed for just this reason.

5.2.2 Usage

The syntax for the sed command is:

```
sed [-n] [-e sedcommand[-e sedcommand...]] [-f scriptfile] [filelist]
```

or

```
sed "sed command(s)" [filelist]
```

where -n means no print; sed does not copy files to stdout except as specified by the p command.
-e sedcommand allows you to enter multiple sed commands on the command line without having to create a file.
-f scriptfile specifies a sed command script.
filelist is a list of files separated by blanks to be processed; if filelist is not specified, standard input (stdin) is used, which means the keyboard.

Simple and short, sed commands are usually entered on the command line, while more complex and lengthy sed scripts are typically invoked from a file containing multiple sed commands.

The sed command uses standard ed commands (see Chap. 3) and performs substitutions as you would normally expect to enter within an editor. For example, examine the file named file.text below:

```
john is great
pete is good
gerard is cranky
sam is bad
joe is good
frank is frank, what can you say
```

If you want to change a simple string within the above file, you could issue the command:

```
$ sed "s/john/kevin/" file.txt
```

The resultant output is:

```
kevin is great
pete is good
gerard is cranky
sam is bad
joe is good
frank is frank, what can you say
```

The above command substitutes the first occurrence of john in every line with kevin. To substitute for good, you would use:

```
$ sed "s/good/okay/" file.txt
```

The resulting output is:

```
kevin is great
pete is okay
```

```
gerard is cranky
sam is bad
joe is okay
frank is frank, what can you say
```

You can issue all of the commands in the ed editor, such as deletes, copies, and moves and can include lines numbers for ranges, etc. For example:

```
$ sed "1,3s/is/is not/" file.txt
kevin is not great
pete is not okay
gerard is not cranky
sam is bad
joe is okay
frank is frank, what can you say
```

Finally, if you want to replace multiple instances on the same line, you would use the /g switch as follows:

```
sed "s/frank/kevin/g" file.txt
john is great
pete is good
gerard is cranky
sam is bad
joe is good
kevin is kevin, what can you say
```

If you had not included the /g option (for global), it would have only substituted kevin for the first occurrence of frank and the subsequent line would have been:

```
kevin is frank, what can you say
```

Note that the sed command is included in double quotes to prevent the shell from interpreting the contents before passing them to the sed executable. This is a common requirement in UNIX since the shells like C and Bourne parse and process any command line information before passing it to any commands or utilities. To ensure that there is no shell preprocessing, simply include any information in double quotes.

sed scripts. sed command files typically consist of lines of the following format:

```
[address[,address]] instruction [arguments]
```

where address consists of line numbers (and special characters such as $ and ^) separated by commands to denote a range.
instruction is an editing instruction that modifies the text.

arguments are commands dependent on the instruction; see ed syntax for more information.

You can include all sed commands in a file and invoke the file from the command line to provide the sed commands. For example, the sed input file (named sed.input) might look like:

```
s/oldstring/newstring/
/newstring/d
```

The example data file called file.data looks like this:

```
this contains oldstring
this doesn't contain oldstring
this contains oldstring
this doesn't contain oldstring
```

To invoke the sed script file on the above data file, you would type:

```
$ sed -f sed.input file.data
this doesn't contain oldstring
this doesn't contain oldstring
```

To understand what sed did in this context, you must understand how sed processes sed scripts and input data files. sed first reads in the first line of data.file and processes the entire sed script file against this line before moving to the second line of file.data. This means that sed reads in the first line:

```
this contains oldstring
```

and performs a string substitution resulting in the string:

```
this contains newstring
```

It then performs the next command in the sed script file, which deletes the line which contains the string newstring, which this line does. It deletes the line. sed has reached the end of the sed script file and reads the next line in the input file file.data. It then replicates the above procedure; however, because there is no string substitution, the line is not deleted. The line is printed out and sed moves to the next line in the input file. This occurs for all lines in the input data file.

The above discussion may concern you; if it doesn't, it should. It is often very difficult to predict exactly what is going to happen when you apply multiple edits to a file with sed. Because of this, sed has the additional safeguard of writing the resultant lines to standard output and not to the original input file. If you want to write the resultant output to a file, you simply redirect standard output as you would with any other command:

```
$ sed "s/oldstring/newstring/" file.txt  newfile.txt
```

will generate a file called newfile.txt with the resultant output. It is a good idea, however, to first save a copy of the file you are modifying before performing a sed on it; this will ensure that you get the results you are expecting. If you have a backup copy, you can always recover from a mistake, but if you don't. . . .

Basic sed commands. Some of the basic sed commands are:

`a` Appends one or more lines to the current line. Append has a special format where the address must consist of a single number or defaults to the entire file and the insertion text must be continued with backslashes (see examples):

```
[address] a\
text\
text\
text
```

`#` Comment line and must occur on the the first line only; the comment can be continued onto the next line with a backslash.

`c` Changes selected lines and replaces them with new text.

`d` Deletes the current line. Note that this causes sed to read the next line in the input data file since it is done processing the line even if there are other sed commands in the sed script file.

`i` Insert is exactly the same as append except that it places the insertion text before the current line instead of in front of it.

`l` Lists nonprintable characters as their ASCII code equivalents.

`n` Next reads the next input line from the input data file. It also writes out the current line.

`p` Prints current line as is with no future changes caused by sed script commands.

`q` Quits processing in sed.

`r` Reads the contents of a specified file and appends them to the current line.

`s` Substitute works exactly as in ed and vi; see examples above and below.

`t` Transforms a character in a given position to another (see transform section).

`w` Writes output to a specified file.

Blank lines and spaces. A useful example is the following:

```
$ sed "/^$/d" file.txt
```

This will remove all blank lines in the file named file.txt. The ^ represents the beginning of the line, while the $ represents the end. The lack of address means that this command will act on all lines, and the d means delete any lines that match the pattern of a blank line.

Note that, just as in ed, blank spaces within substitute strings are honored. For example, to remove a leading blank on each line, you could use the command:

```
$ sed "s/ //" file.txt
```

This would remove the first blank on each line in the file file.txt.

More about addresses. It is important to note that, just as in ed, sed can use strings matches as addresses. For example, if you have the following input file named input.dat:

```
this is stuff before the .include macro
blah blah blah
.include
this is an include part of the file because
it is in the include macro section contained by a .include directive
and a ..
..
this is other stuff not related to the include macro section
blah blah blah...
```

you can print out the include macro section with the command:

```
$ sed -n "/^\.include/,/^\.\./p" input.dat
.include
this is an include part of the file because
it is in the include macro section contained by a .include directive
and a ..
..
```

Note that the first address is derived by the resultant match of the .include macro and the last address to close the range is derived by the match of ... Note also that the .s must be backslashed (\), which escapes them from the sed interpreter and ensures that they are interpreted literally.

Append, change, and insert. The append, change, and insert commands all have a similar syntax:

```
append [line]a\
text\
text

change [line,line]c\
text\
text

insert [line]i\
text\
text
```

where the text to be appended, changed, or inserted ends in a line without a backslash. Note also that the line cannot be a range of lines but must be a single line for both append and insert, while the change command can accept a range of lines.

Insert inserts any text before the line is matched. Append appends text to the end of the line matched in the line statement. Finally, change outputs the text *once* and deletes all line in the range specified in the command.

An example data file called file.data might look something like:

```
root:S9KIMi9QQ4f8U:0:1:Operator:/:/bin/csh
nobody:*:65534:65534::/:
daemon:*:1:1::/:
sys:*:2:2::/:/bin/csh
bin:*:3:3::/bin:
uucp:*:4:8::/var/spool/uucppublic:
news:*:6:6::/var/spool/news:/bin/csh
```

You can use the insert command to insert information before the lines to be processed. An example sed script (sample.sed) might look like:

```
1i\
# This is the Password File for this Machine
```

you would get:

```
$ sed -f sample.sed data.input
# This is the Password File for this Machine
root:S9KIMi9QQ4f8U:0:1:Operator:/:/bin/csh
nobody:*:65534:65534::/:
daemon:*:1:1::/:
sys:*:2:2::/:/bin/csh
bin:*:3:3::/bin:
uucp:*:4:8::/var/spool/uucppublic:
news:*:6:6::/var/spool/news:/bin/csh
```

Transform. Transform is structured as follows:

```
[address]y/abc/xyz/
```

where the replacement is made character by character without regard to any characters around it. In other words, the above sed command will replace all characters with an x character regardless of its position or surrounding characters. Where this is particularly useful is in changing uppercase to lowercase and vica versa. For example:

```
/.*/y/abcdefghijklmnopqrstuvwxyz/ABCDEFGHIJKLMNOPQRSTUVWXYZ/
```

will transform all lowercase letters in a file to uppercase.

Reading and writing files with sed. You can use the w and r commands to include files and write intermediate files with sed. The read command can be used as follows:

```
[address]r file
```

where you can specify an address to include a file to be processed. For example, if you have the following input data file named data.file:

```
this is not line1
this is not line2
this is not line3
```

and another file named data.file2 which contains:

```
this is line4
this is line5
this is line6
```

you can combine the files and process them as follows:

```
$ sed '$r data.file2' data.file
this is not line1
this is not line2
this is not line3
this is line4
this is line5
this is line6
```

The write command allows you to create multiple files from a single input data file. For example, if you have a data input file containing the following information:

```
sun gerard
ibm kevin
sun betty
sun carol
ibm john
ibm jeff
```

and you want to create separate files containing information broken down as machine types and names, you could build a script like:

```
/^sun/w sun.out
/^bm/w ibm.out
```

This would create two separate files called sun.out and ibm.out, one containing a list of sun users and one, a list of ibm users.

5.2.3 Conclusion

sed is an extremely powerful stream editor which allows you to perform quick and easy changes to a file without entering an editor. It can be applied within shell scripts and other environments to provide incredible functionality and power. This chapter touched briefly on most of the commands and techniques you would use with sed, but there is much more capability which has not been explored. Techniques such as pattern and hold space are key to utilizing the more powerful aspects of sed. Finally, scripts can contain branching and conditional information which can provide for more functionality inside the sed script files. See both the sed documentation and the books in Sec. C.1 in the back of this book for more details.

5.3 make

5.3.1 Introduction

The make utility is one of the most powerful and complex of all tools in the UNIX environment. Because of its tremendous complexity, this chapter will not address all of the functionality of make but instead will attempt to introduce you to the essential concepts and power of the make utility so that you can understand, modify, and use the make facility to build all Internet software products described in this book as well as products of your own.

You will find that once you understand make and all it can do, you will use it for all of your software development. make is most useful in large projects which involve a lot of source code files and have a somewhat complex compilation and linking environment.

5.3.2 Usage

make allows you to define a set of dependencies between files and object code and executables which define the compilation process. It ensures the minimum compilation necessary to rebuild a product which reflects all changes since the last rebuild. make can call any source compilers including FORTRAN, C, and COBOL and can rebuild the associated products. make can also be used with noncompiled code such as documentation text to maintain dependencies between files.

Let's assume you have a program which consists of 100 source code files. Ninety of those files are contained an an archive library. You also need to link in four other libraries from a different product. You may find a bug or want to enhance some functionality of the product. This may require changes to several source code files. When you have made those changes, you will need to recompile and relink your executable.

Because of the large number of files and libraries, it would take quite a while to recompile, rearchive, and relink all source files into a new executable. What you would like to do is recompile only those files that were affected by your changes. make allows you to do this by defining all relationships and dependencies between all files and libraries at the beginning of the project in a makefile. Once this is done, you can simply invoke make after making changes, and the make facility will only recompile and relink only those files which were changed.

make requires an investment of time at the front of the development process in terms of building the makefile and testing it. However, once it is finished, you will save a tremendous amount of time when making changes since make will handle all rebuilds for you automatically. This is the power of make and why most UNIX software developers use it.

The syntax for make is:

```
make [-d] [-e] [-i] [-k] [-n] [-p] [-q] [-r] [-S] [-s] [-t] [-f
file] [target ...] [macro ...]
```

where -d is debug mode.
- -e overrides assignments with environmental variables.
- -i ignores errors and continues processing.
- -k stops processing current target if error occurs but continues with other unrelated targets.
- -n displays commands but doesn't execute them. Useful when debugging.
- -p displays set of default macros and dependencies.
- -q checks to see if current executable is up to date.
- -r doesn't use default rules.
- -S terminates if any command receives an error.
- -s doesn't display commands as they are executed. Silent mode.
- -t touches files without recompiling anything. Used to fool make.
- -f file is used to use a makefile other than the default.
- -target ... specifies a target or targets contained in the makefile to execute.
- -macro ... You can specify one or more macros.

The makefile. When make is invoked, it looks for a file in the current directory unless otherwise directed. This file is typically named makefile or Makefile, and they are searched for in that order. Both are equivalent and define dependencies and actions which control make's behavior.

The typical makefiles contain targets, associated files, and actions. The basic structure is:

```
target [target] ... :[:] [file] ... ['commands'] ... [;command]
[(tab) command]
```

where the first line is known as the dependency line. The dependency line contains a target which is used by make to direct execution, a colon, and a list of files and commands on which the target is dependent. Note that the commands are contained within backquotes; in UNIX and in make, this means that make will treat the output of the command enclosed in backquotes as the input to the current context. All commands on the lines following the dependency line contain commands which will be executed to build the target. All command lines *must* be preceded with a tab. Blanks are *not* a substitute for a tab and will cause make to fail. This is one of the many idiosyncracies of make.

The significance of the second colon is to represent a target that is used more than once. In other words, if you have a target that is defined more than once in a makefile, you must follow each target occurrence with two colons to inform make that you are using the target more than once. The format for each occurrence of the targets is the same as for the single occurrence.

Comments are preceded with a pound (#) sign and occur until the end of a line. You must precede each command line with a #, or make will interpret the line. Blank lines can also be used and will be ignored by make except in a command list under a dependency.

Commands are each executed in their own shells and therefore communication between commands is not possible. As is standard with UNIX, each command gets its own process context and variable space, and this will not be maintained even within a command list under a dependency. Keep this in mind when you are building makefiles and are thinking about dependencies between commands under a dependency line. You can execute more than one command in a single shell by placing a \ at the end of a command line. This continues the command onto the next line. You can place multiple commands separated by \s, and they will run in a single shell. Therefore communication between them will be possible through the use of variables and other process-context-sensitive information.

There are three special characters which control the behavior of commands within the makefile:

+	Executes this command even if the -n, -q, or -t commands are specified
-	Ignores errors returned from this command line
@	Does not print out this command when executing

These, in conjunction with command line switches, control the behavior and output of make and the makefile.

Commands can be continued onto the next line with a \ placed at the end of a line.

A simple makefile. An example of a simple makefile is as follows:

```
kevin.o: kevin.c
     cc -c kevin.c
```

This tells make that there is a dependency between kevin.o and kevin.c. To generate the target kevin.o from the input file kevin.c, make needs to issue the command cc -c to compile the C source file and generate an object output file.

To execute this file named makefile, you would simply type:

```
$ make
```

in the directory which contained the makefile. This example happens to be a default rule (see the section below on default rules) and is unnecessary; however, it is a good example of a simple makefile and how to use make. Note that the tab before the cc command is essential since the make command will not work without this exact structure. For more complex makefiles, see the examples section.

Environment. Environmental variables play a key role in determining how make behaves. By altering these variables, you can change the characteristics of make and its behavior. You need to understand which variables to use and how to use them.

When you run make, it reads the environment and treats all variables as macro definitions. The order of processing of those macro definitions is as follows:

1. Make's own default rules
2. Environmental variables
3. Description files
4. Command line

Note that the last definition of a macro overrides the previous. This means that the command line macro definitions will override all previous definitions and that description file definitions will override environmental variables, etc.

The behavior of make is determined as much by command line switches as by definitions in files. You can use the MAKEFLAGS or MFLAGS variables, which will be examined, in that order, for make switches. For example:

```
$ export MAKEFLAGS=-n
$ make
```

will display commands but not run them. Remember that, because of the definition order described above, if there is a conflicting switch in the definition makefile, the -n will be overridden. You can also override this variable with a command line option.

When commands are invoked, a default shell is used. make first looks for the environmental variable MAKESHELL and then for SHELL. If neither are defined, the Bourne shell (/bin/sh) is used. To change to the Korn shell, for example, you would type:

```
$export MAKESHELL=/bin/ksh
```

and all subsequent commands executed within the context of the make procedure would be executed in the Korn shell. The same is true for the C shell.

The environment is also important relative to your current file searches and contexts. If you issue commands which rely on the existence of unqualified filenames, you will need to be concerned with your current working directory and the existence and accessibility of your files.

Default (internal) rules. make has default rules and dependencies which govern the behavior of make when no explicit dependencies and rules are defined in the makefile. You can use the -p command to view some of these rules:

```
     $ make -p
{kevin@devtech}76: make -p
.PRECIOUS:
.SCCS_GET:
.sccs $(SCCSFLAGS) get $(SCCSGETFLAGS) $@ -G$@
.SUFFIXES: .o .c .cc .s .S .ln .f .F .l .mod .sym .def .p .r .y .h
.sh .cps
.c.ln:
$(LINT.c) $(OUTPUT_OPTION) -i $<
.def.sym:
$(COMPILE.def) -o $@ $<
.mod:
$(COMPILE.mod) -o $@ -e $@ $<
.y.o:
$(YACC.y) $<
$(COMPILE.c) $@ $%
$(RM) $%
.F.o:
$(COMPILE.F) $(OUTPUT_OPTION) $<
.F.a:
$(COMPILE.F) -o $% $<
$(AR) $(ARFLAGS) $@ $%
$(RM) $%
```

```
.mod.o:
$(COMPILE.mod) -o $@ $<
.mod.a:
$(COMPILE.mod) -o $% $<
$(AR) $(ARFLAGS) $@ $%
$(RM) $%
...
```

The above is only a partial listing of the output of the make -p command but is representative of the kind of default, or built-in, rules make contains. All definitions for compilers and library formats have a default format for make which determines how things will be compiled and linked. Keep in mind that this differs from system to system. It is generally a good idea to do a make -p before invoking make on your makefile to understand any default rules that may affect your desired result.

The above describes the default dependencies and rules defined in make without any explicit definitions. Keep them in mind when you are building your makefile. You can disable the internal rules of make with the -r command. Each machine typically stores internal rules in a file which you can examine. On AIX, this file is /usr/ccs/lib/make.cfg; on SunOS, it is /usr/include/make/default.mk. See your make documentation for more details about your system.

Suffixes and dependencies. Suffix rules consist of default definitions and predetermined behaviors based on file suffixes. For example, the .c suffix tells make that this is a C source input file; the default action to produce a .o file is the cc -c command. This default rule tells you why the above simple makefile is unnecessary since this rule is already predefined. You could have built the makefile like:

```
kevin.o: kevin.c
```

without a command and make would have known what to do.

You can modify or include suffix rules in the default list of suffix rules by including a .SUFFIXES section in your makefile. For example:

```
.SUFFIXES: .o .kev
```

defines an additional suffix rule that says that to create a .o file you can look, in addition to the default rules, for a file ending in .kev. Note that later you must define what you want this rule to entail by defining commands to execute for this rule.

The default suffix rules are:

```
.SUFFIXES: .o .c .c\~ .f .f\~ .y .y\~ .l .l\~ .s .s\~ .sh .sh\~ .h
.h\~ .a
```

This defines the order in which files are searched to produce a nonexplicitly defined behavior for a given file suffix. The \~ on the end of some of the suffixes allows for the use of Source Code Control System (SCCS), which is the standard way to maintain and control versions of software in UNIX. The rest of the suffixes are:

`.o`	Object code
`.c`	C source code
`.c\~`	C source code in SCCS
`.f`	Fortran source code
`.f\~`	Fortran source code in SCCS
`.y`	yacc code
`.y\~`	yacc code in SCCS
`.l`	lex code
`.l\~`	lex code in SCCS
`.s`	Assembler
`.s\~`	Assembler in SCCS
`.sh`	Shell source
`.sh\~`	Shell in SCCS
`.h`	Header file source
`.h\~`	Header file source in SCCS
`.a`	Archive library

If you want to clear the default suffix list, simply use the .SUFFIXES command with no suffixes. For example:

```
.SUFFIXES:
```

will clear all default suffix rules.

The order of the SUFFIXES rules is important since make interprets the SUFFIXES lines from left to right. This means that make will first try to find an associated C source input file before a Fortran source file before a yacc, etc. Be careful when placing files with the same name in the directory in which make is going to build a product. Always remember the order of the SUFFIXES default list.

Suffix rules which are explicitly contained in your makefile override default rules. For example, if you define a .c.o suffix rule and an associated set of commands, this will override the default rule. As an example:

```
.c.o:
	f77 $<
```

tells make to invoke the Fortran compiler to translate a .c file into a .o file. You should get a lot of syntax errors if you try this one. Obviously this doesn't make sense; however, you can do this and override the default cc invocation if you would like.

make is extremely flexible and allows you to define any relationship you would like based on your needs. Don't forget that make maintains various default rules and relationships, and these must be considered when defining your own.

Targets. Targets define how make will behave. You can specify a target on the command line which will force make to begin execution of the makefile at that target line, skipping any previous commands and targets. This is used to give the makefile different behaviors based on which target you choose. For example, it is common in Internet software to provide a target called clean. This will delete all object files and executables from the current product. This ensures that when you issue a new build command (make), you get completely new executables independent of the relationship between the source code dates and the object and executable dates. This is necessary when recompiling a product on a different architecture than the executables were originally built on.

There are default targets which perform special functions. Some of these are:

`.DEFAULT`	Commands following this target tell make what to do if it can find no commands or rules to generate a specific file or files.
`.IGNORE`	Tells make to ignore errors in the commands and continue processing.
`.POSIX`	Processes the makefile as the POSIX standard specifies.
`.PRECIOUS [file ...]`	Files named on this line are not removed if make is interrupted. If no file is specified, all files are the default.
`.SILENT`	Make does not display any commands during the make.
`.SUFFIXES`	Adds suffixes to the suffix list (see above section).

If you do not specify a target on the make command line, the first target in the makefile will be executed. Note that a target can call make recursively to build other dependent products. Note also that a target can use other targets to build products, and, in fact, this is often the case when building more sophisticated makefiles for large products.

Targets can appear more than once in a makefile; however, only the first occurrence of the target can contain a command section. The dependency list between the two can and should be different, but the commands to operate on the target will be the same. Remember that make processes the first target it sees if not given an explicit target and will therefore find the first target and then the second. If you need to use more than one set of commands for the same target, you must use the double colon option described in the makefile section above.

Macros. Macros are like traditional variables. The basic syntax for a macro definition is:

```
oldstring = newstring
```

This defines oldstring to be replaced by newstring every time it occurs. To designate that you want a replacement, use the syntax:

```
$(oldstring)
```

Every time the $(oldstring) occurs in the file, it is replaced by newstring. This allows you to code your makefile with a symbol and create one single macro definition at the beginning of the makefile. Using this, you can change one line in your makefile, and the change is reflected throughout the entire makefile.

make has the following set of default macros:

`$*`	Filename without the suffix of the input file
`$@`	Full target name of the current target
`$<`	Source files of an out-of-date module
`$$`	Represents an actual dollar sign
`$$@`	Represents the current target name
`$%`	Name of an archive library member
`$?`	List of out-of-date files; used with explicit rules
`CC`	Default C compiler on the system
`AS`	Default assembler on the system
`CFLAGS`	Default flags for C compiler

These default macros are used constantly throughout most makefiles since they make it much easier to define a set of files and associated behaviors. The most commonly changed macros are the final three. While you can change their definition in the beginning of the makefile with a definition statement like those defined above, you can also change the macro definition from the command line. For example:

```
$ make "CC=gcc"
```

will cause make to invoke the GNU C compiler instead of the standard C compiler which comes with the system. The other most commonly used macro is the CFLAGS macro. You can use this on the command line to change the compiler flags used by make when building object codes. For example, you may want to run the debugger on the resultant executable. For this you need to use the -g switch on the cc command:

```
$ make "CFLAGS=-g"
```

This will enable debugging for the resultant executable.

Macros are most often used much as you would use an environmental variable in a shell. By creating a macro at the beginning of the makefile, you can issue a change to the value of the macro once, and it is reflected through the entire makefile instantly. For example:

```
KEVDIR = /usr/kevin
INCDIR = $(KEVDIR)/include
LIBDIR = $(KEVDIR)/lib
CFLAGS = -O -c -g

kevin: kevin.o
     $(CC) $(CFLAGS) -o kevin kevin.o
kevin.o: kevin.c $(LIBDIR)/kevin.lib $(INCDIR)/kevin.inc
```

This will use the default rules to compile kevin.o and the explicit rules stated as macros to link kevin. This is a strange example; can you find anything wrong with it?

Library archives and related issues. Archives are groups of executable files placed together in a library for ease of linking and maintenance. Most archives use the suffix .a to signify their type. The command to use with archives is ar (see Sec. 4.4 for more information on ar). Archives are a special entity to make since they are used so often when developing software in a UNIX environment. Because of the history of archives, they are well understood, and, therefore, there are default rules and behavior within make related to archives.

make has several default rules which apply to archive libraries:

`.c.a`	C source code to an archive library (described below)
`.c\~.a`	SCCS C source code to archive library
`.s\~.a`	SCCS assembler source to archive library
`.f.a`	Fortran source to archive library
`.f\~.a`	SCCS Fortran source to archive library

These rules give you default behavior for taking both SCCS and normal source code and placing compiled objects into a library. This saves you from having to write the commands section to compile and archive the resultant object code.

If a target contains parentheses, make assumes you are using an archive. The string within the parenthesis denotes a member within the archive. The basic structure is:

```
lib(kevin.o)
```

This denotes an archive library named lib and a member within this library named kevin.o. You typically want to build entire archives consisting of compiled subroutines. There is a default rule for the construction of archive libraries. It is:

```
.c.a:
     $(CC) -c $(CFLAGS) $<
          ar rv $@ $*.o
          rm -f $*.o
```

This rule breaks down as follows:

`.c.a`	Target which denotes that the translation from a .c file to a .a file is determined by the commands that follow the target
`$(CC) -c $(CFLAGS) $<`	The net result of the $(CC) command is to recompile any C source code files that have a more recent modification date than their associated member in the archive where: $(CC)--the CC macro has been previously defined and is, by default, the cc command. $(CFLAGS)--the CFLAGS macro has been predefined and contains C compiler switches. $< says that you should use any .c file with the same name as a module in the archive with the same filename.
`ar rv $@ $*.o`	Uses the archive (ar) command to replace all object modules with a more current .c source code file. This is done one member at a time.
`$@`	Denotes the target in process.
`$*.o`	Denotes the current .o file in process rm -f $*.o.

This default rule for archives describes a significant amount of the power of make and shows how you can use it to control your software development process. Typically, the way you would see the dependencies and targets structures for an archive is as follows:

```
library: library(file1.o) library(file2.o) library(file3.o)
library(file4.o)
```

The target is library, the archive name is library, and the members within the library are named file1.o through file4.o. If you run make on a makefile which contains the line above, the default rule described earlier will be invoke, and make will examine the current directory for an archive named library.a. It will then examine file1.o's modification date and compare it to file1.c in the current directory. If file1.c's modification date is newer than file1.o in the archive library, make will invoke the C compiler, archive (with the replace option) the new module, and remove the resultant file1.o from the compilation. It will then do the same for file2.o through file4.o sequentially. This is a very powerful capability and allows you to save a tremendous amount of time when maintaining large software libraries and packages.

Include files. Include files are the most commonly changed and used aspect of a makefile. In most programming languages you include files which contain header and variable information that is common to more than one source code file. Dependencies between source code files and header/include files should also be described in the makefile. For example, let's assume we have a program which consists of four source code files named file1.f through file4.f and two header files named file1.h and file2.h. You should describe the dependencies between these files in the makefile. For example:

```
files: file1.o file2.o file3.o file4.o
# create file executable files
     f77 file1.o file2.o file3.o file4.o -o files
# now build targets referenced above
file1.o: file1.f
     f77 -c file1.f file1.h
file2.o: file2.f
     f77 -c file2.f file1.h
file3.o: file3.f
     f77 -c file3.f file2.h
file4.o: file4.f
     f77 -c file4.f file2.h
```

Note that in the above example, the first two object files (file1.o and file2.o) depend not only on their respective source code files but on an include file (file1.h) as well. You have told the make facility that this dependency exists by including the name of the include file in the dependency statement. Therefore, make will automatically build only those executables that are effected when an include file is changed.

For example, if you change file2.h and reissue the make command, only file3.f and file4.f will be recompiled. After these have been recompiled, files will be relinked with the original file1.o and file2.o and with the new file3.o and file4.o. While this is a fairly simple example, you can see how very complex systems can be described with the makefile and how make can save you a significant amount of time in rebuilding a product.

Examples. You have seen most of the techniques used by makefile developers in structuring the makefile. Once you understand these basic techniques, the biggest part of constructing a makefile is the tedious work of understanding all of the relationships and workings of your development environment. Now that you have seen some simple examples, the best way to understand make is to see a relatively complex example. Once you study this example, much of the above information will begin to make sense as a whole.

This example is taken directly from the AIX manual page shipped with AIX on an RS/6000. It is the makefile used to maintain make itself.

```
# Description file for the Make program
# Macro def: send to be printed
P = qprt
# Macro def: source filenames used
FILES = Makefile version.c defs main.c \
        doname.c misc.c files.c \
        dosy.c gram.y lex.c gcos.c
# Macro def: object filenames used
OBJECTS = versio .o main.o doname.o \
        misc.o files.o dosys.o \
        gram.o
# Macro def: lint program and flags
LINT = lint -p
# Macro def: C compiler flags
CFLAGS = -O
# make depends on the files specified
# in the OBJECTS macro definition
make: $(OBJECTS)
# Build make with the cc program
        cc $(CFLAGS) $(OBJECTS) -o make
# Show the file sizes
        @size make
# The object files depend on a file
# named defs
$(OBJECTS): defs
# The file gram.o depends on lex.c
# uses internal rules to build gram.o
gram.o: lex.c
clean:
        rm *.o gram.c
        -du
# Copy the newly created program
# to /usr/bin and delete the program
# from the current directory
install:
        @size make /usr/bin/make
        cp make /usr/bin/make; rm make
# Empty file ":print" depends on the
# files included in the macro FILES
print: #(FILES)
# Print the recently changed files
        pr $? | $P
# Change the date on the empty file,
# print, to show the date of the last
# printing
        touch print
# Check the date of the old
# file against the date
# of the newly created file
test:
        make -dp | grep -v TIME > 1zap
        /usr/bin/make -dp | grep -v TIME > 2zap
        diff 1zap 2zap
        rm 1zap 2zap
# The program, lint, depends on the
```

```
# files that are listed
lint:   dosys.c doname.c files.c main.c misc.c \
        version.c gram.c
# Run lint on the files listed
# LINT is an internal macro
        $(LINT) dosys.c doname.c files.c main.c \
        misc.c version.c gram.c
        rm gram.c
# Archive the files that build make
arch:
        ar uv /sys/source/s2/make.a $(FILES)
```

There are several things to note about this makefile. First is the macro definitions. There are spaces surrounding the = sign, but this is not required. Unlike most other UNIX utilities, you can either put spaces around the = signs or not, at your discretion. Several macros are used to define lists of files and commands. FILES and OBJECTS define lists of files to be used in a later command, while LINT and P define commands themselves. Remember, macros are simply strings which will be substituted before execution of the line in the makefile, so they can be anything you would like.

The extensive use of comments is excellent practice since makefiles tend to end up being maintained by someone other than the original author. Documenting the makefile is just as important as documenting the code itself. Note that the commands are each executed in their own shell, one per command line, except for the case of the command "cp make /usr/bin/make ; rm make." Two commands will be executed in the same shell because of the use of a semicolon. This is a powerful technique you can employ if you want to execute more than one command in a single shell.

As the make begins, the first target is make. When make reaches this target, it begins to process the makefile. The objects listed in the OBJECTS macro are substituted on the line, and dependencies are built. The OBJECTS files are dependent on defs, which is another target which make finds. grame.o depends on a file lex.c and make will use default rules to build gram.o from lex.c. Note that this is a special case; make has internal rules for yacc and lex files. In this case, gram.c is dependent on gram.y, which is a yacc file. First make invokes the yacc compiler on gram.y to create gram.c Then make invokes the C compiler on gram.c to create gram.o. This chapter will not detail this; see make, yacc, and lex documentation for more details. Finally, all dependencies are established, and the make executable is built.

The output of the make command would be something like:

```
$ make
cc -O -c version.c
cc -O -c main.c
cc -O -c doname.c
```

```
cc -O -c misc.c
cc -O -c files.c
cc -O -c dosys.c
yacc gram.y
mv y.tab.c gram.c
cc -O -c gram.c
cc version.o main.o doname.o misc.o files.o dosys.o
gram.o -o make
13188+3348+3044 = 19580b = 046174b
```

Note that targets like print, test, and lint are not executed. To run lint on all files to check for syntax errors, you would use:

```
$ make lint
```

This would run lint on all files and generate the proper output for syntax checking. Once the first target (in this case make) is done, execution is stopped. Changed files can be printed by issuing the command:

```
$ make print
```

This command outlines a sophisticated makefile. If you understand all that occurred with this makefile, you are ready to use make for your project. If you aren't comfortable with this example, see your make man page and a book such as the O'Reilly & Associates make book.

5.3.3 Conclusion

make is a very powerful tool for building and maintaining software systems on a variety of platforms, including UNIX. It is used by virtually every tool on UNIX that consists of more than just a few source files to be built. By using make, you significantly reduce the maintenance load on your developers while at the same time increasing the quality of your code. It is certainly a tool you will read more about as you go through this book.

5.4 lex

5.4.1 Introduction

lex stands for lexical analysis program generator. It uses its own language and syntax to generate programs called scanners. These programs read data and parse according to the rules structured in the lex input file. These are typically used as parsers and scanner programs for input data. You can generate a relatively simple lex input program which will scan input for regular expression patterns and generate an action coded in C. This gives you a relatively simple way to structure code for input structures while at the same time having the power of the C language to execute an action based on some string or expression. This is the real power of lex and why many sophisticated UNIX users use it.

From the lex input file, a C source code file is created named lex.yy.c. This file is known as a scanner and is compiled with a special lex library which contains functions which lex uses. The resultant executable is what you use to scan input and generate the appropriate actions.

There is a GNU program known as flex which is used by most UNIX power users to replace lex. See Sec. 11.12 for more details on the lex syntax itself since flex is backward compatible with respect to most lex functionality.

Lexical analysis is the process of taking information and dividing it into units typically called tokens. This process requires a great deal of complexity in terms of analysis and coding to provide the "tokenization" of text. This is what lex excels at.

lex is often used with an associated product called yacc, which is a parsing language. yacc is described more fully in the next section. lex and yacc work together to provide a significant fourth-generation/RAD capability which is not found in many other systems. In fact, many UNIX tools are written with lex and/or yacc.

5.4.2 Usage

lex takes input syntax and converts it to C source code which can then be compiled and executed just as you would any other C program. lex creates a routine named yylex in the output file lex.yy.c. This can then be linked and executed to achieve the lexical analysis desired.

Figure 5.1 describes very well what process that creates a sophisticated program using lex and yacc. The figure is taken directly from *lex & yacc* written by Tony Mason and Doug Brown (O'Reilly & Associates, Inc.). This is a great book and a must for any lex/yacc developer.

Figure 5.1 accurately describes the process of generating both lex output (lex.yy.c), yacc output (y.tab.c), and your own C routines to combine into a single executable. This is a very powerful yet complex process which involves a large amount of knowledge about languages and parsers. Keep this in mind as you examine lex and yacc.

The basic synax for lex is:

```
lex [-fntv] [file ...]
```

where -f specifies faster compilation and larger scanner tables.
-n doesn't display output.
-t displays results on standard output instead of lex.yy.c.
-v is verbose mode.
file ... is one or more files to treat as input to lex.

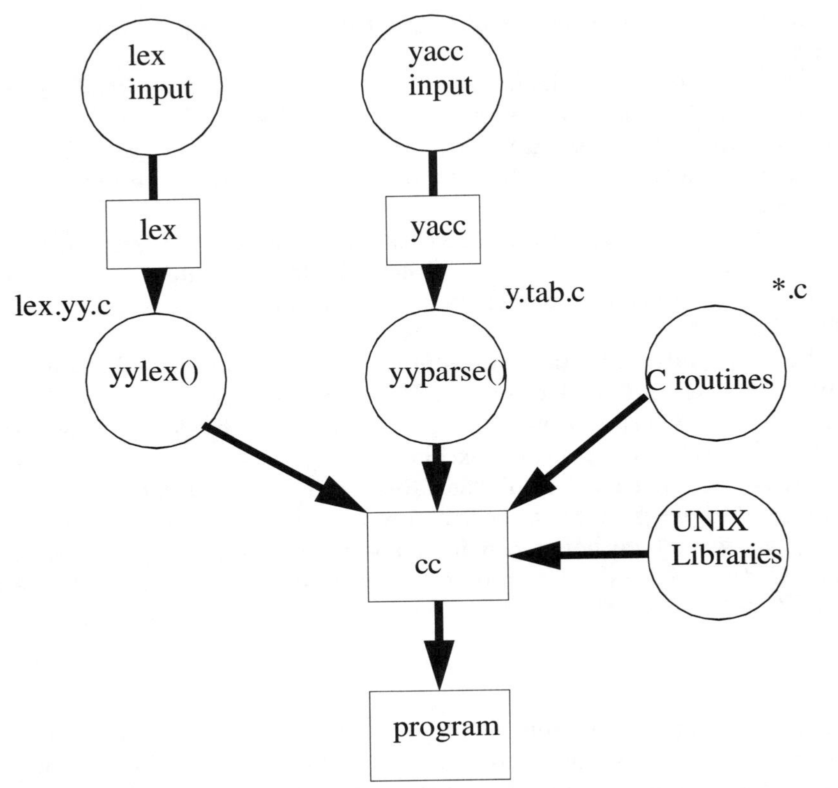

Figure 5.1 The lex and yacc process. ("lex & yacc," *Tony Mason and Doug Brown, © 1992, O'Reilly & Associates, Inc., p. 137. For orders and information, call 800-998-9938.)*

The lex language. lex input files consist of sections based on rules and actions as well as on descriptions separated by %%'s. The basic format is:

```
definitions
%%
rules
%%
user defined functions
```

The definitions section allows you to specify definitions which can define token values to pass to yacc as well as other routines in lex and C. The rules section defines the rules and associated actions which your parser will use to parse and tokenize input. Finally, the user-defined functions allow you to write your own C routines to interface with the lex analyzer.

Often the user-defined functions consist solely of a main routine which takes some input and calls yylex. A simple example of this is:

```
extern int num;
...rules using num to determine behavior and possible
modifying num in the code...
%%
int num;

main(argc,argv)
int argc;
char *argv[];
{
if (argc != 0)
     num=atoi(argv[1]);
else
     printf("You need some command line arguments\n");
yylex();
}
```

This example demonstrates that you may create your own main routine and call yylex to do the lexical analysis. You are sharing the variable num, which you can access and modify in both the rules section and the user-defined function section.

A slightly more complex example is given in the Sun man page for lex as:

```
%% [A-Z] putchar (yytext[0]+'a'-'A'); []+$;[]+putchar(' ');
```

The above lex input file will replace all uppercase letters with lowercase letters and remove all blanks at the end of a line. Finally, it will replace all multiple blank occurrences with a single blank.

The [A-Z] is the pattern lex uses to match against. This means that a match will occur on any uppercase letter. The resulting C functions work as follows:

`putchar(yytext[0]+'a'-'A');`	Standard algorithm used to replace uppercase with lowercase letters by subtracting the difference between the ASCII representations of the characters themselves.
`[]+$;`	Removes all blanks at the end of the line.
`[]+putchar(' ');`	Replaces all multiple character occurrences with a single space.

yytext[0] is a special lex function which provides the current tokenized string of information to output. If you don't use yytext, you will get the token value and not the token itself in the output stream. See the next example for this.

If you assume the name of this file is uptolower.lex, you could execute the command:

```
$ lex uptolower.lex
```

The resulting file is named lex.yy.c and consists, on a Sun platform, of some 572 lines of C code. The code is not included here for obvious reasons; however, take one minute and key this into your local system and execute the commands as listed above. You should get something similar.

Note that if you want to compile this system, you should use a command like:

```
$ cc lex.yy.c -ll
```

This will generate an executable a.out, which can be executed normally and which uses standard input and output during its operation. Note that the -ll on the command line is necessary because the lexical analyzer yylex() needs a dummy main routine to initiate the program. Without the libl library, the program will not link. Issue a command like:

```
$ ./a.out < datainput
```

and the a.out executable will modify the appropriate data input and take the actions determined by the match to an uppercase character.

Another simple example is the following simple lexical analyzer named caps.l:

```
%{
#define NUMBER 400
#define COMMENT 401
#define TE402
#define COMMAND 403
%}
%%
[ \t]+       ;
[0-9]+       |
[0-9]+       |
\.[0-9]+               {return NUMBER;}
#*                     {return COMMENT;}
\"[^\"\n]*\"           {return TEXT;}
[a-zA-Z][a-zA-Z0-9]+   {return COMMAND;}
\n                     {return '\n';}
#include <stdio.h>
main(argc,argv)
int argc;
char *argv[];
{
int val;
while (val = yylex()) printf("value is %d\n",val);
}
```

This example is taken directly from *lex & yacc* by Tony Mason and Doug Brown (O'Reilly & Associates, Inc.).

This example illustrates the relative simplicity of the lex syntax. If you generated equivalent C code, it would be much more sophisticated and complex to provide the function which you receive from the above lex example.

Anything between %{ and %} is copied directly into the resulting C source code. This allows you to embed any information in the declarations section that you want, and it will appear exactly as written in the resulting C source code file.

Something to note about the lex syntax is that the first pieces of information on a line are simply UNIX regular expressions which allow you to express just about any type of expression without too much difficulty. This is the rules part of the lex input file, which is designated by surrounding %%'s. This specifies what you want to match and has an associated action to execute if a match occurs.

If you look at the above example and take a line to examine, you might use the following:

```
[0-9]+\.[0-9]+        |
```

The [] denotes an exclusive choice of one character 0–9, and the + denotes one or more occurrences of the match. The \ is the escape character and ensures that the . (dot) is taken literally and not as a position holder to match any single character (as is the default case if the . is not escaped). The second [0-9]+ has the same meaning as the first occurrence. Therefore, this will match any string like:

```
1.1
0.0
11.11
100.100
etc.
```

Note that this, taken in context with the other three lines representing different regular expression syntax, will match to a *number.* Note also that the | is a continuation line which allows you to specify alternate rules for each specific action. This is exactly what is done in this example to ensure that we get all the kinds of numbers we are looking for.

The other part of the lex input file is the actions section. Each rule has an associated action which will be performed when a rule is matched.

To use the above example, issue the series of commands:

```
$ lex caps.l
```

This will create a file lex.yy.c which contains all the C source code created from the lex input file. Next compile and link the code:

```
$ cc -o caps lex.yy.c -ll
```

This will create an executable caps which you can then execute as you normally would. If you take an input file named caps.input which looks like:

```
This is a test of the caps (or CAPS) program. It has UPPERCASE
and lowercase words from which to CHOOSE. OKAY ...bye..
```

and run the lex analyzer above, you would use a command like:

```
$ caps < caps.input
UPPERCASE
OKAY
```

Note that only the uppercase tokens followed by a blank, tab, or newline character will be displayed.

The #define statements define tokens and associated token numbers to the parser routine yyparse. Both yacc and lex must share the same routines and tokens to ensure that the parser and lexical analyzer are communicating correctly and can recognize each other's tokens. See Sec. 5.5 for more details on parsers.

This section is a very brief introduction to lex. For more information and before you get serious about using lex, see the already referenced Nutshell book *lex & yacc* by Tony Mason and Doug Brown from O'Reilly & Associates; it is the de facto standard documentation for these tools and contains much more information than is presented here.

Flex and its differences. flex is a lex equivalent available from GNU software. See Sec. 11.12 for more examples and information on both lex and flex. In summary, the basic differences between flex and lex are:

flex generates faster code.

flex provides larger table sizes.

flex has no external library libl.a.

flex doesn't support RATFOR.

flex supports more flexible grouping with parenthesis.

flex reads in one file; lex reads in many files and concatenates them together.

flex doesn't support lex input and output functions.

There are other functions that flex provides. See Sec.11.12 for more information.

5.4.3 Conclusion

lex is a very powerful language which supports many different programs. This section is relatively short because of a similar discussion in Sec. 11.12 as well as the sheer complexity and power of lex. flex is the GNU version of lex and provides enhanced functionality as well as greater speed and reliability. Because of this, it is recommended that you take a look at flex as an alternative to lex. More discussion of lex input files occurs in Sec. 11.12.

Some good examples of lex files exist in the groff distribution. See this distribution for working lex input files and associated scanners.

5.5 yacc

5.5.1 Introduction

yacc is an acronym for "yet another compiler compiler." yacc is very similar to lex in that it provides a context-free grammar which it converts to C code which must be compiled and executed as you normally would C code. yacc generates a system called a parser. The parser is responsible for taking tokens generated from a lexical analyzer (typically) and generating an action based on the parsing of the input data. This is typically the second phase in the processing of an input stream and occurs immediately after the lexical analyzer has broken the input stream into independent pieces called tokens. The tokens are then analyzed for patterns and matches and processed according to actions defined based on the result of the parsing. If this seems complicated, it is. However, it is also extremely powerful and lends itself to techniques like rapid prototyping and rapid application development. Using lex and yacc often speeds up the development of an application interface by orders of magnitude and is in fact used in many tools in UNIX, including some on the CD that accompanies this book.

yacc is commonly used to generate parsing routines in conjunction with lex. See the previous section for more details on lex itself. There is a GNU equivalent called bison which is discussed in Sec. 11.13. See this for more information on bison and other aspects of yacc, including differences between different implementation of yacc itself.

5.5.2 Usage

The basic syntax for yacc is:

```
yacc [-dvlt] grammar
```

where -d generates y.tab.h with the define statements that assign token codes with the user-declared token names.
-v is verbose mode. Creates file y.output which contains table and conflict reports.
-l generates y.tab.c containing no numbered line directives.
-t sets y.tab.c so that it will be compiled with debug mode enabled.
grammar is grammar which determines the structure of the generated parser.

While this section does not discuss the yacc grammar in detail, there are some good examples in the distributions on the CD accompanying this book. See the groff distribution for some good examples of yacc grammar files and lex parser interaction.

You typically create a yacc input file named *.y. You also need a lexical program to pass your tokenized information (yylex). Once you have created both of these, you run yacc on the *.y yacc input file to generate the C source code file. This file is typically named y.tab.c. Finally, you compile and link the resulting C source code files into an executable which you can execute as you normally would.

The C source code file contains a routine yyparse(). This is very similar to lex's yylex and simply performs operations on tokens it gets from yylex(). Each time yyparse needs a token, it calls yylex and is passed the next token. yyparse() must be called from a main routine. Neither yacc nor lex generate a main function, and therefore you must link in with other libraries to complete the build.

The yacc language. While this section in no way pretends to be a real reference for yacc, it outlines some very basic information and examples of yacc to illustrate the power of these tools. The basic structure of a yacc input file is very similar to a lex input file, namely:

```
declarations
%%
rules
%%
C routines
```

The declarations section consists of recognized keywords and associated definitions as well as C code. The basic keywords are:

`%left`	Declares left associative operators
`%nonassoc`	Defines operators which may not associate with themselves
`%right`	Declares right associative operators
`%start`	Defines the start symbol
`%token`	Declares token names
`%type`	Declares the type of nonterminals

Just as with lex, the rules section defines the grammar of the parser, and, finally, the C routines section contains any C source code you may want to include in your final C source code routine.

Again, we will use a simple example file named print-int.y from the *lex & yacc* O'Reilly & Associates book:

```
%token INTEGER

%%
lines: /* empty */
      | lines line
      { printf("= %d\n",$2);}
      ;
line: INTEGER '\n'
      { $$ = $1;}
      ;
%%
#include "lex.yy.c"
```

The first part of this file contains a token definition INTEGER. This is made available from the lex.yy.c lexical analyzer which is included at the bottom of the file. The %% denotes the beginning of the rules section of the file. The lines: line tells us that, as is convention, the first of the two alternative definitions is empty. This is a yacc convention and says that an empty string is legitimate. The alternative definition (lines line) specifies that the input consists of one or more lines. Note that line is recursive and is in fact defined below as an INTEGER followed by a newline character.

The characters contained within the curly braces are the action items. These specify what should be done given a match of the rule. In the case of lines, a printf is specified which displays an equals sign and the integer on the input line. The line action sets the value of the return of the function to the first token. Note that yacc supports special syntax pertaining to the $ sign. $$ denotes the value that is returned from the action, while $n specifies the value of the *n*th token. Therefore, $1 is the value of the first token, $2 the second, and so on.

Given this, the line action sets its return value as the value of the INTEGER on the input line and passes this back to the lines rule as the value line. The lines action takes the value of the second toke (denoted by $2 and line in this case) and prints it to standard output. Finally, the included file lex.yy.c contains a lexical analyzer which must know about and determine what an INTEGER is.

If you assume that you have both the appropriate yacc and lex files as described above, you would build and use them as follows:

```
$ yacc print-int.y
$ lex print-int.l
$ cc -o print-int y.tab.c -ly -ll
```

There are several important things to notice about the above series of commands. First is that you can invoke yacc and lex in any order to create the resulting executable. Because print-int.y includes lex.yy.c, it is not necessary to invoke lex.yy.c on the cc command line. Finally, it is necessary to include both the libl.a and liby.a archive libraries to ensure that all the proper yacc and lex files and a main routine are included so that the program will build properly.

This section does not do justice to the power of yacc and its possible interaction with lex. It does, however, present you with some of yacc's basic capabilities and should give you some idea of how you could use a tool like this in your development work. There are several examples in the systems on the accompanying CD. See in particular the groff distribution for some very sophisticated examples of lex and yacc files. Sun systems also have an example system in /usr/lib/yaccpar. Examine this for another good example of a yacc grammar file.

5.5.3 Conclusion

yacc, while very briefly discussed here, is a very powerful parser generator which provides capabilities well beyond most UNIX commands. The combination of lex and yacc provide a very sophisticated and powerful way to build complex parsing systems quickly and easily. This is how several of the compiler systems available were built. Keep these tools in mind for your development efforts.

Much of the functionality of yacc has been replaced and improved with a tool like bison from GNU. There is more information on some syntax and capabilities in Sec. 11.13.

Chapter

6

General UNIX Utilities

UNIX is filled with small powerful utilities which provide significant functionality. This chapter reviews a significant number of power utilities which come with UNIX. If you master the tools discussed in this chapter, you will certainly be well ahead of many users of UNIX systems and will be amazed at what you can accomplish with a small number of commands.

6.1 grep

6.1.1 Introduction

grep is a tool that allows you to search files for patterns. Patterns can be strings or any other regular expression that you may want to search for. Many try to understand what the grep command name means. It turns out that when the authors of grep began to write the tools, they had a history of development and knowledge of the ed editor. Within the ed editor, the typical structure of a command was g/re/p where the g meant that the command was to work on the entire line and not just the first occurrence, and the p meant to print the resultant output. The re stood for regular expression, which basically entails string and symbol substitution sorts of activities. So the grep command was born out of the ed environment. grep stands for "global regular expression print," which searches for regular expressions within a file and prints them out. This is exactly what grep does without requiring you to enter the ed editor; instead it invokes these commands from the command line.

6.1.2 Usage

The syntax for the grep command is:

```
$ grep [-E | -F ] [-i] [-h] [-q] [-s] [-v] [-w] [-x] [-y] [[[-b]
[-n]] |
[-c | -l]] [-p [separator]] { [-e patternlist...] [-f pattern-
file...] | patternlist }
[file...]
```

where -E matches every expression as an extended regular expression. It makes grep act like egrep.
- -F treats each pattern as a string and not a regular expression.
- -i ignores case.
- -h suppresses filenames when multiple filenames are used.
- -q suppresses all standard output.
- -s suppresses error messages written for nonexistent files.
- -v displays all lines not matching pattern.
- -w does word search.
- -x displays exact matches only.
- -y ignores case. It is the same as -i.
- -b precedes each matched line with a block number.
- -n precedes each line with relative number in the file.
- -c displays count of matching lines.
- -l lists filenames only when lines are matched.
- -p separator displays an entire segment beginning with matched text. Segments are separated by a blank line unless included as the separator parameter with -p.
- -e patternlist specifies patterns to match separated by newlines.
- -f patternfile specifies a file containing patternlists.
- patternlist can be used in place of the -e patternlist switch.
- file specifies the name of a file to search. Standard input is the default.

While the above syntax looks somewhat confusing, you will find that grep is one of the easiest commands to use.

6.1.3 Examples

The best way to see grep is to look at some examples. A simple example of grep is:

```
$ grep kevin file.input
```

which will cause the grep command to search for the string kevin in the file file.input.

Another useful command with grep is as follows:

```
$ grep "\^[a-zA-Z]" *.c
```

This command will search all files with the .c suffix in the current directory and print out lines that begin with a character. This can be useful to pull command lines out of C source code, for example.

The command:

```
$ grep "\^#" *.sh
```

prints out all lines within the current directory from files with a suffix of .sh that have a # in the first column. This is useful to see what, if any, specific shells are being invoked inside shell scripts in the current directory.

One of the most common uses of grep is at the end of a pipe from a previous command. A classic example is something like:

```
$ ps -ef | grep kevin
```

This will list all processes on a system owned by kevin (technically this command will show you any process with the string kevin in it). Note that on a Berkeley system the command would be:

```
$ ps -aux | grep kevin
```

but would give the same result.

Another common use of the grep command is the command:

```
$ ls -l | grep ^d
```

This lists only the directory files in the current directory. Remember the ^ denotes the beginning of a line, so the command searches for all lines beginning with a d and therefore displays only the directories.

6.1.4 Conclusion

grep is a very powerful command which you can use to search for regular expressions in files and perform operations on the results. There are other tools which provide similar functionality. egrep (extended grep) works with extended regular expressions which contain more special characters; however, you are punished with slower performance than with grep. There is also a tool called fgrep (fast grep) which works more quickly than grep but handles only strings and not regular expressions (it also seems that fast grep is sometimes slower than grep, so watch out). See your local man pages for more information.

6.2 diff

6.2.1 Introduction

The diff command allows you to compare files for changes. You can compare single files or contents of directories. Differences are displayed on a line-by-line basis. The output also contains commands which you can use to alter the lines to make them the same.

6.2.2 Usage

The syntax for the diff command is:

```
$ diff [-c [lines] | -C lines | -D [string] | -e | -f | [-b] [-i]
[-t] [-w] file1 file2
```

where -c lines produce diff command with lines of context. The default is three. The default structure for output consists of the first line containing the filename and creation dates; the second line contains a line of asterisks. Then lines removed from file1 are marked with a -, and lines added to file2 are marked with a +. Finally, lines changed are marked with a !. Changes within the specified context lines are grouped together.

-C lines are similar to -c lines, but the lines variable is required with -C.

-D string creates a merged version of file1 and file2 on standard output.

-e produces output in ed format for editing file1 to file2.

-f is similar to -e; however, it produces ed commands in reverse order of -e.

-b ignores leading spaces and tabs.

-i ignores case of letters.

-t expands tabs in output lines. Maintains original text structure on output.

-w ignores spaces and tabs.

file1 file2 specifies two files or directories to compare.

When you compare two files, the output is simply the difference between the two files. When the two filenames are directories, the files within the directory are compared. Finally, if one filename is a file and the other is a directory, the diff command searches the directory for a filename which matches the filename in the other file input parameter and compares the files.

6.2.3 Examples

The best way to understand the diff command is to see some examples. Let's assume we have the following two files:

```
file1                       file2
this is line1 of file1      this is line1 of file2
this is line2 of file1      this is line2 of file2
```

When you execute the command:

```
$ diff file1 file2
```

you get the output:

```
1,2c1,2
< this is line1 of file1
< this is line2 of file1
---
> this is line1 of file2
> this is line2 of file2
```

This says that the lines differing between the two files are lines 1 and 2. The < denotes the first file, and the > denotes the second.

If you change the first file to contain:

```
this is line1 of file1
this is line2 of file2
```

and run the same command, you would get:

```
1c1
< this is line1 of file1
---
> this is line1 of file2
```

This says that only the first lines of the file are different. Note that the files are separated by a dashed line.

6.2.4 Conclusion

The diff command compares all text files and generates a listing which displays all differences between files. There are utilities which take the output of the diff command and recreate a merged version. See Part 3 of this book for more details on some of these tools.

The diff command is certainly not complex since this is really all there is to it. Experiment with it more and you will quickly get the hang of it. It is important to note that the diff command only works on text files. If you wish to compare binaries files, you must use a command like sum or cksum. See Sec. 6.12 for more details on these commands.

6.3 tr

6.3.1 Introduction

tr is short for translation. The tr command allows you to substitute characters with different characters from standard input and output. This is a very powerful capability which allows you to replace characters, including nonprintable characters, in a file from the command line. A common example is the replacement of the carriage return/linefeed end of lines from DOS machines with newline characters for UNIX.

As with many commands, there are two distinct versions of the tr command: Berkeley and AT&T; however, they are very similar, both in behavior and syntax, and therefore only the Berkeley version will be discussed. See your local system documentation for more details on your particular implementation.

6.3.2 Berkeley usage

The basic command syntax is:

```
tr [-A] { [-c -s] string1 [string2] | { -d | } string1}
```

where -A performs operations using ASCII collation order instead of current locale collation order.
-c specifies the complement of string1. The complement of string1 is all the characters in the character set not represented in string1.
-s deletes from standard input all but the first occurrence of any characters in string2.
-d deletes each character in string1 from standard input.
string1 is a string of characters (see the string section below).
string2 is a string of characters (see the string section below).

If string1 and string2 are both specified without a -d switch, tr replaces all characters in string2 with their matching characters in string1. You can use the -d switch to remove characters from the standard input stream.

Strings. Strings can be represented in a number of special ways, which is what makes the tr command so powerful. Below is a sample of the possible representations for string1 or string2:

`\-`	Denotes the minus sign
`\octal`	Denotes a one-, two-, or three-character octal number
`char1-char2`	Specifies a string of characters in the collation sequence between char1 and char2

6.3.3 Examples

A simple example to remove all the characters in a file is:

```
$ tr -d a < infile > outfile
```

Note that with the tr command, as with many UNIX commands, you must simply redirect standard input and standard output with the <> symbols to act on files and not on terminal input. This is a very powerful technique which can be employed by many UNIX utilities.

Another example translates curly braces to parentheses:

```
$ tr '{}' '()' < infile > outfile
```

A common use is to change the case of letters in a file. For example, to translate a DOS file from all uppercase to all lowercase letters, use:

```
$ tr 'A-Z' 'a-z' < upperfile > lowerfile
```

Finally, to remove all repeated blank lines in a UNIX file, use the command:

```
$ tr -s '\012' < oldfile > newfile
```

Octal 12 represents a newline character in UNIX. This command replaces all single and multiple occurrences of the newline character with a single occurrence of the newline character.

6.3.4 Conclusion

The tr command is extremely useful, especially when moving files from platform to platform. Because of the capability to transpose and remove characters from any file to any file, including their actual octal representation, the tr command is one of the most often used UNIX power commands.

6.4 compress

6.4.1 Introduction

The compress command is the most commonly used command when distributing software in the UNIX environment. compress is useful for compressing files for disk storage and network bandwidth savings. The uncompress command is used to uncompress the compressed data file, and the zcat command is used to expand the file to standard output.

6.4.2 Usage

The syntax of the compress command is:

```
$ compress [-c] [-d] [-f] [-F] [-n] [-q] [-v] [file...]
```

where -c directs output to standard output.
-d makes compress function as uncompress.
-f forces compression and file overwrite if there is a conflict.
-F is same as -f.
-n omits the compressed file header. Used for backward compatibility.
-q suppresses display of compression statistics.
-v writes compression statistics to standard error.
file specifies file(s) to compress.

Note that the compress command takes an input file and compresses it to generate a file that may or may not be smaller and gives it a file extension of .Z. For example:

```
$ compress kevin
```

will take the input file named kevin and create a file named kevin.Z which is in compressed format. Note that the file kevin is removed. All permission and ownership information is maintained.

The compression performed will typically save 50 to 60 percent in disk space for text files and something slightly smaller for binary files. Note that for small files, however, you may see the file size actually increase. This is because of the compression algorithm, and there is nothing you can do to change this. If the compress determines that the compressed file will actually be larger than the original file, it will not compress the file unless forced to do so with the -f flag. It is a good idea to use the -v flag whenever you use the compress command since it will give you more information on what it is doing. For example:

```
$ compress -v small
small: Compression: -28.57% -- file unchanged
```

This tells you that the file small would actually be increased by 28.57 percent if you compressed it with the compress command. With the -v switch, compress will tell you how much disk space it saved you. For example:

```
$ compress -v medium
medium: Compression: 15.57% -- replaced with medium.Z
```

This means that the file medium was compressed to approximately 85 percent of its original size, and the resulting compressed file was named medium.Z. Note that as the file size increases, you will approach the 50 to 60 percent compression numbers.

6.4.3 uncompress

The uncompress command is used to uncompress the compressed file.

Usage. The syntax for uncompress is:

```
$ uncompress [-c] [-f] [-F] [-n] [-q] [-v] [file...]
```

where the options are exactly as described for compress. The uncompress command assumes that the file name ends with a .Z suffix, and it therefore requires the filename without the .Z suffix. For example, to uncompress one of the files created above, you would type:

```
$ uncompress -v medium
medium.Z -- replaced with medium
```

Note that even though the actual compressed filename was medium.Z, the uncompress command expected the filename medium and *not* medium.Z. This is always true.

It is often the case that tar files are compressed for network distribution. The convention for tar files is to end the filename with a .tar extension. The following example illustrates how to compress and uncompress a tar file.

```
$ compress -v files.tar
files.tar: Compression: 45.24% -- file replaced with files.tar.Z
```

Now move the compressed file or do whatever you want with it:

```
$ uncompress -v files.tar
files.tar.Z -- replaced with files.tar
```

Note that in UNIX you can have as many file extensions as you would like because the period (.) is just another character in the filename. Keep this in mind when you are compressing and uncompressing files.

6.4.4 zcat

The zcat is simply a special flavor of the uncompress command.

Usage. The syntax for the zcat command is:

```
zcat [-f] [-F] [-n] [file...]
```

where the arguments are again the same as the compress command. Note that zcat is exactly like the uncompress command except that the output is directed to standard output instead of a file. This is useful for previewing the contents of files before uncompressing them. For example:

```
$ zcat files.tar | tar tvf -
```

will uncompress the files.tar.Z file and pass the output directly to the tar command. The hyphen in the tar command says to take the input from standard input; the result of this command is a table of contents of the compressed tar file. This can be very useful; it is a way to see the contents of compressed tar files before wasting disk space uncompressing files you don't want. Note that there is nothing to stop you from then issuing the extraction on the tar command to extract a command from the compressed tar file without actually uncompressing the entire tar file.

6.4.5 A brief discussion of the pack command

There is a command called pack/unpack/pcat which accomplishes the same thing as the compress tools; however, it is used less frequently for mostly historical reasons and will, therefore, not be discussed. Note that packed files have a suffix of .z; if you see a file with this extension, you should look at the documentation on the pack command. If you are unsure of a file's format, try the file command since it will attempt to tell you what kind of file you are using. See Sec. 6.16 for more information.

6.4.6 Conclusion

The compress command and associated uncompress and zcat commands are extremely useful when sharing information or trying to conserve disk space. This is the way many files are transported on the

Internet, and you will see specific examples of the compress techniques in the other sections of this book.

compress is well known as containing a proprietary compression algorithm and is rapidly being replaced on the Internet with GNU gzip which supports uncompress but not the compress commands. See Sec. 11.2 and Chap. 9 for more information.

6.5 tar

6.5.1 Introduction

There are many ways to move files and data around in UNIX. While there are commands like cp, mv, backup, cpio, and dd to move data, by far the most commonly used technique for moving data is the tar command. tar stands for tape archive. As is apparent from the name, it is mostly used to move data from disk to tape, but it is also very useful for moving data from disk to disk. Most of the software from the Internet comes in compressed tar format. tar is easily the most powerful and simple tool for moving data from one medium to another, such as from disk to tape and vice versa.

6.5.2 Usage

The basic syntax for the tar command is:

```
tar [-c | -r | -t | -u | -x] [ -b block] [-B] [-C dir ...] [-d] [-F]
[-h] [-i]
[-L inputlist] [-l] [-m] [-N blocks] [-p] [-s] [-v] [-w] [-number]
[-f archive] [-S blocksb | -S feet | -S feet@density] [file... |
directory...]
```

where -c creates a new archive.
- -r writes file at end of archive. Valid for disk (nonstreaming) devices only.
- -t is table of contents.
- -u adds file to end of archive only if it is not already in the archive. Valid for disk (nonstreaming) devices only.
- -x extracts file from archive. If you don't specify a file parameter, the entire archive is extracted.
- -b block specifies the number of 512-byte blocks per record. Default is 20.
- -B forces input and output blocking to 20 (see -b option).
- -C dir allows files from different directories to be placed in same archive. See examples.
- -d places special files and FIFO named pipes in archive. Default is these are not saved.

-F specifies that a.out, sccs, rcs, core, errs, and .o files are not archived.
-f archive is archive to be read or written. If - is used, the standard input and output are used.
-h forces tar to follow symbolic links.
-i ignores header checksum errors. Useful for multivolume tars and large tar files.
-L - inputlist writes files listed in inputlist to the archive.
-l writes error messages to standard output if tar command cannot resolve all links.
-m uses time of extraction as modification time. Default is to preserve modification time.
-N blocks allows for large clusters of blocks in a record. Without this, the largest block size supported is 20.
-p restores files with original permissions, ignoring current umask setting.
-s tries to create a symbolic link.
-S Blocksb specifies the number of 512-byte blocks per volume.
-S feet specifies the size of the tape in feet.
-S feet@density specifies both length and density.
-v is verbose mode. Lists all files as they are processed.
-w displays file and action to be taken and waits for confirmation before proceeding.
-number uses the /dev/rmt0 number file instead of the default (0).
file is filename of active file.
directory is directory containing one or more files to operate on.

Pathnames. Pathnames are critical to the structure of tar archives because they directly affect how the archive can be "unwound." It is strongly recommended that you build archives with relative pathnames (begin with a .) rather than to using fully qualified pathnames (begin with a /). This allows you to extract files to a relative directory from your current location and not from an absolution location where you may not have access or permissions to perform the unwind.

Blocking factors. The issue of blocking factors is important since it can prevent you from accessing data on streaming devices such as tape devices. Most often the standard block size is 20. This means that you are placing 10,240 bytes in each record, which is separated from other records on a tape by an interrecord gap. This interrecord gap is determined by your tape device and consists of either a normal tape mark or an extended tape mark. Consult your vendor for more information, but you normally use extended filemarks to ensure data integrity.

You may get tapes with different block sizes, and while this should be documented on the tape label, it often is not. You may get a message like:

```
Error reading tape...incorrect block size or corrupted information
on the tape
```

If you get this, consult your documentation to see how to change the default block size of your tape device. To get more information on your tape devices and their characteristics, see the mt, tctl, and rmt man pages. See also the section below on tape devices.

Tapes. When using tapes, as is normally the case when you are using tar, there are several issues you must be aware of. The command you would normally use is the mt command to manipulate the tape position and status.

Tapes are streaming devices which only support serial access, and therefore tar makes certain assumptions with regard to generating archives on tapes. Remember, to UNIX everything is a bit stream, and, therefore, every file and device is treated the same as far as UNIX is concerned. This leads to most of the power of UNIX. It also leads to confusion when choosing a device and using commands which manipulate them.

With respect to the tar command, tar will begin to write the tape archive from the current tape position so you must ensure that you are not overwriting critical system information. The command to check the status of a tape device is:

```
$ mt -f /dev/rmt0 status
Exabyte EXB-8500 8mm tape drive:
sense key(0x0) = no sense residual = 0 retries = 0
file no = 0 block no = 0
```

There are many subtleties to the tar command, most of which you will never have to worry about. However, if you are having trouble with your tars to tape, consult Sec. 2.10.

Simple examples. To create a standard archive of a directory and its subdirectories and files, it is typically best to place the beginning directory as a subdirectory to your current location when you invoke the tar command. For example, to create an archive of the directory kevin and all files contained in this directory, I would typically do the following:

```
$ pwd
/home/chicago/kevin
$ cd ..
$tar -c -v -f /dev/rmt0.1 kevin
```

This will create an archive on the tape device rmt0 that contains the kevin directory and all related files. Note that if you examine the archive with the -t option, you see:

```
$ tar -t -v -f /dev/rmt0.1
./.cshrc
./file1
./file2
./dir1/file1
./dir1/file2
```

Note the preceding . on the filenames. This means the pathnames are relative. When you unwind the archive, the restored files will begin from your current working directory. For example, the command to unwind the file might be:

```
$ cd /home/newyork
$ tar -x -v -f /dev/rmt0.1
x .cshrc
x file1
x file2
x dir1/file1
x dir2/file2
```

As you will notice, all files are extracted into a directory relative to the current working directory. If you use absolute pathnames in the creation of the archive, you must extract them in the same place in the hierarchy when you unwind the archive. This can be a problem and should be avoided if possible. Note that if you are distributing a product that requires a certain directory, the absolute pathname method may be exactly what you need, but this is not normally the case.

For more information on files and devices, see Secs. 2.6 and 2.10.

To create an archive of two different subdirectories on the disk, you use a command like:

```
$ tar -c -v -f /dev/rmt0.1 /usr/home/kevin /usr/chicago/kevin
```

All files and subdirectories from both the /usr/home/kevin and /usr/chicago/kevin directories will be placed in one tar archive. Note that the pathnames are absolute; they will therefore only be able to be restored in this same directory when extracted. If you need more flexibility and relative pathnames, use the -C command.

You can also reload specific files by simply specifying their names on the extract command. For example:

```
$ tar -x -v -f /dev/rmt0.1 /usr/home/kevin/.cshrc
/usr/home/kevin/.profile
```

will restore two files in the /usr/home/kevin directory, overwriting any files that currently exist there. Remember that UNIX doesn't have versioning of files, and you therefore must be extremely careful when restoring files since preexisting files will be overwritten.

Creating multiarchives on a single tape. You can create multiple archives on a single tape with the following set of commands:

```
$ mt -f /dev/rmt0 rewind
$ tar -cvf /dev/rmt0.1 /usr/lpp
...backs up all files in /usr/lpp subdirectory...
$ tar -cvf /dev/rmt0.1 /home/lpp
...backs up all files in /home/lpp subdirectory...
```

Note that there is nothing special about the tar commands, but what is special is the choice of the device. This particular example comes from AIX on an RS/6000 from IBM; however, it would work the same on other UNIX operating systems. The difference may come in the device name.

Figure 6.1 shows three files separated by tape marks (tm). The end of the data on the tape consists of two sequential tape marks which denote the logical end of the volume. Each individual file on the tape is separated by a single tape mark. To append to the end of the tape, you skip the first three files and begin to write between the first and second tape mark at the end of the volume. Not all devices support this append operation. This is also related to the particular filemarks you are using: long or short. See your local documentation for more information.

In this example, the device /dev/rmt0.1 is a no-rewind device. This means that after the command is finished executing, the tape is not rewound. The default device /dev/rmt0 rewinds the device at the end of the command. This means that if you issued the above sequence of commands using the /dve/rmt0 devices, you would have overwritten the first tar file with the second, and the end result would have been only one tar file. Understanding these concepts is key to the successful use of UNIX and input/output devices. See Sec. 2.10 for more information.

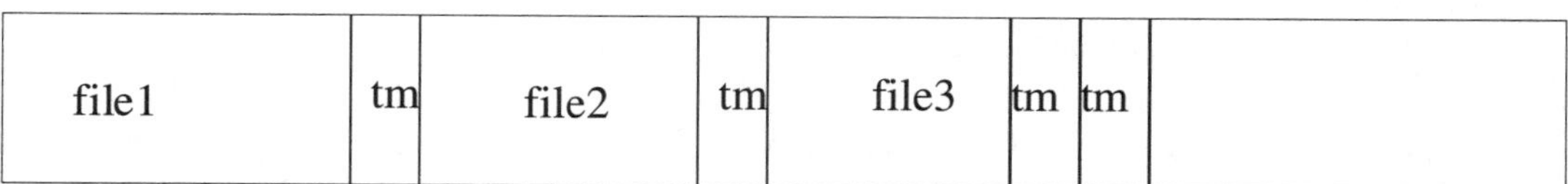

Figure 6.1 Multifile tape.

Reading multiarchive tapes. To access the first archive, you may issue the tar command as you normally would:

```
$ mt -f /dev/rmt0 rewind /* this is just a good idea but not
necessary */
$ tar -tvf /dev/rmt0 /home/lpp
```

Note that because we chose the /dev/rmt0 device, when the tar command is finished, the tape is rewound, and the results of the following command are:

```
$ tar -tvf /dev/rmt0 /home/lpp
```

exactly the same as the previous tar command.

Note that this is the same as above because the tape was rewound. To access the second archive, you can do any of the following:

```
$ mt -f /dev/rmt0.1 fsf 1
$ tar -tvf /dev/rmt0.1
```

or

```
$ tar -tvf /dev/rmt0.1
file1
file2

$ tar -tvf /dev/rmt0
file3
file4
```

Note that the second alternative is somewhat wasteful if you are not interested in the first archive; however, both will allow you to list the contents of the second archive on the tape. Remember that the end of the last tar command in each example above will result in the tape being rewound.

Using tar to move file hierarchies from one disk location to another. One of the most powerful aspects of the tar command is its ability to use the standard input and output capabilities of UNIX to move file hierarchies within UNIX directory structures. The syntax of a tar command which will accomplish this is as follows:

```
$ tar cvf - files | (cd newdir; tar xvf -;)
```

This is one of the most powerful uses of tar and is the primary way to move file hierarchies within and across filesystems. You can also use the command to move entire file hierarchies between systems. See Sec. 4.8 for more information.

Potential problems. Remember that media such as tapes have a finite life span and should be replaced appropriately and maintained at the proper humidity and temperature to ensure the longest possible shelf life. Also, don't forget about the blocking factor issues, and you may need to experiment with blocking factors (with the -b switch) before finding the right combination of parameters to read your data. Always remember to write as much information on the tape labels as possible since it will almost certainly be useful to the next person to use the tape.

Most versions of tar will not support multiple tape volume, and as such you are limited in what you can place in a single tar archive. Today, the largest tape media is 5GB 8-mm tape. While this is certainly a significant amount of data, it may not be sufficient to back up your entire system. The tar command should not be used to back up and restore your system. Other commands such as dump, back up, and restore should be used. They support multiple output volumes to ensure that you have enough output capacity to store and retrieve all backup information.

Most other problems relate to the correct choice of a device for the resulting archive. In UNIX, each device file has different characteristics which control the behavior of the device. You must ensure that you choose the correct device before performing any work with tapes and other output devices. See Sec. 2.10 for more information.

6.5.3 Conclusions

The tar command is one of the most powerful commands in the UNIX environment. It allows you to transparently move file hierarchies from one medium and location to another. While moving from disk to tape can involve some of the complexities discussed above, most often the tar command will work without any problems and will produce a transportable file which can be unwound on any machine which supports the tar archive format.

6.6 find

6.6.1 Introduction

The find command is one of the most useful commands in the UNIX environment. With find, you can search directory structures and locate files. You can operate on all files found with expressions which direct the find command to do something with the resultant output.

6.6.2 Usage

The basic syntax for the find command is:

```
find dir-list expression
```

where dir-list contains one or more pathnames on which to search. Note that all subdirectories under the directories in the dir-list are searched as well.

expression contains a set of commands on which to base the search and resultant output.

Expressions. There are several commands which can be used in the expression part of the find command. Some of the most useful are:

`-name filename`	Filename is the name of the file to search for.
`-links +-n`	Specifies the number of links to match.
`-user username`	Owned by username.
`-group groupname`	Owned by groupname group.
`-type filetype`	Filetype is one of the following: b--block special file c--character special file d--directory f--ordinary file l--symbolic link p--fifo pipe s--socket
`-inum n`	Inode number is *n*.
`-size +-n[m]`	Size of file is *n* blocks and *m* characters.
`-atime +-n`	File last accessed plus or minus *n* days ago.
`-mtime +-n`	File last modified plus or minus *n* days ago.
`-newer filename`	File matches if modified more recently than filename.
`-print`	Prints results to standard output.
`-exec command \;`	If command returns a zero value as an exit status, filename being evaluated must be enclosed in curly braces {}.
`-nouser`	File matches criteria if owner of file is not in the passwd file.
`-ls`	Causes the current path to be printed along with inode, size, mode, number of links, user, group, and modification time.

Expressions consist of commands separated by spaces and chosen from the list above. Evaluation of the commands proceed from left to right, and if a criteria is not satisfied on one condition, the next criteria to the right is not even evaluated.

You can alter the way expressions are evaluated by using the -o and -a options. These are boolean operators between find expressions directives. The -o is a logical OR, and the -a is a logical AND. See the examples for more detail.

You can also negate an operator with the !. Note that the ! must be surrounded by spaces and will negate the next operator in the command. See the examples for more detail.

find operates in the tradition of UNIX, which is not to tell you when you are doing something stupid. For example, if you don't use the -print option, the command will execute and print nothing to the screen. Even if it finds a match, you won't see anything on your terminal. This is used to allow find to be used in other ways and most often in combination with other commands.

6.6.3 Examples

Examples are the best way to understand the find command. To search the entire filesystem for a particular file, you can issue the command:

```
$ find / -name ls -print
```

This will search the entire filesystem starting at the root directory for a file named ls and print the result to the screen.

To search the current directory for a file or files, use the command:

```
$ find . -name "*kevin*" -print
```

This command will search the current directory and all subdirectories for any files with the string kevin in them. Note that you must enclose the *kevin* in double quotes to ensure that the shell does not interpret it before passing the string to the find command. If you did not enclose the *kevin* in double quotes, the shell would expand the string to any files that matched in the current directory and pass those exact matches to the find command before executing the find command. In other words, you would only match the files in the current directory that have the string kevin in them. This technique is key to understanding how UNIX works with commands in passing parameters.

To search a set of directories and subdirectories for a file, you might use a command like:

```
$ find sub1 sub2 sub3 -perm -0600 -print
```

This command searches three subdirectories (sub1, sub2, and sub3) for files which have the file permission structure of 0600. Note that the - before the 0600 string is necessary if you are testing the uppermost bits (sticky and setuid).

You can use the find command to count the number of files in a directory with something like:

```
$ find . -print | wc -l
```

This will count the number of files starting in your current working directory.

An example of using the negate (!) capability of find is:

```
$ find . ! -user kevin -print
```

This will search the current directory and subdirectories for any files not owned by user kevin and will print them to the screen. Note that the ! can act before any operator and must be separated on both sides by white space.

Another common use for the find command is to change file permissions on certain classes of files. For example:

```
$ find . -exec -name "*.sh" -exec chmod +x {} \; -print
```

will find all files with the suffix .sh and ensure that they have execute capabilities.

A good example of using the boolean operator -o is:

```
$ find / \( -name core -o name junk \) -print -exec rm {} \;
```

This command searches the entire filesystem from the root directory and removes all files named core and junk. Note that the backslashes before the parenthesis are used to prevent the shell from interpreting the parentheses. The -o options says to satisfy the expression if the filename is either junk or core. Finally, the print command prints the results to the screen, and the exec command removes any files which match the expression. The curly braces denote the current file being acted on from the expression. Note that this will take quite a while if the filesystem is big, so you may want to think about starting at a different search subdirectory to save time in your search.

6.6.4 Conclusion

The find command is one of the least used and most powerful commands in the UNIX environment. It allows you to write simple commands to locate and perform operations on files in any part of your filesystems. It is often used by system administrators to purge optional files in filesystems with cron. It is also used by programmers who know their way around a UNIX system to find and act on multiple files in unknown locations. find is one of the UNIX power user commands.

6.7 whereis

6.7.1 Introduction

The whereis command locates files in the standard directories and can be very useful to find the location of commands and manual pages. It is often the case that more than one executable with the same name is in your path and therefore accessible. With the whereis command, you can discover where the command is located and gain a better understanding of any other references to the command available in your environment.

6.7.2 Usage

The command syntax is:

```
whereis [-s] [-b] [-m] [-u] [-S] [-B] [-M] [directory...] [-f]
file...
```

where -s searches for source sections of the file.
-b searches for binary sections of the file.
-m searches for manual sections of the file.
-u searches for unusual files. A file is unusual if it does not have a matching file of each requested type (see examples).
-S is like s but adds a search directory for the file.
-B is like b but adds a search directory for the file.
-M is like m but adds a search directory for the file.
directory... is directory or directories separated by spaces used by S, B, or M.
-f is used to terminate search directories.
file is file or files to search for.

Note that the search directories should be fully qualified paths (this means they must begin with a /). The filename(s) are stripped of any leading path information and any training extensions before the search is executed. For example, the filename:

```
/usr/local/devtech/ghostscript.exe
```

would be reduced to ghostscript before the search is executed.

The directories searched are different for every UNIX flavor; however, all the standard directories including:

```
/usr,/usr/bin,/usr/ucb/bin,/usr/sysV/bin,/usr/man,/usr/share,.,/ etc
```

are searched. Note that the . directory is your current directory, and this is often searched for filename. Note that this is not a substitute for the find command. whereis is only useful for finding system-level files and commands and should not be used for general file searches since it will not search most directories for the existence of filename.

6.7.3 Examples

To search for the existence of any files related to the ls command, you would execute:

```
$ whereis ls
/usr/5bin/ls /usr/bin/ls /usr/man/man1/ls.1
```

You typically use the whereis command to find documentation for a particular command. For example:

```
$ whereis man
/bin/man /usr/man/man1/man.1
```

tells you that the man page is in /usr/man/man1. You can then run nroff or do anything else with the man page that you would like. See Sec. 2.8 for more information.

You can use the whereis command to search for commands without documentation with the -u switch. For example:

```
$ whereis -u -M /usr/share/man/man1 -S /usr/ucb/cmd -f *
```

will search for files in the current directory that are not documented in the /usr/share/man/man1 directory with matching source in the /usr/ucb/cmd directory.

6.7.4 Conclusion

whereis is an extremely useful command when trying to understand the structure of commands on a particular flavor of UNIX machine. With whereis you can understand where external commands are and where the associated documentation is located. Remember that whereis not a substitute for the find command primarily because of its assumptions as to directories to search. Because of this limitation, it should be used sparingly for things other than system commands and manual pages.

6.8 cron

6.8.1 Introduction

cron is short for chronograph. The cron facility is a pseudo batch/background processing facility which provides a scheduling and execution facility for jobs submitted either once or many times.

cron is actually a system daemon which executes in the background and references a file called the crontab file to check for possible command execution. cron typically wakes up every minute and checks its crontab file for any jobs to be executed during this minute; however, some newer systems only execute the cron daemon at process initialization and when the crontab file changes.

Regularly scheduled jobs are contained in the crontab file. There are other commands such as the at command which allow you to schedule a job to be executed once based on a time you specify.

6.8.2 The crontabs file

The crontabs file is typically contained in /usr/spool/cron/crontabs. This is an area in which all users can typically write. This allows all users to submit jobs for execution at regular intervals. However, this is typically used by system administrators (not general users) to schedule regular system management jobs.

If you do a directory of the crontab directory, you will see:

```
$ ls /usr/spool/cron/crontabs
adm root sys sysadm uucp
```

These are directories which contain files with scheduled events submitted by a specific user. In the above case, adm, root, sys, sysadm, and uucp have submitted jobs to cron to be scheduled at some regular interval.

The number and names of the files in the /usr/spool/cron/crontabs directory varies between implementations of UNIX, but most will have the above, which collect information pertaining to accounting and monitoring of the system as well as to periodic cleanup of the disk subsystems. Some versions of UNIX also use /var/spool/cron/crontabs as their crontab directory. See your system documentation for your specific implementation.

A typical example of a crontab file named uucp is:

```
#
#ident "@(#)uudemon.crontab 1.1 88/05/16"
#
48 8,12,16 * * * /etc/uucp/uudemon.admin
45 23 * * * /etc/uucp/uudemon.cleanup
0 * * * * /etc/uucp/uudemon.poll
11,41 * * * * /etc/uucp/uudemon.hour
```

The lines preceded by a # are comment lines and serve only to document the crontab file. The basic syntax of the crontab line is as follows: the first field specifies the minute (0–60), the second field specifies the hour in 24-hour format (0=12:00 a.m., 23=11:00 p.m.), the third field specifies the day of the month (1–31), the fourth field specifies the month (1–12), and the fifth field specifies the day of week (0=Sunday, 6=Saturday.) You can combine these specifications in any given order or format. The final field in the file contains the command to be executed. This can be either an executable or a shell script. Remember that the cron daemon is running the command and therefore all permissions and capabilities of the command will be determined by cron's ability to execute them. cron is actually owned by bin, and therefore all commands will be executed as bin.

An asterisk represents all possible values. Every field must be represented by either a number or an asterisk since this is how the lines are parsed. Groups of numbers can be specified within a single field by separating them with commas. No spaces are allowed within a field, and therefore the number lists must be separated by commas and have no spaces.

Examining the first line above tells us that an administration command /etc/uucp/uudemon.admin is going to be run 8:48 a.m., 12:48 p.m., and 16:48 p.m. (or 4:48 p.m.) every day. This is common for an administration script which performs system-level commands. The second line executes once per day at 23:45 p.m. (11:45 p.m.) and cleans up the uucp area. The third line executes a poll once per hour at the beginning of every hour. The final line issues an hour command every half-hour. This is typical of a uucp script file.

You can set scripts to execute at noon on every Saturday with a command like:

```
0 12 * * 6 /usr/home/kevin/fulldump
```

This may be useful for execution of a full dump of a script such as a full system dump every Saturday.

At times you may want to execute your cron script as something other than bin. To do this, you might use a command like:

```
0 0 * * 0 su root % /etc/cleanup > /dev/null
```

This runs a script /etc/cleanup at 12:00 a.m. every Sunday as root and directs any standard output to the null device. Note that the % sign says pass all commands following the % as standard input to the command preceding the % sign. This is very useful when using the su command to execute a command as some process other than bin.

6.8.3 crontab

The command to create, list, remove, and edit crontab files is the crontab command. The basic syntax is:

```
crontab [-e | -l | -r | -v | file]
```

where -e edits the user's crontab file or creates a new one if none exists.
-l lists the user's crontab file.
-r removes a user's crontab file.

-v provides a status of the user's crontab jobs.
file provides a filename. The default is standard input.

crontab copies a file specified by file to the /usr/spool/cron/crontabs area with your userid as the file to determine regularly scheduled jobs that you wish to submit. To submit a file you have created with a simple editor or the crontab -e command, use the command:

```
$ crontab file
```

To check that your file was submitted to cron, issue the command:

```
$ crontab -v
```

or

```
$ crontab -l
```

to get a listing of jobs or a listing of the cron file you submitted.

To remove your cron file, issue the command:

```
$ crontab -r
```

The cron daemon mails you all output from standard output and standard error unless you redirect these streams.

Security of the crontab command is controlled by two files: /usr/spool/cron/cron.allow and /usr/spool/cron/cron.deny. When you issue a crontab command, cron checks first to see if your id is in the cron.allow file. If it is, it executes the command. If your id is not in the cron.allow, it checks the cron.deny file. If your id is in this file, you are explicitly denied access to the crontab area. If neither cron.allow or cron.deny exist, only root can submit commands to the cron daemon. This allows the system administrator to control access to the cron subsystem. These files also vary in their locations. For example, on an RS/6000 they are in the /var/adm/cron directory, while on a Sun they are in /usr/spool/cron. See your local system documentation for specific information on file locations.

The basic syntax of the cron.allow and cron.deny file is one userid per line. For example:

```
kevin
beb
gch
johnjr
```

in the cron.allow file specifically allows kevin, beb, gch, and johnjr access to the cron subsystem. The same structure can be used in the cron.deny file to deny specific access.

6.8.4 at

The at command allows you to execute a given command once at a specified time. The basic syntax is:

```
at [-c | -k | -s | -qqueue] [-m] [-l [job...| -qqueue] [-r job ...]
{-t date | time [day]
[increment]}
```

where -c uses the csh for execution.
-k uses the ksh for execution.
-s uses the bsh for execution.
-qqueue specifies a queuename.
-m mails a message to your userid upon completion of the job.
-l reports on scheduled jobs.
job... specifies one or more jobs using the job number assigned by the at command.
-r job removes a job or jobs.
-t date/time/day specifies job execution at a specific time (see time specification section below for more information).

The at command is just a subset of the functionality of the cron subsystem. By using the at command, you can execute a job at some later time. This is very useful for running large jobs which will consume a significant portion of the machine or a job which should not be executed while users are on the system.

When the at command is executed, it maintains the current process environment including shell variables and context.

The security mechanism used for at is the same as that used by cron. Two files named at.allow and at.deny control access on a userid basis. These are typically in the same directory as cron.allow and cron.deny. See you local system for more details.

Time specification. There are several ways to specify a time of execution. The basic format is:

```
[CC]YY]MMDDhhmm[.ss]
```

where CC specifies the first two digits of the year.
YY specifies the second two digits of the year.
MM specifies the month (01–12).
DD specifies the day of the month (01–31).

hh specifies the hour of the day (00–23).
mm specifies the minute of the hour (00–59).
ss specifies the second of the minute (00–59).

The at command interprets numbers from right to left in the above syntax. This means that if you specify only two digits on the at command line, it assumes that you mean minutes. For example, the command:

```
at 45 < /tmp/script
```

will execute the script /tmp/script at 45 minutes after the current hour. If you specify four digits, the at command assumes you mean hour and minutes. For example:

```
$ at 1145 < /tmp/script
```

would execute the /tmp/script file at 11:45 a.m. on the current day.

There are keywords which makes the time specification easier. Some of the more basic are:

am

pm

noon

midnight

M for midnight

now

A for a.m.

N for noon

P for p.m.

Some basic examples with the above keywords follow:

```
$ at 3:15pm < /bin/rm -R /
```

will delete every file on the disk at 3:15 of the current day. Probably not a good idea.

```
$ at noon < /bin/hello "world"
```

will execute the hello command at noon today.

If the time specified is earlier than that available on the current day, the default is for execution on the following day (denoted as tomorrow).

If the time listed is available later on the current day, it will be executed then.

There is an ability to use a time increment to specify job execution. This allows you to specify a time relative to either the current time or a specified time. The basic commands are:

```
+num keyword
```

where num is a number to denote a relative measure.
keyword is one of the following:
- minute
- hour
- day
- week
- month
- year

```
next keyword
```

where keyword is the same as for +num.

More examples. Some simple examples of the capabilities of the at command follow:

```
$ at 5pm Friday /bin/reboot -Fr
```

This will reboot the machine Friday at 5 p.m.

```
$ at now + 1 day /bin/ls -l /
```

will display all files in the / filesystem exactly 1 day from time of execution.

A common trick to create a script that resubmits and reexecutes itself in perpetuity is to place the following line at the end of a shell script:

```
at now + 1 day < $0
```

This takes the name of the shell script (denoted by $0) and resubmits itself for execution exactly 24 hours later. This is a useful technique, but you may want to consider cron if you have this kind of need. There are advantages to the cron methodology in terms of logging and recoverability that need to be considered.

To list the jobs you have submitted for future execution, use the command:

```
$ at -l
```

To remove a job, issue the command:

```
$ at -r jobid
```

The jobid can be determined from the at -l command.

6.8.5 batch

The batch command is similar to the at now command. When you submit a command with the batch command, the system queues the job and executes it when the system load becomes sufficiently low. There is an internal algorithm used by batch to determine when the system load is light enough to schedule the submitted job. batch is most often used to submit a series of large jobs at the same time. This permits any constant thrashing since all of these processes attempt to get to the CPU at the same time. This can improve the overall throughput of your machine by allowing the system to more efficiently schedule jobs to the CPU.

The basic syntax is:

```
batch
```

Note that there are no options; batch merely processes standard input at a time when the system determines load is light. All removal, monitoring, and security features of the batch command are exactly those of the at command. The commands at -r, at -l, at.allow, and at.deny are used by batch as well to determine the characteristics of the batch command.

6.8.6 Conclusion

The cron subsystem is a very powerful system which provides some of the capabilities you might expect from a batch scheduling system. Certainly it is not as powerful as a JES or VMS batch processing subsystem, but it does provide capabilities of specific job execution times and also the load balancing capabilities of the batch command.

You can also submit regular jobs to the cron system with the crontab command and provide regular job submission capabilities. There are other tools which provide a more function-rich batch environment. If you are interested in these tools, you should investigate some of them further.

6.9 script

6.9.1 Introduction

The script command is a very useful command and is often one of the most requested of all functions on any machine. script logs an interactive session including all input and output from a terminal. This is extremely useful for tracking and logging software installations and system configuration changes. By creating a script log of all activities, you can later review all activities and determine exactly what occurred.

6.9.2 Usage

The basic usage for the script command is:

```
script [-a] [file]
```

where -a appends the log to a previous script log file.
file determines the name of the script log file. Default is typescript.

If you do not specify a filename or the -a, a file in the current working directory named typescript will be overwritten. It is recommended that you save a script log with a filename which pertains to the activity logged.

To exit the script command and close the log file, use the command:

```
$ exit
```

This will place you back on the command line in exactly the place you were before; however, the script file will be closed and no further input or output will be saved to the script log file.

The only activity which may not be represented accurately in the script log is any activity that occurs in a full-screen mode. For example, any vi activity will be confusing in the log file. Keep this in mind when you are using the script command.

6.9.3 Examples

A basic example of saving all input and output to a script log file is:

```
$ script
```

This will save all subsequently typed input and output in a file in the current working directory named typescript. You can later edit, display, or print this file as you would any other text file.

To append the results to another existing script log file named install.log, use:

```
$ script -a install.log
```

After finishing the installation you want to log, type the command:

```
$ exit
```

This will place you in the back at the command prompt and will close and save the log file install.log. No further input and output will be saved to this file.

6.9.4 Conclusion

The script command is often used by system administrators and application managers to log all installation and maintenance activities. The script command, which provides an interactive logging facility to all users, is an often overlooked but very powerful tool that can make you more effective in a UNIX environment.

6.10 umask

6.10.1 Introduction

umask is both a tool and an environmental characteristic; it defines and reports your default file creation characteristics. It allows you to change the default protections on files you create within your current process. Each system has a default, which is most often 022. This is directly related to security on your system and allows you to set a default file creation mechanism for yourself and for anyone else on the system, if you have the authority to do so.

6.10.2 Usage

The syntax of the umask command is:

```
umask [mask]
```

where mask consists of a three-digit octal number which is the mask to be subtracted from the default file creation permissions.

If you issue the umask command without the mask option, it will tell you the current umask setting. Normally the umask is set on login in the .profile or .cshrc files, depending on which shell you are using.

6.10.3 File permissions and umask

When you create a file in UNIX, it is assigned certain file permissions defined by the system. The permission structure looks like:

```
rwxrwxrwx
```

where r means read.
w means write.
x means execute.

The first three characters (left to right) relate to the owner's access to the file. The next three relate to the group's access permissions, and the last three relate to the world's access permission (which means everyone on the system).

This set of three characteristics for each set of users (rwx) can be represented by an octal (base 8) number from 0–7. Each position in the nine-character string describing a file's access is either on or off. If it is on, it is represented by a 1, and if it is off, it is represented by a 0, which is base 2. Octal takes base 2 representation and makes it base 8. The mapping between binary and octal is:

binary	octal
111	7
110	6
101	5
100	4
011	3
010	2
001	1
000	0

For example, to represent all three characters being on (which means read, write, and execute are permitted), you would use:

```
111 (binary)
```

or

```
7 (base 8 or octal)
```

To represent only read and write but no execute privilege, you would use:

```
110 (binary)
```

or

```
6 (octal)
```

Therefore, you would represent the following file permission as:

```
rwxr--r-- == 744
```

The umask is the difference between 777 (all permissions allowed for everyone) and what you would like the permission structure to be. For example, if you want to allow only read access to the group and the world but nothing else, you would choose:

```
want 744 (rwxr--r--)
all permissions are 777, therefore
umask 033
```

Note that 033 is the difference between 777 and 744. The umask sets a mask which is subtracted to give the resultant actual file permissions. This is the standard way a mask works. Let's take a look at a few more examples:

want only read privileges for everyone for all files: want 444; therefore umask is 333

want only execute privileges for everyone but owner: want 711; therefore umask is 066

Note that the umask is in effect until you either exit your shell or change it with an explicit umask command. This means that all files you create will use the umask command to determine file permission and access characteristics. Keep this in mind when you are creating files in your environment.

umask may be set by the system administrator in the /etc/profile file if your system supports this.

6.10.4 Conclusion

The umask command provides control over file creation and access characteristics for your environment. By using umask, you can control access to files that you create and maintain.

6.11 strings

6.11.1 Introduction

The strings command is a little known and used command in the UNIX environment that can provide very useful function to a developer. You may receive an executable that you either don't know what it contains or are not sure of its construction. The strings command can help you with this. The strings command looks for ASCII strings in a binary file. A string is defined by four or more printable ASCII characters in sequence ending with either a newline or NULL.

6.11.2 Usage

The syntax of the strings command is:

```
strings [-] [-o] [-number] filename ...
```

where - looks everywhere in the file for strings rather than just the data space of the executable.
-o precedes each string with its offset in the file.
-number uses number as the minimum string length rather than four.
filename ... - is a list of files to search separated by spaces.

6.11.3 Examples

You can use the strings command to search for strings in any executable. For example:

```
$ strings a.out
waiting %d for char %s
pread select failed
a.out printf
```

As you can see, you may get some useful information out of the executable to help you better understand what the file contains.

6.11.4 Conclusion

The strings command is useful when attempting to determine what is contained in a binary file. It may help you in understanding more about the binary file that you are examining.

6.12 cksum and sum

6.12.1 Introduction

The cksum command generates a checksum based on the cyclical redundancy check (CRC) and the byte count for the file. cksum is typically used to compare files bit by bit.

6.12.2 Usage

The basic syntax is:

```
cksum [file ...]
```

If you don't specify a file, standard input is assumed. Checksums can be generated and are unique based on an algorithm applied to all bits in the file. This is typically used to compare binary files after a file transfer over a network or after uncompression.

Typically, with Internet software, there is a file named README which contains checksums for files split for easy network transfer. You can issue the cksum command against the files and compare them with the checksums listed in the README file. If everything matches, you can continue with your product build; if there are differences, you may want to retransmit the differing files.

This is also used to compare binary executable files when you are unsure of the exact contents of a file. You can build a binary file and use a checksum comparison with the unknown file to ensure they are the same.

On some UNIX machines, the cksum command is actually sum. The algorithm used by the sum command is different from that used by cksum, and it is therefore not compatible to compare checksums. Keep this in mind if you cannot find a cksum command.

6.12.3 Examples

To generate a checksum for a file, issue the command:

```
$ cksum file
12345 95 file
```

The first number is the checksum and the second is the number of bytes in the file. The final item is the filename.

6.12.4 Conclusion

The cksum and sum commands give a power user the ability to confirm the similarity or differences between files. By providing a bit-for-bit comparison, the cksum command provides a way to compare both text and binary files on any UNIX machine. Use this after file transfer and construction of network distribution files.

6.13 uname

6.13.1 Introduction

The uname command provides information on a machine's hardware and software architecture. It is typically used to determine what UNIX operating system you are currently using as well as the hardware architecture. Shell scripts and makefiles often employ this command to determine characteristics for execution on a variety of platforms.

6.13.2 Usage

The basic syntax of the uname command is:

```
uname [-a | -x | -Sname] | [-l] [-m] [-n] [-r] [-s] [-v]
```

where -a displays all available information excluding the network number.
-x displays all information including the network number.
-Sname sets the nodename.
-l displays the network number.
-m displays the machine hardware id.
-n displays the nodename.
-r displays the release number of the operating system.
-s displays the system name (this is the default).
-v displays the operating system version.

6.13.3 Examples

To get a general listing of system information, type:

```
$ uname -a
```

To get the current version of the operating system, use:

```
$ uname -v
```

6.13.4 Conclusion

While uname is a simple command, it can be quite useful when determining what architecture and operating system version you are running. This is particularly useful to shell scripts in determining current execution environments.

6.14 xargs

6.14.1 Introduction

The xargs command is a little known or understood command but is, in fact, one of the most powerful UNIX commands available. xargs creates a dynamic command line by combining standard input with a specified command string to generate one or more composite commands. You can use this to generate a series of commands from very basic syntax.

6.14.2 Usage

The basic syntax of the xargs command is:

```
xargs [-p] [-t] [-n num] [-l [num]] [-x] [-e [endoffile]]
   [-i[string]]
[-ssize] [commandline]
```

where -p provides a confirmation capability for each constructed commandline.
-t echoes commandline and each constructed parameter list to standard error.
-n num runs commandline using as many input parameters as possible up to a maximum of num.
-l [num] executes commandline with num nonempty parameter lines read from standard input. Default value is 1.
-x stops the execution of commandline if the parameter list is greater than the number of bytes specified in the -s option.
-e [endoffile] sets the end of file string. If you don't specify an end of file string, xargs treats the underline (_) as a literal and not an end of file, which is the default interpretation for an underline (_).
-i[string] inserts an entire line into each instance of the string variable found in commandline. xargs ignores spaces and tabs at the beginning of each line. The default string is curly braces {}.
-ssize sets the total line size for the parameter list. Default is the default line length.
commandline is any command which you wish to modify.

Parameters are delimited by one or more spaces, tabs, or newline characters. If any special or unusual characters are included in the string or if you have embedded spaces, you should enclose the strings in double quotes. This will prevent the shell from interpreting the string before passing it to xargs and will provide xargs with the intended string including any special characters.

6.14.3 Examples

The best way to understand the operation of the xargs command is to see a few examples. Let us assume that you have a list of files named files.compile which contains a listing of files you wish to compile into a single executable. Assume the files.compile file contains the following information:

```
file1.f file2.f file3.f
file4.f
file5.f
```

You can use xargs to generate a compilation of all files with something like:

```
$ xargs -t f77 <files.compile
f77 file1.f file2.f file3.f file4.f file5.f
```

xargs simply took standard input redirected from a file and appended it to the f77 command. The -t switch told xargs to display the resulting command to standard error which is, by default, mapped to the terminal screen.

If you had a large number of files such that the filenames would be longer than the default 255 characters which most UNIX systems support, you would generate two lines of f77. For example, you might get something like:

```
$ f77 file1.f file2.f ...
$ f77 file15.f file16.f ...
```

This, of course, would defeat the purpose of the compilation since you would not get the desired executable. If you need the resulting command to include all standard input in one command or nothing, use the -x option. For example:

```
$ xargs -t -x f77 <files.compile
```

will prevent more than one invocation of the f77 command. If the input files from files.compile stretch beyond one line in length, you will get an error message, and the f77 will not occur.

You can use xargs to take standard input and redirect it into parts of the constructed command lines. For example, to rename a select group of files and confirm each rename, use the command:

```
$ ls | xargs -p -i mv {}.new {}.old
```

This will allow you to selectively rename all files with the suffix .new in the current directory to .old. To confirm the change, type y; to reject the rename, type ENTER. This is a classic technique for renaming selected files in a directory.

The -n option provides the ability to specify the maximum number of variables that can be processed on a given invocation of the command line. Assume we have a file containing a listing of filenames which we would like to compare in pairs. An example is:

```
file1 file1a
file2 file2a
file3
file3a
```

An example of an operation on this file is:

```
$ xargs -t -n2 diff <diff.file
diff file1 file1a
diff file2 file2a
diff file3 file3a
```

Note that the -n2 option told xargs to use at most two arguments for a given invocation of the command line. This is a very powerful technique which can be used to build structured shell scripts and programs.

6.14.4 Conclusion

The xargs command allows you to dynamically build command lines by providing both a redirection and a pseudo-parsing capability of standard input along with a merge to a given command line parameter. With this you can generate a set of very powerful commands which operate on standard input and on some arbitrary command in an almost infinite number of ways.

6.15 Signals and the kill command

6.15.1 Introduction

You may find that you have a process running and are unable to stop or restart the command. This is when the kill command and an understanding of UNIX signals become useful. The kill command in combination with the right signal will provide you with a range of outcomes. You can kill a process immediately, or you can simply restart a process, both with the kill command.

6.15.2 Usage

The kill command syntax is:

```
kill [signal] PID ...
```

where signal is chosen from the following list:
- -1—restarts the process rereading all initialization files.
- -2—terminal interrupt (like a CTRL-C).

-3—quits (like a CTRL-\).
-9—kills (cannot be trapped; kills immediately).
-15—software terminates (kills gracefully, closes files, etc. This is the default).

PID... is a list of process ids (probably discovered with the ps command).

Signals range from 1 to 22, with those listed above being by far the most common. You can get more information on signals not listed above in the signals man page.

Note that you can only issue the kill command against processes which you own. The exception, of course, is root, which can kill any process on the machine. The best way to see which processes you own on a system, and therefore which processes you can control and kill, is to issue the ps command piped to a grep containing your username.

6.15.3 Examples

There are many times when a daemon or process gets in a loop or simply fails to respond to your demands. When this happens, you probably want to kill the process or restart it. It is a good idea to use the default signal (15) since this kills the process gracefully. It closes all files and associated file handles and kills any associated processes. If you restart the process later, you shouldn't have any problems. An example of this is:

```
$ ps -aux | grep kevin
kevin 943 23.1 1.9 196 440 p1 R 02:39 0:00 ps -aux
kevin 732 6.6 8.4 1876 1904 co S 01:31 7:51 /usr/openwin/bin/xnews :
kevin 752 2.3 2.9 312 652 p1 S 01:31 0:54 cmdtool -Wp 6 11 -Ws 102
kevin 748 0.0 1.1 208 252 co S 01:31 0:06 olwm -3
kevin 719 0.0 0.0 68 0 co IW 01:30 0:00 -csh (csh)
kevin 731 0.0 0.0 44 0 co IW 01:31 0:00 /usr/openwin/bin/xinit -
kevin 739 0.0 0.0 28 0 co IW 01:31 0:00 sh /home/chicago/kevin/.
kevin 765 0.0 0.7 88 168 p1 S 01:31 0:00 -bin/csh (csh)
kevin 751 0.0 5.4 568 1212 co S 01:31 0:03 mailtool -Wp 0 0 -Ws 589
$ kill
$ ps -ef | grep kevin
```

Note that this process has been killed.

If you want to restart a process, you may want to use the -1 signal. This is often the case when you change the configuration of a daemon's initialization files and want to restart the daemon with the new characteristics. Take the following example:

```
$ ps -ef | grep tty
root 2345 1 0 12:01:43 hft/0 0:00 /etc/getty /dev/console
$/* now modify some characteristic of the getty subsystem */
$ kill -1 1 /* this restarts init and causes reinitialization */
```

Note that this is a special example that is often used to change the configuration of terminal lines. If you issue the kill -1 1 command, init [which is always process id (PID)] 1 is restarted and rereads all its initialization files including the getty files and subsystems. This is an old UNIX trick which allows you to change any init related daemon's characteristics and restart the daemons without interrupting the normal operation of your machine. Note, however, that since the daemons are restarted, any current activity related to that process is lost. Keep this in mind when you are changing these configurations since only the system administrator should be using the kill -1 1 command.

The kill -15 command is often used to kill a hung window manager. Window managers sometimes seem to hang and are impossible to kill. If you lose your window manager, you will have a very difficult time freeing your screen. To fix this without rebooting, simply move to another workstation, telnet into your workstation, and issue the command:

```
$ ps -ef | grep X11 /* works on most Motif systems */
```

or

```
$ ps -aux | grep Xnews /*works on a Sun */
```

This will print out the local X11 server. Once you have this process id, you can issue the kill command:

```
$ kill -15 PID
```

This will kill the window server and free up the screen. This doesn't always work, but it does seem to work most of the time.

Finally, if other kill commands are unsuccessful, you can issue the command:

```
$ kill -9 PID
```

This will kill the process immediately without allowing any cleanup of the process. You may have problems later when you attempt to restart the process if it left temporary files and other "junk" laying around either in memory or on disk. Keep this in mind and only use the kill -9 as a last resort.

6.15.4 Conclusion

The kill command in combination with the proper signal will allow you to kill or restart any process for which you have the privilege. This is a very powerful way of fixing things like runaway processes and hung workstation screens. See the signals and kill man pages for more information.

6.16 file

6.16.1 Introduction

The file command generates a best guess as to the contents of the given file. It is very useful when you are looking at files about which you have no information.

6.16.2 Usage

The basic syntax is:

```
file [-f file] [-cL] [-m file] file...
```

where -L tests the actual file and not the symbolic link.
-c checks for format errors in the magic number file.
-f file gets a list of files from file.
-m file uses file as the magic number file.
file... is one or more files to analyze.

file generates its best guess as to what type of file you asked it to analyze. Binary, text, nroff, and other files are recognized by the first byte of the file, which is called the magic number. This magic number is consistent for similar file types between files and systems. The correlation between magic numbers and file types is contained in the file /etc/magic. You can append your own information in the /etc/magic file to create your own types of files.

Some simple examples of the file command are:

```
$ file /etc/passwd
/etc/passwd: ascii text

$ file /bin/ls
/bin/ls: sparc pure dynamically linked executable

$ file /usr/man/man1/kill.1
/usr/man/man1/kill.1: [nt]roff, tbl, or eqn input text
```

6.16.3 Conclusion

file is a very powerful command which can assist you in understanding file types. You can also create your own file types by adding them to the /etc/magic file.

6.17 ascii

6.17.1 Introduction

You often need to understand the mapping between ASCII characters and their actual numeric representation. There is a file which provides this information to you. Its location varies from platform to platform, but its name is usually the same.

The basic locations of the file which contains the translations are:

```
/usr/pub/ascii
```

or

```
/usr/share/lib/pub/ascii
```

These are text files, and you can simply cat them to standard output.

6.17.2 Conclusion

This little file will become very useful the next time you want to make a character substitution in sed or a specific nonprintable character search in grep or simply substitute for a character in a program. There is no direct command to operate on this file; however, you can very quickly write a shell script to display the information in a way you would like.

6.18 split

6.18.1 Introduction

The split command allows you to split a file into pieces. This is often used to split large files into smaller chunks for either editing or file transfer.

6.18.2 Usage

The basic syntax for split is:

```
split [-number] [-infile [outfile]]
```

where -number is the number of lines to split into individual files.
-infile is the input file. Default is standard input.
-outfile is the output filename consisting of infile followed by an aa, then ab, then ac, etc.

If there is no outfile given, the output filename is x followed by aa, ab, ac, etc.

6.18.3 Conclusion

split is used by many utilities to break apart large files either for editing or file transfer. A commonly used public domain version of this program is known as bsplit. bsplit handles binary files as well and is discussed in Sec. 12.16.

Chapter

7

Output Formatting and Display

There are several key text formatting and display tools that come with most UNIX implementations. The standard UNIX text formatting utilities are nroff and troff. These are command-driven word processing and output formatting tools which provide professional looking output which can be printed on a large number of devices.

The other tool discussed in this chapter is xwd. This stands for X window dump and provides you with the ability to capture the screen and either print or display it at some later time. This is a very powerful tool which allows you to save graphical images as well as text in a file for later display.

7.1 nroff

7.1.1 Introduction

nroff, which stands for nontypesetting runoff, is the standard tool for word processing and output formatting for UNIX. It is the format in which man commands as well as many internal UNIX documents come. Many Internet software products also come with a nroff document which can be formatted and either displayed or printed to get more information on the particular product distribution.

nroff is both a language and a command. Sections which discuss each aspect of nroff follow.

7.1.2 Usage

nroff, the command. The basic syntax for the nroff command is:

```
nroff [-ehiq] [-mname] [-nN] [-opage] [-raN] [-sN] [-Tname] [file...]
```

where -e produces equally spaced words.
-h uses TABS on output instead of spaces to speed output.
-i reads standard input after all input files are processed.
-q invokes simultaneous request rd.
-mname prepends /usr/share/lib/tmac/tmac.name to the input files.
-nN is the page number of the first page.
-opage prints only pages on the comma separated list page.
-raN sets register a to N.
-sN stops every N pages.
-Tname is the output device (see local man page for specific devices supported).
file ... is one or more files to process.

nroff, the language. nroff provides command-driven capabilities to put output into user-chosen formats. Things such as margins, indentations, and spacings are all defaulted to reasonable values. nroff can also do things like generate footnotes, automatically number headings, and put default date and time information on each page and can produce things like numbered lists.

nroff was the predecessor to a tool called troff (see the next section) and provides output streams for both display devices and many printers. troff provides a much higher quality of output for higher-resolution output devices such as newer laser printers or phototypesetters. nroff is more commonly used because of its heritage as well as the high level of portability of nroff codes.

There are a variety of associated tools which work with nroff, such as eqn and tbl, which generate equations and tables respectively. These will be mentioned in this chapter but not in any great detail. See your local system documentation for more details.

Because of the somewhat repetitive nature of most word processing jobs, there are a few sets of commonly used macros which work with nroff and troff. The most common are mm (memorandum) and ms (manuscript).

All nroff commands and macros begin with a period. Some of the most basic nroff commands are:

`.ad b`	Justifies lines.
`.bp`	New page.
`.br`	Breaks line.
`.ce n`	Centers next n lines.
`.fi`	Fills lines.
`.in[+|-]n`	Sets left margin plus or minus n inches. If no plus or minus is present, n is an absolute left margin number.

`.ll[+|-]`	Sets line length to plus or minus n or n if no plus or minus is used.
`.na`	Don't justify lines.
`.nf`	Don't fill lines.
`.so file`	Gets file and includes in line.
`.sp n`	Creates n blank lines.
`.ti[+|-]n`	Sets left margin for next line only (see .in).
`.tl 'left'center'right'`	Creates three-part heading.

All of these commands must begin in the first column of the input file and will generate the requested output when the nroff command is executed. A simple example is:

```
.ce 1
This is an nroff file
.tl 'kevin'doc'help'
.sp 3
This is the beginning of the text.
This is the end of text.
```

If you assume the name of the above file is kevin.nroff, you would process it with the command:

```
$ nroff kevin.nroff
```

The output of the above command is:

```
This is an nroff file
kevin doc help

This is the beginning of text. This is the end of text.
```

There are several things to note about the output format. The first line is centered with the .ce command, the next line is divided equally across the page, there are three blank lines as a result of the .sp command, and finally, the text of the document is filled in. Note that this means that nroff takes the input text and fills the appropriate margins and justifies and fills the text accordingly. This is a very nice feature of nroff that lets you worry about entering the text and having nroff generate the output appropriate for the chosen margins and output device size.

Once you have explored the basic nroff command set, you will want to begin to look at macros which are provided with most nroff systems. Some of the more basic mm macros are:

`.AL [type][indentation][separation]`	Starts automatic list
`.B`	Uses the Roman bold font family
`.BI`	Alternates bold and underline fonts

`.BR`	Alternates bold and Roman fonts
`.DE`	Ends display
`.DF [position][fill][position]`	Starts floating display
`.DL [indentation][separation]`	Starts dashed list
`.DS [position][fill][position]`	Starts static display
`.H level [text]`	Displays a numbered heading
`.FE`	Ends footnote
`.FS`	Starts footnote
`.I`	Uses the Roman italic font family
`.IB`	Alternates underline and bold fonts
`.IR`	Alternates underline and Roman fonts
`.ML mark[indentation][separation]`	Starts marked list
`.LE [separation]`	Ends list
`.LI [mark][prefix]`	Starts new list item
`.P [type]`	Sets type to 0 for a left block paragraph, sets type to 1 for indent paragraph
`.PH "'left'center'right'"`	Generates a running header and footer
`.RB`	Alternates Roman and bold fonts
`.RI`	Alternates Roman and underline fonts
`.SK n`	Skips n pages
`.SP n`	displays n blank lines
`.TC`	Generates a table of contents
`.VL indentation [mark][separation]`	Starts variable item list
`.R`	Uses the Roman font family

Most of the above commands will operate on the line on which they are specified. For example, to italicize a phrase you might use:

```
.I this is italicized
```

With the mm macros, you must use number registers. There are default values for most of the macros described above such as indentation and font. Many of these can be changed by using the number register command. A simple example is:

```
.nr Ej 1
.nr Pt 1
```

The first command causes first-level headings to be preceded by a new-page instead of the default newline. The second .nr command causes the default paragraph type to be 1 instead of 0 for the rest of the document.

The mm macros use a concept of a register to represent an area that is in memory and contains a number which describes the default characteristics of the mm macro command. With the .nr command, you can modify the contents of this register and, therefore, modify the characteristics of the mm macro command.

Once you issue an .nr command, it stays in effect until changed explicitly by another .nr command. This provides you with the ability to change the characteristics and behavior of a given mm macro for the entire length of the document or for merely a portion.

When you use the mm macro package, you must invoke nroff with the -mm option. A simple example is:

```
$ nroff -mm kevin.nroff
```

This generates output to standard output, and, therefore, the output can be redirected with either a pipe or redirect symbol to any other UNIX process or tool.

A simple example input file is:

```
.AL
.LI
item1
.LI
item2
.LI
item3
.LE
```

Applying the nroff command:

```
$ nroff -mm file.input
```

to the above file produces the output:

```
1. item1
2. item2
3. item3
```

This is a numbered list, and many of the characteristics of this list array can be changed with the .nr command. You can also use the .AL command to modify some characteristics of the numbered list as well. For example, the type variable can be set to:

`1`	Arabic numbers
`A`	Uppercase letters
`I`	Uppercase Roman numbers
`a`	Lowercase letters
`i`	Lowercase Roman numbers

Indentation defines the number of spaces to indent and the separation is defined as:

0	Single blank line between items
1	No blank lines between items

To modify a variable other than the first in the list, you must issue null commands for those intervening variables. For example, to change the type of the numbers to uppercase Roman, use the command:

```
.AL "" A ""
```

The heading commands are very useful. They allow you to generate a variety of headings and subheadings. The .H command is a numbered heading; it automatically generates the correct number and increments correctly. The heading level consists of 1 through 6, where 1 and 2 are bold and followed by a blank line. Heading levels 3 through 6 are lowercase with initial capital letters and are underlined and indented. You can use the .nr command to change many characteristics of the headings.

```
.nr Ej 1
```

forces a major heading to the top of the next page.

One nice feature of nroff and the mm macros is that a table of contents is generated at the end of the document based on levels 1 and 2 heading information. Note, however, that this is not printed to standard output unless you use the .TC command.

The concept of a display is another feature of nroff which adds significant value to the system. A display is an atomic unit of text that is also known as a keep. In other words, it is a unit of information which cannot be separated. Items such as tables and graphs are typical examples of displays. There are two kinds of displays: static and floating.

The static display commands place text only on a page that will accept the entire block. If the block will not fit on the current page, it will begin on the next page. A simple example of this is:

```
.DS
contents of a table are here
.DE
```

This will position the table on the current page if it will fit; otherwise, it will move to the next page and display the table there.

Floating displays work slightly differently. With a floating display, you can have nroff place text following the display on a page. If the floating display will not fit, it will merely place the floating display at the top of the next page. This is useful for graphics and images which can be referenced in the text but don't necessarily need to be immediately next to the associated text. It preserves page space and removes potential large blank spaces in your document.

There are many other commands, some of which are in the table above. However, many of the nroff native commands as well as macros are not documented here. See your local system nroff documentation as well as the nroff/troff Nutshell book by O'Reilly & Associates for more detail on nroff commands.

man pages. There are also macros shipped with most machines which contain information and knowledge about manual (man) pages. The macro package is known as an. This way, when you process a man page with nroff, you would use the command:

```
$ man -man file
```

Remember that the -m option tells nroff to use the macro package which follows. In this case, it is an, thus the option -man. Clever, huh? These macros contain many defaults for the structure of a typical man page, including running header formats as well as headers and command lines. These macros are what cause man pages from many different sources to look similar. As long as the vendor or supplier of the man page used the an macro package, the output will be the same. Keep this in mind if you distribute software and associated man page documentation. There are many man page input files on the CD distributed with this book. See one of these for a good example of a man page using the an macro package.

7.1.3 Conclusion

The best way to learn nroff is to experiment with it. nroff is a powerful formatting system which provides significant functionality and portability across UNIX platforms. It is the traditional system for man pages and most other UNIX documentation. While there is significant functionality and power in the standard nroff commands, most people use the mm macro package to generate more complex and powerful output formats.

There are many nroff commands, but only a few basic ones were discussed in this chapter. For a more complete discussion, see the nroff/troff Nutshell book by O'Reilly & Associates.

7.2 troff

7.2.1 Introduction

troff stands for typesetting runoff and provides a higher level of output quality than nroff. It is typically used for output devices like high-quality and high-resolution laser printers, phototypesetters, and film makers.

While troff exists on most UNIX systems, it is not as widely used as nroff, and, subsequently, this book will spend less time discussing it.

7.2.2 Usage

troff, like nroff, consists of language and command components. Each is discussed below.

troff, the command. The basic syntax for troff is:

```
troff [-abiqtwz] [-mmacro] [-nN] [-olist] [-pN] [-raN] [-sN]
[files]...
```

where -a sends approximate ASCII representation to standard output.
-b reports on CAT/4 typesetter availability.
-i reads from standard input after all files are read in.
-q disables echoing.
-t directs output to standard output (be careful).
-w waits until CAT/4 typesetter is available.
-z suppresses all CAT/4 typesetter output.
-mmacro prepends the macro file /usr/lib/tmac/tmac.macro to the input filenames.
-nN numbers first page N.
-olist prints only pages in the comma-separated list.
-pN prints all characters in point size N on CAT/4.
-raN sets register a to N.
-sN stops CAT/4 every N pages.
files input files to be processed.

Note that the CAT/4 device is an old device which provided typesetting capabilities to traditional UNIX machines. These commands are preserved for backward compatibility; however, many UNIX platforms and troff versions do not support this device. See your local system documentation for more information.

As was mentioned above, most macro packages exist in the /usr/lib/tmac directory on most machines. Most have a filename of tmac.* where the * is the macro name. Remember that the macro string begins with a -m, and therefore the string -man uses the macro package an. If you look in the /usr/lib/tmac directory, you will see the associated m, an, and s macro packages. You can look at these for more details about the macros supported on your platform.

troff, the language. troff supports much the same language as nroff. In fact, nroff is often used today to preview a document before submitting it to troff for higher-quality output generation. It should be stated that, much like nroff, troff has no real support for graphics and images. troff is a text manipulation facility. There are related tools to do more sophisticated manipulation such as eqn and tbl; however, these are not discussed in any detail in this section. See your local system for additional information.

troff commands begin with periods just as nroff commands do. With troff, there are a variety of commands which can be "escaped" directly into the input text stream which control the format of the output. These commands become quite complex and provide incredibly powerful text formatting capabilities. This is possible because of the higher quality and enhanced functionality of output devices used by troff.

There are macro packages used by troff which are, by and large, the same as those used by nroff. The most commonly used macro packages are an and mm. troff provides exactly the same functionality as that described in Sec. 7.1. See it for example commands.

troff also has the ability to use eqn and table commands more effectively than nroff. By interfacing eqn and table directly into the input stream of a troff command, you can produce documentation with integrated tables and sophisticated equations.

The basic structure of these commands is:

```
$ tbl input.file | troff -mm -Ti10 | lpr
```

This will first run the file input.file through the tbl preprocessor, which will take all tbl-related commands and execute them to build the appropriate tables within the document. Once this is finished, the resulting output stream is sent to troff where it is processed for standard troff and macro commands. Once this is finished, it is passed directly to lp. Note that this is often the case with troff, unlike nroff, because the output is generated for a particular device. If you attempted to look at the output of this command on the display by viewing standard output, you would see gibberish on your screen. By selecting the typesetting device with the -T command, you determine the format of the output. The eqn command works the same way.

7.2.3 Conclusion

This section is a very brief introduction to troff and its capabilities as well as to its related tools eqn and tbl. The thing to remember is that troff can use exactly the same commands as those documented in the nroff section but can produce a higher-quality output because of the different devices supported. nroff is often used to preview documents, while troff is often used to produce the final copy.

There is a tool from GNU which provides the functionality of troff and much more called groff. See Sec. 14.3 for more information.

7.3 xwd, xwud, and xpr

7.3.1 Introduction

xwd and xwud allow for image storage and display in an X11 windowing environment. Using these two commands in combination allows you to dump and display contents of X11 windows. You can generate a graphic- or text-based X11 window, dump it to a file which contains all screen information in a special format known only to the xwd and xwud commands, and, at a later time, display that window exactly as it was originally displayed. xpr allows you to redirect the xwd file to a printer for hard-copy output.

7.3.2 Usage

The xwd command dumps an image of an X11 window to a file in a special format which can be viewed at a later time with the xwud command. For more information on how to use X11 windows systems most effectively, see Chap. 8.

xwd command. The syntax of the xwd command is:

```
xwd [-add] [-bitmap] [-display display] [-help] [-nobdrs] [-xy]
[-out file]
```

where -add specifies a value to be added to every pixel.
-bitmap specifies that only the first plane of a color image be used. Note that this is required for an image that is to be sent to a printer with xpr.
-display display sets the X11 window display to control output.
-help prints out usage summary.
-nobdrs specifies that the dump should not include the window border.
-xy selects xy format instead of z format.
-out file redirects the output dump to a file named file.

To dump a window, you would generate an X11 window containing any information you would like dumped. This could be graphics, text, or anything as long as it is contained within the X11 window border.

From another window, you would invoke the xwd command. For example:

```
$ xwd -out window.xwd
```

Once you invoke this command, the cursor changes type to indicate xwd has taken over control of the screen. At this point, move the cursor to the window that you want to dump and press the left mouse button. You will hear an audible beep when the dump is finished. You now have a file named window.xwd which contains an exact pixel-for-pixel dump of the X11 window you dumped. You can now print it out with the xpr command or redisplay it with the xwud command. See the following sections for more information on these commands.

Note that with the use of the display variable, you can actually capture a window on another X display. This is a very powerful feature which, if used effectively, can increase your ability to communicate and share information with other people.

xwud command. The xwud command allows you to display a previously dumped image. The syntax is:

```
$ xwud [-in file] [-noclick] [-geometry geom] [-display display]
  [-new]
[-std maptype] [-raw] [-help] [-rv] [-fg color] [-bg color]
```

where -in file specifies the xwd input file.
-noclick turns off clicking termination. The default action is that any button click in the window will terminate the application and kill the displayed window.
-geometry geom specifies the location and size of the window in the standard format for X11 windows.
-display display specifies an X11 display on which to display the image.
-new creates a new color map for the displayed image.
-std maptype specifies a color map type to use. See xcmap for more information.
-raw uses current colors on the screen.
-help prints out options for xwud command.
-rv—if image is a bitmap, swaps foreground and background colors.
-fg color specifies foreground color.
-bg color specifies background color.

If you have not explicitly set the DISPLAY environmental variable, you can use the -display option to display the xwud window on any other X11 display that you have access to. Remember, that, as with all other X11 window commands, the X11 server must have allowed access to the display with the xhost command before you can display on the server. See Chap. 8 for more information.

xpr command. The xpr command prints the output of the xwd dump. The output printers supported vary from machine to machine; however, the most common of Postscript, HP-PCL, HP-GL, and ASCII printers are supported. The syntax of the xpr command is:

```
$ xpr [-append file | -output file] [-noff] [-landscape | -portrait]
  [-compact]
[-cutoff level] [-header string] [-height inches] [-left inches]
  [-noposition]
[-plane planenumber] [-psfig] [-rv] [-scale scale] [-split number]
  [-top inches]
[-trailer string] [-width inches] [-device device]
```

where -append file specifies a file previously created with xpr to append to. Note that this is not supported with Postscript printers.
-output file specifies output file for results of xpr command.
-noff—when used with -append, merges page with previous page.
-landscape specifies landspace format (window wider than high).
-portrait specifies portrait format (window higher than wide).
-compact uses compact encoding for file space conservation.
-cutoff level generates output in monochrome. Expressed as a percentage full brightness.
-header string specifies a string to print above the window.
-height inches specifies maximum height of window in inches.
-left inches specifies the left margin.
-noposition is used to bypass header, image, and trailer positioning commands for Laserjet printer.
-plane planenumber specifies which bit plane to use to store intensities.
-psfig suppresses translation of Postscript picture to center of page.
-rv prints window in reverse video.
-scale scale—for Postscript, allows you to choose bit to grid translations. You can make each pixel translate to a number of grids in Postscript with the scale option. By default the window size is maximized.
-split number allows you to split window into several pages.
-top inches specifies top margin in inches.
-trailer string specifies a trailer string for the window.

-width inches specifies maximum width of window.
-device device—see the local man page for the devices supported on your particular variant of UNIX. The most commonly supported are Postscript (ps), HP Laserjet (ljet), HP Paintjet (pjet), and the DEC LN03 (ln03).

While there are many options for the xpr command, you will probably use a couple of them on a regular basis and never use the rest. Once you understand your printing environment, you can generate a script which contains the correct syntax and simply invoke the script whenever you want to print out an X11 window dump.

xpr uses standard input and output unless otherwise directed with the -output command and/or redirection commands (< and >). For input, you must have generated an xwd file with the wxd command to use as input to the xpr command. For example, using the xwd file generated in the xwd section:

```
$ xpr -device ps -output window.ps < window.xwd
```

will generate a Postscript file called window.ps which you can then print or display with Ghostscript or some other display Postscript interpreter.

To avoid using unnecessary disk space, you can use the standard output capability to route directly to the printer with the command:

```
$ xpr -device ps < window.xwd | lpr
```

which will generate the graphic and send it directly to the default Postscript printer. You can experiment with moving the picture around on the output page with the -height, -width, -top, and -left options. Each device will react a little differently based on its characteristics. Experiment with your configuration before committing to a large output stream which may waste lots of paper before you can stop it.

7.3.3 Conclusion

You can dump and display contents of X11 windows with the xwd and xwud commands. The format of the file is special and known only to the xwd and xwud commands. For more information on the format, see the XWDFile.h header file in the X11 include directory.

xwd and xwud give you the ability to share screens of information with others at a later time or on another display. With this capability, you can utilize output more effectively and share information more efficiently. With the xpr command, you can generate hard-copy output from the xwd files.

Chapter

8

Windowing Systems

There are several windowing system standards in existence today: NeWS, X11, Microsoft Windows, Macintosh Finder, and a host of others. While Microsoft Windows continues to hold the overall desktop lead due to the large installed base of DOS PCs, X11 has become the standard for the heterogeneous desktop environment. Windows and other windowing environments won't work across the network, but X11 is a fully networked, extensible windowing environment which runs on virtually every hardware and software platform in existence. This portability and extensibility are what have driven X11 to be the most widely used windowing environment in heterogeneous environments. We will start with an overview of X11 technology and then outline some issues that one should consider when making a purchase decision.

8.1 X11 Technology Overview

X11 windows is a graphical user-interface (GUI) package written at M.I.T. and was designed to allow graphical interaction across platforms in a client/server configuration. The current most widely used release of X11 is called X11R4, which is MIT X11 Release 4. X11R5 is available from M.I.T.; and most vendors have completed and released the port as a production release. This will soon be the de facto standard.

The X11 system is controlled by two pieces of software, each running on one end of a client/server connection. The application runs on top of the X11 protocol which is really just an interface to network services between machines (see Fig. 8.1). This figure is adapted from *XWindows Systems Administrators Guide* by Linda Mui and Eric Pearce, published by O'Reilly & Associates. By running an application that uses

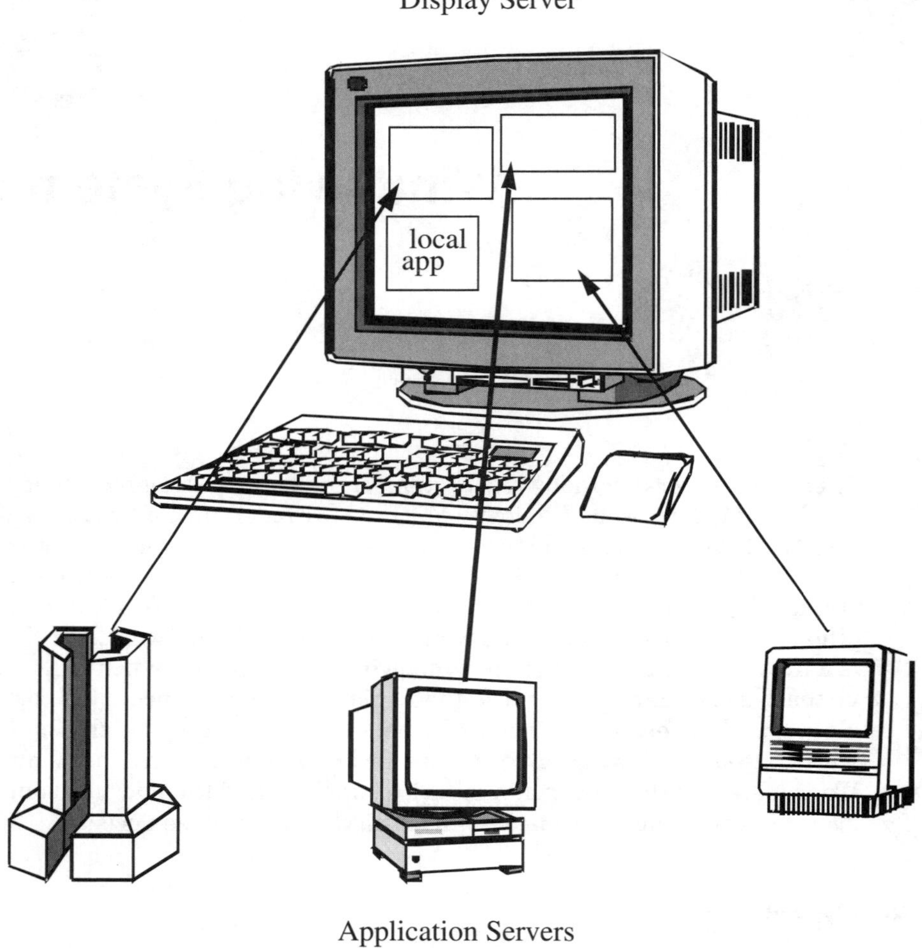

Figure 8.1 The X11 client/server model. *("XWindows Systems Administrators Guide," Linda Mui and Eric Pearce, © 1992, O'Reilly & Associates, Inc., p. 206. For orders and information, call 800-998-9938.)*

X11 windows calls, you can distribute your application on a display other than the one at which you are currently sitting. Unfortunately, X11 windows reverses the standard client/server nomenclature convention and calls the machine on which you display the application the server and the machine from which you run the application the client. This is because the X11 paradigm thinks of the display server and the application client and not the application server and display client as do most applications. This is often the cause of some confusion; however, once you understand this, you won't forget it.

You can have multiple applications running on different machines (clients) and displayed on a single screen or on multiple displays for the same application, although you will normally use only one display. This is the kind of flexibility and power X11 brings to the graphical environment which no other windowing system offers.

Before going much further with this discussion, it is important to define the terms that are commonly used in this environment. The display is the screen on which you wish to display the application output. The client is the application which is generating output to be displayed. Since X11 is a network windowing system, these can be on the same or different machines. To display the results of an application to another machine on a network, it is a simple matter of setting an environmental variable as described below. It requires no code changes or additions to take full advantage of this true client/server model. In fact, X11 is roughly an ISO OSI layer 5 protocol which utilizes layers 1 through 4 to provide transport of packets and frames. This is why you can run X11 over virtually any transport layer including DDCMP and TCP as well as SNA equivalent protocols. This is what provides heterogeneous machine and network support.

There are two issues that you must address before you can access a display. The first is that each display has a protection associated with it that the user must explicitly allow users to access. By issuing the command

```
$ xhost +hostname
```

where hostname is the name of the machine that you would like to access your display, you permit the X11 application to display on your local screen. Note that the xhost command must be executed on the machine on which you would like to display and not the machine from which you will run the application part of the X11 session. This command must be executed for every login session on your display, or access will be denied. Another point to note is that you can allow all machines access by issuing the following command:

```
$ xhost +
```

The alternative to this is to permanently change the access protection by editing the file /etc/X0.hosts. By inserting a line like:

```
hostname
```

in the /etc/X0.hosts file, you will allow access to your display by the machine hostname until this line is removed from the file. Note that to insert multiple hostnames, you simply insert additional hostnames, beginning in the first column of the file, one hostname per line. Note that it is also important to fully qualify the hostname if you are in a domain that is subdivided. This means that your hostnames contain periods. For example, snoopy.fnal.gov is a hostname that should be fully typed into the file since this may avoid some problems later on.

As you have probably noticed, there is no way to give specific users access to your display in standard X11. This is an issue that is being addressed in X11R5. An algorithm called the magic cookie is used to distribute encrypted keys to determine who owns the display and to ensure that others cannot use it. Many X11R4 servers support this; however, it will not be fully exploited and utilized until X11R5.

The other issue is related to defining where you would like the application to be displayed. By setting the environmental variable DISPLAY with a fully qualified hostname followed by a :0, you define where the X11 application should display itself. For example, the command would look as follows:

```
$ set DISPLAY=hostname:0
$ export DISPLAY
```

As an example of this entire process, a classic X11 application is called xcalc, and it is normally installed with the release of X11 on your machine. Let's assume you are sitting at your local display named snoopy and want to remotely execute xcalc from a machine named linus to display on your local display. You would do the following things. On local display (snoopy), the commands would be:

```
$ xhost + hostname
$ telnet hostname
```

Log in as you normally would. On the remote machine (linus), the commands would be:

```
$ set DISPLAY=snoopy:0
$ /usr/openwin/bin/xcalc &
```

A computer calculator should pop up on your local display under the control of your local window manager. To kill it, simply press the mouse button while placing the mouse over the calculator's top border, and you will see an exit choice. Select it, and the application is terminated. Note that the path for the xcalc executable is dependent on the machine and installation choices made for the X11 software. On many machines the command to execute xcalc will be:

```
$ /usr/bin/X11/xcalc &
```

See the manual page on xcalc or X11 for more information.

You can also use a command like:

```
$ /usr/bin/X11/xterm &
```

which will display an xterm window along with associated keyboard mappings and other escape sequence processing. By using xterm, you will often avoid many of the terminal emulation and keyboard mapping problems that you may encounter if you use a standard vendor-supplied terminal window such as cmdtool on a Sun or aixterm on an IBM RS/6000. By invoking an xterm and then running an application, you often avoid many keyboard problems you may be experiencing.

8.2 X11R4 and X11R5

While it is true that X11R4 is the current production version on most machines, X11R5 is on the way. Some of the differences between X11R4 and X11R5 are significant. X11R5 supports scaleable fonts. This provides applications with a much wider choice of fonts with respect to a given application and lets the application programmer worry more about the application logic and less about making the fonts fit in the window. X11R5 also comes with a much larger number of fonts and utilities. Security and authentication are also significantly enhanced in X11R5. This is key as X11R5 makes its way into the commercial market.

In addition to the scaleable fonts, X11R5 delivers a font server capability. Because of the large storage requirements of fonts, you would like to store them in a single location on your LAN and access them only when needed across the network. X11R5 gives you this capability by defining a font server for the network. Every time a machine wants to get a font, it merely initiates a call on the network for the nearest font server and loads the appropriate fonts from there. This alleviates the need to store multiple copies of the fonts on the same LAN.

X11R5 also supports 3-D extensions called PEX (Phigs Extensions to X.) These extensions are new to X11R5 and will support true 3-D representation with native X11. Up until the PEX extensions, there was no standard way, and in fact no way at all, to do 3-D representation in a true X11 window. X11R5 changes all this.

Finally, there is a new color system called Xcms which allows X11 programmers to take better advantage of standard color offerings native with X11.

While it is clear that things like scaleable fonts and more powerful and flexible authentication and security are useful, it still does not change the underlying paradigm of X11. Most of the changes between X11R4 and X11R5 will be important to the programmer but not the user. Because of its scaleability and portability, X11 is clearly the windowing system of choice for the foreseeable future in the UNIX world and in the entire world of heterogeneous computing.

8.3 GUIs

GUIs are the things that users see and "feel" when they use a windowing environment. There are standards for "look and feel" for windowing environments which describe how the interface should look in terms of what the user should expect after pressing a certain button or dragging the mouse across an object on the screen. This is documented in a book called a style guide. This is used by developers to build GUIs on their programs and to ensure that their programs look and feel the same as those of all other vendors on that platform.

The GUI exists as a layer above the base X11 tool kit that provides basic windowing functionality. The GUI relies on the underlying X11 utilities and protocols to provide the network access and behavior that defines the X11 protocol. Each GUI has a style guide associated with it which describes how the buttons, keyboard, and windows behave. This differs between the two primary X GUIs today: Motif and OpenLook. The GUI wars have been one of the most hotly contested of all areas related to UNIX. Sun Microsystems is the only large proponent of OpenLook (it's theirs), while all the other major computer vendors provide Motif. In fact, Motif is running on over 50 percent of the Sun workstations running today.

A major direction has recently been adopted by both the OpenLook and Motif camps called common open software environment (COSE). This is an attempt to unify the GUI for all variants of UNIX including Sun, HP, and IBM. This is in direct response to Microsoft NT, which is poised to gobble up a significant portion of the desktop operating system market. By unifying the GUI for UNIX, vendors have taken a large step toward competing effectively against Microsoft and others for the desktop marketplace. Watch the trade magazines as COSE becomes a real product.

Motif is a specification developed and maintained by the Open Software Foundation (OSF). The OSF, working in collaboration with MIT, DEC, IBM, and others, continues to develop and distribute the Motif tool kit which individual vendors then port to their particular platform. The current distribution is Motif 1.2, but version 1.3 is well on its way and will be made available shortly.

Motif got its look and feel from IBM's Presentation Manager, which is the windowing interface running on IBM OS/2 PCs. IBM submitted this technology to OSF several years ago and provided source code and documentation for standardization. OSF adopted this technology as the GUI of choice and has continued to enhance it.

OpenLook is Sun Microsystem's GUI equivalent to Motif from OSF. It has a different look and feel than Motif does; however, many of the skills needed to use one environment are transportable to the other. OpenLook supports both the X11 protocol and Sun's own proprietary NeWS protocol, which is very similar, to display postscript. NeWS is being phased out in favor of X11 and will be unsupported in the near future.

COSE is clearly the direction of the GUI for UNIX vendors, and you should ask your vendor about their support of this environment. One thing to watch out for with respect to COSE is that the initial work is being done on Motif 1.1, so there may be some initial incompatibilities between COSE and later versions of motif.

8.4 The X11 Distribution

The X11 distribution currently occupies well over 200MB of disk or tape space if you get everything. This is why it is not generally available from bulletin boards and servers. Because of its large size and subsequent high costs of transmission over the network (probably over $100 in connect time), you typically have to order it on a tape or pay a firm to download it to your network. The best way to get X11R5, if not from your vendor, is from:

Software Center
Technology Licensing Office
28 Carleton Street
Room E32-300
Cambridge, MA 02142-1324
(617)258-8330

You can also get it from a network service provider such as UUNET for a nominal fee.

X11R4 and X11R5 are available from a variety of sources including the Internet. Some of the sources are:

Integrated Computer Solutions
(617)621-0060

Free Software Foundation
(617)876-3296

Non Standard Logics
+33 (1) 43 36 77 50

IXI Limited
+44 223 462 131

There are several others. X11R5 is also very large, and it is not, therefore, recommended that you get it over the network. Purchase it from one of the providers listed above or any of several others who can provide it to you on tape.

Neither X11R4 or X11R5 is on the CD included with this book. When you get the X11 distribution, you should also ensure that you get the contributed software for X11 as well. This will be well over 100MB in size, so you will also need to get it on tape.

There are two articles entitled x.faq and x-faq in the X11 directory on the CD. These contain answers to frequently asked questions related to X11. There is a standard in the Internet world which is called the faq (frequently asked questions) document. This contains lists of answers to questions that are frequently asked on a particular topic. The X11 faqs are very helpful and contain significant amounts of information concerning X11 software, its distribution, and its use. In fact, there is even a discussion on how to build X11 distributions. See these files and the section on FAQs in the next chapter for more information.

Patches to X11R5 are often placed on bulletin boards and network gateway boxes such as the UUNET box. You can certainly download these and apply for the distribution at your leisure. However, the general distribution of X11 software over the network is limited by its size.

8.5 Fonts and X11 Windows

Fonts and their use are intimately related to the execution of X11 applications. By choosing the proper fonts and positioning them on the screen correctly, the X11 server provides the primary interface to any applications relying on X11 for display.

Fonts, while reasonably transparent to the user when they are working correctly, can also be the cause of many strange and unexplainable problems. This is largely due to the nature of the X11 client and server applications and their use of the fonts themselves. Each application is responsible for calling the appropriate fonts in the appropriate sizes and locations. If the font families of the X11 server are not what the application expects, you may get strange-looking results. In some cases, you may get a fatal error which will cause the application to exit. If this occurs, there are several ways you can bypass this problem, some of which are described below.

Fonts are stored in a variety of formats including bitmap distribution format (BDF), server normal font (SNF), and portable compiled format (PCF). These formats represent different ways of storing font information.

Each font must be represented as a bitmap before it can be displayed but does not necessarily have to be stored as a bitmap. The BDF format consists of ASCII information which is interpreted by the X11 server before being displayed. This slows the display server down since it has to interpret the ASCII information. These files typically have a suffix of .bdf. Most X11 servers can read and utilize BDF files.

The SNF format is a format specific to a particular X11 server and is created with a thing called a font compiler. The compiler you would use to move from BDF to SNF files is bdftosnf. This is typically shipped with the particular X11 server software and should be utilized to create a more efficient font format to increase the performance of the X11 server. SNF files are binary files and typically have a suffix of .snf.

Finally, the PCF format is a binary format introduced with the X11R5 version of the X11 software. It also contains a font compiler named bdftopcf which creates PC from BDF files. This format is a X11 server neutral binary format which all X11 servers at R5 and beyond understand. Because of the binary nature of the files, the interpretation is faster, and thus the X11 server performance is better.

The resolution of your display has a direct relationship to the fonts you wish to use. Within the standard font directory /usr/lib/X11/fonts, there are several directories including 75dpi, 100dpi, and misc (miscellaneous). These represent 75-dots-per-inch, 100 dots-per-inch, and miscellaneous fixed-width fonts.

Within each directory are several special files. The first is the fonts.dir file which contains a mapping from the actual font name to the filename in which the font is contained. An example is:

```
courBO08.snf.Z -adobe-courier-bold-o-normal--11-80-100-100-m-60-
  iso8859-1
```

This denotes that the font adobe-courier . . . is in compressed format and is stored in the file courBO08.snf.Z. Every time an application references this font, this file is read in by the server and is used to generate the proper bitmaps to display on the screen. All fonts known to the X11 server are documented in the fonts.dir file in the appropriate directories for the font families.

The fonts.dir file must be rebuilt every time you add a new font to a directory. After placing the font files in the correct directory, you must issue the command:

```
$ mkfontdir
```

This will update the fonts.dir file. Do not edit the fonts.dir file directly. If you do not run the mkfontdir command, your font will not be known to the server. Note also that you must restart the X11 server after you have added fonts, or the X11 server will not know of their existence since it reads all fonts.dir files on start. There are other commands you may use to reread this information into the font server, but these are well beyond the scope of this book. See your X11 documentation for more information. Also see the man page on mkfontdir.

The other important file in each font family directory is the fonts.aliases file. This contains a shorthand notation for each font file. For example:

```
lucidasans-14 -b&h-lucida-medium-r-normal-sans-20-140-100-100-p-114-
  iso8859-1
```

creates a font alias lucidasans-14 to represent the actual font, which has a much longer name. This allows the applications to use the shorthand notation and call the appropriate file. The fonts.alias file provides a means of tricking an X11 server into using different fonts than were intended. By creating an alias of the requested font to a font which you choose to use, you force the X11 server to use the aliased font instead of the one it expects. This is a common method for tricking the X11 server into displaying results on a X11 server which does not have the appropriate fonts for the application.

There is a path known as the font path which determines how the X11 server searches for fonts. This is generated when the X11 software is created. You can modify this path with the command:

```
$ xset fp pathname
```

where pathname is the pathname you wish. You separate multiple directories in the pathname with commas. An example is:

```
$ xset fp /usr/lib/X11/fonts/misc,/usr/lib/X11/fonts/75dpi
$ xset fp rehash
```

This sets the fontpath first to the miscellaneous fonts and then to the 75dpi fonts. The rehash command is necessary to tell the X11 server to rehash the fontpath. Without this, the new path will not be entered into the X11 server for proper execution. This must be executed after each fontpath change.

Many of the problems with fonts and X11 windows have come from the tremendous amounts of storage required to store fonts on each display server. With X11R5, the concept of a font server has emerged. You can designate a machine as a font server for your network and simply point the fontpath to the machine and the appropriate directories on this machine. This provides you with a single repository for fonts and saves a tremendous amount of disk space and management.

The basic syntax for the fontpath is:

```
$ xset +fp tcp/hostname:7000
```

where tcp designates the transport layer, hostname is the actual hostname of the font server machine, and 7000 is the port number on which the hostname listens for font requests. This is all documented in the X11R5 release notes and is one of the key differences between X11R4 and X11R5.

The other key issue related to fonts is the basic structure of the fonts themselves. With the new SNF format, fonts are outline fonts and therefore can be scaled. This is very different from the older fonts in X11R4 which were predominantly bitmap fonts which could not be scaled. One of the most common problems in the older versions of X11 was that when you resized a window, the fonts did not scale with the new window size and thus looked awkward. With X11R5, the fonts are scaleable and should be automatically scaled with the display window. This adds a dramatically improved interface to X11 applications and is probably the other key user difference between X11R4 and X11R5.

8.6 X Terminals versus Workstations

A fairly recent entry into the X arena is the X terminal. This is a standalone display that has some local computing power; however, this computing power is only used to run the X server software and is incapable of general-purpose computing. This solution is most often used for display stations that have low interactive use and little graphical manipulation.

The debate raging on X terminals versus diskless or dataless workstations is growing. The question of whether you should be using X terminals or workstations on the desktop is not black and white but is dependent on context and requirements. Note that the distinction between diskless and dataless workstations is one of a local disk used for page and swap. The diskless workstation has no local disk and must page and swap across the network from the operating system server, which imposes severe performance loads on both the server and network. The dataless workstation has a local disk for page and swap but is still primarily served by another workstation for its operating system and other software.

It is generally recommended to utilize a local disk wherever possible since it significantly enhances overall system performance not only on the local workstation but on the server as well. The merits of clustering systems together is only relevant to this discussion as a management issue. Therefore, it will not be discussed except to say that one of the primary arguments for the use of X terminals is that they decrease the amount of system management that is required. Because of font tape and PROM issues as well as a variety of setup issues, it is not clear that X terminals provide a significantly lower maintenance load than dataless workstations. The only thing that is certain is that the performance of these X terminals is application dependent, and this should be considered carefully when choosing the architecture for your environment.

8.6.1 Issues to consider before making a purchase

Many studies have been done on the performance and cost-effectiveness of X terminals versus workstations by vendors and users alike. This section presents general recommendations on what are the most critical issues to consider when making this decision and suggestions for configuration:

1. *Study the type of application that you will be running on these displays.* The type of application that you are going to run will have a big impact on the type of display device that you should buy. If you are going to do compute-intensive or highly graphically interactive work such as CAD/CAM or CASE work, you should buy a dataless workstation (this is a workstation with a small, local disk) since you will need the local compute power as well as the local graphics manipulation capability. If you are going to do work where there is little interaction with the display and it is primarily a display device, this may be an application where an X terminal is sufficient. Finally, whether you are running a GUI such as Open Look from Sun Microsystems or Motif from the Open Software Foundation determines how much computing power you will need, and this should have some bearing on your decision about the local compute power needed.

2. *Network load and configuration issues.* Additional network load is often an argument made by workstation vendors to discourage people from purchasing X terminals. While it is certainly true that network load is a factor to be considered, it is not clear that this is as important as is often stated. Of the studies available, network load was not significantly different between workstations running X and X terminals running X. Of course, because the workstation can run applications locally and therefore avoid any X traffic on the network, it will have a distinct response and network-load advantage. However, the network load and compute cycles required are so dependent on how the X application was written that much of this discussion is irrelevant or at least unclear.

If you are considering an X terminal, there are a variety of technical issues to be aware of. X terminals have a variety of ways in which they can be configured and maintained. The window manager can be resident on the local display X terminal or downloaded from a remote node at X terminal boot time. For reasons of upgrades and control, most consultants recommend that the X server software (window manager) be downloadable from the remote node rather than resident since a hardware change for each X terminal would be required if the server software were local. In other words, every time you need to change your X11 server software, you may need to upgrade your firmware in all X terminals that you own. This is tremendously time consuming and can cost a great deal of money. While not all X terminal vendors force you to do this, it is something to be wary of.

3. *Cost-effectiveness.* It has been discovered that the peak usage (defined as the maximum number of simultaneous users) is the most important factor determining what kind of device is the most cost-effective on the desktop. If the intended peak usage is high, the work is general in nature, or the graphical interaction high, workstations are more cost-effective. The largest cost associated with X terminals is the central host. As you add more X terminals, the central server is required to do more and more not only in terms of CPU but disk and network control as well. At some point you will experience rapid degradation in performance levels and will have to purchase more central resources at relatively high cost.

Licensing is certainly one area that has caused much confusion and concern not only within the ranks of the users but of vendors as well. X will allow you to remotely display virtually any application on any machine that will support the X protocol. How this relates to licensing of products and control of access of these products is an issue that has yet to be resolved. Certainly an X terminal will typically provide a hardware-only solution (almost) while a workstation implies much more in terms of software, licensing of third party products, etc. Vendors are addressing this issue, and solutions will be in place in the next few years to make sure that all applications are run only on machines that are licensed to use them.

It appears that the NetLS license manager is the de facto license manager of choice, and most software vendors are endorsing this for their products. This is a token-based license manager which provides per user licensing capabilities independent of the network or local use. See your vendor for more details on their implementation.

4. *System management.* The standard arguments related to centralized versus distributed computing can apply here. X terminals allow for a more centralized computing style while distributed workstations allow for more decentralized computing. This has significantly more to do with corporate culture and competitive environment than anything else; however, it is clear that distributed computing offers the potential to gain significant competitive advantage and act as an enabler of corporate change that may be badly needed within an organization.

With the significant advances in UNIX cluster management and the relative ease of adding new workstations and software across a cluster, the argument that X terminals are easier to manage and install is becoming less powerful. While it is true that X terminals can be powered up "out of the box," you must configure them on the network, discuss system and configuration issues with your chosen system's manager, and then figure out how to use it. You can now buy workstations that can be powered up and will run out of the box without any issues related to networks, communications, servers, etc. Again, there is trade-off that you will have to make regarding the level of expertise that you expect your organization to have.

While it is clear that X terminals have some limited potential, the application for which they are purchased must be clearly understood. If we simply buy the cheapest solution to allow access to centralized cycles, we will soon run into the same problems that decentralized computing is attempting to solve, namely the lack of control and cheap cycles to do what needs to be done. The cost of X terminals is dependent on two main issues: (1) level of use, where the increasing level of usage dictates the need for a workstation, and (2) central compute cycles are relatively more expensive and limited in what they can handle.

There are applications where X terminals would be sufficient; however, it is important to remember that anything an X terminal can do, a workstation can do. This statement is certainly not true in the reverse.

8.7 The Relation and Interaction of X11 Windows with Microsoft Windows

There are a variety of tools which provide X11 server capabilities for PCs running Microsoft Windows. Companies like Hummingbird, IBM, and NCD offer PC X servers. Most of these tools provide more than enough functionality to run X11 applications and treat a PC as an X11 server. The minimum PC configuration recommended by most vendors is 8MB of RAM and a 386 processor or faster. While you can get by with a slightly lower-powered machine, it is not a good idea and will cause performance problems.

Most X11 server software packages require an additional package which provides TCP/IP networking functionality to the PC. This is often called a transport layer because the layer 4 networking protocol is the transport layer. This kind of package can be purchased from a variety of vendors including FTP Software and IBM. These packages provide you with TCP/IP and the associated tools such as telnet (interactive login), ftp (file transfer), and, often, Network File System (transparent file sharing.)

Once you have a transport layer on your PC, you install an X server package and begin to run X11 applications as you normally would, displaying them on your local PC. Typically, the X11 server software provides additional tools to create icons which you can simply click and invoke a remote X11 application to display on the local workstation. This provides relatively seamless X11 and Windows integration on your desktop.

The general modes of operation for X11 server software on PCs are single window and window coexistence. This means that X11 can take over your entire display or coexist with Microsoft Windows. The simplest and most efficient method for using this kind of software is to run in coexistence mode. This gives you the ability to run X11 and Windows applications side by side. This is very powerful and seems to work fairly well on properly configured PCs.

It cannot be stressed enough that to effectively run this kind of software, your PC must be configured with large amounts of memory (8MB or more) and be at least a 386 processor. If you attempt to run X11 server software on anything less, you will be disappointed. It should also be noted that you should not treat your PC as either an X terminal or UNIX workstation because the performance will simply be much slower. The Windows PC makes an effective X terminal if you are currently using a PC for other tasks which require DOS and/or Windows software on your PC. Many of the packages which run in this environment now run on UNIX. If you are interested in using X11 applications in your environment and need performance and speed, you may want to consider moving to a UNIX environment on the desktop to fill some of your needs.

The coexistence of Windows and X11 is fairly well understood and actually works quite well. If you have an environment which requires both tools, a PC X server package with an associated transport layer should meet your needs and will provide relatively transparent and seamless GUIs for both windowing environments.

Part

3

Nonnative UNIX Power Tools

While there are a wealth of tools available on the native UNIX platform which provide tremendous power and flexibility when using UNIX, there are just as many if not more power tools that don't come native with a UNIX platform. Some of the more powerful of those tools are documented in this section.

Editors, compilers, debuggers, object-oriented compilers and analyzers, text formatters, and many native UNIX power tool replacement tools are just some of the tools discussed in this section of the book. Keep in mind that a large portion of this section is dedicated to GNU tools. GNU is reengineering most of the tools that come with native UNIX and, in fact, is rewriting a freely distributable UNIX kernel based on the Mach microkernel architecture from Carnegie Mellon. Many of the tools discussed are part of the GNU paradigm which is attempting to replace UNIX with a freely distributable version of the same environment.

Tools such as GNU's C compiler called gcc are considered better than what you can typically get from your vendor. Unlike many shareware and free tools you can get for DOS and Mac platforms, these tools are of the highest quality. Support is usually excellent and, since most products discussed in this book are free, the price is right. Keep in mind that all of these tools are freely available from the Internet as well as in the distribution that accompanies this book.

Chapter

9

The Internet

UNIX and the Internet used to be synonymous; however, with the explosion of growth on the Internet, many other types of machines are beginning to access it. Because of the correlation between UNIX tools distribution and the Internet, this chapter presents a background on the history and distribution of power tools for UNIX.

The Internet is now being used to deliver not only UNIX power tools but MS-DOS, Macintosh, VMS, and many other types of application development tools. The Internet is already the information superhighway that many people are talking about today. This chapter presents just a portion of the capabilities and power of the Internet.

9.1 What Is the Internet?

The Internet is simply the largest computer network in the world. With millions of nodes, it surpasses even the largest of corporate networks by many orders of magnitude. It is a collection of many networks bridged and gatewayed together to provide a relatively seamless network which spans the entire world. At one time the Internet was a large network consisting of the IP protocol exclusively; however, today it consists of many networks and protocols.

The Internet started out as the ARPAnet, which was an experimental network designed to support government research for the Defense Department. Because of the disparities of hardware and software platforms among the participants, there was an immediate need to develop an architecture which supported all. The protocol known as IP (Internet Protocol) was invented as an ISO layer 3 protocol that would run on both LANs and WANs while the ISO organizations debated their own layer 3 protocol.

Berkeley began distributing IP with their UNIX kernels, and an entirely new network protocol de facto standard was born. Along with Berkeley, a number of new agencies were beginning to build computing centers, and the only economical way for them to connect everyone together was through the ARPAnet since most universities and research labs were then on the ARPAnet.

In the mid 1980s, the National Science Foundation (NSF) put a 56Kb architecture in place based on regional supercomputer centers that ran IP. This allowed not only universities and research labs access to their network (known as NSFnet) but the ARPAnet as well. NSF promotes educational access and helps defer costs in an effort to place all educational institutions on the NSFnet. This has been extremely successful, and as a result, demand is growing dramatically not only in the educational market but the commercial one as well. As people left their educational environments, they convinced corporations to connect to the Internet.

There are several volunteer groups which govern and maintain the Internet. The presiding body responsible for guiding Internet development and direction is the Internet Society (ISOC). They appoint members to a group known as the Internet Architecture Board (IAB) who are responsible for setting standards for communications and architecture to sustain the tremendous growth seen in the Internet in the last few years. The IAB meets regularly to discuss these issues and hear proposals for change and growth.

Finally, the Internet Engineering Task Force (IETF) is responsible for short-term goals and deliverables on the Internet. They hold regular meetings to which everyone who is interested in the Internet is invited. By splitting into working groups, different problems are solved based on volunteers' experience and interest. The typical output of a working group is a report to the IETF and often the IAB to be set as standards.

Because of the regional nature of the Internet, a Network Operations Center (NOC) was established to handle each region or backbone. For example, NASA has a set of backbones which are managed by a NOC, while the NSF backbones are managed by another NOC. If you connect to the Internet, you will get an NOC that is responsible for your connection. If it cannot solve your problems, it escalates to the next NOC that can solve them.

Beyond providing the NOC, most agencies are responsible for paying for their segment of the Internet (e.g., NASA, NSF). The Internet was developed to share research and engineering data and not commercial data; however, this is changing as corporations and individuals realize the potential of the Internet for sharing information quickly and inexpensively. As this commercial access has grown, several companies have sprung up to provide commercial access to the Internet for a price. These companies purchase a segment of the capacity of the Internet and resell access to commercial customers. Companies like PSInet from Performance Systems Internation and Uunet provide commercial users access to the Internet. The price ranges from just a few dollars a month for a simple dial-up line to thousands of dollars a month for full-function leased-line capacity running IP.

The Internet is simply an extension of the phone and leased line infrastructure. There are gateways and routers which connect a large number of disparate networks around the world (see Fig. 9.1). As the figure shows, you can access the Internet with a variety of components including modems, routers, and bridges. The Internet uses both the public telephone network and a variety of leased lines from government organizations and private access providers such as PSI.

There are protocols which run between the routers and gateways which allow each to understand who it is responsible for based on a concept called a domain. A domain is established by a place called the Network Information Center (NIC) which has been responsible for distribution of addresses and domains since the inception of the Internet.

Internet addresses are IP addresses that are represented by four

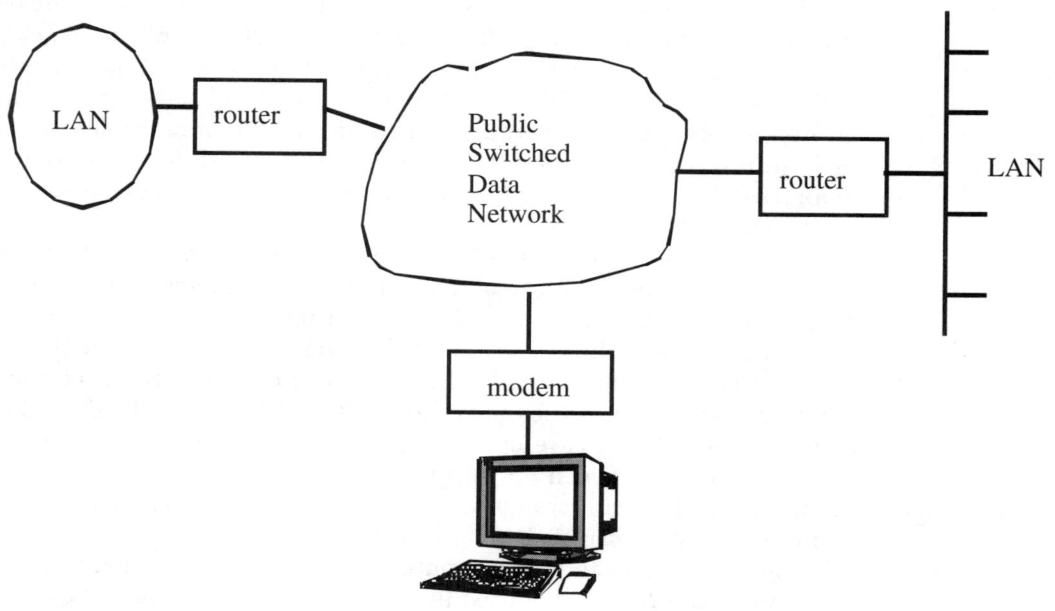

Figure 9.1 The Internet.

groups of numbers separated by periods. An example of an IP address is:

```
191.9.200.1
```

Each number left to right represents a subnetwork of the higher-level represented to the left. In this example, there is a large network represented by 191. Within this network, there is a subnetwork represented by 191.9. Inside this is 191.9.200, and finally the actual node IP address is 191.9.200.1. The NIC is responsible for providing IP (e.g., Internet) addresses based on dividing customers by geography or organization. These numbers allow routers and gateways to section off certain portions of the Internet to reduce the packet loads on individual segments of the network. For example, if you want to send a message to address 192.10.10.10, the initial router you contact through your part of the Internet maintains a table containing who is responsible for the 192 subnetwork and then figures out the quickest way to get your information to this subnetwork. It may have to route it through several gateways and routers; however, the algorithm used by the routers ensures the most efficient path at the time it calculates this. It is important to note that this path may be different at any given time based on network congestion and router and/or gateway availability.

Figure 9.2 shows a network which consists of a gateway machine between two networks. If a packet from the 191 network wants to get to the 192 network, it must be routed through the gateway. Note that the gateway can be a UNIX computer or a specialized device such as a router or brouter (bridge/router.) This device contains tables which help to route the packets to the appropriate network based on the IP address. The Internet works very similarly to this. A rough schematic is shown in Fig. 9.3.

Figure 9.3 represents the telecommunication links between the interior gateway routers. Most of these lines are high-speed T1 and T3 lines, but there are still lines which run at much slower speeds on the Internet network. Suffice it to say that you must connect to the Internet network either directly through a router to the Internet backbone or through an access provider such as UUNET or PSINet. The Internet itself takes care of routing packets through the network by communicating between all routers on the network. This ensures redundancy and reliability on the network and increases its stability.

Because remembering IP addresses is virtually impossible for people, the NIC began to give computers names people could remember. Originally, the NIC distributed all IP addresses and names; however, as the Internet began to grow, this became impossible. A new scheme known as the Domain Name System (DNS) was developed. This gave

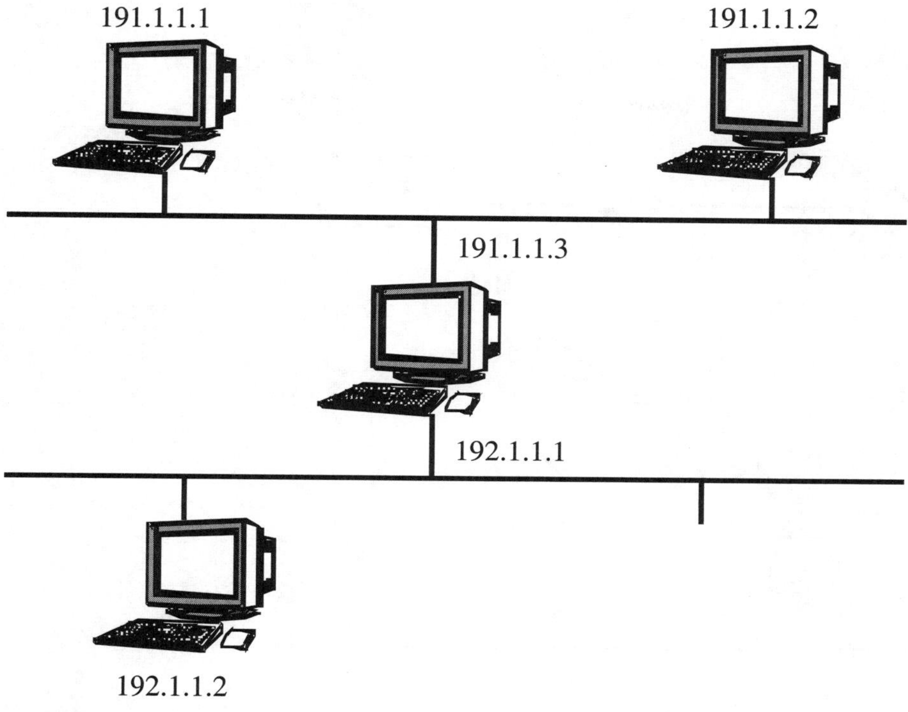

Figure 9.2 Hosts and the routing of packets.

each group of users on the Internet the responsibility to manage its own machine names and IP addresses. The naming structure was based on the success of the IP addressing scheme and therefore is divided into subgroups separated by periods. Each level in this system is called a domain. An example is:

```
fnalb.fnal.gov
nic.ddn.mil
fred.csu,upenn.edu
```

This works in exactly the opposite way from the IP addresses. The major domain is the farthest to the right in this address (known as domain name). There are six main domains: gov (government), mil (military), com (commercial), net (network resources), org (other organizations), and edu (educational institutions). Within a given domain, there exist machines and groups of machines. For example, take the name:

```
fred.cs.uchi.edu
```

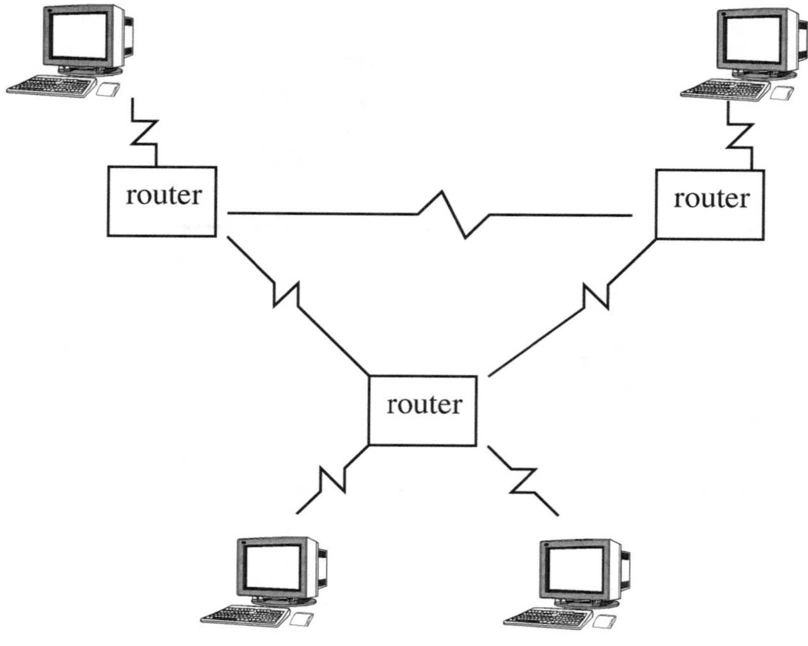

Figure 9.3 The Internet and its routers.

The machine exists in an educational institution, probably at the University of Chicago (uchi), perhaps in the computer science department (cs), and the actual machine name is fred, who is probably the graduate student who uses the machine. This domain name may translate to an address of 192.9.200.1. There is probably a correlation between the uchi and the subnetwork addresses of 192.9 since the NIC probably gave the University of Chicago all addresses within 192.9. This correlation is maintained by the NIC and is crucial since IP addresses and domain names cannot be duplicated on the Internet. If this occurs, major problems result and therefore must be avoided at all costs.

You can have two machines with the same name, but they must be in different domains. For example, fred.cs.upenn.edu would be perfectly fine. Even fred.bio.uchi.edu is fine as long as they are not exactly the same. Note also that the IP addresses of these machines will be very different depending on their domains. Most likely fred.cs.upenn.edu has a different major IP address, while fred.bio.uchi.edu probably starts with 192.9.

Due to the international nature of the Internet, there are international standards for domain names. Typically, the domain name ends with a country code (e.g., ca is Canada); however, these are not yet widely used.

9.2 Tools of the Internet

Note that this is not entitled "Tools on the Internet" but "Tools of the Internet." These are tools that allow the Internet user to be most productive and reap the most benefit from the Internet. There are really three fundamental tools of the Internet which enable users to maximize its usefulness:

1. News
2. anonymous ftp
3. mail

9.2.1 News

News is the Internet bulletin board system. News consists of groups of information and exchanges based on a topic known as a newsgroup. Newsgroups consist of readers that present a menulike interface to newsgroups and allow you to browse and interact with any newsgroups of your choice. You get information on "newsfeeds," which consist of many megabytes of information per day depending on which newsgroups you intend to read. The full newsfeed daily traffic is in the hundreds of megabytes per day and is a tremendous effort to manage. Most users subscribe to a small subset of newsgroups in an effort to minimize the traffic as well as the management aspects of the newsfeeds.

Newsgroups are hierarchical in nature and consist of what look very similar to domain names. An example is:

```
comp.os.aix
```

The largest group is the comp (computer) group, followed by the os (operating system) group and finally the aix operating system division of this newsgroup.

By far the largest set of newsgroups and information comes from the USENET. The USENET consists of seven primary newsgroups:

1. comp—computer science and related topics
2. misc—miscellaneous
3. news—questions relating the news network itself
4. rec—recreational activities
5. sci—scientific and research activities
6. soc—social activities
7. task—controversial topics such as religion, politics, and the like

There are other sources for newsgroup feeds; however, they are beyond the scope of this book. See App. C for sources of books and information on this topic. In addition to the core USENET newsgroups, there are several alternative newsgroups, including:

1. alt
2. bit
3. biz
4. ieee
5. gnu
6. k12
7. vmsnet

These and other newsgroups like them contain much lively discussion and information. You should carefully choose which newsgroups you would like to receive since you will quickly be overwhelmed by information if you aren't careful. Finally, there are other sources such as Clarinet, which is run by the United Press International (UPI) and contains up to the minute news and information.

To get a better understanding of the USENET network, you must examine its origins. When the USENET began, it consisted of people primarily using PCs connected with modems. They would periodically dial each other up and trade information. As the group grew, they developed methodologies for sharing information which involved known locations and flows for the shared information. A person or persons agreed to be the distributor of certain types of information by allowing others to dial into their computers and download information that they required. This was known as a newsfeed. As this matured and the number of newsfeeds grew exponentially, a large network consisting of complex and confusing architecture evolved. With the adoption of high-speed WAN technology, much of this transfer is now occurring over leased lines. However, there are still many informal newsfeeds occurring around the world.

Figure 9.4 is from *The Whole Internet User's Guide & Catalog* by Ed Krol. It is representative of the kind of network that News typically travels through. News servers use the base telephone network to transfer information.

Different news servers provide different newsfeeds based on the needs and usage of that particular node's users. Administrators must choose which newsfeeds they wish to accept and those they wish to distribute. If administrators choose to distribute newsfeeds, they accept the fact that others may call and wish to connect to them, and they need to be responsive and give those requesters access.

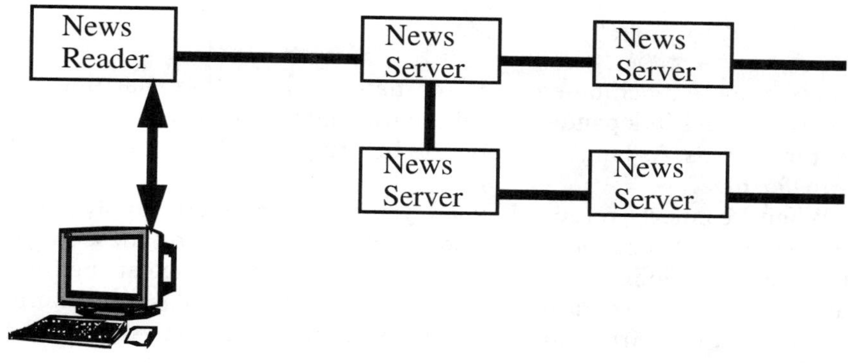

Figure 9.4 The News network. (The Whole Internet User's Guide & Catalog, *Ed Krol, 1992, O'Reilly & Associates. For orders and information, call 800-998-9938.)*

By providing transparent network access to users on the network, the newsreader can access newsgroups transparently. The newsreader has the responsibility not only to act as the menulike front end but to attach to the news server and download lists of articles as well as actual articles selected. It acts as the router to control access to newsgroup information. There are several prominent readers:

1. nn
2. rn
3. trn
4. tin

Since the man pages for each of these tools are some 40 to 50 pages, this book will not discuss individual readers. Suffice it to say that reader choice is religion, and each person prefers one or another. Each reader has disadvantages and advantages, but nn is certainly as good as any other and provides certain benefits such as more control when reading information and tracking. You can change readers at any time, so feel free to experiment with each of the readers you can get.

9.2.2 ftp

The second core technology of the Internet is the anonymous ftp capabilities. ftp stands for File Transfer Protocol and is the core utility that works with TCP/IP to provide file transfer capabilities between nodes on a network. By utilizing login security checks, users can transfer files based on the existence of their accounts on each machine.

The general syntax of the ftp command is:

```
$ ftp remote-machine-name
```

where remote-machine-name is the name of any other machine that you can access independent of where the machine is or what operating system it runs. As long as it supports the ftp protocol, you can use ftp to transfer files.

When a connection is established, you are prompted to supply a username and password for the remote machine. After typing these in, you are placed at the interactive ftp prompt ftp. Once you are at the interactive ftp prompt, you are ready to begin transferring files. An example is a file transfer from your current machine named paris to another machine named rome:

```
paris>$ ftp rome
Connected to rome.
username: kevin
Password required for rome.
passwd: password
User kevin logged in.
Welcome to rome running SunOS 4.1.
ftp> put /tmp/stuff
200 PORT command successful.
150 ASCII data connection for stuff (55 bytes).
226 ASCII Transfer complete.
83 bytes sent in .02 seconds (4k bytes/sec)
ftp> quit
221 Goodbye.
paris> $
```

This example transfers a file named /tmp/stuff from a machine named paris to a file in your home directory named stuff on a remote machine named rome. ftp allows for file transfer in both directions. To transfer a file from a remote machine named rome to the local machine named paris, use the get command. For example:

```
paris>$ ftp rome
Connected to rome.
username: kevin
Password required for rome.
passwd: password
User kevin logged in.
Welcome to rome running SunOS 4.1.
ftp> get /tmp/stuff
200 PORT command successful.
150 ASCII data connection for stuff (55 bytes).
226 ASCII Transfer complete.
83 bytes sent in .02 seconds (4k bytes/sec)
ftp> quit
221 Goodbye.
paris> $
```

Here are a variety of commands within ftp that may be of some use:

`binary`	Transfers a file in binary mode and performs no translation
`ascii`	Transfers a file in ASCII mode; performs any necessary translation to maintain an accurate representation
`put local-file-name remote-file-name`	Puts file from your local machine to the remote machine
`mput filelist`	Multiple file put
`get remote-file-name local-file-name`	Gets a file from the remote machine to your local machine
`mget filelist`	Multiple file get
`user username`	Logs in to remote machine
`help`	Prints list of all ftp commands
`lcd dir`	Local change directory
`cd remote-dir`	Changes remote directory
`close`	Closes current ftp session on remote machine and returns to ftp mode
`delete remote-file-name`	Deletes remote-file-name on the remote machine
`dir filename`	Shows remote filename listing (wildcards supported)
`open machine`	Opens a connection to a remote machine
`pwd`	Prints the name of the current working directory
`quit`	Closes any open connections and exit ftp

If you are interested in transferring multiple files with the mput and mget commands, you will be prompted for each file before transfer unless you invoke ftp with the -i switch. Keep this in mind before you invoke ftp for file transfer.

Also, to interrupt file transfer, you can use the CTRL-C sequence. This will halt file transfer after the server has had time to process the interrupt. It usually takes some time before the data stops flowing into or out of the local machine based on network load and file server performance and load. Be patient.

You will note the lack of a cat command in the ftp subcommand listing above. If you want to examine a file before transfer, you must be a little clever and remember UNIX and its standard I/O structure as described in Sec. 2.5. To examine a file on the screen before transferring it, use:

```
ftp> get file1 -
```

where the - represents standard out. If this doesn't work try:

```
ftp> get file1 /dev/tty
```

which uses the standard terminal device name as the output file. Remember, everything in UNIX is a file, and as such, redirection is as simple as that shown above.

9.2.3 Anonymous ftp

The ftp utility relies on usernames and passwords for ensuring integrity of filesystems and machines. However, there is a de facto standard in the UNIX and Internet worked for using ftp for general-purpose file sharing and transfer. It is known as anonymous ftp. This means that when you connect to the remote machine and you are prompted for your username, you type anonymous. The password can be left blank; however, it is generally accepted that you type your mail address so that you can be tracked and notified in the case of a problem. After logging on, you typically have access only to a small area of files which are explicitly permitted to you. This is how almost all Internet software is shared and propagated. All commands are maintained as in formal ftp; the only difference is that you now don't have to have an account on a machine to access its files. This allows millions of users to share ideas and software without requiring any maintenance and overhead associated with managing large groups of users and software systems. Anonymous ftp is the way general users interact with the Internet for almost all tasks.

9.2.4 Internet mail

Electronic mail (e-mail) to the Internet is one of its primary benefits. Beyond the capabilities of file transfer via anonymous ftp and telnet capabilities which allow for machine sharing, e-mail is by far the most useful feature of Internet access. By acquiring Internet access, you gain the ability to send mail to millions of computers users, not only those directly attached to the Internet but through gateways to those on other networks such as MCI Mail and Compuserve as well. Mail is clearly of great benefit as a way to communicate and exchange information without requiring expensive and high-maintenance options such as leased lines and IP access to the Internet.

Limitations of the e-mail system are time and cost. It clearly costs you something to send a message to someone on the Internet; however, the cost is a matter of cents, depending on where you send the information and how large the message is. Suffice it to say that the cost is very low compared to the increased functionality received. It also costs you something in terms of time. The Internet is a store and forward network, which means that packets of information are gathered at a node and then, at some later time, are forwarded to the next node in the chain. There may be zero to many nodes in between your sending node and the receiving node, depending on the physical topology of the networks and node configurations. This is transparent to the end user since the underlying mail subsystem handles the routing of this information; however, it does affect the transfer times of the mail.

The store and forward nature of the Internet mail subsystem means that information such as mail messages may take some time to reach their final destination. While the time required to receive a message from the Internet is usually seconds, it may take minutes or hours for a message to reach its final destination, depending on the status of links and machines on the path from initiator to final destination. This is clearly not as convenient as using an interactive access method in some instances; however, the many conveniences of mail often outweigh the costs.

Addressing. Mail addressing is based on the domain naming conventions described earlier in this chapter. The general format of a mail address is:

```
usename@machine-name
```

where username is the username of the person to whom you want to send mail and the machine-name is the hostname of the machine. For example, to send mail to a user named kevin on a machine named devtech.devtech.com, you would structure the mail name as:

```
kevin@devtech.devtech.com
```

This uniquely identifies me on the Internet, and it is guaranteed that there is no other person with exactly that same address on the Internet. You do not need to worry about including any other information than the username and node name to which you want the mail sent. There may well be nodes that this information will pass through in between the authoring node and the receiving node, but this is hidden from you by the Internet mailing subsystem.

To send a mail message to the above user, you could use the following:

```
$ Mail kevin\@devtech.devtech.com
Subject: test
this is a test of the Internet mailing stuff. Please reply if you
  get this.
thanx...kevin
.
```

There are several things to note about the above mail. First note that the @ is preceded by a backslash. This is because the @ is a special shell character and should be “escaped” to avoid shell translation. Remember, in UNIX, the shell interprets the entire command line before passing it to the program to be executed. In this case, if you do not precede the @ with a \, the shell will interpret the @ as a shell metacharacter and perform actions before passing the command line information to the Mail executable. Another thing to note is that all mail is terminated with a . in the first column on the last line of the text input area. This will take you out of text input mode and back into command mode. Finally, note that the command Mail was used to invoke a mail subsystem. Remember that UNIX is case sensitive and in this case there is a difference between mail and Mail. The Mail interface is a Berkeley interface, which has slightly more features than the mail interface; however, it does not matter which interface you use to address Internet mail.

There are many gateways to other networks beyond the standard Internet, such as MCI Mail and Compuserve, which you may want to access. Your access provider will give you information on how to address mail to ensure that it reaches those connected networks. There are a few standard naming and addressing conventions, however, that allow you to send mail through gateways to these networks; they are discussed below.

Bitnet. Bitnet addresses are in the form user@host.bitnet. To route from the Internet to a node on a Bitnet network, use user%host from above and follow this with a standard gateway from Internet to Bitnet. For example:

```
kevin%fnal@fnal.fnal.gov for the Bitnet address kevin@fnal.bitnet
```

Ask your access provider for more information on how to access the Bitnet network.

Compuserve. Standard Compuserve addresses consist of two numbers separated by commas (12345,123). To route to Compuserve from the Internet, use the syntax:

```
12345.123@compuserve.com
```

Note that the Compuserve addresses' comma is replaced with a period and followed with a hostname of compuserve.com.

MCI Mail. MCI Mail uses two different kinds of addresses: number and name. If you are sending to a number, simply following the number with the standard hostname syntax:

```
1234567@mcimail.com
```

If you are addressing a name, use the syntax firstname_lastname followed by the hostname:

```
Kevin_Leininger@micmail.com
```

There are other networks which you may want to access; ask your Internet access provider for more information on how to access them.

Sending binary data. Most mailers are structured to send text files only. If you are interested in sending nontextual information such as executables, audio files, etc., you must first encode these files before correct transmission can occur.

The utilities used most often to accomplish this are uuencode and uudecode. The uuencode is provided on most UNIX platforms and converts binary information to text. Once you have done this, you can then mail it as you normally would any text file. The person receiving the file must uudecode the file before accessing it. For example, to send an executable file named runit to user joe on hostname galaxy@ devtech.devtech.com, use:

```
$ uuencode runit < a.out > runit /*takes a.out and makes a text file
  runit*/
$ Mail joe@devtech.devtech.com
Subject: uuencoded program
Here is the runit program, have fun...
~r runit /* mail command to include a file*/
.
```

This creates a file with the first line text and then the uuencoded file following. When joe receives the mail, he will see something like:

```
$ Mail
begin 644 runit
```

Joe first must save the mail message as an external file and then run uudecode on it. The uudecode command will ignore any information before the begin command and will rebuild the executable to be exactly as before it was uuencoded. Joe now has a program named runit which he can execute normally.

Note that for an executable, you must be running on the same type of machine as that on which the executable file was originally built. uuencode and uudecode do not provide binary compatibility but are merely dumb tools to allow for binary transmission from one machine to another.

It should be noted that there are a variety of standards discussions occurring with respect to sending binary files, and standards for mailers and binary files will be adopted in the very near future.

Returned mail. There are many reasons that you may receive returned mail: The address was incorrect, the receiving node was down, the remote host was unknown, or the remote machine is not configured correctly. Any one of these will cause mail to be returned with a message like this one in your mail file:

```
$ Mail
Subject: returned mail for bogusid
Status: R

Mail error was: 550 <bogusid>...User unknown

-- returned mail follows ---
To: bogusid
Subject: test

this is a test
```

If the remote host was unknown, you would receive all information in the returned message which documents the path the mail message took before being returned. An example is:

```
Subject: returned mail for bogusid
Status: R

Mail error was: 5110 <host!bogusid>...Unknown host host

-- returned mail follows ---
To: host!bogusid
Subject: test

this is a test
```

By tracking the path of the returned mail, you can see which machine failed in the store and forward mail network. Check the hostname and full address. If it is correct and the mail will not go through, contact your Internet access provider with a detailed description of the problem.

You will also see a returned mail message with the "User unknown" message. Check that this user does in fact exist; if he or she does, contact your Internet access provider for more information.

If the receiving machine has significant downtime, you may see returned mail with a Subject line describing the condition. If this occurs, contact that machine's system administrator for more information. Note that due to the store and forward nature of the Internet mail subsystem, your mail message will be retransmitted several times to the receiving node before failing. This will avoid having this kind of problem with a short-term downtime for a machine.

If you send mail to more than one person and you get a returned mail message, check to see who received the mail and who didn't, and resend to only those who did not receive the message. All mail messages that can be sent will be, and only those unreachable addresses will be returned.

Getting files with mail. If you don't have direct access to the Internet and want to get files and archives, you can use mail to accomplish this. While interactive methods such as ftp and telnet are more convenient, there are a variety of reasons for using mail to access and retrieve files.

There are two general kinds of mail servers available via e-mail:

1. Generic Internet mail servers
2. ftpmail servers

Generic Internet mail servers provide a mail server daemon which waits for incoming mail with a specific subject or text heading addressed to it and processes the information contained in the mail message. Depending on the included information, it performs different actions from sending help information on its commands to getting files from a local directory and sending them to the mail originator. The standard syntax for these servers is to include a command on the Subject: line such as:

```
$ Mail mail-server@devtec.devtech.com
Subject: help
.
```

which will provide help on the commands and capabilities of the mail server. Note that text for the message is not required since only the Subject: line is examined to determine an action for the mail server. The other common command is the send command. The syntax is:

```
Subject: send filename
```

where filename is a filename which may include a relative or fully qualified directory name. For example:

```
$ Mail mail-server@uunet.uu.net
Subject: send ls-lR.Z
.
```

will retrieve a file named ls-lR.Z from the machine named uunet.uu.net. This file just happens to be the compressed index of all files on the UUNET machine.

The ftpmail server provides the capability for a remote machine to ftp a file to itself and then mail it to your machine. This provides unlimited access to Internet archives through one of these ftpmail servers. The ftpmail machine most commonly used is decwrl.dec.com. To address commands to this machine, use:

```
$ Mail ftpmail@decwrl.dec.com
Subject: junk
connect devtech.devtech.com
chdir pub/physics/hep
binary
get intro
quit
.
```

As shown above, you build an ftp script in your mail text which is executed on the decwrl machine. In the above script, decwrl connects to devtech.devtech.com, changes directories to the pub/physics/hep directory, sets mode to binary, and transfers a file named intro back to your machine via e-mail. The Subject: line is ignored with this server, but you can use it to document your activities. There are many commands available on this server; send the command help to the server for complete details.

9.3 Who Uses the Internet?

As the Internet grows and gains more commercial users, questions arise about who is paying for traffic on different parts of the Internet. What began as an educational and research network is rapidly becoming a commercial network. When you establish a connection to the Internet, you must specify whether you will be using it for research and education or commercial traffic. If you choose research and education, you will be routed over preferred routes using government-subsidized links on what is known today as the National Research and Education Network (NREN). NREN was recently federally funded to allow all Internet research and education users to access a common backbone. However, if you establish your access as commercial, you will need to use a value-added Internet access provider such as Performance Systems International (PSI) or UUNET. See App. D for more information on how to contact these organizations.

Most computer hardware and software vendors have begun using the Internet for distribution of software updates and patches. Because of the lower cost of distribution and access to more timely information, the Internet makes the most sense for them. Of course, the biggest users are still research laboratories and universities; however, commercial users are beginning to utilize the Internet for collaboration between their engineering and research business and among other parts of their organizations such as marketing and sales. The complexion of the Internet is changing rapidly, driven by the commercialization of UNIX and the entire open systems paradigm.

9.4 Why Use the Internet?

The question is really not "why use the Internet?" but, more importantly, "Why not use the Internet?" The Internet provides tremendous access to information that is vital to the efficient operation of computers and computer specialists around the world.

There are two primary reasons to use the Internet: (1) access to information newsgroups and (2) access to software via anonymous ftp. Both have been discussed and, based on discussions in the rest of this chapter, we will see why the Internet is such a powerful resource and why you will use it more and more in your daily life.

9.5 How to Access the Internet

There are a variety of services that provide both partial and full access to the Internet. As discussed before, you must decide what kind of access you need before contracting with a service provider for Internet access.

There are rules and forms that must be filled out before access to the Internet will be allowed. If you choose dedicated Internet access, you will be assigned an Internet addresses and a domain based on information you provide to your service provider. This information will be registered with the NIC and will be made available on the Internet worldwide through the primary routers and gateways. This allows anyone on the Internet to route to you with things like anonymous ftp and mail. Keep this in mind when you talk to your service provider, and make sure you have thought through the ramifications of the "world" having this kind of access to your machine. This is not intended to scare you away from getting access to the Internet. There are many ways to secure your network against network violations; however, by accessing the Internet, you are opening up an entirely new set of issues when discussing security of your machines and networks.

9.5.1 Dedicated Internet access

For dedicated Internet access which provides leased line capability, you will pay several thousand dollars up front for a company to give you a leased line and a router/modem device at your site. This typically consists of a Telebit Netblazer device, which is the standard in the UNIX arena for high-speed modem communications. You will also incur fairly high costs relating to leasing the line, probably $1000 or more per month depending on line speed.

Dedicated access provides you with full IP capabilities, and it is clearly the most high-function solution available. This means anonymous ftp and complete peer-to-peer access to other machines on the network. You will have the Internet as a WAN which looks just like your LAN.

9.5.2 Partial Internet access

There are several kinds of partial Internet access ranging from Serial Line Interface Protocol (SLIP) and Point to Point Protocol (PPP) solutions, which look very similar to dedicated access, to Unix-to-Unix Copy Program (UUCP) access, which is of much lower function.

SLIP/PPP. SLIP allows for IP datastream to run over standard phone lines. You can use SLIP to run a LAN protocol over a standard phone line and use tools like telnet, ftp, NFS, etc., just as though you were connected to a higher-speed LAN such as token ring or Ethernet. SLIP is freely available on the Internet and can be ported to virtually every platform. You may contact a service provider listed in App. D for more information on SLIP access. PPP is the successor to SLIP and contains SLIP functionality and much more. PPP is a better solution if your access provider supports it.

The SLIP/PPP solution will allow you to look as though you have a dedicated connection to the Internet only when you bring SLIP/PPP active. This allows you to avoid the cost of a leased line while still realizing all the benefits of running as a dedicated peer-level node on the Internet.

Typical costs for this are a few hundred dollars a month for unlimited access from a service provider. There are other packages which have lower fixed costs and associated connect time charges. Talk to a service provider for more details.

UUCP. UUCP is a tradition in UNIX which was invented to allow UNIX machines to transfer files over phone lines. It later added support for remote login and became the WAN protocol of choice between UNIX machines over phone lines. As high-speed networks proliferated, UUCP has become much less commonly used; however, it is still used by many Internet access providers to provide a class of Internet connection known as UUCP access.

The cost of this kind of connection is tens of dollars a month and an inexpensive modem. However, you do not get any IP capabilities and therefore don't get anonymous ftp capabilities. You can get News as before, but it must be set up with UUCP for polling on a predefined schedule. All access to files is done through mail. You must send mail to a mailserver on your access provider's machine; they are responsible for sending your requested files to you in the form of mail. You must then use mail to manipulate and control your files from the Internet. This is clearly a lower-function way of interacting with the Internet; however, it does work and is certainly the lowest-cost solution around.

9.5.3 Gateways

There are other ways to gain access to the Internet such as Bitnet, Compuserve, and MCI Mail. If you have accounts on these networks, you have mail access to the Internet and can send mail and exchange information via gateways between these networks. However, you do not have the kind of access that is provided in the other access methods, and this should not be your primary interface to the Internet if you intend on using it in any serious way.

9.5.4 Listing of service providers

There is a listing of service providers for Internet access in App. D of this book. As you can see there are many, and they provide many different types of services. Contact them directly for more information on their products and services.

9.6 The Structure of Internet Software

Software from the Internet is structured in a way that is similar among packages. Most packages are large enough to comprise several files which are typically transferred separately and simply appended to each other before being uncompressed. Compression techniques consist of the following:

1. compress/uncompress—This creates a file with a .Z extension.
2. pack/unpack—This creates a file with a .z extension.
3. gzip—This is a GNU compression algorithm. It also creates a file with a .z or .gz extension.

These algorithms are the three most common and should describe most files you find on the Internet. You typically save anywhere from 30 to 60 percent on file size using these algorithms depending on the file structure and size. The smaller the size, the less efficient the algorithms typically are. For example:

```
$ ls -l stuff*
-rwxr--r-- 1 kevin 61400 Jan 29 12:00 stuff.txt
$ compress stuff
$ ls -l stuff*
-rwxr--r-- 1 kevin 26100 Jan 29 12:00 stuff.txt.Z
```

Note that the compress algorithm renames the file appending a .Z to the original filename and saves approximately 55 percent file space. To uncompress the file, use:

```
$ uncompress stuff.txt
$ ls -l stuff*
-rwx-r--r-- 1 kevin 61400 Jan 29 12:01 stuff.txt
```

Note that the original file is restored and the input filename to the uncompress is the original filename without the extension. The pack algorithm works the same way, and both pack and compress are equally utilized on the Internet. If you look on a remote system with anonymous ftp and see extensions like .Z or .z, you can be sure that these are compressed or packed files and should be transferred and uncompressed or unpacked at the local machine.

gzip is a GNU product which contains no copyrighted source code but is compatible with both pack and compress. There are options on the gzip command line which document how to handle both packed and compressed files as well as its own gzip format. Most, if not all, GNU software is now distributed in gzip format. See Secs. 9.7 and 11.2 for more information.

If the files come separated into named parts such as PART01, PART02, etc., you must append them together with a simple command like:

```
$ cp PART* >> newfile.tar.z
```

where newfile.tar.z is the name of the compressed file you can now uncompress. It is common that a file named README contains checksums of the PART* files. This allows you to check and see that the file transfer occurred correctly. Run either the sum or the cksum command on the PART* files and compare against the files and associated numbers in the README file. One note of caution: There are two primary algorithms used to generate the checksum numbers and they will *not* produce the same result. If you run the checksum on several files, and they are wildly different, it is a pretty safe bet that you have a sum or cksum command that is not the same as that used to compute the checksums in the README file. See Sec. 6.12 for more details.

The most common directory structure on an anonymous ftp machine is the pub, or public, directory. This typically contains all public domain software and is the first place you should look for software. The other common directory is the gnu or GNU directory. This contains software from GNU which is available at no cost as well. See Sec. 9.7 for more information. At the top of the pub directory, there is typically a file called ls-lR or index on an anonymous ftp machine. You should examine this to understand what is on that particular machine and choose what you would like to transfer.

9.6.1 Tar file archives

Often entire directory structures are stored in tar files and then compressed using the pack or compress algorithm. This example illustrates the process of getting such a file and restoring it to a local directory:

```
$ ftp rome
Connected to rome
220 rome ftp servers awaits your command
Name: anonymous
230 Guest login okay, send ident as password
password:
331 Guest login ok, access restrictions apply
ftp> binary
ftp> cd pub
ftp> ls
200 PORT command successful.
150 Opening ASCII mode data connection for /bin/ls.
total 4096
drwxr-s-r-x 2 root 120 512 Nov 10 12:05 dir1
-rw-rw-r-- 1 lib 120 47400 Jan 20 05:45 package1.tar.Z
-rw-rw-r-- 1 lib 120 32300 Jan 18 09:00 package2.Z
226 transfer compete.
220 bytes received in 0.1 seconds.
ftp> get package1
200 PORT command successful.
150 Opening BINARY mode data connection for package1.tar.Z (47400
  bytes)
226 Transfer complete.
47400 bytes received in 1.0 seconds (47k bytes/sec)
ftp> quit
221 Goodbye.
```

You must now uncompress the file and tar it into its proper form:

```
$ uncompress package1.tar
$ tar -xvf package1.tar   (See Sec. 6.5 for more details.)
$ ls -l
-rw-r--r-- 1 kevin 4600 Sep 1 README
-rw-r--r-- 1 kevin 50001 Aug 20 package1.c
-rwxr--r-- 1 kevin 59000 Aug 20 package1
```

You may want to use the tar -tvf command as well to see the table of contents of the tar file before unwinding it since things such as pathnames and file sizes may determine how and where you untar the file.

Inside tar files you will typically see a file named README or

READ.ME or some other variation. This should be the first file you look at after unwinding the tar file. In fact, you should extract the README file separately before unwinding the entire tar file to examine it for any issues relating to disk space, installation procedures, etc. There is also a Makefile which contains all necessary commands and information to build the product on a particular machine. Frequently there is also an Imake file which allows you to make a Makefile for a particular machine. You should examine the tar file for these before using the product since you may have to rebuild the product before correct execution will occur.

As mentioned earlier, you may also see compressed files broken into parts to allow for easier transmission. Each piece is typically 100KB in size and numbered sequentially beginning with 01 as an extension. For example, if package1 consisted of three pieces—package1.tar.Z.01, package1.tar.Z.02, and package1.tar.Z.03—you would bring over each file separately and put them back together using the cat command and its append capabilities. For example:

```
$ cat package1.tar.Z.* > package1.tar.Z
```

would place all files back into a single file named package1.tar.Z, assuming the files were numbered sequentially. Then you would proceed as above.

The other common file naming convention for Internet files is partnn where nn is an integer between 01 and some number. To generate a combined file from these files, use a command like:

```
$ cat part* > newfile
```

where newfile is the name of the resultant file you would like to generate.

9.6.2 Shell archives

Shell archives consist of files which are merely shell scripts which unwind themselves by invoking themselves. To unwind a file called kevin.shar, use:

```
$ sh kevin.shar
```

You may see this divided as before, and you should apply previously discussed techniques before invoking the shell to unwind this archive. Be careful with these since they have been known to contain Trojan horses; you should examine each shell archive before unwinding it. As a general rule, you should also do all work related to the Internet as a nonroot account to ensure local system integrity.

9.6.3 Manual pages

Most software packages come with one or more manual pages to describe the usage of the tool. You can typically find the manual pages by looking in the main source directory for a file with a single-digit file extension such as .1 or .2. A quick and dirty command to look for these files is:

```
$ ls *.?
```

which tells UNIX to look for a file with a single character file extension. If you see anything with a numeric extension (1 to 8), it is probably a man page. Man pages are written in nroff format, which is a command-driven text processing language.

Every time you invoke the man command, man searches for a matching man page in a certain area on the filesystem, and, if it finds it, it executes an nroff command on the file. This displays the man pages in a formatted way on standard output (which is most often your terminal screen). You can issue this nroff command manually on a man page file. For example:

```
$ nroff -man gcc.1 | more
```

will print out the manual page for the GNU C compiler on your screen and pipe the output to more so you can page through at your own speed. The an macros (note that with the -m switch they spell man . . . clever, huh?), you can format almost any manual page for preview on your screen. The other nice thing about this is that you can print out the man page by simply piping standard output. For example:

```
$ nroff -man gcc.1 | lpr
```

By using a pipe to the printer system, you will see the formatted manual page on your default printer. This is one of the first things you should do when you begin looking at and using a new product, whether it is from the Internet or is already installed on the system you are using.

9.7 GNU and Their Paradigm

GNU stands for GNU's Not UNIX and is the brainchild of a man named Richard Stallman. While at MIT, Mr. Stallman wrote much of emacs and many other tools which are widely used in the UNIX community today. After getting frustrated with organizational and legal barriers to creating free software, he left MIT and formed GNU. Today, GNU and the associated Free Software Foundation (FSF) are clearly the leaders in providing high-quality free software on the Internet. The FSF provides for the distribution of code and maintenance and some support of the GNU software. They can be contacted at:

Free Software Foundation
675 Massachusetts Avenue
Cambridge, MA 02139

They are interested in any support they can receive, particularly with respect to free hardware, labor, and money. This helps them in their effort to continue to develop and distribute quality free software.

Originally, GNU was a project to create a replacement for the UNIX operating system and environment. In doing this, hundreds of tools have been written ranging from text processing systems to editors and compilers. Most are excellent and none are poor. Mr. Stallman is seen as somewhat of a radical, particularly by those who want to sell software. There is an article in the GNU section on most Internet machines called the GNU Manifesto. You should read this if you are interested in getting a better understanding of Mr. Stallman's philosophy and, subsequently, GNU's philosophy on software (it is included on the CD with this book). It doesn't take long to understand that Mr Stallman has some pretty radical ideas about intellectual property and software. This philosophy has driven him to develop and distribute free software on the Internet.

The quality of the GNU software is high, and the support and maintenance are good. There is much fear, uncertainty, and doubt (FUD) about free software, most created by software vendors who sell products. They claim that support and quality of free products are low. This is simply not true. emacs is one of the best, if not the best, editors available today on every platform it runs on. Keep this in mind when you are thinking about using free software in your environment. Free software, particularly GNU software, is of excellent quality, and you will have very little trouble with these products.

A few of the more popular GNU utilities are outlined in this book; however, there are many more available. See Sec. 9.9 for more information on how to get listings of GNU and other free software from the Internet.

GNU and the FSF don't have copyrights on their software; instead they have what they call a copyleft. This provides that the software can be distributed for a fee; however, it also says that anyone who distributes the software cannot stop it from being distributed again for whatever cost and in whatever manner anyone sees fit. This fits in with their philosophy of freely sharing software and information in the hopes that this will only improve the product and make it accessible to everyone who wants it. A copy of the GNU Manifesto, their COPYING information, and the GNU General Public License are included on the CD with this book as well as in App. B. These documents are included with all GNU software in this book and must be included in all distributions of their software.

9.8 The Recommended Structure of Installed Software

The structure of software is a topic of much debate today in the software industry. Based on the structure of software from the Internet and the structure of the Makefiles, recommendations for the software structure follow.

Traditionally UNIX has placed executables in the /bin and /usr/bin directories independent of their release or function. In other words, all applications placed their executables in these directories for execution. This works well when you are running a simple configuration with simple software systems; however, when you begin to get into the use and support of multiple versions of multiple software packages, you begin to see significant limitations in this methodology. How, for example, can you run multiple versions of a single software package with the same executable name? You could change the executable name to include the version number, but this is dangerous since it will require changes to documentation which you may not control (such as vendor documentation).

A better way to structure and support software is through the /usr/local filesystem. For a variety of reasons, it makes sense to create a separate filesystem which is mounted as /usr/local. This contains all versions of local software which can then be exported to the network with NFS. Under the /usr/local directory, you can create directories for each of the products you install (see Fig. 9.5). Under the specific product directory you should create version subdirectories. Finally the underlying structure for a particular version of a product should contain

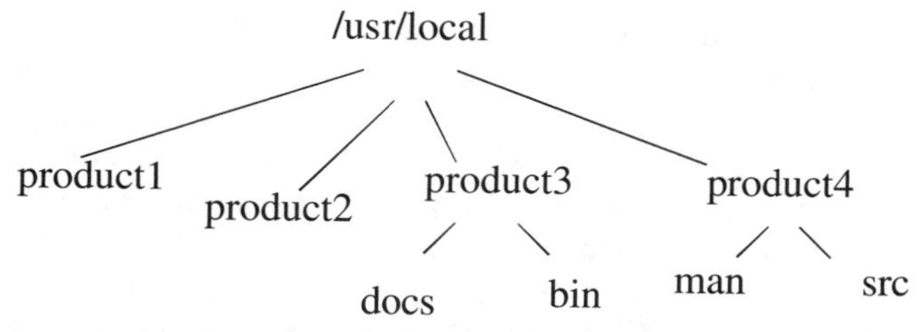

Figure 9.5 Internet product structure.

several standard subdirectories which contain different pieces of the software product. They consist of:

`bin`	Contains executables
`docs`	Contains documentation
`src`	Contains source code
`man`	Contains manual pages

An example of the structure of a product file is as follows:

```
/usr/local/frame/v3_1/README
                      SETUP
                      docs
                      bin
                      src
                      man
```

The README contains documentation on which release of the product is contained in the directory structure and basic information on the product itself. The SETUP file contains commands that should be invoked before the product is invoked. For many products, variables must be set and path changed before they can be executed. To execute this SETUP file, you must either execute it with a source or . statement or build a utility which will do this for you. While this is nontrivial, it will save time and confusion in the long run.

This book is not about software maintenance and structure; however, it is important to understand how best to structure software. Most products that come from the Internet will build correctly under any given subdirectory (e.g., /usr/local/product/version); however, they may have difficulty with the structure containing subdirectories and other files. Keep this in mind when structuring your software architecture. Modifications to the Makefiles are often nontrivial; however, the benefits of this structure often outweigh the initial costs. In fact, with the new GNU products, there are configuration files which generate the appropriate make commands to support virtually any directory structure. See the documentation on make and gmake (GNU make) for more details.

One point to note is that most GNU and other free software packages like to be in /usr/local subdirectories like bin, lib, and include. While this works fine if it is managed correctly, you can run into problems when you are running large machines with a complex and sophisticated user base. For example, if people want to use different versions of a single piece of software (e.g., emacs), it becomes difficult to support them in /usr/local/bin. There are a variety of ways around this, including defining your own prefix (see Sec. 11.1) directory; however, this only addresses part of the problem. Some tools still look for files in hard-coded directories (bad idea), and others need to be placed in a particular directory to execute properly. While this is changing, it is still something to watch out for as you install the packages from this CD as well as others you may acquire.

9.9 How to Locate and Retrieve Software from the Internet

For years, the location of software on the Internet was communicated through information networks of people who were "in the know." Because of the tremendous growth of the Internet in the last few years, this methodology is no longer sufficient to allow all Internet users to know where all the software they are interested in exists. Because of this, a new system called archie was developed.

9.9.1 archie

archie was developed by several people at McGill University in an effort to consolidate file information on a few servers located around the world. By periodically polling servers which are contained in a list which the archie people maintain, they create a list which can be accessed and searched with either telnet or mail. This list is an index of all files on those polled servers with additional information which describes the contents of the files.

In other words, archie provides an index to files on the Internet. This is a wonderful feature when you are looking for particular products or tools and are not sure of their location. With this tool, you can find files virtually anywhere on the Internet. Once you have found them, you can use one of the tools described in this chapter to retrieve them.

There are several archie servers around the world:

Server name	Geographical area covered
archie.ans.net	Sites connected to ANS access provider
archie.au	Australia and the Pacific Basin
archie.doc.ic.ac.uk	United Kingdom
archie.funet.fi	Europe
archie.mcgill.ca	Canada
archie.rutgers.edu	Northeastern United States
archie.sura.net	Southeastern United States
archie.unl.edu	Western United States

Note that you should try to use the server closest to your geographical area since this will minimize both network traffic as well as load on the archie server.

Telnet support for archie. If you have IP and telnet capabilities to the Internet, you can use telnet to access the archie servers. For example:

```
$ telnet archie.rutgers.edu
...
Connected to archie.rutgers.edu
Escape character is '^]'.
SunOS Release 4.1.3 (ARCHIE): Thur Feb 12:05:00 EST 1993

Welcome to the ARCHIE server
archie>
```

There are a variety of commands within archie to search the database and print results:

`help`	Prints out help menus.
`list`	Lists anonymous ftp servers used by archie.
`maxhits number`	Sets the maximum number of matches allowed.
`prog string`	String is the string to match against the files in the database. Probably a filename or substring within a filename.
`servers`	Lists all current archie servers.
`set variable`	Sets a boolean variable. Use show to see possibilities.
`show variable`	Shows boolean variable. If you don't use variable, it will list all variables.
`set search type`	Type can be: exact—exact string match. regex—string is regular expression. sub—string is a substring, case independent. subcase—string is a substring, case must match.
`sho search`	Shows search type.
`unset variable`	Unsets a boolean variable.
`whatis string`	Matches string against index entries in database.

The most common way to use archie is to search by filename. All products will contain files which are named in a way that is related to the product name. This allows you to search filenames collected by the archie server by a string using the prog command:

```
ARCHIE> set search exact
ARCHIE> prog physics
physics: nothing appropriate

no matches
```

You can use the whatis command to search the associated index database. When software is added to the archie database, the author can include information which archie uses to index the files. This allows you to search for information that may or may not be included in the filenames for the product. This is a nice way to narrow a search; however, the information is often out of date and should be used cautiously. Once you get this information, you can access the server referenced with anonymous ftp as described earlier in this chapter.

Mail support for archie. If you do not have full IP access to the Internet, you will not have telnet access to the archie servers; however, you still have mail support. Support for archie that is available through the mail interface is very similar to that offered by telnet, and you will not suffer much loss of functionality. You may wish to submit a mail message to an archie server and view the results the next day or simply not have time or the inclination to peruse the archie databases in real time. Many people who have full telnet access to the Internet still use the mail interface to access and search the archie servers.

To access the archie server via e-mail, simply address the mail to:

```
archie@server
```

where server is one of the servers listed earlier in this chapter.

archie supports what is known as a mail server, which runs as a mail background process. When invoked, it processes incoming mail without human intervention. Many organizations on the Internet use this to serve files and information via e-mail. Often the command to the mail server is contained in the subject line. archie requires no subject line information but instead expects the commands in the text of the message, beginning in the first column. You can simply build commands in the text field of the mail message beginning in the first column. Any command that is not recognized is treated as a help command, and you will get a help file returned for that command in the mail message.

Commands supported by the archie server are a subset of the telnet archie commands:

`compress`	Causes returned mail to be compressed and uuencoded before being sent
`help`	Causes a help guide to be returned
`list expression`	Causes a return list of servers matching expression
`path address`	Gives return e-mail path other than that contained in the from: field
`prog expression`	Searches for filenames matching the regular expression
`servers`	Causes a list of archie servers to be returned
`whatis string`	Causes a list of possible files with string matched in the index database
`quit`	Ends session

To get a help file on using archie via e-mail, issue the commands:

```
$ mail archie@archie.rutgers.edu
Subject:
help
.
```

Sometime later you will receive a file containing help information on archie and supported commands. For example, the following is an exact duplicate of the message received when you issue the help command to an archie server. You should get something similar.

```
From uunet!dorm.rutgers.edu!archie-error Wed Feb 17 08:14:23 1993
Return-Path: <uunet!dorm.rutgers.edu!archie-error>
Received: from uunet.UUCP by devtech.devtech.com (4.1/SMI-4.1)
      id AA07236; Wed, 17 Feb 93 08:14:22 CST
Received: from dorm.rutgers.edu by relay1.UU.NET with SMTP
      (5.61/UUNET-Internet-primary) id AA07571; Wed, 17 Feb 93
      01:14:38 -0500
Received: by dorm.rutgers.edu (5.59/SMI4.0/RU1.5/3.08)
      id AA17094; Wed, 17 Feb 93 01:14:34 EST
Date: Wed, 17 Feb 93 01:14:34 EST
Message-Id: <9302170614.AA17094@dorm.rutgers.edu>
From: uunet!dorm.rutgers.edu!archie
To: devtech!kevin (Kevin Leininger)
Subject: archie reply: for 'help' request
Status: RO

         The ARCHIE Mail Server

HELP for the archie mail server, as of 9 April, 1991 (modified from
the KISS help file)

Requests to this server should be addressed to
archie@archie.rutgers.edu

To contact us humans, mail to archie-l@archie.rutgers.edu
For your information anonymous ftp may be performed through the mail
by various ftp-mail servers. Send a message with the word 'help' in
it to:

      bitftp@pucc.princeton.edu

or

      ftpmail@decwrl.dec.com

for an explanations on how to use them.

NOTE: The Subject: line is processed as if it were part of the main
message body. No special keywords are required.

Note that the "help" command is exclusive. All other commands in the
same message are ignored.

Command lines begin in the first column. All lines that do not match
a valid commands are ignored.

Results are now sorted by archive hostname in lexical order.

An archie UNIX man page and it's straight ASCII text file equivalent
are available on quiche.cs.mcgill.ca in the ~ftp/archie/doc
directory as archie.man.roff and archie.man.txt respectively. If you
would like it mailed to you send mail to bajan@cs.mcgill.ca asking
for it.

The server recognizes six commands. If a message not containing any
valid requests or an empty message is received, it will be
considered to be a 'help' request.

path <path> This lets the requestor override the address that would
      normally be extracted from the header. If you do not hear from
      the archive server within oh, about 2 days, you might consider
      adding a "path" command to your request. The path describes how
      to mail a message from cs.mcgill.ca to your address.
      cs.mcgill.ca is fully connected to the Internet.

      BITNET users can use the convention
```

```
      user@site.BITNET

      UUCP user can use the convention

      user@site.uucp

 help Will send you this message.

 prog <reg expr1> [<reg exp2> ...]

      A search of the "archie" database is performed with each <reg
      exp> (a regular expression as defined by ed(1)) in turn, and
      any matches found are returned to the requestor. Note that
      multiple <reg exp> may be placed on one line, in which case the
      results will be mailed back to you in one message. If you have
      multiple "prog" lines, then multiple messages will be returned,
      one for each line [This doesn't work as expected at the
      moment... stay tuned].

      Any regular expression containing spaces must be quoted with
      single (') or double (") quotes. ALL OTHER ed(1) rules must be
      followed.

      NOTE: The searches are CASE SENSITIVE. The ability to change
      this will hopefully be added soon.

 site <site name> | <site IP address>

      A listing of the given <site name> will be returned. The fully
      qualified domain name or IP address may be used.

 compress ALL of your files in the current mail message will be
      "compressed" and "uuencoded". When you receive the reply,
      remove everything before the "begin" line and run it through
      "uudecode". This will produce a .Z file. You can then run
      "uncompress" on this file and get the results of your request.

 quit Nothing past this point is interpreted. This is provided so
      that the occasional lost soul whose signature contains a line
      that looks like a command can still use the server without
      getting a bogus response.
```

If you want to find all the information related to physics, you would use something like:

```
$ mail archie@archie.rutgers.edu
Subject:
whatis physics
.
```

You would receive information with all files found with the corresponding index keyword of physics, for example:

```
From uunet!dorm.rutgers.edu!archie-error Wed Feb 17 08:14:21 1993
Return-Path: <uunet!dorm.rutgers.edu!archie-error>
Received: from uunet.UUCP by devtech.devtech.com (4.1/SMI-4.1)
     id AA07230; Wed, 17 Feb 93 08:14:20 CST
Received: from dorm.rutgers.edu by relay1.UU.NET with SMTP
     (5.61/UUNET-Internet-primary) id AA07569; Wed, 17 Feb 93
     01:14:37 -0500
Received: by dorm.rutgers.edu (5.59/SMI4.0/RU1.5/3.08)
     id AA17079; Wed, 17 Feb 93 01:14:21 EST
Date: Wed, 17 Feb 93 01:14:21 EST
Message-Id: <9302170614.AA17079@dorm.rutgers.edu>
```

```
From: uunet!dorm.rutgers.edu!archie
To: devtech!kevin (Kevin Leininger)
Subject: archie reply: whatis physics
Status: RO

physics: nothing appropriate

Matches for 'physics'
```

In the above example, there were no matches found. An example with a match might look like:

```
$ mail archie@archie.rutgers.edu
Subject:
whatis
.
```

You could then search for information on a particular file within the whatis returned list:

```
$ mail archie@archie.rutgers.edu
Subject:
prog
.
```

You now have information describing the location and contents of an archive on the Internet. You can retrieve it based on ftp or another method supported by your Internet access provider.

9.9.2 ftp servers

As mentioned earlier in this chapter, you can use mail to access ftp servers if you do not have IP access to the Internet. To do this you issue a set of commands which essentially build a script to be executed on a remote mail server. The basic set of commands available within the mail message is:

`binary`	Specifies that the file is binary and needs to be encoded with btoa before transmission begins
`chdir dir`	Specifies a directory to cd to
`chunksize size`	Specifies a maximum file size for transmission
`compress`	Uses compress to compress the file before transmission
`connect [hostname [login [passwd]]]`	Specifies hostname to connect to and account to use
`dir [dir]`	Generates a directory listing of the current or specified directory
`get file`	Specifies the file to be sent to you via electronic mail

`quit`	Ends the request
`uuencode`	Specifies that the file be uuencoded before transmission instead of btoa

The ftpmail server will follow all commands as you place them in the mail message. The Subject: field is ignored, so begin your script at the beginning of the mail text. The result of the query will be mailed to you electronically. It may take some time for the request to be serviced (a matter of hours) since the ftpmail server that you may use may be heavily loaded with requests or other tasks and may take some time before it gets to your request. The help file tells you where to send mail if you have problems.

The only other thing to note about the ftpmail server is that it breaks files into 64,000-byte files. If the file to be transmitted is larger than 64,000 bytes, the ftpmail server will break it into as many 64,000-byte chunks as necessary and transmit these files one by one. You can change this chunk size with the chunk size command as described above. Note also that you have to tell the ftpmail server that you are transferring a binary file if you don't want any translation to occur. A simple example of this is:

```
$ mail ftpmail@decwrl.dec.com
Subject:
ls
quit
```

This will list all files in the working directory on the default machine decwrl.dec.com. Note that the userid is anonymous unless specified otherwise.

A slightly more sophisticated example is:

```
$ mail ftpmail@decwrl.dec.com
Subject: anything goes
connect uunet.uu.net
chdir /index/networking
get by-name.Z
ls
quit
```

This will retrieve a file named by-name.Z on the UUNET machine in the directory /index/networking. It will also generate a listing of the directory contents after the file inclusion. All of this is in the mail message you will receive from the ftpmail server machine. The other point to note is that you can only issue the chdir command once within a ftpmail script. Therefore, if you want to get more than one file from different directories, you must send separate mail messages.

Be careful not to confuse the ftpmail server syntax with archie syntax since they are clearly not the same. Keep this in mind if you get some confusing error messages back from either server.

9.10 How to Build Software from the Internet

Each chapter on tools from the Internet contains a section on building the product on the particular machine on which you are running. However, there is a commonality between all build procedures ranging from UNIX machines to VAXes and mainframes.

Typically, an archive contains a build procedure for the type of machine it is intended to run on. For UNIX machines, build procedures are typically makefiles which consist of commands to build all necessary files for the particular UNIX "flavor" you are running on. For other machines, there are similar files which contain build procedures provided by the software developer to ensure that the product builds properly and runs correctly the first time. Since the focus of this book is UNIX, the discussion of the formats and procedures is limited, but keep in mind that procedures for other non-UNIX platforms are similar, based on the functionality of the underlying platform.

Traditionally, when you got the software from the Internet, you had to look through the makefile and make modifications depending on what UNIX architecture you were running on. Different versions of UNIX have different C compilers, different library locations, and different versions of make, just to name a few differences. Consequently, it has sometimes been difficult to build software from the Internet for certain platforms.

GNU have made great strides in this area; they are now providing a shell script called configure. Along with most GNU software distributions, there is a file called INSTALL which details much of what you need to know regarding the installation and compilation of all software in the distribution. Now, instead of having to edit the makefile, you simply type:

```
./configure
```

from the main directory and the configure script creates a correct makefile. Note that it assumes you have your software in the /usr/local directory and attempts to place executables in /usr/local/bin, libraries in /usr/local/lib, and man pages in /usr/local/man/man1. If you wish, and you probably should, to place the resulting files in some other directory, you need to specify a series of commands to the configure and/or make commands so that the appropriate files will be generated in a different subdirectory than the default. More about this later.

All Internet tools described in this book have a discussion of how to build them which shows how to build a particular tool into recommended directory structures. See Sec. 11.1 for more information on the build process.

9.10.1 Distribution format

UNIX archives are typically in one of two formats: tar or cpio. Both are standard UNIX utilities which have their own behaviors and characteristics. The structure of software from the Internet was discussed in a previous section; suffice it to say that you "unwind" the file in whatever format you receive it in. Compression is also an issue, and you must ensure that you have unpacked or uncompressed the file appropriately before beginning installation. See Sec. 9.6 for more information.

Once the software has been restored, it must be built. There are several "standard" files with each software distribution. There is typically a README or README.1ST or something similar contained within the directory structure. This should be the first thing read before beginning any compilations building. It contains release information and other information pertinent to the building of the product.

9.11 Understanding Internet Software Documentation

Most Internet packages have software documentation distributed with them in the form of nroff man pages and/or texinfo documents. Each of these tools is discussed in a separate section of this book; however, it is worth mentioning here the basic structure of these files in a typical distribution.

Most tools come with manual pages which typically end in either .1 or .man. These are usually in nroff format and can be viewed with the command:

```
$ nroff -man file.man | more
```

There is also often a texinfo file distributed with most Internet products. This file typically ends in .texinfo and consists of input formatted for the texinfo reader in emacs. This provides a pseudo-hyptertext-based system which allows you to jump between points in the document. You can also use TeX to process the texinfo file into printed output. This allows you to use one file for both screen display and paper output. You can also use the stand-alone texinfo reader included on the accompanying CD to view the texinfo documents even if you don't have emacs.

The final way you may see documentation is in Postscript. These files typically end in .PS or .ps. You can print these out or display them on your screen with a tool like Ghostscript and ghostview.

Sometimes there are doc and man directories and sometimes there aren't. This is up to the person constructing the distribution, and there are no hard and fast rules. Simply scan for these files and directories when you unwind the product.

Much of the information in this book is available in the documentation delivered with most of the products; you just have to know where to look. As you use Internet software and other UNIX power tools more frequently, you will learn how to find your way around the system.

9.12 FAQ

Related to the documentation of a tool is the FAQ, or Frequently Asked Questions, files. These files contain questions and answers to frequently asked questions on a particular topic or tool. Several are included on the CD-ROM included in this book, ranging from emacs to gnuplot. There are other FAQ files, and you can peruse the Internet for more of these on your particular topic. The files may also be named faq or some combination of product name and faq or FAQ. Search for faq or FAQ to get more information about products on the Internet.

9.13 ls-lR.Z

There is a file named ls-lR.Z at the top of many anonymous ftp servers and mail servers. This contains a fairly current file which is a directory listing of the current system. This provides access to the entire directory structure of the software available on a machine. This is typically the first thing you download when you are using either anonymous ftp or UUCP. Keep this file in mind and use grep and vi on it to more efficiently find what you are searching for. An example ls-lR.Z file from uunet.uu.net is on the CD included with this book. Examine it for more details as to its structure and content.

Chapter 10

The GNU emacs Editor

There are very few editors available from the Internet which warrant discussion in this book. The one exception is GNU emacs. emacs is simply the most powerful editor available today and provides complete extensibility and portability across many platforms and architectures.

Editors are religious in nature and become, along with a command interpreter, most people's primary interface to an operating system. While there are other editors available today, such as elvis, which is a vi/ed rewrite from the GNU people, by far the most pervasive nonnative editor is emacs. The most important thing about an editor is its portability and availability. While these other editors exist, they probably are not on any platform you have and therefore won't be very useful when moving onto a new machine. Because of this, this book limits itself to a discussion of emacs.

10.1 Introduction

emacs is the premier editor available in the UNIX market today. It has capabilities far beyond most free editors and, in fact, most editors that cost significant amounts of money. It was written by Richard Stallman of GNU fame and continues to be one of the best and most widely used editors available on the UNIX platform today. In fact, ports of emacs have been made to Macs, PCs, VAX/VMS, and many other platforms. It is clearly the most widely ported editor available for almost any platform today.

Because of the popularity of emacs, it has been widely ported and is supported and distributed by several companies. emacs is written in LISP, and, because of its complexity, some companies have made enhancements and charge a fee for emacs. Companies like Unipress Software and CCA provide emacs for a fee, but there is still a free version of emacs called GNU emacs. This is the version that will be discussed in this chapter.

emacs stands for "editing macros" and was originally designed as a set of editing macros for an ancient editor known as TECO. This editor has since become obsolete, but emacs has continued to grow and thrive. This is a tribute to its power and flexibility. It is somewhat misleading to call emacs an editor. In fact, emacs is an entire working environment and has integrated mail, shell capabilities, and knowledge of your environment which allows it to help you in programming and compiling. emacs is an extremely sophisticated programming environment and, because of its sophistication, is a favorite of software developers and power users.

GNU emacs, as you would expect, is developed and distributed by the GNU Free Software Foundation. See Chap. 9 for more information on this organization. This means that it is freely available and of very high quality. In fact, most people consider the GNU emacs implementation the best of all emacs versions including those sold by other organizations.

The version of emacs discussed in this chapter is 19.17. Because of the constantly changing nature and complexity of emacs, this chapter will focus on discussing the main capabilities and power of emacs and leave the complexities and advanced capabilities of emacs for another book. The purpose of this chapter is to get you familiar with emacs and to provide basic capabilities and knowledge of the product.

10.2 Installation

With version 19 of emacs, the installation has been greatly simplified and the functionality of the install procedure has been enhanced. Through the use of configure, you can select many options related to the compilation and installation of emacs on a single command line.

There are many files in the emacs distribution, several of which are key to the emacs installation process. This chapter will discuss each in turn as they are needed for the installation process.

The first file to examine is the INSTALL file. It documents much of what you need to know to configure and build emacs. The first thing it mentions is to ensure that you have enough swap space on your machine since it requires approximately 8MB or more of swap. If you get an error from the temacs command or when executing the dumped emacs, increase your swap space and try the build again. Note that temacs uses a file called lisp/paths.el, which references several files related to other nonemacs utilities. You may encounter problems related to these, so be careful.

Once you have examined the INSTALL file, you will need to carefully examine the etc/MACHINES file for details on your particular UNIX implementation and the issues related to the building of emacs on your particular platform. Read your specific architecture section carefully since there are often very specific notes about installation problems and issues. For example, on a Sun spare machine, the file specifies that you need to be explicit in your choice of platforms. This is key to the success of building the product.

The first command you will issue is the configure command. The basic syntax is:

```
configure architecture [options...]
```

where architecture is the architecture of your machine chosen from the etc/MACHINES file.

options consists of one or more of the following:

—exec-prefix=EXECDIR—specifies a directory where the architecture-dependent executable files will be placed (EXECDIR/bin). The nonarchitecture-dependent files such as source code will be left in their normal directories. Other architecture-dependent files will be placed in EXECDIR/lib/emacs/VERSION/CONFIGURATION.

—prefix=DIR—specifies the directories in which to place generated emacs files.

—run-in-place—specifies that you would like to maintain the emacs directory structure just as in the distribution and not install it in the /usr/local default directories.

—srcdir=DIR—specifies the emacs source directory.

—with-gcc—uses the GNU C compiler.

—with-x11, with-x=no—specifies whether you would like the X interface or not.

—x-includes=DIR—specifies the X include file directories.

—x-libraries=DIR—specifies the directories for the X library files.

The configure command is documented in more detail in the following chapter. See Sec. 11.1 for more information if you have trouble with the emacs installation.

The first section in the INSTALL file goes into more detail on this, so reference it if you need more information.

The best way to learn to use configure for emacs is to try it a few times and see what happens. Note that when you run configure, you do not compile or build anything but instead create the appropriate makefile and associated build files which you can then execute to build the product.

A simple example of running configure on a Sun SPARC machine is:

```
$ configure sparc-sun-sunos4.1.3 --with-x-11 -- prefix=/usr/
local/emacs/emacs-19.17 \ --run-in-place
```

This will generate the appropriate makefile from which you can build emacs. Issues such as compilers, libraries, utility commands, and many other details are correctly arranged so that the makefile will execute correctly.

To configure emacs on an RS/6000 machine, you would issue a command like:

```
$ configure rs6000-ibm-aix32 --with-x11 -- prefix=/usr/
local2/emacs/emacs-19.17 \ --run-in-place
```

The resulting file from the configure command is config.status. Look at this if you want to see exactly what happened during the configure process.

There are a variety of files including ./list/paths.el, which contains information which tells emacs where to find executables like newsreaders and sendmail, which you can use in conjunction with emacs. A corresponding file ./lisp/site-init.el is the file you need to edit if you want to change the configuration of the paths.el file. You should *not* edit the paths.el file directly because of the nature of the complex syntax. You may need to edit the ./listp/site-init.el file, depending on the configuration of your machine. Use the seq command in site-init.el instead of defvar as used in ./lisp/paths.el as described in the ./list/site-init.el file.

Once you have configured the new makefile, you can execute the make command. There are several options on the make command which will give you quite a bit of control over the build process. The basic syntax for the make is:

```
make [install] [option=value, option=value, ...]
```

where install is optional and tells the make to place all resultant executables, libraries, man pages, and other special files in the default location, which is /usr/local/bin, /usr/local/lib/emacs/VERSION/lisp, etc.

options consist of:

- bindir—location of binary files
- datadir—architecture-independent emacs data files directory
- libdir—emacs library directory
- prefix as described for configure, the directory which is the root for all emacs files instead of the default /usr/local
- statedir—architecture-independent shared emacs files directory

There are several other variables that are emacs specific. These variables are documented in the INSTALL file.

The other files that will be of interest are contained in several different directories. The first is the PROBLEMS file. This lists many of the known problems with emacs and documents either a work around or a fix. View this before you begin to use emacs since it will save you time as you proceed. In fact, there are README files in all directories as well as ChangeLog files in most. The ChangeLog files document the changes in the files in each particular subdirectory from version to version. These are important to view if you are interested in seeing what changes have taken place in the new version.

Finally, there are a variety of files in the etc subdirectory which may be of interest to you, files ranging from specific information on a particular kind of computer to cookie recipes to man pages. Note that the man pages end, as is the norm, with a .1 suffix. Simply nroff the man page for more information. See Sec. 7.2 if you need more information. Probably the most interesting file in the etc subdirectory is the FAQ (Frequently Asked Questions) file. This contains many of the most commonly asked questions about emacs and is extremely useful for the new emacs user to read before beginning to use emacs. See this file before you read the rest of this chapter.

One of the keys for the generation of the executables is to ensure that you have installed the development files for X11. This means that all of the appropriate include and library files are in the proper X11 directories. If you have not done this, you will see the errors which either allude to the fact that the build can't find a file with a .h extension or that there are unresolved symbol references. This probably means that you haven't installed all the appropriate files for the X11 portion of emacs to compile correctly.

If you are interested in service and assistance with the emacs product, see the file etc/SERVICE for a listing of consultants and others who will provide maintenance and other support for emacs and a variety of other free software products.

10.3 Usage

The basic emacs syntax is:

```
emacs [-q] [file]
```

where -q begins emacs without reading any initialization files (.emacs). If you invoke emacs without a file, you are automatically dropped into the help screen. From here you can invoke any emacs command. An initialization file named $HOME/.emacs is read upon invocation.

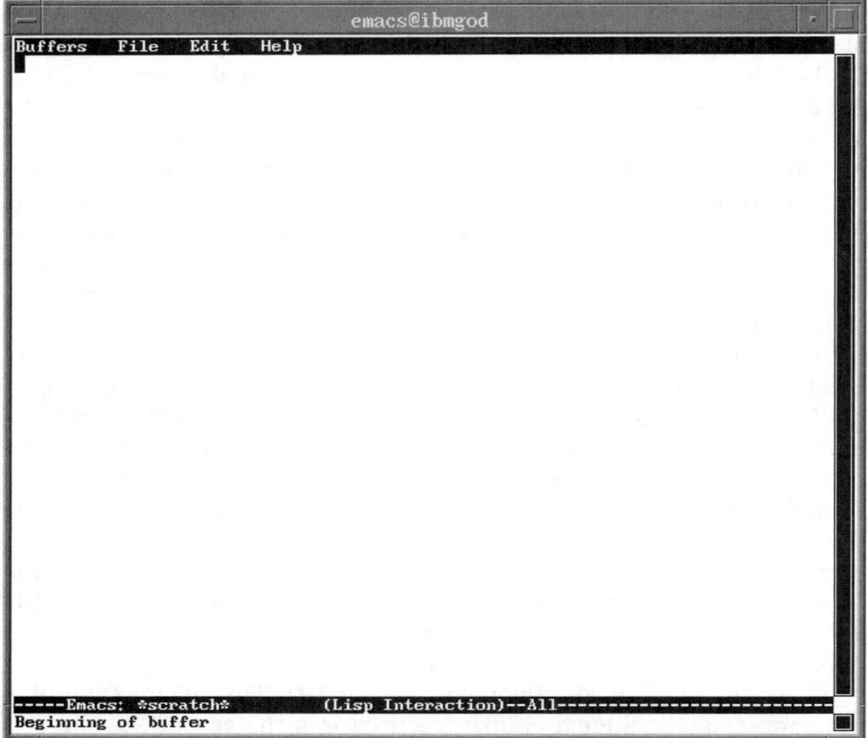

Figure 10.1 Standard emacs screen.

emacs is primarily a command-driven editor which responds to keystrokes in some combination with the CTRL key. These keystrokes execute a corresponding LISP function. Based on the long and cryptic name of commands, you will want to learn the keystrokes and forget about the command names.

There is both a built-in tutorial for emacs and a file named etc/TUTORIAL which you should reference if you are interested in learning more about emacs.

10.4 The emacs Screen

emacs is a full-screen editor and supports many different types of terminals and keyboards. The standard of screen is shown in Fig. 10.1. The main area of the screen is the input area which is where all typed text will be placed. This is a full-screen area, and you can move the cursor freely from one area to another. The line second to the bottom is the mode line. It contains ** if you have made changes to the file since it was last changed. To the right of this is the string emacs:. Following this is the name of the buffer (which may or may not match the name of the file). In parenthesis is the name of the mode (see Sec. 10.5) which shows you which mode you are in. Finally, your position in the file is displayed as a percentage from the first to last line. If the entire file is displayed, the string All is displayed. The last line on the screen is the minibuffer. It displays all commands and filenames that you enter.

10.5 emacs Modes

emacs has a series of modes which dictate how it behaves when certain keystrokes are executed. Modes give emacs knowledge of your particular environment and provide you with enhanced capabilities that will make you more productive. The basic modes are:

Mode	Useful when
C	Writing C code
emacs LISP	Writing emacs LISP
Fortran	Writing Fortran
Fundamental	Default mode, no special behavior
Indented text	Indents all text
LaTeX	Formatting LaTex files
LISP	Writing LISP programs
LISP interaction	Writing and executing LISP
Outline	Writing outlines
Picture	Creating simple drawings
Scribe	Formatting Scribe files
Text	Writing text
TeX	Formatting TeX files
View	Viewing files in read-only mode
nroff	Formatting nroff files

Modes are determined by emacs on invocation. emacs examines the file extension and determines which mode to enter. If it cannot determine the mode from the file extension, it examines the contents of the file. If it cannot determine the mode, it places you in the default mode, Fundamental. This mode assumes no special characteristics.

To move from one mode to another simply type:

```
ESC x modename RETURN
```

where modename is one of the above mode names. This allows you to jump back and forth between modes easily.

There are several minor modes which determine certain default behaviors inside a particular major mode. Minor modes are things like Abbrev, Fill, Overwrite, and Autosave. These provide default characteristics within a major mode.

10.6 Commands in emacs

The commands in emacs are primarily written in LISP and consist of powerful but cryptic commands which are invoked either by command name or keystroke. The keystrokes are by far the most common way to invoke emacs commands because of the cryptic nature of the command names.

The keystrokes for emacs are commonly begun with ESC or CTRL. The basic keystroke operations look something like:

`C-x`	Where x is any character.
`C-c string`	Where string consists of a string or additional control sequence; generally related to modes.
`C-x string`	Where string consists of a string or additional control sequence; generally file-related commands use the C-x string.
`ESC x`	Where x is any character.
`ESC x string`	Where string is any emacs command name. This is the general-purpose way to invoke an emacs command.

Note that the notation C-x means that the CTRL key must be held down while the appropriate key is pressed. Both are then simultaneously released. This method of depressing two keys simultaneously is fundamental to the operation of emacs. While this leads to the need to use two hands to type and use emacs effectively, it also removes most of the confusion and inconsistency of keyboard mapping and differences. This is particularly important in heterogeneous environments with multiple operating environments and keyboard layouts. emacs is certainly the most portable multiplatform editor available today. Don't let the method of multikey operation deter you from using emacs and appreciating its full power and potential. For the ESC key, on the other hand, you simply press it and then the appropriate key. It is not necessary to continue to hold down the ESC key when depressing the other key. This is fundamental to the operation of the keyboard, and you will rapidly become used to this mode of operation. Your fingers will learn where to go.

10.7 Help and the Tutorial

The most important thing to learn when moving to a new environment, particularly something as interactive as an editor, is where to go for more information and help. Interactive help is one of the most powerful of the features in emacs. There is a very sophisticated on-line tutorial which will introduce you to the emacs editor. This is probably the best place to start. To invoke the tutorial, type:

```
C-h t
```

This invokes a tutorial which leads you through much of the basics of emacs. Once you are through with the tutorial, you will be much better prepared to work in emacs and, therefore, much more productive. The screen for C-h-t looks like that shown in Fig. 10.2

Along with the tutorial, there is a general help facility which provides an enormous amount of documentation on the emacs system. To invoke the help facility, type:

```
C-h command
```

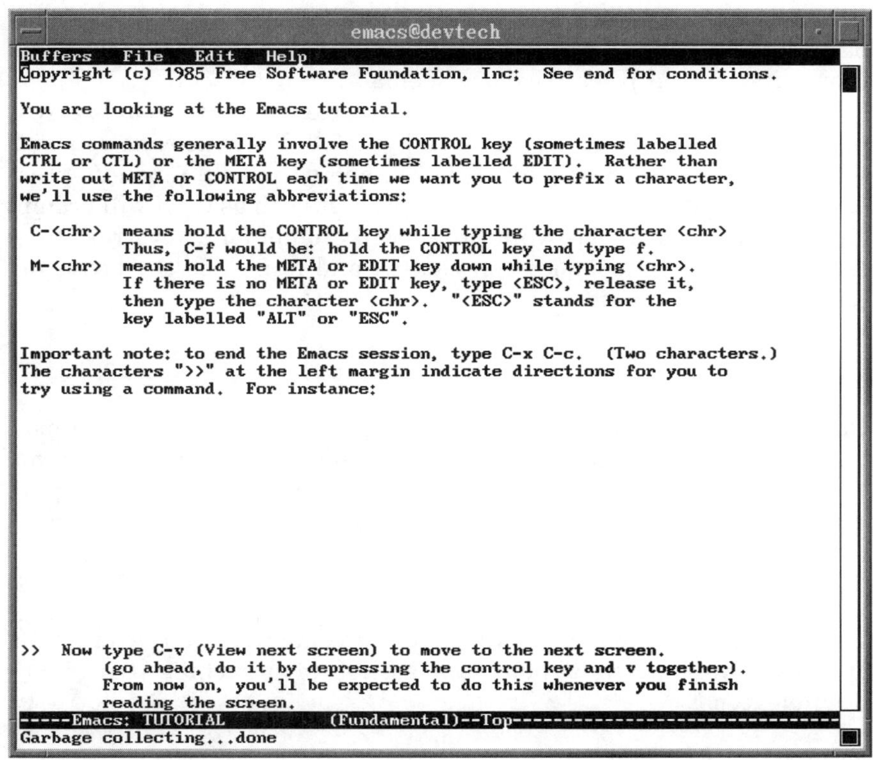

Figure 10.2 Screen for C-h-t.

where command is:

`C-h`	Displays help on the help facility
`b`	Lists all key bindings for current buffer
`c`	Describes the command sequence executed by the keystroke
`f`	Displays actions of function
`k`	Describes the command sequence and what happens when the key is pressed
`l`	Lists last 100 characters typed
`m`	Displays current mode
`s`	Displays syntax table for current buffer
`v`	Displays variable value and its definition
`w`	Displays key binding for command

These commands all prompt for input after execution.

The best way to learn more about emacs help is to type:

```
C-h C-h
```

This places you in a help facility which describes the help facility itself. Once you have gone through this, you will know how to get help in most situations. This is very important because you will probably never know all emacs commands and actions, and the help facility will prove vital in your productive use of emacs.

When you press C-h ?, you get a list of letters and commands across the bottom of the screen as shown in Fig. 10.3. These provide you with some of the choices described above. To abort the help function, press any key except one of those listed. Keystrokes such as C-h f will prompt for a function to describe, while others will prompt for a keystroke to be executed. Each is dependent on context and form. See the above descriptions for more information.

10.8 emacs apropos

On some UNIX systems there is a help system known as apropos. Loosely interpreted, this means "sounds like." apropos provides you with a facility which you can search for something when you don't quite know what you're looking for. To execute apropos, type:

```
C-h a
```

This will place you in a mode where you can enter a regular expression, and emacs will search its help database for any matching strings. For example, type:

```
C-h a (reg-exp) compile
```

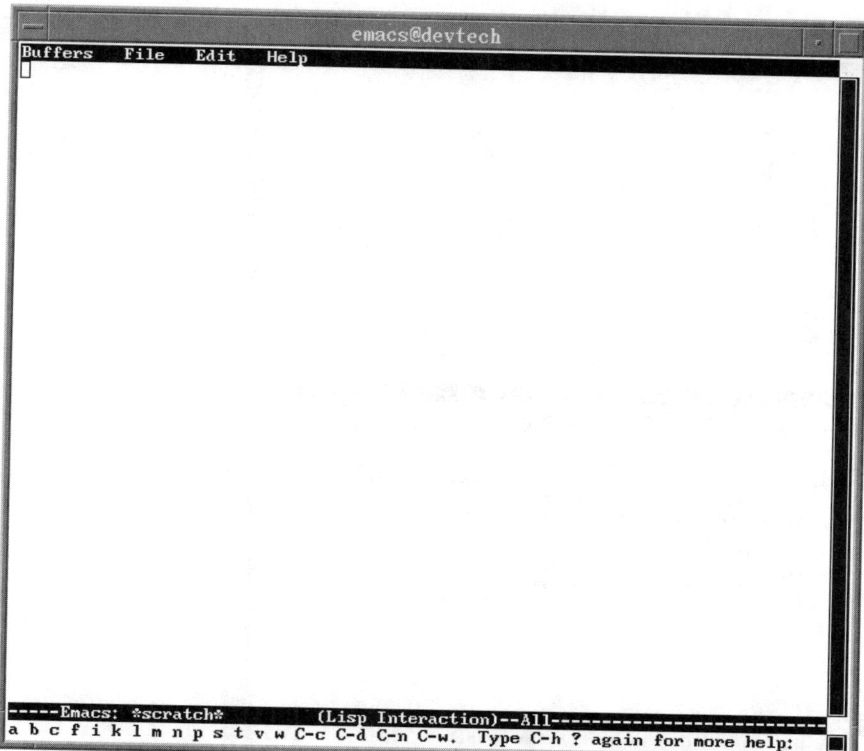

Figure 10.3 The emacs help screen.

It will generate a screen like the one shown in Fig. 10.4. Note that it tells you exactly what it has that relates to the compile string. Use this when you can't remember how to do things but have some idea of what you want to do.

There is one other tool within emacs that you should know about. It is called info and really consists of a hypertext database of text containing information about emacs and related tools. To invoke info, type:

```
C-h i
```

Once inside info, you can type h to get an on-line tutorial. Try this to learn more about info. A full discussion of info is beyond the scope of this book; see related emacs documentation for more information on it.

Figure 10.4 Example of regular expression help.

10.9 Getting Current Information

You can get current information on emacs by pressing the command sequence:

```
C-h n
```

to invoke the news feature of emacs. This will provide "up to the release" information on emacs and associated products. See the C-h minibuffer line for more possible commands.

10.10 Reading in a File

To begin editing a file, type:

```
$ emacs file
```

Once you are in emacs, you are actually in a buffer named file. If you want to read in a different file, issue the command:

```
C-x C-f
```

emacs will prompt you for the filename to read in and issue a command to read the correct file into a new buffer with a matching name. emacs uses the current working directory as a default.

emacs has a nifty feature called command completion. This allows you to type abbreviated command which emacs will finish for you. You simply type the shortest unique string and press TAB, and emacs will finish the string for you. Note that the string must be unique; if it is not, emacs will prompt you with a list of possibilities. You must type enough characters to make it unique and again press TAB. emacs will finish the string for you. This is particularly useful for long filenames. For example:

```
C-x C-f get TAB
```

will expand the file get to any full filename in my current working directory. If the file is named gethostbyname and it is the only filename beginning with a get in my current working directory, emacs will read in the correct file. This can be a real timesaver and is something you will use more and more as you use emacs.

10.11 Making Changes in a File

emacs, unlike many other editors, is in insert mode by default. This means that when you move the cursor to the text input area and begin to type, you insert text, and current text is simply moved to accommodate the inserted text. If you are more comfortable working in the more normal overstrike mode, type the command:

```
ESC x overwrite-mode
```

emacs works as you would expect a full-screen editor to work. With respect to things like word wrap, you can set the fill mode with the command:

```
ESC x auto-fill-mode
```

This will cause word wrapping as you might expect it to work. You can issue the above command again to toggle out of fill mode. If you don't use fill mode, emacs places a backslash at the end of every line as a reminder that the line is continued below.

After using emacs, you will notice that most commands that begin with an ESC operate on words or other groups of characters, while commands preceded by a CTRL operate on single characters. Keep this in mind as you proceed.

There are basic commands to move the cursor within the text window:

`C-f`	Moves forward one space
`C-b`	Moves backward one space
`C-n`	Moves to next line
`C-p`	Moves to previous line
`C-a`	Moves to the beginning of the line
`C-e`	Moves to the end of the line
`ESC f`	Moves forward one word
`ESC b`	Moves backward one word
`ESC e`	Moves forward one sentence
`ESC a`	Moves backward one sentence
`ESC ]`	Moves forward one paragraph
`ESC [`	Moves backward one paragraph

Definitions of sentences and paragraphs default to two spaces after a punctuation mark and blank lines, respectively. You can modify these definitions with the sentence-end and paragraph-end variables. See Sec. 10.24 for more details.

There are basic commands to move and manipulate screens:

`C-v`	Moves forward one screen.
`C-l`	Places the current line at the top of the screen and scrolls the rest.
`ESC v`	Moves backward one screen.
`ESC >`	Moves to end of file.
`ESC <`	Moves to beginning of file.
`ESC x goto-line n`	N is the line number you wish to go to.
`ESC x goto-char n`	N is the character number in the file you wish to go to.

With emacs, you can also issue a command and tell it to execute a certain number of times with the commands:

```
ESC n command
```

where n is the number of times to execute command. In other words, the ESC n command must precede any emacs command which you wish to execute n times in succession.

There are also simple commands which perform text manipulation shortcuts. For example:

`C-t`	Transposes two letters
`ESC t`	Transposes two words
`C-x C-t`	Transposes two lines
`ESC c`	Capitalizes the first character of the current word
`ESC l`	Puts current word in lowercase
`ESC u`	Puts current word in uppercase

There are various other commands which allow you to manipulate the screen and your text. See the interactive help for more details.

`ESC s`	Centers current line
`ESC x center-paragraph`	Centers current paragraph

10.12 Undoing Commands

You can undo a previous command with the emacs command:

```
ESC x u
```

This will prove invaluable at some point in your emacs usage . . . don't forget it.

There are also ways to move text around in and between buffers. Some of the more common commands are:

`C-d`	Deletes the character under the cursor.
`ESC d`	Deletes what remains of the current word.
`C-k`	Deletes what remains of the line. Note that it takes two C-ks to remove an entire line: the first to remove the text and the second to remove the newline.
`DEL`	Deletes the character preceding the cursor.
`ESC DEL`	Deletes the previous word.
`ESC k`	Deletes the current sentence.
`C-y`	Yank. Restores what you have deleted.
`C-w`	Deletes marked region.

When you delete things with any of the above commands except the DEL and C-d commands, emacs saves them in a buffer known as a kill ring. You can issue the C-y command to restore all that has been deleted. emacs is smart enough to restore them in the order you deleted them. This means that you can delete two consecutive lines with C-k C-k C-k C-k, move the cursor somewhere else, and issue a C-y command. The two lines are restored at the position of the cursor, and other lines are adjusted accordingly.

10.13 Working with Text Blocks

One of the most common things you will do is to move blocks of text around in a buffer. The commands to accomplish this are:

`C-@or C-SPACE`	Marks beginning or end of a region
`C-x C-x`	Exchanges location of cursor and mark
`ESC h`	Marks paragraph
`C-x C-p`	Marks page
`C-x h`	Marks buffer
`C-w`	Deletes marked region
`ESC h`	Marks current paragraph
`ESC w`	Copies region into kill ring without removing region in current buffer

To mark a region for manipulation in emacs, merely position the cursor to the beginning of the region and press:

```
C-@
```

or

```
C-SPACE
```

whichever is most convenient. Once this mark has been set, you can move the cursor (also known as the point) to the end of the region using any emacs command. Once you have reached the end of the region, there is nothing special that you have to do. emacs assumes the region begins with the mark and ends with current cursor position. You can verify the position of the mark by issuing the command:

```
C-x C-x
```

This will place the cursor (point) at the current mark position and the mark position at the previous cursor location. This is useful to remind you exactly what you are deleting. Note, however, that it is not necessary to do this. At this point, you can delete the region with the command:

```
C-w
```

Remember that you can undo your deletion with the C-y command.

To copy a block of information, you can mark the region as described before and, once the region is marked, issue the command:

```
ESC w
```

This copies the current marked region to the kill ring. Next, move the cursor to the desired location and issue the C-y (yank) command. This will insert the contents of the last deletion stored in the kill ring in the current location.

You can manipulate the contents of the kill ring with commands like:

```
ESC y
```

which deletes the most recent text in the kill ring. The kill ring is essentially a last in first out (LIFO) queue which acts much as a traditional stack operates. With commands like those listed above, you can manipulate the next block of information in the kill ring to be operated on. For example, you can use the ESC y command to remove the last item from the kill ring until you are at the item you wish to yank with C-y.

The default size of the kill ring is the last 30 deletions. This can be modified with the command:

```
ESC x set-variable RETURN kill-ring-max RETURN value RETURN
```

where value is the numbers of deletion items to save in the kill ring.

10.14 Using Multiple Buffers

You can also use multiple buffers in emacs to move blocks of information around. Each buffer has a major mode associated with it which determines its state. You can have any number of buffers, each containing any amount of information. You can move around within buffers and move between buffers at will. You can merge and cut buffers from one to another and save the resultant buffer to a disk file. There is almost no limit to what you can do with buffers in emacs.

Buffers are a good way to save some but not all information from one file to another. Let's take an example of how we could do this. We have a file named test1 which contains the following information:

```
This is line 1
This is line 2
This is line 3
This is line 4
This is line 5
```

To invoke emacs on this file, type:

```
$ emacs test1
```

To cut lines 3 and 4 out of this file, issue the commands, position the cursor at the beginning of line 3, and press:

```
C-SPACE
```

This marks the first line of the region to be copied. Move the cursor to the beginning of line 4 and press ESC w. This copies lines 3 and 4 to the kill ring. Now you need to open a new buffer. Use the command:

```
C-x b buffername
```

where buffername is the name of the new buffer you want to create. Note that it is probably a good idea to have the buffer name match the filename. Once you type this, a new buffer is created and a blank screen is presented. To yank the last contents of the kill ring into the current buffer, type:

```
C-y
```

which yanks the last kill ring contents to the current buffer. From here you can save and manipulate this buffer as you would any other.

You can list the buffers in your session with the command:

```
C-x C-b
```

This produces a screen which contains information on the current list of buffers and associated information while leaving a portion of the screen as your current buffer. To move to the buffer list, use the command:

```
C-x o
```

Once you are in the buffer list, there is a variety of commands which you can issue to act upon buffers in the list. Some of the more basic are:

`C-n`	Moves down a line
`C-p`	Moves up a line
`SPACE`	Moves to the next buffer in the list
`dx`	Marks the buffer for deletion
`sx`	Saves buffer
`1`	Displays buffer
`2`	Displays buffer in a portion of the window

10.15 Halting the Execution of emacs Commands

You can halt the execution of any emacs command with the command:

```
C-g
```

This will place you back in input mode and stop the execution of the current command.

10.16 Saving a File

To save a file, issue the command:

```
C-x C-s
```

This will save the contents of the current buffer to a file of the same name. If you have any problem with terminal hang-ups, it is probably related to the C-s sequence, which may stop flow control to your terminal. If this occurs, type a C-q to unlock the screen and allow data to begin to flow again.

If you want to save the buffer contents as something other than its buffer name, issue the command:

```
C-x C-w
```

and type the filename under which to save the buffer.

10.17 Exiting emacs

To exit emacs type:

```
C-x C-c
```

emacs will ask you if you want to save any unsaved changes. Answer y or n as appropriate.

10.18 Suspending emacs

You can temporarily suspend emacs with the command:

```
C-z
```

This is a function of the job control of the system and will not work on all systems. If you successfully return to the shell prompt, you can reenter the emacs editor exactly where you left it by typing:

```
$ fg
```

You can also use the standard job control commands to control more than one background process.

10.19 Autosave Files

emacs, by default, creates an autosave file every 300 keystrokes. The name of the autosave file is simply the original filename preceded and followed by # marks. For example, if you issue the command:

```
$ emacs kevin
```

after the first 300 keystrokes, a file named #kevin# would be saved. This will be the place, if a crash occurs, you can recover from. You can force a flush of the current buffer back to the last autosave with the command:

```
ESC x revert-buffer
```

You will then be asked whether you want to revert to the most recent autosave buffer (y or n) and then revert-buffer from file filename (yes or no). This means that you can either go back to the last complete group of 300 keystrokes or to the beginning of your edit session. Note that emacs expects exact matching answers, so type y, n, yes, or no, respectively.

emacs also creates a backup file when you begin an edit session on an existing file. The file is named the filename followed by a ~. For example, if you entered the command:

```
$ emacs kevin
```

and kevin existed, a file named kevin~ would be created which contained the contents of kevin before any changes were made. This allows you to keep a backup copy in case you want to disregard any committed changes.

10.20 Multiple Windows in emacs

emacs provides for multiple window support on most platforms. While many workstations have moved to bitmap support and use windowing systems, you may want to split a current window into multiple screens. From within each screen you can perform any task you could from any full function emacs screen. For example, you can issue email and shell commands and edit other files.

The basic command to split the screen is:

```
C-x 2
```

This will split your current window into two segments as shown in Fig. 10.5. While you can use a mouse and windowing systems capabilities to create multiple windows, it is often more efficient to simply issue the above command and perform the task at hand then finding your mouse, creating a new window, entering the editor, etc.

To move from one window to another, use the command:

```
C-x o
```

To delete a window, type:

```
C-x 0
```

Note you have all the consequences and behaviors of each of the split windows being a full-function editing session. Keep this in mind when you are killing buffers and moving back and forth between them.

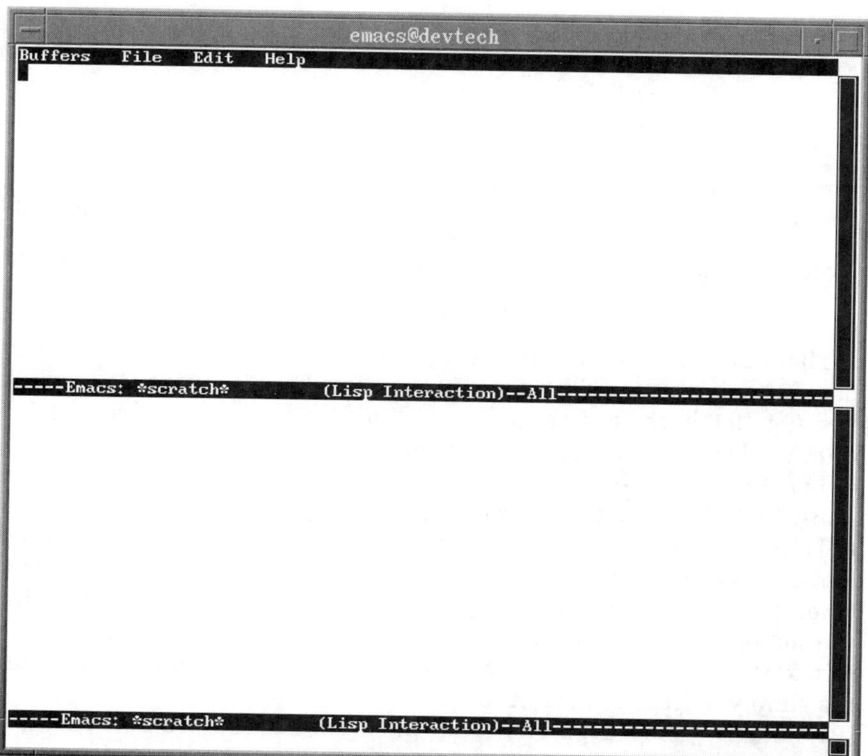

Figure 10.5 emacs split screen.

You can alter the size of windows within a screen with the following commands:

`C-x ^`	Makes the current window taller
`C-x {`	Makes the current window wider

These commands alter the current window size by one line.

10.21 Searching for and Replacing Text

Every editor has a basic search and replace capability. emacs, as you are probably coming to expect, has a variety of search and replace capabilities. They range from simple searches to complete regular expression searches. Keep in mind that the flexibility of emacs allows you to write your own search and replace algorithms, and this may be something you want to do when you have become more familiar with emacs.

The basic search categories are:

`Simple search forward`	C-s ESC string
`Simple search backward`	C-r ESC string
`Incremental search`	C-s string
`Exact string search`	C-s ESC C-w string
`ESC x re-search-forward`	Regular expression search (see below)
`ESC x re-search-backward`	Regular expression search (see below)
`Search and replace`	ESC x replace-string RETURN oldstring RETURN newstring
`Query-replace`	ESC % RETURN oldstring RETURN newstring RETURN

There is commonality among all search command syntax. All commands begin with a CTRL sequence such as C-s (for forward searches) and C-r (for backward searches) and end with a carriage return. All commands can also be repeated to find the next occurrence by pressing either the C-s or C-r command sequence without entering a string. Finally, to end any string search or replace operations, type ESC. This tells emacs you are finished with any search and replace operations and clears the buffer from which to search. It is important to type ESC when you are finished searching to ensure that you are not continuing the actions of the last executed search command. Because the keystroke syntax for regular expressions searches is so complex, most users simply use the re-search command listed above.

Remember also that emacs works from current cursor position; therefore if you want to execute commands from the beginning of the file, you should first position yourself at the beginning of the file and then execute any necessary commands.

Finally, emacs is case independent. When you issue commands related to case, emacs ignores it for the purpose of search and matches it for the purpose of replace. In other words, emacs attempts to match case character by character when replacing text so as to minimize the side effects of the word change. For example if you have a file which contains:

```
I have a file which has several occurrences of oldstring. Oldstring
really consists of a bunch of gibberish which really has no meaning
or context. I hope the OLDSTRING in all caps will not confuse any-
thing I do in the emacs editor.
```

and you issue the command:

```
ESC x replace-string RETURN oldstring RETURN newstring
```

the result would be a file which contained:

```
I have a file which has several occurrences of newstring. Newstring
really consists of a bunch of gibberish which really has no meaning
or context. I hope the NEWSTRING in all caps will not confuse any-
thing I do in the emacs editor.
```

As you can see, the emacs editor attempts to maintain case on a character by character basis. This is useful, particularly when programming since languages such as C are case sensitive.

10.21.1 The simple search

The simple search consists of entering a string and telling emacs to find the next occurrence. For example, to find the next occurrence of the string emacs, use:

```
C-s ESC emacs
```

This will find the next forward occurrence in the file from the current insertion point. emacs may be a string inside a longer string and the match will still occur. If the string gnuemacs occurred next, the cursor would be positioned at the e in the string gnuemacs. The exact string match will look for a unique occurrence of the string emacs if that is what you are after.

To repeat the forward find, type the command:

```
C-s
```

To do a backward find, issue the command:

```
C-r ESC emacs
```

and emacs will search backward from the current position for any occurrence of the string emacs. To repeat the backward find, issue the command:

```
C-r
```

10.21.2 The exact string search

If you are looking for a unique word and not a string, you need to use the exact string (or word) match capability of emacs. To search for the word emacs, issue the command:

```
C-s ESC C-w emacs
```

To find the next occurrence, issue the command:

```
C-s
```

You can also issue backward searches with the C-r version of this command. For example, to find the previous occurrence of the word emacs, issue the command:

```
C-r ESC C-w emacs
```

To repeat the find, issue the command:

```
C-r
```

10.21.3 The incremental search

The incremental search allows you to enter a string, and emacs will begin matching the string with the first letter. This means that you can continue to narrow the search for your match by entering characters in the string you wish to match.

To match the first string that begins with a, type:

```
C-s a
```

The first occurrence of the character a will become the current position. If you are looking for the occurrence of abc, you would simply type a b and a c and watch as emacs continues to narrow the results of your search. This command is most useful to programmers since they may not remember the exact string but know how it begins in the program.

Remember to type ESC when you are finished with your search and replace activity since this will ensure that you are not telling emacs something you don't intend. Note that you can also end the search with another CTRL sequence. Since emacs is CTRL command driven, this is normally how the search is ended; keep in mind that if you don't issue an ESC or CTRL command sequence after you have finished searching, emacs assumes you are still in search mode and will act as such.

10.21.4 Search and replace

Many times you are interested in replacing one or all occurrences of a string in a given file. To replace all occurrences of a word in your current file, type:

```
ESC x replace-string RETURN oldstring RETURN newstring RETURN
```

Remember that the ESC x sequence tells emacs to execute a typed command. In this case the command is replace-string, and the oldstring will be replaced with the newstring in all occurrences of the file. Remember also that emacs works from the current position and only those occurrences following the cursor position will be changed.

10.21.5 Query search

If you want to replace only certain occurrences of a string, you must use the query search capability of emacs. To enter a query search, type the command:

```
ESC % RETURN oldstring RETURN newstring RETURN
```

Once emacs finds the first occurrence of oldstring, a question appears at the bottom of the screen:

```
Query replacing oldstring with newstring.
```

At this point, emacs waits for you to tell it whether to replace the string or perform any of a variety of other options on the string. Some of the available options are:

`DEL`	Doesn't replace; moves to next occurrence of oldstring
`n`	Same as DEL
`SPACE`	Replaces and moves to next occurrence of oldstring
`y`	Same as SPACE
`.`	Replaces current occurrence and quits

,	Replaces current occurrence but doesn't go to next occurrence
^	Moves back to previous occurrence
!	Replaces all following occurrences and doesn't ask for assistance
ESC	Quits query replace

By far the most common answer is SPACE (space bar) or y. Note that UNIX and emacs are case sensitive, and therefore Y is not the same as y. Keep this in mind if you have any troubles in emacs.

10.21.6 Regular expression searches

Regular expressions are typically used when you want to perform a general substitution from a predetermined pattern. Through the use of wildcards substitutions, you can generate strings which can be matched according to your specifications. See Chap. 2 for more information on regular expressions.

emacs can use regular expressions to locate strings and words in any of the basic search and replace operations. For example, to find a word that is at the end of a line, issue the command:

```
C-s ESC C-w last$
```

This will search for the next occurrence of the word last that is the last word on a line. The most basic characters that can be used in regular expressions are:

*	Matches any number of characters
.	Matches a single character
$	Matches the end of line
^	Matches the beginning of line

The regular expression commands react similarly to those described earlier. These commands should be invoked from the command-level interface. The basic syntax is:

`ESC x re-search-forward`	Simple search regular expression
`ESC x re-search-backward`	Simple search regular expression
`ESC x isearch-forward-regexp`	Incremental search regular expression
`ESC x isearch-backward-regexp`	Incremental search regular expression
`ESC x query-replace-regexp`	Query replace regular expression
`ESC x replace-regexp`	Replace regular expression

With these commands, you can execute all the commands described above but have the added flexibility of using regular expressions to match multiple strings with substitution capabilities.

10.22 Text Formatting and Its Relation to emacs

emacs has several modes which support a variety of text formatting utilities. Tools such as troff, nroff, and TeX are supported within emacs. You can use emacs to assist you with writing these types of files, and it provides basic syntax checking and generation for each of the text formatting languages described above.

There are high levels of support for troff and nroff and exceptional levels of support for TeX and LaTeX. emacs provides syntax checkers and generators for these mark-up languages and, in addition, processes them into files which can be processed at a later time if necessary.

Each of the major text formatters is represented by a major mode in emacs. This gives you the ability to simply enter a major mode and have emacs assist you with formatting and syntax. For example, the most common type of standard text formatting system on UNIX is nroff. This is the format which man pages and some Internet documentation come in. Therefore, some of the basic capabilities of the nroff major mode in emacs will be discussed. It should be noted that the nroff mode is very similar to troff, and most of the commands will work in both modes.

To enter nroff major mode, type:

```
ESC x nroff-mode
```

You can now use certain defined behaviors in the nroff major mode to assist you with moving around in the file and formatting it, and it will also assist with syntax. For example, you can use emacs to automatically insert the ending part of a macro. To place emacs in the mode known as electric-nroff-mode, type the command:

```
ESC x electric-nroff-mode
```

An example of this is shown in Fig. 10.6. When you type .PP, you then press C-j. This creates a duplicate .PP with a blank line in between and positions the cursor at the beginning of the blank line. From here you can type your paragraph text. Another example is to type .LG and press C-j; the corresponding .NL will be placed below with a blank line in between. This function is very useful for building macros in nroff or troff format in the nroff major mode of emacs.

You can also use emacs to assist with moving around in the file. Because nroff uses a special file format which does not include blank lines, you may have trouble moving around in the file easily. nroff major mode provides commands which move you both forward and backward with respect to text files. They bypass the interceding macro commands. They are:

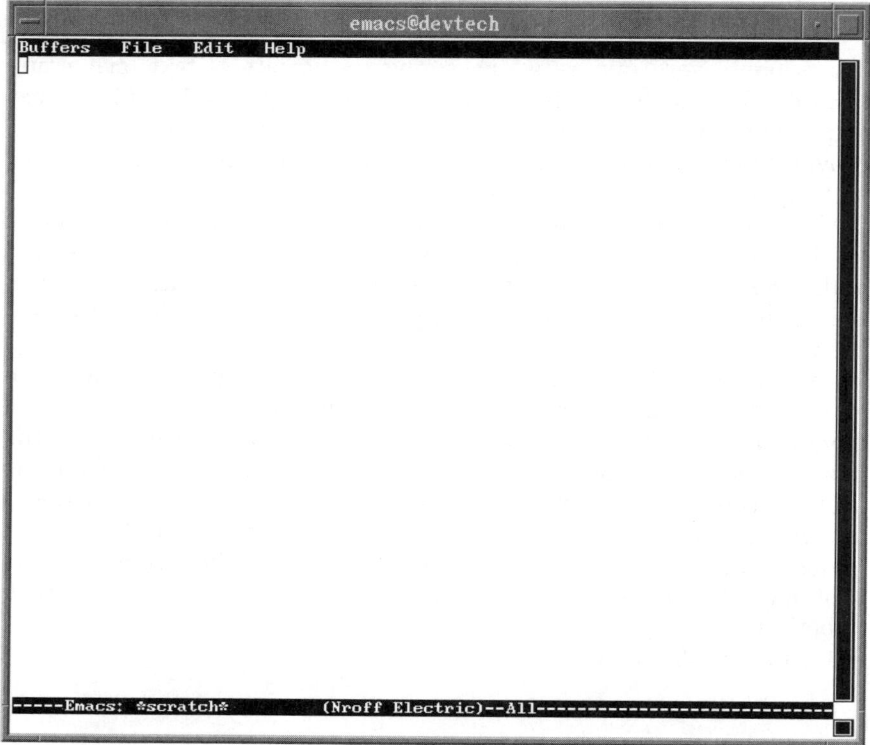

Figure 10.6 electric-nroff-mode.

`ESC n`	Moves forward to next text line
`ESC p`	Moves backward to next previous text line

With these commands, you can save yourself quite a bit of time by not having to move, one line at a time, over all macro commands to get to the next line of text.

There are other commands in the nroff mode; see the on-line help for more information.

10.22.1 TeX and LaTeX support

Similar support exists for TeX and LaTeX. The three major modes are:

`tex-mode`	emacs determines whether the file is TeX or LaTeX and places you in the correct mode.
`latex-mode`	emacs is placed in LaTeX mode.
`plain-tex-mode`	emacs is placed in TeX mode.

emacs will verify curly braces and quotes as well as provides comment capabilities.

emacs also provides additional support for TeX in the form of processing. You can process the contents of your TeX or LaTeX input file with the command:

```
C-c C-b - process current buffer
```

All output messages from this command are placed in the TeX shell buffer. This should come up automatically; if it doesn't, press:

```
C-c C-l
```

This will process your file and produce a .dvi file (device independent file). You can then process the .dvi file and send it to the default printer with the command:

```
C-c C-p
```

This will queue the processed .dvi file to the default printer. To check the queue status, use the command:

```
C-c C-q
```

Finally, to stop processing of a TeX or LaTeX file, type the command:

```
C-c C-k
```

10.23 Shell Commands

You can escape directly from emacs into a shell window with the command:

```
ESC x shell
```

This forks a new shell and places you at the command prompt. From here you can issue any shell commands as you normally would. To exit the shell, type:

```
$ exit
```

This places you back in emacs at the place you left.

You may only want to execute a single command and reenter the emacs editor at the conclusion of this command. To do this, type:

```
ESC ! command
```

emacs opens a window with the results of this command. To kill the window, type:

```
C-x 1
```

Because the output of the command is in a buffer, you can perform any emacs command on the results from within emacs.

10.24 emacs Customization

emacs is one of the most easily customized editors available today. By learning a small amount of LISP, you can create your own command language and essentially build your own editor interface. Some companies have gone so far as to structure editor commands to emulate an old editor from which they are migrating in an effort to minimize the migration pain for the developers. This has been very successful, at least in terms of their ability to create an editor which fits their needs.

There are many variables in emacs which control almost every aspect of its behavior. The primary way to change the state of variables is with the command:

```
ESC x set-variable RETURN variable RETURN value RETURN
```

The set-variable command allows you to enter a variable name and a subsequent value for that variable. This command works in almost every instance and allows you to customize emacs to behavior that you expect.

10.25 X Windows Support

There are several newer versions of emacs which support X windows. Namely, 19.17 has support for X windows. Support is determined when you build the emacs product. You can choose to provide X windows support when the emacs executable is built.

If you choose to provide X windows support, you gain the ability to create multiple windows and utilize the full power of emacs. You will know if X windows support is included by simply invoking the emacs editor from an xterm window (or some derivative). If a new window appears, you are running with X windows support; if it doesn't, you probably aren't.

10.26 Spell Checking

You can perform basic spell checking on the current word in emacs with the command:

```
ESC $
```

emacs processes the current word and prompts for an action. The action list is the same as that presented for the query search capability in emacs. You would typically type one of:

`RETURN`	Word is correct, store in the dictionary.
`SPACE`	Begins a query replace responses to correct word.
`C-g`	Quits without changes.
`n`	Goes to next occurrence without changes.

To check the spelling of an entire file use the command:

```
ESC x spell-buffer
```

This is one of the few commands that will begin its execution at the beginning of the buffer without respect to the current cursor position. It will scan through the entire file, stopping at each occurrence of a word it does not know, and will ask for a response as described above.

10.27 Printing from within emacs

You can issue certain commands to print from within emacs. Some of the most basic are:

`print-buffer`	Prints contents of current buffer to default printer
`lpr-buffer`	Prints contents of current buffer without any preprocessing by pr
`print-region`	Prints contents of current region

You invoke the above commands as any other emacs command:

```
ESC x command RETURN
```

You can configure emacs to issue the print commands with certain characteristics with the command:

```
ESC x lpr-switches -Pibm_laser RETURN
```

This example sets the output queue to ibm_laser. You can use any combination of switches you normally place on the lpr command.

10.28 Other Things That You Can Do in emacs

There are many things you can do within emacs such as invoke mail and execute commands. Although this chapter has discussed how to invoke commands, it will not discuss mail since this interface, while functional, is not as sophisticated as most mail interfaces today.

One interesting thing you can do is read manual pages and nroff documents in general from within the emacs editor. To read a man page, issue the command:

```
ESC x manual-entry RETURN command RETURN
```

This will bring up the manual page for command. To exit, simply exit the buffer as you normally would.

10.29 emacs and Programming Languages

Just as emacs supports several text formatters, it also supports and understands several programming languages. Languages with their own major modes include C, Fortran, and LISP. This book will only discuss C and Fortran since they are the main languages in use with emacs today. You can also create your own language-support modes with the autoload command. See interactive help for more information on this macro.

10.29.1 C language support

emacs has support for automatic recognition of mode based on file extensions. For example, emacs will place you in C mode if you read in a file with an extension of .c, .h, or .y. emacs has an understanding of how the C syntax looks and can assist you with things like semicolons, curly braces, and quotation marks. It can also help you format your code so that you can read it more clearly months or years after you wrote it. To enter this mode manually, type:

```
ESC x c-mode
```

You can preserve indentation of your code by simply pressing LINEFEED (C-j) instead of RETURN at the end of a text line, and emacs will indent to the first character of the previous line. This is very useful when writing in a structured language such as C, and saves it keystrokes and time.

You can also format an entire region with the command:

```
ESC C-\
```

Simply mark the beginning of a region as described earlier in this chapter, place the cursor at the end of the desired region, and press the above sequence. This will indent all interceding lines appropriately. Note the use of the word *appropriately.* emacs has some knowledge of the form and syntax of C and will make indentations based on blocks and structures (curly braces, conditional loops, etc.) which significantly increase the readability of the code. You can alter the indentation defaults for C source code with the standard ESC x command macro. Some of the more basic variables available are:

`c-argdecl-indent`	Indentation for type declarations of functions (default 5)
`c-auto-newline`	Inserts a newline before and after {} and after ; and : (default nil)
`c-brace-offset`	Indentation for line that begins with { (default 0)
`c-continued-statement-offset`	Extra indentation on continuation lines (default 2)

There are other variables. See the on-line help for more information. Many programmers alter these with C since it can save a tremendous amount of time and resources as you key in the code itself.

You can insert comment lines either at the end of a current line of text or at the beginning of a blank line with the command:

```
ESC ;
```

This places the correct comment line syntax (for C it is a /* */) structure and places the cursor in the blank part of the comment string. Use this to place a large number of comments in your code since this will increase maintainability.

There are other commands which move you within your source code file. Some of the more basic are:

`ESC C-a`	Moves to beginning of function body
`ESC C-e`	Moves to end of function body

These allow you to jump between functions, bypassing the rest of the body with one key sequence.

etags (external tags). There is another function in emacs related to moving between functions quickly and easily. With the etags command, you can generate an etags file which contains function references generated from a listing of files. This is useful when your program is contained in more than one source code file. Instead of being forced to move between files and buffers, you can generate a tags file which contains file and function mappings for emacs. This allows you to act on a function name which is not in the current buffer and automatically reference that function and move it into the current screen.

You must invoke etags as a separate command with a syntax of:

```
etags -f outfile infile ...
```

where -f outfile saves the output tag file in the file outfile. The default is a file named TAGS.
infile ... is one or more .c, .h, or .y files which contain information related to your C program.

You can use wildcards in any filename on the etags command line just as you can with any other command. One possible invocation of etags is the following:

```
$ etags *.[chy]
```

which will build the tags file and which contains all function references in all files in the current directory which end in .c, .h, and .y. You could create a tags file with the command:

```
$ etags *.[chy] /usr/local/kevin/*.[chy}
```

This creates a tags file from all possible C source files in both the current directory and the /usr/local/kevin directory.

Once you have created a tags file, you can act on it from within emacs with the following commands:

`ESC x visit-tags-table RETURN filename RETURN`	Reads in the tag file.
`ESC . [tag]`	Where tag is the function you want to find. If you don't enter a tag, emacs will use the word the cursor is currently on.
`ESC ,`	Finds the next occurrence of tag.
`ESC x list-tags`	Generates a list of all tags in current file.
`ESC x tags-apropos`	Generates a list of all matched strings.
`ESC x tags-query-replace`	Allows a search and replace much as described in an earlier section.
`ESC x tags-search`	Allows you to enter a regular expression on which to search.

10.29.2 Fortran language support

Just as with C, there is support for the Fortran language in emacs. Many of the functions are similar and, as you will see, are invoked in much the same way.

When you invoke emacs with a filename which contains an extension .f, you will be placed in Fortran mode by default. By selecting a major mode of Fortran, emacs provides support for syntax and structural checking much the same as is supported for C. Some of the most basic commands are:

`ESC ^`	Joins current line to the previous one
`ESC C-j`	Splits current line at cursor position

`ESC C-a`	Moves to beginning of current subprogram
`ESC C-e`	Moves to end of current subprogram
`C-c C-n`	Moves forward to next statement
`C-c C-p`	Moves backward to previous statement
`C-c C-w`	Creates window 72 columns wide to aid in entering source

There are also variables similar to those supported by C. Some of the most basic are:

`fortran-do-indent`	Additional indentation used in do statements (default 3)
`fortran-if-indent`	Additional indentation used in if statement (default 3)
`fortran-line-number-indent`	Indentation of line numbers (default 1)
`fortran-minimum-statement-indent`	Position beginning of statement (default 6)

With respect to line numbers in Fortran, you can simply type the line number at the beginning of the line, and emacs will move your cursor to column 7 or the column indicated by the variable fortran-minimum-statement-indent.

10.29.3 LISP language support

LISP is a language which is supported by a major mode of emacs. Because emacs is written in LISP, there is strong support for syntax and development of LISP in emacs. Using LISP and its relation to emacs is beyond the scope of this book; however, suffice it to say that LISP may well be emac's best-supported language. See related books and on-line help for more information.

10.29.4 Compiling programs

One of the main benefits of emacs for programmers is the ability to compile code from within emacs itself. The basic command to invoke the compilation system is:

```
ESC x compile
```

This will prompt you with a series of questions relating to the compilation process. The default command is:

```
make -k
```

where -k continues with compilation after errors (this is not the make default).

You can enter your own compilation command, which becomes the default for the session, by using the compile command as described above.

emacs gives you the ability to move from one error to the next with the command:

```
C-x `
```

When you issue the above command, emacs places your cursor at the location where the error occurred. You can then fix the problem and either move to the next error by again issuing a C-x ‘ or reissue the compilation command with ESC x compile.

Each time you issue the C-x ‘ command, you are placed on the next error message in the compilation buffer. To begin at the first error again, use the command:

```
C-u C-x `
```

You can then cycle through the error messages again using the standard C-x ‘ command.

10.30 Multiuser File-Level Locking Support

One of the problems with editing in a UNIX environment is that there is no support for multiple users editing the same file at the same time. Because of the nature of UNIX, there was never this kind of logic built into the file management system. This can cause problems with editors like vi since two or more people can edit the same file at the same time and the one who saves the file last will overwrite any changes made by the other users editing the file.

emacs supports file-level locking such that when a user begins to edit a file, if another person is already editing this file, a warning message is issued notifying you that there are others editing the same file. This can occur either when you read in the file or attempt to save it. Either way, you are made aware of others editing the same file that you are working on. This kind of functionality is critical to business and is one of the most powerful and important features of emacs in a business environment.

10.31 Conclusion

emacs is simply the most powerful and extensible editor available today. While the commands may initially seem awkward, you will quickly get productive and will soon grow to love the emacs editor.

Most professional UNIX people, particularly those who work on multiple platforms and architectures, use emacs for all editing tasks.

While there are other tools which may provide a better partial solution, it is difficult to find a tool which provides more power and flexibility than emacs. With its all encompassing environment, including syntax checking, structure assistance, and mail and compilation capabilities, emacs provides a unified environment for working in UNIX. Once you enter emacs, you may not ever have to leave to accomplish your goals. This is the real power of emacs.

There are many emacs features which have not been discussed in this chapter. See the on-line help or other books for more information. See also the recommended book list in App. C.

Chapter

11

Nonnative Software Development Tools

The primary use of nonnative software for UNIX is for software development. While there are tools that are general purpose in nature and not directly related to software development, they are definitely in the minority. Tools are available that both replace delivered native functionality and add additional functionality to the software development process on UNIX.

This book discusses some of the most commonly used nonnative software development tools. However, there are many tools which are not discussed here. See Chap. 9 for more information on how to find out what tools are available and how to get some of these tools from the Internet itself. It is not the intention of this book to provide all the information on a product and its functionality but instead to introduce the basic function of a product and its basic syntax. Keep this in mind as you read this chapter.

There are also a number of commercial tools which provide functionality similar to that delivered by tools on the Internet. While there are no commercial products discussed or included in this book, there certainly are many good commercial products available for UNIX developers. The intention of this book is to describe information about *free* software, discussing what and where it is and how to get it. If you are interested in commercial software, see your vendors for more information on functional product areas and associated vendors.

It is important to note that most of the documentation in this chapter is available from one source or another and is often included with the tool itself. Much of the syntax and basic functionality documentation contained in this chapter is taken from documentation included with the individual products. README, Install.Notes, man pages, and texinfo documentation are often included with the product distributions. If documentation comes with the product, it is included on the accompanying CD for your reference. The first thing you should do after reading a product section in this book is to look at the product documentation itself. It often contains more information than is described here.

Finally, because of the way most free software packages are licensed, the entire distribution as it comes from the Internet is included on the CD. In some cases, it would have been easier and taken less disk space to included one copy of shared information; however, because of the licensing constraints, everything in the distribution is included. Binaries are included for Sun and IBM RS/6000 workstations. See App. A for more information.

11.1 configure

11.1.1 Introduction

GNU has begun distributing most of their software with a tool called configure, a tool which examines your machine and structures all appropriate build tools such as makefiles and install scripts for the proper machine and software type. One of the biggest problems with Internet software has been the installation. Because of the differences between UNIX implementations, building software for a particular "flavor" of UNIX has often been difficult if not impossible. Only with great modifications to either the source code or the makefiles were you able to build the software or a given platform. GNU has attempted to fix much of this problem with their configure tool.

configure prepares a source code system for building. This tool will save hours of activity and frustration by providing a consistent and robust software building interface.

11.1.2 Usage

The basic syntax for the configure command is:

```
configure HOST [--target=TARGET] [--srcdir=DIR] [--rm] [--site=SITE]
[--prefix=DIR] [--exec_prefix=DIR] [-- program_prefix=DIR]
  [--tmpdir=DIR]
[--with-PACKAGE[=YES | NO] ] [-- norecursion] [--nfp] [-s] [-vV]
[--version] [--help]
```

where HOST is the name of the host machine on which to target.

—target=TARGET are build sources for TARGET and not the default of the current machine.

—srcdir=DIR looks for source code in DIR directory.
—rm removes the current configuration; doesn't create one.
—site=SITE uses specific makefiles for SITE.
—prefix=DIR defines location of install files (default is /usr/local).
—exec_prefix=DIR sets the root directory for host-dependent files.
—program_prefix=DIR configures installation files to install programs in DIR.
—tmpdir=DIR defines directory for temporary file creation.
—with-PACKAGE[=YES/NO] sets a flag for the build to recognize the existence of PACKAGE (default is yes).
—norecursion configures only current directory.
—nfp specifies the lack of floating point units.
-s suppresses status messages.
-v is the verbose option.
-V displays configure version number.
—version is the same as -V.
-help displays usage summary.

Most INSTALL files describe the correct usage of configure for each GNU package distributed.

TARGET descriptions. The basic format of the TARGET descriptions for the different supported platforms is CPU-COMPANY-SYSTEM, where each of the three fields can be represented by one of a set of values. The values for the CPU field are:

```
a29k, alpha, arm, cN, elxsi, hppa1.0, hppa1.1, i386, i860, i960,
m68000, m88k, mips, ns32k, pyramid, romp, rs6000, sparc, vax, we23k
```

For COMPANY, they are:

```
alliant, altos, apollo, att, cbm, convergent, convex, ards, dec, dg,
encore, harris, hp, ibm, mips, motorola, ncr, next, ns, omron,
sequent, sgi, sony, sun, tti, unicom
```

For SYSTEM, they are:

```
aix, aos, bsd, ctix, dgux, dynix, genix, hpux, isc, linux, luna,
mach, minix, newsos, osf, osfrose, riscos, sco, sunos, sysv, ultrix,
unos, vms
```

The COMPANY field can be ignored if you can uniquely identify the target system with the CPU and SYSTEM fields. For example, rs6000-aix is unique and ibm is not required.

You can add version numbers to the end of SYSTEM to more specifically define a particular target system. For example, you can use rs6000-ibm-aix3.2. There is no guarantee that specifying a particular version of an operating system will generate a different result than nonspecification, but it can't hurt.

There are also aliases for the CPU-COMPANY combination. Some of the more popular are:

```
3300, 3b1, 7300, altos, apollo68, att-7300, crds, decstation-3100,
decstation, fx2800, hp7NN, hp8NN, hp9k2NN, hp9k3NN, hp9k7NN,
hp9k8NN, iris, news, next, pmax, ps2, risc-news, sun386i, sun3,
sun4, tower-32, tower
```

There are a variety of bugs and behaviors for each of the possible configurations which are documented in the INSTALL file which comes with the documentation. Some of the more relevant are:

- elxsi-elxsi-bsd	There are current known problems building gcc; contact mrs@cygnus.com for more details.
- m88k-svr3	There are problems with the typically shipped Green Hills C compiler which suggest you should use a previous version of GNU C to generate V2.
- m88k-svr4 - ns32k-sequent	You need to create a file called string.h containing #include <string.h>.
- rs6000-*-aix	There is a problem with the IBM assembler. See the file README.RS6000 for more information on this problem.

You can check for the existence of a particular machine configuration type with the command:

```
$ config.sub name
```

where name is a machine name such as sun, ibm, hp, etc. This is a very useful test before beginning the build process on your system.

The other important feature to focus on is the -exec_prefix option. This provides you with the ability to place the binary files in a different directory structure from the non-architecture-dependent files that can either be in /usr/local or in a directory specified by the -prefix option. This is useful if you are exporting a filesystems which contains these programs in a heterogeneous environment. For example, exporting /usr/local to Sun, HP, and IBM machines can be easily supported with the exec_dir option.

Finally, there is a common makefile label throughout most of the free software packages that use configure. After you have used configure to build a system, you may want to install it. Most packages will support this methodology, and it is well described in the coming sections and chapters. But to summarize, the recommended methodology in most cases is:

```
$ ./configure
$ make clean
$ make target-machine
$ make prefix=/usr/local/tool install
```

The configure builds the appropriate makefile. Next, the make clean removes any possible files which have been built on other machines. This ensures that you get a clean compile and that everything is rebuilt from scratch. Next, the make with the target-machine option will create any binaries and library files which are necessary to run the product. Usually, these files are created in the local subdirectory hierarchy (e.g., /usr/local2/ghostscript/ghostscript-3.6). This allows you to test the executable before installing it in a directory for public use. The final command installs the product in a specified directory (the prefix variable) or in the default /usr/local subdirectory.

Some makefiles are different; you should see the appropriate makefile before you build your product to ensure that you are placing files where you want them to go.

11.1.3 Installation

Since configure comes with most newer GNU systems, there is no need to install it as a separate product. Therefore, this section is really unnecessary; in fact, configure is not distributed as a separate product.

11.1.4 Example

There are many examples in this book which use configure, and, in fact, a fairly standard methodology for using configure is established. Because of its frequency, a simple example using configure is displayed here for demonstration purposes. You will learn more as you build and configure other tools from GNU in other sections of this book.

To configure a product for an RS/6000 machine and include the executables in a subdirectory named bin, use a command like:

```
$ configure --target=rs6000-aix --prefix=/usr/local/product
$ make clean
$ make
$ make install
```

The first line generates the appropriate makefile for an RS/6000. The $ make clean command removes any executables and libraries which may cause the make to function improperly. The $ make will build the product and potentially move files into the prefix directory structure.

Finally, the $ make install command causes the product to be copied into the /usr/local/product subdirectory and causes the manual pages as well as the libraries and executables to be generated and stored in the appropriate subdirectory. This is a slightly different methodology than documented earlier; however, the results should be the same. Note that the $ make command will have the prefix directory defined in it due to its definition in the configure command. This is why the prefix option is not necessary on the make command line. Remember that most of the time, the $ make command will not copy (install) the resultant files unless you explicitly use the install option; however, this is not always the case, so beware.

Note that, as this example shows, you can use configure in combination with make to generate the appropriate executables and library files. You can either issue options like prefix with the configure or the make command. Both are equally correct and will accomplish the same thing.

The final thing to note about the install with configure is that it seems to have trouble with directories that aren't there. This means that if you need any subdirectories, particularly those related to your prefix path, you should create them before you issue the $ make install command, or you may get some nasty error message that install failed. If you see these, look carefully at the directory in which install was trying to operate and make sure it exists.

The configure command will become clearer as you use it to build products throughout this and other chapters. See the following sections for more examples.

11.1.5 Conclusion

configure is a very powerful tool that is distributed by GNU to ease the porting and building of tools on multiple platforms. By removing and hiding inconsistencies between UNIX platforms and compilers, configure makes porting and building software on different architectures simple.

Some older versions of GNU tools don't have the configure programs, and you will have to check makefiles and source code for compatibilities and inconsistencies. While configure will not fix all problems related to multiplatform support, it removes the majority of them and makes porting relatively straightforward.

It is a good idea to check for the existence of newer versions of software if the program does not build correctly the first time on a machine. Most Internet products have been ported to a large variety of UNIX platforms and, if you experience trouble with the build, check for a newer version of the product before wasting too much time messing with the build procedures of the current product.

11.2 gzip

11.2.1 Introduction

gzip is the GNU compression algorithm used to compress most GNU software products for distribution. gzip supports both compression and uncompression of its own format, but it also supports the decompression of pack and compress files. This makes it the ideal tool for compressing and uncompressing files on a UNIX platform. Note that gzip and the often-used PC program called zip are in no way related to each other.

The history of the gzip product is that the pack and compress routines that ship with UNIX contain an algorithm which is proprietary in nature. Because of this, it is necessary to pay royalties to the owner when these tools are acquired. As is often the case with Internet software, someone decided he or she didn't want to pay royalties to these people and created another algorithm for compression and decompression.

It turns out that the compression algorithm for pack and compress is proprietary, but the decompression algorithm is not. Therefore, gzip supports the decompression of both pack and compressed files as well as its own gzip format. This means that there is virtually no file from the Internet that gzip cannot unwind. This makes it a very powerful tool for use with Internet tools.

gzip contains associated tools for viewing compressed files without uncompressing, changing compressed files from one format to another (pack to gzip, etc.), and comparison of compressed files without performing uncompression. These tools make it much easier to work with compressed files, especially when disk space is limited.

Since gzip is a GNU product, it is fully covered by the GNU General Public License, and this is how it is distributed.

11.2.2 Usage

The basic syntax of the gzip command is:

```
gzip [-c][-d][-f][-h][-l][-L][-r][-S string] [-t][-v][-V] [-#]
[file ...]
```

where -c writes output to standard output.
-d decompresses.
-f forces compression or decompression.
-h displays help.
-l lists file sizes before and after compression.
-L displays gzip license.
-r follows all directories and uncompress or compress files in subdirectories as well as the current directory.

-S string uses string as the file suffix instead of the default .gz.
-t checks compress file integrity.
-v is verbose.
-V displays gzip version.
-# is number 1 through 9 for compression levels; 1 performs the compression the fastest but does the worst job, while 9 takes the longest but maximizes the compression. The default is 5.
file ... is one or more files to compress or decompress.

You can place gzip default options in the environmental variable GZIP. These will be overridden by any command line options that conflict with those in GZIP.

gzip reduces the size of files anywhere from 50 to 70 percent depending on the structure and size of the file. Small files are not as effectively compressed due to the efficiency of the compression algorithm.

When you use gzip to compress a file, it is replaced with a file of the same name followed by a .gz. When you uncompress a file, a file with a .gz extension is searched for and replaced with an uncompressed version without the .gz extension.

Another command you can use is gunzip. The basic syntax is essentially the same as for gzip. In fact, they are symbolic links to each other. The syntax is:

```
gunzip [-cfhlLrtvV] [-S string] [file ...]
```

where the options are exactly the same as for gzip except for the -d, which is the uncompress option. gunzip is exactly the same as gzip -d.

You can also view files without actually uncompressing them with the command:

```
zcat [-fhLV] [file ...]
```

where the options are again the same as above. zcat will perform a cat (listing) of the information by uncompressing and piping the results to standard output, which is most often the screen. This is useful when you want to see what is contained in the file before uncompressing it, especially when disk space is limited.

You would typically pipe the output of the zcat command to a pager like more or pg. Because of the frequency of this need, there is the zmore tool. The syntax is:

```
zmore [file...]
```

zmore uses its own pager but does consult the PAGER environmental variable if you want to define a different pager such as pg or less. Its basic default pager behavior is that of more. Some of the more basic commands available with this pager are:

`=`	Displays the current line number.
`/string`	Finds the next occurrence of string and positions this on top of the screen.
`!command`	Invokes a shell command and returns to current location.
`.`	Repeats previous command.
`i-space`	i is a number which represents the number of lines to display. A space bar by itself displays a page defined by the TERM environmental variable.
`iz`	i lines is the new default window size.
`is`	Skips i lines and displays a screenful.
`if`	Skips i screenfuls and displays a screenful.
`q`	Quits.

These are fairly standard pager commands and provide much of the functionality you will need when previewing a file. If you need more, use an editor.

gzip and related commands will automatically detect the structure of the compressed file and generate the correct action to uncompress the file. pack and compress files are automatically recognized and processed correctly, as is gzip's own format for compressed files.

Keep in mind that gzip creates compressed files with a .z extension, which is the same as the pack command. You may use gzip to work with packed files, but not the reverse. You will discover this if you attempt to run the unpack command on a gzip format file.

If you want to compare compressed files, use the commands:

```
zcmp [coptions] file [file...]
zdiff [doptions] file [file...]
```

where coptions are options defined by your implementation of cmp.
doptions are options defined by your implementation of diff.
file—if only one file is specified, it is compared with a matching .z file; if more than one file is specified, it is compared with previous files.

zcmp and zdiff invoke cmp and diff, respectively. All zcmp and zdiff do is uncompress files and pass them to the cmp and diff utilities.

You can control the default behavior of gzip through the use of an environmental variable GZIP. You can define the default options for gzip by setting these in the GZIP variable. For example:

```
$ export GZIP="-r -v -9"
```

When you next invoke gzip, it will work with recursive and verbose modes enabled and will perform maximum compression, even if you don't explicitly specify them.

To move a file from compressed format (compress) to gzip format, use the command:

```
znew [-t][-v][-9][-K][-P] [file.Z ...]
```

where -t tests new file before deleting original.
-v is verbose mode.
-9 uses maximum compression.
-K keeps the .Z file when it is smaller than the new .z file.
-P uses pipes to bypass disk utilization, thus saving temporary disk space needs.
file.Z ... is one or more compressed files to convert.

11.2.3 Installation

gzip, as with most other newer GNU utilities, contains a configure script. To configure for the proper build sequence, move into the proper directory with the configure script and execute it. Note that the following command assumes you have placed the gzip files in a directory /usr/local/gzip/gzip-1.2.3:

```
$ configure --prefix=/usr/local/gzip/gzip-1.2.3
```

If you have problems on your particular platform, see Sec. 11.1 for more details.

After you have configured your system, type:

```
$ make clean
$ make install
```

The first make removes all executables and previously constructed build files. This ensures that you get a complete build for your particular platform. The second make compiles all executables for your platform and places them in the default install directories. The make install command installs the man pages and executables in the /usr/local/bin and /usr/local/man directories by default. If you want to override the location of these files, use a command like:

```
$ make prefix=/usr/local/gzip/gzip-1.2.3 all
```

or

```
$ configure --prefix=/usr/local/gzip/gzip-1.2.3
$ make install
```

They will cause all executables, libraries, and manual pages to be placed in a root directory of /usr/local/gzip/gzip-1.2.3 instead of the default /usr/local. Use this capability to place files according to your local product specifications.

There are a variety of macro variables (typically represented by uppercase characters in a makefile or build procedure) which can be changed based on your needs. While the configure script does a fairly good job of configuring the makefiles for your particular platform, you may need to change compiler optimization levels or other parameters related to the build procedure.

There is more information on the installation process for gzip in the INSTALL file in the main directory for the distribution of the product. Much of the information reviewed in the INSTALL file is covered in Sec. 11.1 and will not be discussed here. The installation of gzip is very straightforward and should not require any modification to the above procedure; however, if something does not work correctly, consult the INSTALL file for more details. There is also a file NEWS which contains information on recent capabilities and needs for the gzip product. See this for current and future release information.

Some of the basic warnings from the README file are:

> On the Mips R4000, the gcc (GNU C compiler) generates bad code; use the native C compiler instead.
>
> On the SGI Indigo, the gcc 2.3.3 compiler generates bad code; use the native C compiler instead.
>
> On SunOS 4.1.1, -O3 works, but -O4 does not, so don't maximize optimization.

These are some examples of information in the README file. Consult it for more information not only about the gzip product but about all Internet software products that have a README file.

11.2.4 Conclusion

gzip is a very powerful package for generation, control, and manipulation of compressed files. It will handle compressed and packed files as well as its own gzip format. Along with gzip and gunzip come a variety of utilities to manipulate compressed files. gzip is needed for almost all GNU distribution files since they are in gzip format and need to be uncompressed before use. gzip is clearly one of the most powerful and widely used Internet tools.

11.3 patch

11.3.1 Introduction

patch is a GNU application which is responsible for providing and installing patches to GNU software systems. patch supports the various outputs from diff as well as the diff output from the GNU diff executable.

By simply distributing a diff file, you can use patch to generate any required changes from one version to the next. An example of that is included on the CD with Ghostscript. If you look in the tar subdirectory for Ghostscript, you will see four compressed patch files. Uncompress (gzip -d) and examine them to learn more about the structure of the patch input files.

11.3.2 Usage

The basic syntax for the patch command is:

```
patch [-d dir] [-Eefsv][-o file] [origfile [patchfile]]
[+[options][origfile]]...
```

where -d dir changes directory to dir before executing any patch commands.
-E removes empty files after patches are applied.
-e causes patch to treat patch file as an ed script.
-f forces mode for patch.
-s is silent mode.
-v displays patch version.
-o file generates output file named file.
origfile is original file to be patched.
[options] are options listed above.
patchfile is file containing patch information.

There are many other options which allow you to change the structure of your patch files and change the default behavior of the patch command; however, since you will probably never use them, they are not documented here. For exact information on the syntax of the patch command and all associated options, see the manual page patch.man in the main patch directory.

As stated above, patch applies the results of diff commands to files. This provides a simple and consistent way of providing software patches to systems currently in use. patch is the most common way Internet software is patched and is therefore widely used.

The default behavior of patch is to apply the diffs to a given file and replace the original with the updated file. The original file is given an extension of .orig in the same directory. If the backup already exists, patch creates a copy of the backup file by changing the first lowercase letter in the file extension to uppercase. If all characters in the backup filename are uppercase, it begins removing a letter from the name until it creates a unique filename. This is then the second-level backup file.

patch supports several different types of patch files and is intelligent enough to determine which type of patch file it is operating on. You can override this with command line options, but it is not recommended unless you know what you are doing. patch also has some intelligence to help it determine when a patch file is corrupted. It then attempts to fix the patch file to ensure that the correct updates are made to the original files. If it cannot, you will get an error, and patch will fail.

If you are patching large files, you may want to set the TMPDIR variable, which specifies the location of all temporary files. The default location is /tmp. Finally, you can set the variable SIMPLE_ BACKUP_SUFFIX to change the default backup file suffix from .orig to anything you want.

The most common use of patch is without command line arguments and without origfiles. The basic syntax is:

```
$ patch <file
```

where file is the patchfile. This will apply all patches within file to all corresponding files in the current directory, creating new original files and renaming the original file with a .orig file extension.

Ghostscript 2.6.1 on the accompanying CD contains four patches which are contained in the tar subdirectory for Ghostscript itself. A piece of one of the patches, Ghostscript 2.6.1 Patch #1, is included here to illustrate the structure of a patch file. To apply this patch, cd to the directory containing the Ghostscript source and do:

```
patch -s < ThisFile
```

patch will work silently unless an error occurs. If you want to watch patch do its thing, leave out the -s argument to patch. See the readme.fix file, which follows, for a summary of the fixes.

```
*** /dev/null Sun Jun 27 07:26:01 1993
--- readme.fix Thu Jun 17 11:18:48 1993
***************
*** 0 ****
--- 1,118 ----
+ Copyright (C) 1993 Aladdin Enterprises. All rights reserved.
+
+ This file is part of Ghostscript; it is licensed under the same
+ terms as the rest of Ghostscript. If you do not have Ghostscript,
+ you do not have the right to have this file.
+
+ Fixes for Ghostscript 2.6.1
+ --------------------------
+
+ (last update: 6/14/93)
```

```
+
+ This file summarizes a number of important quality fixes for
+ Ghostscript 2.6.1. The fixes are supplied in the form of
+ replacements for corresponding files in the 2.6.1 release. Please
+ report any problems.
+
+ 6/5/93
+ ------
+
+ Problem:
+    The Unix install script used gs rather than $(GS) as the name of
+    the executable.
+    The Unix install script didn't copy gs_dbt_e.ps to $(gsdatadir).
+ Files affected:
+    unixtail.mak (and unix-*.mak, built from it using tar_cat)
+
+ Problem:
+    The ps2ascii script still referenced ps2ascii.ps under its
+    old name gs_2asc.ps.
+ Files affected:
+    ps2ascii
+
+ Problem:
+    ps2image.ps had a 'pop' missing in the written-out definition of
+    'max' in the boilerplate code it put at the beginning of
+    compressed files.
+    ps2image.ps got a typecheck if a scan line had no repeated
+    data in it anywhere.
+ Files affected:
+    ps2image.ps
+
+ Problem:
+    rectfill drew rectangles with vertices specified in clockwise
+    order as 0-width lines.
+ Files affected:
+    gsdps1.c
+    gdevx.c
...
*** 1.1 1993/06/27 12:24:14
--- devs.mak 1993/06/09 08:27:08
***************
*** 108,113 ****
--- 108,114 ----
# gifmono Monochrome GIF file format
# gif8 8-bit color GIF file format
# pcxmono Monochrome PCX file format
+ # pcxgray 8-bit gray scale PCX file format
# pcx16 Older color PCX file format (EGA/VGA, 16-color)
# pcx256 Newer color PCX file format (256-color)
# pbm Portable Bitmap (plain format)
***************
*** 756,765 ****

pcx_=gdevpcx.$(OBJ) gdevpccm.$(OBJ) gdevprn.$(OBJ)

! gdevpcx.$(OBJ): gdevpcx.c $(PDEVH) $(gdevpccm_h)

pcxmono.dev: $(pcx_)
      $(SHP)gssetdev pcxmono $(pcx_)

pcx16.dev: $(pcx_)
      $(SHP)gssetdev pcx16 $(pcx_)
-- 757,769 ----

x_=gdevpcx.$(OBJ) gdevpccm.$(OBJ) gdevprn.$(OBJ)
```

```
! gdevpcx.$(OBJ): gdevpcx.c $(PDEVH) $(gdevpccm_h) $(gxlum_h)
pcxmono.dev: $(pcx_)
     $(SHP)gssetdev pcxmono $(pcx_)
+
+ pcxgray.dev: $(pcx_)
+      $(SHP)gssetdev pcxgray $(pcx_)
pcx16.dev: $(pcx_)
     $(SHP)gssetdev pcx16 $(pcx_)?
*** 1.1 1993/06/27 12:24:14
--- gdevpcx.c 1993/06/01 12:21:26
***************
*** 1,4 ****
! /* Copyright (C) 1992 Aladdin Enterprises. All rights reserved.
This file is part of Ghostscript.
--- 1,4 ----
! /* Copyright (C) 1992, 1993 Aladdin Enterprises. All rights
reserved.
This file is part of Ghostscript.
***************
*** 20,25 ****
--- 20,26 ----
/* PCX file format devices for Ghostscript */
#include "gdevprn.h"
#include "gdevpccm.h"
+ #include "gxlum.h"
/* Thanks to Phil Conrad for donating the original version */
/* of these drivers to Aladdin Enterprises. */
***************
```

The first part of the above patch contains documentation which is inserted into the file readme.fix. This is documented by the section:

```
*** /dev/null Sun Jun 27 07:26:01 1993
--- readme.fix Thu Jun 17 11:18:48 1993
***************
*** 0 ****
--- 1,118 ----
```

The original file to be modified is surrounded by ***s, and the modified file information is surrounded by ---. In this case there is no original file, and a new file readme.fix is created with 118 lines (denoted by 1,118.)

The second file to be modified is devs.mak. The section:

```
*** 1.1 1993/06/27 12:24:14
--- devs.mak 1993/06/09 08:27:08
***************
*** 108,113 ****
--- 108,114 ----
```

says that devs.mak's original lines 108 through 113 should be replaced by lines 108 through 114 which are documented directly below the --- 108, 114 ---- line.

This is the standard output structure from a diff command. See the diff manual page for more information and also create some simple examples to understand more clearly how this patch system works. However, unless you are going to create patches, it will probably be unnecessary for you to understand the structure of the patch files to use them.

Most often the syntax is:

```
$ patch < patchfile
```

used in the proper directory; the rest is magic.

11.3.3 Installation

The installation of patch is very simple. patch uses the configure system to create a relatively straightforward makefile which can then be executed normally. The basic commands are:

```
$ ./configure
$ make
```

Note that configure is intelligent enough to generate the appropriate makefile, and the makefile works without any additional option. If you want to place the binaries in some other directory than the main patch subdirectory, use the make install option (for more details see Sec. 11.1).

There are no problems with this simple methodology on the IBM RS/6000 or on Sun running SunOS 4.1.3. You may have to change a compilation or linking variable if you encounter problems on your machine, but it is unlikely.

11.3.4 Conclusion

patch is a very powerful tool which allows you to distribute software updates easily and cleanly. It is also the way most Internet tools are now updated and should be another tool in your personal UNIX tool kit.

By supporting both standard diff and GNU diff, patch allows diff files to be used to support distributed file maintenance and updates.

11.4 imake

11.4.1 Introduction

imake is a facility which generates makefiles in conjunction with the C preprocessor (cpp). It allows you to generate different makefiles based on cpp directives such as #define and #include. It provides you with the ability to include and define the appropriate information into your makefiles so they will build correctly. When you use a heterogeneous environment, this becomes a very powerful tool to build portable makefiles where you can have imake determine what type of machine you are on and build the appropriate makefile. This is a very powerful feature and is often used by the more complex and sophisticated packages on the Internet.

imake is used by older software systems from the Internet; it became fairly widely used because the X11 distributions used it to generate their makefiles. In fact, imake still comes with distributions of X11. The distribution included with this book is a subset of those commands directly related to the imake and associated commands. It contains some imake-related files for X11R4 as well as a separate directory for X11R5 files. See the imake subdirectory on the CD for more information.

imake is part of the X11 distribution and as such is copyrighted by Massachusetts Institute of Technology (M.I.T.). They have provided this technology free given the M.I.T. copyright notice in App. B. See this or the software distribution itself for more details.

11.4.2 Usage

The basic syntax for imake is:

```
imake [-Ddefine] [-Idir] [-Ttemplate] [-f file] [-s file] [-e] [-v]
```

where -Ddefine allows you to issue #define definitions to pass to cpp.
-Idir—dir is the directory of the Imakefile templates.
-Ttemplate—template is used to give the name of the template files.
-f file—file is the per directory input template (default Imakefile).
-s file—file is the name of the output file (default is Makefile).
-e executes the makefile after it is generated (this is not the default).
-v is verbose mode.

imake uses a variety of files to generate the final makefile. It works by placing a preprocessor file named Imakefile in each directory which contains something to be built. imake also uses a generic template file named Imake.tmpl to get generic machine-specific information. Finally, Imake.rules contain information on a specific platform which will provide imake with the ability to generate the exact makefile necessary to build on a particular platform. All files are passed first through cpp to preprocess any cpp directives. The results of this preprocessing pass are incorporated into the resulting file makefile.

When you invoke imake, it passes all variables contained in the -I and -D command line options as well as the following lines:

```
#define IMAKE_TEMPLATE "Imake.tmpl"
#define INCLUDE_IMAKEFILE "Imakefile"
#include IMAKE_TEMPLATE
```

The convention for variable definitions is that imake variables are mixed case, while make variables are uppercase.

The Imake.rules file contains cpp preprocessor macros of the form:

```
string(s) @@\
```

An example, as outlined in the imake man page, might be something like:

```
#define   program_target(program, objlist)  @@\
program:  objlist                           @@\
          $(CC) -o $@ objlist $(LDFLAGS)
```

When you call it with a command like program_target(foo, foo1.o, foo2.o), it will be expanded to:

```
foo:  foo1.o foo2.o
      $(CC) -o $@ foo1.o foo2.o $(LDFLAGS)
```

You can see that the rules file is important in that it allows you to define your own cpp macros in your Imakefiles. For a good example of a complex Imake.rules, see the ./config subdirectory on the CD.

There are several environmental variables which can be used to alter the default behavior of imake. Some of the most important are:

IMAKEINCLUDE	Any valid directory for include files to cpp
IMAKECPP	Cpp to use including fully qualified pathname
IMAKEMAKE	Make to use including fully qualified pathname

You can use macro definitions and redirections as you normally would with any cpp file and directives.

For more information on imake and its associated files, see the manual page for imake in the config subdirectory included with the X11R5 imake distribution. This directory also contains a variety of configuration (cf) files for different architectures which help to define variables for several different kinds of UNIX machines.

The misc subdirectory contains a variety of files which contain notes for porting imake and its associated files to a variety of different platforms. While this provides much of the capabilities for a limited number of machines, you will probably need to use some of your own definitions and learning as you move imake to your particular platform.

One file to examine in this distribution is the XNotes.ps (Postscript) or XNotes.txt (ASCII text) file which contains a variety of information related to X11R5 and its compilation; it will show you what is involved in the build of X11R5.

There are a variety of other tools in the scripts subdirectory, including the xmkmf command. The basic syntax of this command is:

```
xmkmf [-a] [topdir [curdir]]
```

where -a builds the makefile in the current directory and invokes any subdirectory makefiles automatically.
topdir is the root directory where makefile search should begin.
curdir—you can set this to allows xmkmf to reference any directory as its current directory.

xmkxf is an easy command interface to imake. It makes assumptions as to its directory structure and the location of imake template files. This is often run by X11 distributions to generate the proper makefiles from the Imakefiles. A simple example of how xmkmf and imake are related follows:

```
$ ../../config/imake -I../../config -DTOPDIR=../../.
- DCURDIR=./lib/X
```

or

```
$ xmkmf ../../. ./lib/X
```

These two commands accomplish the same thing. They are taken directly from the man page for xmkmf and demonstrate the simplicity of xmkmf. Most machines that run X Windows come with this command, although they may not have a man page. Look in the X11 area for the file xmkmf and the subsequent man page for more information.

Another command that is often useful is imdent. This is a script contained in the scripts subdirectory. imdent lists all cpp directives and their associated nesting level. This allows you to see how your Imakefiles are structured and to ensure that you don't have any nesting problems. The basic syntax is:

```
imdent [-n] [file...]
```

where -n specifies the number of spaces used to designate indentation between nesting levels. Default is two spaces.
file... is one or more files to analyze. Default is standard input.

The final command of interest with this distribution is the mkdirhier command. This will create any directory hierarchy including any intermediate subdirectories as necessary. This is different from the mkdir command, which forces you to create all intermediate subdirectories. The basic syntax is:

```
mkdirhier file
```

where file is any directory you wish to create. This command is very useful when creating nested subdirectories. Unlike the mkdir command, it is not necessary to create any intervening subdirectories before creating the file subdirectory. An example is:

```
$ ls -R
file1 file2
$ mkdirhier ./sub1/sub2
$ ls -R
fil1 file2
./sub1:
sub2
```

Note that, unlike mkdir, it was unnecessary to create the sub1 directory and then create the sub2 directory. This is very useful when installing software and building complex systems.

11.4.3 Installation

Most platforms that have X11 distributions have imake on them. Issue a command like:

```
$ find /usr/X11 -name imake -print
```

on the proper directory for your X11 software, and you will probably see the imake distribution. If you do not have it, you either need to get an X11 distribution such as X11R4 or X11R5 or to examine the file distributed on this CD. This was taken from the Internet under the systems/apollo section and has not actually been built on anything other than an apollo. There is probably a version built for your system included with your X11 files. Check there for a version for your system.

If you want to build the imake distributed with this book, simply move to the installation directory and type:

```
$ make clean
$ make World
```

This will generate ./config/imake, which you can then execute on your particular platform. This also generates the makedepend executable in the ./util /makedepend subdirectory. See the next section for more information on this tool.

In the ./util/msub, the msub executable is generated. The msub command is an executable which substitutes make variables into a script which can be used to propagate other files. If you would like more information, see the man page in the ./util/msub directory.

11.4.4 Conclusion

imake is a very powerful facility which is typically shipped with X11 distributions because of their dependency on them. This book includes both a tar file of some X11R4 imake files and a larger distribution of X11R5-related files.

imake allows you to use cpp directives within a makefile and preprocess the appropriate information into the resulting makefile for a specific platform. It is a very powerful tool and is something to consider when distributing software systems to heterogeneous environments.

11.5 makedepend

11.5.1 Introduction

makedepend is a tool which allows you to automatically generate makefiles from source files. Instead of manually scanning through all source files and dependencies and generating the makefile manually, you can issue the makedepend command and have it automatically build one for you. Instead of the tedious job of creating and typing makefiles, which is not only boring but prone to mistakes, you can use the makedepend command to generate makefiles for you. While it is not always perfect, it is very reliable and will generate correct and working makefiles in many cases.

makedepend has been delivered with X11 distributions since X11R3. First check in your X11 area for the existence of a makedepend executable in the bin subdirectory. If you don't have this, you will need to get the tar file from the included CD. This software is included in the imake directory described in the previous section. However, the makedepend software is what this section focuses on.

11.5.2 Usage

The basic syntax for makedepend is:

```
makedepend [-Dname=def] [-Dname] [-Idir] [- fmakefile] [-oobjsuffix]
[-sstring] [-wwidth] [- - options - -] file ...
```

where -Dname=def defines name as def as a macro for make.
-Dname defines name as 1.
-Idir searches dir for include files when building the makefile.
-ffile places all output from makedepend in file (the default is Makefile unless there is a makefile in the current directory).
-oobjsuffix is the object file suffix.
-sstring is the starting string delimiter.
-wwidth is the line width of output file (default is 78).
- - options—options between double hyphens are silently ignored.
file ... is one or more files to scan as input files.

makedepend scans each file on the input line for each of the following statements:

```
#include, #define, #undef, #ifdef, #ifndef, #endif, #if, #else
```

All include files will be scanned for any nested # statements, and these will be built and reflected in the resulting makefile. All include files are called dependencies. These match the dependency statements in the resulting makefile. The basic format of the output is:

```
file.o: dfile
```

where file.o is the file from the makedepend command line and dfile is the filename from the #include statements within file.

If a file named makefile exists, makedepend uses this file and searches for the line:

```
# DO NOT DELETE THIS LINE -- makedepend depends on it.
```

It replaces information following the above line with the output from the current makedepend run. You can change the above line with the -s option.

11.5.3 A simple example

Assume you have a main file named main.c which includes the following statements:

```
#include def.h
#include num.h

main() {
...
```

The include file def.h consists of the following text:

```
#include string.h
#include exp.h
...
```

and the file num.h includes the following text:

```
#include int.h
#include float.h
...
```

If you issue the command:

```
$ makedepend main.c
```

you will get a new makefile with input from the above main.c consisting of dependencies and targets.

11.5.4 Installation

The installation of this product is exactly the same as imake, which was described in the previous section. In fact, the commands documented in the installation section for imake will build makedepend as well.

There is a man page called mkdepend.man in the imake.X11R5/util/makedepend directory. Issue the command:

```
$ nroff -man mkdepend.man | more
```

to see it displayed on your screen.

11.5.5 Conclusions

makedepend is a powerful tool for building makefiles automatically; it removes the monotonous and error-prone activity of generating your makefiles manually. makedepend generates fairly reliable and robust makefiles and can be counted on to generate usable makefiles.

makedepend comes with most X11 distributions, and you should use the version distributed with your machine if you have it. See the imake distribution on the CD included with this book for makedepend distributions that are not part of X11.

11.6 gcc and g++

11.6.1 Introduction

gcc is the GNU C compiler and is widely considered to be the best available, better than those available directly from the vendors. Because of the wide acceptance of the gcc, it has become the de facto standard in many makefile and build procedures. This chapter cannot cover all aspects of gcc; however, it will discuss its most important aspects and will describe where and how to get more information. Much of the information in this section is taken directly from files delivered with the gcc product. See below for more information.

With the version 2 release of the gcc system, the C compiler (gcc) and C++ compiler (g++) have been put together. This provides a compiler and preprocessor for both the object-oriented C++ environment and the C language environment. This is the only compiler system available today which has this capability. Note, however, that the run-time libraries for the g++ system are not delivered with this distribution and must be retrieved and installed separately.

Another thing important to note is that because of changes in gcc 2.4, the newly created binaries are incompatible with earlier binaries created by earlier versions of gcc. Keep this in mind if you attempt to link or use cross-compiled binaries. gcc 2.4 also supports a floating-point emulation subsystem, which makes it possible to use longer floating-point types as well as support both big and little endian environments in a cross-compiler mode. gcc 2.4 now supports Objective C, which is another object-oriented environment which provides significant value to object-oriented programmers. Finally, there are many features for C++ which are documented in the NEW file. Remember that to effectively use the C++ capability of gcc, you should also use the libg++ files. These files are contained on the CD included with this book.

It is not the intention of this chapter to provide programming information or tips but instead to present some of the capabilities and options that the GNU compilation system provides. While many options are discussed in this chapter, they are by no means all options that are available. See the GNU documentation in *Using and Porting GNU CC,* which are available from a variety of sources including the Free Software Foundation and the gcc distribution in texinfo format. See Sec. 11.15 to learn how to get this information.

gcc is a GNU product and as such is subject to the GNU General Public license as included both in the product distribution and App. B of this book.

11.6.2 Usage

The basic usage of the gcc compiler is:

```
gcc [options | file] ...
g++ [options | file] ...
```

where - option is one of a list of many options, some of which are described below.
- file ... is one or more source input files.

gcc invokes the C compiler and uses defaults a standard C compiler would.
g++ invokes the C++ compiler and uses defaults a standard C++ compiler would.

The options for gcc and g++ are many and can be divided into major sections which are determined by functionality. The basic areas of option functionality, as defined by the GNU documentation, are:

1. Overall options
2. Language options
3. Warning options
4. Debugging options
5. Optimization options
6. Preprocessor options
7. Linker options
8. Directory options
9. Target options
10. Machine-dependent options
11. Code generation options

Each section will be reviewed, and some of the more powerful options will be discussed.

Overall options. The overall options section describes options which apply to the entire command line and compilation process. Some of the options are:

`-E`	Stops after preprocessing
`-S`	Creates an assembler file for each source code input file
`-c`	Creates object files but does not link to create the executable
`-o file`	Places the output in file instead of the standard a.out or *.o
`-pipe`	Uses pipes to communicate between phases of the compilation process instead of using temporary files
`-v`	Verbose mode
`-x language`	Specifies a specific language to compile where the possibilities for language are: assembler assembler-with-cpp c c-header c++ cpp-output objective-c

Language options. These options provide different levels of support for different versions and syntax of the various supported GNU languages. Some of the possible options are:

`-ansi`	Supports ANSI standard syntax.
`-fdollars-in-identifiers`	Supports $ signs in identifiers. This is the default when the -ANSI switch is not used.
`-fall-virtual`	C++ only. All member functions declared in the same class with a method-call operator method are treated as a virtual function of the given class (except constructor functions nd new/delete member operators).
`-fenum-int-equiv`	C++ only. Allows conversion of enum to int datatype.
`-fno-builtin`	Turns off support for non-ANSI built-in functions.
`-fno-strict-prototype`	This is supported for g++ only. Causes declaration statements to specifically not type function arguments.
`-fsigned-bitfields`	Specifies signed bitfields for all machine types.
`-funsigned-bitfields`	Specifies unsigned bitfields for all machine types.
`-funsigned-char`	Defines the type char to be unsigned for all machine types.
`-fsigned-char`	Defines the type char to be signed for all machine types.
`-traditional`	Includes support for Kernighan and Ritchie C syntax.
`-traditional-cpp`	Includes support for original cpp syntax.
`-trigraph`	Includes support for ANSI C trigraphs.

Preprocessor options. These options control the preprocessor phase of the compilation process. Some of the options available are:

`-C`	Keeps comments.
`-Dmacro`	Defines macro macro.
`-Dmacro=string`	Defines macro macro as string.
`-Umacro`	Undefines macro.
`-E`	Runs only the preprocessor phase.
`-H`	Displays each header file as used.
`-M`	Generates a rule which describes the relationship between all files in the compilation process. This can be used by make as a dependency listing.
`-MM`	Like -M but only describes header files included with #include.
`-P`	Does not create #line commands.
`-dM`	Outputs list of macros.
`-i file`	Processes file as input discarding all output. This makes macros available to a later part of the preprocessor process.
`-nostdinc`	Uses only include directories specified on the command line and not the standard directories.

Linker options. Linker options pertain to the link editor processing which generates executables from one or more object files. Some of the more basic are:

`-llib`	Links with the library lib. lib files are normally archive libraries (see Sec. 4.4 for more details).
`-nostdlib`	Doesn't use any standard system libraries; uses only those specified.
`-static`	Uses static libraries. Dynamic libraries are not used.

Directory options. Directory options specify directories on which to operate. Most compilation phases have default directories and areas in which they look. These commands modify the default behavior of the compilation commands. Some of the most basic are:

`-Bdir`	Specifies a directory to search for all compilation process executables (e.g., cpp, cc1, and ld).
`-I-`	Directories specified with -I- and with -Idir before -I- are searched only for #include "file" and not #include <file>.
`-Idir`	Searches for include files in dir.
`-Ldir`	Searches directory for archive library files.

Warning options. Warning options control the output of all diagnostic messages. Some of the most basic are:

`-W`	Displays extra warning messages pertaining to optimization problems, function prototyping, and possible type problems.
`-Wall`	all -W switches documented below.
`-Wformat`	Checks all output statement formats and ensures that output variables match output type definitions.
`-Wimplicit`	Warns when a function is implicitly declared.
`-Wswitch`	Warns when a switch statement is not constructed with all possible types.
`-Wuninitialized`	Warns when an automatic variable is used without being initialized.
`-Wunused`	Warns when a variable or function is not used.
`-fsyntax-only`	Runs a syntax check on the code but doesn't compile.
`-pedantic`	Issues all non-ANSI warning messages as appropriate.
`-w`	Suppresses all warning messages.

There are many other possible warnings you can set when compiling and building programs with gcc and g++. See the man page gcc.1 in the main directory for more detail on these warning triggers.

Debugging options. Options which support the debugging of your codes are important and are therefore the focus of one section of this chapter. The GNU compiler provides many, some of which are described below:

`-dx`	Where x is one of the following: L—dump after loop analysis M—dump all macro definitions N—dump all macro names f—dump after flow analysis l—dump after local register allocation

	m—dump memory usage statistics at end of run y—dump debugging information The dump commands provide information for stages of the compilation process. This may be used to debug gcc itself.
`-g`	Includes debugging information which can be used by gdb or dbx or DWARF. The GNU system allows you to use -g with optimization. This is the only system available which does this, and it can be a timesaver when you are moving and porting large amounts of code. The native debugging format is determined at build time for gcc. See the installation section for more details.
`-gcoff`	Produces debugging information in COFF format.
`-dgdbx`	Produces debugging information for dbx.
`-gdwarf`	Produces debugging information for DWARF.
`-ggdb`	Produces debugging information for gdb.
`-gsdb`	Produces debugging information for sdb.
`-gxcoff`	Produces debugging information in xcoff format.
`-p`	Includes information for the prof command.
`-pg`	Includes information for the gprog command.
`-save-temps`	Saves all temporary files including .cpp and .s files.

Optimization options. Optimization will make your code run more quickly by rearranging statements and reorganizing the way your code works. This provide significant enhancements in the performance of your code while requiring almost no work on your part. It does have one side effect, however. By rearranging the code, you may have problems with interactive debugging because debugging information in the executable may or may not match what is being executed. GNU has addressed this and provides the capability to debug optimized code.

With optimization options, there are many commands that begin with -f. The basic structure of these options is:

```
-foption
-fno-option
```

where the no- precedes and turns off option. For every - foption, there is a -fno-option which is exactly the opposite. Because of this, GNU documentation only describes one or the other. The option described is *not* the default. Obviously, to get the default behavior you simply add or remove the no- options as described, and you can understand the default behavior of the compiler.

Some of the more basic options are (remember they are *not* the default):

`-O`	Optimizes.
`-O2`	Highly optimizes.
`-ffloat-store`	Doesn't store floating-point variables in registers.
`-fno-default-inline`	C++ only. With this option you must member functions as in-line explicitly rather than assuming it is the default.

`-finline`	Expands functions in-line instead of the default of - fno-inline.
`-finline-functions`	Expands all functions into their callers.

There are many other -f options related to code optimization; however, they are beyond the scope of this book. They assume a great understanding of the compilation process and machine architectures, which most people do not have. Examine the manual page for gcc for more information if you are interested.

Target options. You can specify a different compiler, including version and machine architecture, by generating a different target environment. This allows you to generate code for a machine architecture that is different from your current one and to use older or newer versions of the GNU compiler to generate the appropriate code. This is a very powerful feature of the GNU compiler.

Some of the basic options related to this are:

`-b machine`	Machine specifies a target machine for which to build the executable. This relates directly to the gcc installation process and its generation as a cross-compiler. See Sec. 11.6.3 for more details.
`-V version`	Specifies which version of the GNU compiler to run. This is useful when you have installed multiple versions in a cross-compiler environment.

Machine-dependent options. gcc and g++ have many features that are tuned to maximize performance on a particular hardware platform. Because of this, there are many options which control the exact compilation process for any given architecture. There are sets of -m options pertinent to several different hardware architectures. Some of the more basic for the Motorola 6980x0 processors are:

`-m68000`	Compiles for a 68000 processor
`-m68881`	Compiles for a 68881 floating-point processor
`-mfpa`	Compiles for a Sun floating-point processor
`-mshort`	Makes int 16 bits wide
`-mbitfield`	Uses the bitfield instruction (this is the default)
`-mnobitfield`	Doesn't use the bitfield instruction

For the Sun SPARC processors, they are:

`-mfpu`	Compiles using floating-point instructions
`-mno-epilogue`	Generates separate return instructions for return statements

For the Motorola 88x00 processors, they are:

--mbig-pic	Compiles position independent code
-midentify-revision	Includes ident information in the assembler output
-mno-underscores	Generates symbol names without a preceding underscore (_)
-mcheck-zero-division	Generates software traps for divide by zero exceptions
-mno-ocs-debug-info	Omits debugging information as specified by the 88open Object Compatibility Standard
-msvr4	Turns on compiler extensions which are supported in System V Release 4
-msvr3	Turns on compiler extensions which are supported in System V Release 3

For the RS/6000 machine, the option is:

-mno-fp-in-toc	Defines no floating-point constants in the table of contents; the default is -mfp-in-toc.

There are other machine-specific options for MIPS, IBM RT, Convex, and C2. See the documentation delivered with gcc for more information.

Code generation options. Code generation options determine interface options for code generation including function call definitions and variable and structure definitions. Some of the most basic are:

+eN	Where N is 0 or 1. +e0 declares virtual function definitions as extern and is used as an interface definition. No code is generated for this virtual function. +e1 actually generates virtual function code.
-fshort-enums	Allocates on as many bytes to an enum as are required.
-fshort-double	Makes double same size as float.
-fno-common	Places global variables in bss section rather than generating them as common blocks.
-fvolatile	Defines all memory references through pointers to be volatile.
-fpic	Generates position-independent code.

There are many other options relating to most major compiler options areas discussed in this section. See the man page gcc.1 or documentation from GNU for more information.

The GNU C preprocessor. One of the tools distributed with gcc and g++ is the GNU C preprocessor known as cccp. This is a replacement tool for the standard ccp which comes with most C compilers. It allows you to include precompiler directives such as #include and #define to control the behavior of the code and the compiler as well as to build conditional code based on predefined macros. The basic syntax of the command is:

```
cccp [-$] [-Apredicate[(value)]] [-C] [-Dname[=def]] [-dD] [dM]
  [-I dir] [-H] [-I-]
[-idirafer dir] [-imacros file] [-include file] [-lang-c]
  [-lang-c++] [-lang-objc]
[-lang-objc++] [-lint] [-M] [-MD] [-MM] [-MMD] [-nostdinc] [-P]
  [-pedantic]
[-pedantic-errors] [-trigraphs][-Uname][-undef][-Wtrigraphs]
  [-Wcomment] [-Wall] [-Wtraditional] [infile | -] [output | -]
```

where -$ doesn't support the use of $ in identifiers.

-Apredicate(value) asserts the predicate with value (much like #assert).

-C preserves comments.

-Dname[=def] predefines name as a macro with a definition of def.

-dD generates list of #define commands and the results of C preprocessing except for predefined macros.

-dM generates list of #define commands without any results from any other commands.

-I dir defines dir as a place to search for include files.

-H displays the name of each included header file.

-I—if any -I dir options follow the -I- all specified directories are searched for both the #include "file" and #include <file> directives. Any -I dir options specified before the -I-option cause only the #include "file" directives to search in dir and not #include <file>.

-idirafter dir adds dir to the secondary include search path.

-imacros file preprocesses file and discards all output except macros which are made available to the rest of the preprocessor process.

-include file includes file in the compilation process.

-lang-c turns off C++-specific features.

-lang-c++ turns on C++ support including comment support and extra default include directories.

-lang-objc turns on the Objective C #import directive.

-lang-objc++ turns on both -lang-c++ and lang-objc.

-lint examines input code for lint command and precedes with a #pragma directive.

-M outputs a rule for a makefile including all dependencies.

-MD—like -M but output is written to files with a .d extension instead of a .c with the same filename as the input files.

-MM—like -M but only outputs include files included with #include "file".

-MMD—like -MD except only include files are processed.

-nostdinc doesn't use standard include directories.

-P doesn't generate any # lines as output.

-pedantic checks for ANSI C compliance and issues warnings.
-pedantic-errors issues errors rather than warning as above.
-trigraphs supports trigraph sequences.
-Uname doesn't predefine the macro name.
-undef doesn't predefine any of the standard macros.
-Wtrigraphs issues a warning if any trigraphs are encountered.
-Wcomment issues a warning when a comment is encountered.
-Wall is the same as both -Wtrigraphs and -Wcomment.
-Wtraditional issues a warning when it encounters constructs which behave differently between ANSI C and traditional C.
infile | - —infile is the file to be processed. A hyphen (-) denotes standard input.
outfile | - —output is the output file. A hyphen (-) denotes standard output

The C preprocessor is the first link in the compilation chain. It is typically invoked by the cc command but can be invoked separately with the ccp or cccp command. cccp provides the function of including header files, expanding macros, and providing for conditional compilation. It is often used to generate machine-dependent sections in source programs where the end result is that only the appropriate lines of code are passed to the C compiler itself.

There is a man pages cccp.1 included in the gcc distribution which has more detailed information about the options and cccp itself. See this for more documentation.

g++. g++ is the C++ compiler which comes with gcc. It is essentially a script which passes the correct options to gcc to invoke the C++ portion of the gcc compiler. Its options are very similar to those supported by gcc, with a few exceptions. The man page g++.1 is a good listing of the issues and brief commands related to the g++ compiler. See this for more details on g++.

The other issue related to g++ is your need for libg++. This is a group of class libraries which complement gcc and g++. There are other directories including libiberty which contain a variety of commonly used GNU files. See Sec. 11.7 for more information.

Debugging issues and gcc/g++. GNU distributes a debugger known as gdb. Section 11.9 outlines the structure of how gdb works and what kind of information it expects. This is relevant to the gcc section because the gcc system is responsible for generation of the appropriate information so that gdb can function correctly.

The standard debugging system on UNIX is dbx, which comes native with most flavors of UNIX. You can use dbx on code compiled with gcc;

however, gdb has certain features which work better and more effectively with gcc-generated code.

One issue directly related to this is the special debugging output format known as DWARF. DWARF is a standard being developed by Unix International to define standard debugging formats. Version 1 is done and Version 2 is nearly done. gcc supports DWARF V1 except in some instances which may cause incompatibilities with SVR4 SDB. These are documented in the file README.DWARF in the gcc distribution. There is work in progress to finish the DWARF V2 specification. When this is finished, you can bet that gcc will work toward support of this standard. In fact many of the features of the early work on DWARF V2 are already incorporated in gcc.

There is not compatibility for DWARF with g++ and there may be none in the near future since there is some considerable debate about the need for DWARF and its relevance to C++. Watch the distribution information with new versions of g++ for more details.

Using gcc/g++ as a cross-compiler. One of the most powerful features of the gcc/g++ system is its ability to act as a cross-compiler. This means that gcc on one machine can generate code for a different machine architecture. For example, if you are running on a Sun, you can generate an executable that runs on an IBM RS/6000. This is extremely powerful and provides multiplatform support from a single machine architecture for not only source code but object and executable code as well. A simple example of this is given in the Examples section, and some discussion is made in the Installation section on how this is accomplished.

For each machine architecture you wish to support, you must install a version with the configure command and note the target or host architecture. This means that you will have a completely separate version of gcc/g++ for each architecture you wish to compile code for. For example, if you are running on an HP machine and plan to distribute executable code for a SUN and IBM RS/6000 as well, you will need to install and configure three separate versions of gcc on the HP machine if you wish to perform cross-compilations from one HP.

Now that you are excited about the possibility of performing cross-compilation, let's have a brief discussion of what you need to accomplish this. In addition to the gcc system, you need to provide both a cross-assembler and a cross-linker. These tools are available from a variety of vendors and can be used with gcc to create cross-compiles. You also need the appropriate header files for a particular machine so that linking can occur correctly. None of these is a "show stopper" but will require some additional work with respect to getting the appropriate tools to provide the cross-compilation capabilities. See the section on cross-compilation in the INSTALL document distributed with gcc for more guidance.

This is a very powerful feature of the gcc system and one which you should take advantage of if you are running in a heterogeneous environment of UNIX platforms. There are several ways you can get the proper tools assembled to create this capability. Don't let the complexity stop you from pursuing this capability if it is one you really need. See the Installation and Examples sections for more information.

11.6.3 Installation

gcc v2.4.5 comes as 23 files named part1 through part23. These must first be combined and then gunzipped before you can unwind the resulting tar file. If you are not familiar with this process, see Sec. 9.10 for more details.

The installation of gcc will create various directories including /usr/local/lib/gcc and /usr/local/bin if they don't already exist. You can redirect the result of the builds with specific commands; however, the default is to write to the /usr/local area. Check your product specifications and standards before installing gcc.

Once you have unwound the tar file, you will notice that there are several files related to the installation of gcc. Some of the more important are:

INSTALL

README

README.* where * stands for a variety of supported platforms including ALTOS, APOLLO, DWARF, ENCAP, MIPS, NS32K, RS6000, TRAD, and X11

ChangeLog.1-5

NEWS

The INSTALL file contains notes relevant to the building of gcc, while the README files contain specific information on particular platform issues. Inside the INSTALL file, there is a discussion of a variety of machine-specific issues. The ChangeLog files contain release and functionality information. The NEWS file contains "noteworthy changes" in the more recent versions of gcc and g++. Examine these files before proceeding.

The general build recommendation for gcc is the same as for most other GNU commands. First ensure that you have removed all executables and machine-dependent scripts with the command:

```
$ make clean
```

Next run the configure tool, which will build the appropriate makefiles and install scripts for your platform. There are a variety of platforms for which you can configure gcc. See Sec. 11.1 for more information about exact options and machine types for the configure command.

For an RS/6000 you need to be careful that, if you are going to use the -g option on the cc, you have PTF U416277 installed on your machine, or the build will not proceed correctly. If you are not interested in debug information, remote the -g option from the CFLAGS macro and the -g1 in the LIBGCC2_CFLAGS macro in Makefile.in before you run the configure command. You also need to remove the two occurrences of -g0 in the crtbegin.o (line 739) and crtend.o (line 743) targets. If you do not do this, you will get an assembler error that only the PTF mentioned above will fix. This change is not necessary in the Sun or HP environment.

For example, to configure gcc on an RS/6000, you might use a command like:

```
$ configure --prefix=/usr/local2/gcc/gcc-2.4.5 rs6000-aix
```

On a Sun machine, you might use a command like:

```
$ configure --prefix=/usr/local2/gcc/gcc-2.4.5 sparc-sun- sunos4.1
```

If you don't use the --prefix option, the configure will set up the default directories for the binaries and library files that result from the build to be in /usr/local/bin and /usr/local/lib. If you don't want to do this, use the --prefix and tell configure where you want the make to create the files.

Once you have created the proper build files, you need to examine the dates on the files c-parse.y, c-parse.c, cexp.y, and cexp.c. If the dates on the .c files are later than the dates on the .y files, you can proceed. If this is not the case, you need to either invoke yacc to rebuild the .c files or use the bison system, which is the GNU equivalent to yacc. See Sec. 11.13 for more details on GNU bison.

Build the compiler by first moving to the main directory and invoking the make command. For example:

```
$ make LANGUAGES=c
```

This builds only the C component of the compiler. This is the recommended technique if you are using anything other than previous version of GNU C compilers to build gcc. Many vendor-supplied compilers will not build gcc and g++, and therefore you may want to first build only the C compiler to minimize the number of possible build problems. If you are using a previous version of gcc, make sure you fully quality the gcc pathname to the makefile to ensure that you don't get a partially built version of gcc from the current directory.

Once you have built gcc with the above commands, you have built what is called the stage 1 group of the compiler system. This builds a minimal implementation of the gcc system which you can then use to build the entire gcc and g++ system. To take the results of the phase 1 compilation and move them to proper subdirectory, issue the command:

```
$ make stage1
```

This will create a stage1 subdirectory which contains all the necessary files to continue the gcc installation. At this stage, it is appropriate to create and move any other GNU executables that you may need to build the rest of the products into the stage1 subdirectory. An example tool is gas (GNU assembler and GNU linker). If you don't want to do this, you can modify the PATH variables to ensure that the GNU tools (as and ld) precede the standard vendors' versions of these products. This ensures that gcc finds these tools as it continues to build.

Next you should recompile the gcc compiler itself with a full implementation of the stage1 object files and executables. To do this, type:

```
$ make CC="stage1/xgcc -Bstage1/" CFLAGS="-g-O" LANGUAGE="c c++
objective-c"
```

Note that the default is to build everything; however, you can specify one or more of c, c++, or objective-c to build those individual products. This means that the LANGUAGE variable above is unnecessary since this is the default. However, you can specify one or more of the LANGUAGES listed above to build only those languages.

This generates what is known as the stage2 version of the products. With this you can generate what GNU calls the stage3 products by issuing the same make command above but substituting stage2 for stage1 in the above string. For example:

```
$ make stage2
$ make CC"stage1/xgcc -Bstage1/" CFLAGS="-g-O" LANGUAGE="c c++
objective-c"
```

This will create a stage3 subdirectory which contains identical information to the stage2 subdirectory. With this you can compare the stage2 and stage3 subdirectories with the command:

```
$ make compare
```

If there are any differences, you have a problem. If there are no differences, you can remove the stage3 subdirectory.

To install the created files, issue the command:

```
$ make install CC="stage2/xgcc -Bstage2/" CFLAGS="-g -O"
LANGUAGES="c c++
objective-c"
```

This installation procedure copies the gcc executable to the /usr/local/bin directory and cc1, cpp, and libgcc.a to /usr/local/lib/gcc-lib/TARGET/VERSION where TARGET is that specified to configure and VERSION is the version of gcc you are building unless you specified a --prefix on the configure or make command above. If you used the --prefix directory, the make install will install the binaries in the prefix directory in a bin subdirectory, the libraries in the prefix directory in a lib subdirectory, and so forth. This is a powerful capability which allows the products to be grouped closely with the source code. It fits with the overall software structure and philosophy discussed in this book. It will be necessary to include the correct directory in the PATH variable for the gcc executable to ensure that all other scripts and product builds know of the existence of gcc.

You can specify a different directory for these files with the libdir and prefix switches on the make statement as documented above. Experiment with these variables if you need to modify the location of these files to conform to your product standards.

If you have problems with the installation related to include file syntax, try the command:

```
$ make install-fixincludes
```

Install the objective-c portion of the compiler with the command:

```
$ make install-libobjc CC="stage2/xgcc -Bstage2/" CFLAGS="-g -O"
```

If you want to use the g++ capability of this distribution, you need to install the libg++ run-time libraries. See Chap. 9 for more information on how to get this distribution. If you have problems, you can always type:

```
$ make clean
```

and begin the build process again. It is generally not recommended to place things in /usr/local/bin since there are a variety of benefits to keeping products together. Even though this is not in the "UNIX tradition," it is beneficial to keep executables closely grouped with their source files. Even though the new configure methodology will allow for multiple versions of the same binary by creating directories under /usr/local/lib and other directories, you can still have unanticipated side effects, so be careful.

If you want to use gcc as a cross-compiler system, you must repeat the above process using a different target architecture in a different directory structure to create a gcc version which will generate code for this different architecture. Note that there are several problems with this, not the least of which is that you need to provide cross-linkers and cross-assemblers. gcc generates assembler code which must be assembled and linked for the appropriate platform. You must provide those cross-assembler and cross-linker files. These are available from a variety of vendors including those who develop embedded control systems and on-line systems. If you can get this technology, gcc will provide a transparent executable portability and cross-compilation system. See the INSTALL document distributed with gcc for more information on cross-compilation.

One you have installed the version for the particular architecture, you can use machine-specific options (-m...) for that platform as you would if that were the native implementation for your current hardware platform.

Once you have successfully installed the product, you will want to remove any excess directories because of their large size. Issue the command:

```
$ rm -r stage1
```

stage2 will contain the correct executables for gcc and will ensure that you have the minimum numbers of files to reconstruct gcc should you need to.

Other known problems. You can install this system on an HP machine, but you may need gas and gdb, which are the GNU assembler and debugger, respectively. There is an incompatibility between debugging formats on the HP machines which requires the use of GNU tools when building gcc. See the INSTALL file distributed with gcc for more information.

There is also a potential bug when compiling gcc on a Sun with the native Sun C compiler in that you may run out of environmental variable space. If this occurs, see the INSTALL page for more details on how to avoid this problem.

There are other problems with AT&T 3b machines and VMS but these are beyond the scope of this book. See the INSTALL file for more details on these platforms. Also remember to look at the README.*

files where the * is ALTOS, APOLLO, DWARF, ENCAP, MIPS, NS32K, RS6000, TRAD, and X11. Information specific to these implementations is contained in these documents.

Examples. Some simple examples of invoking gcc follow. To invoke the compiler with ANSI C language support, type:

```
$ gcc -ansi -o kevin.exe kevin.c
```

which processes kevin.c and generates an executable named kevin.exe. Note that the directory must be in your path or fully qualified on the command line.

To invoke the compiler and build object files without linking the final executable, type:

```
$ gcc -c file1.c file2.c
```

The result of the above command is file1.o and file2.o.

If you want to see the preprocessed code as it would be passed to the compiler, use the command:

```
$ gcc -E kevin.c > kevin.output
```

and examine kevin.output, which will contain all preprocessed information and the original source code.

To use directories that are different from the standard for include files, use a command like:

```
$ gcc -I /usr/local/kevin/lib kevin.c
```

which will cause gcc to search in /usr/local/kevin/lib for include files instead of in the standard directories.

To generate files used for debugging, type:

```
$ gcc -g kevin.c
```

which will create a file a.out which includes debugging information which can be used by gdb, dbx, or other debuggers.

Finally, if you want to highly optimize your code after you are confident it is working correctly, type:

```
$ gcc -O2 kevin.c
```

This will generate an a.out which runs faster than the nonoptimized version.

To invoke gcc as a cross-compiler, use the -b switch as follows:

```
$ gcc -b sparc-sun-sunos4.1 kevin.c
```

This will create an a.out file which can run on a Sun machine even though you may have compiled it on a non-Sun platform. See the section "Using gcc/gtt as a cross-compiler," above, for more details.

Service. There is a file named SERVICE which provides a listing of people and organizations which provide support and assistance with gcc. See this file if you are interested in additional support for your gcc system above and beyond what you get from GNU and the Internet community.

11.6.4 Conclusion

Much of the above information was gleaned from the manual page that comes with gcc. See this manual page and the associated texinfo documentation for more details.

gcc is one of the best C compilers available today, and it runs on virtually every platform. With the Version 2 distribution, you get both a C compiler and a C++ compiler. This provides incredible functionality while maintaining relative simplicity in terms of use and installation. It should be noted that g++ is a real C++ compiler and not simply a front-end tool which converts C++ to C and then compiles it. This provides a much better and more powerful capability and subsequent code than some of the other C++ front ends available on the market today.

There are many options, most of which you will never use. However, it is nice to know that this kind of functionality is available if you do need it. There are more options available than are documented in this chapter. See the delivered documentation for more information. gcc/g++ is one tool which you should definitely investigate.

11.7 libg++

11.7.1 Introduction

libg++ is a collection of libraries which are commonly used by g++ and gcc for compilation and construction of programs. Several other libraries are included with this distribution, including the liberty library of free software. This consists of a collection of commonly used GNU routines and class libraries. There is a significant amount of documentation included with this distribution in the form of texinfo files. See Sec. 11.15 for more information on texinfo and how to access this information.

libg++ is a GNU product and as such is subject to its GNU Library General Public license as included both in the product distribution as well as in App. B of this book.

11.7.2 Usage

The usage of libg++ is really from tools like g++. There are no interactive commands which you can execute to produce anything of value. The value of libg++ is the class libraries included with the distribution. There are many class libraries and examples of C++ source code contained in this distribution. Some of the classes in libg++ 2.4 are:

IOStream	List
Stream	LinkList
Obstack	Vector
AllocRing	Plex
String	Stack
Integer	Queue
Rational	Deque
Complex	PQ
Fix	Set
Bit	Bag
Random	Map
Data	GetOpt
Curses	Projects

These classes provide numerous capabilities to work with a variety of different objects with the g++ compiler. There is more documentation in the .info files in the libg++ subdirectory. See these and Sec. 11.15 for more details.

11.7.3 Installation

The first file to examine in the distribution is the ./libg++/README file. This contains various pieces of important advice that you should be aware of before attempting to build the product. Some of the more important points are:

Use gcc to compile libg++ and use a version of gcc that is at least as high as the version of libg++, in this case gcc 2.4 or greater.

If you haven't installed the gcc compiler in the expected /usr/local area, you must create a symbolic link in the main directory (one level above the libg++ subdirectory which points directly to the gcc executable so that the make can find gcc.

Don't use GNU sed 1.12, or you will have build problems.

The installation of libg++ is very straightforward and uses configure as most other GNU programs do. At the top directory of the libg++ distribution (probably libg++-2.4), type the following to see what configuration configure thinks your machine is:

```
$ config.guess
```

From this, type the proper configure and TARGET command. The other issue is to make sure configure can find the gcc compiler since this is important to a successful build. If you have used the make install for gcc, the configure will know where to look; however, if you have placed gcc in a directory other than /usr/local//bin, you will need to create a symbolic link in the libg++-2.4 subdirectory (one level above the libg++ directory). An example of an ln to create a symbolic link is:

```
$ ln -s /usr/local2/gcc/rs6000/gcc-2.4.4/bin/gcc gcc
```

This creates a symbolic link in the current directory (in this case /usr/local2/libg++/rs6000/libg++2.4.4) named gcc which points to the gcc compiler created in the previous section of this chapter. It appears, on the surface, that this may not always work and that you may have to place a similar symbolic link in the /usr/local/bin for gcc to ensure that configure for libg++ finds gcc to include in the makefile. Without this, libg++ may not use gcc and may not compile correctly. Watch out for this.

Once you have made the gcc compiler available to configure, you can configure your machine. For example, on an RS/6000, you would type:

```
$ ./configure rs6000-ibm-aix3.2 -- prefix=/usr/local2/libg++/libg++-
2.4
```

This will create a Makefile which you can then execute. If you are using an RS/6000, you will run into the same compilation problem you had with gcc related to the use of the -g debug option. You must remove all references to the -g options in the resultant makefile or Makefile.in. If you don't, you will get a fatal compiler error. You can eliminate this error by calling IBM and requesting TF U416277. Once you have fixed this issue, you can proceed with the commands:

```
$ make clean
$ make all
```

They will compile all included libraries in libg++. Optionally, you can now type:

```
$ make install
```

if you want to place the resultant files in the /usr/local/lib areas. This is the recommended area since many tools look for libg++ in usr/local/lib.

Finally, you can test your results with the command:

```
$ make check
```

This will generate and execute some test to ensure that your build process was successful. If you have errors, you may need to rebuild from scratch. If you continue to get errors, see the documentation for potential problems.

11.7.4 Conclusion

libg+ contains a variety of class libraries from Curses to IOstream to Data. By using these class libraries as well as the other library files provided with libg++, you will get a good look at some excellent class libraries and applications you can build with them.

11.8 gas

11.8.1 Introduction

gas is the GNU assembler, which compiles and creates binary files from assembler code. It also provides a cross-compiler capability for assemblers. This means that you can compile assembler code to run on a different architecture machine from that on which it is compiled. This is a powerful feature and is often used by software engineers to support heterogeneous platforms as easily as possible.

Even though it can be used as a stand-alone assembler package, its primary function is to serve as an assembler for many of the other GNU packages. While there are assemblers distributed with vendor systems, gas is a very sophisticated package which supports all of the kind of things GNU products tend to do. You may want to reference this and install it before you begin to install and configure most of the other GNU products described in this book.

gas is a GNU product and as such is subject to its GNU General Public license as included both in the product distribution and in App. B of this book.

11.8.2 Usage

The basic syntax of gas is:

```
as [-a|-al|-as] [-D] [-f] [-Idir] [-L] [-ofile] [-Rvw] [-- | file
...]
```

where -a creates an assembly listing file including symbols.
-al creates assembly listing only.
-as creates symbol listing only.
-D is ignored by as; used for as compatibility.
-f does not perform any preprocessing.
-Idir uses dir for include files.
-L keeps local symbols.
-ofile—output file is file.
-R merges data section into text section.
-v displays as version.
-w suppresses warning messages.
-- is standard input.
file... is one or more files to assemble.

Much of the above information was taken from the as man page named ./gas/doc/as.1 included in the distribution on the CD included with this book. See this file for more information.

There is also information in texinfo format which can be viewed with either texinfo mode in emacs or with the info program available with the texinfo distribution on the CD. There is also a section on documentation in the ./gas/README file in this distribution. If you want to create tex output files, you will need to install TeX on your machine.

If you want to build the TeX dvi (device independent) files, you must use a command like:

```
$ cd gas-2.1.1/gas/doc
$ make as.dvi
```

and have TeX installed and available. If you want to build the texinfo files, use a command like:

```
$ make info
```

instead of the make as.dvi as listed above. Note that here you must have the texinfo available. See Sec. 11.15 for more information.

11.8.3 Installation

The installation of gas is very straightforward and consists of moving to the main directory of the gas distribution and typing:

```
$ ./configure TARGET --prefix=dir
```

where TARGET is the target architecture of the current machine. If you don't know your current target, type the command:

```
$ ./config.guess
```

This will generate a target string for you. For example, on an RS/6000 with software in the /usr/local/gas/gas-2.1.1 subdirectory, you might type:

```
$ ./configure rs6000-ibm-aix3.2 -- prefix=/usr/local/gas/gas-2.1.1
```

Then you simply issue the make command:

```
$ make
```

This will build all the proper executables and libraries for gas. There are a few additional notes in the NEWS and the associated README files in the gas subdirectory. See these if you want more information. Of particular interest is the file README.coff which describes support for COFF and "vanilla" linkers. See this if you are interested in coff support.

11.8.4 Conclusion

gas provides an assembler for many machines and tools including gcc, gdb, g++, emacs, and many others. If you use gas, you will be assured of minimal problems when building these tools. You can also use gas as a very powerful assembler which supports multiple architectures and machines. Take a look at this technology if you are interested in assembler technology since it is a fairly good implementation of a cross-platform assembler.

11.9 gdb

11.9.1 Introduction

gdb is the GNU debugger which you can use to interactively debug executable applications in a UNIX environment. gdb works much like dbx. It provides interactive debugging capabilities for languages such as C. C++. gdb also supports remote debugging and cross-debugging capabilities that allow you to debug a remote application on a hardware architecture that is different from the local one. The interface for remote debugging is still somewhat primitive and will require some effort to configure. There are stubs which can be modified including m68k-stub.c, i386-stub.c, and sparc-stub.c. Examine these for more details on how to perform remote debugging over a serial line.

gdb is a GNU product and as such is subject to its GNU General Public license as included both in the product distribution and in App. B of this book.

11.9.2 Usage

The basic syntax of the gdb command is:

```
gdb [-help] [-nx] [-q] [-batch] [-cd=dir] [-f] [-b bps] [-tty=dev]
   [-s file]
 [-e prog] [-se prog] [-x file] [-d dir] [-c file] [prog [core | ID]]
```

where -help displays interactive help screens.
-nx doesn't run any initialization files such as .gdbinit.
--q is quiet mode. Doesn't print introductory message.
-batch executes all commands given by the -x option and return.
-cd=dir uses dir as the working directory.
-f is used with emacs to output current position information within the file.
-b bps sets line speed of any serial line used for remote debugging.
-tty=dev defines dev as standard input and output.
-s file reads symbol table from file.
-e prog uses prog as the executable file.
-se prog uses prog as the executable file and reads the symbol table from it.
-x file is the file containing gdb interactive commands to be executed.
-d=dir searches dir for executable files.
-c file uses file as a core file to examine. Normally, this is in the core file itself.
prog is the executable to run with gdb.
core is the core dump to analyze.
ID is the process ID to attach session to.

gdb gives you the ability to debug executable programs, analyze core dumps, and attach to running processes and analyze their operation. As with all interactive debuggers, gdb provides basic capabilities to monitor variables and program operation and to alter execution by changing values and conditions during execution.

Basic interactive operation. The basic commands available to gdb are very similar to dbx. Some of them are:

break

bt

continue

help

print

next

quit

run

step

These are all documented both in the manual page shipped with gdb and in the Postscript reference card refcard.ps. See these for more documentation and more commands for gdb. See also Sec. 4.1 for more information on debugging techniques and topics.

There have been many enhancements to the gdb product in the last few months, most of which are documented in the file ./gdb/NEWS. See this file for changes to gdb listed by release for the last few versions. The other file of interest is the ./gdb/README file which documents many of the issues you will encounter when building gdb and looking at the documentation.

The build of gdb is straightforward and consists of the configure and make commands. An example on an RS/6000 might look like:

```
$ configure rs6000-ibm-aix3.2 --prefix=/usr/local2/gdb/rs6000
  - gdb-4.9
$ make
```

If you use gmake, you might want to issue the command:

```
$ make -j5
```

to multithread the build process. This will speed it up considerably.

A prebuilt info file (for the Info system and emacs) is contained in this release as ./gdb/gdb.info. Use emacs or some other tool to examine this. See Sec. 4.1 for more information on this.

11.9.3 Installation

The installation of gdb is very simple. First uncompress the distribution file with gzip -d or gunzip. Next unwind the tar file into a local software directory. The directory structure created begins with a root directory of gdb-4.9 and includes several subdirectories such as library directories, help directories, a texinfo subdirectory, and a README file.

To build gdb, use the commands:

```
$ cd gdb-4.9
$ configure TARGET --prefix=dir
```

where TARGET is the architecture you are currently using, and the dir is the prefix where you would like the resulting files placed. If you have questions about the configure and build process, see Sec. 11.1.

A simple example of building on a Sun machine might be:

```
$ ./configure sparc-sun-sunos4.1.3
$ make
```

If you are using gmake, you might multithread the build with a command like:

```
$ make -j5
```

This creates the gdb executable in the gdb subdirectory. You can move this into any directory according to your product structure specifications. You can create different versions of gdb for different target machines based on the --target option on the configure command. This gives you the ability to debug a program on a remote machine that is not of the same architecture as the local machine. See Sec. 11.1 and the gdb/README file in the gdb subdirectory for more information on building cross-compiling capabilities with configure and gdb.

There is a premade reference card in a file named ./gdb/refcard.ps, which is a Postscript file and can be printed to any Postscript printer. You can also preview this document and view it on-line with a tool like Ghostscript. You will make use of this quite often until you get more familiar with the gdb tool. There is TeX-formatted output in the gdb.info file which can be built and used by emacs; other tools can be used to manipulate and view this information.

Finally, there is a gdb testsuite which requires the presence of a tool called dejagnu, which is available from any Internet source. If you are interested in this, see the ./gdb/README file for more information.

Known problems. There are several known problems including problems with backtraces on the RS/6000, incorrect reporting of struct values on SunOS, and breakpoint problems when watchpoints are enabled. See the gdb/README file for more details.

Examples. To debug a file named kevin.out, use the command:

```
$ gdb kevin.out
```

To analyze a core file and determine where the crash occurred, use the command:

```
$ gdb core
```

You can also attach to a running process with a command like:

```
$ gdb kevin.out 1111
```

which will attach to a process with an ID of 1111. You can attach and detach to a number of processes during a gdb session. See on-line help for more information. See also Sec. 4.1 for more details on similar debugging techniques.

11.9.4 Conclusion

gdb is a very powerful debugger which provides most of the capability you would want in an interactive debugger. It also works well with other GNU products such as gcc and gas and allows for advanced techniques such as cross-compilation and cross-debugging.

For more information than is available in this book and in delivered documentation, see *Using GDB: A Guide to the GNU Source Level Debugger* by Richard Stallman and Roland Pesch, available from the Free Software Foundation.

11.10 gawk

11.10.1 Introduction

gawk is an acronym for GNU awk. It is upwardly compatible with SVR4's awk and supports nawk and awk features. The release that this chapter is based on is gawk 2.15.2. With gawk, you can run awk on almost every UNIX platforms and be sure that you are running the same awk on every platform. Therefore, the performance will be the same. gawk supports awk as described in the book *The AWK Programming Language* by Aho, Kernighan, and Weinberger, along with some GNU-specific extensions.

One of the problems with awk on different platforms has been inconsistencies in the performance of this tool on different flavors of UNIX. With gawk, as with other GNU products, you eliminate the inconsistencies and provide a stable awk development platform for most flavors of UNIX.

With gawk 2.11 and beyond, there is full DOS support, so you can begin to take your gawk scripts from UNIX to DOS without portability problems.

For a more complete discussion of the awk syntax, see Sec. 5.1, which contains a variety of examples and more discussion of the awk language itself. They are directly applicable to gawk and in fact should be transparent to whether you use gawk or awk.

gawk is a GNU product and as such is subject to its GNU General Public license as included both in the product distribution and in App. B of this book.

11.10.2 Installation

gawk comes in standard Internet compressed tar file format. If you get the file from the Internet, you must first uncompress the received file. After uncompressing the file with the uncompress command, you can issue the tar command to see the contents of the file.

```
$ uncompress gawk.tar # This is not necessary if you are using the
  file from the CD
$ tar tvf gawk.tar | more
```

This will give you a table of contents from which you will see a variety of files in subdirectories. Note that the tar file is relative and therefore will be unwound relative to your current working directory. This is important, and you should see Sec. 6.5 and Chap. 9 for more information.

Create a directory and unwind the tar file:

```
$ mkdir /usr/local/gawk
$ tar xvf gawk.tar
```

All the files in the tar archive will be unwound and placed in directories under your current working directory. You are now ready to examine files and build the product for your platform. Note that this process is unnecessary for the files on the included CD since they are unwound by the installation process (see App. A). However, you may need to follow this procedure if you get a different version from the Internet or some other source.

Files. As is standard with most Internet products, the first file to look for is the README file. Once you find this, print it out and examine it in detail. It contains information on the current release features and functionality as well as on bugs and installation notes.

Along with the README file, there are two files, FUTURES and PROBLEMS, which describe future enhancements and features of the product and known problems with the current gawk, respectively. Consult these two files for more information.

The other file of immediate interest is the Makefile. As is standard with most Internet software products, the Makefile is tailored for the Sun environment. With gawk, they have also built in some dependencies on gcc (GNU's C compiler) which you must watch out for. Different C compilers support different functions within C. This is discussed in more detail in Sec. 11.6; however, suffice it to say that you will need to change switches on the make compiles for different C compilers to work correctly.

Release 2.15.2 of gawk includes a simple version of the GNU configure tool which supports only the architecture option and none of the -- options that most other tools use. Because of this, you may have to edit the Makefile.in file which configure uses to create the Makefile. Some of the variables you may have to modify are:

prefix=

CC

PARSER

Once you have modified the appropriate lines in Makefile.in, run the configure command. On a Sun, the command would look like:

```
$ configure sunos41
```

To see what configurations are supported, simply type:

```
$ configure
```

This will list all supported machine types.

In Makefile.in, there are sections outlined by comments which tell you which platforms are supported with which commands in the Makefile. Because of the changing standards in the C language, several flavors are shown. If you are running a compiler which is ANSI-compliant, you should select the ANSI sections of the Makefile and make sure that the ANSI-compliant switch on your C compiler is invoked by the Makefile. If this is a problem, consult your C compiler documentation for more detail. After configuring as explained above, issue the following command to build the product:

```
$ make
```

You can rebuild from scratch if you would like by issuing the commands:

```
$ make clean
$ make
```

The make clean command cleans out any previously existing executables. This ensures that you have a new set of executables specifically for your environment. See Sec. 5.3 for more details on this process.

There are machine-specific README files for a variety of machines. For example, there is a file README.rs6000 which documents an issue with the alloca routine. For the most part, you can ignore this for the build. To build this product on the RS/6000, you would first edit the Makefile.in file as discussed above and then use commands like:

```
$ configure rs6000
$ make
```

Finally, you will find documentation in the form of gawk.1 files in the directories. The file extension .1 normally means that the file is a help file and comes from section 1 of the UNIX documentation, which is general user commands. You can access and print this file to the screen or a printer with the nroff commands. For example:

```
$ nroff -man gawk.1 | more /* prints out manual page to the screen */
```

or

```
$ nroff -man gawk.1 | lpr /* prints out command to default printer */
```

Printing out the manual page for future reference is one of the best ways to use Internet software products; it allows you to understand a product's exact functions relatively quickly. See Sec. 9.11 and other sections in Chap. 9 for more information. Other documentation is supplied in TeX format. TeX is a macro language which provides very sophisticated command-driven word processing and typesetting capabilities.

There are a variety of sources listed in the README file for bug reports and fixes as well as general information for the gawk product. Reference these for more detail on the gawk product.

11.10.3 Usage

gawk can use either POSIX-style commands, which are preceded by a single hyphen, or GNU-style options, which are preceded by two hyphens. To simply see the documentation, we will use the POSIX-style syntax. See the manual page (gawk.1) if you want more information on the GNU syntax.

The syntax for the gawk command is:

```
gawk [-a] [-e] [-W compat] [-W copyleft] [-W help] [-W lint]
  [-W posix]
[-V] [-Fsep][-v var=value] -f prog [--] file ...

gawk [-a] [-e] [-W compat] [-W copyleft] [-W help] [-W lint]
  [-W posix]
[-V] [-Fsep][-v var=value] [--] progtext ...
```

where -a uses awk-style regular expressions. This is the default.
-e uses egrep expressions as documented in the POSIX standard.
-W compat is the compatibility mode. gawk runs just like awk.
-W copyleft prints GNU copyright.
-W help displays options.
-W lint runs lint to check potential programming problems.
-W posix enables compatibility mode with awk.
-V prints current version of awk to standard error.
-Fsep defines field separator.
-v var=value defines BEGIN block variables.
-f prog is the awk command input file.
-- signals the end of options. Used to separate options from files.
progtext is awk commands included in-line instead of in a file prog as with the -f switch.
I file is awk input file.

gawk looks very similar to awk in terms of syntax and command structure. There are some things to point out, however. There have been many changes in gawk in the last few months, many of which are documented in the NEWS file. See this for more information on gawk functionality.

When searching for files to be used with the -f switch, the AWKPATH variable is examined to determine fully qualified paths. The default, if no AWKPATH is defined, is .:/usr/lib/awk:/usr/local/lib/awk.

As mentioned earlier, gawk is compatible with SVR4 awk and supports features such as preexecution variable definition with the -v var=val, multiple -f option concatenation, ANSI C printf support, and the \a, \v and \x escape sequences. See the README file for more information.

Finally, GNU added some extensions which are unique to gawk, such as:

IGNORECASE variable which allows for character-case independence

AWKPATH variable

-a, -e, -c, -C, and -V options

11.10.4 Conclusion

gawk is a powerful tool which not only provides awk and nawk compatibility but also provides its own set of features and functions that add value to the original awk functionality. It also runs on multiple platforms and provides a stable and uniform environment for developing and running awk scripts.

11.11 gmake

11.11.1 Introduction

gmake (now called make) is, as you would expect, GNU's version of make. make is a tool used for software development and maintenance. It allows you to build only the parts of a program which have changed. By building a makefile which contains information on which files are a part of the final executable and describing the structure of those files and how they fit together, make can save you a considerable amount of errors and inconsistencies later in the software development process. When you change one piece of an application, make rebuilds only those pieces that changed and leaves the rest untouched. This saves a considerable amount of time over rebuilding the entire executable after each change. make is extremely powerful for software developers and GNU fully supports make functionality. See Sec. 5.3 for more details on make.

gmake (or make) is subject to its GNU General Public license as included both in the product distribution and in App. B of this book.

11.11.2 Installation

First uncompress the file and unwind it as follows:

```
$ uncompress gmake.tar
$ tar xvf /* note tar will unwind starting in the current directory
  */
```

As is often the case with Internet software products, you should first print out the README file in the main directory. As is the case with most GNU products, you must first configure the products for your particular environment:

```
$ configure TARGET --prefix=dir
```

where TARGET and dir are determined by your environment. For example, on a Sun you might type:

```
$ ./configure sun-sparc-sunos4.1 -- prefix=/usr/local/gmake/make-3.68
```

Once you have configured the correct makefile, type the command:

```
$ make install
```

or

```
$ make
```

The first will compile gmake and install it in the default directory /usr/local. The second command will simply build the gmake executable in the current working directory. Note that this may be preferable, depending on your software environment. This is all there is to building gmake.

There are a few other subtle things you can do with the configure if you want. See the INSTALL file for more information.

11.11.3 Usage

The syntax for the gmake command is:

```
gmake [-f makefile] [option] ... target ...
```

where -f makefile defines a makefile other than the default makefile or Makefile files.

option consists of one or more of the following options:

- -C dir changes directory to dir before searching for makefile.
- -d is debugging mode; gives more information about files and processing.
- -f file uses file as makefile input.
- -i ignores all errors.
- -I dir is similar to compiles; uses dir to search for included makefiles; can be used more than once on a single make command to search multiple directories.
- -j jobs specifies the number of jobs you want to run simultaneously.
- -k continues after an error has occurred. Files unrelated to the failed target will still be made.
- -l load—no new jobs will be run if there are other jobs running, and the average load on the systems is load (in percent).
- -n prints out commands and results but doesn't execute them; useful for debugging.
- -o file doesn't remake file even if the .o file is older than its associated source file.
- -p prints database that results from reading makefiles. This generates a schema for the building and structure of your

program. To print the default database, use the -f/dev/null with the -p switch.
-q prints zero if targets are up to date, and nonzero if they are not; does not execute any commands.
-r doesn't use implicit rules including suffixes.
-s is silent mode; doesn't print out any commands as they are executed.
-t touches files to fool make and prevent recompilation.
-v prints the current version of make.
-w prints working directory.
-W file tells make that file has been modified even if it hasn't.
target is label within the makefile to begin build.

One of the big differences between gmake and most other make facilities is its support of the concept of relative path builds. The variable VPATH is often discussed in many of the configure scripts used to build many of the products discussed in this book. The configure utility uses this capability to generate binaries in directories other than where the source lives. gmake also has much richer support for substitution reference functionality.

The other very nice feature is the jobs support (-j). gmake will allow you to create and execute multiple jobs or commands at the same time. It will automatically generate a number of job streams to execute the build more quickly by splitting the compilation job into multiple streams which are independent of each other. You can limit the load on the machine with the -l option. Explore this feature if you have the opportunity to create multiple job streams from a single makefile.

A simple example of creating a multistream job is the following command:

```
$ make -j 3 all
```

This will attempt to create up to three jobs to compile all executables and link for a final executable. If you have a large number of file compilations which must occur before a link, this is a good strategy to speed up the build process since you can be busy compiling while another compile job is waiting for I/O. This can significantly speed up a build if used properly. Note that you don't need to do anything special to your Makefile in order to take advantage of this capability. gmake will do as much as it can transparently. This is a simple example of the power of gmake.

11.11.4 Conclusion

make is a fully compatible version of make that runs on a variety of platforms. It is generally seen as at least as good as the default version of make and oftentimes is better. There are often subtle differences in make functionality and behavior between machines and operating systems that are not discovered until after a project has begun. With make, you can avoid many of the pitfalls and problems associated with different flavors of UNIX by using make on all platforms associated with your software development.

Finally, by using advanced functions of gmake, such as multiple job stream support and relative path support (VPATH), you can make your build processes quicker and better.

11.12 flex

11.12.1 Introduction

flex is a replacement for lex. While it is significantly faster than standard lex, it does not maintain complete backward compatibility with lex, and, therefore, you must be careful.

flex stands for fast lex, which is a fast lexical analyzer. It allows you to scan and operate on input and look for patterns on which to operate. A typical use of lex and flex is to generate parsers of text which allow you to write relatively simple and straightforward routines which will analyze input information and structure the corresponding output according to rules defined in the flex input file.

The output of a flex input file is a C source code routine named lex.yy.c which defines a routine yylex(). This routine can be compiled with a standard C compiler and the -lfl option on the C compilation statement. When the resulting code is executed, it parses the input and applies the rules from the flex input file to process the input and generate the appropriate output.

This chapter will not cover lex and flex syntax in depth; however, it will present the basic syntax and operations of flex to familiarize you with its basic operation and functionality. See Secs. 5.4 and 5.5 for more information about them.

flex is a BSD-related product and as such is subject to the copyright restrictions of The Regents of the University of California. A copy of the license is included both in the product distribution and in App. B of this book.

11.12.2 Usage

The basic syntax for flex is:

```
flex [-FILT8bcdfinpstv -C[Fefm] -Sskeleton] [file...]
```

where -F uses the fast scanner table.
-I generates an interactive scanner.

-L tells flex not to generate #line directives in lex.yy.c.
-T is the trace mode.
-8 generates an 8-bit scanner.
-b generates backtracking information to lex.backtrack.
-c is the null option (useful for backward compliance only).
-d is the debug mode.
-f is the full table or fast scanner mode.
-i generates a case-insensitive scanner.
-n is the null option (useful for backward compliance only).
-p is the performance report to standard error.
-s suppresses unmatched scanner input to standard output.
-t displays output to standard output instead of default lex.yy.c.
-v generates a summary statistics to standard error.
-C[Fefm] are table compression commands where:
  F uses alternate fast scanner representation.
  e generates equivalence classes.
  f specifies that full scanner tables should be generated.
  m generates meta-equivalence classes.
  no option generates compressed tables but no equivalence or meta-equivalence classes.
-Sskeleton overrides default skeleton scanners file.
file... is one or more files on which to operate.

flex generates programs it calls scanners. These scanners (typically named lex.yy.c) contain code which recognizes lexical patterns. The input file to flex is called the rules file. It contains pairs of directives which consist of regular expressions called patterns and corresponding C code sequences called actions. When the resulting scanner is compiled and executed, it scans input for matching regular expressions and executes the corresponding C code.

flex is typically used for input parsing and manipulation. See Sec. 11.12.3 for some examples.

Although regular expressions have been discussed in other sections of this book, flex uses an extended set of regular expressions for its rules file; therefore, it is useful to summarize their basic syntax here:

`c`	Matches any character (e.g., 'x').
`.`	Matches any character except newline.
`[abc]`	Matches either a, b, or c in that order.
`[abd-f]`	Matches either a, b, or any character from d through f.
`[^A-Z\t]`	Negated character class. This means any character except A through Z and a tab.
`regexp*`	Zero or more regular expressions.
`regexp+`	One or more regular expressions.
`regexp?`	Zero or one regular expressions.

regexp{2,5}	Two to five regular expressions.
regexp{2,}	Two or more regular expressions.
"string"	Literal match of string.
\num	Where num is an octal number.
\xnum	Where num is a hex number.
regexp1regexp2	Regular expression 1 followed immediately by regular expression 2.
^regexp	Regular expression at the beginning of a line.
regexp$	Regular expression at the end of a line.
<<EOF>>	End of file.
<s1,s2>regexp	Regular expression when start condition s1 or s2 is realized.

There is precedence in these operators exactly as in other regular expression operators, and they are listed above in order from highest to lowest precedence.

The basic format of the rules file is:

```
definitions
%%
rules
%%
code
```

where definitions consist of the variables and function definitions that you would normally place in the global declaration section of your code. You can also include name definitions which allow you to define symbolic names for regular expressions. For example, the following are common name definitions:

```
DIGITS [0-9]
LOWCHARS [a-z]
```

They can later be referenced with:

```
{name}
```

syntax. For example:

```
{DIGITS}
```

would reference the regular expression (0-9). There are almost an infinite number of things you can do with this section. It is really application dependent.

The rules section consists of pairs of patterns and actions. Patterns must begin in the first column, and the associated action must begin on the same line as the pattern. There are a variety of rules pertaining to the pattern matching, including negated character classes matching newline characters unless explicitly stated and the unique occurrence of beginning of line and end of line operators. See the flexdoc.1 file for more details.

The actions part of the rules section consists of pure C code. You can also include several flex directives such as:

`ECHO`	Displays token on the screen.
`BEGIN`	Places scanner in a start condition.
`yymore()`	Appends matched token to current yytext value.
`yyless(n)`	Returns all but first n characters of the current matched token to the input stream to be rescanned.
`yyterminate()`	Acts as a RETURN statement.
`unput(c)`	Places character c back to the input stream.
`input()`	Reads the next character from standard input.

flex uses a token-based mechanism which defines the token by strings separated by white space. This is a common methodology for a parser such as flex. All commands in the resulting scanner work on the current token. The token is made available to the program as a pointer yytext. The length of the token is contained in yyleng. This mechanism can be effected with the -I option, which generates what is known as an interactive scanner. This means that instead of the default action to read ahead one character before matching a pattern, the scanner will only do this when absolutely necessary. This saves processing time and makes interactive usage more efficient. The general rule stated with respect to this is to use -I if the input is going to be interactive; otherwise, don't use -I.

The default rule is that of simply displaying input text on the output stream. The flex input file looks like:

```
%%
```

Note that if you compile and execute this, it will simply echo all that you type in.

Finally, the code section consist of C code which can make use of the flex-generated scanner to manipulate input files. This section contains the logic of your program and the largest part of the processing capacity of the resulting scanner.

The resulting lex.yy.c file is large relative to the flex input file. A simple example of a flex input file is:

```
%%
```

If you run flex on this, you get the file:

```
# include "stdio.h"
# define U(x) x
# define NLSTATE yyprevious=YYNEWLINE
```

```
# define BEGIN yybgin = yysvec + 1 +
# define INITIAL 0
# define YYLERR yysvec
...
struct yysvf *yyestate;
extern struct yysvf yysvec[], *yybgin;
# define YYNEWLINE 10
yylex(){
int nstr; extern int yyprevious;
while((nstr = yylook()) >= 0)
yyfussy: switch(nstr){
case 0:
if(yywrap()) return(0); break;
case -1:
break;
default:
fprintf(yyout,"bad switch yylook %d",nstr);
} return(0); }
/* end of yylex */
int yyvstop[] = {
0,
0};
# define YYTYPE char
struct yywork { YYTYPE verify, advance; } yycrank[] = {
0,0, 0,0, 0,0, 0,0,
0,0};
struct yysvf yysvec[] = {
0, 0, 0,
...
yyunput(c)
int c; {
unput(c);
}
```

The ellipses (...) represent large pieces of missing code. In the interests of space, several hundred lines of code have been removed. The thing to realize is the complexity and size of this file. The power of flex is that it generates much of the parsing logic that you would have to write if you were to generate these routines yourself. You can effect the size and speed of the parsing by using the -C option. You can use a command like -Cem and generate the smallest table and, therefore, the slowest execution, or you can use the -CF option to generate the largest table and the fastest execution. This entire issue is related to tricks that flex does to increase parsing speed.

flex builds equivalence classes which are merely equivalent representations for patterns. For example, you can use the regular expression [a-c] which is equivalent to a b c. flex creates tables of information which store these equivalencies. The more equivalencies you store, the larger the table, but the faster the processing time. This is the tradeoff relative to the -C option.

Start conditions allow you to define conditional rules. To create a rule with a start condition, use the syntax:

```
<string>regexp
```

where <string> is any string which represents that start condition.
regexp is any regular expression.

For example, you can create a start condition known as KEVIN with a command like:

```
<KEVIN>"kevin"
```

This rule will be activated when you place the scanner in KEVIN start condition with a command like:

```
%s KEVIN
```

in the definitions section of the flex input file. You can also use the keyword BEGIN to define a start condition within your code. The typical implementation is to use a global boolean variable and test its value to define a start condition.

For example, you might see a section of code like:

```
if (name="KEVIN") then
BEGIN(KEVIN)
etc....
```

This will execute the start condition KEVIN for the scanner.

There is a very good section on performance in the flexdoc.1 document included with flex. See this for more details on how to get the maximum performance out of your flex system.

There are a variety of macros which you can redefine with flex. The most basic are:

YY_DECL	Declaration of yylex
YY_INPUT	Redefines the way yylex gets it input
YY_USER_ACTION	Defines a user action to be executed before an action
YY_USR_INIT	Defines a user action to be executed before scan begins
yywrap()	Redefines the end of file condition return code

11.12.3 Examples

One of the simple ways you can use flex to manipulate text is to let the scanner remove any specified text strings from the input file. An example rules file name example.flex might look like:

```
%%
"string to remove"
```

You can first run flex on this file with the command:

```
$ flex example.flex
```

This generates a file lex.yy.c which is the scanner file. This is a C code file which can be compiled and executed. Note that lex.yy.c does not have a main function declaration and therefore must be compiled and linked with the command:

```
$ cc -lfl lex.yy.c
```

This generates a file a.out which can then be executed as you would any other executable. Note that if you use lex (and not flex), you need to use the option -ll instead of -lfl to generate the same resulting executable.

Assume you have an input file named example.input which contains the following information:

```
line1
line2
line3
line4
string to remove
line6
```

When you execute the command:

```
$ a.out < example.input
```

the resulting output will be:

```
line1
line2
line3
line4
line6
```

You can redirect this as you normally would with the command:

```
$ a.out < example.input > example.output
```

Now the file example.output contains the above output.

11.12.4 Differences between lex and flex

The basic differences documented between flex and lex are:

yylineno lex variable is not supported by flex.

input() is not redefinable in flex at least in accordance with POSIX specifications.

output() is not supported.

flex supports exclusive start conditions.

flex expands definitions with enclosing parens, while standard lex does not.

%r (ratfor) is not supported by flex.

After a call to unput(), yytext and yyleng are undefined.

The precedence of {} and ^ are different with flex.

To reference yytext outside of the scanner, you declare yytext as "extern char. *yytext" in flex instead of "extern char yytext[]".

yyin is not defined until the first scanner execution with flex, unlike lex which defines yyin to stdin.

Special table size declarations required by lex are not needed by flex and are ignored.

Multiple actions on the same line are supported by flex.

yyrestart() is available in flex.

yyterminate() is available in flex.

There are other subtle differences and most are documented in flexdoc.1. See this document if you need more details. Certainly performance is better with flex than with most lex implementations. As your rules files get large, this becomes a significant benefit.

11.12.5 Installation

The installation of flex is very straightforward. There is a very basic makefile which contains a few comments at the beginning that discuss POSIX and SystemV support issues. By including a macro definition on the make command line, you can override any possible definitions, and the make should run successfully.

For the first make on a platform like a Sun, you should use the command:

```
$ make first_flex
```

If you are building a system on a more System V-based system, you should first edit the Makefile and add the -DUSG flag to the CFLAGS macro definition. Then issue the above command to build flex on a System V system. This will generate the flex executable, which you can then execute appropriately.

For example, on an RS/6000 it is necessary to place the -DUSG in the CFLAGS macro definition in the Makefile. Then issue the make first_flex command. For this Sun, it is not necessary to change the Makefile before issuing the make first_flex command.

To ensure that the build process occurred correctly, issue the command:

```
$ make test
```

There should be no results from the diff command. If there are, you have a problem, and you need to go back and review your Makefile for potential problems on your system. Otherwise, you can install the executable in the /usr/local default directories with the command:

```
$ make install
```

if you want; otherwise, simply place the resulting flex executable in your path and have at it.

You may also want to modify the macros BINDIR, LIBDIR, AUXDIR, and MANDIR to point to some location other than the default /usr/local. Any choice should be consistent with your product support methodology.

11.12.6 Conclusions

flex is a very powerful tool which provides additional function above and beyond most vendor implementations of lex. One of its most powerful features is in its relationship to yacc, which was not discussed in this section. See the documentation accompanying flex for more details. There are several flex input files in the software on the accompanying CD. See the groff distribution for a good example of both a lex/flex file and of a yacc/bison file.

Much of the information in the section was taken from the files flex.1 and flexdoc.1. flexdoc.1 contains a lengthy and comprehensive overview of flex and must be read before attempting any real use of flex. Several of the examples in this section were taken directly from these documents, and they will prove invaluable as you become more proficient with flex.

11.13 bison

11.13.1 Introduction

bison is the GNU replacement for yacc (yet another compiler compiler). The standard input file has a standard suffix of .y and the output is C source code. bison is really a language and precompiler system which allows you to parse and modify input according to formats specified in the bison input file.

bison is backward compatible with yacc and supports yacc input files. It is a GNU product and as such is subject to its GNU General Public license as included both in the product distribution and in App. B of this book.

11.13.2 Installation

The basic installation of bison is straightforward. As with most of the other newer GNU packages, you must first configure the software for your particular machine with the configure command.

The same problem that occurred with gcc on the RS/6000 may occur when building bison. Namely, if the PTF U416277 is not installed, you will get a compilation error on the first file compilation referring to a file /tmp/xxx.s where the .s suffix refers to a temporary assembler file. To fix this, you must remove the -g references from the Makefile.in file and then run the configure command. Once you have modified the Makefile.in file, run the configure. On an RS/6000 this might look like:

```
$ configure rs6000-ibm-aix3.2 -- prefix=/usr/local/bison/bison-1.21
```

You also might use a command like:

```
$ configure rs6000-ibm-aix3.2 --prefix = /usr/local/bison/bison-1.21
--CFLAGS
```

This will construct the Makefile without the -q option. If you have trouble with the configure command, see Sec. 11.1 for more information.

It appears that the bison Makefile assumes that you have the proper subdirectories created before it can correctly create files in them. This works well for /usr/local; however, if you change the path of the final executables with the --prefix as shown above, you need to manually create the following directories before executing the make command:

```
bin, man/man1,info,lib
```

Once you have done this and configured your machine, you can build the software. To do this, use commands like:

```
$ make clean
$ make install
```

This will generate all executables and place them in lib, bin, and man directories under the /usr/local/bison/bison-1.21 directory. If you don't specify the install option, the executables and other files will be copied into the directories specified with the prefix option on the configure command. Using the install option is not a recommended practice in large environments since you may unintentionally overwrite software. See Sec. 9.6 for more information.

You can override macros and options with either configure or make. See Sec. 11.1 for more information.

Once you have compiled and linked bison, you are ready to execute as described in the rest of this chapter. If you have questions or needs, reference the INSTALL file in the bison distribution; it contains more information specific to configure and make which may help with the bison installation.

11.13.3 Usage

The basic syntax for bison is:

```
bison [-b file-prefix] [--file-prefix=file-prefix] [-d] [--defines]
  [-l] [--no-lines]
[-o outfile] [--output-file=output-file] [-p prefix] [--name
  -prefix=prefix] [-t]
[--debug] [-v] [--verbose] [-V] [--version] [-y] [--yacc] [--fixed
  -output-files] file
```

where -b file-prefix defines a prefix to be used by all bison output files.
--file-prefix=file-prefix is same as -b file-prefix.
-d generates an additional output file containing macro definitions for the token type names defined in the grammar and the semantic value type YYSTYPE. This file has an extension of .h and a filename which is the same as file.
--defines is the same as -d.
-l does not place #lines in the bison output file.
--no-lines is the same as -l.
-o outfile specifies output filename.
--output-file=outfile is the same as -o outfile.
-p prefix renames external symbols used by the parser to use prefix instead of the default yy.
--name-prefix=prefix is the same as -p prefix.
-t outputs YYDEBUG so debugging is enabled.
--debug is the same as -t.
-v is the verbose option. The output file containing the verbose information has the same filename as the input file with an extension of .output instead of .tab.c.
--verbose is the same as -v.
-V displays version of bison.
--version is the same as -V.

-y makes output filename y.tab.c to maintain backward compatibility with yacc.
--yacc is the same as -y.
--fixed-output-files is same as -y.
file is the bison input file to be operated on.

As you can see, most commands have two options that accomplish the same thing. This is historical and has to do with different parsing mechanisms on UNIX and how you might establish your input parsing. There should be no differences to the bison command between the single and double hyphen options.

See the bison.1 manual page and bison.texinfo file for more information since much of this information was taken directly from there.

11.13.4 Differences between yacc and bison

bison is very compatible with yacc, including support for yacc input files. The only differences are in the output naming conventions and the @N operator.

bison will create an output file with the same filename as the input file except for replacing the .y input file suffix with a .c. In other words, yacc always creates an output file named y.tab.c regardless of the input filename. bison, on the other hand, will keep the original filename. If you have a bison input file named kevin.y, when you execute bison, you will get an output filename of kevin.tab.c. This is a nice advantage, but it does tend to confuse make since it has default rules about yacc output filenames. Keep this in mind when you are building your software systems.

The other key differences are in bison's support of @N, which gives you access to the character number, beginning line number, and ending line number of symbols in the current rule. This is not available with yacc.

11.13.5 Differences between yacc and yacc

There are several versions of yacc available, including Berkeley and AT&T versions, which provide slightly different functionality. You need to be extremely careful as to which one you are using because you may or may not get different behavior. This is dependent not only on which version of UNIX you are using but on your path on a given machine. For example, on some versions of SunOS, you have two versions of yacc, one in /usr/bin and the other in /usr/5bin. Keep this in mind when building makefiles and developing software systems.

The differences between tools on different UNIX platforms are some of the main reasons to use a tool like bison; it buys you complete portability between heterogeneous platforms. This becomes essential as you distribute your software systems to more than one UNIX architecture.

11.13.6 Conclusion

bison is a parser generator which makes it easy to parse and interpret command input lines as well as file contents of a given structure. Parsing is one of the most time consuming of all software development activities, and bison gives you a faster interface and development cycle for generating this parsing code.

11.14 f2c

11.14.1 Introduction

f2c is a program which attempts to convert Fortran to C. It is not clear how good this software is; however, it has been recently updated on the network, so there is work going on at BellCore and AT&T. There is a disclaimer issued with the product which is contained both in the product and in App. B. While the author has not personally used this product, it does look interesting and, if it works, could be quite useful. The best way to check the usefulness of this system is to try it and see what kind of code it produces.

f2c is a AT&T/Bellcore product and as such is subject to the AT&T/Bellcore copyright as included both in the product distribution and in App. B of this book.

11.14.2 Usage

Much of the information in this section is taken from the file f2c.1, which is a formatted manual page. You can print this out or view it on-line for more information.

The basic usage of f2c is simple:

```
f2c [-C] [-I2] [-onetrip] [-C++] [-ec] [-ext] [-i2] [-r8] [-Tdir]
  [-w8] [-Wn]
[-!c] [-!I] [-!it] [-!P] [-AEPRUacgpuwz] file ...
```

where -C ensures subscripts are within array boundaries.
-I2 defines INTEGER and LOGICAL as 2 bytes.
-onetrip compiles DO loops that are executed at least once.
-c++ generates C++ code instead of C.
-ec—uninitialized COMMON is placed in separate files.
-ext issues messages concerning non-f77 Fortran code.

-i2 is similar to -I2, only INTEGER and LOGICAL may be assigned by INQUIRE.
-r8 promotes REAL to DOUBLE and COMPLEX to DOUBLE COMPLEX.
-Tdir places temp files in dir.
-w8 suppresses warnings when COMMON or EQUIVALENCE forces odd word alignment of doubles.
-Wn defines n characters per word.
-!c - Doesn't produce C code.
-!I - Doesn't include include statements.
-!it - Doesn't infer type of untyped EXTERNALs based on their use as parameters to previously defined or prototyped procedures.
-!P doesn't infer ANSI or C++ prototypes from usage.
-A produces ANSI C (default is K&R C).
-R doesn't make REAL become DOUBLE PRECISION.
-P creates file.P continuing prototypes.
-E declares uninitialized COMMON to be extern.
-U maintains case of variables and external names.
-a makes local variables automatic.
-c includes original Fortran source code as comments.
-g includes original Fortran line numbers as comments.
-p includes preprocessor definitions to make COMMON block members look like local variables.
-u makes the default type undefined.
-w suppresses all warning messages.
-z doesn't implicitly recognize DOUBLE COMPLEX.
file... is one or more files to be processed.

The input files are scanned for .f and .F files with a filename matching file. An output file is created with the name file.c. You should be able to compile this resultant file.c with your C compiler and proceed as you normally would.

Note that the resulting C routines require both the libI77 and libF77 archive libraries when they are linked. This means that you need to use the -lF77 -lI77 -lm options on the ld or cc command to ensure that these programs are properly linked.

A simple example consists of a file named test.f, which is a Fortran file as shown below:

```
      PROGRAM MAIN
C
C     THIS IS PROGRAM TEST
C     IT CALCULATES THE SUM OF UP TO N VALUES OF X**3 WHERE
C     NEGATIVE VALUES ARE IGNORED
C
```

```
      READ(5,*) N
      SUM=0
      DO 10 I=1,N
           READ(5,*) X
           IF (X.GE.0) THEN
                Y=X**3
                IF (SUM.GE.0) THEN
                     SUM=SUM+Y
                ELSE
                     GOTO 20
                END IF
                END IF
10    CONTINUE
20    CONTINUE
      WRITE(6,*) 'This is the sum:',SUM
      STOP
      END
```

You invoke the f2c converter program on it with the command:

```
$ f2c test.f
```

This creates a file test.c which looks like:

```
* test.f -- translated by f2c (version of 23 April 1993 18:34:30).
   You must link the resulting object file with the libraries:
      -lf2c -lm (in that order)
*/

#include "f2c.h"

/* Table of constant values */

static integer c__3 = 3;
static integer c__1 = 1;
static integer c__4 = 4;
static integer c__9 = 9;

/* Main program */ MAIN__()
{
   /* System generated locals */
   integer i__1;
   real r__1, r__2;

   /* Built-in functions */
   integer s_rsle(), do_lio(), e_rsle(), s_wsle(), e_wsle();
   /* Subroutine */ int s_stop();

   /* Local variables */
   static integer i, n;
   static real x, y, sum;

   /* Fortran I/O blocks */
   static cilist io___1 = { 0, 5, 0, 0, 0 };
   static cilist io___5 = { 0, 5, 0, 0, 0 };
   static cilist io___8 = { 0, 6, 0, 0, 0 };
/*      THIS IS PROGRAM TEST */
/*      IT CALCULATES THE SUM OF UP TO N VALUES OF X**3 WHERE */
/*      NEGATIVE VALUES ARE IGNORED */
s_rsle(&io___);
do_lio(&c__3, &c__1, (char *)&n, (ftnlen)sizeof(integer));
e_rsle();
```

```
sum = (float)0.;
i__1 = n;
for (i = 1; i <= i__1; ++i) {
     s_rsle(&io___5);
     do_lio(&c__4, &c__1, (char *)&x, (ftnlen)sizeof(real));
     e_rsle();
     if (x >= (float)0.) {
/* Computing 3rd power */
          r__1 = x, r__2 = r__1;
          y = r__2 * (r__1 * r__1);
          if (sum >= (float)0.) {
               sum += y;
          } else {
               goto L20;
          }
     }
/* L10: */
     }
L20:
     s_wsle(&io___8);
     do_lio(&c__9, &c__1, "This is the sum:", 16L);
     do_lio(&c__4, &c__1, (char *)&sum, (ftnlen)sizeof(real));
     e_wsle();
     s_stop("", 0L);
} /* MAIN__ */
/* Main program alias */ int main_ () { MAIN__ (); }
```

Once you have created the test.c file, you need to compile and link the resulting executable with a command like:

```
$ gcc -o test test.c -lF77 -lI77 -lm
```

Note that the F77 and I77 library archives must either be in the default /usr/lib, or you must include the -L command like:

```
$ gcc -o test test.c -L/usr/local/f2c/libF77 -lF77 - L/usr/
local/f2c/libI77 -lI77 -lm
```

Note that the -L directories must be wherever you have built the archive libraries included with this distribution.

The best set of examples and discussion of feature/function for f2c is in the document f2c.ps, which is a Postscript document included with this distribution. If you have Ghostscript installed, you can preview it. You can also print it to any Postscript printer for review.

If you have problems with unresolved references, they may be the result of the way your compiler generates labels and the necessary conversion to link C and Fortran routines together into a single executable. See your compiler documentation for more details. It is important to use the same compiler to generate both the libraries and the final executable. gcc is a good compiler, and it works well on Sun and IBM machines. Other machines were not tried but are supported. Keep this in mind as you attempt to build final executables.

The above example file is included in the CD distribution in the ./src/example directory. This is something the author added to the CD and in no way is related to the original distribution of the f2c system.

You should examine the README file since it has some information related to the function of f2c, including a discussion of bug reports, machine dependencies, and system call issues. See this file before building the product. See also a file named fixes, which contains information on fixes and functionality in various versions of the product.

11.14.3 Installation

This product was built on several UNIX machines including an RS/6000 and a Sun. As with most products, there are some subtleties to watch out for. The first recommendation is to use the GNU C compiler since this will ensure that ANSI file headers and other constructs will be supported by your compiler. You can try to build the products with your native compiler, but if you have trouble, try the GNU C compiler.

First move to the ./src subdirectory and build the xsum and f2c executables with the commands:

```
$ make clean
$ make all
```

If you want to use the GNU C compiler, you must invoke commands like:

```
$ make clean
$ make all CC=gcc
```

You cannot change the makefile contained in the ./src subdirectory because the makefile itself checks the contents of the makefile to ensure that it was transmitted over the network correctly. While this is unfortunate, you can modify the C compiler choice by using the macro command line substitution with make as described above.

Next you should move to the ./libF77 subdirectory to compile this library. As is documented in the ./libF77 README file, the makefile assumes that the f2c.h header file is contained in /usr/include. As before, ensure that there are no files in the directories which can change the results of the makefile by using the command:

```
$ make clean
```

The next issue is to create the proper f2c.h file in the ./libF77 subdirectory. Unfortunately, the makefile hard codes the location of f2c.h as

/usr/include. If you do not want to place f2c.h in this directory, you must first issue the following command:

```
$ cat /usr/local/f2c/f2c-1993.04.28/src f2ch.add > f2c.h
```

This assumes that your f2c is installed in /usr/local. If you have placed the distribution in some directory other than this, you must substitute your path for /usr/local in the above command. Note also that you need to be sitting in the ./libF77 subdirectory when you issue the cat command. This command creates a new f2c.h in the local directory which you will use to create the libF77.a archive library. Use the make command to build the archive library:

```
$ make CC=gcc
```

Remember that you can use your default C compiler by simply issuing the make command without the CC macro definition.

On an RS/6000 there is a bug with the assembler unless you have PTF U416277 installed. If you do not have this installed you need to override the -g option on the compile statement with a command like:

```
$ make CC=gcc CFLAGS=
```

This will override the default in the makefile and build the f2c system without debug information. In fact, this is a good idea anyway since it creates a more efficient system without the -g option. Note that you must do the same thing for the other subdirectories (libF77 and libI77).

Finally, move to the ./libI77 subdirectory and issue the same commands you issued to build libF77. There is one change. You must create an empty file named local.h in the ./libI77 subdirectory since the fp.h include file attempts to include it. This file is useful only for VAX and CRAY environments, and you therefore only need to create an empty file with a command like:

```
$touch local.h
```

Now use the make command to create the archive library. Once you have done this, you have completely constructed the f2c distribution. See the corresponding README files for each subdirectory for more information related to their contents.

11.14.4 Conclusion

f2c is a tool which attempts to take Fortran code and automatically convert it to C code. The basic syntax seems to be supported fairly well; however, there is simply not enough experience or information available as of the time of this writing to confirm its stability. Simply try it for yourself on some of your codes and see what happens.

Whatever happens, it may be a very useful tool for you to use in beginning the port of some of your Fortran codes to the C language and environment. See the file f2c.ps in the distribution for more information.

11.15 texinfo

11.15.1 Introduction

texinfo is a documentation system which delivers both on-line and paper documentation from a single input file. texinfo is written and supported by the Free Software Foundation (FSF) and is, therefore, a very robust and well-written product.

texinfo files, often known as info files, are distributed with most GNU products. These files are the documentation you should use to learn about and understand the product. The most common use of the info files is in conjunction with emacs. emacs macros are distributed with texinfo such that you can view info files from within emacs and use emacs as your on-line documentation system. You can also generate dvi (device independent) files for use with TeX and LaTeX pre- and postprocessor software.

There is a stand-alone tool called info that is distributed with texinfo. It will allow you to view documents interactively. See Sec. 11.15.3 for more details.

Finally, texinfo will eventually be merged into the emacs distribution and will disappear as an individual distribution. Keep this in mind if you plan to use texinfo and are not a big emacs user.

texinfo is a GNU product and as such is subject to its GNU General Public license as included both in the product distribution and in App. B of this book.

11.15.2 Installation

The basic installation of texinfo is similar to many other tools from GNU:

```
$ configure --prefix=/usr/local/texinfo/rs6000/texinfo-3.1
```

This will create the proper Makefile. From this you can run make. Remember that without PTF U416277 on your RS/6000, you will get an assembler error related to the -g command, so you should issue the make as follows:

```
$ make CFLAGS=
```

This is not necessary on other platforms.

The make will generate several executables in all subdirectories. It will install a variety of LISP macro files and build several programs, including texi2dvi and makeinfo, which reformat TeX input files to device-independent files and create info files from text files, respectively. These programs and especially the macros can be used by emacs and TeX to generate display and formatted printable output from the same texinfo document.

The README file contains a listing of files in the distribution and their contents. The most interesting is the texinfo.texi file. This contains all the documentation for texinfo itself and can be viewed either with emacs or as stand-alone program info.

The other file of interest is the NEWS file. This contains a variety of information on changes and enhancements to the texinfo product for the last few versions. Take a look at this before you begin using the product.

11.15.3 Usage

texinfo consists of a variety of different types of files. The basic texinfo input file has a .texi or .texinfo suffix. Usually the subject of the texinfo document is the prefix. For example, the texinfo document for gawk is entitled gawk.texinfo. The most common way of using texinfo and texinfo files is with emacs. You can format and display a texinfo file with a few simple keystrokes within emacs. You can also format and display texinfo files with the info subsystem distributed with this book. Finally, you can use TeX to format the texinfo files for printed output.

There are also several scripts distributed with texinfo 3.1 including texi2dvi, which takes texinfo input and generates a dvi for later TeX processing.

This distribution also contains several LISP files which are used by emacs to format a texinfo file. There are a couple of utility files which are not contained in the ./lisp subdirectory with emacs 19.17. To take advantage of these, simply move them into the ./lisp subdirectory and begin to use them.

Finally, there are makeinfo and info files which are executables which create an info file from texinfo files and view them, respectively.

Makeinfo. The makeinfo application takes texinfo input files and generates info output files which can be viewed with the info viewing system. The basic syntax is:

```
makeinfo [options...] file...
```

where options consist of:

`-Idir`	Specifies dir as a directory to search for @include files
`-Dvar`	Defines a variable
`-Uvar`	Undefines a variable
`--no-validate`	Suppresses cross-reference validation
`--no-warn`	Suppresses warnings
`--no-split`	Doesn't split large files
`--no-headers`	Doesn't generate Node: headers
`--verbose`	Verbose option.
`--version`	Displays makeinfo version
`--output file`	Specifies an output filename other than the one specified in the texinfo input file with the @setfilename command
`--paragraph-indent num`	Specifies the default paragraph indent as num

and file... is one or more files to process.

You simply move to the directory where the .texinfo or .texi input file is and issue the makeinfo command. A simple example is:

```
$ makeinfo gawk.texi
```

This will generates a gawk.info file which can then be viewed with the info viewer. If you are in a directory other than the one in which the file is being built, you can use the -I option to specify a directory for any include files.

Info. Once you have generated an info file, you can view it with the info command. The basic syntax is:

```
info [options...] menu-item...
```

where options are:

`--directory dir`	Specifies a directory to search for input files. You can specify a default search path with the INFOPATH environmental variable.
`-f filename`	Specifies a file to use as the initial file (default is dir).
`-n node`	Specifies a node within the input file to move to.
`-o file`	Sends output to file instead of to the default standard output.
`-h`	Produces help.
`--version`	Displays info version.

and menu-item specifies a menu item within the info display file.

Info is essentially a very limited version of emacs which gives you a small set of commands with which you can manipulate the viewing of an info file. The basic command set is:

`f`	Follows a cross-reference
`h`	Invokes tutorial
`?`	Gets summary of info commands
`h`	Selects a node
`Ctrl-g`	Aborts the current command
`Ctrl-l`	Refreshes the screen
`m`	Specifies a menu item by name
`n`	Moves to the next node
`p`	Moves to the previous node
`u`	Moves up a node
`Space`	Scrolls forward a page
`Delete`	Scrolls backward a page
`b`	Goes to beginning of current node
`q`	Quits
`g`	Moves to a specified nodename
`s`	Searches for a specified string
`ESC-x print-node`	Prints the current node to lpr

The basic screen looks like that shown in Fig. 11.1. The window in the figure is the result of the command:

```
$ info -f info.info
```

in the ./info subdirectory of the texinfo distribution. From here you can execute any of the above-mentioned commands to move around within the info file.

texinfo syntax. texinfo syntax is not the same as TeX but replaces TeX to create a file which can be used by both info and TeX to create output. The basic syntax for a texinfo file is commands preceded by a @. A short sample texinfo file, texi.info, is included in the texinfo 3.1 distribution under info. To examine it, use the info system. This short example explains how you would construct a texinfo file. From this you can create almost any kind of file you would like. The texinfo files in the texinfo distribution contain an example of virtually every kind of texinfo command. See these for more details on the actual language.

To get more information on the texinfo system, type these commands when sitting in the top directory of the texinfo 3.1 distribution:

```
$ cd info
$ ./info -f info
```

Note that info is also the default help system on the RS/6000, so you need to be a little careful as to your PATH and which info gets invoked.

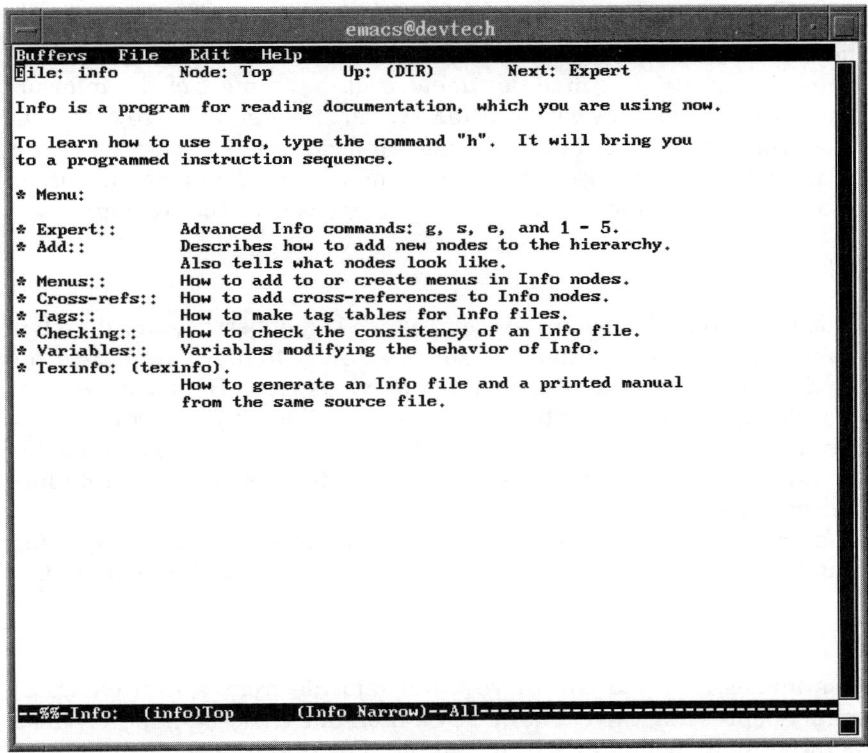

emacs@devtech
Buffers File Edit Help
File: info Node: Top Up: (DIR) Next: Expert
Info is a program for reading documentation, which you are using now.
To learn how to use Info, type the command "h". It will bring you
to a programmed instruction sequence.
* Menu:
* Expert:: Advanced Info commands: g, s, e, and 1 - 5.
* Add:: Describes how to add new nodes to the hierarchy.
Also tells what nodes look like.
* Menus:: How to add to or create menus in Info nodes.
* Cross-refs:: How to add cross-references to Info nodes.
* Tags:: How to make tag tables for Info files.
* Checking:: How to check the consistency of an Info file.
* Variables:: Variables modifying the behavior of Info.
* Texinfo: (texinfo).
How to generate an Info file and a printed manual
from the same source file.
--%%-Info: (info)Top (Info Narrow)--All---

Figure 11.1 Example info window.

It is a good idea to specify ./ at the beginning of the command to ensure that you are getting the info in the current directory.

Once you have played with this and learned a little about the info system, you can use info to get more information on texinfo itself with the commands:

```
$ cd ..
$ ./info/info -f texi
```

Note that some of this information is in the INTRODUCTION; however, the documentation of the above commands in the INTRODUCTION file is incorrect. You should use the above commands to get into the info system and get more information about texinfo.

Finally, to get detailed information about the info system, type:

```
$ ./info/info -f info-stnd
```

Note that the default input filetype is .info for the info system, and it is therefore redundant to include the file suffix.

You can create a printed document containing most of the information in the texinfo files with the TeX system. See the INTRODUCTION file in the texinfo distribution for more information.

The other way to use texinfo is from within emacs. texinfo is an emacs mode and is invoked from within emacs with the command:

```
C-h i
```

This drops you into the info system, which is a hypertext-based system providing access to information and the ability to move around within the documents as well as return to a previous page. By placing all texinfo files in the emacs/info directory, you can access these files transparently with the above command. Note that you have to also modify the dir file in the ./emacs/info subdirectory to make the new info files known to emacs.

You can also access a texinfo file through emacs in a directory other than the default texinfo emacs directory by executing the command:

```
g(filename)nodename<return>
```

This means that you can move to an info file from within emacs by simply depressing the g followed by a filename enclosed in parenthesis followed by a nodename within the file. For example you can move to the gawk info file by typing:

```
g(/usr/local2/gawk/rs6000/gawk-2.15.2/gawk.info)
```

This will produce a screen which looks like the one shown in Fig. 11.2.

You can make anything the default upon invocation of the emacs info mode by placing the appropriate info files into the ./info subdirectory in emacs and editing the dir file in the same directory to contain the nodename for the new info files.

Most software distributions from GNU come with texinfo files; they are very useful when learning a new product. See the help for texinfo within emacs for more information.

11.15.4 Conclusion

There is a tremendous amount of information contained within the texinfo files distributed with many free software products on the Internet. texinfo has its own syntax and methods for constructing files. It is beyond the scope of this book to provide information on the syntax of the language; however, all the information you need is contained in the info files in the texinfo distribution on the CD with this book. By taking

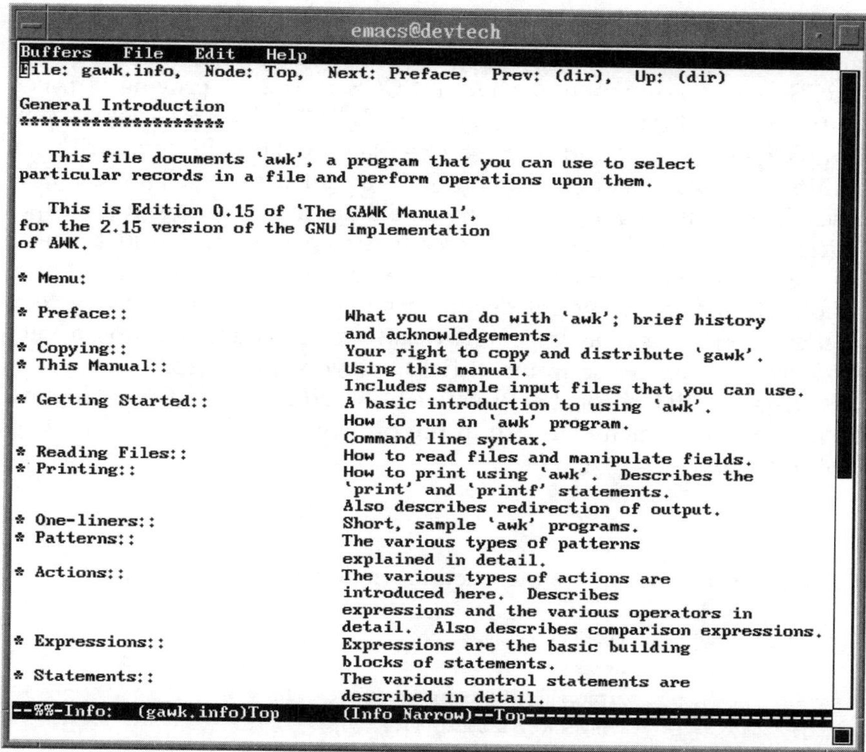

Figure 11.2 gawk info screen.

some time and reviewing this information using the info system described above, you will very quickly become a power texinfo user.

emacs is a very powerful editor and texinfo is one of the reasons why. By providing a hypertext-like system from the same document from which you produce hard-copy documentation, you are saving a significant amount of developer time and cost. Because of the power of texinfo, you can use on-line documentation in a way that really enhances your productivity and effectiveness on a given system.

Finally, texinfo files are written in a format familiar to TeX. In fact, TeX is what you use to produce the texinfo in a printed format.

11.16 RCS

11.16.1 Introduction

RCS stands for Revision Control System. The version discussed in this chapter is 5.6. RCS is written and maintained by Walter F. Tichy at Purdue University. GNU distributes it along with their MANIFEST, which describes the copyleft licensing arrangement. Because of this, you can freely distribute RCS, and thus it is included in this book.

RCS provides function similar to SCCS in that it provides version control and configuration management. By providing a series of commands which control and track source files, RCS provides you with the ability to better control and monitor your software development processes. This chapter is by no means an exhaustive overview of the capabilities and subtleties of RCS. Consult the documentation distributed with RCS for more information. There are manual pages in the man subdirectory and Postscript documents (*.ps) in the doc subdirectory. Specifically, there is a document titled rcs.ps which contains a very good overview and description of RCS and version control.

RCS is a GNU product and as such is subject to its GNU General Public license as included both in the product distribution and in App. B of this book.

11.16.2 Usage

The basic usage of RCS is included in the following commands:

`ci`	Checks in revisions
`co`	Checks out revisions
`ident`	Extracts identification markers
`rcs`	Changes RCS file attributes
`rcsclean`	Cleans working directory
`rcsdiff`	Compares revisions
`rcsfreeze`	Freezes a configuration
`rcsmerge`	Merges revisions
`rlog`	Reads log messages

Each command is discussed in more detail below.

Checking in a file. The basic syntax is:

```
ci [{-lrufkqIM} [rev]] [-ddate] [-mmsg] [-nname] [-Nname] [-sstate]
[-tfile] [-t-string] [-wlogin] [-Vn] [-xsuff] file ...
```

where -l[rev] checks in file(s) and automatically recheck this file out and lock for future editing.
- -r[rev] checks in file(s) and releases the lock.
- -u[rev] checks in file(s) and immediately rechecks this file out but doesn't lock.
- -f[rev] forces the file checkin even if the file hasn't changed.
- -k[rev] searches the checkin file for information keywords containing author, change time, state, etc., to place in RCS instead of computing them locally upon checkin.

-q[rev] is quiet mode.
-I[rev] is interactive mode.
-M[rev] sets the modification time for checkin file.
-d[date] uses current date for checkin.
-mmsg uses string as the message for checkin log.
-nname assigns name to name of revision instead of simply using a number to represent the revision number.
-Nname is the same as -nname except that it will override any previous definition of name.
-sstate sets state of checkin file(s).
-tfile writes text contained in file to RCS.
-t-string writes text contained in string to RCS.
-wlogin assigns login as owner of checkin rather than current userid.
-Vn emulates RCS version *n* instead of the current version.
-xsuff specifies information regarding location of file(s) to be checked in.
file ... is one or more files specified to operate on.

ci is the command which checks files into RCS. You must either own or be the supervisor of the branch for that particular revision. You can override protections and locks with switches on the ci command line.

You control all checked-in files with a concept called a revision. The revision tracks all file releases and relates them to other files. The default revision is 1.1 if no previous matching RCS file exists. ci works with files it calls working files. Working files are the files to be checked in, while the files stored in RCS are called RCS files.

Both the working file and RCS files can be specified explicitly. For example:

```
$ ci test.c
```

will create a file ./RCS/test.c and remove test.c. Placing the RCS file in the RCS subdirectory is the default action for ci. You can specify a resulting RCS filename explicitly. For example:

```
$ ci test.c testing/RCS/test.c
```

takes the file test.c and checks it into RCS in the subdirectory ./testing/RCS as the filenamed test.c.

You can also specify file suffixes for the resulting RCS files. For example:

```
$ ci test.c testing/RCS/test.c,1
```

where ,1 is the suffix for the RCS file. You can check in a file named test.c in the current directory by merely specifying the RCS file. For example:

```
$ ci RCS/test.c,1
```

will look in the current working directory for a file named test.c and check it in. There are several other ways you can manipulate filenames. See the ci man page for more information.

Checking out a file. The basic syntax is:

```
co [{-lrufpqIM} [rev]] [-kkv] [-kkvl] [-kk] [-ko] [krev] [-kv]
   [-d[date]] [-sstate] [-w[login]]
[-jlist] [-Vn] [-xsuff] file ...
```

where -l[rev] checks out file(s) and automatically locks them for future editing.
-r[rev] retrieves latest file or one which matches rev.
-u[rev] retrieves the latest file or the one specified by rev unless the file is locked; then it unlocks and retrieves the file.
-f[rev] forces the working file overwrite.
-p[rev] displays retrieved revision on standard output instead of including in the file.
-q[rev] is quiet mode.
-I[rev] is interactive mode.
-M[rev] sets the modification time for the new working file.
-kkv generates keyword strings based on default information. Username is not included unless the retrieved file is locked.
-kkvl is the same as -kkv except that username is always included.
-kk generates keyword strings without substitution.
-ko generates old keyword string as it existed before the file was checked in.
-k[rev] searches the checkin file for information keywords containing author, change time, state, etc., to place in RCS instead of computing them locally upon checkin.
-kv generates only keyword substitutions and not keyword strings.
-d[date] retrieves file whose date is equal to or later than that specified by date (date can be specified in free format; (see co man page for more information).
-sstate retrieves latest version whose state is state.
-w[login] checks out latest revision owned by login.

-jlist joins revisions together by taking first comma-separated pair from list and generates output passed to the next pair (see rcsmerge).
-Vn emulates RCS version n instead of the current version.
-xsuff specifies information regarding location of file(s) to be checked in.
file ... is one or more files specified to operate on.

There are a variety of keywords which are placed either in the check out file or displayed to standard output. Some of the most important are:

```
$Author$
$Date$
$Header$
$Locker$
$Log$
$Revision$
$Source$
$State$
```

Most of these keywords are self-explanatory. For more information and more keywords, see the co man page. Files are manipulated much the same as with ci. See the previous section for more information.

Searching for keywords. The basic syntax is:

```
ident [-q] [file ...]
```

where -q is quiet mode.
file ... is one or more files to search.

ident searches all named files for all RCS keywords. These are designated by $string$. The result is displayed to standard output.

Change RCS file attributes. The basic syntax is:

```
rcs [-ILUiq] [-alogins] [-Aoldfile] [-e[logins]] [-b[rev]]
  [-cstring] [-kstring] [-l[rev]]
[-u[rev]] [-Mn:log] [-[-nname[:[rev]] [-Nname[:[rev]] [-orange]
  [-sstate[:rev]]
[-t[file]] [-t-string] [-Vn] [-xsuff] file ...
```

where -I is interactive mode.
-L sets strict check in, which is useful for shared files. Enforces locking even for the file's owner.
-U sets nonstrict check in, which means that the owner of a file can check in and check out without locking restrictions.

-i creates and revisions a new RCS file but doesn't deposit anything.
-q is quiet mode.
-alogins appends login list (comma-separated usernames) to the access control list for a file.
-Aoldfile appends login list for oldfile to file.
-e[logins] removes named or all names on the access control list for file.
-b[rev] sets the default branch to rev or the highest if rev not specified.
-cstring makes string the comment displayed before each Log display.
-kstring sets the default keyword substitution to string.
-l[rev] locks the revision rev.
-u[rev] unlocks the revision rev.
-mn:log replaces revision n's log message with log.
-nname:[rev] sets the revision specified to the symbol name. If rev is not specified, the symbolic name is deleted.
-Nname:rev is the same as -nname but overrides any previously defined symbolic names.
-oranges removes revisions specified by range of the form rev1[:rev2], etc.
-sstate:rev sets revision rev to state where state is merely a symbolic name which represents the state of the revision.
-tfile replaces contents of specified RCS file with file.
-t-string replaces descriptive log text of specified RCS file with string.
-Vn emulates RCS version *n*.
-xsuff uses suffixes (see the ci section).
file ... is one or more files to operate on.

RCS either creates a new RCS system or modifies the attributes of an existing one. This is the first command you will execute to begin an RCS library for a software system.

Clean up working files. The basic syntax is:

```
rcsclean [-kstring] [-n[rev]] [-q[rev]] [-u[rev]] [-Vn] [-xsuff]
  [file...]
```

where -kstring uses subst keyword substitution (see co for more details).
-nrev displays the results of the rcsclean command without actually executing it.
-qrev is quiet mode.
-urev unlocks rev if no difference is found.

-Vn emulates RCS version *n*.
-xsuff uses suffixes to control RCS files.
file ... is file or files to be operated on.

rcsclean removes any files that have been checked in since they were last modified. You can either specify files to be checked and removed, or, if no files are specified, all files in the subdirectory RCS are checked against working files in the current directory and removed.

Compare revision differences. The basic syntax is:

```
rcsdiff [-kstring] [-q] [-rrev1 [- rrev2]] [-Vn] [-xsuff] [diff
  options] file ...
```

where -kstring is keyword substitution (see co section).
-q is quiet mode.
-rrev1 -rrev2—if only rev1 is specified, its contents are compared with its working file; if both are specified, the corresponding files are compared between revisions; and if no revisions are specified, the latest revision is compared with its corresponding working files.
-Vn emulates RCS version *n*.
-xsuff uses suffix notation for RCS files.
diff options includes all options from the diff command.
file ... is one or more files to operate on.

rcsdiff generates diff commands on various specified revision files and/or working files outside of RCS. You can even specify diff options to the rcsdiff command. The output of this command looks much like that of the diff command and can be used with other commands to merge file changes.

Freezing configurations. The basic syntax is:

```
rcsfreeze [name]
```

where name is the symbolic name for a revision.

rcsfreeze freezes a configuration (revision) in RCS and, optionally, assigns a symbolic name to this revision. A configuration consists of one or more RCS file revisions grouped together. This is something like a release of a software system. By grouping files together in a configuration, you can later extract these files as a group for manipulation.

Merging files and revisions. The basic syntax is:

```
rcsmerge [-kstring] [-p[rev]] [-q[rev]] [-r[rev]] [-Vn] [-xsuff] file
```

where -kstring uses keyword substitution (see the co section).
-p[rev] displays results on standard output instead of replacing working file.
-q[rev] is quiet mode.
-r[rev] merges file in revision rev.
-Vn emulates version *n*.
-xsuff uses suffix to characterize RCS files.
file is file to merge in.

rcsmerge places the changes between two RCS revisions into a working file specified as file. If you specify two revisions with the -r option, these are the revisions specified; if you specify one revision, it compares these files with those of the latest revision in the RCS library. Finally, if you don't specify a revision, it will merge the results of the latest two revisions into the working file.

This command is useful for seeing what revisions have occurred and how the two specified revisions differ. You can also use this to merge changes that are received after a revision is released and changes have been made.

Displaying log information. The basic syntax is:

```
rlog [-LRbht] [-ddate] [-l[lockers]] [-r[revs]] [-sstates]
  [-w[logins]] [-Vn] [-xsuff]
file ...
```

where -L ignores RCS files without locks.
-R displays only RCS filename without path.
-b displays information about the highest branch.
-h displays RCS information.
-t is same as -h and includes descriptive text.
-ddate displays revision activities within given dates where dates are specified by ranges separated by colons.
-l[lockers] displays information about locked revisions. If lockers is specified as a comma-separated list of usernames, only those revisions owned by these users are displayed.
-r[revs] displays information about revision specified in a comma-separated list.
-sstates displays revision information that is in state.
-w[logins] displays all revisions checked in by usernames in the login comma-separated list.
-Vn emulates RCS version *n*.
-xsuff uses suffixes to specify RCS files.
file ... is file or files to display information about.

rlog displays information relating to those files specified in file(s). With various switches, you can control the display of information and manipulate it accordingly. A simple and common example of using this command is:

```
$ log RCS/*
```

This will display information on all files in the RCS subdirectory.

There are basic themes which run through the above commands. One of the most important is the -xsuffix option. Suffixes are merely ways to control the search order of RCS when looking for RCS files. The default is determined when RCS is installed but is usually ,v. This means that RCS will looks for files ending in ,v as RCS files. You can modify this with the use of suffixes. For example:

```
$ ci -x.rcs test.c
```

will generate and search for RCS files which end in .rcs. When you executed the above command, RCS created a file RCS/test.c.rcs which is the RCS file created with the ci command. You can specify more than one suffix by separating them with forward slashes. For example, to create and use RCS files with suffixes .rcs and ,v, use a command like:

```
$ ci -x.rcs/,v test.c
```

This will create a file test.c.rcs. However, if you had a file named test.c,v, RCS would find this with a command like:

```
$ co -xrcs/,v test.c
```

and retrieve the file correctly. Suffixes allow you to choose your file-naming conventions according to your needs.

The above commands form the base set of commands with which you can perform RCS operations. The basic user needs to only use ci and co to maintain and use the RCS system. Basic functions of RCS as outlined in the accompanying documentation are:

Store and retrieve multiple versions of text

Maintain a history of changes

Lock files and control user access

Support hierarchical versioning

Merge revisions

Provide user-friendly release and configuration control mechanisms

Minimize disk space required by storing only deltas

While most points above are self-explanatory, the last is worth brief mention. RCS, like SCCS, stores only the differences between file revisions (commonly called deltas), which minimizes the amount of disk space required while maintaining the proper relationships between file versions.

There is a manual page named rcsintro.1 which describes in some detail the operation of RCS. There are linkages between RCS and some versions of make, particularly GNU make. See the accompanying rcs.ps file for more details on this interface.

11.16.3 Examples

A simple example of the use of RCS will explain most of the functions you will need to know to use RCS effectively. Assume you have a Fortran source file named test.f and you want to check it into RCS. First create an RCS subdirectory:

```
$ mkdir RCS
```

Then check the file into RCS with the command:

```
$ ci test.f
```

This will create a file in the RCS subdirectory and remove test.f from the current directory. Remember, the default first revision is 1.1. If you want to check in the file but not remove it from the current directory, use the command:

```
$ ci -l test.f
```

or

```
$ ci -u test.f
```

The first does an implicit checkout after the checkin and locks the file for editing. The second does an implicit checkout after checkin but does not lock the file.

Next, you may want to check out the file for modifications. Use the command:

```
$ co -l test.f
```

This will take the latest version of test.f from the RCS subdirectory and create a test.f file in your current working directory. Note that if you co without the -l option, you will not be able to check the file back in with a subsequent ci command. This is useful when you want to compile or examine a file without making changes.

Once you have edited the file, you can check it back in with the command:

```
$ ci test.f
```

This will remove the file test.f from your current working directory and save it as test.f revision 1.2. If you have not locked the file with co -l, you will get an error message relating to the fact that you don't own the lock on test.f. If this is the case, you can force a lock with the command:

```
$ rcs -l test.f
```

This grabs the lock without actually checking out the file. Note also that if someone else has the lock, this command will fail, and you will have to see the person who has the lock and coordinate your checkin with him or her.

You can also compare a working file to an RCS file with a command like:

```
$ rcsdiff test.f
```

This will generate a diff command between your current test.f working file and the highest revision test.f in the RCS system.

There are other commands provided with RCS; however, your need for them will probably be minimal, at least initially. Keep these simple examples in mind when beginning to use RCS.

11.16.4 Installation

There are several issues to note when installing RCS. You need a diff command that supports the -n option. If yours does not, get GNU diff from the included CD and use it. There is a README file in the main RCS directory which has an in-depth discussion of the history of features and functions of RCS. See this for related information.

The information on how to build RCS is contained in the ./src/ README file. A synopsis of that file follows. There is no configure as is part of standard delivery with most newer GNU products. There is instead a shell script named conf.sh. This is executed from within the Makefile and builds the proper configuration as well as it can. Note that the initial section of the Makefile is called the configuration section. This is the place you may have to change some variables and macro definitions based on your machine architecture and what pieces of software you have installed. For example, if you don't have the GNU diff command installed, you need to comment out the line DIFF and remove the commend for the previous line which defines standard diff. There is a section in the README file entitled Makefile notes. See this for more details on possible problems or notes for your particular platform.

The first command to type is:

```
$ make conf.h
```

This generates a new conf.h that is appropriate for your machine. If you get an error message, see the README file section entitled conf.h notes. This contains some brief comments as to possible problems or issues with the conf.h. There should be very little problem since conf.sh seems to be fairly conservative in its construction of conf.h and assumes very little about your machine.

Once you have built conf.h, issue the command:

```
$ make install
```

This generates all the appropriate executables for RCS. It also issues the install command by default, which will install all binaries in the /usr/local directory structure for access by all users on the system. This is also what you typically export to the network; therefore, this will provide RCS to the network. You can change this by modifying the appropriate Makefile or conf.h macros.

You can test the installation with the command:

```
$ make installtest
```

This will test the installation and produce diff commands for all commands in RCS. Note that you must have an RCS subdirectory created for the makeinstall to use. You must also have installed the correct diff based on the macro definition discussed earlier.

This is all there is to installing RCS. It is really quite simple. If you find any bugs, report them to rcs-bugs@cs.purdue.edu.

11.16.5 Conclusion

RCS has many of the features of SCCS and other more attractive features. It also has an easier interface which provides a more feature-rich and user-friendly interface. By providing a configuration management capability, RCS can assist you with your software development projects. With the ability to track and control file manipulation and modification and provide a history of all changes, RCS will quickly become a required part of your software development processes.

Chapter

12

Nonnative General Utilities

This section contains tools which are general in nature but are available only from the Internet or some other source. These tools range from shells to shell utilities and tools which provide additional functionality to your existing workstations such as fax.

These tools are not directly related to software development. For more information on tools related to software see Chap. 11.

12.1 bash

12.1.1 Introduction

bash is the GNU Bourne-Again Shell and is a sh-compatible shell interpreter which provides significantly enhanced functionality over sh (Bourne shell), csh (C shell), and ksh (Korn shell). While sh and csh are provided on most UNIX platforms, ksh is not and therefore is not as widely used as the other two shells.

You can purchase ksh from AT&T for use on any system; however, you may not be willing to provide additional funding for a shell for your version of UNIX and, therefore, are limited to sh and csh. ksh has more functionality than either sh or csh and, in fact, combines the best functionality from both sh and csh in its implementation. But because of its lack of general availability, because of its cost, there is a need for additional shell functionality that bash can provide.

bash is intended to be POSIX compliant and to provide consistent and documented interfaces and command structures as well as heterogeneous support of UNIX platforms. This is important as you get larger and more heterogeneous environments and need to support and use systems with diverse UNIX flavors. bash utilizes the best functions from sh, csh, and ksh and provides significant functionality above and beyond sh, csh, or ksh, all at no cost.

bash is a GNU product and as such is subject to its GNU General Public license as included both in the product distribution and in App. B of this book.

12.1.2 Usage

The basic syntax of bash is as follows:

```
bash [options] [file]
```

where options consist of both internal (built-in) and external options which are documented in some detail below:

`-, --`	Disables further command line option processing. All strings following - or -- are filenames or arguments.
`-c commands`	Reads commands from commands.
`-i`	Makes shell interactive.
`-login`	Invokes bash as if invoked by login.
`-nobraceexpansion`	Doesn't perform curly brace expansion.
`-noprofile`	Doesn't load /etc/profile or .bash_profile.
`-norc`	Doesn't load personal initialization file .bashrc.
`--quiet`	Doesn't display start-up information.
`rcfile file`	Uses file as personal initialization file instead of .bashrc.
`-s`	Reads commands from standard input.
`-version`	Displays current version of bash.
`file`	Is file containing shell commands to be executed on bash invocation.

Shell programming. This chapter will not discuss all the functionality provided by bash; however, some discussion of the shell programming characteristics as well as built-in commands is necessary to understand the context of the shell and its capabilities.

Many of the same functions supported in the other shell are supported in bash. Things like reserved words, pipes, metacharacters, and other similar functions are fully supported. In fact, it is a good assumption that sh programming syntax will create the proper framework for developing shell scripts and executing commands.

There are ways to control the execution of shell programs and commands with basic syntax provided with bash. The standard throughout the bash command documentation is the use of the word list separated by semicolons to represent a series of one or more commands. An example is:

```
list1 = (command1;command2; command3; ...)
```

where commandn is simply a regular UNIX command or internal shell command. As with sh, this allows you to create multiple commands on the same command line. This is a powerful feature for interactive use and for scripting.

Some examples of command syntax are:

<table>
<tr><td><code>#</code></td><td>In first column, denotes a comment</td></tr>
<tr><td><code>(command;command;...)</code></td><td>Executes all given commands in a single subshell</td></tr>
<tr><td><code>{command;command;...}</code></td><td>Executes all given commands in current shell</td></tr>
<tr><td><code>for name [in word;] do list; done</code></td><td>Standard loop syntax</td></tr>
<tr><td><code>case word in [patttern [|pattern] ...list;;] ...esac</code></td><td>Standard case syntax</td></tr>
<tr><td><code>if list then list [elif list then list] ...[else list] fi</code></td><td>Standard if command syntax</td></tr>
<tr><td><code>while list do list done</code></td><td>Standard while syntax</td></tr>
<tr><td><code>until list do list done</code></td><td>Somewhat unique until command syntax</td></tr>
</table>

There are metacharacters which mean special things to the bash interpreter. They are |, &, ;, ( ), < >, <space>, and <tab>. If you want to physically represent the shell metacharacters on a command line, you must “escape” them much as you have to in the other shells. In other words, if you have a string:

```
kevin( )
```

which you want to represent on the command line as a literal and not have bash interpret the ( ) to mean something special, you would use:

```
kevin\(\)
```

where the \ (backslash) escapes the metacharacters from interpretation.

There are two other ways to affect command line interpretation: the single quote and the double quote. They behave differently; therefore it is important to understand how they work in bash.

The single quote maintains the literal string with no command substitution or shell interpretation. For example:

```
'string1;$string2;!string3'
```

will present the literal string as displayed above as the result of the command interpretation. The only exception to this is the single quote itself, which may not be placed within a pair of single quotes.

Double quotes maintain the literal string with the exception of $, ‘, and \ interpretation. This is useful to provide literal metacharacters other than those listed. The same string as above:

```
"string1;$string2;!string3"
```

will provide the output:

```
string;someotherstring;!string3
```

where someotherstring is the interpreted value of string2. Note that this provides basic string-level substitution without interfering with your ability to pass most literal strings directly to the program invoked from the shell.

This brings us to a discussion of shell variables and parameters. The basic syntax for viewing and setting variable values is:

```
name=[value]
```

where name is the name of the variable to set.
value is the value to set for name. If value is not set, the default is NULL.

Simple display of the value of name is with the metacharacter $. For example, to set and view the value of the variable of author to kevin, use:

```
$ author=kevin
$ echo $author
author=kevin
```

There are special predefined variables in bash which are very similar to sh and ksh. They are:

BASH	Full pathname of current bash invocation.
CDPATH	Searches path for cd command.
ENV	If set, provides bash initialization file.
EUID	Effective user id.
HISTFILE	File to save history command.
HISTSIZE	Size of history recall list.
HOSTTYPE	Automatically set to current system type.
IGNOREEOF	If set, specifies the number of EOFs that must be received before bash exits. The default value is 10.
LINENO	Current line number in a script.
MAIL	Set to a specific filename; bash notifies you when you receive mail to this file.
MAILCHECK	Sets time in seconds to check for new mail.

MAILPATH	Specifies a path to check for new mail. Default is system mail area.
OLDPWD	Previous working directory.
OPTARG	Last option argument processed by built-in command.
OPTIND	Last option index processed by built-in command.
PPID	Parent process id.
PWD	Current working directory.
RANDOM	Each time RANDOM is used it generates a random number.
SECONDS	Equates to the number of seconds since bash invocation.
SHLVL	Is incremented each time bash is invoked.
TMOUT	Time in seconds to wait for terminal input before timing out.
UID	Current user id.
command_oriented_history	Attempts to save multiple command line commands as a single-history entry for later easier use.
noclobber	Doesn't overwrite existing files with redirection commands.
nolinks	Doesn't follow symbolic link paths for command execution.
notify	Notifies the user of job control issues immediately.

There are many other variables in bash, but these are the most commonly used ones. See the documentation for more details, specifically the man page delivered with bash (bash.1).

Many of the things you have come to expect from a shell interpreter in UNIX are available and supported in bash. Things like redirection, command line expansion and substitution, built-in commands, aliases, and job control are fully supported. Many of these functions such as job control and aliases operate much the same as csh, while functions such as redirection and substitution operate much as sh does.

There are a variety of ways you can structure the command line within bash. There are also a variety of ways you can define bash to interact with respect to command line editing and terminal emulation. Much of the functionality of bash is derived from emacs, and therefore command documentation is similar to emacs. For example, the syntax C-c means to depress the CTRL key and the lowercase c key at the same time. The documentation delivered with bash uses syntax like M-c to denote pressing the ESC key and the lowercase c key in sequence. To be consistent, this section will use the same syntax.

Some of the more basic bash capabilities and commands are:

set editing-mode vi	Establishes command line editing with vi commands (similar to ksh)
C-a	Moves to beginning of line
C-b	Moves back one character
C-d	Deletes text under cursor

`C-e`	Moves to end of line
`C-f`	Moves forward one character
`C-k`	Removes text following cursor
`C-l`	Refreshes the screen
`C-n`	Recalls the next command from the history list
`C-p`	Recalls the previous command from the history list
`C-r`	Moves sequentially through the history list in reverse order
`C-s`	Moves sequentially through the history list in forward order
`C-u`	Kills the current line
`C-v`	Adds the character following C-v as a literal (good way to enter ESC, etc.)
`M-/`	Attempts filename completion
`M-~`	Attempts userid completion
`M-<`	Moves to the first command in the history list
`M->`	Moves to the last line in the history list
`M-b`	Moves back one word
`M-c`	Capitalizes first character of current word
`M-d`	Removes text in the current word following the cursor
`M-f`	Moves forward one word
`M-l`	Lowercases the current word
`M-u`	Uppercases the current word

All of the above keystroke sequences can be executed at the command line to provide the documented functionality. bash has by far the most flexible and powerful user interface for a shell since it combines all the best from sh, csh, and ksh. The above listing is a sample of that functionality. See the documentation for more details.

Most of the built-in commands are similar to those of the other shells. Commands such as echo, eal, exec, fg, jobs, popd, pushd, set, test, trap, ulimit, umask, and wait are fully supported. There are some unique commands which deserve specific mention. Some of these are:

`builtin [shell-builtin [args]`	Executes shell-builtin with args. This is used to redefine a built-in command for execution of itself.
`dirs [-l]`	Lists directories in current remembered directories created and manipulated by pushd and popd.
`help [pattern]`	Provides bash-specific help on built-in commands or those matching pattern.
`times`	Displays user and system times since shell invocation.
`ulimit [-HSacdfmstpn [limit]]`	Displays and manipulates process resources: -H—specifies a hard limit on the resource which says that it cannot be increased at a later time. -S—specifies a soft limit on the resource which says that it can be increased to the hard limit at a later time. -a—displays all current limits.

-c—core file maximum size.
-d—data segment maximum size.
-f—maximum file size.
-m—maximum resident size.
-s—maximum stack size.
-t—maximum CPU time.
-p—pipe size.
-n—number of open file descriptors.
limit—specifies a limit to set. If limit is not specified, all above options cause the current variable value to be displayed.

Some systems may not support the ulimit command. Try it on your system and see.

12.1.3 Installation

There are a variety of files associated with bash and its installation and usage. One of the first to examine is the ChangeLog file, which contains information that describes changes to the current version. This is important since bash is undergoing constant development and change, and new features and bug fixes will be documented here.

bash does not use the configure subsystem to assist with the build; however, it does have the capability to determine which machine you are on based on information and logic placed in the makefile itself. While this may not always be accurate, it does provide a good first guess as to machine type and the necessary files for the correct build to occur.

The basic syntax to build bash is:

```
$ make clean
$ make
```

Once you have done this, the documentation recommends that you attempt to run bash with the command:

```
./bash
```

This should invoke an interactive bash shell. If it does not, see the file INSTALL for information regarding specific machine information.

There are a variety of product- and machine-specific issues which may need to be addressed when you build bash. The file machines.h contains both a general macro definition section and a specific section for a variety of machine types. Look in this file for your machine type and ensure that the build agrees that this is the machine type you are using. Once you have invoked the make command, it creates a file named .machine which tells you what type of machine it thinks you are using.

If you are using tools other than the standard ones shipped with your machine, you may need to edit the Makefile to use these tools. For example, if you are using the GNU C compiler, you should uncomment the related lines in the beginning of the cpp-Makefile file. You should also uncomment the bison line in the same file since the yacc compiler may have problems with building bash. So, install bison before you install yacc.

For example, it was necessary to change the prototype definitions for both rindex and index in general.c to avoid a prototype conflict on the RS/6000 using gcc. These are the kind of things which sometimes occur when building these types of products. See the documentation with bash for more details on building and using bash.

When make executes, it displays what it thinks is the current machine type and stores it in a file named .machine in the current build directory. Check this file to see what machine type bash was built for if you don't see it displayed on your screen. See also the file machines.h which contains information regarding compilation parameters for all defined machine types. In fact, if you are porting to a machine that is not in machines.h, you should create your own block of information for your particular architecture and make based on these parameters.

Bug reports should be mailed to bash-maintainers@ai.mit.edu. See the file INSTALL for more information on bug reporting.

12.1.4 Conclusion

bash is a very powerful tool which provides shell functionality from sh, ksh, and csh as well as some of its own unique functionality. By providing this functionality at no cost and the ability to run the same shell on various UNIX platforms, you can significantly enhance the portability of your environment while at the same time reducing costs. bash is backward compatible with sh, csh, and ksh and will support most shell scripts, commands, and functional subsystems to ensure protection of your current investments.

Much of this documentation was taken directly from the GNU bash man page; see it for more information. Note also that, as with most newer GNU products, there is a texinfo file in the documentation subdirectory which you can view with info or emacs to get more information than is in the man page.

12.2 perl

12.2.1 Introduction

perl stands for practical extraction and report language (but is better known as pathologically eclectic rubbish lister). perl really consists of the best of many structures and constructs from C, sed, and awk as well as many of the functions of shell programming. It is a language unlike any other you have seen and, subsequently, has a significant amount of power and capability for doing work on a UNIX platform.

perl is a massive and powerful utility that is fairly new in the UNIX community. Because of its power, this section will not spend very much time on its use and syntax but will focus more on its overall capabilities and uses. There is a lengthy manual page included with the perl distribution that covers all perl capabilities and syntax in great detail.

perl really provides functionality that combines the best of C programming with the best of shell programming. It provides a rich data manipulation capability as well as data display capability. As perl matured, it gained the capability to use sockets for network and interprocess communication as well as for file and process manipulation.

perl makes easy what has traditionally been difficult to do in the past: combine interactive applications to manipulate and display information not only on the local machine but on remote machines as well. It provides a conglomeration of many UNIX functions in one C-like language. If you are familiar with C syntax, perl will look very familiar and should be relatively easy to learn. However, because of the complexity, it will take some time to learn all of its functions, so be ready to dedicate a few days to become proficient.

perl supports many of the structures and functions of sed and awk and in fact contains tools to covert your old awk and sed scripts to perl scripts. This is a very useful first step in learning perl since it provides you with a direct translation from something you are familiar with to something you are trying to learn. From this, you can see how perl functions and the advantages it can provide.

perl also delivers a debugging system which allows you to trace a program in real time and see its behavior one line at a time.

The benefits of perl in a heterogeneous computing environment are clear: one consistent development interface across all platforms. There are many differences between point tools in a UNIX solution. Some machines use ksh while others use sh. Some machines use awk while others use nawk. Because of UNIX's ability to pipe tools together, developers tend to string single tools together in a long chain to accomplish their desired results. As the heterogeneity of the environment increases, this chain begins to break down since different point tools behave differently on different platforms. perl fixes this by providing a single, consistent interface across all platforms, including most of the point tools within its domain. This is probably the biggest single benefit to perl for most power users and is the main reason perl is so widely accepted.

perl is a GNU product and as such is subject to its GNU General Public license as included both in the product distribution and in App. B of this book.

12.2.3 Installation

perl comes in a compressed tar file. First unzip the file and unwind the resulting tar file. Once this is done, run the configure command:

```
$ ./configure
```

This is not the typical configure system which generates makefiles and determines the type of machine you are running on by itself. It is a script which prompts you for input at a variety of places and lets you help it figure out what kind of machine it is on. configure provides a nice set of default operating systems from which to choose. If you choose one of these, you will get nice default prompts as you run the script; however, if you don't, you will have to answer many questions about the structure of your operating environment.

In building the executables contained on the CD included with this book, most of the defaults were chosen, including default directories in which to place binaries. However, they were not installed. If you wish to install them in a particular directory, either enter the desired directories in the ./configure session or edit the makefile and change the first few macro definitions which define where the binaries and libraries go. This will only be used when you issue the $make install command. This means that the binaries were created in the main perl directory. By creating the files in this manner, the build seemed to proceed much more smoothly. Look at the CD for more information.

configure will generate the appropriate files from which you can build perl. The basic command is similar to others using the configure utility (see Sec. 11.1 for more information). The basic command might be:

```
$ make clean
$ make
```

This will generate the appropriate perl executables, including utilities to convert awk and sed scripts to perl scripts. perl runs on many platforms, and you shouldn't have any problems with the installation.

All answers given to the ./configure tool are contained in the config.sh files in each machine's directory. View this to determine what responses to give to configure to build these products.

12.2.4 Conclusion

This section did not introduce you to either the syntax or the functionality of perl. Instead it attempted to whet your appetite for more information about it. By providing information about its basic capabilities and functions, this section may have prodded you into further action.

The best introduction to perl is in the Nutshell Book *Programming Perl* from O'Reilly & Associates. The other document to study is the manual page included with the perl distribution perl.1. This is 100+ pages of in-depth information on perl and its syntax and functionality. Study these two items before proceeding with perl.

perl is the most powerful language to emerge for a long time. It provides many functions that fourth-generation languages purport to provide, but at the same time it provides the power of second- and third-generation languages. perl 4.035 is on the included CD. Dump it to your hard disk and have fun.

12.3 shellutils

12.3.1 Introduction

shellutils is a collection of shell utilities which enhance your effectiveness within the shell environment. They are distributed by the Free Software Foundation (FSF). The commands shipped with shellutils 1.8 are:

```
basename, date, dirname, echo, env, expr, false, groups, id,
logname, nice, nohup, pathchk, printenv, printf, sleep, stty, su,
tee, test, true, tty, uname, who, whoami, yes
```

For more detail on specific commands see the usage section. Some of the commands are identical to those available on most UNIX platforms; however, there are utilities such as basename and dirname which are not available on all UNIX flavors, and, therefore, they are worth investigating. There is also an advantage to portability across UNIX flavors, and providing a tool such as printenv that is the same across all of your UNIX platforms has large benefits, especially when you are distributing software and other systems in a heterogeneous environment.

Also, GNU is attempting to deliver noncopyrighted software which provides the same function as that delivered by UNIX vendors and also conforms to the POSIX interface specifications so that all implementations will be the same.

There is a small subsection below on each command included in the shellutils distribution version 1.8. See your local Internet distribution for more current information if it is available.

shellutils is a GNU product and as such is subject to its GNU General Public license as included both in the product distribution and in App. B of this book. Also see the GNU Library General Public License in the distribution and in App. B.

12.3.2 Installation

shellutils come with the standard configure capability that ships with most newer GNU tools. The basic commands you use to build shellutils are:

```
$ configure --prefix=/usr/local/shellutils/shellutils-1.8
$ make clean
$ make
```

This will generate all files in directories under /usr/local/shellutils-1.8 such as lib, man, and bin. Make sure these subdirectories exist, or you will have problems with the final phase of the build process. The default is to create these files in the same directories under /usr/local and therefore to share directories with other tools. As your environment grows large, this can cause problems, so this book recommends that you separate all tools into their own subdirectories to keep from overwriting files and other information. See Sec. 11.1 for more information on this tool.

Files are created in man/man1, bin, and lib subdirectories under either the prefix variable or the default directories.

12.3.3 Usage

There are something like 26 commands which are provided in the shellutils tar file. These are briefly described below.

basename. The syntax is:

```
basename string [suffix]
```

where string is any string, usually a qualified filename.
suffix is string to remove as a suffix.

basename strips any prefix up to the last / from a given string. It will also remove any suffix defined by a string suffix. The output is directed to standard output. For example:

```
$ basename /usr/local/kevin
kevin
```

To remove a suffix, you might use a command like:

```
$ basename /usr/local/kevin.tar.Z .Z
kevin.tar
```

This function can be very useful when scripting or generating utilities which manipulate filenames and you only want the filename and not the fully qualified path or suffix information.

date. The syntax is:

```
date [-u] [-d date] [-s date] [+FORMAT] [MMDDhhmm[[CC]YY][.ss]]
```

where -u sets the time in Greenwich Mean Time (or Universal Coordinated Time).
-d date displays the date as calculated from date.
-s date sets the date as specified in date.
+FORMAT specifies the relative format.
[MMDDhhmm[[CC]YY][.ss]]... specifies the date in months, days, hours, minutes, centuries, years, and seconds, respectively.

date returns the current time and date when executed with no parameters. See either the man page for more information on date or the cron section for more information on time parameters.

dirname. The syntax for dirname is:

```
dirname filename
```

where filename is a fully or partially qualified filename.
dirname strips the filename following the last / and returns only the fully qualified pathname. For example:

```
$ dirname /usr/local/kevin/test.file
/usr/local/kevin
```

This is useful when scripting and is basically the opposite of the basename command.

echo. The syntax is:

```
echo [-ne] [string ...]
```

where -n doesn't output trailing newline.
-e interprets escaped (backslashed) characters in string.
string ... is one or more strings to be echoed to standard output.

The most common use of echo is to examine the results of a command before actually executing it. For example:

```
$ echo ls *
```

will print the results of the command ls * to standard output without executing ls *. The * will be replaced by all files in the current directory before the ls command is executed.

env. The basic syntax is:

```
env [-] [-i] [-u name] [--ignore-env]
[--unset=name][name=value]...[command [args...]]
```

where - ignores inherited environment.
-i is the same as -.
-u name unsets environmental variable name before command execution.
--ignore-env is the same as -.
--unset=name is the same as -u name.
-name=value defines variable as value for command execution.
command [args...] is the command to be executed including any passed arguments.

This command is useful when you either want to pass no information from the current environment because of a different required behavior of a command or want to pass environment information only to a subprocess. In UNIX, only certain information is passed from a parent to its child process. If you want to ensure the existence of a variable only for the life of a child process, use the env command to accomplish this. A basic example of this might be:

```
$ env -TERM=vt100 curses.application
```

This runs the application curses.application with the TERM environmental variable set to vt100, which is what the curses application needs to function properly.

expr. The syntax is:

```
expr expression
```

where expression represents a number of expressions ranging from boolean to arithmetic to string oriented.

You can use expr to evaluate expressions which support the following basic operators:

`|`	Logical OR
`&`	Logical AND
`< <= > >=`	Less than, less than equal to, greater than, greater than equal to; returns a 1 if relation is true and 0 otherwise
`+ - * /`	Add, subtract, multiply, and divide
`:`	String comparison

Spaces must separate all operators and operands. The best way to understand this function is to see a couple of examples:

```
$ expr 1 + 2
3
$ expr $a == $b
```

will compare the contents of a and b and return 1 if they match and 0 if they don't.

false. The syntax is:

```
false
```

This only sets the status environmental variable to 1, which represents false.

groups. The syntax is:

```
groups [username...]
```

where username... is one or more username. groups prints out all groups the current user or any user specified by username belongs to.

id. The syntax is:

```
id [-gnruG] [--group] [--name] [--real] [--user] [--groups]
[username]
```

where -g, --group display only group information.
-n, --name display username and not id. Requires -n, -g, or -G.
-r, --real display real userid and not effective userid. Requires -n, -g, or -G.
-u, --user display only the userid.
-G, --groups display only supplementary groups.
username is username of user.

logname. The syntax is:

```
logname
```

This displays the user's login name.

nice. The syntax is:

```
nice [-n adj] [-adj] [--adj=adj] [command [arg...]]
```

where -n adj, -adj, --adj=adj specify that adj be the adjustment to the process priority instead of the default +10.
command [arg...] is command to be effected.

nice adjusts the process priority to the UNIX scheduler. This effects how much CPU time the process or command gets. The higher the number, the lower the priority. The range is from –20 (the highest priority) to 19 (the lowest priority). General users cannot bump their command priority up but can bump it down. For example:

```
$ nice -adj=15 batchjob
```

will execute the command batchjob at a lower priority level by a factor of 15. To get a listing of the current scheduling priorities, simply type:

```
$ nice
0
```

The default nice setting is 0.

Only the superuser (root) can increase command execution priority with a command like:

```
$ nice -adj=-20 batchjob
```

This will execute batchjob with the highest priority possible on the system.

Use this command when the system gets loaded and response time gets slow. nice allows you to decrease the amount of CPU time your jobs are getting and lets you focus on getting your interactive processes more CPU time and, one hopes, better response.

nohup. The syntax is:

```
nohup command [args...]
```

where command [args...] is a command to be executed with optional arguments.

nohup allows you to execute a job even after you hang up or log off. This is very useful since the default is to kill any background jobs when you log off and the parent process goes away. Keep in mind that standard output is typically a tty, so when you log off, the standard output is redirected to nohup.out. Standard input, however, is queued, and the job will hang if it is expecting input from a terminal device. Make sure to redefine standard input if you are going to use nohup. Note also that nohup doesn't automatically put the command in the background. You should do this explicitly with & before logging off.

pathchk. The syntax is:

```
pathchk [-p] [--portability] path...
```

where -p, --portability check path for length related to the POSIX spec and also to see if they contain only characters in the portable character set.
path... is one or more pathname to check.

pathchk is a compatibility tester for directory systems in heterogeneous environments. It is very useful when you are distributing complex and sophisticated software systems to heterogeneous environments which may have different specifications for path characteristics.

pathchk checks to see if the pathnames are within the filesystem's maximum as well as if all directories and subdirectories within path have execute permission. pathchk prints out a 0 if all tests are passed and a 1 if one or more test failed.

printenv. The syntax is:

```
printenv [var...]
```

where var... is one or more environmental variables to be displayed.

printenv displays the value of any specified or all (if no variables specified) variables in the current process context. This is very similar to printenv, which exists on most UNIX systems.

printf. The syntax is:

```
printf format [arg...]
```

where format specifies the format of the output string.
arg... is one or more arguments to display.

printf functions exactly as the C function printf, including its support of formats and arguments. For example:

```
$ printf "%s\n" string1
string1
```

Note that the format is enclosed in quotes to bypass shell interpretation. Try this command without the quotes and see what you get.

sleep. The syntax is:

```
sleep number[smhd]
```

where number is an alphanumeric number followed by:

s—seconds (default)

m—minutes

h—hours

d—days

sleep puts your current process context to sleep for a specified period of time. For example:

```
$ sleep 10s
```

will put your current process to sleep for 10 seconds.

stty. The syntax is:

```
stty [-ag] [--all] [--save] [setting...]
```

where -a, --all display all current settings.
-g, --save is save all current settings.
setting... is one or more settings passed to stty. See information below.

stty is a very powerful and cryptic terminal line display and control facility. There are many parameters which determine the behavior of your terminal, most of which can be controlled through stty.

su. The syntax is:

```
su [-flmp] [-c command] [-s shell] [--login] [--fast]
[--preserve-env]
[--command=command] [--shell=shell] [-] [user name[arg...]]
```

where -f is fast start-up. Prevents /bin/csh from reading its start-up file .cshrc.
-c command, --command=nd invoke shell and run command as the first executable.
-, -l, --login run as an entirely new login, which means environmental variables and other process related variables and states are not preserved.
-m, -p, --preserve-env preserve the current environment, including using the SHELL variable to create the new shell.

-s shell, --shell=shell invoke the new process with shell instead of the default shell from /etc/passwd.
username[arg...] is the option userid and arguments to be passed to the login shell. Note that the default is to su to root if no userid is given.

su allows you to switch user and move freely from one real userid to another while either maintaining your current process context or inheriting one from the user you su to. If you want to execute as another, you can either telnet localhost to loop back into the current address or simply su to the username in question. su is typically easier and supports more function than the telnet command.

tee. The syntax is:

```
tee [-ai] [--append] [--ignore-interrupts] [file...]
```

where -a, --append append to a preexisting file.
-i, --ignore-interrupts ignore interrupts during the processing of output to the tee command.
file... is one or more files to write to.

The tee command is useful to append or create a file taking standard output and redirecting both standard output and a file. This allows you to view standard output information while at the same time creating a file for future reference and logging. For example:

```
$ ls | tee ls.out
```

will generate both an output listing of files in the current directory to the standard output, which is probably the terminal, and will create a file with the same information called ls.out. Simply list the contents of ls.out with the cat command to prove this to yourself.

test. The syntax is:

```
test [expr]
```

where expr is an expression which consists of a variety of boolean and other operations on files. The typical syntax is:

```
operator file
```

Some of the basic expressions which exist are:

`-G file`	File exists and is owned by your effective groupid.
`-L file`	File exists and has symbolic link.

`-O file`	File exists and is owned by your effective userid.
`-S file`	File exists and is a socket.
`-b file`	File exists and is a block mode file.
`-c file`	File exists and is a character mode.
`-d file`	File exists and is a directory.
`-e file`	File exists.
`-f file`	Files exists and is a regular file.
`-g file`	File exists and is a gid file.
`-k file`	File exists and has sticky bit set.
`-n string`	True means that string length is nonzero.
`-p file`	File exists and is a pipe.
`-r file`	File exists and is readable.
`-s file`	File exists and has a size greater than 0.
`-u file`	File exists and sid bit is set.
`-w file`	File exists and is writeable.
`-x file`	File exists and is executable.
`-z string`	True if string length is zero.
`! expr`	True if expression is false.

In addition to the above unary operations, you can support binary operations as expressions. Some of the possibilities are:

`file1 -nt file2`	True if file1 is newer than file2
`file1 -ot file2`	True if file1 is older than file2
`file1 -ef file2`	True if file1 and file2 have the same inode and device numbers
`string1 = string2`	True if string1 equals string2
`string1 != string2`	True if string1 is not equal to string2
`expr1 -a expr2`	True if expression1 and expression2 are true (logical AND)
`expr1 -o expr2`	True if expression1 or expression2 are true (logical OR)
`num1 -eq num2`	True if num1 equals num2
`num1 -ne num2`	True if num1 is not equal to num2
`num1 -ge num2`	True if num1 is greater than or equal to num2
`num1 -gt num2`	True if num1 is greater than num2
`num1 -lt num2`	True if num1 is less than num2
`num1 -le num2`	True if nun1 is less than or equal to num2

These functions are most useful when script programming. For example, you can test for the existence of a file with a command like:

```
if (test -f kevin) then
...
```

This will check to see if the file kevin exists and is a regular file. The result of the test command is a 0 if the expression is true and 1 if it is false. This corresponds to the expression evaluation in script programming.

You can also use this function to check arithmetic information with a command like:

```
if (test $num1 -eq $num2) then
```

where $num1 and $num2 could be numeric arguments you want to compare. There are almost an unlimited number of possibilities with this test command.

It should be noted that in some shell programming languages, including Bourne and Korn, the test is implicit in the parenthesis () and therefore redundant.

true. The syntax is:

```
true
```

This returns a status of 0, which means that the expression is true. A classic example of the use of this is in a loop that you want to be continuous. For example:

```
if (true) then
.....
```

The line under this expression will always be executed. You can also use an expression like:

```
while (true)
....
```

and accomplish an endless loop. Be careful of this one since you have to break out of this some other way than with a conditional evaluation of the expression in the while statement.

tty. The syntax is:

```
tty [-s]
```

where -s is silent mode. It displays nothing.

tty displays the current terminal line you are connected to. This can determine which output device you want to use to direct output. For example:

```
$ tty
/dev/ttyp0
```

This reports that your current terminal line is /dev/ttyp0. You can then use this to ensure that all output you want on your screen is directed to /dev/ttyp0 with a command like:

```
$ shell.script > /dev/ttyp0
```

which will direct all output from the shell.script to /dev/ttyp0.

uname. The syntax is:

```
uname [-snrvma] [--sysname] [--nodename] [--release] [--version]
[--machine] [--all]
```

where -s, --sysname display the system name.
-n, --nodename display the nodename.
-r, --release display the current release of the operating system.
-v, --version display the current version of the operating system.
-m, --machine display the machine type.
-a, --all display all above information.

The uname command is very useful when you are trying to determine what type of machine you are on and what release and version of the operating system you are using. Scripts typically use this to determine which files they should use to compile and which utilities and environments are there by default. This is a quick and easy way to see what kind of architecture you are currently running on. For example:

```
$ uname -a
SunOS devtech 4.1.2 1 sun4c
```

is generated on a Sun machine running 4.1.2 on a SPARC (sun4c) architecture. The same command on an RS/6000 generates:

```
$ uname -a
AIX ibmgod 2 3 000040113700
```

This tells you that you are running AIX 3.2 on a machine named ibmgod. Note that the final number represents a machine name. Each operating environment has a different representation of its current version and release levels as well as architecture; however, these are fairly standard for each different type of machine. See your machine's uname documentation for more information.

To see a hostname for a script file or some other utility, use a command like:

```
$ uname
```

This will generate the hostname only.

who. The syntax is:

```
who [-HTimqsuw] [--count] [--idle] [-- heading] [--message] [--mesg]
[--writeable] [file]
[am i]
```

where -H, --heading display column headings.
-T, -w, --message, --mesg, --writeable display a + after each userid who can receive a message and a - after those userids who cannot (see the mesg command).
-i, --idle, -u display the length of time a user or users have been idle.
-m displays current username.
-q, --count display usernames and number of users logged in.
-s is ignored by gnu who.
file is file to look at for login list (default is /etc/utmp).
am i displays current username.

The who command is typically used to see who is logged on to the system and to monitor their activity. Many systems have watchdog daemons which monitor terminal activity and automatically log people off the system after an amount of inactive time. The command often used to monitor the status of account activity is the who -i command. A typical output looks something like:

```
$ who -i
root pts/0 May 18 23:56 . 11632
root tty0 May 18 08:48 16 11995
kevin pts/1 May 16 01:01 old 10110
```

This shows that root is logged on twice, once through a virtual window (pts) and once through a serial line (tty0). We can also see that the first instance of root has been active in the last minute since the sixth field is a ., which means that the account has been active in the last minute. The second instance has been idle for 16 hours, and the third instance (kevin) has been idle for more than 24 hours; this id is designated by the phrase old.

To see your current username type:

```
$ whoami
kevin
```

yes. The syntax is:

```
yes [string...]
```

where string... is one or more optional strings to output.

The yes command outputs strings until interrupted. If you don't include string, you will get a y on every line. You can interrupt with the standard interrupt signal such as C-c or anything you have defined as the intr signal. See the stty command above and Sec. 2.4 for more information on this setting.

This tool is useful to test a variety of things about scripts and your terminal definition. It is often used to test terminal performance as well.

12.3.4 Conclusion

shellutils consists of a variety of tools and scripts which provide additional and/or replacement functionality for certain tools in your current environment. While many of the functions provided in shellutils may exist in your environment, they may differ from platform to platform. The power of shellutils is that it provides the same functionality across heterogeneous platforms. At the same time, many of the utilities provide additional functionality over their vendor-supplied counterparts, such as increased speed or additional function. Keep these in mind as your distribute systems that depend on one of these systems. It may be that you want to distribute the core function delivered with this package with your systems to ensure similar behavior across disparate platforms.

12.4 textutils

12.4.1 Introduction

textutils is the GNU distribution of their text-processing utilities. While there are many utilities distributed with standard vendor versions of UNIX, most of the GNU utilities have additional functionality and speed.

The tools in this distribution also attempt to maintain consistency with the POSIX standards. This is an advantage for the user, particularly where portability and heterogeneity are issues.

textutils is a GNU product and as such is subject to its GNU General Public license as included both in the product distribution and in App. B of this book. Also see the GNU Library General Public License in both the distribution and in App. B.

12.4.2 Usage

As with the shellutils distribution, the textutils distribution consists of a variety of commands which provide replacement and additional functionality to UNIX systems. The basic set of commands delivered with textutils is:

```
cat, cksum, comm, csplit, cut, expand, fold, head, join, nl, od,
paste, pr, sort, split, sum, tac, tail, unexpand, uniq, and wc
```

The basic function of the above commands is similar to that of the vendor-delivered tools. There are a few differences, however, and these related tools will be discussed below.

comm. The syntax is:

```
comm [-123] file1 file2
```

where -123 suppresses columns 1, 2, and 3, respectively.
file1 file2 are two files to compare.

comm generates a three-column listing of a file compare. The first column contains unique lines in file1, column 2 contains unique lines in file2, and column 3 contains lines common to both files.

csplit. The syntax is:

```
csplit [-sk] [-f prefix] [-n digits] [--prefix=prefix]
[--digits=digits] [--quiet]
[--silent] [--keep-files] file pattern...
```

where -s, --silent don't display output file sizes.
-k, -keep-files don't delete output files.
-f prefix, --prefix=prefix use prefix as the output file name prefix.
-n digits,--digits=digits increment output filenames with digit numbers and not the default of two.
file is file to split.
pattern is string to determine where to split file.

This command is useful when splitting files into separate pieces. Files which contain programming text or chapters seperated by some consistent identifier are perfect for csplit. This is a fairly powerful tool and can be used to split text files of any type.

head. The syntax is:

```
head [-c N[bkm]] [-n N] [-qv] [--bytes=N[bkm]] [--lines=N] [--quiet]
[--silent] [--verbose] [file...]
```

where -c N[bkm], --bytes=N[bkm] specify the number of characters to display specified as N bytes(b), kilobytes(k), or megabytes(m).
-n N, --lines=N display N lines instead of the default 10.
-q, --quiet don't display filename headers.
-v, --verbose display filename headers.

The head command displays the first 10 lines of a file by default. You can change the default dislay size with the appropriate option. head is a very useful command to see what the contents of an unknown file are.

od. the syntax is:

```
od [-abcdfhijloxv] [-s[bytes]] [-w[bytes]] [-A radix] [-h bytes]
   [-N bytes] [-t type]
[--skip-bytes=bytes] [--address-radix=radix] [-- read-bytes=bytes]
   [--format=type]
[--output-duplicates] [--strings[=bytes]] [--width[=bytes]]
   [files ...]
```

where -A radix, --address-radix=radix specify the output base of file offsets:
d—decimal
o—octal (the default)
x—hex
n—none
-N bytes, --read-bytes=bytes output only N bytes of each input file.
-j, --skip-bytes=bytes skip byte input bytes before processing.
-t type, --format=type determines output type chosen from:
a—named character
c—ASCII character
d—signed decimal
f—floating point
o—octal
u—unsigned decimal
x—hex
-v, --output-duplicates output identical lines (the default is to output the first and place an asterisk to denote additional consecutive lines).
-s, --strings[=bytes] output ASCII strings and no other information.
-w, -width[=bytes] determine input bytes per output line (default is 16).

The other single-digit options denote old option formats and are there to support backward compatibility with older versions of od. See the man pages for more information.

od stands for output dump and consists of a facility to dump files in any format you would like such as hex, octal, or decimal. You can also output information as its representative ASCII characters. This command is very useful for examining nontext files for textual information and structure.

tac. The syntax is:

```
tac [-br] [-s sep] [--before] [[-regex] [--separator=separator]
[file...]
```

where -b, --before place separator before record it precedes it in the file.
-r, --regex--separator is a regular expression.
-s sep, --separator=separator define separator between records.
file... is one or more files to reorder.

The tac command takes one or more files and sends the records to standard output in the reverse order from which they were read. This allows you to combine files and reverse the record structure of the entire group of files if you wish.

There are several other utilities distributed with this package; however, in the interest of space, they are not documented here. They do provide functionality that is very useful and powerful and deserve to be investigated. Examine the man pages shipped with the distribution for more information on the individual tools. Depending on how you installed this package, these files will probably be in the man directory with .1 filename extensions. To view them, use a command like:

```
$ nroff -man file.1 | more
```

which will output the man page to the current terminal.

See the NEWS file for more information on current changes to the code.

12.4.3 Installation

textutils comes with the configure subsystem, and, therefore, porting is well documented and understood for most systems. As with other systems, to build and install textutils, you should use a series of commands like:

```
$ configure --prefix=/usr/local/textutils/textutils-1.8
$ make clean
$ make install
```

This will generate all files in directories under /usr/local/textutils/textutils-1.8 such as lib, man, and bin. Make sure these subdirectories exist, or you will have problems with the final phase of the build process. The default is to create these files in the same directories under /usr/local and therefore share directories with other tools. As your environment grows large, this can cause problems, so this book recommends you separate all tools into their own subdirectories to keep from overwriting files and other information. See Sec. 11.1 for more information on this tool.

Files are created in man/man1, bin, and lib subdirectories under either the prefix variable or the default directories.

12.4.4 Conclusion

textutils provide significant functionality and portability enhancements over those tools provided with most vendor implementations of UNIX. Along with better performance, most of these utilities provide enhanced functionality.

textutils might be something you want to distribute with your systems to ensure portability and compatibility between diverse platforms.

12.5 binutils

12.5.1 Introduction

As with the other utilities, textutils and shellutils, binutils consists of tools to provide significant additional functionality beyond those provided by most vendor's implementation of UNIX. These tools provide functionality related to binary files on UNIX. Tools like ld, strip, size, ar, nm, gprof, and others provide very powerful tools to manipulate binary files on a UNIX platform.

This chapter discusses release 2.2.1, which is a completely rewritten distribution of binutils. At the time of this book, it is still in beta release and, therefore, slightly unstable. binutils 2.2.1 is contained in the software distribution as something you can look at. It provides similar functionality to 1.9 but includes updated build facilities and better ports of all tools in the binutils distribution.

binutils is a GNU product and as such is subject to its GNU General Public license as included both in the product distribution and in App. B of this book.

12.5.2 Usage

The basic group of commands is documented below. See the individual tool manual pages for more information on each tool. The basic tools available in binutils are:

```
gprof, ar, ld, nm, strip, size, ranlib
```

These tools perform similar functions to those distributed by the vendors but often perform better and provide better portability. Unfortunately, there are no man pages shipped with this distribution; however, there is a very good profiling discussion in the gprof.texinfo file. See Sec. 11.15 for more information on how to access this.

These tools do not support COFF format files but do support COFF encapsulation, which provides a workaround for moving the results of these files to other COFF-compatible platforms. To get COFF encapsulation, however, you must use all GNU tools to build all components. The basic GNU tools you need are gcc, gdb, and gas. You also need to convert the library formats to support this encapsulation. See the README and README.ENCAP files for more information.

12.5.3 Installation

binutils 2.2.1 comes with the configure utility and therefore should be relatively straightforward to build. However, there seem to be several problems with the build procedures as provided in the distribution. It was necessary to first build from the top directory and then build in the binutils directory separately. There was also a strange reference to byacc in the distribution binutils Makefile which caused the build to fail. Finally, you must have makeinfo built and installed on your system if you want to install the product.

At the simplest level, you can type the commands:

```
$ configure --prefix=/usr/local/binutils/binutils-2.2.1/binutils
$ make clean
$ make
```

Note that the prefix represents one directory below the root of the distribution directory structure and is representative of how this distribution is structured. Normally you would place the binaries and libraries in directories under the root directory; however, because of the behavior of the makefile with respect to the install procedure, it is necessary to place the resulting files in directories other than those directly below the root of the distribution. This is a subtle bug and certainly one to watch out for. Keeping this restriction in mind, you can use any directory you would like. See Sec. 11.1 for more information.

If you want to use the native C compiler, either modify the resulting Makefile or use the CC macro command on the make invocation line. You can also use gcc with a command like:

```
$ make CC=gcc
```

which ensures that gcc is in your path.

The most important thing is to choose the proper CFLAGS and CC macros to determine how the binutils programs will be built. There are sections for a variety of systems; uncomment the system that most closely matches your own. The other issue is that the makefile defaults to using bison and flex instead of yacc and lex, if you have these.

The make will generate seven executables and a host of other files which can be used for encapsulation purposes related to COFF. See the file README.ENCAP for more information. You can now execute all generated commands by simply invoking them by name.

The beta version of release 2.2.1 has several problems with it. However, this section does give you a flavor for what the binutils distribution is all about. See the Internet or some other source to get an updated version if you are interested in production.

12.5.4 Conclusion

binutils contains a variety of tools which allow you to manipulate binary files on a UNIX platform. These tools often perform better than their vendor-supplied counterparts and function similarly on all UNIX platforms. This is the big advantage to using this distribution and why it is often shipped with software system distributions.

12.6 Netfax

12.6.1 Introduction

The Netfax facility provides a distributed fax server capability which allows you to preview, send, and receive Group 3 faxes from any machine on a LAN. The software is free, and the only hardware required is a EIA-592 Asynchronous Facsimile DCE Control Standard, Service Class 2. An example given in the associated documentation is the Everfax 24/96D, which currently retails for $499. The main phone number for Everfax is 1-800-821-0806. There are other modems that will satisfy the hardware requirements as well. See your UNIX vendor for more information.

The primary server is a process known as a fax spooler which runs on a machine which is accessible by all other fax client machines. By posting either mail or flat files to a spooler directory, the server will scan the queue periodically and distribute the fax material appropriately. You can receive Group 3 faxes, and they will be stored in the appropriate directories for receipt. There are programs delivered which allow you to modify the format of these files into tiff and other formats for use by other tools and utilities.

The files to be faxed support ASCII, postscript, and TeX dvi files as input. The fax spooling subsystem will generate the appropriate Group 3 fax output automatically. This provides many tools and utilities with the ability to send faxes transparently by merely creating an output file in one of the supported fax server input formats.

This is a very powerful tool which will provide fax capabilities for very low cost.

fax is a GNU product and as such is subject to its GNU General Public license as included both in the product distribution and in App. B of this book. There is also an associated copyright from M.I.T. which is distributed with the product on the CD. See this for more information.

12.6.2 Usage

There are several commands related to the Netfax spooling system. The basic ones follow:

fax. The syntax is:

```
fax -p phone [-c] [-h host] [-m] [-r rec] [-s send] [-S phone]
  [-u user][file]
faxps -p phone [-c] [-h host] [-m] [-r rec] [-s send] [-S phone]
  [-u user][file]
```

where -p phone is the phone number of fax receiver machine (uses Hayes string formats).
-c sends fax using information in -r, -s, and -S options.
-h host specifies host acting as fax spooler.
-m sends mail to you when fax is delivered.
-r rec is the name of receiver.
-s send is the name of sender.
-S phone is the phone number of sending fax board.
-u user uses name to queue the job instead of your local userid.
file is file to fax (format is different depending on whether you are using fax or faxps).

The fax command is the primary command to send a plain ASCII file as a fax. The faxps command takes a Postscript file as its input file and sends it as a Group 3 fax. The input file format is the only difference between fax and faxps.

The phone number sequence is Hayes compatible. For example, to dial a fax at the number 555-1212, you would use a command like:

```
fax -p 5551212 ...
```

You can use other dial characters such as T for tone dialing and , for pause. If you are disabling call waiting on your phone, you might use a command like:

```
fax -p *70,,5551212 ...
```

This will dial *70, wait 4 seconds, and dial 555-1212.

A full-blown command might look something like:

```
$ fax -p *70,5551212 -c -r "John" -s "Kevin" -S "5552020" fax.txt
```

faxps uses exactly the same syntax as fax, only the input files are Postscript and not plain text as with the fax command. A sample command might look like:

```
$ faxps -p 5551212 -c -r "Joe" -s "Kevin" -S "5552040" fax.ps
```

where fax.ps is a Postscript file. faxps uses Ghostscript to convert the input file (in this case fax.ps) from Postscript to Group 3.

faxenq. The syntax is:

```
faxenq phone1 phone2 ... [---file1 file2 ...] [-m] [-u user]
[-h host]
```

where phonen is one or more phone numbers to send the fax to.
filen is one or more files to be queued to the fax spooler.
-m sends mail when the fax is sent.
-u user specifies user as the sender of the fax.
-h host specifies fax spooler server.

faxenq is a command which queues your faxes to the fax spooler server for later distribution. This provides an asynchronous fax capability. This is especially nice to use as a fax server when you have multiple faxes to send to different locations and you want this to happen while you continue to work on other things.

faxmail. faxmail allows you to send mail as a fax by transmitting standard input mail as a fax. When you enter faxmail, it asks you for all pertinent information such as sender, receiver, phone number, etc., which will allow it to queue it to the fax spooler server for later transmission.

faxrm. The syntax is:

```
faxrm job [-h host]
```

where job is job as specified in the job spooler queue.
-h host specifies spooler host.

faxrm removes a fax job from the spooler queue. Once the job has started you cannot remove the job from the queue.

faxspooler. The syntax is:

```
faxspooler [-lloglevel] [-fdev] [-dmaxtime] [-rwaittime] [-D] [-Idir]
[-Odir] [-Eaddress]
```

where -lloglevel specifies loglevel as the debug log level from 0 (least verbose) to 7 (most verbose).
-fdev specifies dev as the fax board.
-dmaxtime is maximum time to try sending a fax.
-rwaittime specifies wait time between fax retries.
-D runs the spooler as a daemon.
-Idir is incoming fax spool directory.
-Odir is outgoing fax spool directory.
-Eaddress is e-mail notification address for incoming faxes.

faxspooler is the daemon which serves all fax activities to the network. Faxes are received by the host, and they are spooled in an incoming directory numbered sequentially. Each page of a fax is given its own subdirectory within the created directory. E-mail is sent when the fax is received.

faxq. The syntax is:

```
faxq [-hhost]
```

where -hhost specifies the host of the master fax spooler. faxq lists all jobs in the queue on host.

These basic commands are all you need to send and monitor faxes on your LAN. With Netfax, you can provide network access to a central fax-serving facility for minimal cost and maintenance.

12.6.3 Installation

Netfax comes with a standard makefile which builds fax and the associated executables. The makefile is formated to use gmake by default; however, you can use standard make if you don't have gmake installed.

The three files that may need modification are:

```
./include/conf.h
./include/conf.mk
./include/fax_prog.mk
```

These files consist of header information, a base configuration makefile, and a makefile which will build the appropriate executables, respectively. conf.h contains information pertaining to the actual device names for the fax board and commands which determine the default behavior of the fax server such as retry times, maximum retries, and the Postscript converter to use when converting from Postscript to G3 fax standards. Look carefully at this file before building.

The conf.mak and fax_prog.mk are template files which document the makefile features that are needed to build Netfax. These *.mk files are in subdirectories which will be automatically built when the original make is executed. Netfax requires gmake because of its use of subdirectories. To build, move the main Netfax directories and issue the command:

```
$ gmake
```

If you don't have gmake installed, you will have to move the *.mk template makefiles into the current working directory with the main makefile before issuing the make command. It would be better if you simply take gmake from the included CD to build Netfax.

The other requirement for the best use of Netfax is Ghostscript 2.41 or greater. This provides a Postscript interface and the ability to display Postscript on a bitmapped display. See Sec. 14.1 more information. The device to use for Ghostscript and fax is dfaxhigh. See the INSTALL file for exact details on how to build the correct fax driver for Ghostscript.

There are subdirectories containing manual pages (man), documentation files (doc), Postscript programs (ps), and others. This system was not delivered compiled on the CD because you need to link it to your particular fax board. You will need to build it yourself. Have fun.

12.6.4 Conclusion

Netfax provides the capability of LAN fax serving at a very low cost. By providing software which allows distributed fax server management,

Netfax provides your LAN with the ability to fax ASCII or Postscript files as well as TeX files.

Netfax provides most of what you can get from expensive commercial packages without the cost or complexity. Give it a try and see how it works.

12.7 oleo

12.7.1 Introduction

oleo is a very sophisticated and powerful spreadsheet package provided by GNU for most UNIX flavors. It works much as other spreadsheets work with cells referenced by characters and numbers and using macros to perform common functions.

oleo supports both dumb terminals through a curses interface and X11. You can generate embedded Postscript files which are snapshots of all or a portion of the spreadsheet. This can then be printed, displayed, or faxed with other tools such as ghostscript and Netfax.

oleo is a GNU product and as such is subject to its GNU General Public license as included both in the product distribution and in App. B of this book.

12.7.2 Usage

oleo looks very much like other spreadsheets on the surface but has much more capability than other similar products. The basic input screen is shown in Fig. 12.1. There is a listing of main commands in the USING file. See this for a detailed breakdown of basic commands.

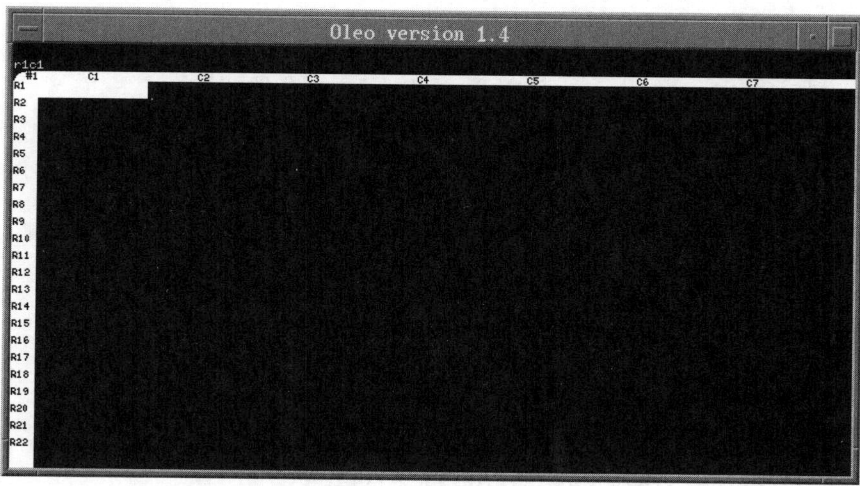

Figure 12.1 The oleo spreadsheet.

The other file which contains useful information is the KEYS file. This contains a description of all keystrokes and their associated commands. The syntax used below is the same as that used in Chap. 10. Namely, the C-n represents any CTRL character held down while the n key is pressed. This is the same nomenclature as that used by emacs.

The basic oleo commands are:

`C-g`	Aborts the current command
`C-X C-C`	Ends the session
`C-Z`	Suspends oleo
`C-x !`	Recalculates
`C-H`	Help mode
`C-h C`	Helps with a command
`C-X j`	Moves the cursor to a specific address
`C-P`	Moves cell cursor up
`C-N`	Moves cell cursor down
`C-F`	Moves cell cursor right
`C-B`	Moves cell cursor left
`C-[ p`	Scans up
`C-[ n`	Scans down
`C-[ f`	Scans right
`C-[ b`	Scans left
`C-[ v`	Scrolls up
`C-V`	Scrolls down
`C-X >`	Scrolls right
`C-X <`	Scrolls left
`C-X (`	Begins entering a macro
`C-X )`	Ends entering a macro
`C-h o`	Displays options
`C-[ C-P a`	Saves region as ASCII
`C-[ C-P p p`	Saves region as Postscript
`C-[ C-P p s`	Saves page size for Postscript printer
`C-[ g`	Interfaces to gnuplot, if installed, so you can plot results
`C-[ c`	Copies region
`C-[ m`	Moves region
`C-O`	Inserts row
`C-[ o`	Inserts column
`C-K`	Deletes row
`C-[ k`	Deletes column
`M-x clear-spreadsheet`	Clears the spreadsheet
`C-X 5`	Splits window horizontally
`C-X 2`	Splits window vertically

There are a variety of other commands which provide more sophisticated function. See the KEYS file for a complete listing.

There is a file named USING which contains a description of basic oleo operations and functionality. See it for more detailed information on oleo. This section will provide a very brief overview merely to introduce you to basic oleo capabilities. The basic oleo command structure looks similar to emacs and uses both the ESC and CTRL keys.

oleo operates on a cell basis much like Lotus or Excel, and the command syntax is virtually identical. Keyboard mapping can be controlled and changed based on user need. You toggle between input and command mode.

oleo supports a variety of input and output formats including integer, float, hidden, graph, general, dollar, comma, percent, and several others. Because of the power of the underlying UNIX architecture, oleo has a variety of functions beyond what most spreadsheets provide. For example, you can have the spreadsheet automatically calculated while continuing to enter input. You can also have automatic backup generation, automatic update of various functions such as rnd(), cell(), my(), and others.

12.7.3 Installation

oleo uses the standard configure package that comes with most GNU utilities. As with other configure utilities, you should use a series of commands like:

```
$ configure --prefix=/usr/local/oleo/oleo-1.4
$ make clean
$ make install
```

again ensuring that you have the proper subdirectories (man/man1, src, bin, etc.) under the prefix specified directories. See Sec. 11.1 for more information on this build process.

There are a few special instructions for the build of oleo documented in a file INSTALL.OLEO. See this for detailed information. The main options for compilation include spreadsheet size, X11 support, and a few machine-specific instructions regarding include files.

One thing to note is a bug which exists on AIX. You need to have the same PTF that needs to be insalled for gcc and some other programs (PTF U416277) from IBM. If you don't have this on your system, you will need to either remove the -g option from the CFLAGS macro in the makefile or issue the make like:

```
$ make CFLAGS=
```

This will fix the related problem on the RS/6000.

This installation is fairly straightforward and presents no real problems. If it does, see the GNU people for more information. Also see the README file for possible contacts and mail addresses.

12.7.4 Conclusion

oleo is simply one of the most powerful spreadsheet programs available today. While it supports syntax used by tools like Lotus and Excel, it provides additional functionality that you may want in a spreadsheet. Plus it's *free.*

This chapter has certainly not been an exhaustive presentation of oleo and its capabilities. However, it has presented some of its basic capabilities and characteristics. Keep oleo in mind when you are evaluating spreedsheets. By using oleo, you can significantly reduce your need to purchase spreadsheet tools and facilities.

12.8 mtools

12.8.1 Introduction

mtools contains a variety of tools which allows you to manipulate DOS filesystems and disks. This gives you the ability to write, read, copy, and format DOS files and disks to and from UNIX machines. This section discusses mtools 2.0.7. There may be newer releases, but as of this writing, they were not readily available.

12.8.2 Usage

There are several commands which come in the mtools command set. The basic commands included are:

```
mattrib, mcd, mcopy, mdel, mdir, mformat, mkmanifest, mlabel, mmd,
mrd, mread, mren, mtype, and mwrite
```

Each command and basic syntax is outlined below.

mattrib. The syntax is:

```
mattrib [-a|+a] [-h|+h] [-r|+r] [-s|+s] dosfile ...
```

where -a, +a remove or add attribute bit.
-h, +h remove or add hidden bit.
-r, +r remove or add read-only bit.
-s, +s remove or add system bit.
dosfile... is one or more DOS files to operate on.

Note that for all m commands in the mtools toolkit you can specify pathnames with either the UNIXlike forward slash (/) or the DOS backslash (\). Note that you must quote the \ if you don't want the shell to interpret it as an escape for the following character. For example:

```
$ mattrib +a file.dos
$ mattrib -s "a:\subdir\file.dos"
```

See the following commands for a discussion of a: and how you can manipulate this.

mcd. The syntax is:

```
mcd [dir]
```

where dir is directory to change to.

Without a specified dir, you will get the current working directory displayed.

mcopy. The syntax is:

```
mcopy [-mntv] file1 file2
```

or

```
mcopy [-mntv] file1 ... dir
```

where -m preserves file modification time.
-n—no warning is displayed when overwriting an existing file.
-t copies as a text file (converts CR/LF to LF or vice versa).
-v is verbose mode.
file1, file2 specifies files to be copied.
dir specifies a directory to copy files to.

This command copies files and performs the proper file modifications if specified.

mdel. The syntax is:

```
mdel [-v] file...
```

where -v is verbose mode.
file... is one or more files to delete.

The command deletes DOS files.

mdir. The syntax is:

```
mdir [-w] dir
```

where -w is wide output.
dir is directory to be displayed.

mdir displays the contents of a DOS directory.

mformat. The syntax is:

```
mformat [-t tracks] [-h heads] [-s sectors] [-l label] drive:
```

where -t tracks specifies the number of tracks on the device.
-h heads specifies the number of sides on the device.
-s sectors specifies the number of sectors on the device.
-l label writes a label on the device.
drive: is device to be operated on.

One thing to note with mformat is that you must preformat the disk with the UNIX format command. mformat will place DOS information such as boot sector, FAT, and root directories on a preformatted UNIX disk. Once mformat has been run, you can use this device on any DOS machine.

mkmanifest. The syntax is:

```
mkmanifest [files]
```

where files are long-named files to be shortened.

mkmanifest provides you with a listing of the shortened names of long UNIX files that may be written out with a command like mwrite. When you write files from a UNIX filesystem to a DOS filesystem, the filenames may need to be shortened to support DOS filename conventions (8+3). If this occurs, you will want to use mkmanifest as follows:

```
mkmanifest file1 file2 ... > manifest.out
```

which will place the shortened names of file1, file2, etc., in the file manifest.out. You can then copy this to the DOS output device for later execution as a script. The manifest.out file will look something like:

```
mv short1 long1
mv short2 long2
```

where shortn and longn are the converted filenames. In other words, this creates a script which you can use later to move the files back from a DOS filesystem to a UNIX filesystem and preserve their original long names.

mlabel. The syntax is:

```
mlabel [-v] drive:
```

where -v is verbose mode.
drive: is drive to operate on.

mlabel generates a label on a DOS output device. You are prompted for a new label.

mmd. The syntax is:

```
mmd [-v] dir ...
```

where -v is verbose mode.
dir... is one or more directories to create.

mmd stands for make MS-DOS directory and will create MS-DOS directories on a DOS output device.

mrd. The syntax is:

```
mrd [-v] dir ...
```

where -v is verbose mode.
dir is one or more directories to remove.

mrd stands for MS-DOS remove directory.

mread. The syntax is:

```
mread [-mnt] dosfile unixfile
```

or

```
mread [-mnt] dosfile1 [...] unixdir
```

where -m preserves file modification times.
-n doesn't display a warning when overwriting a file.
-t transfers as a text file (change CR/LF for LF and vice versa as necessary).
dosfile is DOS file to read.
unixfile is UNIX file to write.
unixdir places to copy one or more DOS files.

mren. The syntax is:

```
mren [-v] file1 file2
```

where -v is verbose mode.
file1 is file to rename.
file2 is name of renamed file.

mren renames a file from file1 to file2.

mtype. The syntax is:

```
mtype [-st] file [...]
```

where -s strips high bit.
-t is text line viewing.
file ... is one or more files to operate on.

mtype displays the file(s) on standard output.

These are the basic commands included in mtools. More information is available for each command in the specific man page included in the mtools distribution in the main directory with a suffix of .1. See also the release.notes file for more information on current release information. This is important since new features provide significantly enhanced function.

mwrite. The syntax is:

```
mwrite [-tnvm] unixfile dosfile
```

or

```
mwrite [-tnvm] unixfile [unixfile...] dosdirectory
```

where -t is text file transfer. It translates all linefeeds to carriage return/linefeed.
-n is m file overwrite warning.
-v is verbose mode.
-m is preserve file modification times on write.
unixfile is the UNIX name of the file following standard UNIX conversions.
dosfile is the DOS name of the file following standard DOS conversions.

12.8.3 Installation

There is a standard makefile included with the mtools distribution which needs some modification based on your machine architecture. Much of this is documented in the file Configure. See this file for more information if this section is not sufficient to build mtools correctly.

Once you select the correct values for your machine, type the command:

```
$ make
```

This should be sufficient to build mtools for your platform.

For example, on the RS/6000 the best choice seems to be the RT_ACIS, which defines a floppy drive at /dev/rfd0 addressible as A:. However, the first default floppy device sector information is 15, while on the RS/6000 it should be 18. Make this change and rebuild with the make command. Note also that gcc seems to work better with this than CC does, so you might use a command like:

```
$ make CC=gcc
```

This is useful and seems to work correctly on the RS/6000 used to build the included CD's software. Note that you also need to create the CFLAGS with the definitions:

```
CFLAGS=-O -DRT_ACIS -DLOCKF
```

This will create the correct system on the RS/6000.

On a Sun, all that is necessary is to define -DLOCKF and the CFLAGS definitions and build the programs.

Note that if you need to define additional DOS devices to support, you need to edit the devices.c file which is the devices database. See the Configure file for exact information on the syntax of the devices.c file.

12.8.4 Conclusion

The utility programs included in the mtools distribution have proven invaluable to many users of UNIX and DOS machines. This gives you the ability to transparently transfer information between DOS and UNIX machines. The capability to read, write, and manipulate DOS files on a UNIX platform provides significant functionality and eases the transition from DOS to UNIX.

12.9 cpio

12.9.1 Introduction

cpio is one tool that comes with most standard versions of UNIX and is fairly portable between platforms. Because of this and the fact that it is less and less used by UNIX users, it was not discussed as a power tool in the native tools section of this book (Part 2). However, because of its power and the implementation written by GNU, a brief introduction is included in this section.

cpio is an archive utility much like tar and was traditionally used to create archives for transmission on the Internet and other places. It is still used; however, its frequency of use has dropped over the last few years as the use of tar has increased. With the 2.2 version of GNU cpio, you have the ability to manipulate tar files as well as cpio archives with the cpio command.

GNU cpio has documented advantages over most vendor's implementations of cpio, including network tape drive support and symbolic link support.

cpio is a GNU product and as such is subject to its GNU General Public license as included both in the product distribution and in App. B of this book.

12.9.2 Usage

The basic syntax for cpio is:

```
cpio {-o|--create} [-0ABLVacv] [-C bytes] [-H format] [-M string]
  [-O [[user@host:]
archive] < list [>archive]

cpio {-i |--extract} [-BSVbcdfmnrtsuv] [-C bytes] [-E file]
  [-H format] [-M message]
[-R [user][:.][group]] [-I [[user@]host:]archive]
  [-F [[user[@host:]archive]
[pattern...] [< archive]

cpio {-p|--pass-through} [-0LVadlmuv] [-R [user][:.][group]] dir
  < list
```

where -0 reads list of files terminated by a null instead of the standard newline character.

-A appends to existing archive.

-B sets blocksize to 5120 bytes instead of the standard 512 bytes.

-C bytes sets blocksize to bytes.

-E file reads from file the names of more files to be used as input to cpio.

-F user@host:archive specifies an archive name to use as input and output. You can specify a remote hostname and device as show above. Protection is done with .rhosts (rsh command).

-H format uses format for archive from list below:

bin—obsolete binary format

crc—SVR4 portable format with checksum

newc—SVR4 portable format

odc—old POSIX portable format

tar—old tar format

ustart—new POSIX.1 tar format

-I user@host:archive specifies an archive name to use as input. You can specify a remote hostname and device as shown above. Protection is done with .rhosts (rsh command).

-L copies actual files pointed to by symbolic links instead of link itself.

-M string displays string at end of volume requesting additional volume.

-O user@host:archive specifies an archive name to use as output. You can specify a remote hostname and device as shown above. Protection is done with .rhosts (rsh command).

-R user:.group sets the created files' ownership to user and group.

-S swaps the halfwords of each word (see -b).

-V displays a dot as each file is processed.

-a preserves original access times.

-b swaps order of bytes and halfwords (converts big endian to little endian).

-c uses old archive format (for backward compatibility).

-d makes appropriate directories as needed.

-f copies only those files, *not* machine-specified patterns.

-i,--extract is copy-in mode.

-l maintains links instead of using actual files.

-m preserves file modification times.

-n displays uid and gid instead of username.

-o, --create is copy-out mode.

-p,--pass-through is copy-pass mode.

-r interactively renames files with prompting.

-s swaps bytes with a halfword.

-t is table of contents.

-u replaces all files disregarding date information.

-v is verbose mode.

archive is archive to manipulate.

dir is output directory.

list is list of filenames (can be used similarly to patterns).

patterns are regular expressions to determine files matched.

There are three basic modes of operation for cpio: copy-out(-o), copy-in(-i), and copy-pass(-p). copy-out mode transfers file input one line at a time into an archive, copy-in mode transfers a file from an archive to files, and copy-pass transfers files from one directory structure to another.

These three modes provide all access to cpio and its associated archives. Actually, cpio is one of the easiest archive commands of any available on UNIX. The most common way for cpio to be used is with the find command. A simple example of cpio archive creation is:

```
$ find . -name "file*" -print | cpio -o > /dev/rmt0
81 blocks
```

This command will search starting in the current directory for any files starting with the string file and move them to a tape device /dev/rmt0. You could just as easily move them to an archive file with a command like:

```
$ find . -name "file*" -print | cpio -o > ../file.cpio
```

This will create a file named file.cpio in the directory above the current working directory. Note that you want to be careful if you use the same directory to create the archive since you may get a copy of the archive inside the archive itself. *Be careful.*

Some other simple examples of this command are:

```
$ cpio -itv files.cpio
```

This will generate a table of contents listing to your screen.

To move an entire directory hierarchy, use a command group like:

```
$ find . -print | cpio -p /newrootdir
```

This will move the entire directory structure (including subdirectories and their contents) beginning with your current working directory into /newrootdir and preserve the current structure. This is a very useful command and is often simpler than the tar command that performs the equivalent functionality.

With respect to tar support, cpio will fully support most vendor's tar archives. For example, if you have created a file named kevin.tar and you want to see a table of contents, you could use a command like:

```
$ cpio -itv -H tar < kevin.tar
```

This will generate a standard listing just as the tar command would. You can create and extract from tar files with exactly the same syntax.

As you can see, there are many ways to use the cpio command, all of which are fairly easy. Keep in mind that there are various formats, and you may have to use a format other than the default for portability purposes. However, if you use GNU cpio, it will support all formats, and you shouldn't have to worry about portability.

12.9.3 Installation

The cpio installation is very straightforward and consists of the standard GNU configure subsystem. This means you can simply run the commands:

```
$ configure
$ make prefix=/usr/local/cpio install
```

This will generate three exectables: cpio, mt, and rmt. The mt and rmt commands are included to support cpio's operation on your machine. If you want to use a remote tape device, the rmt command will support this function if one is not available on your machine. The mt command is used to manipulate a local tape device if this is necessary. The usage of this should be transparent to you; however, you can simply type:

```
$ mt
```

to get a listing of available options for the mt command. This does not work for rmt since this is merely an interface to mt on another system.

If you are building this product on an RS/6000, you want to issue the command:

```
$ make CFLAGS=
```

unless you have the PFT U211273 installed since you will get a compiler error otherwise. It also seemed to work well with gcc, so you might try this as well as your native compiler.

12.9.4 Conclusion

cpio from GNU has advantages over the vendor-supplied cpio, including remote device and tar file support. These features as well as the increased portability of having one cpio on all vendor platforms makes GNU cpio a good choice if you are using archives in a heterogeneous environment.

See the man pages for more information on both cpio and mt.

12.10 elvis

12.10.1 Introduction

elvis 1.7 is the GNU version of vi and ex and not only replaces the functionality provided by vi and ex, but five other utilities, including ctags, elvprsv, elvrec, fmt, and ref, provide additional functionality. elvis also runs on platforms from UNIX to DOS to Amiga to VAX. The real power of elvis is that you can run vi-like editors on many diverse platforms.

Because of elvis's similarities to vi and ex (which are discussed in Chap. 3), this section will not discuss much of the functionality of elvis but instead will briefly discuss its user-interface and installation procedures.

12.10.2 Usage

The syntax is:

```
elvis [-Reirv] [-c command] [-m [file]] [-t tag] [-w size] [file...]
```

where -R enters elvis in read-only mode.
-e starts up in colon command mode.
-i starts up in input mode.
-r is flag which notifies you to run elvrec to recover a crash file.
-v starts up in visual command mode.
-c command executes command after file is loaded.
-m file searches through file for a compiler error message and places cursor there.
-t tag places cursor at tag.
-w size sets window option's value to size.
file... is one or more files to edit.

elvis uses the standard environment variables such as TERMCAP, TERM, LINES, COLUMNS, and HOME, to determine its behavior. The default initialization file for elvis is elvis.rc. Place any initialization files there. Figure 12.2 shows the initial elvis screen with the INSTALL document from its distribution. The basic functions of the five other executables included with the elvis distribution are described below.

ctags. The syntax is:

```
ctags [-arstv] file...
```

where -a appends the output file instead of replacing it.
-r generates both tags and refs.
-s includes static tags.

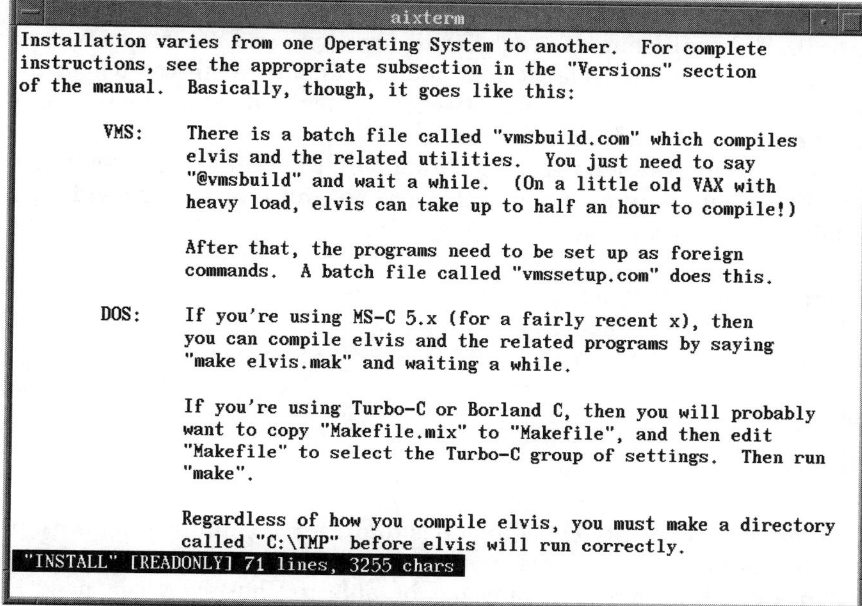
```
aixterm
Installation varies from one Operating System to another.  For complete
instructions, see the appropriate subsection in the "Versions" section
of the manual.  Basically, though, it goes like this:

        VMS:    There is a batch file called "vmsbuild.com" which compiles
                elvis and the related utilities.  You just need to say
                "@vmsbuild" and wait a while.  (On a little old VAX with
                heavy load, elvis can take up to half an hour to compile!)

                After that, the programs need to be set up as foreign
                commands.  A batch file called "vmssetup.com" does this.

        DOS:    If you're using MS-C 5.x (for a fairly recent x), then
                you can compile elvis and the related programs by saying
                "make elvis.mak" and waiting a while.

                If you're using Turbo-C or Borland C, then you will probably
                want to copy "Makefile.mix" to "Makefile", and then edit
                "Makefile" to select the Turbo-C group of settings.  Then run
                "make".

                Regardless of how you compile elvis, you must make a directory
                called "C:\TMP" before elvis will run correctly.
"INSTALL" [READONLY] 71 lines, 3255 chars
```

Figure 12.2 The elvis screen.

-t includes typedefs.
-v includes variables declarations.
file... is one or more files to process.

ctags provides a function which scans C source and include files and generates two special files: tags and refs which contain information on the structure and contents of these input files. With these two special files, you can use elvis to more efficiently trace through and modify the code based on information provided by the ctags program.

tags are basically function names and macro definitions. The tags file contains a cross-reference that lists tag names and their associated filenames. The refs file contains the definitions for each tag in the tags file. These two files are generated by ctags to be used by elvis for later work on the code.

The :tag command in elvis allows you to move from tag to tag within your source code system. In other words, by typing :tag, you will automatically move to that tag, even if it is in a different file. This provides you with the ability to move between functions and not worry about the files involved.

The basic use of this command is as follows:

```
$ ctags -stv *.[ch]
```

which tells ctags to process all files in the current directory that end in .c or .h. This will generate tags for all functions and macros as well as static tags, variable declarations, and typedefs through the use of the proper options. It will generate two files: tags and refs, which will be used by the :tag command in elvis.

Use this when you are tracing through an unfamiliar new system. It will save you significant amounts of time and effort by providing a "fileless" interface to the software system.

elvprsv. The syntax is:

```
elvprsv ["-why elvis died"] /tmp/filename...
```

or

```
elvprsv -T /tmp/filename...
```

elvprsv is the utility called by elvis to preserve your current work in the event of a system or edit crash. You should not need to execute this when a crash occurs (you may not be able to); however, you need to execute this when you want to recover the information. The documentation's recommendation is to run this upon reboot. It will automatically generate e-mail to the appropriate user saying that there is a "recoverable" elvis file in the /tmp directory. The default place where elvis preserves files is /usr/preserve/p*. Check here for more details on your current preserved files.

elvrec. The syntax is:

```
elvrec [preservedfile [newfile]]
```

where preservedfile is the file which was preserved on system crash.
newfile is the new file to create which you can then edit normally.

If you don't use any parameters with elvrec, you will get a listing of all recoverable files. The default place to save preserved files is /usr/preserve/p*. Check here for more possibilities.

ref. The syntax is:

```
ref [-t] [-c class] ... [-f file] ...tag
```

where -t outputs tag information.
-c class places tag in class "class."

-f file checks that tag is a static function in file.
tag is tag to search for.

ref displays matching header information for a given tag. It uses a slightly different algorithm depending on which option you use; however, it will generate a listing for you if it can find a matching tag in the current tags and refs files. See the manual page for more information on this function since it is somewhat complex. Note that you can run this function from within elvis with the Shift-K command.

The above provides a basic discussion of elvis and the tools distributed with it. Take a look at the associated documentation for more details since most of this information was taken from the delivered documentation, which is in the doc subdirectory and can be printed and appended at any time. Simply print the .doc files and append them in the order described in the INSTALL file.

12.10.3 Installation

The installation of elvis consists of the following steps:

1. $ cp Makefile.mix Makefile
2. edit Makefile
3. $ make clean
4. $ make prefix=/usr/local/elvis install

The Makefile consists of a variety of environments, one of which needs to be selected before the make will proceed correctly. The systems documented in the Makefile range from SCO XENIX to Sun to Coherent to DOS. Select the one that best approximates your environment and uncomment this section. Proceed with steps 3 and 4.

The Sun build is simple; merely use the settings in the SunOS section of Makefile. If you don't get a clean build, you may have to send mail to the author at kirkenda@cs.pdx.edu or contact the appropriate support person for more information.

There is no explicit section for the RS/6000; however, the System V section will work quite nicely.

12.10.4 Conclusion

elvis is a very powerful vi and ex clone which provides homogeneous function across a heterogeneous environment. It also provides tools which make elvis a powerful tool for software developers. By using elvis with other tools such as ctag and ref, you can create a powerful software development environment that you can distribute with your system if you so desire.

12.11 gptx

12.11.1 Introduction

gptx is GNU ptx, which is a permuted index generator. A permuted index is a listing of "sounds like" commands and keywords which are related to the actual UNIX commands. If you are used to displaying a listing of the file contents of a directory with a dir command and not ls, the permuted index will show both dir and ls and relate the two. Berkley systems come with an apropos command which displays a permuted index. See your system for more details.

A typical permuted index looks something like:

```
uustat(1C) uucp tatus inquiry      job control..................uustat(1)
and operator                       join(1) relational database.....join(1)
terminal                           jterm(1) reset layer of window.jterm(1)
makekey(1) generate encryption     key........................makekey(1)
a UNIX system command              keywords locate(1) identify...locate(1)
```

This is a small sampling, but you can see the relationship between keywords and UNIX commands. This allows you to search a file (namely the permuted index) for a common and/or related keyword and find the appropriate UNIX command. This was the original way UNIX documentation was delivered.

This is an alpha release 0.2 of gptx which emulates ptx while adding additional function. There is no manual page, but there is a texinfo file which documents some of the basic function of gptx. Reference this for more information.

gptx is a GNU product and as such is subject to its GNU General Public license as included both in the product distribution and in App. B of this book.

12.11.2 Usage

The basic syntax of gptx is:

```
gptx [-ACORTfr] [-bio{file}] [-SW{regexp}] [-gw{num}]
[inputfile...] >outputfile
```

where -A selects automatic references.
-C displays copyright information.
-O generates output in nroff/troff format.
-R—when used with default output, references are displayed at

the beginning of the line rather than at the right as is the default.
-T generates output in TeX format.
-f ignores case.
-r treats the first nonwhite character string as the reference keyword in the output.
-bfile—file contains characters that cannot be parts of words.
-ifile—file contains words which will not be treated as keywords.
-ofile—file contains words to be retained in concordance output.
-Sregexp specifies the regular expression that represents the end of line and end of sentence characters.
-Wregexp specifies the regular expression which describes the keyword.
-gnum specifies the size of whitespace between words.
-wnum specifies the maximum width of output file lines.
inputfile is file(s) to be processed.
>outputfile is redirected standard output which contains the permuted index.

There is a compatibility mode which can be invoked with the standard ptx command. The options are similar but some are not supported. Simply invoke the gptx command with ptx. This will provide ptx-like function using gptx.

12.11.3 Installation

The basic installation of gptx follows the basic configure-type installation:

```
$ configure
$ make clean
$ make install
```

Note that you can use the prefix variable on the make command if you want to generate the binaries in a directory other than where the source code resides. There are additional minor issues which are documented in the INSTALL file.

On a Sun machine, you should use gcc with the -traditional option. The easiest way to permanently configure this is by defining the CC environmental variable on the command line before invoking the configure command. For example:

```
$ CC="gcc -traditional";configure
$ make
```

This will build gptx correctly on a Sun. Note that there is no special requirements on an RS/6000.

12.11.4 Conclusion

gptx and ptx are commands which generate permuted index files in dumb terminal output format. gptx replaces and enhances ptx and doesn't require nroff or troff to examine the index itself. While the distribution included with this book is in alpha mode, it is demonstrative of what the gptx system is attempting to do. After you have looked at this, go to the Internet and get a more recent version if one is available.

12.12 less

12.12.1 Introduction

less is a pager, which controls the output of information to the screen. The most common example of a pager is the more command. There is also a pg command; however, this is not as commonly used in the UNIX environment.

less is a pager much like more but allows both forward and backward movement through a file. less has a command structure very similar to that of more and, therefore, is very easy for most people to use. Clearly the biggest advantage to less is the ability to move backward through a file; however, because of its design, less does not have to read an entire file into memory like more and, therefore, comes up much faster. Many advanced UNIX users use the less pager instead of the other vendor-delivered pager tools.

12.12.2 Usage

The basic syntax of the less command is:

```
less [-[+]?aBCcdEefHiMmNnqQrSsuUw] [-bn] [-hn] [-jn] [-kfile]
[-{oO]file] [-p pattern] [-P prompt] [-t tag] [-Ttagfile] [-xtag]
  [-ytag] [-[z]tag]
[+[+]cmd] [filename]...
```

where +—in front of an option tells less to execute this command before entering the file.

-? displays a list of commands.

-a begins search *after* last line on current screen.

-B disables automatic allocation of additional buffers for old data storage.

-bn uses n buffers instead of the default 10.

-C clears screen, then repaints.

-c repaints screen.

-d suppresses all error messages due to lack of terminal capability.
-E automatically exits less at first end of file.
-e automatically exits less at second end of file.
-f opens nonregular file.
-hn scrolls n lines backward.
-i ignores case for searches.
-jn specifies n as the line number where target results are placed (e.g., search matches).
-kfile—file is a lesskey file which contains key mappings.
-M is verbose mode.
-m is verbose mode.
-N displays line numbers.
-n supresses line numbers.
-Ofile copies output to file and display, overwriting existing file.
-ofile copies output to file and display.
-Pprompt changes prompt.
-ppattern starts at first matching pattern in file upon less invocation.
-Q is totally quiet mode.
-q is quiet mode.
-r displays raw control characters.
-S doesn't wrap lines.
-s compresses consecutive blank lines into one blank line.
-ttag is related to the ctags command.
-Ttagfile specifies a tagfile for -ttag.
-U treats backspaces and carriage returns as control characters.
-u treats backspaces and carriage returns as printable characters.
-w uses blank lines to represent anything beyond the end of file.
-xn sets tabs every n characters.
-yn scrolls forward a maximum of n lines.
-[z]n sets default window scrolling size to n lines.
comd is command to execute.
file is file to page through.

You can define any options using the environmental variable LESS. This is examined at every invocation of less.

Once you have entered a file and are using the less pager, you can issue a variety of commands, some of which are listed below.

`=`	Displays information about the current file
`! command`	Shell escape
`SPACE`	Scrolls forward one screen

`h`	Displays help summary
`RETURN`	Scrolls forward one line
`d`	Scrolls forward one line
`b`	Scrolls backward one line
`v`	Invokes an editor on the current file
`w`	Sets window size
`y`	Scrolls backward one line and resizes window as necessary
`R`	Repaints the screen
`g`	Goes to line n (default is 1)
`G`	Goes to line n (default is end of file)
`p`	Goes to percent n in the file
`/string`	Goes to the first matching occurrence of string
`?string`	Goes backward to the first matching occurrence of string
`n`	Repeats previous search
`N`	Repeats previous search but in opposite direction
`:e [file]`	Examines new file
`:n`	Examines next file in filelist from command line
`:p`	Examines previous file in the filelist from the command line

Almost all of the above commands can be followed by an integer which represents the number of lines on which to act. Most of the commands have a default value of 1.

You can use a program called lesskey to define all the keys you may wish to use with less. Keep in mind that this will change the mapping for your keys, and the fundamental behavior of less may change depending on the redefinition of your keyboard. lesskey is beyond the scope of this book. See the man pages less.man and lesskey.man for more information.

12.12.3 Installation

The less distribution has a very unusual installation script called linstall distributed with it. There is no makefile distributed with less, and you must use the following command to build it:

```
$ sh linstall
```

This will ask you a series of questions from which it builds a makefile and defines.h file. The questions are very straightforward and should not be difficult for you to answer. Once you have executed this script, you can issue the command:

```
$ make
```

This will build the less executable to the specifications you determined when running the linstall script. If you have problems, examine the makefile for potential problems with your system. The build is fairly straightforward, and you shouldn't have any real problems with it. If you do, use the mailing address in the README file of the distribution for help.

12.12.4 Conclusions

less is a very powerful tool which allows you to examine a file and move back and forth within that file with ease. You can also move into an editing function if you so desire. Through the use of keypad definitions (lesskey) and environmental variables, you can modify less's behavior to match your specific needs. See the man pages included with its distribution for more details.

12.13 ispell

12.13.1 Introduction

ispell is an interactive spell checker which presents its best guesses as to the correct spelling of a misspelled word. You can either use it in an integrated fashion with emacs or by itself. If you have need for a spell checker to check ASCII files for typos and misspelled words, ispell is probably the best way to go.

ispell is a GNU product and as such is subject to its GNU General Public license as included both in the product distribution and in App. B of this book.

12.13.2 Usage

The basic syntax for ispell is:

```
ispell [-l | -D | -E] [file...]
```

where -l displays misspelled words from standard input.
-D displays system dictionary flags.
-E displays system dictionary expanded.
file ... is one or more files to spell check. If no file is entered, ispell uses standard input.

The most common way to use ispell is on a flat ASCII file. Once you enter the ispell command, it begins to scan the file until it finds a word that is not in its dictionary. At this time it places the unknown word at the top of the screen and prints a series of "near miss" words below it. At the bottom of the screen, the two lines surrounding and including the line with the unknown word are displayed.

Once the words are displayed, you can select from the following options:

?	Displays help
SPACE	Accepts the word this time
A	Accepts the word for the rest of the file
I	Accepts the word and places it in the user's private dictionary
R	Prompts for a replacement word
num	Where num is the number of the near miss that is correct

12.13.3 Installation

Because ispell is a GNU product, it comes with the standard configure capability which all users have come to expect from GNU. The methodology used to build ispell is no different than that described for other GNU products in this book.

```
$ ./configure
$ make clean
$ make prefix=/usr/local/ispell
```

This will build ispell and place the bin and man pages in the appropriate directory. The other file of interest is the file ispell.dict. This is the dictionary file which is created by the build procedure. It is placed in a lib directory, and ispell is compiled with a hard-coded path for this file. You will see the path on the first execution of ispell. In the above example, ispell will expect ispell.dict to be in /usr/local/ispell/lib. If it is not, ispell will fail. Keep this in mind as you build ispell.

The other aspect to this is that you may want to build your own dictionaries. This is beyond the scope of this section; however, it is documented in the INSTALL file contained with the distribution. See the end of it for assistance with developing and building your own dictionaries.

12.13.4 Conclusion

ispell is a relatively simple tool to understand and use that provides value when you need to check the accuracy of your typing or spelling. If you can extract information into a flat ASCII file, you can use ispell very effectively. You can also use the integrated ispell with emacs. See Chap. 10 for more information on this capability.

12.14 screen

12.14.1 Introduction

screen is a utility which provides a full-screen window manager that allows a dumb terminal to support multiple terminal sessions. Full vt100 support is included, and there are history buffers and copy and paste capabilities between window sessions. This is similar to the new alphawindows protocol which is coming into vogue; however, it is free and runs on dumb vt100-style devices.

Each screen session has a UNIX command associated with it, and as you toggle back and forth between screens, you are automatically attached to the UNIX command assigned to that window. The most common UNIX command within a window is a shell command such as /bin/csh, /bin/sh, or /bin/ksh. This provides a terminal window just as if you were logging into the machine in a single-session mode.

screen is a GNU product and as such is subject to its GNU General Public license as included both in the product distribution and in App. B of this book.

12.14.2 Usage

The basic command line use for screen is:

```
screen [-A] [-L] [-O] [-R] [-a] [-c file] [-D|d [pid.ty.host]]
  [-e xy] [-f,-fn,-fa]
[-h] [-i] [-l,-ln] [-ls,-list] [-t name,-k name] [-r [pid.tty.host]]
  [-s] [-wipe]
[command [args]]
```

where -A adapts window size to display size.
-L—last character position on auto-margin terminal is writeable.
-O matches more closely your terminal's characteristics if not a vt100.
-R resumes the first detached window.
-a includes all display capabilities in each window's termcap.
-c file overrides the default configuration file from $HOME/.screenrc to file.
-D | -d [pid.tty.host] begins session as undetached.
-e xy defines the command character x and the literal command character y.
-f, -fn, -fa turn flow control on, off, or to automatic switching mode, respectively.
-h n specifies the size of the history buffer as n lines.
-i causes interrupt key to interrupt display automatically.
-l, -ln turn logon mode on or off.
-ls, -list display a list of screen sessions.
-tname, -kname set the title for the default shell or specified program.
-r [pid.tty.host] resumes a detached screen session.
-s sets the invocation shell to that specified in command.

-wipe is same as -ls but removes sessions instead of simply marking them as dead.
command [args] is command to invoke with associated arguments.

Note that the environmental variable SHELL will determine which shell will be invoked by default and that the tty setting will determine the characteristics of the terminal emulation and what features are utilized and supported.

You can customize the key bindings and other features with the command:

```
C-a : command
```

where command is taken from the list described on page 13 of the screen manual page included with the screen distribution. See this file for more details. With the customization command, you can modify almost every aspect of your terminal emulation and multiwindow environment on the fly.

Command mode. There are a variety of interactive commands you can execute which talk directly to the terminal manager. Some of the more basic are:

`C-a C-\`	Kills all windows and terminates screen.
`C-a [`	Enters copy/scrollback mode, which allows for screen cut and paste. The syntax is very similar to vi.
`C-a ]`	Writes current contents of paste buffer to the current window.
`C-a ?`	Displays a list of available commands.
`C-a n`	Where n is a number between 0 and 9 and represents the window session number.
`C-a C-a`	Switches to previously displayed number.
`C-a c`	Creates a new window with a shell and moves to this window.
`C-a C`	Clears the current screen.
`C-a d`	Detaches the current screen.
`C-a D`	Detaches the current screen and kills all associated processes.
`C-a f`	Cycles flow control from automatic to on or off.
`C-a h`	Generates a hard copy of the current screen.
`C-a H`	Begins logging of current window to hardcopy.n where n is the window number.
`C-a i`	Displays information about current window.
`C-a k`	Kills the current window and switches to previous window.
`C-a l`	Refreshes the current window.
`C-a L`	Determines whether entry in /etc/utmp is generated. This determines whether you are logged in or not.
`C-a M`	Toggles monitoring of the current window. If the window is placed in the background and monitoring is on, you will receive status upon output to that window.

`C-a n`	Switches to next window.
`C-a p`	Switches to previous window.
`C-a q`	Sends CTRL-q to the current process in the current window.
`C-a r`	Toggles automatic line wrap.
`C-a s`	Sends CTRL-s to the current process in the current window.
`C-a t`	Displays the time of day, hostname, and load averages.
`C-a v`	Displays version and generation date.
`C-a w`	Displays a list of all windows. Current window is marked with an *, and the previous window is marked with a -.
`C-a x`	Runs screen lock on the current window.
`C-a z`	Suspends all screen sessions.
`C-a Z`	Resets window to default values.

There is a message line at the bottom of the screen which keeps you informed as to the status and results of an executed command.

To exit screen, you can either type C-a C-\ or exit at the command prompt. When you have exited the final screen, you will see the message "screen is terminating." At this point, you are back at the original session from which you invoked screen.

There is an issue of flow control related to the screen system. When you want to stop the flow of information, you typically press a C-s. When you want to resume the flow, you press C-q. With screen, if you press these, screen will interpret them for you or pass them to the underlying application. By enabling or disabling flow control with the C-a f command, you can change the behavior of the screen subsystem. If you want to ensure that you send C-s and C-q to the application and bypass any processing by screen, use the C-a s and C-a q commands, respectively.

There is much more information in the lengthy man page included with the distribution.

12.14.3 Installation

The first file you must modify is the config.h.in file. This file contains a variety of macro definitions which control a variety of aspects of screen including things like POSIX compliance, whether you are running setuid root for screen as is recommended, and how the detach and screen lock functions. Each macro is described in some detail, and you should have no trouble modifying the file for your particular machine type.

Once you have modified the config.h.in file, you can proceed with a normal configure build just as you do with most GNU products. The typical command set to build using the configure product is:

```
$ configure
$ make clean
$ make prefix=/usr/local/screen
```

where the prefix defines the directory in which to place all executables and man pages. Keep in mind that there are more things you can do with the configure command. See Sec. 11.1 for more details.

12.14.4 Conclusion

screen is a very powerful utility which provides many users of dumb terminals some relief from the limitation of one session. By providing multiple sessions (up to nine sessions at once), you can utilize your dumb vt100-style terminal much more effectively and can dramatically increase your productivity without incurring the expense of purchasing a new windowed device such as an X station or workstation.

12.15 areacode

12.15.1 Introduction

areacode provides a simple interface, although now somewhat out of date, to all the areacodes in the United States. It is a very simple program which provides the geographical match when given an area code. While this hasn't been modified for several years, you can insert the city and state with the appropriate area code directly into the areacode.c file and recompile to generate this mapping.

While it seems a fairly trivial tool, it is amazing how much time it saves if you use the phone and/or bulletin boards quite a bit.

12.15.2 Usage

The basic format of the areacode command is:

```
areacode nnn ...
```

where nnn ... is one or more area codes to scan for. That's it. Remember that you can add your own and recompile to generate more mappings if you wish.

12.15.3 Installation

The beginning of areacode contains text from the uunet mailer as well as text from the author. You need to remove all text up to and including the line which says

```
-----------------cut-here------nothing on the bottom-----
```

Save the resulting file as areacode.c. Once you have done this, you can compile the program as you normally would compile a C program.

There is nothing resembling a makefile or configure in this distribution because of its simplicity.

To compile areacode, use the command:

```
$ cc -o areacode areacode.c
```

This will generate an executable named areacode which you invoke directly.

12.15.4 Conclusion

While areacode is a trivial utility, it can provide significant value if you are involved in the use of a phone system. It is flexible enough that if you want to add your own information, you can do so.

12.16 bsplit

12.16.1 Introduction

bsplit comes as a shell archive and works similarly to split. However, it provides a split which is common among all different platforms. The other key difference is that bsplit works well on binary as well as ASCII files.

12.16.2 Usage

The basic syntax of bsplit is:

```
bsplit [-size][file [prefix]]
```

where -size specifies the size of the file to split out.
file specifies a file to split.
prefix specifies a prefix to add to the output files. The default is x.

This command is very similar to split except for the binary file support. A simple example is:

```
$ ls -l elvis-1.7.tar
... elvis-1.7.tar ..... 227040
$ bsplit elvis-1.7.tar
$ ls -l
...elvis-1.7.tar ...227040
...xaa ... 50000
...xab ... 50000
...xac ... 50000
...xad ... 50000
...xae ... 27040
```

Note that the default split file size is 50,000 bytes, and the file naming convention is to begin with x and cycle up from aa. You can change both the default file size and the prefix by simply including these on the bsplit command line as documented above.

To put the split files back together again, you use a command like:

```
$ cat x* > newfile
```

This will take all the x files and concatenate them, in order, back into the file newfile. From here you can treat it just as you would have before you split it. In this case, you could issue the tar command against it and should notice no differences.

12.16.3 Installation

bsplit comes as a shell archive. This means that you remove all text in the bsplit file up to the line:

```
#! /bin/sh
```

Once you create this file bsplit.c, you simply compile the file with the command:

```
$ cc -o bsplit bsplit.c
```

This creates an executable bsplit which can then be executed just as the split command is.

12.16.4 Conclusion

The bsplit command is used by many Internet utilities to split large binary files to allow for better distribution. You can use the cat command with the append option to recreate the original file as it existed before the bsplit command was executed.

bsplit is the command many people use to split software on the Internet, so you can't go wrong using it yourself.

Chapter

13

Nonnative Communications Tools

There are several very good tools which provide communication interfaces from UNIX platforms to other platforms. This chapter presents some of the best power tools which run on most UNIX platforms.

Kermit provides file transfer and terminal emulation capabilities between most platforms today including PCs, Macs, UNIX, VMS, and others. It is widely used and is often the de facto choice when moving information between different platforms. Because of the tight budgets at Columbia and various other factors, Kermit is not distributed on the CD with this book. However, it is very inexpensive, and the documentation that comes from Columbia is much better and more complete than this section. Contact:

Watson Laboratory
Columbia University Academic Information Systems
612 West 115th Street
New York, New York 10025, USA, Earth
(212)854-5126 (phone)
(212)662-6442 (Fax)
kermit@columbia.edu

for information on the product and how to get it.

xmodem is a protocol which provides basic file transfer capabilities from one platform to another. In fact, xmodem is often supported within larger programs like Kermit and other emulation packages that you can purchase. You can, however, use xmodem by itself for file transfer if this is all you need.

tn3270 provides full screen *all points addressible* (APA) 3270 datastream emulation. With this tool, you can make an asynchronous ASCII device look like a 3270 terminal. This is one of the most powerful tools available and provides most of the functionality you get from very expensive 3270 emulator packages from a variety of vendors.

crttool provides true vtxxx emulation between platforms. While there are several packages available which provide some level of emulation, if you are using a software package which needs complete vtxxx terminal-style support, you may want to investigate crttool.

slip stands for Serial Line Internet Protocol and provides IP protocol on dial-up phone lines. This gives you the ability to run full LAN applications over a standard dial-up phone line. This is a very powerful tool, and you will see it with many vendor's implementations of PC communications software.

There are many other packages which provide communications functionality which are not mentioned here. However, those described here provide most of what you will need in these types of packages and will at least get you started in this area.

13.1 Kermit

13.1.1 Introduction

Kermit is a terminal emulation and file transfer tool which is provided free from a variety of sources including the Internet. Its primary use is as a file transfer tool over telephone lines. It was written and is maintained primarily at Columbia University by Frank da Cruz, Bill Catchings, and Jeff Damens.

There are two primary versions, of which the most popular is C-Kermit. This version is written primarily in C and is, therefore, portable to many platforms including UNIX. The other version is called MS-Kermit and is much less commonly used and will, therefore, not be discussed.

Kermit is structured based on a client/server paradigm which consists of one machine acting as the server while the other machine is the client or remote machine. This allows for two-way file transfer using the "put" and "get" commands. You must first start the server function, then escape back to the client machine, and issue commands. The server can be either local or remote, and it provides the maximum flexibility and power.

The primary advantage of Kermit over many other file transfer and terminal emulation package is it's available on many platforms including UNIX, VMS, Macintosh, DOS, OS/2, and VM. This allows users to use the primary interface and scripts to transfer files and information from any platform to any platform. The other benefit of Kermit is in its file transfer speed. The latest version of Kermit has very sophisticated compression mechanisms which enhance file transfer speed and compatibilities.

13.1.2 Installation

As with all other nonnative UNIX tools in this book, the easiest way to get Kermit is from the Internet. This may mean purchasing a tape or using a direct or indirect Internet connection to get Internet access. See Chap. 9 for more information.

There is a Kermit tar file available for a variety of versions. Check the dates and make sure you get the latest and greatest version since changes and additions are occurring constantly as the product matures. Store the Kermit tar file in /tmp or some other place which will not take up permanent disk space since you will not need it once the tar file is unwound. I will assume the tar file is called kermit.tar and the directory in which it is stored is /tmp.

C-Kermit files all begin with a ck prefix. You should create a directory for Kermit, then cd to this directory. Next you need to unwind the tar file with the commands:

```
$ cd ./kermit
$ tar xvf /tmp/kermit.tar
```

Often the tar file is named ckuxxx.tar where xxx is the version of Kermit. The most recent Kermit is version 189; therefore you may see the file cku189.tar. This is the tar file you need to unwind to get the most current version as of the writing of this book.

The files resulting from the tar command follow the naming syntax:

```
ck<system><what>.<type>
```

where <system> describes the system to which the file applies:

9	OS-9
a	Documentation
c	All systems with C compilers
d	Data General
h	Harris computers
i	Commodore Amiga
m	Macintosh
o	OS/2
p	DOS PC
u	Unix and Unixlike systems
v	VAX/VMS
w	Wart

<what> is a mnemonic for what's in the file:

aaa	README file
cmd	Command parsing

con	Connect command
deb	Debug/transaction log formats
dia	Modem/dialer control
fio	System-dependent file I/O
fns	Protocol support functions
fn2	More protocol support functions
ker	General Kermit definitions
mai	Main program
pro	Protocol
scr	Script command
tio	System-dependent terminal I/O and interrupt handling
usr	User interface
us2	More user interface
us3	More user interface

<type> is the file type:

c	C source
h	Header files
w	Wart preprocessor source
nr	nroff/troff source
mss	Scribe text source
doc	Documentation
ps	Postscript documentation
hlp	Help text
bld	Instructions for building Kermit
bwr	Bug list
upd	Program update log
mak	makefile

For more information on the functionality and content of each file, see C-Kermit documentation which is available within the tar file. Depending on which version of Kermit you get, you may get different groups of the files discussed above. See your distribution and associated documentation for more details.

A makefile is provided, as for all tools from the Internet, in an effort to assist you with the installation and building of the product. This makefile is called ckuker.mak. Rename this file to makefile and issue the make command as follows:

```
$ mv ckubs2.mak makefile
$ make Sys5r3
```

where xxx is the platform for which you are building Kermit. Note that within the makefile there are a variety of platforms for which the UNIX version of Kermit can be built. Choose a platform after reviewing the makefile, which has descriptions of which platforms are available and which you should choose depending on the platform you are on. If your particular platform is not listed, choose between bsd and sys5r3, which denote Berkeley- and AT&T-derived systems, respectively. Most systems will work correctly with the sysV symbol, and therefore the command:

```
$ make sysr3
```

would build a working system for you if your particular system is not specifically listed. The resulting binary will be called wermit. Test this and make sure it works, then rename wermit to kermit and install in the bin subdirectory for general use:

```
$ mv wermit bin/kermit
```

Move the source code into the src directory and the documentation into the doc directory. This again uses the general product structure recommended for nonnative UNIX products in Sec. 9.8.

For the RS/6000 you might use a command like:

```
$ make rs6000c
```

and for a Sun running SunOS 4.1.3, you might use a command like:

```
$ make sunos41c
```

Note that most operating systems and associated machines are supported with reasonable defaults in the makefile. See the makefile for all the different machines supported.

13.1.3 Usage

Kermit provides interactive and command line capabilities. For short and simple file transfers, the command line capabilities will be sufficient; however, for more complex transactions, the command mode will be necessary. Each will be described in detail below.

File transfer. Kermit's primary use is as a file transfer tool over telephone lines. In local mode, stdout is continuously updated to show the progress of the file transfer. A dot is printed to the screen for every four data packets. Other packets are represented by:

`I`	Exchange parameter information
`R`	Receive initiate

S	Send initiate
F	File header
G	Generic server command
C	Remote host command
N	Negative acknowledgment
E	Fatal error
T	Time-out
Q	Damaged packet received
%	Packet retransmitted

You may control the flow and operation of Kermit during this transfer using the following commands:

CTRL-F	Stops transfer of current file and moves onto the next file
CTRL-R	Resends the current packet
CTRL-A	Displays status of the transfer
CTRL-B	Interrupts entire batch of files and terminates the transfer

Note: With System V versions of UNIX, you may have to precede the above interrupt commands with a \ to escape the control sequence. Finally, to regain control in the event of an emergency, type CTRL-C CTRL-C. This should interrupt the Kermit program and take you back to the terminal prompt. This will kill anything that was currently in progress, so only do it as a last resort.

Command line operation. The basic syntax is:

```
$ kermit [-rkxtfcniwqdh} [-s fn] [-a fn1] [-l dev] [-b speed]
[-p parity] [-g rfn] [-e len]
```

where r passively waits for files to receive.
k passively receives files and displays to stdout.
x begins server operation.
t is half-duplex with XON as handshake character.
f sends a "finish" command to the server.
c establishes a terminal connection before any protocol transaction occurs.
n is like -c but after a protocol transaction occurs.
i sends file without any conversions.
w writes protect—avoids filename duplications for incoming files.
q is quiet—suppresses screen update messages.
d is debug—creates debug.log file current directory with debugging information.
h displays help information.

s fn sends filename fn.
a fn1 alternates name for file; cannot use wildcards.
l dev is a terminal line such as /dev/tty1.
b speed specifies line speed.
p parity specifies parity as e,o,m,s,n.
g rfn requests a remote server to send name(d) files.
e len is extended packet length; allows for packets longer than the default 90.

Kermit uses a very standard UNIX command syntax utilizing hyphens and stdin and stdout. It also uses the client/server paradigm which allows for either of the two communicating machines to act as the server. A connection between a server and client must be established before transfers can take place. To establish a connection and a remote server, issue the following command:

```
$ kermit -l /dev/tty1 -b 2400 -n -r
```

This will establish a 2400-baud terminal connection with the remote machine where you will log in and establish the remote machine as the server. To transfer a file, enter the send command, then escape back to the local session using the CTRL-\ C command. You will be able to watch the file transfer occur. When it is finished, you will be reconnected to the remote machine. You can then send another file or log off as you normally would.

The escape sequence to go from remote to local machine is:

```
CTRL-\ C
```

The CTRL-\ is equivalent to an ASCII escape. Therefore the escape sequence to return from remote to local mode is ESC-C. Because the ESC key is rarely mapped correctly, CTRL-\ is often used to simulate ESC. Note that to simulate the ESC, you must hold down the CTRL and \ keys simultaneously. This sends a single ESC character. Once you have done this, press the C key, and you should receive a Kermit prompt.

Local mode really means that you are logged on to a local machine or you are using an external communication line. Remote mode denotes a machine which is logged on and transferring files over an external line that is connected to your local machine. Your local machine is remote unless you explicitly point your Kermit session at an external line with a -l command.

Some other examples are:

```
$ kermit -l /dev/tty1 -b 2400 -c | vt100
```

Note that Kermit provides generic terminal emulation, and you can, if you wish, pipe this through programs which interpret terminal sequences and control access to the screen. A common one is a vt100 program which allows for DEC vt100 terminal emulation.

```
$ kermit -l /dev/tty1 -nf
```

This will shut down the remote server and establish a terminal session to the remote machine. This is particularly useful if you wish to stop file transfer activities and resume interactive use of the remote machine. Note that this works because of the use of the n option which allows the f option protocol to finish before the n option begins. If you were to use -cf, this would not work correctly.

```
$ kermit -l /dev/tty1 -b 9600 -qg kevin.\* &
```

This command will transfer all remote files named kevin.* to your local directory. There are several things to note about this command. Kermit will be invoked in the background by the &. This allows work to continue while the transfer is occurring. The q causes Kermit to suppress any output to the terminal, so you don't get those annoying messages to the screen during transfer and usage. Note also that Kermit understands wildcards for filenames; however, the only ones that are recognized and handled correctly are * and ?. The * will do a multicharacter substitution while the ? will do a single-character substitution. All other shell metacharacters such as [and { are ignored. Finally, note that we had to escape the * with a backslash so that the shell didn't interpret it before passing it to Kermit.

Kermit uses standard input and output, and you can, therefore, use pipes and redirections with Kermit to provide more functionality in the tradition of UNIX.

Terminal emulation and modems. The command

```
$ kermit -l /dev/rty1 -b 9600 -c
```

will provide generic terminal emulation and allow you to log in to a remote machine over a serial line. This will work over any kind of serial line including local and remote connections. If you are using a local connection such as a null modem cable between two RS-232 ports, this will connect you directly to the getty subsystem on the remote machine, and you will get a login prompt. If you are using a switched line with modems, this command will give you control of the modem. Once you have control of the modem, you can issue standard modem commands such as those for Hayes-compatible modems. Assuming you have a phone line with two compatible modems and the remote is set up for autoanswer, you can issue the following commands to log in over the phone line to the remote machine:

```
$ kermit -l /dev/tty -b 9600
```

At this point, you are talking directly to the modem, which has its own command language and syntax. Most modems are Hayes compatible and follow a standardized command syntax. If you have a Hayes-compatible modem and want to now connect to a remote system, issue the following command:

```
ATDTnumber
```

where number is the phone number you wish to dial. For example, 5554404 would be a valid dial string, so the command would read:

```
ATDT5554404
```

This works exactly the same as dialing a phone. For a long distance call, you would again follow the same structure as for the normal phone. For example:

```
ATDT13125554404
```

At this point, the remote modem and your local modem will begin a handshaking sequence to establish baud rates, error correction protocols, and compression techniques. There are many Hayes commands available which control virtually every aspect of your modem. You should read your modem documentation for more information. To print out the configuration of your modem type:

```
AT&V
```

At this point, you will connect to the remote machine and should get a login prompt. Log in as you normally would and proceed as if logged in on a LAN. You now have generic terminal emulation and file transfer capabilities. If you are interested in using the machine in an interactive mode as if you were logged in locally, you can proceed; however, if you would like to transfer files, you must first put the remote machine in server mode and escape back to the local machine with the proper control sequence (probably CTRL\-C). You issue the receive command and your local machine waits for any files to arrive; when the transmission is finished, you are returned to your remote session where you can log off or continue with your work.

An example of this would be as follows:

```
login: kevin
password:xxxxx
Welcome to foobar, AIX 3.2
$ kermit -x
CTRL\-C
$ kermit
kermit> receive remote-file local-file
$ logoff (note we are back at foobar now, so we need to logoff)
$ (we're back at the local host)
```

remote-file from the remote machine is copied to local-file on your local machine. Note that paths can be fully qualified or relative in the standard UNIX way. There are commands to change directories and much more. These are typically available from within Kermit in what is known as interactive mode. This is the most powerful way to use Kermit.

Interactive mode. Interactive mode in Kermit is the preferred way to perform anything but the most simple of tasks. It provides a simple interface to the entire functionality of Kermit. Through the use of simple commands, you can perform logons and file transfers as well as run scripts, redirect files, and perform modem control.

The Kermit prompt is C-Kermit>. At this point, you can type any valid Kermit command and even issue standard UNIX commands. When you invoke Kermit, it first looks in your home directory and then your current directory for a file named .kermrc. This must contain Kermit commands only and cannot contain UNIX commands. An example will appear later in this chapter.

A brief list of Kermit commands is as follows:

`%`	Comment
`!`	Executes a UNIX command from within Kermit
`bye`	Ends session and logs out remote server
`close`	Closes a log file
`connect`	Establishes a session to either a modem or remote machine
`cwd`	Changes working directory
`dial`	Dials a telephone number
`directory`	Displays a directory listing
`echo`	Displays arguments literally
`exit`	Exits from program
`finish`	Exits remote server but doesn't log off
`get`	Gets file(s) from remote server
`hangup`	Hangs up the phone

`help`	Displays help for commands
`log`	Opens a log file
`quit`	Same as exit
`receive`	Receives files from remote server
`remote`	Issues command to remote server
`script`	Executes a login script with remote system
`send`	Sends file(s)
`server`	Begins server operation
`set`	Sets various parameters
`show`	Displays set parameters
`space`	Displays current disk space usage
`statistics`	Displays statistics about most recent transaction
`take`	Executes commands from a file

These commands are the first entered on the Kermit interactive command line. The Kermit command interpreter is relatively sophisticated in that it accepts unique shorthand commands for the above commands. You can also use the ? to prompt for proper responses. This is a very powerful feature that allows Kermit to help you finish commands. For example, if you type set and can't remember which set option you would like to use, you can type:

```
C-Kermit> set ?
```

and Kermit will provide you with a list of possible options from which to choose. This is available for all Kermit commands and is quite helpful. The other useful command is help. If you type help, you will be presented with a listing of all Kermit commands. If you type help command where command is one of the available Kermit commands, you will get additional information on that particular command itself. The other useful feature of the interactive interface is the ESC capability. If you need to fill in the rest of a keyword or request a default value, simply press ESC (again, this may be CTRL\) and Kermit will "fill in the blanks." This is very useful since you will often forget defaults and keywords.

A brief description of each Kermit command follows.

%. This is useful for inserting comments into script files.

! [command]. This allows you to execute shell commands from within the Kermit interpreter. For example, to examine whether a file is in your current directory or not, you could issue the following command:

```
C-Kermit> ! ls
```

This will list all files in the current directory. Note that you can issue any UNIX command; however, you again must be careful of the symbol substitution. Be sure to separate the ! and the command with at least one space. If you want to fork a new interactive shell, issue the ! without any command argument. To exit from this shell, type exit or CTRL-D.

bye. This stops the remote server, and the connection between your local machine and the remote machine is killed. It will return you to your local machine.

close. This closes a log file created by the log command.

connect. This command establishes a session with either the locally attached modem or the remotely attached machine. It works in coordination with the set line command to establish the connection. This is the best way to establish a direct connection to the modem and have access to the Hayes command set directly on the modem. Examples are given below. To get back to the local Kermit prompt after issuing the connect command, you must issue the escape as documented earlier. For example, CTRL\-C will bring you back to the Kermit prompt where you issue any commands as you normally would. To reconnect, issue the connect command again.

cwd [dir-name]. This allows you to change your local current working directory to dir-name.

dial [tele-string]. This issues the dial command through the local modem. You can bypass any direct interaction with the modem and Hayes command structure as described earlier with this command. For example:

```
C-Kermit> dial 13125554404
```

will connect to the modem and issue the command ATDT13125554404 just as documented earlier. This has the disadvantage that you don't have control over other parameters of the modem, and you may have to change other modem properties. This must be done from the Hayes direct modem connection with the connect command. This command is used in coordination with the set line and set modem commands as documented below. Note that you will get a "connected" message when the modems have established a link; however, you will then be placed back in interactive Kermit mode. You next need to type connect to tie into the established link. For example:

```
C-Kermit> dial 13125554404
connected....
C-Kermit> connect
login:....etc.
```

directory [dirname]. This displays a file listing of the current working directory or of the dirname directory.

echo [text]. This provides access to the terminal screen. You would typically use this within a script file to issue messages to the screen.

exit. This exits from the Kermit program and logs off the remote machine and associated processes. It will place you back on your local machine in the same state as before you issued the first Kermit command.

finish. This is the same as bye.

get filename [filename1]. This sends a request to the remote Kermit server to send the file filename. It requires that the remote Kermit server be started and a connection established. You can optionally rename filename to filename1 on the receiving machine. An example of using a modem and getting a remote file named /tmp/foobar and placing it on the local machine as /tmp/kevin follows:

```
$ kermit
C-Kermit> set modem hayes
C-Kermit> set line /dev/cua0
C-Kermit> set speed 9600
C-Kermit> dial 9,13125554404
connected...
C-Kermit> connect
login: kevin
passwd: xxxxx
Welcome to SunOS 4.2, Have a Good Time
$ kermit
C-Kermit> server
Control\-C* (to escape back to local machine) *
C-Kermit> get /tmp/foobar /tmp/kevin* (gets the remote file
/tmp/foobar and places it on the local machine as /tmp/kevin) *
C-Kermit> exit
$
```

You are now back at the local machine with the $ prompt.

hangup. This hangs up the local modem and kills the connection.

help [command]. This provides help on what commands are available and gives more specific help on a particular command.

log {packets, session, transactions, debugging} filename. This establishes a log file of various aspects of Kermit's operation. The packets option allows for a trace of all packets in and out of the communications port. The session option provides for screen trapping. The transactions option keeps a record of all files transferred. Finally, the debugging option provides information on the internal workings and operation of Kermit and is probably only useful to developers and real hacks. You issue the close command to close and save this log file.

quit. This is the same as exit.

receive [filename]. This passively waits for the receipt of a file. Note that this is very different from the get command, which actively gets a file from a remote machine; receive waits for the file to arrive. This means that the remote machine must issue a send before the receive will process any incoming information. If you wanted to send a file to a remote machine, you could use receive as follows:

```
$ kermit
C-Kermit> set modem hayes
C-Kermit> set line /dev/cua0
C-Kermit> set speed 9600
C-Kermit> dial 9,13125554404* (Note that we are using the standard
Hayes dialer string) *
connected...
C-Kermit> connect
login: kevin
passwd: xxxxx
Welcome to SunOS 4.2, Have a Good Time
$ kermit
C-Kermit> receive /tmp/kevin
Control\-C* (to escape back to local machine) *
C-Kermit> send /tmp/foobar
C-Kermit> exit
$
```

This sends the local file /tmp/foobar to the remote machine as /tmp/kevin. Note that we could have typed connect at the local C-Kermit> prompt and reconnected to the terminal session on the remote machine if we wanted to.

remote. This allows you to issue commands to the remote machine. There are several remote commands available.

`remote cwd [directory]`	Changes remote working directory
`remote delete filename`	Deletes remote filename
`remote directory [dirname]`	Lists files in remote dirname or current directory
`remote host command`	Executes command on remote machine
`remote space`	Displays remote disk capacity and usage

`remote type [filename]`	Displays remote filename on screen
`remote who [user]`	Displays remote user(s)
`remote help`	Displays remote server's capabilities

script. This allows for execution of canned scripts using send and respond strings. See Kermit documentation for more information.

send filename [filename1]. This sends the file named filename and, optionally, renames it filename1 on the remote system. Note that the other machine must be either in server mode or have issued the receive command. See the example above.

server. This places Kermit in server mode. All subsequent commands, such as send, the remote commands, and finish, must come from the other Kermit machine. See the above example.

set [variable value]. This allows you to control virtually every aspect of the communication between Kermit machines. There are many options, but only the most important ones will be documented here. See the Kermit documentation for more information.

`duplex {full,half}`	Determines full (two-way) or half (one-way) communication.
`file type {binary,text}`	Determines whether or not translation takes place when the file is transferred. If the file contains text only, use the set file type text command and any necessary file translations will take place; use binary to turn off translation. See example below.
`flow-control {none, xon/xoff}`	Controls flow control based on end-to-end connection.
`incomplete {discard,keep}`	Keeps or discards incomplete file if line goes down.
`line [device]`	Is used to establish line to use for communication.
`modem-dialer {direct,hayes, racalvadic,...}`	Is used to establish type of modem or direct connection. Note this must be used *before* the set line command.
`parity {even,odd,mark,space,none}`	Establishes parity.
`speed {0,300,1200,2400,9600,19200}`	Establishes line speed. Use *after* the set line command.

The set file type command is extremely useful when moving between diverse machines. If you are using an ASCII machine and transferring to or from a non-ASCII machine, Kermit will perform any translations necessary to make the file readable on the other machine. For example, if you are sending a text file from a UNIX machine to an IBM mainframe in text mode, it will automatically translate the ASCII characters to EBCDIC. Do not use the text mode if the file contains any nontextual information. For example, tar files contain nontextual information and you, therefore, must use the set file type binary command, and the remote machine must understand the tar format. This is the same for all nontextual format files.

To display the values of these variables, use the show command.

show [variables]. This is used to display the value of a variable established with set.

space. This displays information on local disk space and usage.

statistics. This displays statistics about the most recent Kermit transaction.

take [filename]. This runs a file containing Kermit commands. Note that it cannot send any information after the connect is issued. For this, use the script command. A typical use of the take command is to establish a connection and get a login prompt from the remote machine. For example:

```
set modem hayes
set line /dev/tty1
set speed 9600
dial 13125554404
connect
```

From here you must log on interactively. Remember that when you enter Kermit, it does a take on the file .kermrc, and this is where you would typically place commands like those above. If the above file were named take.file, you would execute it as follows:

```
C-Kermit> take take.file
```

You would see the connected message and proceed as you normally would.

13.1.4 Conclusion

Kermit is a very powerful tool which provides generic terminal emulation and file transfer capabilities over serial lines. It runs on virtually every platform and provides sufficient granularity of control that you can do almost anything you would like to do when transferring files between diverse machines. Transfers between mainframes, workstations, Macs, and PCs work without a hitch. One of the "gotchas" about UNIX is that there is a newline character at the end of every line instead of the more standard CR/LF. When transferring files between machines, Kermit takes care of this for you. Also, when moving from an ASCII to EBCDIC machine such as an IBM mainframe, Kermit will perform the translation automatically.

For more information, print out the documentation provided with Kermit since it is very good and includes more information than is included here. You can also contact the number provided for Columbia for more information.

13.2 xmodem

13.2.1 Introduction

xmodem is a commonly used protocol which is shipped with most UNIX machines and PC and Mac terminal emulators. It is used by tools like Kermit to transfer files and move information from one platform to another.

xmodem is based on a client/server model where you define one end of a communication link as the server and the other end as the client. User interaction with xmodem is very similar to that of Kermit.

xmodem is in fact a protocol and as such handles data transmission errors and automatically generates retransmission of bad packets. This allows the higher-level applications such as Kermit and the xmodem application itself to assume that all packets received are correct and to proceed accordingly.

The latest version of xmodem (3.4) is probably the last if not one of the last versions of xmodem to be produced since most work on xmodem has stopped. While a good tool, xmodem has been superseded by tools like zmodem and Kermit when file transfer capability is needed. This distribution does seem to work well, however, and is of value to anyone who wants xmodem support and capabilities.

13.2.2 Usage

The basic syntax for the xmodem command is:

```
xmodem [rb|rt|sb|st|][ymkdlx] [file...]
```

where rb receives binary.
rt receives text.
sb sends binary.
st sends text.
y uses ymodem protocol.
m uses MODEM7 batch protocol.
k uses XMODEM-1K file transfer protocol.

d deletes the xmodem.log file before file transfer is begun.
l doesn't create the log file.
x is debug mode.
file... is one or more files to be transferred.

One machine must be set to send a file, while the other must be set to receive a file. To interrupt any file transfer activity use C-x C-x.

A simple example follows. To receive a file named kevin.text, use:

```
$ xmodem rt kevin.text
```

On the serving machine, type:

```
$ xmodem st kevin.text
```

This will transfer the file across the link. Note that you can send multiple files with the Xmodem protocol. A simple example is that on the receiving machine, use:

```
$ xmodem rty file1 file2 file3
```

On the sending machine, type:

```
$ xmodem sty file1 file2 file3
```

Three files will be transferred. See the man page for more information.

13.2.3 Installation

This software comes in three shar archives plus a patch for the part01archive. Simply uncompress the archives (if necessary) and remove all comments up to the first shell command (in this case each begins with an echo command). Once you have removed the preceding comments, issue the command:

```
$ sh partxx
```

where xx is 01, 02, or 03.

Next, you need to shar the patch1 archive with the command:

```
$ sh patch1
```

This will update the files in the current directory.

Finally, you can issue the make command to build xmodem on your system.

13.2.4 Examples

The best way to understand how to use the xmodem command is to view a few simple examples.

Sending a file to a remote machine. To send a file to a remote machine, first log in to the remote machine with any standard terminal emulation program such as Kermit. Move to the appropriate directory to which you want the file transferred. On the remote system, type:

```
$ xmodem -r testfile
```

This starts the xmodem protocol for receive on the remote machine. Now you must interrupt the terminal emulation session with the proper command. For example, with Kermit you would type C-c, and when using Asynchronous Terminal Emulation (ATE), you would type C-v. Each different terminal emulator has some command sequence to interrupt your session and place you back on the local machine. See your documentation for more details on your specific implementation.

Once you are back at your local prompt, you need to initiate a send procedure from your terminal emulation system. For example, with Kermit you would issue a send command from within Kermit; from many emulation programs, you can initiate a send from a pull-down menu or from within a terminal emulation program with a command like send. For example, with ATE you would issue the command:

```
s testfile
```

Each implementation is different. See your documentation for details.

Note that the emulation program must support the xmodem protocol. It will say so explicitly if it does. File transfer occurs and is documented in terms of packets sent and error rates. Once the file transfer occurs, you are returned to the interactive prompt on the local machine. You can then reconnect and log off or do whatever you would like on the remote system.

Receive from a remote machine. Log in to the remote machine as described above and issue the command:

```
$ xmodem -s testfile
```

Return to the local machine and issue a receive command. This will receive the remote file testfile from the remote machine. Keep in mind that you can rename the file on the local machine for the receive if you would like.

Once the transfer is finished, return to the remote machine and log out or perform any activities as you normally would.

13.2.5 Conclusion

xmodem is not only a protocol supported by most emulation and file transfer programs but is an application as well. xmodem is available for most platforms but may not be shipped by the vendor with their implementation of UNIX. If it is not, see the implementation included on the CD with this book.

13.3 tn3270

13.3.1 Introduction

tn3270 is an application which provides 3270 terminal emulation from a UNIX workstation. It requires no special hardware and can run with the tn3270 protocol over a LAN or WAN. All that is required is that a transport such as TCP/IP be present on the connection. It is a tool which constantly amazes people, and after using it, they wonder why they have been buying expensive solutions that provide similar or less functionality.

tn3270 runs on many platforms; however, the version documented in this chapter is 4.1.1, which lacks support for many platforms, including DOS and the Mac. However, these platforms are supported in earlier releases with significantly reduced functionality. These tn3270 clients are also available from sources such as FTP Software, Inc. (North Andover, MA, 508-685-4000) for the DOS platform and from some archives supported by Brown University. See the README under the tn3270 subdirectory for more information.

The tn3270 distribution. The tn3270 distribution consists of a compressed tar file. Once you uncompress and unwind it, you will see several key files:

`README`	File which contains information about files on the distribution and a support person.
`ANNOUNCE`	Announcement of newer functions in the current release.
`curses`	Directory which contains screen manipulation routines called curses. This is a standard UNIX package.
`man`	Directory containing manual pages.
`telnet`	Contains source code for the telnet functionality to build tn3270.
`tn3270`	Code to build the tn3270 product. Note that there is a README file within this directory which we will use.
`transcom`	Tool which allows for Tektronix capabilites from the mainframe.

Within the tn3270 subdirectory there is a README file. This contains information relevant to the building of tn3270. tn3270 is written to build easily on a Berkeley-derived system. This means that it should compile easily on a Sun and ultrix. However, it will compile on platforms such as the HP and IBM RS/6000 given the proper switches to maintain compiler compatibility and so forth.

The basic tn3270 screen is shown in Fig. 13.1. As you can see, this looks like a 3270 display inside a window on the workstation screen. This window can be moved, resized, copied into and from, etc., just like any other standard window on X11. This is a very powerful way to use a mainframe from a UNIX workstation.

13.3.2 Installation

Building tn3270 is very straightforward. Simply move to the tn3270 subdirectory and issue the make command. For example:

```
$ pwd
/usr/local/tn3270/disttn3270
$ cd tn3270
$ make
lots of stuff generated from the make...
```

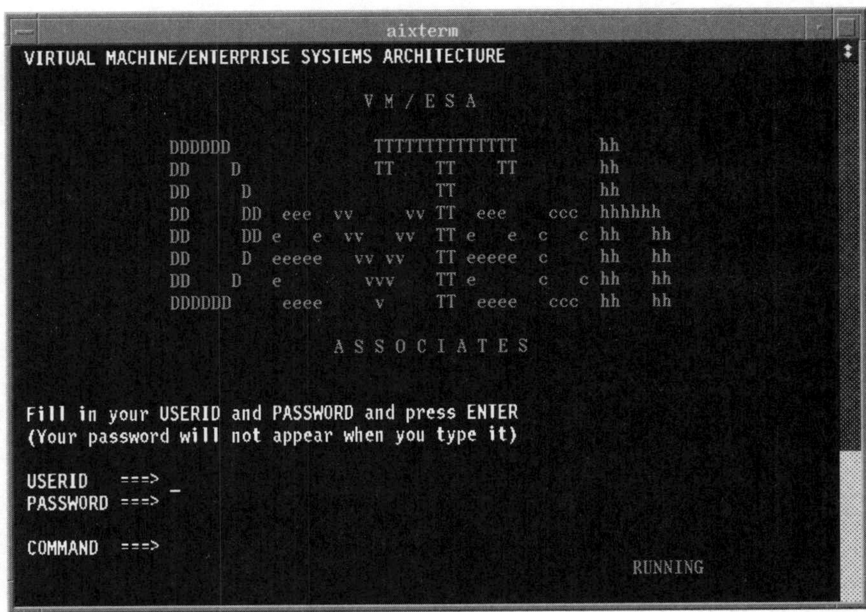

Figure 13.1 The tn3270 window.

If you have compiler problems, there are two optional makefiles: makefile_4.2 and telnet/Makefile_ultrix. Try the makefile_4.2 if you get compiler errors and the telnet/Makefile_ultrix if you have problems with make or the link editor (ld). See the README file for more details.

When the make command is invoked, the makefile builds all appropriate executables and generates a file tn3270. This is the executable used to invoke tn3270. Note that much of the C code in the distribution is Kernighan & Ritchie-style C code and will cause ANSI C compilers trouble. Use the K & R support within your compiler to compile this code to minimize problems with syntax and compilation. I was not able to get this to compile without a significant time investment on the IBM RS/6000; however, IBM is shipping a tn3270 version free with their operating systems, so it is unnecessary to port the tn3270 software to AIX anyway. It is certainly more relevant on the Sun and HP machines where the code compiles without any difficulty. It should also build on SCO UNIX; however, this was not available during the production of this book.

The final step to building the tn3270 product is to move a copy of the map3270 database to the /etc/directory:

```
$ pwd
/usr/local/tn3270/disttn3270
$ cp etc/map3270 /etc/map3270
```

This places the default keyboard mappings for many standard ASCII terminals in a location where the tn3270 application can find it. You can use tn3270 without using the map3270 database; however, it makes it much more complicated. If you do not have privilege to write to the /etc area, see your system administrator and/or the section below on keyboard mapping.

13.3.3 Usage

The tn3270 protocol. The tn3270 protocol is a public domain protocol which runs above the transport layer of your network. It is approximately a layer 5 protocol in the seven-layer ISO model. It is a specification which describes full-screen 3270 data stream emulation on a non-3270 data stream device.

With the tn3270 protocol, you can distribute the 3270 data stream onto LANs and WANs that are running a TCP/IP transport. tn3270 uses the standard ports for telnet to provide this service and merely relies on the tn3270 emulation software package to be on the client end to interpret the contents of the delivered packets, break them apart, and transform them from 3270 to curses packets which UNIX uses to manipulate the screen.

Most implementations of TCP/IP for mainframe support the tn3270 protocol. Certainly IBM's TCP/IP for VM and MVS provide a tn3270 data stream with no additional configuration on the mainframe required. An example of the use of this architecture is shown in Fig. 13.2. Note that the tn3270 product does *not* provide any cluster controller emulation capabilites but instead looks like a 3278 dumb terminal device. There are other products which provide these sorts of capabilities, and they are beyond the scope of this book. Suffice it to say that you can use various vendor products to provide local 317x and 327x cluster controller emulation capabilites, and you can use tn3270 to provide a dumb terminal emulation into these products.

To invoke tn3270, type the command:

```
$ tn3270 [-d] [-n filename] [-t command] [hostname [port]]
```

where -d turns on socket-level tracing.
-n filename is the file to receive tracing information; default is stderror.
-t command specifies UNIX command to process IBM 4994 data.
hostname is the hostname of the remote system.
port is used to specify a port other than the standard port.

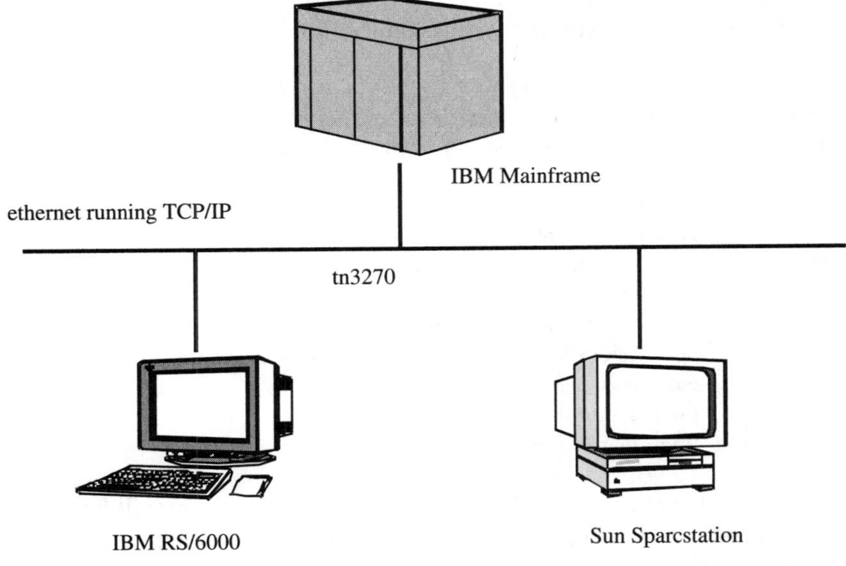

Figure 13.2 The tn3270 architecture.

When you invoke tn3270, a negotiation takes place between your terminal and the mainframe which establishes your terminal characteristics. The tn3270 application looks at your TERM variable and establishes things like rows and columns, keyboard mappings, etc. In all cases, the terminal looks like a 3278 to the mainframe, and the negotiation determines which model within the 3278 family is emulated.

tn3270 uses curses to map keyboard ASCII sequences to the appropriate signals the mainframe is expecting. There is a default file which describes the mapping of all keys on the keyboard to keys and actions expected on the mainframe. etc/map3270 is shipped with the distribution and contains example codes and mappings for the tn3270 product. This describes the default characteristics of the terminal emulation if you make no changes. In addition, tn3270 looks for an environmental variable TN3270 to define the mapping file. There are two additional products shipped with tn3270: mset and map3270. See the section below on keyboard mapping for more information.

Modes of operation. There are two modes of operation with tn3270. One is command mode, which gives you a prompt tn3270>. From here you can issue tn3270 commands which control most aspects of your tn3270 session. A key command is help. To use it, type:

```
tn3270> help
```

Commands may be abbreviated. The following is a listing of the commands available within the tn3270 command mode. Note that they are very similar to the standard telnet commands.

`close`	Closes current connection
`display`	Displays operating parameters
`mode`	Tries to enter line-by-line or character-at-a-time mode
`open`	Connects to a site
`quit`	Exits telnet
`send`	Transmits special characters ('send ?' for more)
`set`	Sets operating parameters ('set ?' for more)
`status`	Prints status information
`toggle`	Toggles operating parameters ('toggle ?' for more)
`transcom`	Specifies Unix command for transparent mode pipe
`z`	Suspends telnet
`!`	Invokes a subshell
`?`	Prints help information

If you don't include a hostname on the tn3270 line, you will be placed in command mode. To open a connection to a remote machine using the 3270 data stream, issue the command:

```
tn3270>open hostname
```

This will connect you to the remote host, negotiate a session and terminal characteristics, and put you at the login screen just as if you were sitting at a 3270 data stream full-screen terminal. You are now in full-screen emulation mode, which is the other tn3270 mode of operation. From this mode, you can execute all commands as you normally would from a full-screen 3278-style terminal. A mapping has occurred, as is discussed in the following section.

You can move from full-screen emulation mode to command mode by typing CTRL-C. This will take you to a tn3270> prompt where you can issue command mode commands as you normally would. To return to full-screen mode, type <return> on a blank line. While you are in command mode, the full-screen session is merely suspended. When you reenter the full-screen session, you should return to your previous full-screen state.

There are many commands within command mode for tn3270. In fact, the full set for telnet is supported. You can use quit and open to quit and open new connections to other machines and ! to escape to a shell, including the !/bin/sh or !/bin/ksh or !/bin/csh commands to fork to a completely new shell. Use the interactive help for more information on which commands may be useful to you.

Terminal emulation issues. The best way to use the tn3270 tool is through X11. Simply move into a terminal shell window on your local machines and invoke the tn3270 exactly as described above. The emulation will be taken care of by your machine.

It gets more interesting, however, when you are accessing a tn3270 server remotely. In other words, the tn3270 application runs on a node other than your local one. There are two ways to use the tn3270 product effectively on a remote station. The first is to use the X11 capability and the xterm terminal emulator to provide remote support:

```
$ TERM=vt100;export TERM /* export the TERM variable as a standard
  vt100 */
$ telnet remotehost /* go to the remote machine which is running
  tn3270 */
login
$ /usr/openwin/bin/xterm -display localhost:0
* this pops up an xterm window on your local display...select this
  window to make it active */
$ tn3270
* now you have invoked the tn3270 and used the X11 server to
 provide terminal emulation */
```

The second way is to set both the local TERM and remote TERM to vt100 and use the existing window:

```
$ TERM=vt100;export TERM
$ telnet remotehost
login
$ TERM=vt100;export TERM
$ tn3270
```

Note that both solutions work, but the first is more elegant in terms of full-screen terminal emulation and support for windowing functions. You could, and probably should, set up a rsh-type command to invoke the shell from a remote machine. For example:

```
$ rsh remotehost -l usename /usr/openwin/bin/xterm
$ tn3270 /* from within the newly created window */
```

For more information on these types of techniques for utilizing the power of X11, see Chap. 8.

Keyboard mapping issues. When tn3270 is invoked, it looks for a file /etc/map3270. This file contains the default keyboard mappings for tn3270. A program called mset allows you to set your keyboard characteristics and associated key mappings. mset is automatically built when you build tn3270. To invoke it, type:

```
$ mset [keyboardname]
```

To avoid having to scan the /etc/map3270 file every time tn3270 is invoked, you can set the environmental variable MAP3270, which is read before tn3270 scans the /etc/map3270 file. MAP3270 contains either a fully qualified path (beginning with a /) which points to a file which contains the keyboard mappings for your particular terminal or contains actual keyboard characteristics and key mappings. The tn3270 tool scans the string contained in MAP3270. If it begins with a /, it looks for a file with a name matching the string which contains the mappings. If the MAP3270 variable does not begin with a /, tn3270 uses the mappings contained within the MAP3270 variable itself to establish mappings for your session.

You can have the mset command establish your MAP3270 variable for you. For example, place the following in your .profile:

```
$ set noglob; export MAP3270="`mset`";unset noglob
$ echo $MAP3270
MAP3270=sun- cmd{BTAB='^B';CLEAR='^Z';DELETE='^?'|'^D';
  DOWN='^-J';EEOF='^E';EINP='^W';ENTER='^M';ESCAPE='^C';
  FERASE='^U';FLINP='^X';INSRT='^[`;LEFT='^H';NL='^N';PA1='^P1';
  PA2='^P2';PA3='^P3';PFK1='^[1';PFK2='^[2';PFK3='^[3';PFK4='^[4';
  PFK5='^[5';PFK6='^[6';PFK7='^[7';PFK8='^[8';PFK9='^[9';PFK10='^[0';
  PFK11='^[-';PFK12='^[=';PFK13='^[!';PFK14='^[@';PFK15='^[#';
  PFK16='^[$';PFK17='^[%';PFK18='^[\^';PFK19='^[&';PFK20='^[*';
  PFK21='^[(`;PFK22='^[)';PFK23='^[_';PFK24='^[+';RESET='^T';
```

```
RESHOW='^V';RIGHT='^L';SYNCH='^R';TAB='^I';UP='^K';XOFF='^S';
XON='^Q' ;}:
```

If the environmental variable MAP3270 is not set, the mset command looks for the /etc/map3270 file. If mset cannot find any of the above information, it researches for a terminal type of unknown. If it cannot find anything for this, it uses its defaults.

The etc/map3270 file is a database file which contains a listing of terminal types and corresponding keyboard mappings. The final step in building tn3270 is to move a copy of this file to the /etc directory. Now let's take a look at the structure of the map3270 file. There are many terminal types represented in the map3270 database. The vt100 section looks as follows:

```
vt100 | vt100nam | pt100 | vt125 | vt102 | direct831 | tek4125 |
pcplot | microvax{ enter = '^m'; clear = '^z' | '\EOM';

nl = '^?'; tab = '^i'; btab = '^b'; left = '^h' | '\EOD'; right
  = '^l' | '\EOC'; up = '^k' | '\EOA';
down = '^j' | '\EOB'; home = '\EOn';
delete = '^d'; eeof = '^e'; einp = '^w'; insrt = '^ ' | '\E ';

# pf keys pfk1 = '\EOq' | '\E1'; pfk2 = '\EOr' | '\E2'; pfk3
= '\EOs' | '\E3'; pfk4 = '\EOt' | '\E4'; pfk5 = '\EOu' | '\E5'; pfk6
= '\EOv' | '\E6'; pfk7 = '\EOw' | '\E7'; pfk8 = '\EOx' | '\E8'; pfk9
= '\EOy' | '\E9'; pfk10 = '\EOP\EOp' | '\E0'; pfk11 = '\EOP\EOq' |
'\E-'; pfk12 = '\EOP\EOr' | '\E='; pfk13 = '\EOP\EOs' | '^f13';
pfk14 = '\EOP\EOt' | '^f14'; pfk15 = '\EOP\EOu' | '^f15'; pfk16
= '\EOP\EOv' | '^f16'; pfk17 = '\EOP\EOw' | '^f17'; pfk18
= '\EOP\EOx' | '^f18'; pfk19 = '\EOP\EOy' | '^f19'; pfk20
= '\EOQ\EOp' | '^f20'; pfk21 = '\EOQ\EOq' | '^f21';

# program attention keys pa1 = '\E\EOP' | '^p1'; pa2 = '\E\EOQ' |
'^p2';

# local control keys
escape = '^c'; # escape to telnet command mode master_reset = '^g';
  centsign = '^\';

# local editing keys settab = '\E;'; deltab = '\E''; clrtab
= '\E:'; setmrg = '\E,'; sethom = '\E.'; coltab = '\E\E[B'; colbak
= '\E\E[A'; indent = '\E\E[C'; undent = '\E\E[D'; } # end of vt100,
  etc.
sun {
```

The first line describes all terminal types supported by the following definitions. The next fields describe characteristics of the ENTER, clear screen, newline (nl), tab, and cursor movement keys. The section entitled pf keys describes how the traditional PF keys are mapped. The vertical bar denotes options that perform the same task. The following characters are also special:

`'/E'`	Escape
`'/n'`	Newline
`'/t'`	Tab

`'/r'`	Carriage return
`^`	CRTL

If you want to understand how to execute a PF1 as you would from a normal 3278-style terminal to access a help function, type:

```
ESCAPE 1
```

In general, the PF keys are mapped with an ESCAPE and the associated numeric key across the top of the keyboard. Note that you should avoid using the keypad since this may be mapped to something else. To generate an interrupt (PA2), you would type:

```
CTRL-p 2
```

Again CTRL-C takes you back to command mode. You can create your own terminal definitions, map the keys appropriately, and simply include it in this file. The file map3270.5 file contains a very nice description of all functions supported and mapped by the map2370 database. See this for more information. The most commonly used keys are (remember, ^ is CTRL):

`^z`	CLEAR
`^p2`	ATTN
`^m`	ENTER
`^t`	RESET
`PF1`	ESC 1
`PF2`	ESC 2
`...etc...`	
`PF13`	ESC !
`PF14`	ESC @
`...etc...`	
`^u`	ERASE

If you have problems with the terminal emulation and keyboard mappings, take a look at the termcap database for a listing of supported ASCII terminals. This should not be necessary since most ASCII terminals support the vt100 emulation, and this should provide reasonable emulation for you. However, if you have a keyboard which has special keys that you would like to utilize, consult the termcap and terminfo databases for more information.

Manual pages. There are three manual pages shipped with the product. In the tn3270 subdirectory, there are the following files:

`map3270.5`	Man page for the map3270 tool
`mset.1`	Man page for the mset tool
`tn3270.1`	Man page for the tn3270 tool

Note that all can be previewed with the command:

```
$ nroff -man filename | more
```

See Chap. 9 for more information on where to put man pages and how to use them.

13.3.4 Conclusion

This kind of tool will allow you to dial in from home with a dumb terminal or PC running ASCII full-screen emulation (vt100 or something similar) and log in to a full-screen 3270 environment. This same tool will allow you to access a full-screen 3270 environment from any workstation on any LAN that is connected to the 3270 environment. This is one of the most heavily used tools by UNIX power users, and tn3270 is truly a power tool.

13.4 crttool

13.4.1 Introduction

The version of crttool described and contained in this book is 2.0 This supports true vt200 emulation, which is supported on most ASCII devices and controllers in existence today. It is extremely useful when you are moving between flavors of UNIX and between UNIX and other platforms such as VMS and mainframe environments.

This emulation provides the capability for applications expecting to run on a true vt terminal to work appropriately. This means that all vt escape sequences will be trapped and emulated correctly. This is important to maintain backward compatibility with most older UNIX applications.

crttool will open up a new window with the characteristics of a vt200 terminal. This terminal window will behave differently from the default shell windows. There is support for things like vt200 escape sequences, double wide characters, cut and paste buffers, and terminal sizes ranging from 80 to 132 columns.

13.4.2 Installation

As with most Internet files, the README files are the most important ones. The first file to examine is the crttool-2.0.README file in the root directory of the distribution. This contains a complete description of the tool and an exhaustive discussion of features and functionality. It also contains information on gotchas and other things to watch out for when building and invoking crttool.

The tar file contains several subdirectories, including fonts, crttool.src, sfonts, vfonts, and xfonts-mod. These contain all the necessary fonts and source codes to build the crttool executable. Note that fonts play a big part of any X11 windows application, and there is a lot of information required before you can become proficient with fonts and X11 windows. Suffice it to say that crttool uses a large number of fonts, and they are all included in the distribution.

Inside the crttool.src directory, there is a Makefile which will build the product. Note again that this Makefile is tuned for a SunOS environment, and you will have to make modifications to the variables to make this work in a non-Sun environment.

This Makefile not only builds all necessary executables, but it also compiles and links in all necessary fonts for crttool to work properly with the windowing environment.

To build crttool, use the following:

```
$ cd /usr/local/crttool/crttool.src
$ make
```

To ensure you make a clean copy, you might want to issue the command:

```
$ make clean
$ make
```

to first clean out any old executables and object files before recompiling and relinking. If you are running a version of the operating system that is compatible with the delivered executables, it should not be necessary to rebuild crttool.

Note that there is not a version for the RS/6000 because this code must be significantly modified to run on anything other than a Sun.

13.4.3 Usage

The syntax of crttool is:

```
crttool [-C] [toolargs] [-Cm] [-Cn color] [-Cb buttons] [-Cw]
   [-Ct  font]
[program [arguments]]
```

where -C sends console message to this console.
toolargs supports arguments from other windowing systems like sunview.
-Cm uses a monochrome display.

-Cn color uses color from the following crttool table:
- -C0—background
- -C1—foreground
- -C2—black
- -C3—red
- -C4—green
- -C5—yellow
- -C6—blue
- -C7—magenta
- -C8—cyan
- -C9—white

-Cb buttons defines function keys to be placed at the top of the window. This can either be a file or an environmental variable.

-Cw enables autowrap.

-Ct font defines fonts for the crttool window from the list:
- 10—10 point regular
- 12—12 point regular
- 14—14 point regular
- 16—16 point regular
- 18—18 point regular
- 24—24 point regular
- 10-bold—10 point bold
- 12-bold—12 point bold
- 14-bold—14 point bold
- 16-bold—16 point bold
- 18-bold—18 point bold
- 24-bold—24 point bold

program arguments—if a program name is present, the crttool executes it. The default is the shell command, which places you at an interactive prompt.

The crttool was written for the Sun environment and works best there. Most of this chapter discusses crttool with respect to the Sun environment.

There is one subtlety when using crttool in the Sun environment. You must set the environmental variable FONTPATH to the fonts subdirectory contained in the crttool distribution *before* invoking the windowing environment. For example, you could issue the commands:

```
% setenv FONTPATH /usr/local/users/soft-
ware/crttool/crttool.src/fonts:/usr/openwin
% openwin
```

They will load the appropriate fonts when openwindows is invoked so that crttool can work properly and find all the appropriate fonts that it

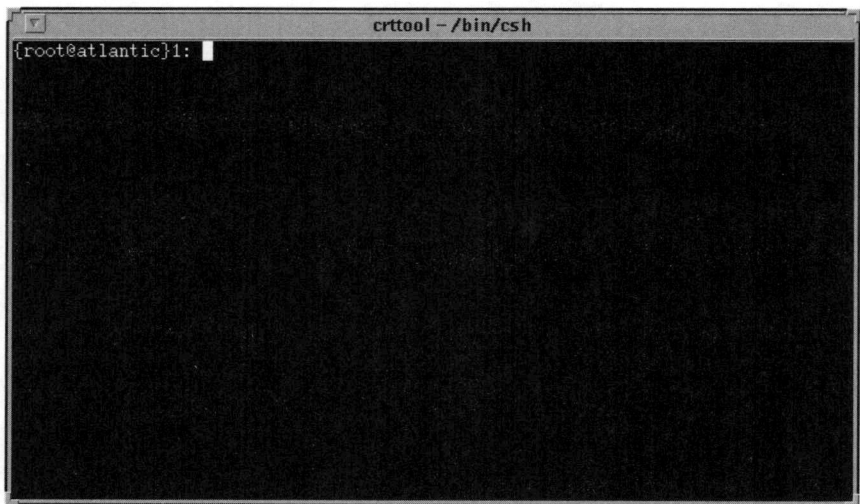

Figure 13.3 The crttool window.

needs. If you don't do this, you will get missing font errors since some of the fonts used by crttool are not standard fonts located in the standard font directories. Fonts will probably be your main problem when moving crttool from machine to machine and when attempting to display across the network. See Sec. 8.5 for more information on fonts.

When crttool opens up a new window, you are emulating a vt200-style terminal. This is shown in Fig. 13.3.

Keyboard mapping. Besides font support, the other primary issue you will need to think about is keyboard mapping. crttool installs its own version of the vt220 terminfo file. This avoids standard problems associated with the incorrect mappings made by the default vt200 termcap file.

crttool is shipped with a variety of default keyboard mappings including Sun Type 3 and Type 4 keyboards. The basic keyboard mapping between the vt-style keyboards and the Sun-style keyboards is:

vt200	Type 3	Type 4
PF1	R4	R4
PF2	R5	R5
PF3	R6	R6
PF4	C-R6	KP-
KP7	R7	R7

vt200	Type 3	Type 4
KP8	R8	R8
KP9	R9	R9
KP-	C-R9	C-KP+
KP4	R10	R10
KP5	R11	R11
KP6	R12	R12
KP,	C-R12	KP+
KP1	R13	R13
KP2	R14	R14
KP3	R15	R15
ENTER	C-R15	ENTER
KP0	C-R13	KP0
KP.	C-R14	KP.
UP	S-R8	S-R8
DOWN	S-R14	S-R14
LEFT	S-R10	S-R10
RIGHT	S-R12	S-R12

where KP represents keypad and R represents the keypad for Sun keyboards and where they begin with R1 in the upper left-hand corner and move left to right, then top to bottom. Note that the top row of keys on the Sun keypad (R1, R2, R3, NUMLOCK) is not used in these keyboard mappings.

You can issue function escape sequences with the mouse as well with the -Cb buttons options as outlined above.

13.4.4 Conclusion

crttool is an extremely powerful tool for accessing heterogeneous platforms and providing good vt-style terminal emulation. Cross-platform support is clearly its strength as a tool, and it certainly works best in a heterogeneous environment with X11 as the primary windowing protocol.

The crttool is a tool available from many sources including the Internet. Many vendors have taken the basic crttool and added slick functionality to enhance its usability and saleability. If you are interested in commercial support and slick and glossy look and feel capabilities, you may want to investigate commercial offerings; however, the crttool as available from the Internet and described in this chapter is very easy to use and is extremely powerful. Remember, it's free, so the price is probably right.

13.5 slip

13.5.1 Introduction

slip standands for serial line internet protocol. It provides an IP connection over a standard dial-up phone line. slip is included with many vendor's implementations of communications software. It allows you to run all LAN-based applications just as if you were directly connected to the LAN. This is a very powerful technology which provides capabilities to make your remote communications as seamless as possible. It is gradually being replaced by PPP (Point to Point) Protocol which is known as "Son of Slip." It is much more robust and reliable than slip and is backward compatible. See the Internet or other services for more information.

13.5.2 Installation

There are a variety of configuration issues most related to network configuration. The main issues with a low-speed protocol are timeout and buffer size. Because IP relies on the timeliness of packet delivery, there are issues related to the performance of the dial-up line which directly affect the performance of the network. cslip 2.6 is tuned to perform and build correctly on Sun machines. Two Sun architectures are defined: sunos3 and sunos4. The sun3 architecture, which consists of Motorola 680x0 chips, is supported. The sun4 architecture consists of the sparc risc architecture chips.

Note that you need to establish a slip line on each end of the potential slip connection. Each end can be on a different type of machine; however, you should attempt to use the same network configurations and versions of slip. The exact configuration of cslip 2.6 is described below. This needs to be performed on each end of the slip connection.

You can reduce the buffer size of slip by modifying tcp_sendspace and tcp_recvspace in the file tcp_usrreq.c. You also need to make the retransmission occur less often than the default by changing the following line in the file netinet/tcp_input.c from:

```
RCPT_RANGESET(tp->r_rxtcur,
((tp->t_srtt > 2)+tp->t_rttvar) >> 1,...
```

to

```
RCPT_RANGESET(tp->t_rxtcur,
tp->t_srtt >> 3) + tp->t_rttvar,
```

There are also kernel configuration issues. Copy all files in common/net into /sys/net. Also copy the files in common/net/*.h and sunos4/net/*.h to /usr/include/net.

Add the following lines to /sys/conf.common/files.cmn:

```
net/if_sl.c optional sl INET
net/slcompress.c options sl INET
net/bpf.c optional bpfilter
net/bpf_filter.c optional bpfilter
```

Under SunOS 4.1, you need to add the following lines to the file /sys/sun/str_conf.c:

```
#include "sl.h"
...
#if NSL > 0
extern struct streamtab if_slinfo;
#endif
....
#if NSL > 0
{slip", &if_slinfo },
#endif
```

Once you have modified the above files, you need to build and configure the kernel. This involves different commands on different versions of the operating system you are using. See your operating system documentation for details on recompiling the kernel.

With respect to the network configuration, create a group named slip for all programs to be created. You need to build sliplogin, slstats, slinfo, myetheraddr, and tip with the appropriate makefiles. It is recommended that you use gmake to build the tools and utilities since the makefiles are nested, and gmake does a better job with this kind of configuration. This tool was not built for the RS/6000 since there is a version which comes prebuilt with AIX. It should be noted, however, that the version that comes with AIX is older, and you may want to take a look at building cslip 2.6 for your RS/6000.

Move the following files to the /etc directory:

slip.hosts

slip.login

slip.logout

You may need to modify the slip.hosts file on your local machine. There is an example slip.hosts in the sliplogin directory.

You may also need to uncomment the line:

```
route set $r $1 mtu 552 ...
```

in the slip.login file. Once you have edited this file and you are in the sliplogin directory, type the command:

```
$ make install-conf
```

This will build the proper executables for slip.

Next, cd to the tip directory and type:

```
$ make install-conf
```

This builds the tip files and places several script files in the /etc directory for future executions. You need to add dialstrings to the /etc/remote file. Some examples are documented in the README file; see this for more information.

Create a slip account which will be used to invoke and execute the slip interface. Next you must configure the serial port for both dial-in and dial-out capabilities. You may need to create the device cua0. Some example commands to create the appropriate device files are:

```
$ mv /dev/ttya /dev/ttyd0
$ mknod /dev/cua0 c 12 128
$ chmod 666 /dev/cua0
```

This creates a device file /dev/cua0 which is the common access device. Then you must edit the /etc/ttytab file and create the line definition.

Once you have configured the programs, see Usage section in the documentation for the exact use of the commands involved in the start-up and use of slip on your machine.

13.5.3 Usage

Once slip is configured and started up, there is no usage discussion necessary. slip merely provides an interface to run a LAN protocol such as TCP/IP over a serial line. See the documentation included with slip for any other details.

13.5.4 Conclusion

slip is a very powerful technology which lets you take advantage of a dial-up line to run a full LAN protocol. While it does perform on very slow links, the performance is not really reasonable until you get to speed of 9600 or 19200 baud. Keep this in mind when you consider using and installing slip on your machine.

There are also versions of slip for DOS, Macs, and a variety of other machines. Once you configure slip for a connection, you can run protocols like NFS, X Windows, and TCP over a standard dial-up phone line.

13.6 zmodem

13.6.1 Introduction

zmodem is first and foremost a file transfer protocol which allows file transfer to occur over serial lines (local and dial-up). It superseded xmodem and ymodem and their associated protocols. While xmodem accomplishes relatively simple file transfers and provides some basic integrity checks, zmodem goes beyond this to provide multifile transfer capabilities as well as a higher level of redundancy checking to ensure file integrity. zmodem is the choice of most PC and UNIX people (perhaps the Kermit people would object) for file transfer.

13.6.2 Installation

The zmodem tar file for the current version (2.6) is simple to unwind with the basic tar command. Once you have done this, you need to compile the two executables related to send and receive. There is a simple Makefile which specifies either System V, Xenix, 386 Xenix, or Berkeley 4.x. If you simply type make, you will see what systems are directly supported. For example:

```
$make
Please study the #ifdef's in rbsb.c, rz.c, and sz.c,
then type 'make system' where system is one of:
  sysv SYSTEM 5 Unix
  xenix System 3/5 Xenix
  x386 386 Xenix
  bsd Berkeley 4.x BSD, and Ultrix
```

The implementation of System V seems to be relative to Version 2, which is somewhat old and out of date; however, it may be useful for a system based on a newer version of System V.

As an example, on a Sun, zmodem installed correctly using:

```
$ make bsd
```

Contrary to what you might think, you need also to use bsd for the RS/6000. The sysv flag causes some problems. The other thing to note is that the makefile is very simple and is hard-coded to use cc. gcc seems to work better, so it is necessary to modify the makefile to use gcc instead of cc.

This is all there is to building zmodem. See the Makefile for more information. There is also a way to interactively get code, see the README file for more information.

13.6.3 Usage

There are two basic executables (rz and sz) and four associated symbolic links to those files (rx, rb, sx, and sb). The r executables refer to receiving a file or files, while the s executables refer to sending one or more files. The z refers to the zmodem protocol, the x to the xmodem protocol, and the b to batch sending of files using either xmodem or ymodem.

The basic syntax for the s commands is:

```
sz [-+abdefkLlNnoprqTtuvyY] file ...
sb [-adfkrqtuv] file...
sx [-akrqtuv] file
sz [-orqtv] -c command
sz [-orqtv] -i command
```

where - denotes standard input.

+ appends transmit data to an existing file.

a converts newline characters to CR/LF for UNIX-to-PC file transfer.

b is binary mode.

c command sends command to receiver for remote execution; returns when command execution is complete.

d changes . to / throughout the transmitted filename.

e escapes all control characters.

f sends full pathname.

i command sends command to receiver for execution; returns when command is received.

k sends files using 1K blocks instead of the default, 128-byte blocks.

L N uses ZMODEM packets of N length.

l N pauses for confirmation of data receipt from receiver every N bytes.

n sends file if destination file does not exist; overwrites destination file if source file is newer than the destination file.

N sends file if destination file does not exist; overwrites destination file if source file is newer or longer than the destination file.

o disables 32-bit *cyclical redundancy check* (CRC).

p does not transfer file if destination file already exists.

q is quiet mode.

r resumes interrupted file transfer.

t tim changes timeout to tim tenths of a second.

u unlinks file after transmission.

v is verbose mode.

y overwrites any preexisting file.

Y overwrites any preexisting files and skips any files which do not have the file with the same pathname on the destination system.

file ... is one or more files to transfer.

The basic s zmodem commands work just as the Kermit commands do.

You must first set up one end of a connection as a sender and then move back to the other system and use the receive function.

A simple example uses Procomm to receive a file. First log in to the UNIX machine with Procomm terminal emulation and then type:

```
$ sz *.c
```

Go back to Procomm and tell it to receive a file using the zmodem protocol. This will transfer all files ending with a .c suffix in the current directory back to your PC.

The receiving end of zmodem works much the same way as the sending side. The basic syntax is:

```
rz [-+abepqtuv]
rb [-+abqtuv]
rz [-1abceqtuv] file
[-] [v] rzCOMMAND
```

where - denotes using standard input.
+ appends transmit to an existing file.
a converts newline characters to CR/LF for UNIX-to-PC file transfer.
b is binary mode.
c requests 16-bit CRC.
e escapes all control characters.
p does not transfer file if destination file already exists.
q is quiet mode.
t tim changes timeout to tim tenths of a second.
u unlinks file after transmission.
v is verbose mode.
file is command file to append transferred information to.

The r commands are the receive-style commands which allow you to receive a file or files from sender.

The rz command allows you to take input to the receiver and execute it as a command file. This is typically used for mail and other remote execution process needs.

zmodem supports a concept called AutoDownload, which means that the other end of a connection is automatically started when it receives the appropriate zmodem command. This is the case with a tool like ProComm; it automatically begins a file transfer when the opposite end (typically on a UNIX machine) is invoked with a zmodem command.

There are several strange behaviors of this package with different types of machines, but the one to watch out for with UNIX machines is that zmodem tends to have problems when used in conjunction with cu. Both attempt to take characters from the input stream, and this can cause problems. You should use some other communications mechanism when using zmodem with UNIX.

Much of this syntax was taken directly from the included manual pages. Just look for *.1 in the directory and print or display them for futher information.

13.6.4 Conclusion

zmodem is a fairly sophisticated protocol which allows you to transfer one or more files to a remote machine over a serial line. While zmodem is both a tool and a protocol, it is included in most terminal emulation and file transfer packages for PCs and other types of workstations. This means that you can use this to transfer files to and from your UNIX machine with a variety of different tools at the other end of the link.

Chapter

14

Nonnative Output Formatting and Display Tools

There are many native tools in UNIX which provide basic text formatting and display capabilities. Most of these tools are based on output for a teletype since this is how UNIX began. Because of this, most native UNIX text formatting tools are somewhat primitive by today's standards.

This chapter outlines several tools which provide significantly enhanced function to a UNIX platform and associated text processing. These packages also work on most UNIX and nonUNIX platforms and provide portable input and output files. This becomes very useful when you want to generate documents for more than one computer architecture.

Finally, these tools provide the capability to preview documents both in a standard tty-type environment and in a windowing environment such as X11. This saves time and paper when building drafts of large documents. Keep in mind that there are several standard text processing tools which come with UNIX, and the tools documented in this chapter merely enhance the overall text processing capabilities of most UNIX machines.

14.1 Ghostscript

14.1.1 Introduction

Ghostscript is a language that very closely resembles Postscript. It contains interpreters and drivers for many machines and operating systems such as:

IBM PC and compatibles running DOS with EGA, VGA, or SVGA

Many UNIX systems running X11R3, X11R4, and X11R5

Apple Macintosh

Sun workstations running Sunview

VAX/VMS running X11R3, X11R4, or X11R5

Ghostscript provides for multiprotocol display of Postscriptlike files across heterogeneous platfoms and displays. It provides output drivers for a variety of cards and display devices as well as Postscript-compatible devices such as printers and plotters. You can preview documents with the Ghostscript previewer to make any necessary corrections before printing.

The primary interface to Ghostscript is the Ghostscript interpreter. This allows you to display, print out, or save interpreted Ghostscript files. The Ghostscript interpreter provides several options to control both input interpretation and output. Many Postscript files will work with this interpreter. The advantage of Ghostscript is not only its cost (free) but its multiplatform capability.

Ghostscript was written by GNU but is actually maintained and distributed by Aladdin Enterprises. Aladdin can be reached at:

Aladdin Enterprises
P.O. Box 60264
Palo Alto, CA 94306
(415) 322-0103
...{uunet,decwrl}!aladdin!ghost
ghost@aladdin.com

Aladdin suggests that you subscribe to the Usenet newsgroup gnu.ghostscript.bug. Because of Ghostscript's widespread distribution, Aladdin makes no claims to support the product fully but will respond to e-mail if they have time. Aladdin is looking for help with modifications to Ghostscript. See the README file for more information. Aladdin also sells commercial licenses for Ghostscript and associated products. Call or write them for more information.

See the readme.doc and NEWS files for information on up-to-the-minute fixes and enhancements to the product.

Ghostscript is a GNU product and as such is subject to its GNU General Public license as included both in the product distribution and in App. B of this book.

14.1.2 Installation

The current version of Ghostscript as of this writing is 2.6.1, which is what was used to generate this chapter. Check for the current version using information provided in Chap. 9.

As is standard with most Internet software packages for UNIX platforms, the build procedures for Ghostscript are contained in the makefile. There is a file called make.doc which describes what needs to be changed within the makefile for Ghostscript to build properly. There is also a file called use.doc which describes how to use the Ghostscript interpreter. There are other doc files which describe different aspects of the Ghostscript distribution. They are:

`README`	Description of files in Ghostscript distribution
`drivers.doc`	Description of interface between drivers and Ghostscript
`history.doc`	Description of the history of product releases
`humor.doc`	Humorous comments on Ghostscript
`fonts.doc`	Information about fonts in distribution
`language.doc`	Description of Ghostscript language
`lib.doc`	Information about Ghostscript libraries
`make.doc`	Description of installation and configuration issues
`man.doc`	Manual page for Ghostscript
`psfiles.doc`	Information about .ps files included
`readme.doc`	Information regarding features
`use.doc`	Information about how to use Ghostscript

First make a copy of the compressed tar file in a directory other than the one in which you are building Ghostscript. This will allow you to start over if things look like they are going in the wrong direction.

Once you have gotten the compressed tar file from the Internet, unwind the tar file into the appropriate directory and begin to build the executables. Ghostscript unwinds the files into one directory known as gs261. While this is not a good practice, it does allow for easiest distribution since all files are in one place. You can modify the structure after you build the product. Note that if you are unsure of how to extract, uncompress, and build an appropriate directory structure for Ghostscript, see Secs. 9.8 and 9.10 for more information.

Examining and modifying the makefiles. There are many makefiles in the Ghostscript distribution. A brief listing is shown below. As you can see, there are many makefiles in this distribution. The ones of interest to UNIX users are:

`gc.mak`	Generic makefile used for all platforms
`devs.mak`	Makefile listing all device drivers
`ansihead.mak`	Initial makefile for ANSI C compilation
`cc-head.mak`	Initial makefile for Kernighan & Ritchie C compilation
`devs.mak`	Makefile for device drivers including printers and displays
`gcc-head.mak`	Initial makefile for GNU C compilation
`unix-ansi.mak`	More of the makefile for ANSI C compilation
`unix-cc.mak`	More of the makefile for Kernighan & Ritchie C compilation

`unix-gcc.mak`	More of the makefile for GNU C compilation
`unixhead.mak`	Generic part of makefile for all UNIX C compilations
`unistail.mak`	Generic part of makefile for all UNIX C compilations

The makefiles are structured using variables. This allows you to simply change the variable at the beginning of the makefile; the rest of the makefile can remain unchanged. The areas that may need to be changed are:

Default search paths for fonts and initialization files

Debugging options

Device drivers to be included

Optional features to be included

The defaults for UNIX machines are:

Current directory where product source code exists

No debug code included

Devices are platform specific

Features are platform specific

Each makefile contains an initial comments section followed by a section entitled Options. The Options section is where you may want to make edits. Do not make edits outside the Options sections without understanding exactly what you are doing.

The first step in building Ghostscript is determining which series of makefiles you are going to use. There are three basic sets of makefiles revolving around different C standards and compilers. Kernighan & Ritchie C is the old standard which was the original C syntax. Most C compilers still support this syntax. If you have a compiler which supports only the K & R standard, use the command:

```
$ln -s unix-cc.mak makefile
```

This creates a symbolic link called makefile. The make utility looks for a file makefile by default.

If you are using the GNU C compiler (known as gcc), you should issue the command:

```
$ln -s unix-gcc.mak makefile
```

Finally, if you can, you should use an ANSI standard C compiler. Most compilers including gcc support the ANSI standard. If you are using an ANSI standard compiler but not gcc, issue the command:

```
$ln -s unix-ansi.mak makefile
```

You must also be concerned with the location of the X11 libraries which are linked to create the Ghostscript executable. The default location for the X libraries is /usr/local/include. If this is not the correct location, you must change the XINCLUDE macro on invocation of the make command or modify the proper makefile for your compiler.

There are issues relating to the X server and screen refreshing methods and tiling. This behavior should be okay. If you have problems, consult the make.doc for more information on some possible fixes.

For specific machine notes, consult the make.doc. An example of building Ghostscript 2.6.1 on an RS/6000 running AIX 3.2 is as follows.

```
$ ln -s unix-ansi.mak makefile
$ make XCFLAGS=-D_POSIX_SOURCE -DSYSV\
> XINCLUDE=-I/usr/lpp/X11/include XLIBDIRS
=-L/usr/lpp/X11/lib
```

You may get a link error on the final link. If so, try simply typing make with no options. The link seems to work correctly this way (your guess is as good as mine). Note that this is different from the notes in the build.doc file in that the paths to the include and library files for X11 are different. This is one of the most common mistakes that must be corrected between machines. The X11 files are in different places on different UNIX implementation, and you should use the XINCLUDE and XLIBDIRS macros to set the correct directory. According to the Ghostscript documentation, people often still have trouble on the RS/6000.

You can also use gcc to build Ghostscript with a command like:

```
$ ln -s unix-gcc.mak makefile
$ make CFLAGS= XINCLUDE=-I/usr/lpp/X11/include XLIBDIRS
=- L/usr/lpp/X11/lib \
GENOPT=SVR4
```

This will build Ghostscript with gcc. Note that because of the way linking is done, you should make sure you have used gcc to create X libraries if you are going to use gcc to create Ghostscript. If you have not done this, you should use the vendor compiler as documented in the first example. Note that the linking conventions may be different between the gcc and vendor C compiler, and you may experience problems with symbol resolution. If you do, try the vendor compiler.

Finally, on the Sun, it is necessary to use the unix-cc.mak file and compile with the following command:

```
$ make XINCLUDE=-I/usr/openwin/include XLIBDIRS=- L/usr/openwin/lib \
XLDFLAGS="-Bstatic -lXmu -Bdynamic"
```

If you still have problems with this command, contact Sun and request the following patches for your machine:

Patch id 100512-02

Patch id 100573-03

These patch problems are with the X11 library files. Without these, you may get an error message related to the loader's inability to find _get_wmShellWidgetClass and _get_applicationShellWidgetClass.

These are examples of how to build a software product and the kinds of things you typically run into. Keep in mind that compiler differences and X11 library and include files are often 95 percent of the battle when porting to a platform. Once you get by these problems, you are off and running. There are several machine-specific comments in the gs.1 manual page. Use nroff -man to preview this and ensure that you understand any machine-specific issues before you begin to build Ghostscript.

Once you have compiled Ghostscript, you may want to install it with the command:

```
$ make install
```

This will place the appropriate executables in /usr/local/bin. Then as long as /usr/local/bin is in PATH, you will have transparent access to it. This is also relevant if you are using Ghostview. Ghostview requires access to Ghostscript, and it, therefore, makes it much easier to use Ghostview with Ghostscript installed in a well-known, common directory.

14.1.3 Usage

To invoke the Ghostscript interpreter, type the command:

```
$ gs [filename...]
```

Other options available are listed below. The interpreter looks for the existence of several initialization files such as:

`gs_*.ps`	Initialization files which configure initial screens for Ghostscript including gs_init.ps, gs_fonts.ps, gs_statd.ps, etc.
`Fontmap`	Contains fontsmaps for all fonts used by Ghostscript

Once the interpreter has processed the files on the input command, it waits for input from standard input, which is the keyboard. The interpreter will interactively interpret the commands you type in. To quit the interpreter, type exit.

As is the standard for most UNIX applications, to get help, invoke the interpreter with a -h or -?. For example:

```
$ gs -h
$ gs -?
```

When you invoke Ghostscript, it opens a window on your display by default using the X11 protocol. Of course, you must be running an X11 windows-compliant window manager and GUI. This means that you can distribute the display of the Ghostscript files across the network to any machine that supports the X11 protocol. In addition to the display window, the original invoking window becomes the Ghostscript control window. You are asked to press a return to continue. If you press the return, the display window is cleared, and you are placed at the Ghostscript (GS>) prompt. From this prompt, you can enter interactive commands conformant with the Ghostscript language for immediate interpretation on the display device. For example, type:

```
$ gs tiger.ps
```

You will get another window open on your screen and a color picture of a tiger's head (see Fig. 14.1). Once the picture is drawn, Ghostscript pauses and waits for you to do something. Typing a return will clear the display window and place you at the interactive prompt. For more information on some of the commands you can type, see the section on the Ghostscript language below.

You input the filename, and Ghostscript searches the current directory, then any specified by the -I switch, any specified by the GS_LIB environmental variable, and finally, directories specified by the GS_LIB_DEFAULT macro in the Ghostscript makefile.

There are several parameters which can be set in your Xdefaults file. They are:

`borderWidth`	Border width in pixels (default 1)
`borderColor`	Border color (default black)
`geometry`	Window size and placement (format WxH+X+Y where W is width in pixels, H is height in pixels, X is numbers of pixels from left hand side of screen, and Y is number of pixels from top of screen)
`xResolution`	Number of x pixels per inch
`yResolution`	Number of y pixels per inch

You can place these in your .Xdefaults file in the format:

```
Ghostscript*geometry: 1280x1024+0+0
```

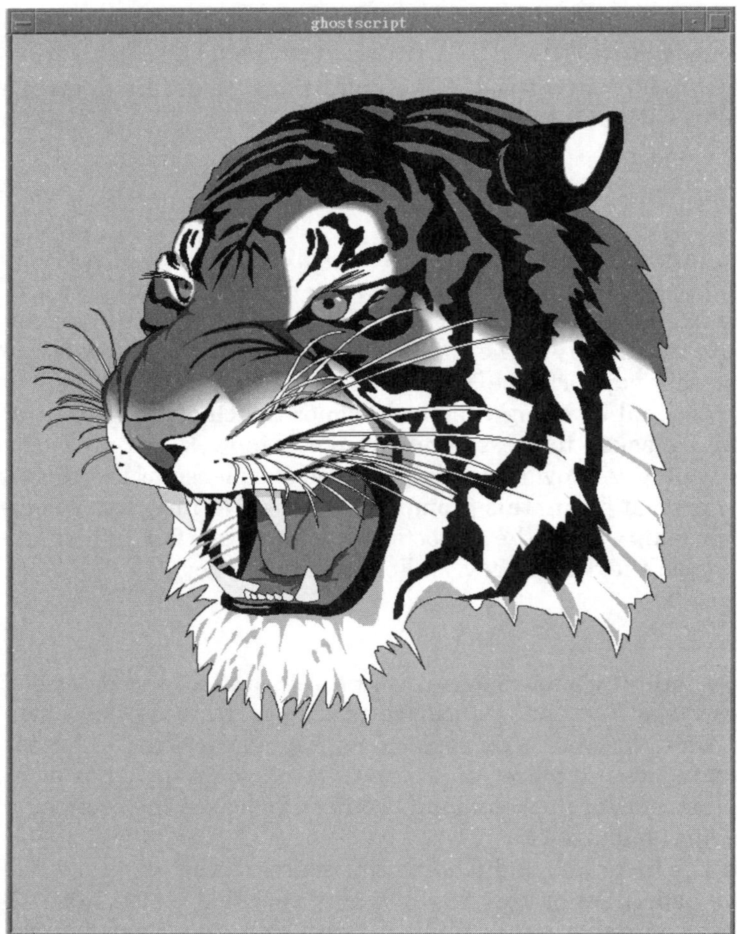

Figure 14.1 The Ghostscript display.

This will make the display window cover your entire display if you have a screen capable of displaying 1280 × 1024 resolution. It probably makes sense to use something a little bit smaller, but feel free to experiment. Note also that it is not necessary to use the xrdb command, which makes these characteristics available to all users of the X server, to load these characteristics into the X server as documented. This may or may not be what you want to do.

There are several other switches available to Ghostscript; however, the only one that is useful to the general user is:

```
-dNOPAUSE
```

which disables the prompt and pause at the end of each page. This allows other applications to use Ghostscript to drive their output and means that you no longer have to press return to clear the display window and end the display of a page. See the use.doc for more information.

Devices. You can choose multiple devices for output from the Ghostscript interpreter. The default for the UNIX environment is the X11 display. There is a switch on the command line which allows you to select the output device on invocation of Ghostscript:

```
-sDEVICE=devicename
```

where devicename is

sonyfb (monochrome Sony display)

sunview (Sunview window system)

X11 (X11R3 or greater)

any of a variety of printers (see the devs.mak for more information)

a variety of graphical ouput formats such as GIF, PCX, and bitmap formats

The other alternative is to set the environmental variable GS_DEVICE to the device you would like to use. Ghostscript will look for this variable on invocation and use this as the default output device. As a result of the build, device files are built with an extension of .dev. If you examine all *.dev files in your Ghostscript directory, you will see which devices are supported on your system. This is determined in part by which makefile you choose for your make procedure. Look for the existence of the *.dev files in your Ghostscript directory. To see what devices names are available for your configuration type:

```
GS> devicenames ==
```

Additional drivers can be inserted and built for specific devices you own.

Manual pages. There are two manual pages distributed with the product: man.doc and man1.doc. The man.doc file contains a very basic man page which can be used to describe syntax, etc. The man1.doc file is a much more complete man page and should be used for the manual page for users of the system. The man page is in nroff an macro format. This means that to view the man page, you should use the command:

```
$ nroff -man man1.doc | more
```

Note that the nroff command interprets the man1.doc file and uses the an macros for assistance. The pipe to more lets you see it exactly as it would appear through the man system. If you have questions concerning the structure of the man system or how best to use the man pages from Internet software, see Chap. 9.

A brief discussion of the Ghostscript language. Ghostscript supports Postscript Level 1 and many of the Display Postscript extensions. It also supports many of the Level 2 operators. It is an interpreter for a language specification that is described in the *Postscript Language Reference* manual (Addison-Wesley, 1985).

Some of the very basic commands, such as the following, allow for file manipulation:

`GS> (filename) run`	Where filename is a Postscript file
`GS> devicenames ==`	Reports what devices are supported
`GS> (devicename) selectdevice`	Where devicename is from list above

The Postscript language itself is a very sophisticated language which contains commands to perform almost any task you could expect from a graphics language. See the standard Postscript documentation above for more information about commands available at the GS> prompt. Also see language.doc for more information.

14.1.4 Conclusion

The Ghostscript interpreter is a very powerful graphics display and interpretation tool that runs on many platforms and is available free of charge from a variety of sources. Full Postscript support and interpretive capabilities make Ghostscript a very powerful tool for viewing documents and graphics before committing them to paper.

14.2 Ghostview

14.2.1 Introduction

Ghostview is a full-function user-interface for Ghostscript. While Ghostscript provides the ability to preview Postscript files by interpreting the Postscript input files, Ghostview provides an interactive interface which allows you to manipulate the Ghostscript and provides a much more interactive and user-friendly interface. In summary, Ghostview creates and manages the X11 interface for Ghostscript.

Ghostview is a GNU product and as such is subject to its GNU General Public license as included both in the product distribution and in App. B of this book.

14.2.2 Installation

There is an Imakefile distributed with Ghostview that you can use to generate the appropriate makefile for your particular platform. See Sec. 11.4 for more details on imake. You may have to modify the IRULESSRC macro in the Imakefile or the makefile if you use imake. This will point imake to the proper template directories.

If you don't have imake installed, you can edit the makefile manually. The areas you may have to modify are primarily the directories which point to the X11 subdirectories. For example, on an RS/6000, you want to define:

```
LIBSRC=/usr/lpp/X11/lib
LIBDIR=/usr/lpp/X11/lib
```

On a Sun platform, you may want to use something like:

```
LIBSRC=/usr/openwin/lib
LIBDIR=/usr/openwin/lib
```

if the xmkmf command does not create the correct makefile. You can use the xmkmf for the Sun, but this doesn't typically ship with xmkmf built on an RS/6000. Because of this, you must manually modify the makefile which comes with Ghostview for the RS/6000. Simply find the DEFINES definition and add:

```
DEFINES = -DSYSV ...
```

This ensures that the system is built as a System V system. If you don't, you may have trouble finding the vfork procedure since it doesn't exist on the RS/6000.

As with many of the delivered makefiles, the defaults are structured according to the standard SVR4 X11 structure, which is /usr/X11/lib, and, in actuality, exists on very few machines. Keep this in mind when you examine the makefile.

Once you have modified the makefile as necessary, issue the command:

```
$ make
```

This will build the software system. If you have errors, examine them and make the appropriate modifications to the makefile and reissue the make command.

14.2.3 Usage

Ghostview provides much the same usage interface as Ghostscript. The basic syntax is:

```
ghostview [--[no]install] [-[no]private] [-[no]center] [-[no]title]
  [-[no]date]
[-[no]locator] [-resolution dpi] [-dpi dpi] [-xdpi dpi] [-ydpi dpi]
[-[no]quiet] [-preload file] [-magstep n] [-portrait] [-landscape]
  [-upsidedown] [-seascape]
[-letter] [-tabloid] [-ledger] [-legal] [-statement] [-executive]
  [-a3] [-a4] [-a5] [-b4]
[-b5] [-folio] [-quarto] [-10x14] [-force] [-forceorientation]
  [-forcemedia] [-[no]swap]
[-[no]openwindows] [-[no]ncdwm] [-page label] [file]
```

where -install installs the standard color map.
-private installs the nonstandard color map.
-center centers the page in the viewport (default).
-title displays the %%title comment (default).
-date displays the %%data comment (default).
-locator displays locator (default).
-resolution dpi sets display resolution at dpi dots per inch.
-dpi dpi is the same as -resolution.
-xdpi dpi, -ydpi dpi sets x and y resolution at dpi dots per inch.
-quiet doesn't produce informational messages (default).
-preload file preloads file which may include fonts, etc.
-magstep n defines document magnification. The formula used to display the document on the screen is (1.2*magstep), and values range from -5 to 5.
-portrait displays in portrait mode.
-landscape displays in landscape mode.
-upsidedown displays upside down.
-seascape displays in seascape mode (this is counterclockwise 90° rotation).
-letter displays page in 8.5 × 11 in.
-tabloid displays page in 11 × 17 in.
-ledger displays page in 17 × 11 in.
-legal displays page in 8.5 × 14 in.
-statement displays page in 5.5 × 8.5 in.
-executive displays page in 7.5 × 10 in.
-a3, -a4, -a5 displays page in 842 × 1190, 595 × 842, and 420 × 595 postscript points, respectively.
-b4, -b5 display page in 729 × 1032 and 516 × 729 Postscripts points, respectively.
-folio displays page in 8.5 × 13 in.
-quarto displays page in 610 × 780 Postscript points.
-10x14 displays page in 10 × 14 in.

-force tells ghostview that orientation or media is being forced and may not be the default.
-forceorientation tells ghostview that orientation is being forced.
-forcemedia tells ghostview that media is being forced.
-swap swaps the meaning of landscape and seascape and uses the %%Orientation comment in the input source file.
-noopenwindows turns off bitmap usage.
-noncdwm ignores bug in window resizing when running the ncdwm.
-page label gives the displayed page a label.
file is input file to be processed.

Most of the options discussed above are the defaults. Note that most options contain opposites which can be enabled by either including or excluding the no prefix to the option. Most of the options above will never be used, but they will be useful if you want to change the default behavior of your Ghostview environment or X11 environment.

Ghostview fully supports the Adobe document structuring conventions which control things like page size and orientation. The basic window is shown in Fig. 14.2. There are five buttons in the window: File, Page, Magstep, Orientation, and Media. Each is a pulldown button which provide specific function related to a major operational area of Ghostview. The File button provides all file level interaction with Ghostview. The Page button gives you the ability to move around within the pages of a Postscript document. Magstep allows you to magnify the document to allow for easier viewing or high resolution of the document. The Orientation button allows you to change the display of the document from landscape to portrait, to flip the document, and to have other orientations of the page. Finally, the Media button provides a list of possible mediums for display including Letter, Tabloid, Ledger, and Legal. There are also keystrokes called Keyboard accelerators which provide faster access to commands than the mouse. Once you have used Ghostview a few times, you will want to use these to speed your interaction with the product. See the ghostview.ps file for more information on these options and their explicit meaning and operations. There is a section on frequently asked questions in the README file. See this if you experience any problems or have questions about a certain behavior.

Because Ghostview is an interactive interface to Ghostscript, there are several ways you can control the integration of the two tools. By setting the environmental variable GHOSTVIEW to the X11 window id of the window you want Ghostscript to use, you cause Ghostscript to draw on an existing window instead of creating its own separate window. This is useful when you want to concentrate all graphics in one

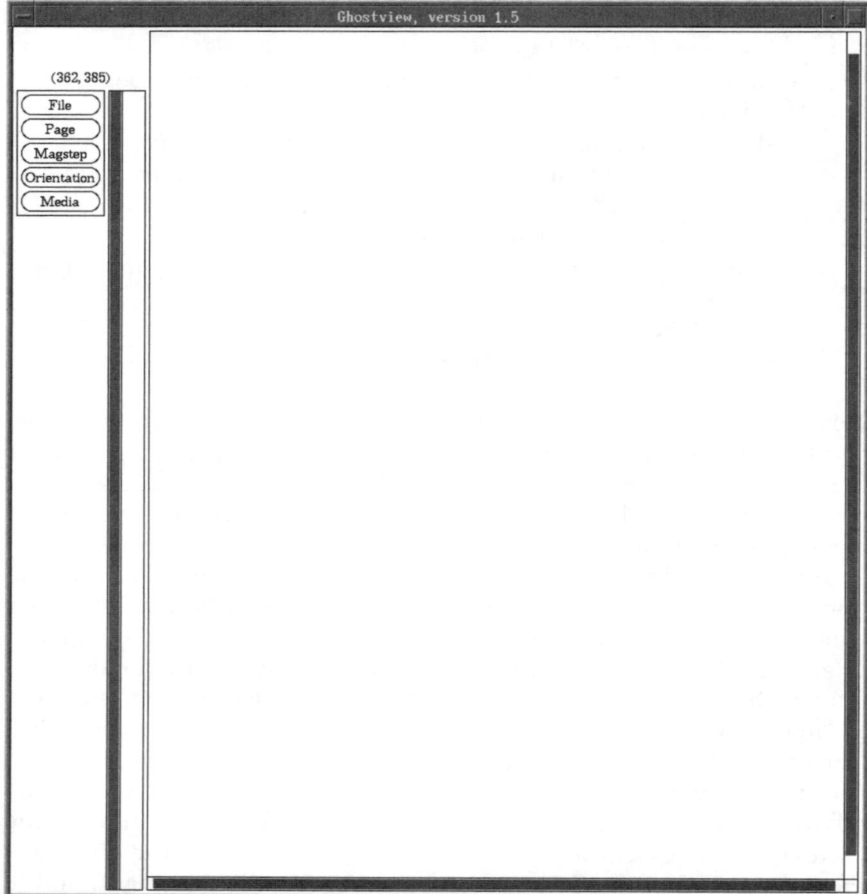

Figure 14.2 The Ghostview window.

window and use the attributes such as size and orientation of the current window to display the graphic you are looking at.

Ghostview invokes Ghostscript as part of its initialization process. It is therefore necessary to have the Ghostscript directories in your path and have them installed and available for use. If you have trouble with Ghostview invocation, you may want to ensure that Ghostscript is installed and functioning properly.

14.2.4 Conclusion

Ghostview is a very user-friendly interface to Ghostscript. While Ghostscript has a variety of cryptic commands with which you display and manipulate commands, Ghostview provides a single command interface which displays documents using the capabilities of Ghostscript. Based on experience, Ghostview is the primary interface you will want to use for displaying and manipulating information on your display.

14.3 groff

14.3.1 Introduction

groff is the GNU equivalent of troff and nroff. It provides support for much of the command set contained in the nroff and troff languages as well as all devices supported by these tools. groff also provides support for additional devices including X11 previewers and Postscript output devices. And it also provides portability across multiple platforms including many varieties of UNIX as well as VMS and other operating systems.

This implementation of groff also contains GNU versions of troff, pic, eqen, tbl, refer, and a variety of macros including an and mm. See the README file for more details on the groff distribution itself.

14.3.2 Usage

The basic syntax of the groff command is:

```
groff [-tpeszaivhblCENRVXZ] [-wname] [-Wname] [-mname] [-Fdir]
  [-Tdev]
[-ffam] [-Mdir] [-dcs] [-rcs] [nnum] [-olist] [-Parg] [file...]
```

where -t preprocesses with gtbl.
-p preprocesses with gpic.
-e preprocesses with geqn.
-s preprocesses with gsoelim.
-z supresses output from groff.
-a—see gtroff.
-i—see gtroff.
-v displays version number.
-h displays help.
-b—see gtroff.
-l sends output to the printer.
-C—see gtroff.
-E—see gtroff.
-N doesn't allow newline with eqn commands.
-R preprocesses with grefer.
-V prints pipeline on standard output.
-X previews with gxditview.
-Z doesn't postprocess output.
-wname, -Wname, -mname, -Fdir—see gtroff.
-Tdev processes output for device dev.

-ffam, -Mdir, -dcs, -rcn, -nnum, -olist—see gtroff.
-Parg passes arg to the postprocessor.
file ... is file or files to process.

Many of the options for groff are the same as those for nroff and troff. Available devices consist of Postscript devices, dvi format for TeX processors, X75 for 75 dpi X11 previewer, and X100 for X100 dpi X11 previewer. To get more information on all available devices, see the directories named devname, where name is the name of the device class

The commands are the same as those used by nroff and troff; for examples see Secs. 7.1 and 7.2.

groff also contains an nroff implementation. The basic syntax is:

```
gnroff [-hi] [-mname] [--nnum] [-olist] [-rcn] [-Tname] [file...]
```

where -h displays help; all the other options are describe in the gtroff doc section below.

gtroff is the fundamental package contained and used by most other tools in the groff distribution. The basic syntax of gtroff is:

```
gtroff [-abivzCER] [-wname] [-Wname] [-dcs] [-ffam] [-mname] [-nnum]
   [-olist]
[-rcn] [-Tname] [-Fdir] [-Mdir] [file...]
```

where -a generates ASCII output.
-b displays a trace with each error message.
-i reads standard input after all input files are processed.
-v displays version.
-z supresses formatted output.
-C enables troff compatibility mode.
-E suppresses error messages.
-R doesn't load troffrc.
-wname enables warning name.
-Wname disables warning name.
-dcs defines c as a string s.
-ffam uses fam as the default font family.
-mname reads in the file tmac.name.
-nnum is the number of the first page num.
-olist outputs comma-separated pages in list.
-rcn sets number register c to n.
-Tname outputs device format.
-Fdir searches dir for directories containing devname, where name is the device name.
-Mdir searches dir for macro files.
file... is one or more files to process.

gtroff works very similarly to troff, with support for more and newer devices such as X11 previewers and high-resolution Postscript printers.

gtroff does have some features in addition to those in troff. Support for fractional point sizes, numeric expressions including boolean logic operators such as < and >, and new escape sequences such as \A‘anything‘, which becomes 0 or 1 depending on the properness of the value of anything. There are other escape sequences which support new gtroff funtionality. gtroff also supports a variety of different commands which manipulate fonts and number registers, provide conditional expressions, and do many other things. See the file troff/troff.man for more details. Remember, to view this file before you have built gtroff, use a command like:

```
$ nroff -man troff/troff.man | more
```

This will display the output just as the man command would.

Another powerful command included in the groff distribution is the grog command. The basic syntax is:

```
grog [-options] [file ...]
```

where -options are gtroff options which will be inserted to the results of the grog command.
file ... is one or more files to process.

The grog commands stand for groff guess. If you run this command on a groff input file, grog will guess which macros need to be used to print the file or files and will insert them into the groff command option automatically. This is very useful when you are not sure what macros are used in a file and simply want grog to tell you and to execute the appropriate command.

There are also subdirectories which contain commands such as refer, which builds a bibliography for groff; eqn, which builds equations; tbl, which builds tables; grotty, which generates standard tty output; and grops, which generates Postscript output. The best way to see what commands are available is to examine the subdirectory structure within the groff directory with a command like:

```
$ ls -l | grep ^d | more
```

This will display and page a listing of the directories within the current working directory.

The other useful way to see the commands in the current groff distribution is to use a command like:

```
$ find . -name "*.man" -print
```

This will generate a listing of all man pages in the current directory structure.

There are a variety of macros and environmental variables which determine the execution characteristics of groff. By settings variables such as GROFF_TMAC_PATH, GROFF_PATH_DIR, and FONTDIR, you can change the way gtroff works. See the associated man pages for each tool to understand which environmental variables you can change to change gtroff output and behavior.

14.3.3 Installation

The first requirement for the installation of groff is a C++ compiler. This will probably mean the g++ compiler, which is documented in Sec. 11.6. Besides g++, you will need the libg++ libraries to provide all class header information so that the compilations and links will proceed normally. See Sec. 11.6 for more details on installing the g++ compiler if you need help.

Once you have installed the C++ files and compiler, you can run the standard configure install, which will build the appropriate makefiles, which can then be executed. The basic format is:

```
$ ./configure
$ make clean
$ make prefix=/usr/local/groff all
```

If you have problems with the make, examine the beginnings of the makefile for the macro definitions, which may be incorrect. There are a variety of makefiles spread throughout various subdirectories. You may want to investigate gmake as an alternative to make to support the VPATH variable and various path distributions. The configure will attempt to see that you have the correct files and headers for your C++ compiler before creating the makefile. If you have trouble with the configure, make sure you have installed and made available all compiler and header/include files for g++ (gcc) before invoking configure.

There is a simple command to test the build of groff:

```
$ test-groff -man -Tascii groff/groff.n | more
```

It should display reasonable-looking output on the display. If it doesn't, something hasn't built correctly. See the makefiles for more details. If you have other problems, see the file named PROBLEMS for potential known problems and solutions.

Be sure to set all appropriate environmental variables such as

FONTDIR when you build the product. See the INSTALL and PROBLEMS files for more details if you have problems. Once the product is built, you shouldn't have any trouble; however, if you do, it is probably a misdefined environmental variable.

Remember also that there are makefiles in each subdirectory which describe the dependencies for that particular tool.

Finally, there is a tool included called gxditview. This is an X11 previewer based on xditview. To build this product, you must cd to the xditview subdirectory and issue the make command. There is an INSTALL file which describes this process in more detail in the xditview subdirectory. As with most X11-related tools, there is an associated Imakefile which may need to be tweeked and remade with the xmkmf command. Once you have done this, rebuild the product with the make command. This will generate the appropriate gxditview executable. If you continue to have problems, check the FONTDIR, XINITDIR, and XDMDIR macro definitions to ensure that these point to the correct directories. Often these files do not exist in the standard /usr/.../X11 directory. This is key to generating a correct build and is classic gotcha when building X11-related tools.

14.3.4 Conclusion

groff is a very powerful environment which consists of both nroff and troff functionality as well as the associated tools eqn, restor, tbl, and others. See the files in doc and man for more details on these commands. groff also comes with a groff X11 previewer called gxditview, which can be built separately to provide bitmapped graphical capabilities.

groff is clearly one of the most powerful environments available on the Internet and should be investigated if you are doing any work with text processing and output formatting.

14.4 pbmplus

14.4.1 Introduction

plmplus is a tool kit which consists of a variety of filters and conversion programs to take one file format and generate another. It also has some tools to manipulate various portable file formats. The distribution is broken down into functional units consisting of:

1. PBM—bitmap manipulation
2. PPM—full color image manipulation
3. PNM—content-independent manipulations

All units are backward compatible, which means that PNM supports both PPM and PBM, and PPM supports PBM. Which units you install is determined when you install the product. See Sec. 14.5.3 for more details.

pbmplus is a free product and as such is subject to its own copyright and license as included both in the product distribution and in App. B of this book.

14.4.2 Usage

The basic usage of the pbmplus package is driven by individual commands contained within the package. The basic mode of operation for pbmplus is to take a given input format and generate a standardized generic output format. From this format, you can generate any other given format with a different tool. pbmplus has four generic (or intermediate) formats:

1. pbm (bitmap)
2. pgm (grayscale)
3. ppm (pixmap)
4. pnm (any format map)

where the bitmap format represents a pixel with a bit, grayscale has additional information to preserve shading, and pixmap preserves color information about each pixel. The pnm format supports all three previous formats as well as a variety of others. Each of these generic formats has a set of associated tools which manipulate these formats and generate the desired output format.

There are manual pages for each of the commands which convert from one format to another. All man pages end with a .1 and exist in the pnm, pbm, pgm, and ppm subdirectories. Because of the large number of man pages and the small number of options to these commands, they are not documented here. The basic format of all commands is:

```
$ command file
```

where command is the conversion or filter program and file is the file to be converted.

There are really two basic kinds of utilities included in pbmplus. The first contains conversion and filter programs which take one kind of information and convert it to another. The second kind of utility program manipulates pnm format files. These are typically used once you have converted a file into pnm format to do things like crop the picture size, enhance a bitmap, and rotate and scale a bitmap. Keep in mind that these operate on the pnm format files which have already been converted to pnm format. Both types of utilities are described in separate tables below.

The following table outlines the conversion and filter commands and their basic functionality.

Format	To	From
Abekas YUV bytes	tuvtoppm	ppmtoyuv
Andrew Toolkit raster object	atktopbm	pbmtoatk
ASCII files		pbmtoascii
Atari degas .pi1	pi1toppm	ppmtopi1
Atari degas .pi3	pi3topbm	pbmtopi3
Atari compressed spectrum file	spctoppm	
Atari uncompress spectrum file	sputoppm	
Bennet Yee face file	ybmtopbm	pbmtoybm
Bitgraph graphics		pbmtobg
CMU window mgr bitmap	cmuwmtopbm	pbmtocmuwm
DEC sixel		ppmtosixel
Doodle brush	brushtopbm	
Epson printer		pbmtoepson
FITS	fitstopgm	pgmtofits
GEM .img file	gemtopbm	pbmtogem
GIF	giftoppm	ppmtogif
Gemini 10X printer graphics		pbmto10x
Gould scanner file	gouldtoppm	
GraphOn compressed graphics		pbmtogo
Group 3 fax	g3topbm	pbmtog3
HIPS	hipstopgm	
HP Laserjet		pbmtolj
HP Paintjet	pjtoppm	ppmtopj
IFF ILBM	ilbmtoppm	ppmtoilbm
Img-whatnot	imgtoppm	
Lisp Machine bitmap	lispmtopgm	pgmtolispm
MGR bitmap	mgrtopbm	pbmtomgr
MacPaint	macptopbm	pbmtomacp
PICT	picttoppm	ppmtopict
Motif UIL icon file		ppmtouil
MTV or PRT ray tracer output	mtvtoppm	
NCSA ICR format		ppmtoicr
PCX	pcxtoppm	ppmtopcx
Portable bitmap		pgmtopbm

Format	To	From
Portable graymap		ppmtopgm
Postscript image data	psidtopgm	
Postscript data		pnmtops
Printronix printer graphics		pbmtoptx
QRT ray tracer output	qrttoppm	
Raw RGB	rawtoppm	
Raw grayscale	rawtopgm	
Sun icon	icontopbm	pbmtoicon
Sun rasterfile	rasttopnm	pnmtorast
Text	pbmtext	
Three portable graymaps	rbg3toppm	ppmtorgb3
TIFF	tifftopnm	pnmtotiff
TrueVision targa file	tgatoppm	ppmtotga
UNIX plot file		pbmtoplot
Unknown		anytopnm
Usenix FaceSaver	fstopgm	pgmtofs
X10 bitmap	xbmtopbm	pbmtox10bm
X11 window dump	xwdtopnm	
X11 puzzle file		ppmtopuzz
X11 bitmap	xbmtopbm	pbmtoxbm
X11 pixmap	xpmtoppm	ppmtoxpm
X11 window dump	xwdtopnm	pnmtoxwd
Xim file	ximtoppm	
Zinc bitmap		pbmtozinc

There are also utilities included with the pbmplus release which operate on these generic bitmap-type files. With these utilities you can enhance, resize, reshape, and reformat the generic bitmap files. It should be noted that many of the techniques used in these utilities are taken from books entitled *Beyond Photography,* written by Holzmann, and *Digital Image Processing,* written by Gonzalez and Wintz. See the individual man pages for more information on the algorithm and its origin.

Utility	Function
pbmlife	Applies Conway's Rules of Life to portable bitmap
pbmmake	Creates a blank bitmap
pbmmask	Creates a mask bitmap
pbmreduce	Reduces portable bitmap n times
pbmupc	Creates a universal product code bitmap
pgmbentley	Utilizes the Bentley effect to smear the bitmap
pgmedge	Edge detects the graymap

Utility	Function
pgmenhance	Edge enhances a portable graymap
pgmhist	Creates a histogram of the graymap
pgmnorm	Normalizes the contrast of the graymap
pgmoil	Creates an oil painting (smearing technique)
pgmramp	Creates a grayscale ramp (useful with other bitmaps)
pnmarith	Performs arithmetic on two anymaps
pnmcat	Concatenates anymaps
pnmconvol	Generates $M \times N$ convolution on anymaps
pnmcrop	Crops an anymap
pnmcut	Cuts a rectangle out of an anymap
pnmdepth	Changes pixel depth on an anymap
pnmenlarge	Enlarges an anymap
pnmfile	Describes an anymap
pnmflip	Flips an anymap in any direction
pnmgamma	Performs gamma correction on an anymap
pnmindex	Builds an index of several anymaps
pnminvert	Inverts an anymap
pnmmargin	Adds a border to an anymap
pnmnoraw	Converts anymap to plain format
pnmpaste	Pastes a rectangle into an anymap
pnmrotate	Rotates an anymap by a given angle
pnmscale	Scales an anymap
pnmshear	Shears an anymap by a given angle
pnmsmooth	Smooths out an anymap
pnmtile	Duplicates an anymap in a specified size
ppmdither	Dithers a color image
ppmhist	Builds a histogram of a pixmap
ppmmake	Creates a pixmap of a specified size and color
ppmpat	Creates a "pretty" pixmap
ppmquant	Quantizes colors down to some chosen number
ppmquantall	Operates on multiple files so they can share a colormap
ppmrelief	Runs a Laplacian relief filter on a pixmap
sxpm	Shows and/or converts XPM2 files to XMP3 files

Assume you have a G3 fax file named kevin.g3 and you want to create a Postscript file of it. You would issue the commands:

```
$ tifftopnm kevin.g3 > kevin.pnm
$ pnmtops kevin.pnm > kevin.ps
```

Note that most, if not all, of the commands generate their output to standard output. You can redirect standard output as you normally would to create the new file.

The utility programs are typically more complex in their syntax and require a brief glance at the man page associated with the command. For example, to use the pnmenlarge command, you might use something like:

```
$ pnmenlarge 2 kevin.pnm > newkevin.pnm
```

This effectively doubles the size of the kevin.pnm bitmap file. You can then create your Postscript file as before with the command:

```
$ pnmtops newkevin.pnm > kevin.ps
```

This generates the Postscript with an image twice as large.

Other utility commands use different syntax. See the man pages for more information. As mentioned in the earlier sections, you can view a man page with the command:

```
$ nroff -man pnmtops.1 | more
```

This is exactly what the man command does, so have at it.

As you can see from the size of the tables above, there are many commands from which to choose and, therefore, many file formats are supported.

14.4.3 Installation

The installation of pbmplus consists of a variety of makefiles, each existing in a directory that contains source files. The main directories are pbm, pgm, ppm, and pnm. These contain all utilities and filters related to the corresponding type of input file format.

Within each makefile, there is a section marked CONFIGURE. These are the sections you must modify to ensure that the build proceeds correctly. For example, ld and cc command options are described, each in its own CONFIGURE section. You can also define which directories will contain the output files and which tools (such as gcc) will be used to configure and build the pbmplus system.

The first step in building pbmplus is building the included tiff libraries. Use the following commands to build libtiff:

```
$ cd libtiff
$ make clean
$ make
```

They will create all necessary files in the libtiff directory. Note that several makefiles for different platforms are included in this directory. Choose the one that is right for your platform. Note that your compiler may or may not support newer C functions such as prototypes, and you may have to change variables such as -DPROTOTYPE=1 to -DPROTOTYPE=0 to disable prototyping capabilities. The other macros you may be interested in are USE_VARARGS and BSDTYPES. See the associated makefile for the correct definition of these macros for your particular platform.

There are a variety of macros which you can add to the definitions within the makefile. These are documented both in the README file in the libtiff subdirectory and in the makefile in the libtiff subdirectory itself. Note that these affect whether tags for JPEG and other algorithms are compiled into the system. Choose the default as the first step to simplify the build process. There is nothing to stop you from going back later and rebuilding the pbmplus distribution with different build flags.

Once you have built the libtiff subdirectory, you are ready to build the rest of the software in the pbmplus distribution. Modify each relevant CONFIGURE section in the makefile in the main pbmplus directory. Once this is finished, type the command:

```
$ make
```

This will generate the appropriate executable files which match those described in the two tables above. Note that if you are using gmake, you may have to modify each makefile in each of the pxm subdirectories (where x can be b, g, p, or n). See each makefile for more details. It is recommended that you use nonGNU make to build these tools since it introduces less complexity to the situation than gmake in this case.

14.4.4 Conclusion

pbmplus is a very powerful tool kit which provides conversion and utility programs for many of the bitmap file formats available today. If you use the tools in pbmplus, there is virtually no file format that you cannot support in full graphical form. By using the ability to convert from one format to many others, you can suddenly share information from a variety of mediums transparently. This is clearly a very powerful UNIX tool kit.

14.5 gnuplot

14.5.1 Introduction

gnuplot is a command-driven plotting package which contains a variety of functions and commands to generate plots on a large number of devices. You can automatically generate labels, define constants and functions, and manipulate plots from an interactive interface. gnuplot is one of the most powerful plotting packages available for UNIX today.

gnuplot is a GNU product and as such is subject to its GNU General Public license as included both in the product distribution and in App. B of this book. It has a slightly different copyright notice than the usual GNU copyright and therefore is separate in App. B.

14.5.2 Usage

The basic syntax of the gnuplot command is:

```
gnuplot [X11 options] [-mono] [-gray] [-clear] [file ...]
```

where X11 options consist of many of the standard options you would expect to use with an X application such as border size, image size, color maps, and aspect ratios.
-mono uses monochrome rendering.
-gray uses grayscale rendering.
-clear clears the device between plots.
file ... is one or more files to plot.

gnuplot supports two basic types of plotting terminals, X11 and x11, where the X11 device supports a different points plotting style than x11. See the man page on X for more details on standard X11 options. Most of these can be applied to the gnuplot utility.

gnuplot has its own interactive language which is case sensitive and emulates the UNIX command syntax. You can use the \ to move beyond one line and the ; to separate multiple commands on a single line. The basic types of output devices supported by gnuplot are:

AED	AED 512 and AED 767
AIFM	Adobe Illustrator Format
AMIGASCREEN	Amiga custom screen
APOLLO	Apollo Graphics
ATT6300	AT&T 6300 graphics
BITGRAPH	BEN Bitgraph
CGI	SCO CGI
CORONA	Corona Graphics
DXY800A	Roland DXY800A plotter
DUMB	Dumb terminal
DXF	AutoCad dxf file format
EEPIC	EEPIC LaTeX driver
EGALIB	EGA/VGA PC graphics
EMTEX	LETeX with emTeX specials
EPS60	Epson 60dpi printers

EPSONP	Epson LX-800, Star NL-10, NX-1000, etc.
FIG	Fig graphics language
GPR	Apollo graphics
HERCULES	Hercules graphics board
HP2648	HP2648, HP2647
HP26	HP2623A
HP75	HP7580
HPGL	HP7475 and other GL printers
HPLJII	Laserjet II
HPLJII	Laserjet III
IMAGEN	Imagen laser printers
IRIS4D	Iris computer
KERMIT	Kermit Textronix 4010 emulator
LATEX	LaTeX picture environment
LN03P	DEC LN03P printer
NEC	NEC CP6 printer
PBM	PBMPLUS pbm, pgm, ppm, and pnm
POSTSCRIPT	Postscript
PRESCRIBE	Kyocera printer
QMS	QMS/QUIC printer
REGIS	DEC ReGis graphics
SELANAR	Selanar
STARC	Star color printer
SUN	Sun workstation
T410X	Textronix 4106, 4107, 4109, and 420x terminals
TANDY60	Tandy DMP-130 series printers
TEK	Tektronix 4010
UNIXPC	AT&T Unix PC
UNIXPLOT	Unixplot
V384	Vectrix 384 color printers
VTTEK	VT-like Tektronix 4010 emulator
X11	X11R4 window system

If you examine the README file, you will see that there are a variety of commands, probably the most important being the help command. From within gnuplot, you can issue the help command to see a listing of all commands available. Rather than duplicate all the information given in the interactive help section, below is a table of commands and their basic function.

autoscale	Automatically scales axis to incorporate all data.
bugs	Displays a list of current bugs.
cd	Changes the current working directory.
clear	Clears the current screen.
comments	Describes comment support.
environment	Describes a number of environmental variables which can be set.
exit	Leaves gnuplot.
expressions	Describes expression support.
help	Describes this help facility.
line-editing	Describes basic line-editing capabilities.
load	Inputs a file for processing.
pause	Causes a pause of a specified time or until the return is pressed.
plot	Displays the plot.
print	Prints expressions to the screen.
pwd	Prints working directory.
quit	Exits gnuplot.
replot	Redraws the current plot.
save	Saves user-defined functions or variables to a file.
set	Sets a variety of options which are described in this help.
shell	Forks and execs to a shell.
show	Shows the values of set commands.
splot	Plots 3-D information.
startup	Defines the start-up file (.gnuplot).
substitution	You can use command line substitution within gnuplot with ''.
userdefined	You can define your own functions and variables within gnuplot.

See the individual help sections for more information on each command. The basic things you need to understand to use gnuplot effectively are plot and expressions.

Expressions consist of functions which are supported by C, BASIC, Fortran, and other third-generation languages. This means that you can use C- or Fortran- or BASIC-like syntax to define a function to plot on the display or print to a printer. An example of a very simple expression to display to the screen is the command:

```
gnuplot> plot cos(x)
```

Note, however, that if you do this without either setting the TERM environmental variable or using the set term command, you will get an error message. The best way to do this is something like:

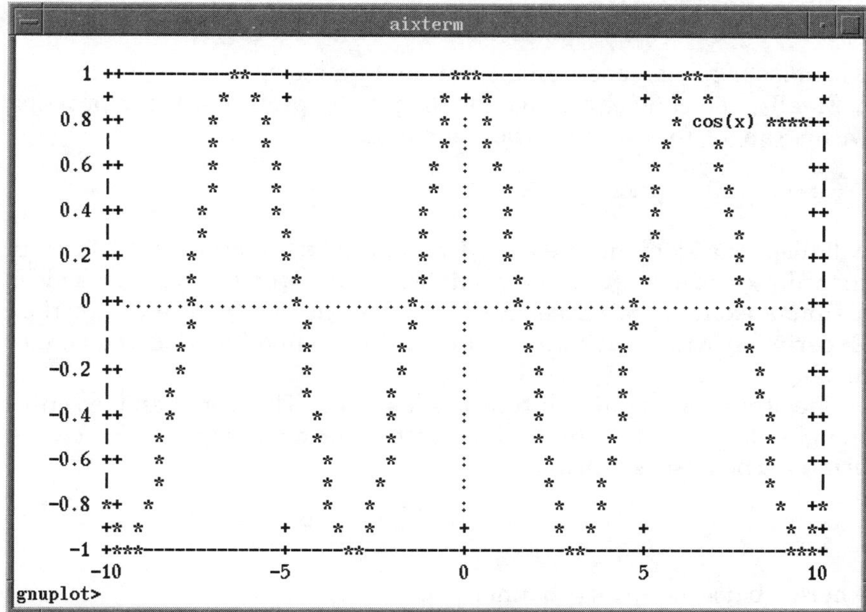

Figure 14.3 gnuplot dumb terminal.

```
gnuplot> set term dumb
gnuplot> plot cos(x)
```

This will display a cosine curve on a dumb device such as a vt100 or other ASCII device. The output will look something like that shown in Fig. 14.3.

If the output device were a Postscript device, you could use:

```
gnuplot> set term postscript
gnuplot> plot cos(x)
```

and you would get Postscript output. To see the current value of term, use the command:

```
gnuplot> show term
terminal type is dumb
```

If you set your term to be X11, you will get a much better looking graph. It may look something like Fig. 14.4.

You can define your own functions (see the plot command for more information) for any function you can dream up. For example, you can graph something like:

```
gnuplot> plot x+5*sin(x)
```

which looks like an ascending sinusoidal function.

Finally, you can set a range for the plot by prefacing the expression with a range. For example, the command:

```
gnuplot> plot [1:5] x+5
```

will display a straight line from 1 to 5 in the x direction and 6 to 10 in the y direction exactly as you would with a piece of graph paper. This is a simple example of range. It can be applied to any type of function. Experiment with your own functions. There is no function you cannot display.

The other command of interest is lasergnu. This command executes the gnuplot command to produce output for an Imagen or Postscript printer. The basic syntax is:

```
lasergnu [-b] [-p] [-P printer] [-f file] [-t title][-help]
plot-command...
```

where -b doesn't print a banner page.
-p generates Postscript output.
-P printer spools output to printer automatically.

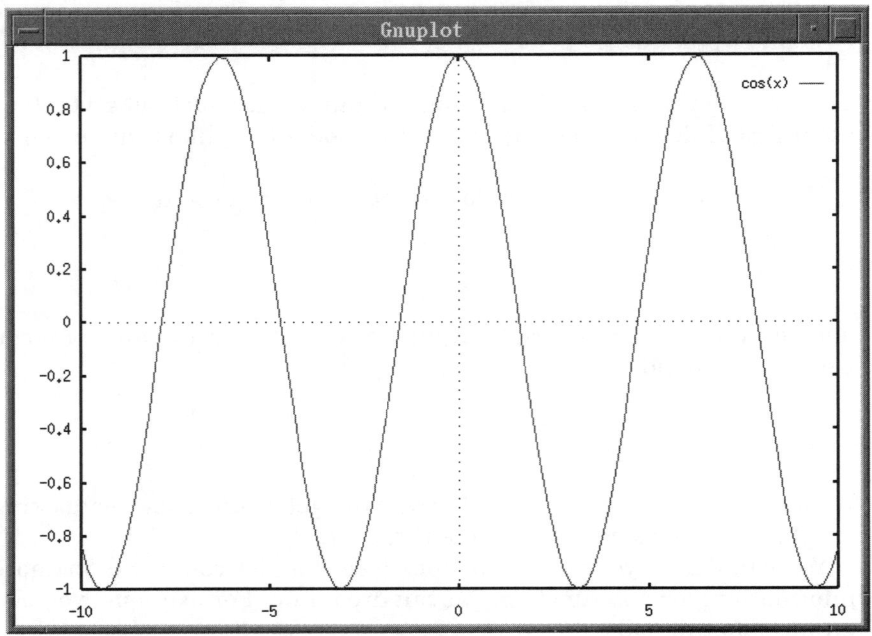

Figure 14.4 gnuplot with X11 window.

-f file takes plot-commands from file as input to lasergnu.
-t title gives the plot a title.
-help display a list of options.
plot-command... is one or more plot commands.

A simple example is:

```
$ lasergnu -p "plot [1:5] x"
```

This will generate Postscript output displaying a straight line from 1 to 5 and will print to the local default printer.

14.5.3 Installation

gnuplot has been tested on many systems, all of which are listed in the file README. See this file for more details on support for a particular platform. There are a variety of definitions you may want to change in the makefile before building gnuplot. The first thing to do is copy the UNIX makefile to the proper default name:

```
$ cp makefile.unx makefile
```

From this you can examine which of the first few sections you may want to change. The only macros you will probably need to change are the destination directories for the binaries, libraries, and man pages. Change definitions such as DEST and MANDEST to determine where you would like to place the binaries and help files. You must also set the TERMFLAGS variable to define which devices you would like gnuplot to support. The basic list of supported devices is listed in the README file.

You can build the appropriate devices for a given machine by simply letting the make choose the defaults for you. The build is fairly straightforward. On a Sun, use the command:

```
$ make sun_x11
```

This will generate the gnuplot executable on a Sun. If you encounter a load error on the build which looks like:

```
ld.so: Undefined symbol: __XtInherit
```

you need to include the -OW_BOTCH macro on the build line to fix this problem.

On the RS/6000 you can type the command:

```
$ make aix32
```

or

```
$ make aix32o
```

The aix32 label will work correctly for a machine running xlc 1.2; the aix32o label will work correctly with a machine running xlc 1.1. You can check which version of xlc you are running with the command:

```
$ lslpp -h > /tmp/lslpp
```

Then edit the file and look for xlc to see which version you are running. See you system manual for more details.

If you are unsure of your machine type, simply type:

```
$ make
```

This will generate a listing of possible machine types and terminals to support. From this list, chose your machine type. A good first attempt is to type a command which builds the ALL target. This will generate the executables with certain macro definitions which gnuplot gives you when it begins the build.

There are several machines which are supported by this distribution of gnuplot. See the makefile for more information.

Note that if you are building the version for X11 support, you may have to modify the X11INCLUDE macros to specify the correct directory for both the include and library files for X11. For example, on an RS/6000 these files exist in the /usr/lpp/X11 directory structure, while on the Sun they exist in /usr/openwin. Keep this in mind if you get "can't find file" error messages. This seems to have been fixed in the newer versions of gnuplot, but keep it in mind if you see the above kind of error.

14.5.4 Conclusion

gnuplot is a very powerful plotting package which provides significant functionality to the UNIX power user. By providing plotting support for many devices, including many newer devices, gnuplot is a very useful tool for data manipulation and display.

14.6 X11R5

There is an X11R5 directory which contains some very brief release notes for X11R5. You may want to look at those to at least learn where to go to get more information on X11R5.

Appendix

How to Get Software from Included CD

Because of a lack of support for Rock Ridge extensions by the AIX CD/ROM device drivers, I was forced to use the standard ISO-9660 format for the CD. This means that all filenames on the CD must be in uppercase and must consist of no more than eight characters plus three following a period (looks like DOS to me). This is extremely limiting in terms of representing UNIX file information; however, due to IBM's lack of extension support, this was necessary to ensure portability across all platforms.

Because of the limitations of the ISO-9660 format, I was forced to change the basic structure of the software on the CD. Therefore, I have provided an installation script which, while very basic, provides you with the basic information necessary to install a software package. Along with the package are some files which provide basic size and installation information as well as any other information you may want concerning the package.

Because of the ISO-9660 compliance, you cannot run the software directly from the CD. You must instead install it on a hard disk and invoke it from there. While most of the software has been precompiled for both RS/6000 AIX 3.2.3 and Sun Solaris 1, it cannot be directly executed from the CD due to the changes that were required to format the CD correctly. This is unfortunate; however, given the nature of the CD structure, necessary.

At the top level of the directory, each product has a directory which reflects its product name. The name used most often directly reflects the name of the product; however, in some cases it has had to be shortened. For example, the Ghostscript product directory is named

GSCRIPT due to ISO-9660 restrictions. At the top directory, there is a file named FILES which contains a listing of products and associated directory names. This will help you pick the product you would like.

The products normally consist of three underlying directories: SUN, RS6000, and GENERIC. The SUN directory contains a compressed tar file with SUN executables. The RS6000 directory contains a tar file with RS/6000 executables. Finally, the GENERIC directory contains the standard distribution of the software package without any modifications or executables. This is the standard release exactly as you would get it from the Internet.

To install any software, you must first mount the CD into a mount point on a local disk. Each operating system syntax is slightly different, so look at the following examples to see how to mount the CD. For the Sun, it is:

```
$ mount -t hsfs -r /dev/sr0 /cdrom
```

For the IBM, it is:

```
$ mount -r -v cdrfs /dev/cd0 /cdrom
```

These examples assume you are using the mount point /cdrom. This can be any directory which is defined.

Once you have mounted the CD on your machine, you can begin to examine and install the software. To install a piece of software, you should first invoke the command:

```
$ cd mount_point
```

where mount_point matches the mount point you specified in the mount command above. Once you have moved to this directory, invoke the installation script with the command:

```
$ ./INSTALL.UDT
```

This will invoke the installation script. This is a very simple script and merely uncompresses and unwinds a tar file in the specified directory. If this script doesn't do what you need, you will have to manipulate the files manually. This should be relatively straightforward.

Each product directory contains a file named SIZE which designates the size of the installed package. INSTALL.UDT reads this and informs you as to the size of the installation, giving you a chance to exit if you don't have sufficient disk space in a filesystem to install the product. You can view this file manually since it is a flat ASCII text file.

I recommend that you install most products in the /usr/local prefix area, since this will create a /usr/local/bin, and place the resulting executables in this area. Then you simply place /usr/local/bin in your PATH and can execute all resulting products. You can use other prefixes, but you must ensure that the resulting bin subdirectories are in your PATH.

An example installation script follows:

```
Welcome to the UNIX Developers Tool Kit Installation Script. This
script performs very basic installation assistance consisting of
basic uncompression and unwinding of associated files on the CD. If
you have any more sophisticated problems than this script will
handle, you must perform them manually.

The author makes no warranty with respect to this installation
script or any on this CD. Good Luck.

Kevin E. Leininger

Note that all information used by this script is CASE SENSITIVE so
be careful and follow the prompts. Most responses should be in
lowercase except for the product names, which are all in uppercase.

Finally, you can abort this installation at any time by pressing
CTRL-C

Enter y to continue: y

Enter the mount point for your CD. This is the fully qualified
directory which contains all product names in uppercase (e.g.,
/cdrom): /usr/local2
Is /usr/local2 correct <y/n>: y

Enter the product name you wish to install. If you are not familiar
with the products on the CD and their associated names, see the
FILES file at the top of this CD (e.g., EMACS, GVIEW): GROFF
Is GROFF correct <y/n>: y

Enter the machine type(SUN, RS6000 or GENERIC): GENERIC
Is GENERIC correct <y/n>: y
Would you like to view the README file for GROFF which runs on the
GENERIC <y/n>: y

This directory contains only a tar file for groff 1.08. To compile
you need a C++ compiler as well as the appropriate libraries to
link. Because of this I didn't generate any binaries. If you are
interested, untar the file and have at it. There is documentation in
the book on how to configure and build groff. Good Luck...

I fully subscribe to the associated GNU General Public License seen
in the COPYING file in this directory and assume no warranty or
responsibility in any way for the software in this distribution. I
also am not responsible for support or maintenance of anything
related to this product or its distribution.

Kevin E. Leininger

Press y to continue <y>: y

The size of the software is 3MB

Ensure you have enough disk space for installation and choose your
installation point wisely. Do you wish to continue <y/n>: y

Now we need an installation directory. Please enter a fully
qualified installation path (e.g.,/usr/local): /tmp
Is /tmp installation directory correct <y/n>: y
Ready to install /usr/local2/GROFF/GENERIC.Z into /tmp
```

```
Is this correct <y/n>: y

Here we go...Please be patient, some of these files are large.
x groff-1.08/include/Makefile.sub, 607 bytes, 2 media blocks.
x groff-1.08/include/assert.h, 1188 bytes, 3 media blocks.
x groff-1.08/include/cmap.h, 1377 bytes, 3 media blocks.
x groff-1.08/include/cset.h, 1769 bytes, 4 media blocks.
x groff-1.08/include/device.h, 833 bytes, 2 media blocks.
x groff-1.08/include/driver.h, 1105 bytes, 3 media blocks.
x groff-1.08/include/errarg.h, 1304 bytes, 3 media blocks.
x groff-1.08/include/error.h, 2070 bytes, 5 media blocks.
x groff-1.08/include/font.h, 3363 bytes, 7 media blocks.
x groff-1.08/include/index.h, 1140 bytes, 3 media blocks.
x groff-1.08/include/lib.h, 2634 bytes, 6 media blocks.
x groff-1.08/include/macropath.h, 837 bytes, 2 media blocks.
x groff-1.08/include/posix.h, 1179 bytes, 3 media blocks.
x groff-1.08/include/printer.h, 1964 bytes, 4 media blocks.
x groff-1.08/include/ptable.h, 5409 bytes, 11 media blocks.
x groff-1.08/include/refid.h, 1298 bytes, 3 media blocks.
x groff-1.08/include/search.h, 2770 bytes, 6 media blocks.
x groff-1.08/include/searchpath.h, 1028 bytes, 3 media blocks.
```

The list of extacted files continues for some time. In the interest of space lets skip to the end:

```
x groff-1.08/acgroff.m4, 9354 bytes, 19 media blocks.
x groff-1.08/bug.PS, 1262 bytes, 3 media blocks.
x groff-1.08/configure, 24510 bytes, 48 media blocks.
x groff-1.08/configure.in, 1063 bytes, 3 media blocks.
x groff-1.08/gendef.sh, 238 bytes, 1 media blocks.
x groff-1.08/mdate.sh, 921 bytes, 2 media blocks.
x groff-1.08/test-groff, 806 bytes, 2 media blocks.

All done with GROFF installation. Would you like to install another
product <y/n>: n
Thanks and have a good time.
```

This is a very simple example of what an installation looks like. After this, you may need to additionally configure a machine for a particular prefix subdirectory or a particular machine.

Because of certain anomalies in older versions of UNIX, you may see all filenames in lowercase. If you do, certain filenames and script responses will have to be different from those shown above. For example, instead of EMACS, you will see emacs, instead of SUN you will see sun, and finally, instead of INSTALL.UDT, you will have to type install.udt to invoke this installation.

If you are unable to access this CD, an alternative medium is available; contact me via e-mail at kevin1@devtech.com.

Good Luck.

Appendix

B

General Licenses

B.1 GNU General Public License

GNU GENERAL PUBLIC LICENSE
Version 2, June 1991

Preamble

The licenses for most software are designed to take away your freedom to share and change it. By contrast, the GNU General Public License is intended to guarantee your freedom to share and change free software—to make sure the software is free for all its users. This General Public License applies to most of the Free Software Foundation's software and to any other program whose authors commit to using it. (Some other Free Software Foundation software is covered by the GNU Library General Public License instead.) You can apply it to your programs, too.

When we speak of free software, we are referring to freedom, not price. Our General Public Licenses are designed to make sure that you have the freedom to distribute copies of free software (and charge for this service if you wish), that you receive source code or can get it if you want it, that you can change the software or use pieces of it in new free programs; and that you know you can do these things.

To protect your rights, we need to make restrictions that forbid anyone to deny you these rights or to ask you to surrender the rights. These restrictions translate to certain responsibilities for you if you distribute copies of the software, or if you modify it.

For example, if you distribute copies of such a program, whether gratis or for a fee, you must give the recipients all the rights that you have. You must make sure that they, too, receive or can get the source code. And you must show them these terms so they know their rights.

We protect your rights with two steps: (1) copyright the software, and (2) offer you this license which gives you legal permission to copy, distribute and/or modify the software.

Also, for each author's protection and ours, we want to make certain that everyone understands that there is no warranty for this free software. If the software is modified by someone else and passed on, we want its recipients to know that what they have is not the original, so that any problems introduced by others will not reflect on the original authors' reputations.

Finally, any free program is threatened constantly by software patents. We wish to avoid the danger that redistributors of a free program will individually obtain patent licenses, in effect making the program proprietary. To prevent this, we have made it clear that any patent must be licensed for everyone's free use or not licensed at all.

The precise terms and conditions for copying, distribution and modification follow.

GNU GENERAL PUBLIC LICENSE
TERMS AND CONDITIONS FOR COPYING,
DISTRIBUTION AND MODIFICATION

0. This License applies to any program or other work which contains a notice placed by the copyright holder saying it may be distributed under the terms of this General Public License. The "Program", below, refers to any such program or work, and a "work based on the Program" means either the Program or any derivative work under copyright law: that is to say, a work containing the Program or a portion of it, either verbatim or with modifications and/or translated into another language. (Hereinafter, translation is included without limitation in the term "modification".) Each licensee is addressed as "you".

Activities other than copying, distribution and modification are not covered by this License; they are outside its scope. The act of running the Program is not restricted, and the output from the Program is covered only if its contents constitute a work based on the Program (independent of having been made by running the Program). Whether that is true depends on what the Program does.

1. You may copy and distribute verbatim copies of the Program's source code as you receive it, in any medium, provided that you conspicuously and appropriately publish on each copy an appropriate copyright notice and disclaimer of warranty; keep intact all the notices that refer to this License and to the absence of any warranty; and give any other recipients of the Program a copy of this License along with the Program.

You may charge a fee for the physical act of transferring a copy, and you may at your option offer warranty protection in exchange for a fee.

2. You may modify your copy or copies of the Program or any portion of it, thus forming a work based on the Program, and copy and distribute such modifications or work under the terms of Section 1 above, provided that you also meet all of these conditions:

a) You must cause the modified files to carry prominent notices stating that you changed the files and the date of any change.

b) You must cause any work that you distribute or publish, that in whole or in part contains or is derived from the Program or any part thereof, to be licensed as a whole at no charge to all third parties under the terms of this License.

c) If the modified program normally reads commands interactively when run, you must cause it, when started running for such interactive use in the most ordinary way, to print or display an announcement including an appropriate copyright notice and a notice that there is no warranty (or else, saying that you provide a warranty) and that users may redistribute the program under these conditions, and telling the user how to view a copy of this License. (Exception: if the Program itself is interactive but does not normally print such an announcement, your work based on the Program is not required to print an announcement.)

These requirements apply to the modified work as a whole. If identifiable sections of that work are not derived from the Program, and can be reasonably considered independent and separate works in themselves, then this License, and its terms, do not apply to those sections when you distribute them as separate works. But when you distribute the same sections as part of a whole which is a work based on the Program, the distribution of the whole must be on the terms of this License, whose permissions for other licensees extend to the entire whole, and thus to each and every part regardless of who wrote it.

Thus, it is not the intent of this section to claim rights or contest your rights to work written entirely by you; rather, the intent is to exercise the right to control the distribution of derivative or collective works based on the Program.

In addition, mere aggregation of another work not based on the Program with the Program (or with a work based on the Program) on a volume of a storage or distribution medium does not bring the other work under the scope of this License.

3. You may copy and distribute the Program (or a work based on it, under Section 2) in object code or executable form under the terms of Sections 1 and 2 above provided that you also do one of the following:

a) Accompany it with the complete corresponding machine-readable source code, which must be distributed under the terms of Sections 1 and 2 above on a medium customarily used for software interchange; or,

b) Accompany it with a written offer, valid for at least three years, to give any third party, for a charge no more than your cost of physically performing source distribution, a complete machine-readable copy of the corresponding source code, to be distributed under the terms of Sections 1 and 2 above on a medium customarily used for software interchange; or,

c) Accompany it with the information you received as to the offer to distribute corresponding source code. (This alternative is allowed only for noncommercial distribution and only if you received the program in object code or executable form with such an offer, in accord with Subsection b above.)

The source code for a work means the preferred form of the work for making modifications to it. For an executable work, complete source code means all the source code for all modules it contains, plus any associated interface definition files, plus the scripts used to control compilation and installation of the executable. However, as a special exception, the source code distributed need not include anything that is normally distributed (in either source or binary form) with the major components (compiler, kernel, and so on) of the operating system on which the executable runs, unless that component itself accompanies the executable.

If distribution of executable or object code is made by offering access to copy from a designated place, then offering equivalent access to copy the source code from the same place counts as distribution of the source code, even though third parties are not compelled to copy the source along with the object code.

4. You may not copy, modify, sublicense, or distribute the Program except as expressly provided under this License. Any attempt otherwise to copy, modify, sublicense or distribute the Program is void, and will automatically terminate your rights under this License. However, parties who have received copies, or rights, from you under this License will not have their licenses terminated so long as such parties remain in full compliance.

5. You are not required to accept this License, since you have not signed it. However, nothing else grants you permission to modify or distribute the Program or its derivative works. These actions are prohibited by law if you do not accept this License. Therefore, by modifying or distributing the Program (or any work based on the Program), you indicate your acceptance of this License to do so, and all its terms and conditions for copying, distributing or modifying the Program or works based on it.

6. Each time you redistribute the Program (or any work based on the Program), the recipient automatically receives a license from the original licensor to copy, distribute or modify the Program subject to these terms and conditions. You may not impose any further restrictions on the recipients' exercise of the rights granted herein. You are not responsible for enforcing compliance by third parties to this License.

7. If, as a consequence of a court judgment or allegation of patent infringement or for any other reason (not limited to patent issues), conditions are imposed on you (whether by court order, agreement or otherwise) that contradict the conditions of this License, they do not excuse you from the conditions of this License. If you cannot distribute so as to satisfy simultaneously your obligations under this License and any other pertinent obligations, then as a consequence you may not distribute the Program at all. For example, if a patent license would not permit royalty-free redistribution of the Program by all those who receive copies directly or indirectly through you, then the only way you could satisfy both it and this License would be to refrain entirely from distribution of the Program.

If any portion of this section is held invalid or unenforceable under any particular circumstance, the balance of the section is intended to apply and the section as a whole is intended to apply in other circumstances.

It is not the purpose of this section to induce you to infringe any patents or other property right claims or to contest validity of any such claims; this section has the sole purpose of protecting the integrity of the free software distribution system, which is implemented by public license practices. Many people have made generous contributions to the wide range of software distributed through that system in reliance on consistent application of that system; it is up to the author/donor to decide if he or she is willing to distribute software through any other system and a licensee cannot impose that choice.

This section is intended to make thoroughly clear what is believed to be a consequence of the rest of this License.

8. If the distribution and/or use of the Program is restricted in certain countries either by patents or by copyrighted interfaces, the original copyright holder who places the Program under this License may add an explicit geographical distribution limitation excluding those countries, so that distribution is permitted only in or among countries not thus excluded. In such case, this License incorporates the limitation as if written in the body of this License.

9. The Free Software Foundation may publish revised and/or new versions of the General Public License from time to time. Such new versions will be similar in spirit to the present version, but may differ in detail to address new problems or concerns.

Each version is given a distinguishing version number. If the Program specifies a version number of this License which applies to it and "any later version", you have the option of following the terms and conditions either of that version or of any later version published by the Free Software Foundation. If the Program does not specify a version number of this License, you may choose any version ever published by the Free Software Foundation.

10. If you wish to incorporate parts of the Program into other free programs whose distribution conditions are different, write to the author to ask for permission. For software which is copyrighted by the Free Software Foundation, write to the Free Software Foundation; we sometimes make exceptions for this. Our decision will be guided by the two goals of preserving the free status of all derivatives of our free software and of promoting the sharing and reuse of software generally.

NO WARRANTY

11. BECAUSE THE PROGRAM IS LICENSED FREE OF CHARGE, THERE IS NO WARRANTY FOR THE PROGRAM, TO THE EXTENT PERMITTED BY APPLICABLE LAW. EXCEPT WHEN OTHERWISE STATED IN WRITING THE COPYRIGHT HOLDERS AND/OR OTHER PARTIES PROVIDE THE PROGRAM "AS IS" WITHOUT WARRANTY OF ANY KIND, EITHER EXPRESSED OR IMPLIED, INCLUDING, BUT NOT LIMITED TO, THE IMPLIED WARRANTIES OF MERCHANTABILITY AND FITNESS FOR A PARTICULAR PURPOSE. THE ENTIRE RISK AS TO THE QUALITY AND PERFORMANCE OF THE PROGRAM IS WITH YOU. SHOULD THE PROGRAM PROVE DEFECTIVE, YOU ASSUME THE COST OF ALL NECESSARY SERVICING, REPAIR OR CORRECTION.

12. IN NO EVENT UNLESS REQUIRED BY APPLICABLE LAW OR AGREED TO IN WRITING WILL ANY COPYRIGHT HOLDER, OR ANY OTHER PARTY WHO MAY MODIFY AND/OR REDISTRIBUTE THE PROGRAM AS PERMITTED ABOVE, BE LIABLE TO YOU FOR DAMAGES, INCLUDING ANY GENERAL, SPECIAL, INCIDENTAL OR CONSEQUENTIAL DAMAGES ARISING OUT OF THE USE OR INABILITY TO USE THE PROGRAM (INCLUDING BUT NOT LIMITED TO LOSS OF DATA OR DATA BEING RENDERED INACCURATE OR LOSSES SUSTAINED BY YOU OR THIRD PARTIES OR A FAILURE OF THE PROGRAM TO OPERATE WITH ANY OTHER PROGRAMS), EVEN IF SUCH HOLDER OR OTHER PARTY HAS BEEN ADVISED OF THE POSSIBILITY OF SUCH DAMAGES.

END OF TERMS AND CONDITIONS

Appendix: How to Apply These Terms to Your New Programs

If you develop a new program, and you want it to be of the greatest possible use to the public, the best way to achieve this is to make it free software which everyone can redistribute and change under these terms.

To do so, attach the following notices to the program. It is safest to attach them to the start of each source file to most effectively convey the exclusion of warranty; and each file should have at least the "copyright" line and a pointer to where the full notice is found.

<one line to give the program's name and a brief idea of what it does.> Copyright (C) 19yy <name of author>

This program is free software; you can redistribute it and/or modify it under the terms of the GNU General Public License as published by the Free Software Foundation; either version 2 of the License, or (at your option) any later version.

This program is distributed in the hope that it will be useful, but WITHOUT ANY WARRANTY; without even the implied warranty of MERCHANTABILITY or FITNESS FOR A PARTICULAR PURPOSE. See the GNU General Public License for more details.

You should have received a copy of the GNU General Public License along with this program; if not, write to the Free Software Foundation, Inc., 675 Mass Ave, Cambridge, MA 02139, USA.

Also add information on how to contact you by electronic and paper mail.

If the program is interactive, make it output a short notice like this when it starts in an interactive mode:

Gnomovision version 69, Copyright (C) 19yy name of author Gnomovision comes with ABSOLUTELY NO WARRANTY; for details type 'show w'. This is free software, and you are welcome to redistribute it under certain conditions; type 'show c' for details.

The hypothetical commands 'show w' and 'show c' should show the appropriate parts of the General Public License. Of course, the commands you use may be called something other than 'show w' and 'show c'; they could even be mouse-clicks or menu items—whatever suits your program.

You should also get your employer (if you work as a programmer) or your school, if any, to sign a "copyright disclaimer" for the program, if necessary. Here is a sample; alter the names:

Yoyodyne, Inc., hereby disclaims all copyright interest in the program 'Gnomovision' (which makes passes at compilers) written by James Hacker.

<signature of Ty Coon>, 1 April 1989 Ty Coon, President of Vice

This General Public License does not permit incorporating your program into proprietary programs. If your program is a subroutine library, you may consider it more useful to permit linking proprietary applications with the library. If this is what you want to do, use the GNU Library General Public License instead of this License.

B.2 GNU Library General Public License

GNU LIBRARY GENERAL PUBLIC LICENSE
Version 2, June 1991

Copyright (C) 1991 Free Software Foundation, Inc. 675 Mass Ave, Cambridge, MA 02139, USA Everyone is permitted to copy and distribute verbatim copies of this license document, but changing it is not allowed.

[This is the first released version of the library GPL. It is numbered 2 because it goes with version 2 of the ordinary GPL.]

Preamble

The licenses for most software are designed to take away your freedom to share and change it. By contrast, the GNU General Public Licenses are intended to guarantee your freedom to share and change free software—to make sure the software is free for all its users.

This license, the Library General Public License, applies to some specially designated

Free Software Foundation software, and to any other libraries whose authors decide to use it. You can use it for your libraries, too.

When we speak of free software, we are referring to freedom, not price. Our General Public Licenses are designed to make sure that you have the freedom to distribute copies of free software (and charge for this service if you wish), that you receive source code or can get it if you want it, that you can change the software or use pieces of it in new free programs; and that you know you can do these things.

To protect your rights, we need to make restrictions that forbid anyone to deny you these rights or to ask you to surrender the rights. These restrictions translate to certain responsibilities for you if you distribute copies of the library, or if you modify it.

For example, if you distribute copies of the library, whether gratis or for a fee, you must give the recipients all the rights that we gave you. You must make sure that they, too, receive or can get the source code. If you link a program with the library, you must provide complete object files to the recipients so that they can relink them with the library, after making changes to the library and recompiling it. And you must show them these terms so they know their rights.

Our method of protecting your rights has two steps: (1) copyright the library, and (2) offer you this license which gives you legal permission to copy, distribute and/or modify the library.

Also, for each distributor's protection, we want to make certain that everyone understands that there is no warranty for this free library. If the library is modified by someone else and passed on, we want its recipients to know that what they have is not the original version, so that any problems introduced by others will not reflect on the original authors' reputations.

Finally, any free program is threatened constantly by software patents. We wish to avoid the danger that companies distributing free software will individually obtain patent licenses, thus in effect transforming the program into proprietary software. To prevent this, we have made it clear that any patent must be licensed for everyone's free use or not licensed at all.

Most GNU software, including some libraries, is covered by the ordinary GNU General Public License, which was designed for utility programs. This license, the GNU Library General Public License, applies to certain designated libraries. This license is quite different from the ordinary one; be sure to read it in full, and don't assume that anything in it is the same as in the ordinary license.

The reason we have a separate public license for some libraries is that they blur the distinction we usually make between modifying or adding to a program and simply using it. Linking a program with a library, without changing the library, is in some sense simply using the library, and is analogous to running a utility program or application program. However, in a textual and legal sense, the linked executable is a combined work, a derivative of the original library, and the ordinary General Public License treats it as such.

Because of this blurred distinction, using the ordinary General Public License for libraries did not effectively promote software sharing, because most developers did not use the libraries. We concluded that weaker conditions might promote sharing better.

However, unrestricted linking of non-free programs would deprive the users of those programs of all benefit from the free status of the libraries themselves. This Library General Public License is intended to permit developers of non-free programs to use free libraries, while preserving your freedom as a user of such programs to change the free libraries that are incorporated in them. (We have not seen how to achieve this as regards changes in header files, but we have achieved it as regards changes in the actual functions of the Library.) The hope is that this will lead to faster development of free libraries.

The precise terms and conditions for copying, distribution and modification follow. Pay close attention to the difference between a "work based on the library" and a "work that uses the library". The former contains code derived from the library, while the latter only works together with the library.

Note that it is possible for a library to be covered by the ordinary General Public License rather than by this special one.

GNU LIBRARY GENERAL PUBLIC LICENSE
TERMS AND CONDITIONS FOR COPYING,
DISTRIBUTION AND MODIFICATION

0. This License Agreement applies to any software library which contains a notice placed by the copyright holder or other authorized party saying it may be distributed under the terms of this Library General Public License (also called "this License"). Each licensee is addressed as "you".

A "library" means a collection of software functions and/or data prepared so as to be conveniently linked with application programs (which use some of those functions and data) to form executables.

The "Library", below, refers to any such software library or work which has been distributed under these terms. A "work based on the Library" means either the Library or any derivative work under copyright law: that is to say, a work containing the Library or a portion of it, either verbatim or with modifications and/or translated straightforwardly into another language. (Hereinafter, translation is included without limitation in the term "modification".)

"Source code" for a work means the preferred form of the work for making modifications to it. For a library, complete source code means all the source code for all modules it contains, plus any associated interface definition files, plus the scripts used to control compilation and installation of the library.

Activities other than copying, distribution and modification are not covered by this License; they are outside its scope. The act of running a program using the Library is not restricted, and output from such a program is covered only if its contents constitute a work based on the Library (independent of the use of the Library in a tool for writing it). Whether that is true depends on what the Library does and what the program that uses the Library does.

1. You may copy and distribute verbatim copies of the Library's complete source code as you receive it, in any medium, provided that you conspicuously and appropriately publish on each copy an appropriate copyright notice and disclaimer of warranty; keep intact all the notices that refer to this License and to the absence of any warranty; and distribute a copy of this License along with the Library.

You may charge a fee for the physical act of transferring a copy, and you may at your option offer warranty protection in exchange for a fee.

2. You may modify your copy or copies of the Library or any portion of it, thus forming a work based on the Library, and copy and distribute such modifications or work under the terms of Section 1 above, provided that you also meet all of these conditions:

a) The modified work must itself be a software library.

b) You must cause the files modified to carry prominent notices stating that you changed the files and the date of any change.

c) You must cause the whole of the work to be licensed at no charge to all third parties under the terms of this License.

d) If a facility in the modified Library refers to a function or a table of data to be supplied by an application program that uses the facility, other than as an argument passed when the facility is invoked, then you must make a good faith effort to ensure that, in the event an application does not supply such function or table, the facility still operates, and performs whatever part of its purpose remains meaningful.

(For example, a function in a library to compute square roots has a purpose that is entirely well-defined independent of the application. Therefore, Subsection 2d requires that any application-supplied function or table used by this function must be optional: if the application does not supply it, the square root function must still compute square roots.)

These requirements apply to the modified work as a whole. If identifiable sections of that work are not derived from the Library, and can be reasonably considered independent and separate works in themselves, then this License, and its terms, do not apply to those sections when you distribute them as separate works. But when you distribute the same sections as part of a whole which is a work based on the Library, the distribution of the whole must be on the terms of this License, whose permissions for other licensees extend to the entire whole, and thus to each and every part regardless of who wrote it.

Thus, it is not the intent of this section to claim rights or contest your rights to work written entirely by you; rather, the intent is to exercise the right to control the distribution of derivative or collective works based on the Library.

In addition, mere aggregation of another work not based on the Library with the Library (or with a work based on the Library) on a volume of a storage or distribution medium does not bring the other work under the scope of this License.

3. You may opt to apply the terms of the ordinary GNU General Public License instead of this License to a given copy of the Library. To do this, you must alter all the notices that refer to this License, so that they refer to the ordinary GNU General Public License, version 2, instead of to this License. (If a newer version than version 2 of the ordinary GNU General Public License has appeared, then you can specify that version instead if you wish.) Do not make any other change in these notices.

Once this change is made in a given copy, it is irreversible for that copy, so the ordinary GNU General Public License applies to all subsequent copies and derivative works made from that copy.

This option is useful when you wish to copy part of the code of the Library into a program that is not a library.

4. You may copy and distribute the Library (or a portion or derivative of it, under Section 2) in object code or executable form under the terms of Sections 1 and 2 above provided that you accompany it with the complete corresponding machine-readable source code, which must be distributed under the terms of Sections 1 and 2 above on a medium customarily used for software interchange.

If distribution of object code is made by offering access to copy from a designated place, then offering equivalent access to copy the source code from the same place satisfies the requirement to distribute the source code, even though third parties are not compelled to copy the source along with the object code.

5. A program that contains no derivative of any portion of the Library, but is designed to work with the Library by being compiled or linked with it, is called a "work that uses the Library". Such a work, in isolation, is not a derivative work of the Library, and therefore falls outside the scope of this License.

However, linking a "work that uses the Library" with the Library creates an executable that is a derivative of the Library (because it contains portions of the Library), rather than a "work that uses the library". The executable is therefore covered by this License. Section 6 states terms for distribution of such executables.

When a "work that uses the Library" uses material from a header file that is part of the Library, the object code for the work may be a derivative work of the Library even though the source code is not. Whether this is true is especially significant if the work can be linked without the Library, or if the work is itself a library. The threshold for this to be true is not precisely defined by law.

If such an object file uses only numerical parameters, data structure layouts and accessors, and small macros and small inline functions (ten lines or less in length), then the use of the object file is unrestricted, regardless of whether it is legally a derivative work. (Executables containing this object code plus portions of the Library will still fall under Section 6.)

Otherwise, if the work is a derivative of the Library, you may distribute the object code for the work under the terms of Section 6. Any executables containing that work also fall under Section 6, whether or not they are linked directly with the Library itself.

6. As an exception to the Sections above, you may also compile or link a "work that

uses the Library" with the Library to produce a work containing portions of the Library, and distribute that work under terms of your choice, provided that the terms permit modification of the work for the customer's own use and reverse engineering for debugging such modifications.

You must give prominent notice with each copy of the work that the Library is used in it and that the Library and its use are covered by this License. You must supply a copy of this License. If the work during execution displays copyright notices, you must include the copyright notice for the Library among them, as well as a reference directing the user to the copy of this License. Also, you must do one of these things:

a) Accompany the work with the complete corresponding machine-readable source code for the Library including whatever changes were used in the work (which must be distributed under Sections 1 and 2 above); and, if the work is an executable linked with the Library, with the complete machine-readable "work that uses the Library", as object code and/or source code, so that the user can modify the Library and then relink to produce a modified executable containing the modified Library. (It is understood that the user who changes the contents of definitions files in the Library will not necessarily be able to recompile the application to use the modified definitions.)

b) Accompany the work with a written offer, valid for at least three years, to give the same user the materials specified in Subsection 6a, above, for a charge no more than the cost of performing this distribution.

c) If distribution of the work is made by offering access to copy from a designated place, offer equivalent access to copy the above specified materials from the same place.

d) Verify that the user has already received a copy of these materials or that you have already sent this user a copy.

For an executable, the required form of the "work that uses the Library" must include any data and utility programs needed for reproducing the executable from it. However, as a special exception, the source code distributed need not include anything that is normally distributed (in either source or binary form) with the major components (compiler, kernel, and so on) of the operating system on which the executable runs, unless that component itself accompanies the executable.

It may happen that this requirement contradicts the license restrictions of other proprietary libraries that do not normally accompany the operating system. Such a contradiction means you cannot use both them and the Library together in an executable that you distribute.

7. You may place library facilities that are a work based on the Library side-by-side in a single library together with other library facilities not covered by this License, and distribute such a combined library, provided that the separate distribution of the work based on the Library and of the other library facilities is otherwise permitted, and provided that you do these two things:

a) Accompany the combined library with a copy of the same work based on the Library, uncombined with any other library facilities. This must be distributed under the terms of the Sections above.

b) Give prominent notice with the combined library of the fact that part of it is a work based on the Library, and explaining where to find the accompanying uncombined form of the same work.

8. You may not copy, modify, sublicense, link with, or distribute the Library except as expressly provided under this License. Any attempt otherwise to copy, modify, sublicense, link with, or distribute the Library is void, and will automatically terminate your rights under this License. However, parties who have received copies, or rights, from you under this License will not have their licenses terminated so long as such parties remain in full compliance.

9. You are not required to accept this License, since you have not signed it. However, nothing else grants you permission to modify or distribute the Library or its derivative works. These actions are prohibited by law if you do not accept this License. Therefore, by modifying or distributing the Library (or any work based on the Library), you indicate

your acceptance of this License to do so, and all its terms and conditions for copying, distributing or modifying the Library or works based on it.

10. Each time you redistribute the Library (or any work based on the Library), the recipient automatically receives a license from the original licensor to copy, distribute, link with or modify the Library subject to these terms and conditions. You may not impose any further restrictions on the recipients' exercise of the rights granted herein. You are not responsible for enforcing compliance by third parties to this License.

11. If, as a consequence of a court judgment or allegation of patent infringement or for any other reason (not limited to patent issues), conditions are imposed on you (whether by court order, agreement or otherwise) that contradict the conditions of this License, they do not excuse you from the conditions of this License. If you cannot distribute so as to satisfy simultaneously your obligations under this License and any other pertinent obligations, then as a consequence you may not distribute the Library at all. For example, if a patent license would not permit royalty-free redistribution of the Library by all those who receive copies directly or indirectly through you, then the only way you could satisfy both it and this License would be to refrain entirely from distribution of the Library.

If any portion of this section is held invalid or unenforceable under any particular circumstance, the balance of the section is intended to apply, and the section as a whole is intended to apply in other circumstances.

It is not the purpose of this section to induce you to infringe any patents or other property right claims or to contest validity of any such claims; this section has the sole purpose of protecting the integrity of the free software distribution system which is implemented by public license practices. Many people have made generous contributions to the wide range of software distributed through that system in reliance on consistent application of that system; it is up to the author/donor to decide if he or she is willing to distribute software through any other system and a licensee cannot impose that choice.

This section is intended to make thoroughly clear what is believed to be a consequence of the rest of this License.

12. If the distribution and/or use of the Library is restricted in certain countries either by patents or by copyrighted interfaces, the original copyright holder who places the Library under this License may add an explicit geographical distribution limitation excluding those countries, so that distribution is permitted only in or among countries not thus excluded. In such case, this License incorporates the limitation as if written in the body of this License.

13. The Free Software Foundation may publish revised and/or new versions of the Library General Public License from time to time. Such new versions will be similar in spirit to the present version, but may differ in detail to address new problems or concerns.

Each version is given a distinguishing version number. If the Library specifies a version number of this License which applies to it and "any later version", you have the option of following the terms and conditions either of that version or of any later version published by the Free Software Foundation. If the Library does not specify a license version number, you may choose any version ever published by the Free Software Foundation.

14. If you wish to incorporate parts of the Library into other free programs whose distribution conditions are incompatible with these, write to the author to ask for permission. For software which is copyrighted by the Free Software Foundation, write to the Free Software Foundation; we sometimes make exceptions for this. Our decision will be guided by the two goals of preserving the free status of all derivatives of our free software and of promoting the sharing and reuse of software generally.

NO WARRANTY

15. BECAUSE THE LIBRARY IS LICENSED FREE OF CHARGE, THERE IS NO WARRANTY FOR THE LIBRARY, TO THE EXTENT PERMITTED BY APPLICABLE

LAW. EXCEPT WHEN OTHERWISE STATED IN WRITING THE COPYRIGHT HOLDERS AND/OR OTHER PARTIES PROVIDE THE LIBRARY "AS IS" WITHOUT WARRANTY OF ANY KIND, EITHER EXPRESSED OR IMPLIED, INCLUDING, BUT NOT LIMITED TO, THE IMPLIED WARRANTIES OF MERCHANTABILITY AND FITNESS FOR A PARTICULAR PURPOSE. THE ENTIRE RISK AS TO THE QUALITY AND PERFORMANCE OF THE LIBRARY IS WITH YOU. SHOULD THE LIBRARY PROVE DEFECTIVE, YOU ASSUME THE COST OF ALL NECESSARY SERVICING, REPAIR OR CORRECTION.

16. IN NO EVENT UNLESS REQUIRED BY APPLICABLE LAW OR AGREED TO IN WRITING WILL ANY COPYRIGHT HOLDER, OR ANY OTHER PARTY WHO MAY MODIFY AND/OR REDISTRIBUTE THE LIBRARY AS PERMITTED ABOVE, BE LIABLE TO YOU FOR DAMAGES, INCLUDING ANY GENERAL, SPECIAL, INCIDENTAL OR CONSEQUENTIAL DAMAGES ARISING OUT OF THE USE OR INABILITY TO USE THE LIBRARY (INCLUDING BUT NOT LIMITED TO LOSS OF DATA OR DATA BEING RENDERED INACCURATE OR LOSSES SUSTAINED BY YOU OR THIRD PARTIES OR A FAILURE OF THE LIBRARY TO OPERATE WITH ANY OTHER SOFTWARE), EVEN IF SUCH HOLDER OR OTHER PARTY HAS BEEN ADVISED OF THE POSSIBILITY OF SUCH DAMAGES.

END OF TERMS AND CONDITIONS

Appendix: How to Apply These Terms to Your New Libraries

If you develop a new library, and you want it to be of the greatest possible use to the public, we recommend making it free software that everyone can redistribute and change. You can do so by permitting redistribution under these terms (or, alternatively, under the terms of the ordinary General Public License).

To apply these terms, attach the following notices to the library. It is safest to attach them to the start of each source file to most effectively convey the exclusion of warranty; and each file should have at least the "copyright" line and a pointer to where the full notice is found.

<one line to give the library's name and a brief idea of what it does.> Copyright (C) <year> <name of author>

This library is free software; you can redistribute it and/or modify it under the terms of the GNU Library General Public License as published by the Free Software Foundation; either version 2 of the License, or (at your option) any later version.

This library is distributed in the hope that it will be useful, but WITHOUT ANY WARRANTY; without even the implied warranty of MERCHANTABILITY or FITNESS FOR A PARTICULAR PURPOSE. See the GNU Library General Public License for more details.

You should have received a copy of the GNU Library General Public License along with this library; if not, write to the Free Software Foundation, Inc., 675 Mass Ave, Cambridge, MA 02139, USA.

Also add information on how to contact you by electronic and paper mail.

You should also get your employer (if you work as a programmer) or your school, if any, to sign a "copyright disclaimer" for the library, if necessary. Here is a sample; alter the names:

Yoyodyne, Inc., hereby disclaims all copyright interest in the library 'Frob' (a library for tweaking knobs) written by James Random Hacker.

<signature of Ty Coon>, 1 April 1990 Ty Coon, President of Vice

That's all there is to it!

B.3 Most Recent GETTING.GNU.SOFTWARE File

-*-text -*- Getting GNU Software, 21 Mar 93 Copyright (C) 1986, 1987, 1988, 1989, 1990, 1992, 1993 Free Software Foundation, Inc.

Permission is granted to anyone to make or distribute verbatim copies of this document provided that the copyright notice and this permission notice are preserved.

* GNU and the Free Software Foundation

Project GNU is organized as part of the Free Software Foundation, Inc. The Free Software Foundation has the following goals: 1) to create GNU as a full development/operating system. 2) to distribute GNU and other useful software with source code and permission to copy and redistribute.

Further information on the rationale for GNU is in file '/pub/gnu/GNUinfo/GNU' (all files referred to are on the Internet host prep.ai.mit.edu).

Information on GNU Internet mailing lists and gnUSENET newsgroups can be found in '/pub/gnu/GNUinfo/MAILINGLISTS'.

* How To Get The Software

The easiest way to get a copy of the distribution is from someone else who has it. You need not ask for permission to do so, or tell any one else; just copy it. The second easiest is to ftp it over the Internet. The third easiest way is to uucp it. Ftp and uucp information is in '/pub/gnu/GNUinfo/FTP'.

If you cannot get a copy any of these ways, or if you would feel more confident getting copies straight from us, or if you would like to get some funds to us to help in our efforts, you can order one from the Free Software Foundation. See '/pub/gnu/GNUinfo/DISTRIB' and '/pub/gnu/GNUinfo/ORDERS'.

* What format are the *.gz files in?

Because the unix 'compress' utility is patented (by two separate patents, in fact), we cannot use it; it's not free software.

Therefore, the GNU Project has chosen a new compression utility, 'gzip', which is free of any known software patents and which tends to compress better anyway. As of March 1993, all compressed files in the GNU anonymous FTP area, 'prep.ai.mit.edu:/pub/gnu', have been converted to the new format. Files compressed with this new compression program end in '.gz' (as opposed to 'compress'-compressed files, which end in '.Z').

Gzip can uncompress 'compress'-compressed files and 'pack' files (which end in '.z'). This is possible because the various decompression algorithms are not patented—only compression is.

The gzip program is available from any GNU mirror site in shar, tar, or gzipped tar format (for those who already have a prior version of gzip and want faster data transmission). It works on virtually every unix system, MSDOS, OS/2, and VMS.

* Available Software

** GNU Emacs

The GNU Emacs distribution includes: - manual source in TeX format. - an enhanced regex (regular expression) library.

See '/pub/gnu/GNUinfo/MACHINES' for the status of porting Emacs to various machines and operating systems.

** C Scheme - a block structured dialect of LISP.

The Free Software Foundation distributes C Scheme for the MIT Scheme Project on it tapes. A partial ftp distribution can be found on prep.ai.mit.edu. The full ftp distribution can be found on zurich.ai.mit.edu.

Problems with the C Scheme distribution and its ftp distribution should be referred to: <bug-cscheme@martigny.ai.mit.edu>. There are two general mailing lists: <info-cscheme @martigny.ai.mit.edu>and <scheme@mc.lcs.mit.edu>. Send requests to join either list to: <info-cscheme-request@martigny.ai.mit.edu> or <scheme-request@mc.lcs.mit.edu>.

** Other GNU Software
A full list of available software are in '/pub/gnu/GNUinfo/ORDERS' and '/pub/gnu/GNUinfo/DESCRIPTIONS'.
** Where is the documentation?
If documentation exists, it is inside each program's source code distribution. Instructions on installing a program are often in files name "README" and "INSTALL". Manuals and on-line documentations are written in GNU's texinfo format and are found in files ending with ".texi" or ".texinfo". Reference cards are usually written in TeX, and TeX files end in ".tex". Unix style man pages only exist, when volunteers supply them (the GNU Project finds the texinfo format to be superior). Man page files usually end in a single digit.

* No Warranties

We distribute software in the hope that it will be useful, but without any warranty. No author or distributor of this software accepts responsibility to anyone for the consequences of using it or for whether it serves any particular purpose or works at all, unless he says so in writing.

* If You Like The Software

If you like the software developed and distributed by the Free Software Foundation, please express your satisfaction with a donation. Your donations will help to support the foundation and make our future efforts successful, including a complete development and operating system, called GNU (Gnu's Not Un*x), which will run Un*x user programs. Please note that donations and funds raise by selling tapes, cd-roms, and floppy diskettes are the major source of funding for our work.

For more information on GNU and the Foundation, contact us at Internet address <gnu@prep.ai.mit.edu> or the foundation's US Mail address found in file '/pub/gnu/GNUinfo/DISTRIB'.

B.4 Author's Disclaimer

The author and distributor of this software are in no way responsible for anything related to either the performance or distribution of the software on the accompanying CD. The author is also not responsible for any maintenance or support activies on anything related to the software or the distribution of the software. The author also stands by all copyright and permission notices of all software on the CD.

B.5 M.I.T.'s Disclaimer

Copyright 1991 by the Massachusetts Institute of Technology.

Permission to use, copy, modify, and distribute this document for any purpose and without fee is hereby granted, provided that the above copyright notice and this permission notice appear in all copies, and that the name of MIT not be used in advertising or publicity pertaining to this document without specific, written prior permission. MIT makes no representations about the suitability of this document for any purpose. It is provided "as is" without express or implied warranty.

B.6 The Regents of the University of California's Disclaimer (Flex)

Flex carries the copyright used for BSD software, slightly modified because it originated at the Lawrence Berkeley (not Livermore!) Laboratory, which operates under a contract with the Department of Energy:

Copyright (c) 1990 The Regents of the University of California. All rights reserved.

This code is derived from software contributed to Berkeley by Vern Paxson.

The United States Government has rights in this work pursuant to contract no. DE-AC03-76SF00098 between the United States Department of Energy and the University of California.

Redistribution and use in source and binary forms are permitted provided that: (1) source distributions retain this entire copyright notice and comment, and (2) distributions including binaries display the following acknowledgement: "This product includes software developed by the University of California, Berkeley and its contributors" in the documentation or other materials provided with the distribution and in all advertising materials mentioning features or use of this software. Neither the name of the University nor the names of its contributors may be used to endorse or promote products derived from this software without specific prior written permission.

THIS SOFTWARE IS PROVIDED "AS IS" AND WITHOUT ANY EXPRESS OR IMPLIED WARRANTIES, INCLUDING, WITHOUT LIMITATION, THE IMPLIED WARRANTIES OF MERCHANTABILITY AND FITNESS FOR A PARTICULAR PURPOSE.

This basically says "do whatever you please with this software except remove this notice or take advantage of the University's (or the flex authors') name".

Note that the "flex.skel" scanner skeleton carries no copyright notice. You are free to do whatever you please with scanners generated using flex; for them, you are not even bound by the above copyright.

B.7 AT&T/BellCore Copyright (f2c)

****

Copyright 1990 by AT&T Bell Laboratories and Bellcore.

Permission to use, copy, modify, and distribute this software and its documentation for any purpose and without fee is hereby granted, provided that the above copyright notice appear in all copies and that both that the copyright notice and this permission notice and warranty disclaimer appear in supporting documentation, and that the names of AT&T Bell Laboratories or Bellcore or any of their entities not be used in advertising or publicity pertaining to distribution of the software without specific, written prior permission.

AT&T and Bellcore disclaim all warranties with regard to this software, including all implied warranties of merchantability and fitness. In no event shall AT&T or Bellcore be liable for any special, indirect or consequential damages or any damages whatsoever resulting from loss of use, data or profits, whether in an action of contract, negligence or other tortious action, arising out of or in connection with the use or performance of this software.

***/

B.8 pbmplus Copyright

COPYRIGHTS

All the software in this package, whether by me or by a contributer, has a copyright similar to this one:

Permission to use, copy, modify, and distribute this software and its documentation for any purpose and without fee is hereby granted, provided that the above copyright notice appear in all copies and that both that copyright notice and this permission notice appear in supporting documentation. This software is provided "as is" without express or implied warranty.

Many people get confused by this legalese, especially the part about "without fee." Does this mean you can't charge for any product that uses PBMPLUS? No. All it means is that you don't have to pay me. You can do what you want with this software. Build it into your package, steal code from it, whatever. Just be sure to let people know where it came from.

B.9 gnuplot Copyright

```
/*
* Copyright (C) 1986 - 1993 Thomas Williams, Colin Kelley
*
* Permission to use, copy, and distribute this software and its
* documentation for any purpose with or without fee is hereby granted,
* provided that the above copyright notice appear in all copies and
* that both that copyright notice and this permission notice appear
* in supporting documentation.
*
* Permission to modify the software is granted, but not the right to
* distribute the modified code. Modifications are to be distributed
* as patches to released version.
*
* This software is provided "as is" without express or implied warranty.
*
*
* AUTHORS
*
* Original Software:
* Thomas Williams, Colin Kelley.
*
* Gnuplot 2.0 additions:
* Russell Lang, Dave Kotz, John Campbell.
*
* Gnuplot 3.0 additions:
* Gershon Elber and many others.
*
* Send your comments or suggestions to
* info-gnuplot@dartmouth.edu.
* This is a mailing list; to join it send a note to
* info-gnuplot-request@dartmouth.edu.
* Send bug reports to
* bug-gnuplot@dartmouth.edu.
*/
```

B.10 The GNU Manifesto

THE GNU MANIFESTO

Copyright (C) 1985 Richard M. Stallman (Copying permission notice at the end.)

What's GNU? Gnu's Not Unix!

GNU, which stands for Gnu's Not Unix, is the name for the complete Unix-compatible software system which I am writing so that I can give it away free to everyone who can use it. Several other volunteers are helping me. Contributions of time, money, programs and equipment are greatly needed.

So far we have an Emacs text editor with Lisp for writing editor commands, a source level debugger, a yacc-compatible parser generator, a linker, and around 35 utilities. A shell (command interpreter) is nearly completed. A new portable optimizing C compiler has compiled itself and may be released this year. An initial kernel exists but many more features are needed to emulate Unix. When the kernel and compiler are finished, it will be possible to distribute a GNU system suitable for program development. We will use @TeX{} as our text formatter, but an nroff is being worked on. We will use the free, portable X window system as well. After this we will add a portable Common Lisp, an Empire game, a spreadsheet, and hundreds of other things, plus on-line documentation. We hope to supply, eventually, everything useful that normally comes with a Unix system, and more.

GNU will be able to run Unix programs, but will not be identical to Unix. We will make all improvements that are convenient, based on our experience with other operating systems. In particular, we plan to have longer filenames, file version numbers, a crashproof file system, filename completion perhaps, terminal-independent display support, and perhaps eventually a Lisp-based window system through which several Lisp programs and ordinary Unix programs can share a screen. Both C and Lisp will be available as system programming languages. We will try to support UUCP, MIT Chaosnet, and Internet protocols for communication.

GNU is aimed initially at machines in the 68000/16000 class with virtual memory, because they are the easiest machines to make it run on. The extra effort to make it run on smaller machines will be left to someone who wants to use it on them.

To avoid horrible confusion, please pronounce the 'G' in the word 'GNU' when it is the name of this project.

Who Am I?

I am Richard Stallman, inventor of the original much-imitated EMACS editor, formerly at the Artificial Intelligence Lab at MIT. I have worked extensively on compilers, editors, debuggers, command interpreters, the Incompatible Timesharing System and the Lisp Machine operating system. I pioneered terminal-independent display support in ITS. Since then I have implemented one crashproof file system and two window systems for Lisp machines, and designed a third window system now being implemented; this one will be ported to many systems including use in GNU. [Historical note: The window system project was not completed; GNU now plans to use the X window system.]

Why I Must Write GNU

I consider that the golden rule requires that if I like a program I must share it with other people who like it. Software sellers want to divide the users and conquer them, making each user agree not to share with others. I refuse to break solidarity with other users in this way. I cannot in good conscience sign a nondisclosure agreement or a software license agreement. For years I worked within the Artificial Intelligence Lab to resist such tendencies and other inhospitalities, but eventually they had gone too far: I could not remain in an institution where such things are done for me against my will.

So that I can continue to use computers without dishonor, I have decided to put together a sufficient body of free software so that I will be able to get along without any software that is not free. I have resigned from the AI lab to deny MIT any legal excuse to prevent me from giving GNU away.

Why GNU Will Be Compatible with Unix

Unix is not my ideal system, but it is not too bad. The essential features of Unix seem to be good ones, and I think I can fill in what Unix lacks without spoiling them. And a system compatible with Unix would be convenient for many other people to adopt.

How GNU Will Be Available

GNU is not in the public domain. Everyone will be permitted to modify and redistribute GNU, but no distributor will be allowed to restrict its further redistribution. That is to say, proprietary modifications will not be allowed. I want to make sure that all versions of GNU remain free.

Why Many Other Programmers Want to Help

I have found many other programmers who are excited about GNU and want to help.

Many programmers are unhappy about the commercialization of system software. It may enable them to make more money, but it requires them to feel in conflict with other programmers in general rather than feel as comrades. The fundamental act of friendship among programmers is the sharing of programs; marketing arrangements now typically used essentially forbid programmers to treat others as friends. The purchaser of software must choose between friendship and obeying the law. Naturally, many decide that friendship is more important. But those who believe in law often do not feel at ease with either choice. They become cynical and think that programming is just a way of making money.

By working on and using GNU rather than proprietary programs, we can be hospitable to everyone and obey the law. In addition, GNU serves as an example to inspire and a banner to rally others to join us in sharing. This can give us a feeling of harmony which is impossible if we use software that is not free. For about half the programmers I talk to, this is an important happiness that money cannot replace.

How You Can Contribute

I am asking computer manufacturers for donations of machines and money. I'm asking individuals for donations of programs and work.

One consequence you can expect if you donate machines is that GNU will run on them at an early date. The machines should be complete, ready to use systems, approved for use in a residential area, and not in need of sophisticated cooling or power.

I have found very many programmers eager to contribute part-time work for GNU. For most projects, such part-time distributed work would be very hard to coordinate; the independently-written parts would not work together. But for the particular task of replacing Unix, this problem is absent. A complete Unix system contains hundreds of utility programs, each of which is documented separately. Most interface specifications are fixed by Unix compatibility. If each contributor can write a compatible replacement for a single Unix utility, and make it work properly in place of the original on a Unix system, then these utilities will work right when put together. Even allowing for Murphy to create a few unexpected problems, assembling these components will be a feasible task. (The kernel will require closer communication and will be worked on by a small, tight group.)

If I get donations of money, I may be able to hire a few people full or part time. The salary won't be high by programmers' standards, but I'm looking for people for whom building community spirit is as important as making money. I view this as a way of enabling dedicated people to devote their full energies to working on GNU by sparing them the need to make a living in another way.

Why All Computer Users Will Benefit

Once GNU is written, everyone will be able to obtain good system software free, just like air.

This means much more than just saving everyone the price of a Unix license. It means that much wasteful duplication of system programming effort will be avoided. This effort can go instead into advancing the state of the art.

Complete system sources will be available to everyone. As a result, a user who needs changes in the system will always be free to make them himself, or hire any available programmer or company to make them for him. Users will no longer be at the mercy of one programmer or company which owns the sources and is in sole position to make changes.

Schools will be able to provide a much more educational environment by encouraging all students to study and improve the system code. Harvard's computer lab used to have the policy that no program could be installed on the system if its sources were not on public display, and upheld it by actually refusing to install certain programs. I was very much inspired by this.

Finally, the overhead of considering who owns the system software and what one is or is not entitled to do with it will be lifted.

Arrangements to make people pay for using a program, including licensing of copies, always incur a tremendous cost to society through the cumbersome mechanisms necessary to figure out how much (that is, which programs) a person must pay for. And only a police state can force everyone to obey them. Consider a space station where air must be manufactured at great cost: charging each breather per liter of air may be fair, but wearing the metered gas mask all day and all night is intolerable even if everyone can afford to pay the air bill. And the TV cameras everywhere to see if you ever take the mask off are outrageous. It's better to support the air plant with a head tax and chuck the masks.

Copying all or parts of a program is as natural to a programmer as breathing, and as productive. It ought to be as free.

Some Easily Rebutted Objections to GNU's Goals

"Nobody will use it if it is free, because that means they can't rely on any support." "You have to charge for the program to pay for providing the support."

If people would rather pay for GNU plus service than get GNU free without service, a company to provide just service to people who have obtained GNU free ought to be profitable.

We must distinguish between support in the form of real programming work and mere handholding. The former is something one cannot rely on from a software vendor. If your problem is not shared by enough people, the vendor will tell you to get lost.

If your business needs to be able to rely on support, the only way is to have all the necessary sources and tools. Then you can hire any available person to fix your problem; you are not at the mercy of any individual. With Unix, the price of sources puts this out of consideration for most businesses. With GNU this will be easy. It is still possible for there to be no available competent person, but this problem cannot be blamed on distribution arrangements. GNU does not eliminate all the world's problems, only some of them.

Meanwhile, the users who know nothing about computers need handholding: doing things for them which they could easily do themselves but don't know how.

Such services could be provided by companies that sell just hand-holding and repair service. If it is true that users would rather spend money and get a product with service, they will also be willing to buy the service having got the product free. The service companies will compete in quality and price; users will not be tied to any particular one. Meanwhile, those of us who don't need the service should be able to use the program without paying for the service.

"You cannot reach many people without advertising, and you must charge for the program to support that." "It's no use advertising a program people can get free."

There are various forms of free or very cheap publicity that can be used to inform numbers of computer users about something like GNU. But it may be true that one can reach more microcomputer users with advertising. If this is really so, a business which advertises the service of copying and mailing GNU for a fee ought to be successful enough to pay for its advertising and more. This way, only the users who benefit from the advertising pay for it.

On the other hand, if many people get GNU from their friends, and such companies don't succeed, this will show that advertising was not really necessary to spread GNU. Why is it that free market advocates don't want to let the free market decide this?

"My company needs a proprietary operating system to get a competitive edge."

GNU will remove operating system software from the realm of competition. You will not be able to get an edge in this area, but neither will your competitors be able to get an edge over you. You and they will compete in other areas, while benefiting mutually in this one. If your business is selling an operating system, you will not like GNU, but that's tough on you. If your business is something else, GNU can save you from being pushed into the expensive business of selling operating systems.

I would like to see GNU development supported by gifts from many manufacturers and users, reducing the cost to each.

"Don't programmers deserve a reward for their creativity?"

If anything deserves a reward, it is social contribution. Creativity can be a social contribution, but only in so far as society is free to use the results. If programmers deserve to be rewarded for creating innovative programs, by the same token they deserve to be punished if they restrict the use of these programs.

"Shouldn't a programmer be able to ask for a reward for his creativity?"

There is nothing wrong with wanting pay for work, or seeking to maximize one's income, as long as one does not use means that are destructive. But the means customary in the field of software today are based on destruction.

Extracting money from users of a program by restricting their use of it is destructive because the restrictions reduce the amount and the ways that the program can be used. This reduces the amount of wealth that humanity derives from the program. When there is a deliberate choice to restrict, the harmful consequences are deliberate destruction.

The reason a good citizen does not use such destructive means to become wealthier is that, if everyone did so, we would all become poorer from the mutual destructiveness. This is Kantian ethics; or, the Golden Rule. Since I do not like the consequences that result if everyone hoards information, I am required to consider it wrong for one to do so. Specifically, the desire to be rewarded for one's creativity does not justify depriving the world in general of all or part of that creativity.

"Won't programmers starve?"

I could answer that nobody is forced to be a programmer. Most of us cannot manage to get any money for standing on the street and making faces. But we are not, as a result, condemned to spend our lives standing on the street making faces, and starving. We do something else.

But that is the wrong answer because it accepts the questioner's implicit assumption: that without ownership of software, programmers cannot possibly be paid a cent. Supposedly it is all or nothing.

The real reason programmers will not starve is that it will still be possible for them to get paid for programming; just not paid as much as now.

Restricting copying is not the only basis for business in software. It is the most common basis because it brings in the most money. If it were prohibited, or rejected by the customer, software business would move to other bases of organization which are now used less often. There are always numerous ways to organize any kind of business.

Probably programming will not be as lucrative on the new basis as it is now. But that is not an argument against the change. It is not considered an injustice that sales clerks make the salaries that they now do. If programmers made the same, that would not be an injustice either. (In practice they would still make considerably more than that.)

"Don't people have a right to control how their creativity is used?"

"Control over the use of one's ideas" really constitutes control over other people's lives; and it is usually used to make their lives more difficult.

People who have studied the issue of intellectual property rights carefully (such as lawyers) say that there is no intrinsic right to intellectual property. The kinds of supposed intellectual property rights that the government recognizes were created by specific acts of legislation for specific purposes.

For example, the patent system was established to encourage inventors to disclose the details of their inventions. Its purpose was to help society rather than to help inventors. At the time, the life span of 17 years for a patent was short compared with the rate of advance of the state of the art. Since patents are an issue only among manufacturers, for whom the cost and effort of a license agreement are small compared with setting up production, the patents often do not do much harm. They do not obstruct most individuals who use patented products.

The idea of copyright did not exist in ancient times, when authors frequently copied other authors at length in works of non-fiction. This practice was useful, and is the only way many authors' works have survived even in part. The copyright system was created expressly for the purpose of encouraging authorship. In the domain for which it was invented—books, which could be copied economically only on a printing press—it did little harm, and did not obstruct most of the individuals who read the books.

All intellectual property rights are just licenses granted by society because it was thought, rightly or wrongly, that society as a whole would benefit by granting them. But in any particular situation, we have to ask: are we really better off granting such license? What kind of act are we licensing a person to do?

The case of programs today is very different from that of books a hundred years ago. The fact that the easiest way to copy a program is from one neighbor to another, the fact that a program has both source code and object code which are distinct, and the fact that a program is used rather than read and enjoyed, combine to create a situation in which a person who enforces a copyright is harming society as a whole both materially and spiritually; in which a person should not do so regardless of whether the law enables him to.

"Competition makes things get done better."

The paradigm of competition is a race: by rewarding the winner, we encourage everyone to run faster. When capitalism really works this way, it does a good job; but its defenders are wrong in assuming it always works this way. If the runners forget why the reward is offered and become intent on winning, no matter how, they may find other strategies—such as, attacking other runners. If the runners get into a fist fight, they will all finish late.

Proprietary and secret software is the moral equivalent of runners in a fist fight. Sad to say, the only referee we've got does not seem to object to fights; he just regulates them ("For every ten yards you run, you are allowed one kick."). He really ought to break them up, and penalize runners for even trying to fight.

"Won't everyone stop programming without a monetary incentive?"

Actually, many people will program with absolutely no monetary incentive. Programming has an irresistible fascination for some people, usually the people who are best at it. There is no shortage of professional musicians who keep at it even though they have no hope of making a living that way.

But really this question, though commonly asked, is not appropriate to the situation. Pay for programmers will not disappear, only become less. So the right question is, will anyone program with a reduced monetary incentive? My experience shows that they will.

For more than ten years, many of the world's best programmers worked at the Artificial Intelligence Lab for far less money than they could have had anywhere else. They got many kinds of non-monetary rewards: fame and appreciation, for example. And creativity is also fun, a reward in itself.

Then most of them left when offered a chance to do the same interesting work for a lot of money.

What the facts show is that people will program for reasons other than riches; but if given a chance to make a lot of money as well, they will come to expect and demand it. Low-paying organizations do poorly in competition with high-paying ones, but they do not have to do badly if the high-paying ones are banned.

"We need the programmers desperately. If they demand that we stop helping our neighbors, we have to obey."

You're never so desperate that you have to obey this sort of demand. Remember: millions for defense, but not a cent for tribute!

"Programmers need to make a living somehow."

In the short run, this is true. However, there are plenty of ways that programmers could make a living without selling the right to use a program. This way is customary now because it brings programmers and businessmen the most money, not because it is the only way to make a living. It is easy to find other ways if you want to find them. Here are a number of examples.

A manufacturer introducing a new computer will pay for the porting of operating systems onto the new hardware.

The sale of teaching, hand-holding and maintenance services could also employ programmers.

People with new ideas could distribute programs as freeware, asking for donations from satisfied users, or selling hand-holding services. I have met people who are already working this way successfully.

Users with related needs can form users' groups, and pay dues. A group would contract with programming companies to write programs that the group's members would like to use.

All sorts of development can be funded with a Software Tax:

Suppose everyone who buys a computer has to pay x percent of the price as a software tax. The government gives this to an agency like the NSF to spend on software development.

But if the computer buyer makes a donation to software development himself, he can take a credit against the tax. He can donate to the project of his own choosing—often, chosen because he hopes to use the results when it is done. He can take a credit for any amount of donation up to the total tax he had to pay.

The total tax rate could be decided by a vote of the payers of the tax, weighted according to the amount they will be taxed on.

The consequences:

* the computer-using community supports software development.
* this community decides what level of support is needed.
* users who care which projects their share is spent on can choose this for themselves.

In the long run, making programs free is a step toward the post-scarcity world, where nobody will have to work very hard just to make a living. People will be free to devote themselves to activities that are fun, such as programming, after spending the necessary ten hours a week on required tasks such as legislation, family counseling, robot repair and asteroid prospecting. There will be no need to be able to make a living from programming.

We have already greatly reduced the amount of work that the whole society must do for its actual productivity, but only a little of this has translated itself into leisure for workers because much nonproductive activity is required to accompany productive activity. The main causes of this are bureaucracy and isometric struggles against competition. Free software will greatly reduce these drains in the area of software production. We must do this, in order for technical gains in productivity to translate into less work for us.

Appendix C
Where to Go to Get More Information

C.1 Some Recommended Books

There are many books available in this market, but I thought it was important to point out a few of the better ones to get you started in the right direction. They are:

Any book written by Andrew Tanenbaum

Any C programming books by Rex Jaeschke

Any Nutshell book (O'Reilly & Associates, Inc.)

Any X Window System book by O'Reilly & Associates

The AWK Programming Language by Alfred Aho, Brian Kernighan, and Peter Weinberger

Essential System Administration by Aeleen Frisch, O'Reilly & Associates, Inc.

Life with UNIX by Don Libes and Sandy Ressler

Korn Shell by Bill Rosenblatt, O'Reilly & Associates, Inc.

The Korn Shell by Morris Bolsky and David Korn

The Matrix by John Quarterman

Solaris 2.X Transition Guides from Sun Microsystems (obviously useful for Sun users only)

The UNIX C Shell by Gail Anderson and Paul Anderson

UNIX Network Programming by W. Richard Stevens

The UNIX Programming Environment by Brian Kernighan and Rob Pike

UNIX System Security by Patrick Wood and Stephen Kochan

There are many others but you can't go wrong with those listed above.

C.2 Where You Can Get Help

Besides the free resources of the Internet, including e-mail to experts and newsfeeds, you can purchase expertise. Lists of consultants exist in a variety of packages and areas on the Internet. See the file in the emacs distribution under the etc subdirectory entitled SERVICE. This has a listing of a variety of people who offer services and support contracts for free software, including most of the packages discussed in this book. If you are a commercial customer, this may not be a bad way to go.

Appendix

D

Internet Access Providers

TABLE D.1 Nationwide and International Service Providers

Provider	Coverage	Services
AARNet AARNet Support GPO Box 1142 Canberra ACT 2601 Australia +61 6 249 3385 +616 2491369 (fax) aarnet@aarnet.edu.au	Australia	Dedicated (9.6KB–2MB) SLIP PPP
ANS (Advanced Networks and Services) 2901 Hubbard Road Ann Arbor, MI 48105 (313) 663-7610 maloff nis . ans . net	Worldwide	Dedicated (1.5MB–45MB)
a2i Communications 1211 Park Avenue #202 San Jose, CA 95132 info@rahul .net	Continental U.S.	Dial-up
CLASS (Cooperative Library Agency for Systems and Services) 1415 Koll Circle, Suite 101 San Jose, CA 95112-4698 (800) 488-4559 (408) 453-0444	National	Dial-up (member libraries only)
Demon Internet Services Demon System Ltd. 42 Hendon Lane London N3 lTT England +44 81 349 0063 internet@demon.co.uk	UK	Dial-up SLIP PPP

TABLE D.1 (*Continued*)

Provider	Coverage	Services
EUnet EUnet Support +31 20 59 25 12 4 glenneu.net	Europe	
PACCOM University of Hawaii, Hawaii ICS 2565 The Mall Honolulu, HI 96822 (808) 956-3499 torben@hawaii.edu	Pacific Rim countries	Dedicated (64KB–1.5KB)
PSI (Performance Systems International) 1180 Sunrise Valley Drive Suite 1100 Reston, VA 22091 (703) 620-6651 (703) 629-4586 (fax) PSlLink info@psi.com	Worldwide	Dedicated (9.6KB–1.5MB) Dial up SLIP PPP/UUI
SprintLink SprintInternational 13221 Woodland Park Drive Herndon, VA 22071 (703) 904-2156 mkisericml .icp.net	Worldwide	Dedicated (9.6 KB–1.5MB)
UKnet UKnet Support +44 227 475497 postmasteruknet.ac.uk	UK countries	Dedicated Dial-up UUCP
UUNET Suite 570 3110 Fairview Park Drive Falls Church, VA 22042 (703) 204-8000 (800) 4UU-NET3 info@uunet.uu.net	Worldwide	Dial-up SLIP PPP UUCP Dedicated (9.6 KB–1.5MB)
The Well 27 Gate Five Road Saulsalito, CA 94965 (415) 332-4335 info@well.sf.ca.us	Access through X.25 and direct dial	Dial-up
The World Software Tool and Die 1330 Beacon Street Brookline, MA 02146 (617) 739-0202	U.S.	Dial-up

TABLE D.2 Regional Service Providers

Provider	Coverage	Services
AccessNB* Computer Science Department University of New Brunswick Fredericton, NB Canada E3BSA4	New Brunswick, Canada	
ARnet* Walter Neilson (403) 450-5188	Alberta, Canada	
BARRNET William Yundt Pine Hall Room 115 Stanford, CA 94305-4122 (415) 723-3104 gd.whyforsythe.stanford.edu	San Francisco, CA area International—Far East	Dedicated Dial-up SLIP PPP
BCnet BCnet Headquarters 419-6356 Agricultural Road Vancouver, BC Canada V6T lZ2 (604) 822-3932 BCnet'ubc.ca	British Columbia	Dedicated (2400–1.5MB)
CERFnet PO Box 85608 San Diego, CA 92186-9784 (800) 876-2373 (619) 455-3990 helpcerf.net	Southern CA International (Korea, Mexico, Brazil)	Dedicated (14.4KB–1.5MB) Dial-up (local & 800) SLIP PPP
CICnet ITI Building 2901 Hubbard Drive, Pod G Ann Arbor, MI 48105 (313) 998-6103 infocic.net	Midwest U.S. (IL IA MN WI MI OH IN)	Dedicated (56KB–1.5MB)
Colorado Supernet CSM ComputerCenter Colorado School of Mines 1500 Illinois Golden, CO 80401 (303) 273-3471 (303) 273-3475 (fax) info'csn.org	Colorado	Dedicated (9.6KB–1.5MB) Dial-up SLIP PPP

TABLE D.2 (*Continued*)

Provider	Coverage	Services
CONCERT P.O. Box 12889 3021 Cornwallis Road Research Triangle Park, NC 27709 (919) 248-1404 jrrconcert.net	North Carolina	Dedicated (56KB–1.5MB) Dial-up SLIP PPP/UU
JVNCnet Sergio Heker 6 von Neuman Hall Princeton University Princeton, NJ 08544 (609) 258-2400 market jvnc.net	Northeastern U.S. International	Dedicated (19.2 KB–1.5MB) Dial-up SLIP
Los Nettos Information Sciences Institute 4676 Admiralty Way Marina del Rey, CA 90292 (310) 822-1511 los-nettos-requestisi.edu	Los Angeles, CA area	Dedicated (1.5MB)
MBnet* Gerry Miller (204) 474-8230	Manitoba, Canada	
Merit 2200 Bonisteel Boulevard Ann Arbor, Ml 48109-2112 (313) 764-9430 jogdenmerit.edu	Michigan	
MIDnet 29 WESC University of Nebraska Lincoln, NE 68588 (402) 472-5032 dmfwestie.unl .edu	Plains States U.S. (NE OK AR SD IA KA MO)	Dedicated (56KB–1.5MB)
MRNet (Minnesota Regional Network) 511 11th Avenue So, Box 212 Minneapolis, MN 55415 (612) 342-2570 (612) 344-1716 (fax)	Minnesota	Dedicated (56KB–l.5MB)
MSEN 628 Brooks Street Ann Arbor, Ml 48103 (313) 998-4562 info@msen.com	Michigan	Dedicated (9.6KB–1.5MB) Dial-up SLIP PPP

TABLE D.2 (*Continued*)

Provider	Coverage	Services
NEARnet BBN Systems and Technologies 10 Moulton Street Cambridge, MA 02138 (617) 873-8730 nearnet-join@nic.near.net	Northeastern U.S. (ME NH VT CT RI MA)	Dedicated (9.6KB–10MB) SLIP PPP
Netcom Online Communication Services 4000 Moorepark Avenue #209 San Jose, CA 95117 (408) 544-8649 ruthann@netcom.com	California (6 locations in major cities)	Dial-up
netIllinois Joel Hartman Bradley University 1501 W. Bradley Avenue Peoria, IL 61625 (309) 677-3100 (309) 677-3092 (fax) joel@lbradley.edu	Illinois	Dedicated (9.6KB–1.5MB)
NevadaNet University of Nevada System Computing Services 4505 Maryland Parkway Las Vegas, NV 89154 (702) 739-3557	Nevada	Dedicated
NLnet* Wilf Bussey (709) 737-8329	Newfoundland Labrador	
NorthWestNet 2435 233rd Place NE Redmond, WA 98053 (206) 562-3000 ehood@nwnet.net	Northwestern U.S. (OR WA WY AK ID MT ND)	Dedicated (56KB–1.5MB)
NSTN* 900 Windmill Road, Suite 107 Dartmouth, NS Canada B3B 137 (902) 468-NSTN parsons@hawk.nstn.ns.ca	Nova Scotia, Canada	Dedicated (9.6KB–56KB) SLIP Dial-up
NYSERNet 111 College Place, Room 3-211 Syracuse, NY 13244 (315) 443-4120 luckett@nysernet.org	New York State	Dedicated (9.6KB–1.5MB) SLIP PPP Dial-up

TABLE D.2 (*Continued*)

Provider	Coverage	Services
OARnet Ohio Supercomputer Center 1224 Kinnear Road Columbus, OH 43085 (614) 292-9248 alisonosc.edu	Ohio	Dedicated SLIP PPP
Onet 4 Bancroft Avenue, Rm. 116 University of Toronto Toronto, Ontario M58 lAl Canada (416) 978-5058 eugenevm.utcs.utoronto.ca	Ontario, Canada	
PEINet* Jim Hancock (902) 566-0450	Prince Edward Island, Canada	
PREPnet 305 S. Craig, 2d Floor Pittsburgh, PA 15213 (412) 268-7870 Dial-up twb+andrew.cmu.edu	Pennsylvania	Dedicated (9.6KB–1.5MB) (Dial-in from outside PA accepted) SLIP PPP
PSCnet Pittsburgh Supercomputing Center 4400 5th Avenue Pittsburgh, PA 15213 (412) 268-4960 hastingspsc.edu	Eastern U.S.	Dedicated
RISQ* 3744 Jean Brillant Bureau 500 Montreal, Quebec Canada H3TIPl (514) 340-5700 turcotteclouso.crim.ca	Quebec	
SASK#net* Dean C. Jones (306) 966-4860 Sesquinet	Saskatchewan	
Office of Networking and Computing Rice University Houston, TX 77251-1892 (713) 527-4988 farrellrice.edu	Texas Latin America	Dedicated (8.6KB–1.5MB) SLIP

TABLE D.2 (*Continued*)

Provider	Coverage	Services
SURAnet 1353 Computer Science Center 8400 Baltimore Boulevard College Park, MD 20740-2498 (301) 982-4600 info@sura.net	Southeastern U.S. Caribbean Islands	Dedicated (56KB–45KB)
THEnet Texas Higher Education Network Information Center Austin, TX 78712 (512) 471-2444 infonic.the.net	Texas Limited Mexico	Dedicated (1.5MB) Dial-up SLIP
VERnet Academic Computing Center Gilmer Hall University of Virginia Charlottesville, VA 22903 (804) 924-0616 jajvirginia.edu	Virginia	Dedicated Dial-up SLIP PPP
Westnet 601 S. Howes, 6th Floor South Colorado State University Fort Collins, CO 80523 (303) 491-7260 pburnsyuma.acns.colostate.edu	Western U.S. (AZ CO ID NM UT WY)	Dedicated
WiscNet 1210 W. Dayton Street Madison, WI 53706 (608) 262-8874 dorlmacc.wisc.edu	Wisconsin	Dedicated (56KB–1.5MB) Limited Dial-up/SLIP PPP
WVnet* Harper Grimm (304) 293-5192 ccO110416)wvnvm.wvnet.edu	West Virginia	Dedicated SLIP PPP

*The information for these providers was not verified by press time.

Index

ABOUT THE AUTHOR

Kevin E. Leininger is a UNIX expert currently working as Director of Reengineering at DevTech Associates, a systems integration firm based in Naperville, Illinois. He has worked for Fermi National Accelerator Labs as an integration expert for UNIX, VAX, IBM, and Macintosh environments. He speaks frequently at major UNIX conferences and has written for *CIO Journal* and *Optiv.* He is currently on the readers' advisory board of *Open Computing.*

CD-ROM WARRANTY

This software is protected by both United States copyright law and international copyright treaty provision. You must treat this software just like a book. By saying "just like a book," McGraw-Hill means, for example, that this software may be used by any number of people and may be freely moved from one computer location to another, so long as there is no possibility of its being used at one location or on one computer while it also is being used at another. Just as a book cannot be read by two different people in two different places at the same time, neither can the software be used by two different people in two different places at the same time (unless, of course, McGraw-Hill's copyright is being violated).

LIMITED WARRANTY

McGraw-Hill takes great care to provide you with top-quality software, thoroughly checked to prevent virus infections. McGraw-Hill warrants the physical CD-ROM contained herein to be free of defects in materials and workmanship for a period of sixty days from the purchase date. If McGraw-Hill receives written notification within the warranty period of defects in materials or workmanship, and such notification is determined by McGraw-Hill to be correct, McGraw-Hill will replace the defective CD-ROM. Send requests to:

Customer Service
TAB/McGraw-Hill
13311 Monterey Lane
Blue Ridge Summit, PA 17294-0850

The entire and exclusive liability and remedy for breach of this Limited Warranty shall be limited to replacement of a defective CD-ROM and shall not include or extend to any claim for or right to cover any other damages, including but not limited to, loss of profit, data, or use of the software, or special, incidental, or consequential damages or other similar claims, even if McGraw-Hill has been specifically advised of the possibility of such damages. In no event will McGraw-Hill's liability for any damages to you or any other person ever exceed the lower of suggested list price or actual price paid for the license to use the software, regardless of any form of the claim.

McGRAW-HILL, INC. SPECIFICALLY DISCLAIMS ALL OTHER WARRANTIES, EXPRESS OR IMPLIED, INCLUDING, BUT NOT LIMITED TO, ANY IMPLIED WARRANTY OF MERCHANTABILITY OR FITNESS FOR A PARTICULAR PURPOSE

Specifically, McGraw-Hill makes no representation or warranty that the software is fit for any particular purpose and any implied warranty of merchantability is limited to the sixty-day duration of the Limited Warranty covering the physical CD-ROM only (and not the software) and is otherwise expressly and specifically disclaimed.

This limited warranty gives you specific legal rights, you may have others which may vary from state to state. Some states do not allow the exclusion of incidental or consequential damages, or the limitation on how long an implied warranty lasts, so some of the above may not apply to you.